ANATOMY OF THE
AUSCHWITZ DEATH CAMP

YISRAEL GUTMAN AND MICHAEL BERENBAUM, editors

Editorial Board
Yehuda Bauer, Raul Hilberg, and
Franciszek Piper

ANATOMY OF THE
AUSCHWITZ
DEATH CAMP

Published in association with the
United States Holocaust Memorial Museum
Washington, D.C.

Indiana University Press
Bloomington and Indianapolis

The paper used in this publication meets the minimum requirements
of American National Standard for Information Sciences—Permanence
of Paper for Printed Library Materials, ANSI Z39.48–1984.

Manufactured in the United States of America

Library of Congress Cataloging-in-Publication Data
Anatomy of the Auschwitz death camp / Yisrael Gutman and Michael
    Berenbaum, editors ; editorial board, Yehuda Bauer, Raul Hilberg,
    Franciszek Piper.
            p.   cm.
    Commissioned by the U.S. Holocaust Research Institute.
    ISBN 0-253-32684-2
        1. Auschwitz (Poland : Concentration camp)   2. Holocaust,
    Jewish (1939–1945)—Poland.   I. Gutman, Israel.   II. Berenbaum,
    Michael, date.   III. U.S. Holocaust Memorial Museum.   IV. U.S.
    Holocaust Research Institute.
    D805.P7A53   1994
    940.54'7243'094386—dc20   93-45729

    1 2 3 4 5 99 98 97 96 95 94

CONTENTS

————————————— *Part IV The Inmates*

————————————— *Part V The Resistance*

————————————— *Part VI Auschwitz and the Outside World*

PREFACE

Auschwitz was the largest and most lethal of the Nazi death camps. Actually it was three camps in one: a killing center, a concentration camp, and a series of slave-labor camps. Long regarded as a symbol of the Holocaust and of the Nazi period, Auschwitz illumines the totality of the Nazi killing machine.

A generation of historians has spent the last half-century studying the Holocaust. These senior scholars are now nearing retirement; their work has reached maturation. Many of their individual works have been published, but never have they collaborated on a comprehensive historical overview of Auschwitz. This volume brings together their individual talents and scholarship on this most important subject.

For much of the past half-century, the study of Auschwitz was centered in Poland, where it was conducted in a constrained political climate that made it impossible for Polish scholars to tell what they knew, and certainly not all that was known. The new political situation in Poland permits Polish scholars to create a depoliticized picture of Auschwitz. For the first time since the Holocaust, Polish scholars can write about the Jewish fate in Auschwitz without constraint. And for the first time, scholars in the West have access to major archival holdings in the former communist countries.

Until now, there has been no single, comprehensive study of Auschwitz in English or any other language. Although various parts of the camp have been studied in detail, no treatment of the whole exists. This work is designed to rectify that situation.

A complete exploration of Auschwitz is not the province of historians alone. Psychologists and sociologists, art historians and students of literature and film, physicians and chemists also participate in this research. Each discipline has a unique perspective to offer. Only by approaching Auschwitz from a multidisciplinary perspective can we understand the full dimensions of the largest and most lethal of the death camps. For example, while historians may document medical experimentation at Auschwitz, only physicians can evaluate the scientific validity of such experimentation and its relationship to medical training and ethics.

Pseudoscholars on three continents have tried to deny that Auschwitz was a death camp, that it had gas chambers and ovens, that lethal Zyklon B was used as a killing agent. That is the climate in which the present work was created, and the presentation of this collective study of Auschwitz should indirectly address some of the issues raised by these charlatans.

The work is the collaborative effort of scholars from the United States, Israel, Germany, Austria, Norway, Poland, and France. The contributors are among the most distinguished scholars of the Holocaust on three continents. All the essays are original, written exclusively for this book. Some are based on research that was published elsewhere but that appears here for the first time in the English language and in a new formulation. The sum total of these individual essays represents a significant original work.

The division of the book is organic. We begin in part I with the camp as an institution—the instrument of death and its history. We learn of its role in the Nazis' "final solution of the Jewish question." We read a detailed study of the statistics of those dead, a meticulous treatment that dispels the mistaken calculation that four million were murdered at Auschwitz but documents the murder of more than 1.1 million—90 percent of whom were Jews. We look at the role the camp played in the use of slave labor and in the German economy, and at the other dimensions of Auschwitz, its satellite camps. And we learn of the dismantling of Auschwitz, the death marches, and the final flames in which the SS sought desperately in a race against time to destroy the evidence of their crimes by shipping out the remaining victims and destroying the camp.

From the institution, we turn in part II to the mechanism of destruction. We present a major study of the gas chambers—which for the first time makes use of German documentation from newly opened archives in the former Soviet Union—by a scholar who demonstrates the economic competitiveness, bureaucratic struggles, and technological sophistication that led to the evolution of means capable of murdering and incinerating thousands of persons a day. We also reexamine Polish and other German documents on the gas chambers. We then learn the fate of those murdered, whose possessions were taken from them and recycled—so too the gold from their teeth, the hair from their heads, even the ashes of their bodies. In sum, this part presents an exhaustive, detailed analysis of the infrastructure of destruction.

From the mechanisms, we turn in part III to the Nazi personnel, the killers. Who was the commandant of Auschwitz and who constituted his staff? What was their background? How did they run the camp? What was their fate in the aftermath?

From the killers, we proceed in part IV to explore the life and fate of the Auschwitz inmates: the inmates forced by the killers to run the camp, the daily life of the ordinary inmate, the special fate of women and children, the family camps, the Gypsies. We learn of a peculiar aspect of Auschwitz, an aspect that appears to be a contradiction in terms, certainly a conflict in experience. We read of "health and hospitals" at Auschwitz, of "medical practice"—legitimate and otherwise—in the shadow of the gas chambers. We approach the specialty killers—the healers turned killers, the physicians of Auschwitz—and the experiments they performed. We turn to the fate of Hungarian Jews who entered Auschwitz in record numbers in the late spring and early summer of 1944 and were killed in a systematic mass destruction during the most lethal weeks of the Holocaust. We also look at the victims of Auschwitz from a psychological perspective through the work of a distinguished psychiatrist who worked as a prisoner-physician at Auschwitz and has since worked with its survivors.

We then learn in part V of the underground resistance at Auschwitz, those prisoners who fought and those who escaped, and those who lived as *Sonderkommando* members, carrying out special assignments at the gas chambers and ovens.

We then leave Auschwitz along with those who escaped and explore some perplexing questions in part VI. What did the Allies—the leaders, diplomats, and military officers, especially of the United States and Britain —know, and when did they know it? What was known in London and New York—and especially in Washington, where the decision not to bomb Auschwitz was finalized? We face an awful truth: the Allies knew what was happening, and those who knew did not act.

We live two generations after the event. Seemingly, we can look retrospectively and gain perspective. And yet, the more historians teach us of the German atrocities, the less we can comprehend their meaning. "In the beginning was testimony," Lawrence Langer writes. In the end, memory does not provide meaning, he adds, but an encounter with its opposite, for "from the perspective of the victims, who far outnumber the survivors, the disorder of meaningless death contradicts the ordering impulses of time. Those who died for nothing in the Holocaust left the living with a paralyzing dilemma of facing a perpetually present grief."

The editors have permitted the diverse scholars wide latitude in the interpretation of Auschwitz. While the overall presentation of the data forms a singular portrait of the camp, from time to time scholars disagree on details, perspectives, and interpretation. We have sought not to harmonize the details of each presentation but to let the self-corrective mechanisms of good scholarship do their task. As much as we respect each individual contribution and contributor, the editors do not agree with each detail in every essay.

This work is one of the initial publications of the United States Holocaust Research Institute, the scholarly and academic wing of the United States Holocaust Memorial Museum. So perhaps a word about the Institute is in order. It has three components: the Library, the Holocaust Archives, and the Academic Programs. As envisioned, the Library and the Archives are the raw material for assisting the further development of Holocaust-related research, a critical task which the Museum took upon itself from its inception. Toward that end, the Institute's Academic Programs will serve as the home of visiting scholars-in-residence in the Museum; provide funding for their stays at the Museum and working facilities to encourage their scholarship; serve as the base for visiting graduate-students-in residence who are working on dissertations and pursuing original research and can avail themselves of the facilities of the Museum; and assist scholars visiting the Museum for periods ranging from days to months to facilitate their research. The Institute will undertake a publications program to disseminate significant works on the Holocaust by publishing books with commercial or university presses, publishing a journal and periodical as resources become available, funding translations into English of important works in many languages, and republishing out-of-print classics or new works of special merit. In addition, the Institute will convene, as appropriate and as resources permit, conferences relating to the Holocaust and publish their proceedings; conduct ongoing seminars and periodic conferences on the state of Holocaust scholarship in the United States and the need for graduate training and faculty; and host periodic conferences for college professors from a variety of disciplines who teach the Holocaust—with or without specialized training—to acquaint them with recent research and to discuss issues relating to the teaching of the Holocaust. The Institute also will serve as a resource for other elements of the Museum, including its permanent and special exhibitions; its educational programs in the Museum, at high schools and elementary schools, and in outreach programs; and its public programs. Finally, the Institute will host an ongoing public seminar program for scholars that will serve as a center for both the dissemination of in-house research and the discussion of major research and will cooperate with similar research institutions in the United States, Israel, Germany, Poland, Czechoslovakia, and other countries.

Michael Berenbaum
Washington, D.C.

CONTRIBUTORS

YEHUDA BAUER is Director of the Vidal Sassoon Institute on the Study of Antisemitism and Professor of Jewish History at the Hebrew University in Jerusalem. A prolific writer and lecturer, he is the author of *The Holocaust in Historical Perspective* and *A History of the Holocaust*, among other works.

MICHAEL BERENBAUM is Director of the United States Holocaust Research Institute and Hymen Goldman Adjunct Professor of Theology at Georgetown University. He is the author of *After Tragedy and Triumph: Modern Jewish Thought and the American Experience*.

RANDOLPH L. BRAHAM is Director of the Emeric and Ilana Csengeri Institute of Holocaust Studies at the City University of New York and the author of *The Holocaust in Hungary* and *The Tragedy of Hungarian Jews*, as well as many other books.

NATHAN COHEN completed B.A. and M.A. degrees at Hebrew University in Jerusalem. His master's thesis dealt with diaries written in Lithuania during the Holocaust, and he is currently preparing a dissertation about Warsaw as a Jewish cultural center, 1920–1942. He teaches in the Yiddish Department at Hebrew University and conducts research at the Institute of Contemporary Jewry there.

DANUTA CZECH, a sociologist, completed her studies in 1952 at the Philosophy Faculty of Jagiellonian University in Krakow. Since 1955 she has been Director of the Research Department at the Auschwitz-Birkenau State Museum. A member during the Second World War of the resistance movement in the Tarnow district of Poland, she is the author of *Kalendarium der Ereignisse im Konzentrationslager Auschwitz-Birkenau* (The calendar of events in concentration camp Auschwitz-Birkenau), as well as many other professional monographs and articles.

LEO EITINGER, a survivor of Auschwitz, is Professor of Psychology at the University of Oslo (Emeritus). The author of several textbooks on neuroses, psychoses, and forensic psychiatry, he has published several monographs and numerous papers on concentration camp survivors in Norway and Israel and has edited *The Psychology and Medical Effects of Concentration Camps and Related Persecution on Survivors: A Research Bibliography*.

MARTIN GILBERT is a Fellow of Merton College, Oxford, and the official biographer of Winston Churchill. He has published more than thirty books, including *Auschwitz and the Allies* and *The Holocaust: A History of the Jews of Europe during the Second World War.*

YISRAEL GUTMAN is Professor of Modern Jewish History at the Hebrew University of Jerusalem and Chairman of Yad Vashem's Academic Committee. He was Editor-in-Chief of the *Macmillan Encyclopedia of the Holocaust.* Among his many books is *The Jews of Warsaw, 1939–1943.*

AMY HACKETT has a Ph.D. in History from Columbia University and has taught at Columbia University, Washington University, and Iona College. She edited the English translation of *The Encyclopedia of the Third Reich.*

RAUL HILBERG is the John G. McCullough Professor of Political Science at the University of Vermont (Emeritus). His work *The Destruction of the European Jews* is widely regarded as a classic in the field.

MIROSLAV KARNY studied History in Prague. During the German occupation of Czechoslovakia he spent three years in Theresienstadt, Auschwitz, and Dachau. After liberation he worked as a journalist in Prague, and for the past fifteen years he has been a free-lance historian of German fascism.

NILI KEREN is Director of Holocaust Studies at the Kibbutz Seminary in Tel Aviv. She received her Ph.D. from Hebrew University after writing a dissertation on Holocaust education in Israel. She has also published a well-received book on education in Theresienstadt (in Hebrew).

SHMUEL KRAKOWSKI is Chief Archivist of Yad Vashem, Israel's national memorial to the Holocaust, and co-author of *Unequal Victims: Poles and Jews during World War II,* among other works.

HELENA KUBICA graduated from the Department of History of the Jagiellonian University. Since 1977 she has worked in the Department of Historical Research at the Auschwitz-Birkenau State Museum. She is leading a research project on the fate of children and juveniles in Auschwitz and is the author of several works on the subject.

HERMANN LANGBEIN, born in Vienna, fled to Spain after the Anschluss to take part in the International Brigade against Fascism. He was interned in a French camp, then in Dachau, Auschwitz, and Neuengamme. Now a free-lance writer in Vienna and secretary of the International Committee of the Camps, he is the author of *Menschen in Auschwitz.*

LAWRENCE LANGER, Alumni Professor of Literature at Simmons College (Emeritus), is the author of *The Holocaust and the Literary Imagination, Versions of Survival: The Holocaust and the Human Spirit,* and *Holocaust Testimonies: The Ruins of Memory.*

ALEKSANDER LASIK graduated from the Department of Sociology at Adam Mickiewicz University in Poznan and received his Ph.D. in 1988 with a thesis on SS troops in Auschwitz. He is preparing a study of the SS in KL Stutthof, as well as another monograph, "SS Totenkopfverbände 1939–1945." He has worked at the College of Pedagogy in Bydgoszcz since 1977.

ROBERT JAY LIFTON, Distinguished Professor of Psychiatry and Psychology at the City University of New York, John Jay College, is the author of *The Nazi Doctors* and *The Genocidal Mentality*.

FRANCISZEK PIPER received his Ph.D. from the Department of History at Jagiellonian University. Since 1965 he has been employed in the Department of Historical Research at the Auschwitz-Birkenau State Museum and now heads the department. He is the author of several monographs about the Auschwitz satellite camps and has led research on the methods of extermination of prisoners (including the use of gas chambers) along with the numerical results of extermination.

JEAN-CLAUDE PRESSAC is a pharmacist and an independent scholar working in La Ville du Bois, France. Since 1982, the work of Mr. Pressac has been promoted and supported on a documentary, editorial, and financial level by the Beate Klarsfeld Foundation, which has published in English the following works of Pressac: *The Stuthoff Album, The Deficiencies and Inconsistencies of the Leuchter Report*, and *Auschwitz: Technique and Operation of the Gas Chambers*. The latter work was sent to hundreds of libraries and documentation centers throughout the world by the Beate Klarsfeld Foundation. Mr. Pressac's chapter is adapted from his book *Les Crématoires d'Auschwitz: La machinerie du meurtre de masse* (Paris: CNRS, 1993).

IRENA STRZELECKA is a graduate of the History and Philosophy Department at Jagiellonian University. Since 1965 she has worked in the Department of Historical Research at the Auschwitz-Birkenau State Museum. She is the author of several monographs and articles dealing with the history of the Auschwitz subcamps, the first transports of Poles to Auschwitz, camp hospitals, and medical experiments.

ANDRZEJ STRZELECKI graduated from the History and Philosophy Department of Jagiellonian University in 1964. Since then he has worked at the Auschwitz-Birkenau State Museum in the Department of Historical Research. In 1979 he received a Ph.D. at the Silesian University in Katowice. He has published several treatises and articles, among them a large work entitled *Evacuation, Liquidation and Liberation of KL Auschwitz* (1974, in Polish).

HENRYK SWIEBOCKI graduated from the Department of History of Jagiellonian University. Employed in the Department of Historical Research of the Auschwitz-Birkenau State Museum, he is the author of historical exhibitions and publications about Auschwitz. His work mainly concerns resistance in the camp, the help extended to prisoners by Poles, and attempts to inform the outside world about Nazi crimes.

ROBERT-JAN VAN PELT is Assistant Professor of Architecture in the Architecture School at the University of Waterloo, Canada. He is the author of three books on architectural history, including a history of Solomon's Temple and a theoretical discourse on the significance of the Auschwitz crematoria for the understanding of architectural history. He is completing a major study of the planning and architectural history of Auschwitz.

DAVID S. WYMAN is the Josiah DuBois Professor of History at the University of Massachusetts (Emeritus) and the author of *The Abandonment of the Jews: America and the Holocaust 1941–1945* and *Paper Walls.*

ACKNOWLEDGMENTS

We wish to acknowledge colleagues and friends who encouraged us along the way to completing this book. First and foremost, we thank the members of the editorial board—Raul Hilberg, Yehuda Bauer, and Franciszek Piper—who cooperated closely in soliciting and evaluating papers. Their insights helped shape the book, and their scholarship informs it.

We wish to thank the contributors, distinguished scholars all, who were generous with their knowledge and talents and almost without exception gracious in the manner in which they cooperated with the publication.

We thank our colleague and friend Jeshajahu Weinberg, Director of the United States Holocaust Memorial Museum in Washington, who supported this project from its inception, and Alfred Gottschalk, Chair of the Academic Committee of the United States Holocaust Memorial Museum, whose encouragement was essential.

Ronald Goldfarb, the Museum's literary agent, demonstrated friendship and patience. His experience and advice were of substantial importance in seeing this work to publication.

Janet Rabinowitch of Indiana University Press, our able editor, has believed in this project and supported it. We have benefited from her meticulous work and sanguine advice. Ken Goodall performed with precision the difficult and unenviable task of copyediting the manuscript.

We wish to thank the translators who contributed to this work. Peter Heinegg translated Jean-Claude Pressac's text from French into English, and Robert-Jan van Pelt worked closely with Mr. Pressac to ensure that a technical article was clear and lucid as well as precise and informed by the latest scholarship. We wish to thank T. Aaron Wachhaus and Charlotte Hebebrand, who translated from German, and Jerzy Michalowicz, who translated from Polish.

Anatomy of the Auschwitz Death Camp is one of the initial publications of the United States Holocaust Research Institute, the scholarly division of the United States Holocaust Memorial Museum. Several of the Research Institute's staff contributed importantly to the publication. Betsy Chock graciously and selflessly assisted with the typing of the manuscript. Linda Harris and Bryan Lazar scanned chapters into the computer. Genya Markon and Teresa Amiel of the Museum's photo archives helped select the photographs and prepared their captions. Dewey Hicks and William Meinecke competently and quickly produced the maps. David Luebke, former Director of Publications at the Museum and now a professor at Bennington College, assisted in the preparation of the book. So, too, did Aleisa Fishman, who had the unenviable task of proofreading the manuscript and who handled other chores with skill and efficiency. Janice Cook and Jeffrey Burridge helped in the editing of this work.

Lydia Perry and Deirdre McCarthy, assistants to Michael Berenbaum, were gracious and able. Their assistance was invaluable. Ms. Perry typed sections of the manuscript, prepared other portions for editing and scanning, and handled difficult correspondence and various negotiations. Ms. McCarthy saw to it that the manuscript was ready for publication, freeing her schedule to perform the work in a timely fashion.

This book is the first joint publication effort of scholars on three continents and from several different countries brought together under the auspices of the United States Holocaust Research Institute. May it be the first of many.

Yisrael Gutman
Jerusalem, Israel
Michael Berenbaum
Washington, D.C.

ANATOMY OF THE
AUSCHWITZ
DEATH CAMP

Part I

A History of the Camp

YISRAEL GUTMAN, presenting a historical overview of Auschwitz, chronicles its development from an army barracks to its emergence as a full-fledged concentration camp and the largest Nazi killing center. He details life inside the concentration camp, from its earliest stages through the mass killing process and its liquidation prior to the long-delayed liberation by Soviet troops on January 18, 1945. Gutman, a survivor of Auschwitz and a participant in its resistance, was also a participant in the Warsaw ghetto uprising. He writes with the authority of a scholar and participant in the events he chronicles. Gutman also explores the scholarly and political controversies that impacted the historians of Auschwitz.

Franciszek Piper explores the role of Auschwitz as a slave-labor camp as it evolved throughout the war, most especially during periods of intense labor shortages. His work depicts the tension between the Nazis' need for slave labor and their effort to achieve a "final solution of the Jewish question." With regard to Birkenau, the relationship between killing and labor was symbiotic, Piper writes. The killing center could operate because deportations—the arrival of new prisoners—maintained a renewable supply of fresh labor.

Piper details the corporate investment in the slave-labor camps by mainstream German firms motivated by profits and spurred on by the SS offerings of unique economic and production opportunities. He clarifies the shift in policy that resulted from the labor shortages and from failures of Heinrich Himmler's great plans for concentration-camp based enterprises. Rather than invest in new facilities, which were expensive and unprofitable, the Nazis situated labor camps adjacent to industrial sites because it was cheaper and organizationally simpler. The need for labor in 1943 resulted for a time in better living conditions in some concentration camps. As for Auschwitz, Piper documents the uniqueness of this extermination, concentration, and slave-labor camp in scale and in task.

Shmuel Krakowski documents through Nazi records the evolution and implementation of the destruction-through-work policy that viewed slave labor as slow extermination. He depicts the German corporate investment in the slave-labor program and the partnership between the SS and private industry. He describes the differences between Jewish and non-Jewish prisoners. The former lived under a sentence of death in virtual isolation from the outside world, while the latter were allowed to send letters and receive packages. From Jewish sources, diaries, letters, memoirs, oral testimony, and trials, he depicts daily life in these camps.

The question of how many people died at Auschwitz has been shrouded in mystery. Figures based on exaggerated estimates were published early on and repeated in the media: four million dead, including two million Jews and two million Poles. With the collapse of the Communist regime in Poland, Polish researchers are now free to publish detailed documentation on the question of numbers. Franciszek Piper reveals the fruits of twenty-five years of historical research that provides figures on deaths of Jews,

Poles, Gypsies, Soviet POWs, and other victims. By documenting those who entered, those who left, and the number that remained, Piper triangulates his figures. Once he calculates how many arrived at Auschwitz, how many departed, and how many remained in the camp, he can detail with precision the number of inmates killed at the camp: 1.1 million. Piper's work could not have been published a few years ago, when the Polish government placed itself squarely behind the figure of four million dead. Although his conclusions challenge common assumptions, they substantiate the claim that Jews were the focus of Nazi mass murder plans and that Auschwitz was the epicenter of the "final solution."

Michael Berenbaum

1

Auschwitz—An Overview

YISRAEL GUTMAN

In the years since the Second World War, the name Auschwitz has become virtually synonymous with the unrestrained tyranny, the power of terror, and the systematic murder of millions of human beings during German Nazi rule.

In *Der SS Staat* (the SS state), a book on the structure of the concentration camp system, Eugen Kogon, a former prisoner of the Buchenwald camp, described almost unlimited totalitarianism in which living arrangements and behavioral norms were imposed on persons deprived of any right to participate in shaping their lives and fate.[1] It was under the unremitting oppression of the concentration camps that the Nazi concept of absolute power over a captive population came closest to full implementation. Thus a survivor, Primo Levi, observed that

> never has there existed a state that was really "totalitarian." . . . Never has some form of reaction, a corrective of the total tyranny, been lacking, not even in the Third Reich or Stalin's Soviet Union: in both cases, public opinion, the magistrature, the foreign press, the churches, the feeling for justice and humanity that ten or twenty years of tyranny were not enough to eradicate, have to a greater or lesser extent acted as a brake. Only in the *Lager* was the restraint from below non-existent, and the power of these small satraps absolute.[2]

In a similar vein, Hannah Arendt argued that "the concentration and extermination camps of totalitarian regimes serve as laboratories in which the fundamental belief of totalitarianism that everything is possible is being verified."[3]

Auschwitz was the largest of the Nazi concentration camps. In the period from May 1940, when German authorities laid the groundwork for its establishment, to January 1945, when most surviving Auschwitz prisoners were marched off by their German captors and Soviet Army troops liberated the camp, approximately 405,000 prisoners of both sexes from nearly every European country were registered, assigned serial numbers, and incarcerated there. Of this number an estimated 200,000 perished.[4] (This figure does not include prisoners who were murdered without being registered.) The proportion of deaths among Auschwitz prisoners was much higher than in other concentration camps, such as Sachsenhausen, Buchenwald, and Mauthausen.[5]

With the expansion and development of the camp complex, Auschwitz and its satellites encompassed more than 40 camps spread over a vast industrial area rich with natural resources. These camps served as a huge pool of prisoner labor for the German war effort, as well as for work in mines, construction, and agriculture.

But the uniqueness and historical significance of Auschwitz do not derive from those features. In January 1941, the head of the RSHA (Reichssicherheitshauptamt, or Reich Main Security Office) of the elite Nazi police unit, the Schutzstaffel (SS), Reinhard Heydrich, second in the SS hierarchy to Heinrich Himmler, classified various concentration camps in accordance with the severity of the offenses committed by their prisoners. Auschwitz was placed in the same category as Dachau and Sachsenhausen as a camp for prisoners whose offenses were "relatively light and definitely correctable." One might conclude that at that time Auschwitz did not differ significantly from other concentration camps.

From May 1940 to January 1942, 36,285 prisoners (26,288 civilians and 9,997 Soviet prisoners of war) were incarcerated in the camp. But not even the mass scale of the camp and the savagery of its regime were fated to become its hallmark.

The gruesome history and enduring horror of Auschwitz can be attributed primarily to the machinery for mass extermination of human beings created by the Nazis at the nearby Birkenau camp, a unit of Auschwitz. The location was designated by Himmler as the centerpiece for "the final solution of the Jewish question in Europe." From spring 1942 until fall 1944, the operation designed to annihilate European Jews functioned almost without letup as transport trains delivered Jews from Nazi-occupied countries and European satellites of the Third Reich.

The overwhelming majority of those victims, designated as "RSHA transports" earmarked for "special treatment" (*Sonderbehandlung*), were ignorant of their destination and their fate. They were moved like cattle and arrived in a state of total exhaustion. It has been said that "there will never be people as innocent as the victims on the threshold of the gas chambers."

"Selections" took place on the railroad siding ramp at the gates of Birkenau. Children, the elderly, the sick, and large numbers of men and women were selected for death and marched immediately to the gas chambers. Other transport arrivals, classified as able-bodied, were selected for work and were registered in the camp as prisoners. According to the best estimates now obtainable, more than one million Jews were murdered in the gas chambers on arrival and their bodies incinerated in the camp's crematoria without the victims ever being registered.

Of those murdered upon arrival, no trace remained: no name, no record, no precise information. In *The Nazi Doctors*, Robert Jay Lifton writes:

> When we think of the crimes of Nazi doctors, what comes to mind are their cruel and sometimes fatal experiments. . . . Yet when we turn to the Nazi doctor's role in Auschwitz, it was not the experiments that were most significant. Rather, it was his participation in the killing process—indeed his supervision of Auschwitz mass murder from beginning to end.[6]

The place that gave its name to the camp was the small Polish district town of Oswiecim, located 50 kilometers (km) southwest of Krakow and 286 km from Warsaw. From the partition and subjugation of Poland in 1772 until the establishment of the independent Polish republic in 1918, Oswiecim, virtually unknown outside Poland, lay within the territory of the Hapsburg Empire. Following the occupation of Poland in September 1939 by the Third Reich, Oswiecim was incorporated into Germany together with Upper Silesia, hitherto under Polish rule, and renamed Auschwitz. On the eve of the war, the town's population stood at 12,000, including nearly 5,000 Jewish residents. The Sola River, a tributary of the Vistula, flows near Oswiecim; yet at this latitude it is little more than a creek. Although Oswiecim is not far from the Tatra mountains, whose peaks remain snowclad year-round, it lies in a humid and foggy valley with swampy soil, an unpleasant climate conducive to disease.

The initiative to establish a concentration camp in Auschwitz in the spring of 1940 came from the SS and the police district command, which argued that the jails and prisons could no longer meet its needs due to the intensification of Polish resistance activities. Martin Broszat, a German historian of National Socialism and Nazi power, writes in his study of the concentration camps:

> Establishment of the camp and the selection of distant Auschwitz in the Kattowitz [Katowice] district, part of the annexed new eastern territories (about 30 km east of Kattowitz, on the juncture of Eastern Upper Silesia, the General Government, and Warthegau) as its site was due above all, though not exclusively, to the large number of Polish prisoners captured by the security

police in these areas. They were incarcerated in congested prisons without any intention of putting them on trial.[7]

The concentration camps, which existed from the time of the Nazi take-over until the collapse of the Third Reich, were conceived as an "iron fist" to circumvent the law as dictated by the regime's changing needs. Initially the camps served as instruments of terror and "reeducation" to frighten, deter, and paralyze the Nazis' opposition, primarily members of left-wing political parties and others with liberal views. As the regime consolidated its grip on power, some of its highly placed functionaries concluded that the camps had fulfilled their purpose and should be abolished. During 1936, some 7,500 prisoners on average were incarcerated in concentration camps in Germany. Eventually the chancellor and Nazi Führer Adolf Hitler decided to continue the camps under Himmler and the SS and consolidated their power.

In the second stage of the camps' history, from 1936–37 to the first years of the war, the camps served as dumping grounds for "work shirkers," "a-social elements," criminals, and Jews (especially in the aftermath of the *Kristallnacht* anti-Jewish violence that erupted on November 9, 1938). Many such prisoners worked as forced laborers, described by the historian Karl Dietrich Bracher as slave laborers impressed for work in Hitler's "megalo-maniac" construction projects.[8] SS-owned plants and other enterprises were created next to existing camps, and two new camps were established at Flossenburg and Mauthausen. On the eve of the war, the prisoner popu-lation of Nazi concentration camps had reached 25,000.

The war brought in its wake "a great change in the life of concentration camps," according to the commander and architect of the Auschwitz camp, Rudolf Ferdinand Höss, who wrote his memoirs in a Polish jail after the war. The growing network of concentration camps began absorbing ever-increasing numbers of nationals of Nazi-occupied countries, mainly under-ground political activists and other suspects. Conditions in the camps deteriorated steadily. As Martin Broszat points out,

> the tendency of the SS to turn concentration camps into the pool of manpower for forced labor at its disposal can be detected as early as the winter of 1941–42. Paradoxically, this tendency ran counter to the desire, which had also gained momentum since the outbreak of the war, to eradicate and drive out certain groups of undesirables.[9]

In practice, this meant that along with planning and promoting productive labor, methods known collectively as "destruction through work" (*Vernichtung durch Arbeit*) were introduced. Destruction through work assumed two main forms: (1) work as punishment in the comprehensive terror system, involving humiliation, brutal treatment, and physical abuse, and (2) backbreaking labor without even the simplest work tools, performed by prisoners living in conditions below subsistence-level.

The growing number of prisoners classified by the Nazis as "racial" inferiors coincided with the attitude that such persons constituted a hostile and expendable element that should be eliminated. Their taskmasters acted as if the supply of prisoner manpower was inexhaustible, requiring no effort to preserve it. This stance changed in 1942, however, as the war on the eastern front dragged on and the shortage of manpower was keenly felt.

In March 1942, concentration camps were placed under the SS Economic-Administrative Main Office (Wirtschafts-Verwaltungshauptamt or WVHA), a move that suggests a more rational approach to prisoner manpower in concentration camps. From the second half of that year, and particularly from 1943 on, this shift was apparent in a modest improvement in the living conditions of prisoners, which in turn somewhat reduced the mortality rate. While this relaxation of prisoner labor policies did not extend to the policy on the extermination of European Jews, which reached its climax during this period, it did affect the conditions of some Jewish victims. Under heavy pressure from officials interested in the most effective use of manpower for the war machine, Himmler consented to the temporary use of some able-bodied, skilled Jewish workers in the production process, while making sure that these prisoners were placed in concentration camps under SS control.

Although the living conditions of Jewish prisoners in the camps generally were much harsher than those of other national and ethnic groups and their mortality rate consequently was higher, it is nonetheless incontrovertible that the few Jews who survived until the end of the war in the camps owe their lives largely to the Germans' desperate need for manpower, which brought a relaxation of camp regime in the later stages of the war.

In the first years of their existence, the camps were populated by German prisoners and, after the annexation of Austria in 1938, by numerous Austrians as well. In the final stages of the war, Germans from the Reich (*Reichsdeutsche*) comprised only 5 percent to 10 percent of the prisoner population, while the overwhelming majority of prisoners were Russians, Poles, French, Dutch, Czechs, Greeks, and Jews from Nazi-occupied European countries.

The growth in the prisoner population was formidable, from 25,000 at the outbreak of the war to 525,000 in 1944. In January 1945, a few months before war's end, the camps held more than 700,000.

The concentration camp system was a relatively small segment of the vast network of more than 2,000 camps in areas under Nazi control, including labor camps, prisoner-of-war (POW) camps, and transit camps for prisoners and Jews awaiting transport to their final destination. Concentration camps differed from other types of camps in that they remained under the control of the central SS authorities and maintained a uniform internal regime and unified command. All SS-controlled concentration camps were bound by the same harsh regulations which governed other prisoners and SS personnel: a daily schedule that regulated prisoners' lives down to the last detail, a hierarchy of SS command with some power handed to functionary-prisoners (those assigned official duties), and a penal system which permitted the hanging of prisoners.

The camp established at Dachau in 1933 by Himmler, then police chief in Munich, served as a model for all subsequent concentration camps. Dachau served also as a training facility for the SS's so-called Death's-Head Unit (Totenkopfverbande), which became the core of SS personnel responsible for running the concentration camp system. Having completed the Dachau "school," they went on to serve as commanders and senior officials in other such facilities.

SS-Oberführer (Colonel) Theodor Eicke, the first Dachau commander and later the inspector for concentration camps, designed the Dachau camp regulations, which served as a model for regulations in all other concentration camps. It was Eicke who determined that "commiseration with the enemy of the state [the prisoner] does not benefit the SS man." At the beginning of the war, Eicke joined the combat SS formation (Waffen SS) and was killed on the eastern front in 1943, but his theory and practice remained in force in Nazi concentration camps until the end.

The site selected to become the core of the future Auschwitz camp lay outside the town of Oswiecim. It included 16 one-story buildings that had served as army barracks. The Inspectorate for Concentration Camps dispatched two commissions to inspect the proposed site. The first, which arrived in January 1940, issued a negative opinion. The second, which arrived in April 1940, was headed by SS-Hauptsturmführer (Captain) Rudolf Höss, whose name was to become permanently linked with the camp. Acting on a report from Höss, Himmler ordered the establishment of the camp on the site and appointed Höss as its commander.

The first order of business was the eviction of about 1,200 persons who lived in shacks and cabins in the vicinity of the projected camp. Next, 300 Jewish residents of Oswiecim were brought in for six weeks to level the terrain and lay foundations. Then, in May 1940, 30 German criminal prisoners arrived from the Sachsenhausen camp. Assigned the first Auschwitz camp serial numbers, these prisoners made up the network of functionary-prisoners holding official posts in the prisoner hierarchy, "the long arm of the SS in the camp," as David Rousset, a French concentration camp survivor, put it.

On June 14, 1940, the first transport carrying 728 Polish inmates from the town of Tarnow in Galicia arrived in the camp. The administration and

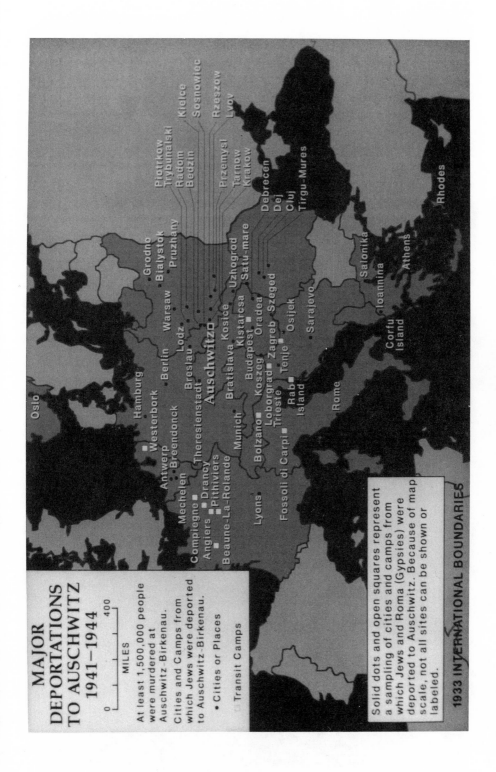

MAJOR DEPORTATIONS TO AUSCHWITZ 1941–1944

MILES
0   400

At least 1,500,000 people were murdered at Auschwitz-Birkenau.

Cities and Camps from which Jews were deported to Auschwitz-Birkenau.

• Cities or Places

□ Transit Camps

Solid dots and open squares represent a sampling of cities and camps from which Jews and Roma (Gypsies) were deported to Auschwitz. Because of map scale, not all sites can be shown or labeled.

1933 INTERNATIONAL BOUNDARIES

Oslo
Hamburg
Westerbork
Antwerp
Breendonck
Mechelen
Compiegne
Drancy
Anglers
Pithiviers
Beaune-La-Rolande
Lyons
Fossoli di Carpi
Bolzano
Loborgrad
Trieste
Trieste
Munich
Berlin
Theresienstadt
Breslau
Lodz
Warsaw
Grodno
Bialystok
Pruzhany
Piotrkow
Trybunalski
Radom
Bedzin
Kielce
Sosnowiec
Rzeszow
Lvov
Przemysl
Tarnow
Krakow
Debrecen
Dej
Cluj
Tirgu-Mures
Uzhogrod
Satu-mare
Kosice
Bratislava
Kistarcsa
Budapest
Koszeg
Oradea
Zagreb
Szeged
Tenje
Rab
Island
Osijek
Sarajevo
Rome
Salonika
Ioannina
Corfu
Island
Athens
Rhodes

Auschwitz

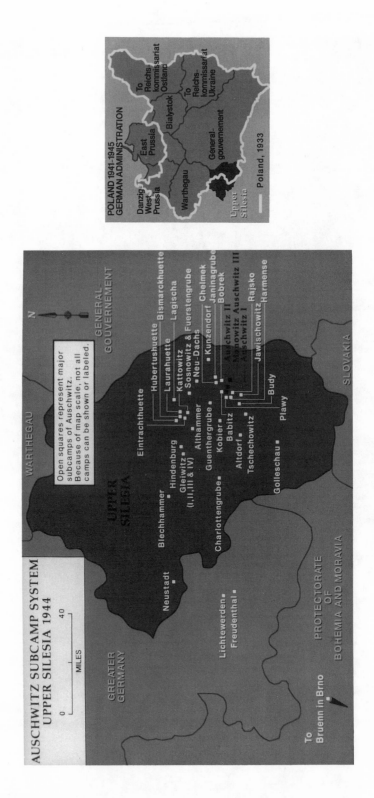

AUSCHWITZ SUBCAMP SYSTEM
UPPER SILESIA 1944

0   40
MILES

GREATER GERMANY

WARTHEGAU

N

Open squares represent major subcamps of Auschwitz. Because of map scale, not all camps can be shown or labeled.

UPPER SILESIA

GENERAL-GOUVERNEMENT

Neustadt

Blechhammer

Eintrachthuette

Hubertushuette

Bismarckhuette

Laurahuette   Lagischa

Kattowitz

Hindenburg

Sosnowitz & Fuerstengrube

Neu-Dachs

Cheimek

Janinagrube

Kunzendorf   Bobrek

Gleiwitz
(I, II, III & IV)

Althammer

Guenthergrube

Auschwitz II

Monowitz Auschwitz III

Kobier   Auschwitz I

Charlottengrube

Babitz   Jawischowitz   Rajsko

Altdorf   Budy   Harmense

Tschechowitz

Lichtewerden

Freudenthal

Gollechau   Plawy

PROTECTORATE
OF
BOHEMIA AND MORAVIA

To
Bruenn in Brno

SLOVAKIA

POLAND 1941-1945
GERMAN ADMINISTRATION

Danzig
West
Prussia

East
Prussia

Warthegau

Bialystok

To
Reichs-
kommissariat
Ostland

General-
gouvernement

To
Reichs-
kommissariat
Ukraine

Upper
Silesia

—— Poland, 1933

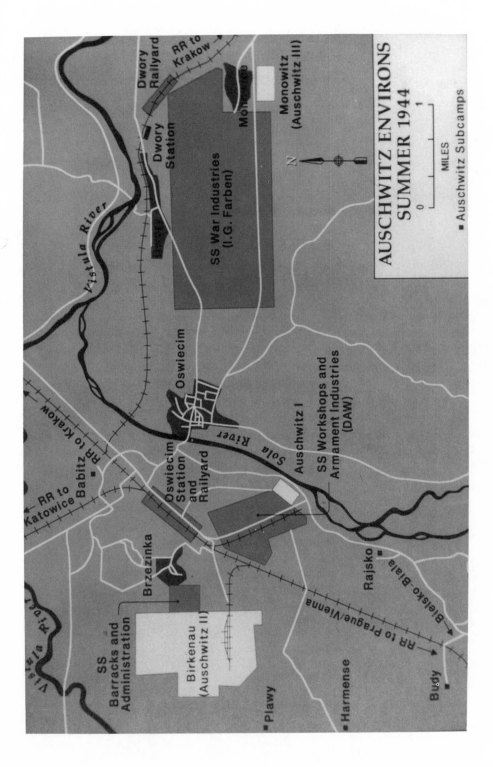

AUSCHWITZ ENVIRONS
SUMMER 1944

■ Auschwitz Subcamps

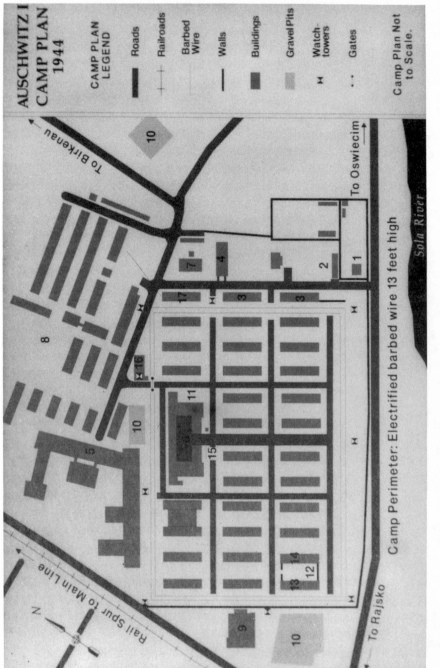

Selected features: 1. Camp commander's house. 2. Main guard house. 3. Camp administrative offices. 4. Gestapo. 5. Reception building and prisoner registration. 6. Kitchen. 7. Gas chamber and crematorium #1. 8. Storage buildings and workshops. 9. Storage of confiscated belongings. 10. Gravel pit, execution site. 11. Camp orchestra. 12. "Black wall," execution site. 13. Block 11, punishment bunker. 14. Block 10, medical experiments. 15. Gallows. 16. Block commander's barracks. 17. SS hospital.

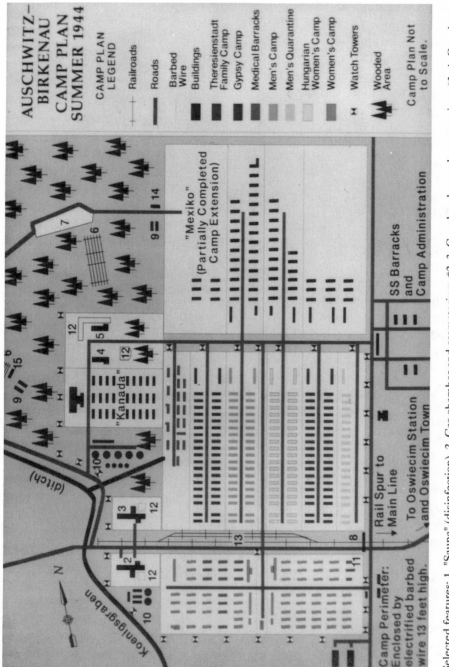

Selected features: 1. "Sauna" (disinfection). 2. Gas chamber and crematorium #3. 4. Gas chamber and crematorium #4. 5. Gas chamber and crematorium #5. 6. Cremation pits. 7. Mass graves for Soviet POWs. 8. Main guard house. 9. Barracks for disrobing. 10. Sewage plant. 11. Medical Experiments barrack. 12. Buried ashes from crematoria. 13. "Rampa" (railroad platform). 14. Provisional gas chamber #1. 15. Provisional gas chamber #2.

management staff was assembled, mostly officials transferred to Auschwitz from other camps. SS-Obersturmführer (First Lieutenant) Josef Kramer from Mauthausen was appointed as Höss's deputy. Karl Fritsch of Dachau was appointed chief of the prisoner camp. A political department (a branch of the Gestapo, the state secret-police organization) was also established.

As the main concentration camp for the occupied Polish territories, the Polish underground, and the Polish intelligentsia, Auschwitz grew steadily and gradually to accommodate prisoners of various categories. To facilitate implementation of plans for the camp, more residents were evicted from several districts of the town and from surrounding areas; all Jewish residents of Oswiecim were evacuated to the nearby town of Chrzanow. By uprooting the local population, the Germans created an empty area measuring 40 sq km designated as "the interest area of the camp."

When Himmler first visited Auschwitz in March 1941, 10,900 prisoners, most of them Poles, had been incarcerated in the camp. After touring the camp with an entourage of senior SS officers, local officials, functionaries of the Inspectorate for Concentration Camps, and officials of the giant industrial conglomerate IG Farbenindustrie who sought to establish a subsidiary on the camp grounds, Himmler laid down expansion plans. They included intensive construction work in the camp area with a view to accommodating 30,000 prisoners and the establishment at Birkenau (Brzezinka), about 3 km away, of a camp for 100,000 prisoners of war. Three months before the Germans attacked the Soviet Union, Himmler was clearly anticipating prisoners from that future campaign. Expansion plans also called for supplying 10,000 prisoner workers to IG Farben for the construction of a large industrial enterprise in the vicinity of Auschwitz and for agricultural development with the help of prisoner manpower, establishment of workshops, and war effort enterprises in the camp.

Himmler's visit inaugurated an upsurge in construction. In 1942, an average of 8,000 prisoners worked daily in construction. The main camp (*Stammlager*), Auschwitz I, expanded so rapidly that by the end of 1941 it could accommodate 18,000 prisoners and in 1943 held as many as 30,000. Living quarters for the SS were built within the perimeter of the camp, together with barracks for SS guards, headquarters for the Auschwitz complex, and a workshop and depot sector. The entire main camp occupied an area 1,000 m long and 400 m wide.

Construction in the Birkenau camp, which was to become Auschwitz II, started in October 1941. The terrible congestion which prevailed in the main camp as a result of the arrival of Soviet prisoners of war toward the end of 1941 forced the Germans to accelerate the pace of construction work in Birkenau. Preparation of the ground necessitated draining swamps. Workers labored under inhuman conditions and suffered cruel treatment. The new camp was completed at a high cost in lives of POWs and civilian prisoners. But ultimately the construction did not go according to plan, and the projected scope of construction and the division of the camp into subcamps had to be modified.

In the second half of 1941, Himmler entrusted Auschwitz authorities with preparations for the projected mass annihilation of European Jews. In the context of this plan, Birkenau was designed to hold various categories of prisoners and to function also as a death camp. The first sectors of Birkenau, subcamps separated by barbed-wire fences and equipped with gates and watchtowers, were completed in 1942. In 1943, the sector designated as BII was completed. It consisted of separate subsectors designed for living quarters (designated BIIb to BIIf) and located in long wooden structures built originally as horse stables. Thus a barrack originally designed for 52 horses served as living quarters for over 400 prisoners.

In March 1942, a women's sector was established in the main camp. It held 999 German women prisoners brought from the Ravensbrück concentration camp and the same number of Jewish women brought from Slovakia. Before long, the population of the women's camp rose to 6,000 prisoners. In August, it was moved to Birkenau. In January 1944, the Birkenau women's sector held 27,053 prisoners, who suffered from a lack of the most basic sanitary and hygienic conditions and were subject to frequent selections for gassings.

The Birkenau camp sectors, both men's and women's, held prisoners of many nationalities, most of them Jews. In January 1944, the total prisoner population of Auschwitz camps reached 80,839.

In February 1943, a separate family camp for Gypsies was created in sector BIIe, and a similar camp for Jews from the Theresienstadt ghetto in Czechoslovakia was opened in September. Later, both family camps were liquidated and most of their inmates murdered in the gas chambers.

In addition to the intensive expansion and construction of sectors of the main camps in the years 1942–45, some 40 camps were established over a wide area around Auschwitz, some of them tens of kilometers from the main camp. These camps were either directly affiliated with Auschwitz or served as branches. Varying in size, their prisoner populations ranging from several dozen to several thousands, these camps were established near mines, foundries, and other industrial enterprises. Establishment of such an extensive network of satellite camps was necessary because prisoners could not march more than several kilometers to work, and mines and other sources of raw materials were often located considerable distances from the main camp. The Germans also sought to avoid concentrating a large number of industrial buildings close to the main camp for security and other reasons.

The various types of satellite camps were designated *Aussenlager* (external camp), *Nebenlager* (extension or subcamp), *Arbeitslager* (labor camp), and others. For the most part, their internal regime was patterned after that of the concentration camp. They were populated mostly by Jewish prisoners living in the utmost deprivation, often under worse conditions than in the main camps. Mines and other industrial enterprises using the slave labor of prisoners (who, of course, were paid nothing, with all the proceeds from their labor going to the SS coffers) belonged to some of the largest German companies, including Hermann Göring Werke, Siemens-Schuckert, and IG Farbenindustrie. Acting in concert with the huge Krupp conglomerate, camp authorities established a large plant owned by Weichsel Union Metallwerke close to the main camp. It employed hundreds of prisoners, including men from Auschwitz I and women from Birkenau. In the last phase of the camp's existence, women workers from this plant were transferred to separate living quarters near the main camp.

In a comprehensive survey of the structure of the camp, Danuta Czech, a Polish scholar on the staff of the Auschwitz-Birkenau State Museum, concludes:

> Twenty-eight of the forty satellite camps of Auschwitz worked either directly or indirectly for the German armaments industry. Nine were established near foundries and other metal works, six near coal mines; six more supplied prisoner labor to chemical plants, three others to light industry; one was situated next to the plant manufacturing construction materials and one near a food processing plant. Prisoners of other camps worked in renovation and construction, in forestry, farmsteads and growing livestock, experimental agricultural stations, and other enterprises.[10]

Prisoners of the Jaworzno and Jawiszowice satellite camps worked in coal mines; of Swietochowice camp, in a foundry; of Lagisze camp, in the construction of a power plant; of Myslowice camp, in a coal mine. The largest satellite camp was Monowice (Monowitz), where IG Farben erected a huge synthetic rubber plant (Buna Werke). Studies conducted after the war indicate that the performance of prisoners working under duress, in conditions of brutal regime, harsh oppression, and extreme deprivation, fell far short of German objectives, and the overall performance of the huge industrial complex near Auschwitz can be considered an abysmal failure in terms of output and efficiency.

In the fall of 1943, sweeping organizational and administrative changes were made in the camp complex. These changes appear to have been precipitated by the discovery of widespread corruption in the Political Department (Politische Abteilung) headed by Maximilian Grabner, perhaps the most feared and cruel SS functionary in Auschwitz. Investigation proceedings instituted against Grabner uncovered unauthorized appropriation of property and other cases of abuse of power involving some senior SS -

officials, including Höss himself. Grabner was relieved of his duties and subsequently put on trial; others were transferred to new posts. In November, Höss was removed as camp commandant and transferred to the Inspectorate for Concentration Camps at Oranienburg. He was replaced by SS-Obersturmbannführer Arthur Liebehenschel.

Simultaneously, the entire camp complex was broken into three parts. Auschwitz I remained the main camp; Birkenau became Auschwitz II; and Auschwitz III, also called Monowitz, the industrial camp, comprised Buna Werke and the network of satellite camps. Liebehenschel was the commander of Auschwitz I. SS-Sturmbannführer Fritz Hartjenstein was the commander of the Birkenau complex, which included the mass-murder installations and crematoria for incinerating the bodies of victims. These changes brought some relative improvement in living conditions in the camp and opened the final phase of its existence, which lasted until its evacuation and liquidation beginning on January 18, 1945.

It is all but impossible to portray the living conditions faced daily by prisoners of the Auschwitz camps. Every day in the life of a prisoner was filled with unbearable tension and superhuman effort, emotional turmoil and terror, continuing without respite for months on end. The prisoner's day was also hollow, empty, and mirthless, lacking any novelty and enveloped in everlasting gloom. Despite the stress, with the ever-present danger the Auschwitz prisoners could never lower their guard, all their energy going to maintain permanent vigilance. Furthermore, the prisoners enjoyed no privacy; day and night they remained in tangible proximity to others. Spoiled food provided no nourishment. Incessant hunger was also a source of ceaseless torment and anguish.

The daily regimen of the prisoner, whose name was replaced by a camp serial number, was punctuated by duties and orders from morning until night which had to be performed quickly and accurately. In addition to personal responsibility for inadequate performance, the prisoner had to bear the burden of collective responsibility. Sleeping and waking were regulated as well. Each morning the prisoner had to draw on every ounce of strength to survive.

It comes as no surprise that memoirs and reminiscences of former prisoners abound with descriptions of terror and superhuman efforts. Despite being surrounded by thousands of fellow inmates, each prisoner remained utterly alone. Only a handful appear to have established ties of friendship, to have considered other prisoners, or to have understood the reality engulfing them. Others drew sustenance from memory in their obstinate effort to go on, to nourish their hope of survival, to eventually reach the shore of the living.

Setting foot on the soil of Auschwitz marked a radical and irrevocable departure from one's previous existence. The camps were surrounded by a double length of barbed wire, an electrified fence illuminated at night and dotted with watchtowers manned by armed SS guards. All around were other camps and kilometers of empty space patrolled by the SS. On entry, the prisoner was stripped not only of all personal possessions but also of his or her identity. Even the prisoner's body was violated, as all body hair was shaven off. A camp serial number was tattooed on the prisoner's left arm (a practice unique to Auschwitz), and a small triangle if the prisoner was Jewish. Name was replaced by number, home by block, room and bed by a three-tiered bunk with a thin layer of straw for a mattress.

Throughout the year, the prisoners wore striped camp fatigues, the fabric stiff with dirt and sweat, without underwear, and their feet shod in wooden shoes without socks. A piece of cloth was attached to the coat and trousers bearing the prisoner's serial number and the symbol of his or her category: red triangle for political prisoners; green triangle for ordinary criminals; black triangle for asocials. There were several other such identifying marks, for homosexuals, for "Bible researchers" (*Bibelforscher,* that is, for Jehovah's Witnesses), and others. All Jewish prisoners were marked by a Star of David composed of red and yellow triangles.

For most prisoners, the first encounter with what one former French prisoner described as *l'univers concentrationnaire* was usually the decisive one. As a rule, adjustment to the camp proved most difficult for persons accustomed to comfort, order, and a predictable social milieu; such individuals either could not or would not become part of camp life. Prisoners who had experienced the harsh living conditions of prisons and ghettos, which served as an antechamber of sorts to the inferno of the concentration camp, were, on the whole, better prepared. Those unwilling or unable to adapt soon sunk into apathy and dejection; they were known as "*Muselmänner*" in the camp slang (the origins of this appellation remain unknown, some surmise that it derived from the alleged resemblance of these prisoners, unable to stand on their feet, to Muslims in supine prayer). Moribund, their senses dulled, such prisoners hovered in the twilight zone between life and death. Before long, their bodies lost their shape, becoming little more than skeletons covered with dry yellowish skin. Gazing aimlessly with their lifeless eyes, they moved slowly, unperturbed by savage cries in German urging them to move on, even after truncheon blows rained hard on their bodies. For their part, veteran prisoners found little pity for these "misfits." We may surmise that the sight of these tragic figures caused fellow inmates considerable fear and anxiety at the prospect of deteriorating into one of them.

The prisoner's day began with reveille at 4:30 A.M. Half an hour was allowed for morning ablutions. At the mandatory roll call, prisoners stood at attention in straight rows to be counted; the number of prisoners had to match the official figures. After roll call, the prisoner work details or labor squads, called *Kommando*, would set off to their places of work. Most prisoners were assigned permanently to a labor squad. In rows of five abreast, they passed through the gate emblazoned with the sign *Arbeit macht frei* (Work makes one free), often to the accompaniment of an orchestra playing near the gate.

Most of the work was performed outdoors in both summer and winter. In summer the workday lasted 12 hours, in winter a little less. Work was performed under the watchful eyes of the *Kapos*—prisoner foremen assigned to oversee the entire squad or parts of it—and the SS escort, who urged on both the Kapos and the working prisoners. No rest was allowed. A prisoner assigned to latrine duty would measure the time taken by workers to relieve themselves.

The squads considered as "good" assignments were those employed in services: kitchen, laundry, and various workshops. Prisoners in such squads worked indoors and enjoyed greater opportunity to "organize" (a camp slang expression for "steal") some extra food, the most precious benefit in the camp. For the most part, only the old-timers and prisoners with "connections" worked in these squads. Relations in the prisoner society, such as they were, originated in prewar ties, solidarity among prisoners from the same transport, and, above all, ties of membership in the political underground and resistance movements.

After returning to camp from work, the prisoners reported to evening roll call, also mandatory. The number of prisoners present again had to match official figures. The failure of even a single prisoner to appear, whether because he or she had fallen asleep or escaped, caused considerable agony to fellow inmates at the evening roll call; they had to remain in their places, standing at attention, regardless of the weather, sometimes for hours until the missing prisoner or the reason for his or her disappearance was discovered.

The evening roll call was often followed by individual or collective punishments. Only after that were the prisoners allowed to retire to their living quarters in the "block" to receive their bread rations with meager supplements and a watery drink. Those with enough strength or will power would leave their block to meet with friends or relatives from another block. At curfew two or three hours later, prisoners were confined to their cold and dark blocks. Prisoners used their rolled-up clothes and shoes as headrests to prevent their theft during the night.

Except for those employed in armaments plants, the prisoners did not work on Sundays. Nevertheless, Sunday was not a day off. Cleaning, shaving, showering in groups, and similar activities were compulsory, keeping the prisoners occupied even on their one day free of work.

Although the prisoner society lived under a uniform regime, it was far from homogeneous in its composition and, to some extent, in conditions.

Some tensions and conflicts, including divisions between different categories of prisoners, resulted from deliberate German policies. Camp authorities created a small though powerful stratum of prisoners in positions of authority: kapos in charge of the work units, *Lagerälteste* in charge of the entire prisoners' camp population, *Blockälteste* and *Stubendienste*—the prisoners commanding the blocks—and many positions in the central administration of the camps. They also divided the prisoner population into ethnic and "racial" groups, as Germans did with all subjugated populations. One important division in the camp set the so-called reds, or political prisoners, against the greens, or criminal prisoners.

Despite their small numbers, German prisoners generally held positions of authority and occupied key posts in the prisoner apparatus. Hermann Langbein, an Austrian political prisoner, wrote in his *Menschen in Auschwitz*, (People in Auschwitz) that

> Höss concealed the fact that his subordinate [SS-Hauptsturmführer] Hans Aumeier, who served as camp director, admitted frankly after his arrest that prisoners with sadistic dispositions were deliberately singled out for the positions of "block elders" [chiefs of prisoner blocks]. "Most of them were professional criminals," Aumeier added.[11]

In Auschwitz I, most official posts held by prisoners were assigned to Poles. In the men's and women's camps at Birkenau, many such posts were held by Jewish prisoners. Contrary to the prevalent opinion, not all prisoners in positions of authority, such as kapos and block elders, maltreated their fellow inmates. Mistreatment was the case mainly in the first two years of the camp's existence. This situation gradually changed, and the urge to harass and torment the prisoners abated somewhat.

Bruno Bettelheim and others argue that the concentration camp system spawned a reality in which all the beliefs, values, and norms of behavior adhered to in the world outside the camps were abandoned. The prisoners came to accept this situation as reality and in a certain sense even identified with the apparatus of brute power, thereby becoming an integral part of the system. Thus Bettelheim maintains that

> even in the concentration camps, belief in the power and justice of the police was so strong that prisoners were not willing to believe that they had been unjustly persecuted. Rather, they searched their mind to find some guilt in themselves. The inner desire to be loved by the superego is extremely strong, and the weaker the ego becomes, the stronger is this desire. Since in the totalitarian system the most powerful superego surrogates are the rules and their representatives—in short the system itself—one can gain approval of the superego surrogates only by going along with the system.[12]

But such arguments chiefly articulate the soul searching that went on among German prisoners in concentration camps in Germany in the 1930s as they witnessed the growing power of the Nazi regime.

Bettelheim also refers to the phenomenon of a weak personality over-awed by power and the desire to bask in its splendor, even to deliver oneself to its "mercies." This phenomenon is in evidence in different aspects of the totalitarian regime, including concentration camps. Some prisoners elevated to positions of official authority at Auschwitz apparently exhibited such behavior, but even at Auschwitz and other concentration camps, this phenomenon was exceptional, not routine. Primo Levi's comments are pertinent in this context:

> I am not an expert on the unconscious and the mind's depths, but I do know that few people are experts in this sphere, and that these few are the most cautious. I do not know, and it does not much interest me to know, whether in my depths there lurks a murderer, but I do know that I was a guiltless victim and I was not a murderer. I know that the murderers existed, not only in Germany, and still exist, retired or on active duty, and that to confuse them with their victims is a moral disease or an aesthetic affectation or a sinister sign of complicity; above all, it is precious service rendered (intentionally or not) to the negators of truth.[13]

When key positions in the lower echelons of the camp hierarchy were held by habitual criminals, the Auschwitz prisoners were often subjected to humiliation, arbitrary punishment, and physical abuse, including torture. This treatment stemmed from a total disregard for human beings and a desire to fulfill the expectations of Nazi taskmasters. This character type outlived its usefulness, however, when productive work assumed critical importance for the beleaguered Third Reich. At that time, most supervisory positions were entrusted to the "politicals," bringing some relief into the lives of prisoners.

A considerable proportion of the political prisoners in positions of authority were linked to the underground and resistance organizations active in Auschwitz, enabling these groups, in the late stages of the camp's existence, to influence conditions in the camp. The underground groups operated through several channels, smuggling out information to the external world, procuring medicines and material assistance for prisoners associated with the underground, attempting to rescue prisoners due to be killed, and assisting in escapes. Although the underground's ability to lead a general uprising and mass escape from Auschwitz fell short of expectations, its activities, especially in preserving invaluable documentation and informing the outside world about the camp, indicate that prisoner subjugation to the overwhelming might of Nazi power was far from complete.

Józef Garlinski, a former Polish Auschwitz prisoner who studied the underground activity in the camp, especially the role of the Poles and their ties with the surrounding Polish population, wrote that

> the earliest threads which linked the camp with the outside world did not have the character of an organized action. The people, seeing the prisoners working nearby, tried to help them. Food, sometimes medicines and dressings, were left in hiding places. The initiative was private and spontaneous, but the circle of those who helped kept growing and began to take the form of a clandestine society. At the end of 1940 the district command of the underground army in Krakow helped to organize the *Akcja Cywilna Pomocy Wiezniom* [Civil Action for Help to Prisoners].[14]

The help of the population was vital in accomplishing many escapes from the camp.

Hunger in Auschwitz was ubiquitous and pervasive. Prisoners were tormented by it before and after meals. Thoughts and fantasies about food haunted the prisoners, even in their sleep. Countless conversations revolved around hunger and ways of appeasing it. Food was uppermost on every prisoner's mind, although not everyone went equally hungry.

Theoretically, each prisoner was entitled to a daily ration of 350 grams of bread, half a liter of ersatz coffee for breakfast, and one liter of turnip and potato soup for lunch. Also, four times a week each prisoner was to receive a soup ration of 20 grams of meat, but in practice meat rarely reached the bowls from which the prisoners ate. The official daily value of food for prisoners employed in light work stood at 1,700 calories and for prisoners doing strenuous work, 2,150 calories. An analysis done after the war of the actual food content ranged from 1,300 calories for light-work prisoners to 1,700 calories for prisoners performing hard labor. The difference was caused by plunder of food by SS personnel and functionary-prisoners. Inequality pervaded the food distribution system. The kapo, or the prisoner entrusted with ladling out the soup, made sure that the thicker, more nourishing contents from the bottom would reach "proper" prisoners, whereas the others had to content themselves with a watery substance from the top of the pot. (The red bowl and tin spoon were the only items of private property the prisoners could have, and they lugged them everwhere they went.)

Under these conditions, supplementary food was tantamount to survival. But other habits sometimes overrode even this paramount concern; prisoners addicted to tobacco went as far as trading part of their daily ration for tobacco. The bread ration thus served as a currency of sorts. The functionaries, who made up perhaps 3 to 5 percent of the prisoner population, exchanged their supplementary bread and soup for higher-quality and tastier victuals.

Prisoners condemned to subsist on the official ration lost weight rapidly, and their survival odds diminished accordingly. Non-Jewish prisoners could receive some money from relatives or sponsors outside and purchase low-quality supplements of food and cigarettes. From the end of 1942, camp authorities allowed prisoners to receive food parcels, which proved of critical importance. The parcels usually contained food of high caloric value, and lucky recipients could even exchange some of it for bread. But the Jewish prisoners, who soon constituted the majority in the two main camps at Auschwitz, received no parcels. Nor did Soviet prisoners.

In *The Drowned and the Saved*, Primo Levi argues that sometimes thirst was even more pervasive, more physically and mentally debilitating, than hunger. The water at Auschwitz was contaminated with various impurities, and members of the SS staff were instructed not to drink it. This warning, of course, did not apply to the prisoners. In Birkenau, the prisoners, especially the women, suffered from chronic shortage and poor quality of water. Levi writes from experience:

> In August of 1944 it was very hot in Auschwitz. . . . There was no drinkable water in the camp or often on the work site . . . as a rule, the evening soup and the ersatz coffee distributed around ten o'clock were abundantly sufficient to quench our thirst, but now they were no longer enough and thirst tormented us. Thirst is more imperative than hunger: hunger obeys the nerves, grants remission, can be temporarily obliterated by an emotion, a pain, a fear . . . not so with thirst which does not give respite . . . in those days it accompanied us day and night: by day, on the work site, whose order . . . was transformed into a chaos of shattered constructions; by night, in the hut without ventilation, as we gasped the air breathed a hundred times before.[15]

Other critical factors affecting prisoners' chances of survival were their national origin and racial classification. In *Values and Violence in Auschwitz*, Polish researcher Anna Pawelczynska, who was also a prisoner in the camp, attempted to rank the prisoners according to their origins. "Pseudo-scientific theories of race," she writes, "began to take drastic effect by ranking the different nationalities of prisoners, thus spelling out their turns to die." Jews and Gypsies, regardless of their citizenship, occupied the bottom of the scale, a position which automatically made them the prime victims of the gas chambers and crematoria. Slightly above them, she adds, were Slavs, especially the Poles and the Russians, who were subjected to different murder methods at different times. The next category comprised persons of various European nationalities for whom no precise extermination plans were developed. The only ones exempt from such plans were persons of German origin.[16]

In point of fact, all the Jews and many of the Gypsies brought to Auschwitz were not only victims of murder but also subjects of plans for annihilation. With few exceptions, Soviet prisoners of war were also annihilated en masse. Prisoners of other national origins were not subjected to systematic murder, even though in some cases they met a gruesome fate. Among the victimized groups were a large number of members of the Polish intelligentsia who had been subjected to mass arrests and violent terror.

The harsh conditions in the camp and the savagery of its regime resulted in an inordinately high mortality rate, particularly in the first years of the camp's existence. Langbein maintains that the periodic savage onslaughts by the German camp command, assisted by functionary-prisoners, were directed against the "new arrivals," or *Zugange*, as they were known in the camp. The first ones to bear the brunt of these murderous assaults were the Poles, followed by the Russians. The Jews' turn also came early.

But the Jews, including those registered and incarcerated in the camp as prisoners, met a different fate from that of victims of other origins. The few Jews who arrived at Auschwitz in the first transports were all murdered forthwith. Polish and other Jews who were deemed unfit for work were put to death mostly by phenol injections administered in the camp hospitals. Langbein, who occupied an official position in the Auschwitz hospital and was a leading figure in the prisoners' underground structure, maintains that reports compiled by the resistance showed that between 25,000 and 30,000 persons were murdered by phenol injections; the proportion of Jews among them was very high. In March 1943, murder by phenol injection was discontinued. But Jews continued to be identified in hospitals as unfit for work and dispatched to the gas chambers.

Camp hospitals evoked fear in prisoners. As long as they could summon enough strength to stand, prisoners avoided sick call, which might place them in the hospital. Even those suffering from high fever, crippling diarrhea, or festering wounds tried to avoid hospitalization as long as possible. At the same time, for some prisoners the prospect of several days' rest in bed, exempt from roll calls, backbreaking work, and physical abuse, could be very alluring.

The mortality rate among prisoners peaked periodically for various reasons. In the early stages, the terroristic regime and the poor living conditions pushed it upward. In those years, however, there were comparatively few prisoners in the camp. During the first two years, up to March 1942, about 27,000 persons were incarcerated in Auschwitz, whereas over the next year, until March 1943, the number of prisoners jumped by 135,000, five times the population of the two preceding years. This large influx marked a turning point in the composition of the prisoner population. According to reports compiled by the resistance, at this time 2.7 percent of the Auschwitz prisoners were Germans, 30.1 percent were Poles, and 57.4 percent were Jews. With time, this trend gained momentum, so that in the middle of 1944, Jews constituted two-thirds of all the Auschwitz prisoners.

Epidemics of lice, typhus, dysentery, and common phlegmon, particularly in Birkenau, resulted in skyrocketing mortality rates in the period from July 1942 to March 1943; according to available data, they ranged from 19 percent to 25 percent per month. The decline that followed can be attributed to some improvement in the camp conditions in general and in hospitals in particular. In May 1943, the monthly mortality rate dropped to 5.2 percent, and in the main Auschwitz camp it dropped even more. Opportunities to help patients were seized by most prisoner-doctors and other members of the medical staff. Otto Kraus and Erich Kulka, authors of *The Death Factory in Auschwitz*, conclude that

> most prisoner-doctors conducted themselves honorably. They succeeded in saving many lives not only by providing medical care but also by deceiving SS men with false diagnoses and examinations, by keeping secret the existence of contagious diseases, etc. In this way they saved a great many patients from gassing, hard work in the camp, and physical punishments.[17]

In addition to the racist policies that classified prisoners into national-ethnic categories, the atmosphere at Auschwitz made conflicts and divisions in the prisoner society inevitable. In a world with all moral norms and restraints lifted and no holds barred, where congestion, severe deprivation, and nervous tension were ubiquitous, the prisoners easily succumbed to violence and rudeness. Conditions of life in the camp managed to undermine any solidarity that might be expected to arise among human beings who found themselves in identical situations. The assumption that common suffering bridges distances separating people was not borne out by camp reality. Tempers were short, and foreign customs and habits, manifestations of religious piety, and the sound of foreign languages kept the prisoners on edge. Deprived of privacy, the prisoners proved especially sensitive to an unfamiliar language which grated on their ears and often gave rise to suspicion that the speakers were mocking those unable to understand it.

National stereotypes gained acceptance. The Germans were described as arrogant and conceited, seeking privileged treatment; the Poles were described as keeping to themselves and xenophobic; the French gained a reputation as unconcerned with personal hygiene. Jews were perceived as inferior by everybody else. Antisemitic stereotypes brought from the outside tended to become entrenched in the camp, though in some cases non-Jewish prisoners discarded their home-grown prejudices. Jewish prisoners were set apart by national origin, cultural and economic background, and language. Thus, for example, the Hungarian Jews who arrived at the camp as late as August 1944 from relatively tolerable conditions accused the Polish Jews, most of them old-timers, of aloofness and selfishness. Perhaps most difficult was the situation of the Greek Jews, who suffered more than others from the harsh northern climate, did not speak any languages spoken in the camp, and often believed that other prisoners were responsible for their troubles and acute distress. Even if these divisions, rivalries, and rifts among the prisoner society were unplanned and did not stem from deliberate German policies, the camp authorities were of course well aware that this phenomenon worked in their favor.

Jewish prisoners in particular lived in the shadow of certainty that their relatives had perished, that their own fate was sealed, and that their incarceration in the camp was but a reprieve granted by the Germans to drain them of their strength through slave labor before sending them to their deaths. Writers of memoirs and researchers of concentration camps usually agree that a source of great anguish and torment for prisoners, even in the period of some improvement in living conditions, was uncertainty as to the timing and circumstances of their liberation. Although no prisoner remained unaffected by it, the shadow of a death that could come at any moment, even on the threshold of liberation, loomed particularly large over the Jewish inmates. Furthermore, unlike the great majority of other prisoners, who still had a home, a homeland, relatives, and friends waiting for them outside, the Jewish prisoners had lost these most precious possessions. Their homes, their entire precamp world, lay in ruins, and their families had perished.

In *Survival in Auschwitz*, Primo Levi writes about January 18, 1945, the day when the evacuation of Auschwitz began.

> Nobody knew what our fate would be. Some SS men had remained, some of the guard towers were still occupied. About midday an SS officer made a tour of the huts. He appointed a chief in each of them, selecting from among the remaining non-Jews. The matter seemed clear. No one was surprised that the Germans preserved their national love of classification until the very end, nor did any Jew seriously expect to live until the following day. The two Frenchmen had not understood and were frightened. I translated the speech of the SS man. I was annoyed that they should be afraid: they had not even experienced a month of the lager, they hardly suffered from hunger yet, they were not even Jews, but they were afraid. . . . Then the bombardment began. It was nothing new: I climbed down to the ground, put my bare foot into my shoes, and waited. It seemed far away, perhaps over Auschwitz, but then it was a near explosion, and before one could think, a second and a third one loud enough to burst one's ear-drums. Windows were breaking, the hut shook, the spook I had fixed in the wall fell down. . . . The Germans were no longer there, the towers were empty.[18]

The first gassings of prisoners in Auschwitz were carried out in September 1941. The victims were thousands of Soviet prisoners of war, subsumed under the category of political activist, consigned to immediate annihilation who were used in some way as guinea pigs in the trial run of the death machinery in the camp.

A great deal of information is now available about mass murder by gas in Auschwitz, the operation of killing installations, dates, the type of victims and their numbers, selections for and methods of murder. There exist precise documents about the construction of the gas chambers and crematoria and the use of the gas Zyklon B. We also have the written and oral testimony of witnesses among prisoners and German personnel, including the most important among them: the memoirs and testimony of the chief organizer and commandant of the Auschwitz camp, Rudolf Höss. Höss gave statements shortly after his capture by the British in March 1946 and appeared as a witness before the International Military Tribunal in Nuremberg. After his extradition to Poland, during his imprisonment before and after the trial, and as he was awaiting execution by hanging on the grounds of the Auschwitz camp, Höss, on his own volition, wrote his biography and various pieces in which he spelled out in great detail the mass murders in Auschwitz.

Another written testimony of critical importance was given by Dr. Johann Paul Kremer, a uniformed SS doctor in the camp, who kept a diary during his duty there and took part in the selection of victims. An affidavit written during his captivity by the British in July 1945 by another SS man, Pery Broad, who served in the Political Department (the Gestapo office) in the camp, contains numerous details about the mass murders there. We also have statements by escaped prisoners, as well as reports from the camp smuggled out by the resistance. A collection of data based on daily resistance and other documents entitled *Kalendarium*, along with other data compiled by the Polish researcher Danuta Czech, offers a systematic and thorough chronological account of events in the camp. The *Kalendarium* includes lists prepared at the behest of the Nazis, lists and reports illegally copied by inmate clerks and preserved, and documents abandoned when the Nazis retreated from Auschwitz.[19]

One important and greatly moving category of documents comprises notes written by Jewish Sonderkommando prisoners assigned to work in the crematoria who carefully buried their accounts in the vicinity of the crematoria. Some of these documents were recovered and deciphered after the war and were published in a few languages. We also have the testimonies of German defendants in the Auschwitz trials, as well as those of the handful of surviving Sonderkommando prisoners.

The critical importance of the Höss testimony stems not just from Höss's unique knowledge of the details and overall picture of the camp. His testimony is crucial mainly because Höss answers the questions not only of who carried out the mass murders, but also when and how, who ordered the conversion of Auschwitz into a death camp, and who backed this order with the necessary authority. Despite some inaccuracies due to tricks of memory, the general reliability of his testimony remains beyond doubt.

Höss relates how in the summer of 1941—he could not give the exact date, but we have reason to assume that it was in July or August—he was suddenly summoned from Auschwitz to the SS headquarters in Berlin. Himmler, contrary to his custom, received Höss outside the company of his aide-de-camp and addressed him as follows:

> The Führer has ordered the final solution of the Jewish question and we, the SS, were assigned this mission. The existing liquidation sites in the East cannot cope with the large operations expected in the future. I have therefore chosen Auschwitz for this purpose, first, because of its convenient location in terms of transportation, and, second, because the site can be easily isolated and concealed.[20]

Höss claims to have been keenly concerned with what kind of gas could be used as an efficient killing agent. During his absence from Auschwitz, Zyklon B, a product usually used for sanitation, was used to kill a large group of Soviet prisoners, and, he learned, it suited the requirements of mass killing.[21]

In early 1942, two peasant cottages near Birkenau whose inhabitants had been evicted began functioning as provisional gas chambers. About 2,000 persons could be squeezed into them at one time. In this phase of the operation, the gas victims were Jews brought in transports from Upper Silesia and Slovakia. Then, from March 1943 on, four gas chambers and crematoria, designed and built specifically for mass murder by German engineers and companies, were in operation at the Birkenau camp. At their top capacity, these installations could "process" 4,416 victims in 24 hours.[22]

It was in these installations at Birkenau that hundreds of thousands of Jews were systematically murdered after being transported from European countries. The chronicle of events, the *Kalendarium*, enables us to follow the transport of Jews rounded up in various "actions," or mass seizures of Jewish nationals, in several countries. Thus in 1942, Jews from Upper Silesia, Slovakia, the Netherlands, France, Belgium, Yugoslavia, and parts of occupied Poland reached Auschwitz. In 1943, Jews from Germany, parts of Poland, Theresienstadt in Czechoslovakia, the Netherlands, France, and Greece (continuous transports), as well as Yugoslavia, the Majdanek camp and ghettos of Zaglebie in Poland, the Bergen-Belsen camp, and Italy, met their fate. In 1944, transports rolled into Auschwitz with Jews from France, the Netherlands, Belgium, Theresienstadt, Italy, Slovakia, and Poland (Lodz, Radom, Galicia); one huge consignment was of several hundred thousand Hungarian Jews. Unlike other victims, Jews, with some exceptions, were not brought to Auschwitz individually, accused of real or imaginary offenses. With the establishment of the death factory, Jews arrived in mass transports from Nazi-occupied countries or satellites of the Third Reich. Most transports carried entire families uprooted from their residences as part of the process of total eradication of Jewish communities, their only offense being their "racial" and national origins.

Designated as RSHA transports, the Jews faced selection immediately upon arrival; those deemed fit to work, usually a small minority of those on the transports, became registered prisoners, whereas all others, including as a rule all children and the elderly, went to their death in the gas chambers. Transport entries in the *Kalendarium* referring to mass transports of Hungarian Jews in May–July 1944 reveal a clear pattern which indicates their fate. Danuta Czech points out that individual deportees, mainly twins (designated as subjects of the Nazi physician Josef Mengele's experiments), were put in the camp as registered prisoners. Furthermore, a certain number of young people and those classified as fit for work were consigned to other camps. The remainder went to the gas chambers. Thus, for example, in an entry of May 2, we read that following the selection of two transports—one carrying 1,800 Jews, "men and women fit for work, ages 16 to 50," and another carrying 2,000 deportees—486 men and 616 women were incarcerated in the camp, whereas the remaining Jews were gassed. The selections among Jews were carried out by SS doctors. Regular transports of non-Jews did not go through the selection process; non-Jews went on to become registered prisoners.

The overwhelming majority of Jews transported to Auschwitz, particularly those from Western Europe, Greece, and Hungary, were unaware of their destination or its nature until the very end. The SS was in charge of the killing process, and SS men poured the gas pellets down the shafts of the gas chambers. The Sonderkommando, comprising mostly Jewish prisoners kept in isolation from the rest of the camp, performed the "dirty work," consisting, as Höss wrote in his biography, of "helping [the victims] to undress, filling the bunker with Jews, removal of the bodies," and burning the corpses. There is no doubt that the Sonderkommando workers were the most wretched of all the Auschwitz prisoners. Not only was their work the incarnation of a nightmare, but also they knew, as witnesses and participants in the labor of death, that their fate was sealed. In autobiographical notes, some wrote descriptions of their deeds; one wrote that no interpretation of the camp's meaning would be complete without their testimonies.

In October 1944, Sonderkommando prisoners staged a doomed uprising against their oppressors; explosives were smuggled in by Jewish women workers from a factory to the Birkenau camp. Their uprising and subsequent attempt to escape, which ended with the murder of all participants, was the only significant act of resistance of its kind in the history of the camp.

On January 18, 1945, ahead of approaching Soviet troops, the Nazis began a hasty and chaotic evacuation of Auschwitz. The last roll call in the main camp listed 48,342 male prisoners, 16,000 women, and 96 prisoners of war. About 58,000 prisoners then started forced marches from stop to stop, from camp to camp. They walked through Austria and Germany in the cold and snow of the winter and early spring months of 1945. Along the way, a large percentage of the last Auschwitz victims perished.

About 6,000 sick and completely exhausted inmates and a few of the hospital personnel remained behind in the camp area waiting for the end. Finally, on January 24, the SS left in a hurry. Levi, who was among the few thousand inmates liberated at Auschwitz, writes:

> January 24th. Liberty. The breach in the barbed wire gave us a concrete image of it. To anyone who stopped to think, it signified no more Germans, no more selections, no work, no blows, no roll-calls, and perhaps, later, the return. But we had to make an effort to convince ourselves of it, and no one had time to enjoy the thought. All around lay destruction and death.[23]

Attempts have been made to classify the survivors according to their behavior or personality traits, in an effort to pinpoint factors that might explain their survival. In some cases, physical fitness, endurance, a capacity to distance oneself mentally from the camp realities, or a callous attitude toward fellow prisoners undoubtedly played some part. But for the majority of survivors, one is hard put to formulate general rules in this regard. Life in the camp resembled walking through a minefield, and the fact that some prisoners managed to brave all the obstacles and dangers was due mostly to pure luck.

NOTES

1. Eugen Kogon, *Der SS Staat: Das System der deutschen Konzentrationslager* (Frankfurt am Main, 1946).

2. Primo Levi, *The Drowned and the Saved* (New York, 1988), p. 47. Published originally in Italian as *I sommersi e i salvati*.

3. Hannah Arendt, *The Origins of Totalitarianism* (Cleveland, 1951), p. 437.

4. The estimate was reached by Franciszek Piper in *Ile ludzi zginelo w KL Auschwitz* (How many people perished in Auschwitz) (Oswiecim, 1992), p. 90. See also the essay on this question by Piper in the present volume (chap. 4).

5. Falk Pingel, *Haftlinge unter SS Herrschaft* (Hamburg, 1978), p. 230. According to Pingel, of the 405,000 persons registered as prisoners of Auschwitz, 265,000 lost their lives in the camp.

6. Robert Jay Lifton, *The Nazi Doctors: Medical Killing and the Psychology of Genocide* (New York, 1986), p. 4.

7. Martin Broszat, "Nationalsozialistische Konzentrationslager 1933–1945," in Martin Broszat, ed., *Anatomie des SS-Staats*, vol. 2 (Freiburg im Breisgau, 1965), pp. 97–98.

8. Karl Dietrich Bracher, *Die deutsche Diktatur-Entstehung Struktur, Folgen des Nationalsozialismus* (Cologne, 1969), p. 393.

9. Broszat, p. 108.

10. Danuta Czech, "KL Auschwitz: An Historical Outline" (in Polish), in *Auschwitz* (Warsaw, 1987), pp. 30–31. I drew heavily on this article for information about the establishment, construction, expansion, and structure of the camp. I also relied on Jan Sehn, *The Auschwitz-Birkenau Concentration Camp* (in Polish) (Warsaw, 1956), and *Konzentrationslager Oswiecim* (Warsaw, 1955); and on *Bulletin of the Main Commission of German Crimes in Poland* (in Polish), vol. 1 (1946), PF-65–130.

11. Hermann Langbein, *Menschen in Auschwitz* (Vienna, 1972), p. 170.

12. Bruno Bettelheim, *Surviving and Other Essays* (New York, 1980), pp. 329–30.

13. Levi, *The Drowned and the Saved*, pp. 48–49.

14. Józef Garlinski, "The Underground Movement in Auschwitz Concentration Camp," in *Resistance in Europe: 1939–1945*, ed. Stephen Hawes and Ralph White (Middlesex, 1976), p. 64.

15. Levi, *The Drowned and the Saved*, p. 79.

16. Anna Pawelczynska, *Values and Violence in Auschwitz: A Sociological Analysis* (Berkeley, 1979), pp. 54–55.

17. Ota Kraus and Erich Kulka, *The Death Factory in Auschwitz* (in Hebrew) (Jerusalem, 1960), p. 8.

18. Primo Levi, *Survival in Auschwitz* (New York, 1958), pp. 141–43.

19. See the German edition of the volume: Danuta Czech, *Kalendarium der Ereignisse im Konzentrationslager Auschwitz-Birkenau 1939–1945* (Reinbek bei Hamburg, 1989).

20. See *Kommandant in Auschwitz: Autobiographische Aufzeichnungen des Rudolf Höss*, ed. Martin Broszat (Munich, 1963), pp. 157–59.

21. Ibid., p. 159.

22. *Nationalsozialistische Massentötungen durch Giftgas*, ed. Eugen Kogon, Hermann Langbein, Adalbert Rückert et al. (Frankfurt, 1986), p. 219.

23. Levi, *Survival in Auschwitz*, p. 153.

2

The System of Prisoner Exploitation

FRANCISZEK PIPER

Auschwitz is known primarily as a site of mass extermination, mainly of Jews. But it also played an integral part in the Nazi system of concentration camps in which exploitation of slave labor assumed considerable importance. Seeking answers to the following questions can lead to a better understanding of the two functions of Auschwitz:

1. What position did the Auschwitz camp, with its dual functions, occupy in the general camp system?
2. What were the specific features of the dual functions of Auschwitz?
3. How were two seemingly mutually exclusive functions (ruthless extermination of prisoners and labor utilization) reconciled?

Concentration camps, including Auschwitz, were set up as one branch of the Nazi power apparatus. Before the Second World War, they functioned primarily as centers for detention of internal political opponents of the regime. Incarcerated dissidents were subjected to temporary isolation, "re-education," and terror. After the outbreak of the war, the function of the camps was expanded to include the extermination of members of the anti-Nazi resistance movement, extermination of whole national groups deemed racially hostile or inferior by the ruling ideology, and extermination of those who stood in the way of the German conquest and occupation apparatus.

Concentration camps also fulfilled other, secondary functions. They served as execution sites for persons sentenced to death under the *Sonderbe-*

handlung (special treatment) procedure, which excluded any juridical act and in which the police authorities were solely responsible for all decisions. They also were used as execution sites for certain categories of prisoners of war, such as Soviet political officers and escaped prisoners. And they were used for criminal medical experiments. But the most important secondary use of the camps was the utilization of prisoner labor.

As a result of the decision to exterminate the European Jews, the Nazis created a new category of camps that operated exclusively as death camps, or killing centers. There were four—Treblinka, Belzec, Sobibór, and Chelmno. In principle, all deportees who were sent to these camps were put to death upon arrival. The exceptions were small groups of prisoners who occasionally were kept alive to help burn bodies and organize and ship the property of victims.

Like all the other concentration camps, Auschwitz and Majdanek practiced isolation and partial destruction of its prisoners through labor and the terrorizing of prisoners who were decreed hostile. But Auschwitz and Majdanek occupied a unique position in the Nazi system of concentration camps. They became centers of total extermination and served as tools to effect the Nazis' "final solution of the Jewish question in Europe."

The Nazi policies on use of the labor of concentration camp prisoners evolved in three distinctive phases. In phase one, 1933–37, prisoner labor was used mainly in the construction, expansion, and maintenance of the camps themselves. Phase two, 1938–41, saw the use of prisoner labor on a mass scale in the construction materials industry (quarries, stone and gravel works, brickyards). In the final phase, 1942–45, prisoner labor was used mainly in the armaments industry and its branches and subsidiaries.

By confining prisoner labor to the camps during the first period, the Nazis were guided less by the needs of the camps or by their own ideological tenets than by the situation that existed in the labor market in the Third Reich. In the mid-1930s, the years of the Great Depression, millions of unemployed Germans still vied for scarce jobs. Any attempts by the Schutzstaffel (SS), the Nazi police unit that ran the camps, to use prisoner labor outside the camps (to drain swamps, for example)[1] was met with resistance from civilian authorities, who regarded such actions as obstacles in the efforts to reduce the country's unemployment.

Employment of prisoners outside the camps also lost its urgency for other reasons. After several years in power, the Nazis concluded that opposition to the National Socialist (Nazi) party in German society and in the party itself had been so weakened that the camps and other institutions of "protective" detention were no longer needed.[2] With time, most of the camps were liquidated and their prisoners released. By 1937, the number of camps had dwindled from several dozen to three, while the prisoner population had declined from several tens of thousands to 8,000.[3]

Establishment of new camps and regrowth of the prisoner population dates to 1938, when Nazi Germany annexed new territories for the first time. It wasn't long before the acquisitions resulted in surpluses in the camps' labor force which significantly exceeded the internal needs of the camps. At the same time, the Germans were intensifying their war preparations. These activities resulted in a reduction in unemployment in some areas of the economy, and shortages of manpower soon began to be felt. This trend was particularly pronounced in the construction materials industry, which faced the task of supplying materials necessary for the realization of grandiose projects conceived by the Nazi Führer, Adolf Hitler, such as autobahns, large public buildings in Berlin and Nuremberg, and other major undertakings.

In 1938, to help supply the materials needed for Hitler's grand plans, SS chief Heinrich Himmler ordered the establishment of the Deutsche Erd- und Steinwerke GmbH (DEST), which began rapidly acquiring quarries, clinker works, and gravel pits where large numbers of concentration camp prisoners were put to work.[4] From then on, most new camps were set up next to such industries, especially quarries (Mauthausen and Flossenburg in 1938, Gross-Rosen in 1940, and Natzweiler in 1941). Work in these camps uniquely combined the advantages of "punishment" with economic benefits. Himmler realized that exploitation of prisoner labor in SS enterprises offered an opportunity to gain financial independence for his organization, and with that would come the prospect of consolidating his position and the independence of the SS within the apparatus of power.[5]

As early as November 1941, Himmler recommended that imprisoned Soviet commissars who were capable of hard work and were subject to execution under established decrees be sent to quarries.[6] At the end of the month, Hitler was so certain of swift victory that he told Albert Speer, his personal architect who was soon to become minister of armaments and war production, that all construction plans remained in effect.[7] The Third Reich's strategies and related economic planning had to be modified in December, however, when the German Army's advance on Moscow was contained and forced to retreat and the United States entered the war. Lightning campaigns gave way to a long-term confrontation that pitted the military and economic might of the rival forces.

Because those who were in the age groups capable of handling weapons had been conscripted, an inadequate supply of manpower became a very serious problem for the German economy. From May 1939 to May 1942, German civilian employment fell by 7.8 million people, due mainly to intensified conscription.[8] As a result, the demand for labor was met by foreign workers and prisoners of war.

Prisoner labor was put under the jurisdiction of the office of General Plenipotentiary for Employment, established on March 21, 1942.[9] Although concentration camps were excluded from its jurisdiction, Hitler directed that the camps be co-opted by the general war-production effort.

The first expression of change in the scope of tasks of concentration camps surfaced in an announcement by Himmler on January 25, 1942. That was just five days after the now-infamous Wannsee Conference at which Reinhard Heydrich, Himmler's chief lieutenant, acting in accordance with directives formulated as early as 1941, presented the SS plan for total extermination of Jews. Himmler's announcement called for 150,000 Jews who were subsumed under the *Endlösung* (final solution) operation to be transported to concentration camps in connection with the "great tasks and economic undertakings" facing the camps. Subsequent organizational and personnel changes furthered the realization of Himmler's scheme.[10] In an order issued on March 3, 1942, Himmler incorporated the existing Inspectorate of Concentration Camps into the SS Economic-Administrative Main Office (WVHA), thereby putting the inspector of the camps, Richard Glücks, under his own economic expert, Oswald Pohl.

Since the money that private enterprises paid to hire prisoner labor had to be transferred to the state treasury, Himmler strove to create his own armaments industry to be run by DEST and the Deutsche Austrüstungswerke (DAW) by adjusting their operations to the new needs.[11]

Conflict between the SS and the agencies of private capital surfaced earliest in Auschwitz, where the state contracted the huge chemical company IG Farbenindustrie to construct a new enterprise to produce synthetic rubber and liquid fuels. The Auschwitz site was selected because of the availability of water, coal, and lime, as well as a supply of labor from the camp. It appears that at first Himmler tried to derail the plan by submitting a proposal for the construction of his own chemical works.[12]

Himmler also proposed to the Reich coal commissar that certain coal mines be transferred to the SS and that prisoners be put to work in them.[13] Neither of Himmler's plans was put into practice, however. In both cases, the private companies emerged victorious from the confrontation. At the time, the private companies enjoyed the backing of the still-powerful Hermann Göring and other Nazi notables and had several important advantages, such as a plentiful supply of prisoner labor, industrial plants that were already in operation, the necessary financial resources, cooperative ties, and skilled personnel. In contrast, the SS had only one asset at its disposal—the labor force, most of which was unskilled. Undeterred, Himmler believed that Pohl would overcome the difficulties and emerge victorious in the drive to bring the industries under the control of the SS.

Meanwhile, unable to openly oppose Hitler's directives and the industry's proposals, Himmler made an effort to gain time by agreeing to hire out prisoner labor on the condition that the industrial plants involved be built in the camps themselves. The expense of building such new plants meant that the enterprises would be unprofitable from the beginning. As a result, several months after the directives concerning the use of prisoner labor in the armaments industry were issued, nothing had changed. The SS neither developed its own armaments industry nor supplied significant contingents of workers to the private sector.

Only a handful of companies with sufficient clout to gain concessions from Himmler made limited use of the labor of concentration camp prisoners. It is not a coincidence that until the end of 1942, the only companies that succeeded in using prisoner labor in Auschwitz were IG Farben and Hermann Göring Werke. IG Faben employed prisoners until April 1941 in construction of the chemical works at Dwory, near Auschwitz, and starting in August 1942, the Göring firm put prisoners to work in the Brzeszcze-Jawiszowice coal mine.

Under these circumstances, Hitler acquiesced in Speer's demands and issued instructions in September 1942 to discontinue construction of industrial works at the camps. From then on, camps were to be established next to already functioning industrial enterprises because it was considerably cheaper and technically and organizationally simpler.[14] Thus one of the chief obstacles to using prisoner labor in the armaments industry and other areas considered vital to the German war effort was removed.

Before long, however, another obstacle presented itself—a shortage of prisoners fit for work. In spring 1942, concurrent with the mobilization of all available manpower and resources for the war effort, decrees were issued aimed at the fullest possible use of the labor of concentration camp prisoners. Ruthless implementation of these decrees, regardless of the fact that prisoner labor at that time had little to do with war production, resulted in a sharp increase in prisoner mortality. Despite the unceasing influx of new transports into the camps, the prisoner population continued to decline. From June to December 1942, 57,503 prisoners died in concentration camps. At a time when the average prisoner population was 96,770, the death rate was about 10,000 per month. From August to November 1942, the prisoner population actually declined from 115,000 to 83,000.[15]

Auschwitz was no exception. On January 4, 1943, there were 29,306 men and women prisoners,[16] even though the serial numbers assigned up to this date had exceeded 123,000 (85,427 men, 27,978 women, and about 10,000 prisoners of war).[17] Taking into account that a few prisoners were released from the camp and some were transferred out, one may conclude that these figures provide a clear picture of the extermination activities of the camp authorities and the consequences of the living conditions created by the camp regime.

It became obvious that the continuing policy of destruction of concentration camp prisoners on such a scale was bound to result in further dwindling of the prisoner population. This realization in turn must have led to the abandonment of Himmler's ambitious economic plans. The consistently pursued implementation of the "destruction through labor" principle turned out to be more effective in the area of destruction than in the area of labor.

In light of the Reich's shrinking labor supply, it was necessary to slow the downward trend in the size of the prisoner population. As a result, the SS authorities decided that the living conditions of prisoners should be improved by better nutrition, improved sanitary conditions, and better treatment and that the number of people systematically placed in the camps should be increased. As part of the new policy, which began in October 1942, the prohibition on sending packages of food to prisoners was lifted. In December 1942, camp doctors were instructed to improve sanitary conditions in the camps. In April 1943, a decree was issued that stopped the practice of euthanasia on prisoners unfit for work, limiting it to the mentally ill and Jews.

In September 1942, Himmler concluded an agreement with the justice minister that sought to increase the influx of new prisoners. The two sides agreed that certain prisoners within the jurisdiction of the justice system would be handed over to the SS with a view to transferring them to the camps. In line with this new plan, Heinrich Müller, chief of the Gestapo secret-police organization, ordered in December 1942 that persons under police custody be transferred to concentration camps. In January 1943, Himmler ordered that children and juveniles captured in clashes with partisan forces be placed in the camps. As a result, the prisoner population nearly tripled—from 88,000 in December 1942 to 224,000 in August 1943. In addition, during this period the prisoner mortality rate dropped from 10 percent to 2.09 percent per month.[18]

It is important to keep in mind that Auschwitz was the largest of the 15 concentration camps in existence in August 1943. One-third (74,000) of the total prisoner population was in Auschwitz. In absolute terms, Auschwitz boasted the highest death rate; in August 1943, deaths reached 2,380. The proportion of deaths also was among the highest (3.3 percent). The only camp with a higher proportion was Lublin-Majdanek (6.04 percent).[19]

Efforts to increase the prisoner population continued over the next 12 months. The result was a doubling of the prisoner population of concentration camps. In August 1944, the prisoner population in all camps reached 524,000. Not counting about 30,000 unregistered prisoners, one-fifth of all prisoners (105,168)[20] were incarcerated in Auschwitz.[21] In January 1945, the total prisoner population exceeded 700,000.[22] But due to a partial evacuation of the camp, the Auschwitz prisoner population fell to 67,000.[23]

No figures are available to indicate the extent to which the labor of this rapidly increasing population was actually used in the German war economy. Indirect data suggest, however, that during 1942 and 1943, less than half of the prisoner population was employed in the war effort. But late in 1944 and early in 1945, according to Pohl, between 400,000 and 420,000 prisoners worked directly for the war effort. Of this number, between 230,000 and 250,000 were employed in private industrial enterprises and about 170,000 prisoners worked directly for the Ministry of Armaments and War Production constructing underground factories for the aviation industry.[24]

Since most of the prisoners who worked in industry were incarcerated in satellite camps, the growth of these camps may serve as an indicator of the degree to which prisoner labor was used outside the camp system. In 1942, only a small number of satellite camps existed. By the end of 1943, however, some camps had over a dozen satellite camps. As late as March 31, 1944, the 20 concentration camps that were in existence (13 in the Reich, three in the General Government, three in Ostland, and one in the Netherlands) had a total of 165 satellite camps, an average of about eight each.[25]

Despite pressure to use concentration camp prisoners for the German war effort, camp realities reflected a compromise between the tasks of exterminating prisoners and exploiting their labor. While the use of prisoner labor continued to expand, the camps remained above all penal institutions. Although the latter function collided with the economic tasks of the camps, the Nazi regime attached too great an importance to it to subordinate it to the needs of economic output.

Because the prisoner labor force was so small (less than one percent of the labor force of the Third Reich), the prisoner manpower could not significantly affect the situation in the labor market in 1942 and 1943—even if it were put to maximum use. The question of prisoner employment remained within the province of the SS and a narrow circle of industrialists who, for one reason or another, took an interest in it. The economic and political factions of the Reich that made policy focused their attention on the employment of foreign workers and prisoners of war, whose numbers exceeded manyfold the size of the camp prisoner population.

In May 1942, the prisoner population numbered 100,000, of which barely 25,000 could be placed at the disposal of war industry after meeting the needs of the camps for prisoner labor.[26] At that time, the German economy employed 2,640,000 foreign workers and 1,470,000 prisoners of war. In the next two years, the number of foreign workers rose to 5.3 million and the number of prisoner-of-war workers to 1,830,000.[27]

The rapacious exploitation and ruthless extermination of concentration camp prisoners no doubt was related to the success of Fritz Sauckel, plenipotentiary for labor recruitment, in recruiting civilians for forced labor. As long as the German economy could meet its demand for labor outside concentration camps, the lives and labor potential of the prisoners were expendable. This correlation is discernible to an even greater extent when considering the treatment of Jews in the camps, to whom no moral or political restraints applied.

In the first half of 1944, the German military situation suddenly took a critical turn for the worse when lost campaigns brought enormous territorial losses. The Soviet Army had all but driven the invading Germans from the Soviet Union; a second front was opened in the west, and the theater of war rapidly approached the prewar Reich borders. Even though a sizable number of personnel who were fit for labor were evacuated from the front line, the territorial losses severely reduced the availability of forced labor. This situation led to a sudden interest by industry in other disposable reserves of labor, including concentration camp prisoners. Many companies began to apply to the SS for prisoners, whose numbers exceeded half a million in the second half of 1944. If the requests were approved, the companies were required to build housing for the prisoners (usually camp barracks) and to construct fences and guard towers. SS officials served as administrative personnel.

In the organizational structure of concentration camps, the satellite camps formed subsidiary units, often called labor camps (*Arbeitslager*), subcamps (*Nebenlager*), or labor parties (*Arbeitskommando*). When growth of the camp system reached its peak in late 1944 and early 1945, the number of large satellite camps exceeded 500,[28] and the number of smaller camps—some housing fewer than 20 prisoners—numbered about 400.[29] That was a sharp increase compared with the 165 satellite camps that were in existence in March 1944. These figures show that more than 80 percent of all satellite camps were established after March 1944. It was then that the employment of prisoners in concentration camps in the German war economy received top priority.

Changes in the use of prisoner labor also were reflected in the practical aspects of the functioning of the Auschwitz concentration camp. We should bear in mind Auschwitz's specific features: in combining the functions of a concentration camp and, beginning in 1942, the function of outright extermination, Auschwitz served as a prototype of sorts for the new generation of camps that combined physical elimination of masses of people with the exploitation of manpower. By concentrating on direct extermination on one hand and ruthless exploitation of the labor of prisoners on the other, the Nazis managed to turn some of the doomed prisoners into instruments of the German war machine while doing away with the need to keep alive thousands of people who could not be productively employed. Accordingly, selections of the newly arrived prisoners focused on the able-bodied who could be put to work until their time ran out.

The extermination component and the exploitation of labor component of the Auschwitz death factory only appear to be strange bedfellows. In reality, they fed off each other, existing in a symbiotic nexus of sorts. Because there was a steady influx of new transports, the killing center could maintain a constant supply of fresh labor. The concentration camp supplied the operation with the technical means of extermination. Prison labor built the gas chambers, the crematoria, and the unloading ramp. SS personnel supervised the killing process, and prisoner labor was used to service the crematoria, to incinerate the bodies, and to prepare the victims' property for shipment. In addition, the camp fulfilled another function—disinformation on a gigantic scale with concealment of its criminal nature from the potential victims and from public opinion.

The Auschwitz concentration camp was set up during the second phase of the policy of using prisoner labor, when enterprises controlled by the SS played a key role, and most prisoners were employed in quarries and brick and gravel works. It was during this phase that the concentration camps were set up near the prisoners' workplaces. In the case of Auschwitz, however, the factor of prisoner labor played no part at all. The most important considerations in choosing the camp site were adequate communication lines[30] and construction constraints, since the camp was originally planned to function only as a local camp or transit and quarantine point for prisoners en route from Silesia to the Reich.

The transformation of Auschwitz into a regular concentration camp did not change the fact that no DEST works could prosper at that location because there were inadequate supplies of raw materials. In fact, only gravel could be mined in abundance. Consequently, in the first years of the camp's existence, Auschwitz prisoners were put to work in administrative tasks, in expanding the camp, and in farming and animal husbandry near the camp. Enlargement of the camp, which at its peak capacity was planned to house about 230,000, continued until 1944, requiring the employment of a considerable portion of the able-bodied prisoners.

Farming was an important consumer of prisoner labor at Auschwitz. After six villages in the camp vicinity were cleared of their inhabitants, the SS administration controlled about 4,000 hectares (10,000 acres) of land. The land was used for a large gardening farm, a poultry farm, fish breeding, and four stock and agricultural farms. In 1940, Himmler planned an agricultural experimental farm, where experiments could be conducted thanks to the suitable soil and climate conditions and the unlimited supply of cheap labor. Laboratories were set up at the camp, and experiments in growing a rubber-yielding plant that was brought from the Soviet Union were undertaken.

Of the four SS enterprises that used Auschwitz prisoner labor (Deutsche Ausrüstungswerke, Deutsch Erd- und Steinwerke GmbH, the Goleszow cement plant, and Deutsche Lebensmittel GmbH), only the DAW and the Goleszow cement plant were important. At first the DAW produced wood-work for construction; then, in 1942, it began producing large quantities of army supplies, such as ammunition crates. Workers there also repaired military vehicles and disassembled disabled aircraft. In 1944, the SS enterprises employed about 4,500 prisoners. Despite Himmler's forecasts, a large armaments production center in Auschwitz never came to be.

Because there was little industry at Auschwitz, a substantial number of prisoners were sent to satellite camps near Silesia, where there was a shortage of workers.

Aside from the SS enterprises and the firms engaged in camp construction, the only industry near Auschwitz was the Krupp fuse plant, which was relocated there in June 1943. Several months later it was taken over by another firm, the Union Metallindustrie. Other firms had their own camps, which came under the jurisdiction of the Auschwitz camp management.

The first satellite camps of Auschwitz were set up in 1942. They were Jawischowitz, Buna at Monowitz, and Chelmek. Five more camps were set up in 1943 and another 19 in 1944. Altogether, 27 satellite camps supplying prisoner labor to private and state firms were established. Nine were built next to steel and metal works (usually armaments), six next to coal mines, and six next to chemical works. The remainder were near other industrial enterprises.

During every year that Auschwitz was in existence, prisoner labor was assigned to outside businesses. In 1941, about 1,000 prisoners (of a total of 10,000) worked for the only firm in the vicinity—the IG Farbenindustrie. In 1942, about 4,600 prisoners (of 24,000) worked for outside establishments. In 1943, about 15,000 prisoners (of 88,000) worked for outside firms. And in 1944, about 37,000 (of 105,000, excluding unregistered prisoners) worked for firms outside the camp. In January 1945, following a partial evacuation of prisoners, outside establishments employed about 35,000 prisoners (of 67,000).[31] The situation in other camps was similar. For example, in January 1945, approximately 20,000 Dachau prisoners (of 50,000 at the camp) worked for outside firms or in work parties that were not part of the camp.[32]

The leading employers of prisoners were chemical plants. In 1944, chemical plants employed over 18,000 prisoners, or nearly 50 percent of all prisoners who worked outside the camps. The largest employer was IG Farbenindustrie, the synthetic rubber and fuel plant near the camp. In the summer of 1944, it had 11,000 Auschwitz prisoners at its disposal. The second largest employer of Auschwitz prisoners was the mining industry, which employed over 8,000 prisoners in 1944. The third largest employer was the steel and metal industry, which employed over 7,000 prisoners in 1944.[33]

The prisoner laborers who contributed to the industrial establishments can be divided into two categories: those employed directly in production (tending machinery, mining coal, etc.) and those employed in the construction and development of industrial plants. From the prisoners' standpoint, the best place to work was in the metallurgic industries. There they worked in closed quarters that were heated in winter and where the pace of work depended less on the zeal of supervisors than on the technological processes involved. The most exhausting work was mining. Since almost all the prisoners who were assigned to work in the mines were doing so for the first time in their lives, they were usually assigned to auxiliary jobs that didn't require skills, such as loading coal and hauling trucks. Such tasks were the most difficult, strenuous, and physically exhausting.

Because most prisoners were unfamiliar with mining, they were often involved in accidents. As one former prisoner, Witold Tokarz, a doctor who worked in the sick bay of the Jawischowitz satellite camp, wrote in his memoirs, "Most of the patients were prisoners who had suffered injuries in work-related accidents." Such accidents often resulted from a lack of suitable protective clothing and a disregard for safety rules. Prisoners usually worked without helmets, rubber boots, or waterproof overcoats. In some cases, they worked in low-ceilinged, flooded gangways, kneeling and sometimes even lying in water.

Working conditions were aggravated further by the brutal treatment that the camp authorities and work supervisors accorded the prisoners. To maintain the highest possible output and attendance, sick and unproductive prisoners were transferred from satellite camps back to Auschwitz, where they were put to death in the gas chambers. Those sent back to Auschwitz were replaced by new prisoners. SS doctors from the Auschwitz main camp performed the selections during inspections of satellite camps. Because the conditions at the satellite camps were so harsh and the mortality rate was so high, the camp authorities regarded the satellite camps as penal camps within the Auschwitz complex.

Severe working conditions also prevailed at construction sites of firms engaged in all kinds of investment projects. Such firms included IG Farbenindustrie AG, Oberschlesische Hydriewerke AG (construction of chemical plants), Energieversorgung Oberschlesien AG (construction of power plants), and Erdol Raffinerie Trzebinia GmbH (development of existing refineries). There too prisoners were employed in assorted unskilled jobs, such as leveling terrain, digging ditches, and reloading. Only a handful of prisoners with skills worked in less strenuous jobs, such as installation and assembly.

Harassment and beatings were daily occurrences. At the Walter power plant in Lagisza, for example, SS men killed prisoners by hitting them with the butts of rifles, trampling them underfoot, or shooting them. At the satellite camp at Trzebinia, beatings and killings also occurred daily. From September 30, 1944, to January 17, 1945, the prisoner population of the Trzebinia camp declined from 819 to 641. To cope with high mortality and the problems associated with transporting bodies to the crematoria in Birkenau, Trzebinia acquired its own crematorium, similar to one built earlier in the Blechhammer satellite camp.

Cheap prisoner labor, combined with low cost of upkeep of prisoners, made the prisoners a source of profits for the state, the SS, and the industrial firms involved. For one prisoner's day of work, the firms paid the state from three to six reichsmarks, a rate much below wages paid to free workers. But because of the poor physical condition of the prisoners and the absence of incentives to perform well, the output of the prisoners was lower than that of civilian employees. The employers made up for the losses by extending work hours and saving on protective clothing and other services required by law for civilian workers.

In their efforts to maximize profits, the firms that employed prisoners strove to squeeze all the productivity they could from their workers. The employers were aware that the prisoners' output was directly related to their tragic situation but did next to nothing to improve living conditions. At best, they paid bonuses that could be redeemed in the camp messroom to workers who achieved better than average output. However, the negligible value of the bonuses and the fact that the messrooms lacked the most sought-after grocery items made the bonuses ineffective as work incentives. More important than bonuses was the emphasis the employers put on discipline, either through their own personnel, who used physical violence to force prisoners to work harder, or by complaining to the camp authorities and requesting that unproductive prisoners be punished. Occasionally the work day was prolonged to over twelve hours to force the prisoners to fulfill set quotas. In other cases, prisoners were held at work so late into the night that shortly after they returned to the camp, they had to go back to work again.

Despite the relatively low payment that the state received for prisoner labor, it more than covered the cost of prisoner upkeep. Since daily upkeep of one prisoner (food, clothing, lodging) cost the state 1.34 reichsmarks and the lowest rate for the labor of an unskilled prisoner employed by private and state monopoly establishments was three to four reichsmarks, more than half the income flowing into state coffers for the hire of prisoners was profit. In the case of skilled workers whose day's work was worth four to six reichsmarks, the profit was even higher.

At the end of 1943, the state's monthly earnings from the hire of Auschwitz prisoners reached two million reichsmarks. Partially preserved bills for seven months of male prisoner labor and nine months of female prisoner labor indicate that the state received over 12 million reichsmarks. Total earnings of the Nazi state from Auschwitz prisoners' labor from 1940 to 1945 are estimated to have reached 60 million reichsmarks.[34]

Of the 1.5 million people taken to Auschwitz, 400,000 were given prisoner status, which meant they were registered and given serial numbers and were left alive for some time. About half of these registered prisoners were Jews and half were non-Jews, mostly Poles. Although the German economy experienced constant labor shortages, especially in the second phase of the war, often half of the prisoner population of the camp remained unemployed. Even in the most critical periods, extermination of thousands of people unfit for work proceeded apace in the Auschwitz camp, as it did in other camps.

Auschwitz became the killing center for Jews from every part of Europe except the east. This factor played a decisive role in the intensification of the extermination process there. In other camps, periodic shortages of manpower imposed constraints on the intensification of mass killings. In contrast, the Auschwitz camp was constantly inundated with masses of arriving deportees, making the problem of labor-force shortages nonexistent from 1942 on. The only problem at Auschwitz was to maintain the prisoners' capacity for work.[35] But the unlimited opportunities to replace prisoners reduced by back-breaking work to nothing more than human wrecks (*Muselmänner*, in the camp slang) with new arrivals still in their prime provided the inducement, if any was needed, to kill prisoners instead of allowing them to recover.

This method of disposing of the used-up and sick prisoners was applied in Auschwitz on a much broader scale than in other camps. The policy of total extermination of Jews was upheld, and deviations from it were limited. This, of course, derived from the fact that the Nazi regime viewed the extermination of Jews as a top political priority, to be realized at all costs, no matter what economic losses it caused. The entire camp was enveloped in the atmosphere of murder on a colossal scale, in which human life counted for nothing and every pair of hands could be replaced by dozens of others at any moment. The consequences were borne not by Jewish prisoners alone but also by non-Jews—especially Poles, Gypsies, and Russians, categorized as "subhumans" in the Nazi "racial" hierarchy.

The sharp deterioration of the German military and economic situation in the first half of 1944, coupled with losses of vast territories whose populations had been regarded as reservoirs of manpower for the German economy, spurred the Nazis' interest in the available reserves of workers, including concentration camp prisoners. This renewed interest was also warranted by a considerable increase in the prisoner population due to intensified deportations and the measures that had been taken earlier to lower prisoner mortality.

In August 1944, the prisoner population of Nazi concentration camps stood at 524,286, with Auschwitz boasting about 105,000 prisoners. But there were limitations on the use of the manpower. Declaration of the Reich territory as "*Judenfrei*" precluded the transfer of Jewish Auschwitz prisoners to camps inside Germany. Since the prohibition did not apply to non-Jewish prisoners, many non-Jews, especially Poles, were moved to camps in the German interior. The result was a further increase in the proportion of Jews in Auschwitz. The subsequent lifting of the prohibition in the spring of 1944 marked the onset of mass transfers of manpower surpluses into the Reich. A new category of prisoners was established. These prisoners were not assigned serial numbers. They were brought to Auschwitz with the sole purpose of putting those who were unfit for work to death in the gas chambers. Auschwitz began to function as a gigantic sieve that sifted out able-bodied prisoners. From then on, it became the center for the distribution of Jewish labor for the entire network of concentration camps.

The rising number of prisoners employed in German industry in 1944 failed to boost productivity. The disciplinary regulations still in effect precluded rational organization of labor. The regulations often stood in the way of matching jobs with appropriate prisoner skills, hindered the introduction of effective incentives to increase prisoners' interest in their work, and precluded physical and mental regeneration of the prisoners. Until the very end, the Nazis pursued the policy of rapacious exploitation of prisoner labor in accordance with the principle of maximum results with minimum investments. The system was most effective in squaring the economic postulates of German industrial circles with the plans to exterminate the Jews and certain categories of Slavs, which had been outlined in the first years of the war by Nazi leaders and put into practice by the SS. Thus despite the unquestionable benefits that prisoner labor could have provided to the German state, the SS, and the private firms involved, the overall effect of prisoner employment was incommensurate with the labor potential that existed in the camps.

Despite Himmler's undisguised ambitions to make his own contribution to the development of the economic potential of the Third Reich by using prisoner labor, his main goals were direct and indirect prisoner extermination. Had the SS wanted to create conditions that were conducive to a productive labor force, they would have set up forced-labor camps in the Reich and the occupied countries. Such camps, however, would not have allowed for the constant turnover of the prisoner population, which always left room for new transports. There would have been no official notifications of premature death of those incarcerated in the camps, and no rumors about horrors taking place.

Just as the defeat of the Third Reich revealed that Nazi ideology was based on myths and prejudices, the negligible effects of the prisoner slave labor rendered absurd the attempts to reactivate in the 20th century a system of production based on slavery. That became strikingly obvious in the last two years of the war, when attempts were made to introduce the system of inexpensive forced labor into highly advanced industrial establishments. Thus Auschwitz and the other concentration camps went down in history not as a gigantic reservoir of labor but as the site of unprecedented crime.

NOTES

1. Andrzej Jozef Kaminski, *Hitlerowskie obozy koncentracyjne i srodki masowej zaglady w polityce imperializmu niemieckiego* (Poznan, 1964), pp. 151–52.
2. Ibid., p. 139.
3. Ibid., p. 149.
4. Ibid., p. 152.
5. Ibid.
6. Reimund Schnabel, *Macht ohne Moral: Eine Dokumentation uber die SS* (Frankfurt am Main, 1957), pp. 207–8.
7. Albert Speer, *Erinnerungen* (Frankfurt am Main and Berlin, 1969), p. 196.
8. Czeslaw Madajczyk, *Polityka III Rzeszy w okupowanej Polsce,* vol. 1 (Warsaw, 1970), p. 256.
9. Artur Eisenbach, *Hitlerowska polityka zaglady Zydow* (Warsaw, 1961), p. 326.
10. Kaminski.
11. Speer, pp. 519, 522.
12. Berthold Puchart, *Dzialalnosc niemieckiej IG Farbenindustrie w Polsce* (Warsaw, 1973), p. 268.
13. Andrzej Strzelecki, "Das Nebenlager Jawischowitz," *Hefte von Auschwitz* 15 (1975), p. 190.
14. Speer.
15. *Trials of War Criminals before the Nuremberg Military Tribunals,* vol. 5 (Washington, D.C., 1950), pp. 379–81.
16. Franciszek Piper, "Zatrudnienie wiezniow KL Auschwitz, organizacja pracy i metody eksploatacji sily roboczej" (Oswiecim, 1981), table 5.
17. Danuta Czech, *Kalendarium der Ereignisse im Konzentrationslager Auschwitz-Birkenau 1939–1945* (Reinbek bei Hamburg, 1989), p. 377.
18. *Trials of War Criminals,* p. 381.
19. Ibid., p. 382.
20. Schnabel, p. 200.
21. Czech, p. 79.
22. Martin Broszat, "Nationalsozialistische Konzentrationslager, 1933–1945," in Martin Broszat, ed., *Anatomie des SS-Staates* (Freiburg im Breisgau, 1965), p. 159.
23. Czech, pp. 114–15.
24. *Trials of War Criminals,* p. 445.
25. Ibid., p. 383.
26. Broszat, p. 116.
27. Alan Milward, *Die Deutsche Kriegswirtschaft 1939–1945* (Stuttgart, 1966), p. 102.

28. Enno Georg, *Die wirtschaftlichen Unternehmungen der SS* (Stuttgart, 1963), p. 41.

29. Jan Sehn, *The Auschwitz-Birkenau Concentration Camp* (Warsaw, 1961), p. 61.

30. Rudolf Höss, *Commandant of Auschwitz* (London, 1959), p. 206.

31. F. Piper, pp. 294–98.

32. Teodor Musiol, "Dachau 1933–1945," *Aneks* 13.

33. Piper, pp. 294–96.

34. Ibid., p. 360.

35. Figures for 1943 indicate that on average about 50 percent of the prisoner population was employed. Some prisoners did not work because of their physical condition or lack of work. Thus, for example, on February 4, 1943, of the total of 42,742 male and female prisoners, only 23,635 worked. By November 4, 1943, the prisoner population had risen to 87,827 men and women, of whom only 45,905 were employed. On April 25, 1944, there were 18,260 men prisoners in Birkenau, but only 7,000 of them, i.e., fewer than 40 percent, were employed; others were either not fit for work or remained unemployed for other reasons. Four months later, on August 22, 1944, the employment situation had slightly improved: of the total of 19,587 male prisoners present, only 10,127, or 51.7 percent, actually worked.

3

The Satellite Camps

SHMUEL KRAKOWSKI

Approximately 50 satellite camps were erected around the two chief Auschwitz camps—Auschwitz I (the *Stammlager* or main camp) and Auschwitz II-Birkenau—from 1942 through 1944. The satellite camps, as noted in chapter 2, were set up for a particular kind of slave labor designed to result in the gradual murder of certain groups of prisoners, according to the Nazi system of *Vernichtung durch Arbeit*, or "destruction through work."

The system was applied first to Jews as a part of the "final solution"—the Nazi plan to eradicate the Jewish people. In the verdict in the trial against Nazis who committed crimes in the satellite camps of Auschwitz, the German court in Bremen stated that "already in the Wannsee Protocol it was determined that the conditions of work for Jews selected for labor would be such that a large proportion would fall victim to a natural selection."[1] The system called for certain Jews, the *Arbeitsfähige* (those able to work), to be temporarily spared from murder in the gas chambers. Instead, they were assigned to labor that was so brutal that they could survive only for a short period.

The adoption of this system was a result of the endeavors of certain German industrial magnates who were interested in continuing the exploitation of cheap Jewish labor that had begun with the Nazis' establishment of Jewish ghettos and slave-labor camps. The dearth of workers in Germany due to the prolonged war also played an important role in the decision to use able prisoners as laborers.

In accordance with accepted policy, SS chief Heinrich Himmler wired a message to Richard Glücks, the inspector of concentration camps, on January 26, 1942, shortly after the Wannsee "final solution" conference:

Because Russian prisoners of war are anticipated in the immediate future, I will send a large number of the Jews and Jewesses who have been deported from Germany into the camps. Within the coming four weeks, you should prepare to receive 100,000 male Jews and up to 50,000 Jewesses into the concentration camps. In the coming weeks, large economic concerns will be approaching you. SS-Gruppenführer [Oswald] Pohl will inform you of the details.[2]

On September 18, 1942, in a meeting at Himmler's headquarters, State Secretary Dr. Rothenberg, SS-Gruppenführer Streckenbach, and SS-Obersturmbannführer Bender decided to expand the system of destruction through work to include some groups of non-Jewish concentration camp prisoners—all Gypsies, Russians, and Ukrainians; Poles with sentences of over three years' imprisonment; and Czechs and Germans with sentences of over eight years. Members of the last two categories could be included only with the approval of the Reich minister of justice. Excluded were Poles who applied to be accepted into the list of German nationals (the so-called *Volksliste*).[3]

In the same spirit, Propaganda Minister Joseph Goebbels expressed the following opinion in a meeting in Berlin on September 14, 1942, regarding which groups of concentration camp prisoners should be exposed to destruction through work:

Jews and Gypsies unconditionally, Poles who have to serve three to four years of penal servitude, and Czechs and Germans who are sentenced to death or penal servitude for life, or to security custody [Sicherungsverwahrung] for life. The idea of exterminating them by labor is the best; for the rest, however, except in the aforementioned cases, every case has to be dealt with individually. In this case, of course, Czechs and Germans have to be judged differently. There may be cases where a German sentenced to 15 years of penal servitude is not to be considered asocial, but in contrast to this a person sentenced up to eight years may be.[4]

Those who were employed within the framework of the destruction-through-work principle became a special category of prisoner. Their plight, as well as the way they were treated by the Nazis, was different from the plight of other kinds of prisoners, such as slave-labor workers and persons deported for compulsory work in Germany. Benjamin Ferencz accurately referred to these special prisoners as "less than slaves."[5]

Because Auschwitz was also a death camp, it was destined to play a significant role in the implementation of the destruction-through-work system. Auschwitz II-Birkenau became the center for selection of the victims who were destined to be murdered by destruction through work. It was there that victims were selected to work in the Auschwitz satellite camps as well as the satellite camps of other concentration camps, including Gross-Rosen, Buchenwald, Stutthof, Dachau, and Mauthausen. The selections were conducted on the arrival ramps of Auschwitz-Birkenau. Those prisoners who were chosen for work were transferred to the quarantine camp, where many of them died shortly after arriving. Surviving prisoners, after a short stay in the quarantine camp, were chosen for work in the various satellite camps.

The Germans did not register the prisoners who were sent to quarantine; nor did they compile statistical data on the number of prisoners sent there. Those who were transferred to other concentration camps were not registered, either. Only those prisoners who were selected for work in the Auschwitz satellite camps were registered and tattooed with Auschwitz concentration camp numbers.

The first and largest Auschwitz satellite camp for slave labor was Auschwitz III. Construction of this camp began near the end of 1941. At first it was called the Buna camp, but after some time it was renamed Auschwitz III-Monowitz. In time it became the seat of command of all the Auschwitz satellite camps.

To date, no comprehensive studies deal with the satellite camps of Auschwitz, although valuable works about specific satellite camps were published by a team of historians from the Auschwitz-Birkenau State Museum. Their studies, based largely on Nazi documentation, contain substantial information about the history of individual camps, including statistical data and details concerning the SS commands of the camps. The Auschwitz satellite camps were spread over a large area, mainly north and west of the main camp. Most were situated in the industrial area of Upper Silesia. A few camps were established close to the main camp. But the prisoners kept there had to be led long distances to their workplaces. The rationale behind setting up satellite camps was to house the prisoners close to their work and thus avoid transporting them long distances every day.

The greatest number of Auschwitz satellite camps were established where the former slave-labor camps for Jews, the Zwangsarbeitslager für Juden (ZAL), had been. An expansive network of slave-labor camps for Jews existed in Silesia between 1940 and 1944. They were run by the so-called Organisation Schmelt, headed by SS-Oberführer Albrecht Schmelt. In early 1943, they employed more than 50,000 Jewish slave laborers. That year, the Nazis started to systematically liquidate these camps. Most of the inmates were deported to Auschwitz, where the majority of them were murdered. Most of the camps became satellite camps of the Gross-Rosen concentration camp, but at least 15 became satellite camps of Auschwitz.

Important satellite camps that had once been slave-labor camps included Lagischa, which became a satellite camp on June 15, 1943; Fürstengrube,

September 2, 1943; and Blechhammer, April 1, 1944. Blechhammer replaced the former Jewish slave-labor camps of Reigersfeld, Sackenhoym, Malapane, and Brande. In April 1944, ZAL Laurahütte slave-labor camp became a satellite camp of Auschwitz, and in May 1944, the ZAL Gleiwitz concentration camp became a satellite camp.[6] Several satellite camps were erected farther away from Auschwitz, mainly the Brunn, Bruntal, and Svetla camps in Czechoslovakia.

The Reich Ministry for Economic Affairs played an important role in the establishment and operation of the satellite camps. In fact, a special Office for Jewish Affairs was established in the ministry to deal with the work of Jews in the satellite camps.[7]

Many German firms were involved in the exploitation of the Auschwitz prisoners. The most important were IG Farbenindustrie and Bismarckhütte, Oberschlesische Hydrierwerke, Siemens-Schuckert, Hermann Göring Werke, Ost Maschinenbau, Grün & Bilfinger, Holzmann, Königshütter Metallwerke, Emmerich Machold, Borsig Koks-Werke, Rheinmetall Borsig, and Schlesische Feinweberei. These firms worked in close partnership with the SS. For example, the prisoners of the Golleschau satellite camp were employed in a cement plant of the Golleschau firm. The German court in Bremen stated that "the cement plant Golleschau [Zementwerk Golleschau] was a joint-stock company. The greater part of stocks belong to a Swiss firm. Since 1940, most of the shares were bought by German firms and taken by SS Bureau 2. At the end of July 1942, a satellite camp was established to employ Jewish prisoners. The director of the Zementwerk Golleschau was, since 1940, Richard Göbel. . . . The board consisted of Göbel, Pohl, and a citizen of Switzerland."[8]

Each satellite camp was run by a *Kommandoführer*, or work leader, who was unofficially called *Lagerführer*. Usually these were senior petty officers in the SS with the rank of Scharführer or Oberscharführer. The Kommandoführer were nominated by the command of the Auschwitz main camp. Each Kommandoführer had a deputy, a staff of SS petty officers, and a contingent of men at his disposal. The size of the staff depended on the size of the camp.

Each camp had a unit of guards, whose numbers also varied according to the size of the prisoner population. Guard units were commanded by a *Postenführer* (guard leader), usually of SS petty officer rank. They were staffed not only by German SS men but also by collaborating French, Croatian, Bulgarian, and Belorussian SS men, as well as members of the Todt Organization.

Prisoners in the satellite camps were very heavily guarded. For example, the Gleiwitz I camp—with an average of 1,300 prisoners—was guarded by a platoon of 50 men from the Sixth SS Guard Company.[9] Fifty SS men also guarded the Janinagrube camp, where the number of prisoners averaged between 700 and 800.[10]

Each SS camp command was augmented by prisoners who were assigned positions in the inner structure of the camp. These positions included *Lagerältester* (camp elder), *Blockältester* (barracks elder), *Vorarbeiter* (work-gang chief), and *Kapo* (work-crew chief). These "prisoner-functionaries" were mostly German prisoners assigned to their positions by the command of the Auschwitz main camp. Rarely were they members of other nationalities. Exceptions were the few cases where the camp commander or the camp elder assigned Jewish prisoners to a prisoner-functionary post.

Jews constituted the vast majority of prisoners in the Auschwitz satellite camps. Franciszek Piper estimated that they made up 95 percent of the Sosnowitz II camp[11] and 80 percent of the Neu-Dachs (Jaworzno) camp.[12] Emeryka Iwaszko estimated that Jews constituted 80 percent of the Janinagrube camp.[13] Tadeusz Iwaszko estimated that Jews made up 85 to 90 percent of the Fürstengrube camp[14] and 95 percent of the Günthergrube camp.[15] According to Irena Strzelecka, the vast majority of the prisoners in the Hindenburg camp were Polish Jews.[16] And except for a small number of German prisoner-functionaries, all the prisoners were Jewish in the Althammer, Czechowice, Trzebinia, Charlottengrube, Gleiwitz, Blechhammer, Bismarckhütte, and Laurahütte camps.

Not only did the Jews make up the majority; they also were in a special category, treated much more harshly than prisoners of other nationalities. Officially, they received only half the amount of food that German prisoners received.[17] And unlike the "Aryan" prisoners, they were not allowed to send letters or to receive packages. But even worse was the special treatment the Jewish prisoners received at the hands of the SS men.

Life in the Auschwitz satellite camps was a constant chain of suffering. Prisoners usually were forced to rise at 4:30 in the morning. The day began with the *Appell* (roll call), which lasted about an hour, regardless of weather conditions. During roll call, the prisoners were almost always tormented and beaten.

Most prisoners were employed in exhausting work without proper clothing or equipment. Zeev Sapir testified that prisoners of the Jaworzno camp worked in the coal mines on three shifts. They were required to fill 45 wagons of coal every day—a normal amount for well-fed workers but an impossible task for starving prisoners. Those who could not do the required work usually were executed.[18] In the Althammer camp, prisoners were forced to dig ditches while standing in water without proper shoes. Those who became too weak to continue were taken to the nearby forest, ordered to run, then were shot by an SS guard.[19] During winter, exposure to the cold added to the prisoners' suffering. Moshe Brandwein testified that in the Blechhammer camp, prisoners tried to save themselves from freezing by fashioning makeshift shirts from paper cement sacks. Anyone caught committing this "offense" was punished with 25 lashes.[20]

Food rations were scanty. Former satellite camp prisoners have testified about the constant sharp hunger that they were forced to endure. For example, the daily food ration that the Jewish prisoners received in the Janinagrube camp consisted of 250 grams of bread, a few grams of margarine, some jam or sausage, one liter of black coffee, and some soup made of cabbage, carrots, and potatoes.[21] Hela Adler testified about hunger in the Hindenburg camp. While working in the factory, women prisoners were given some soup at noontime. Then, after returning to the camp in the evening, they were rationed a small portion of bread and margarine that had to suffice as their supper as well as their breakfast the next morning.[22]

But even more debilitating than the cold weather and the constant hunger was the unrelenting reign of terror in the camps—the sadistic behavior of the SS men and some of the German prisoners, the frequent selections, the executions. Lewis Friedman described in testimony the execution of seven prisoners for allegedly attempting to escape from the Fürstengrube camp in the summer of 1944. They were hanged publicly with the other prisoners present.[23] Dov Levy described a similar public hanging in the Golleschau camp.[24] Moshe Brandwein testified about the public hanging of a Jewish prisoner from Bedzin named Tuchschneider in the Blechhammer camp. His offense was binding the sole of his torn shoe with a piece of wire. Along with him, the Germans hanged the kapo Oksenhendler, a Jew from Paris, because he tried to justify Tuchschneider's "offense."[25]

Zeev Sapir described how prisoners of the Jaworzno camp had to go to work every day in the coal mines—a distance of one and a half kilometers. Each group of 30 prisoners, with their hands chained, was guarded by four SS men and two dogs. The Germans entertained themselves by setting the dogs on the prisoners. They would give the command "Du Mensch, pass' an diesen Hund" ("You human, beat this dog"), the dog would then attack the helpless chained prisoner, and the prisoner would arrive at his workplace bleeding and with clothes torn.[26]

Hela Adler described the terror that women prisoners suffered in the Hindenburg camp, where SS guards maltreated and tormented them and their alleged offenses were used as pretexts for punitive exercises. For example, the women were herded out of the barracks and forced to squat for an hour until their legs became stiff. When an SS guard did not like the way a woman prisoner held a shovel, he would beat her with it until she lost consciousness.[27]

Some SS guards would play with the lives of Jewish prisoners by pulling off the prisoners' caps and throwing them outside the patrolled area. The guards would then order the prisoners to retrieve them because no prisoner was allowed to go without a cap. When the prisoners went to get their caps, the SS guards would shoot them for "attempted escape."[28] Such deadly games were common in the Lagischa camp, where SS guards killed one or more prisoners every day.[29] Shmuel Blumenfeld testified that SS guards in the Jawischowitz camp used to shoot into the camp and kill prisoners, especially during air raid alarms.[30]

The behavior of many of the prisoner-functionaries was often just as brutal and sadistic as that of the SS men. The German court in Bremen stated that

> an explicit right to hit or punish misdeeds with work was never extended to kapos and work-gang leaders. But in the context of the "final solution," it was not only tolerated "from above" but also expected that kapos would "string up," "finish off," or bludgeon Jewish prisoners without regard for the consequences. For this reason Germans were appointed who could be trusted to act brutally or from whom merciless ruthlessness toward the Jews could be expected. In addition to the feared sluggers, there were kapos whom the Jewish prisoners regarded as humane. They also hit, but within measure and only pro forma—when superiors [SS personnel or civilians to whom the work gang was assigned] were near. Such kapos were a minority; they remained the exception.[31]

Many survivors testified about the brutal behavior of the German prisoner-functionaries. Dov Levy described the sadistic behavior of the German kapos in the Golleschau camp. The worst of them was the Kapo Eschmann, who killed some prisoners and struck terror into others.[32] One rare exception was a German political prisoner named Wörl, the camp elder of the Fürstengrube camp, who managed to save a number of lives. He knew how to free sick prisoners from hard work, how to keep them unregistered in the camp infirmary, and when to move them before SS men from the main camp arrived to take the sick to be murdered in the gas chambers. Yad Vashem, Israel's National Memorial to the Holocaust, awarded Wörl the title "Righteous among Nations."[33]

From time to time, the SS men conducted selections of the sick prisoners and transferred them to Auschwitz II-Birkenau to be gassed. The German court in Bremen stated that

> the Jewish workers who were infirm because of the heavy labor or whom mistreatment had rendered unable to work were transported from the satellite camps back to the Auschwitz main camp; in the camp infirmary, they were given a superficial examination by an SS physician, who decided whether it was possible to restore a given prisoner to a physical capacity for work. Prisoners who seemed capable of recovery were admitted to the infirmary and eventually returned to their old satellite camps or to a new one. Prisoners of whom a re-

covery . . . could not be expected were sent immediately to Birkenau, where they met the fate of innumerable comrades in suffering.[34]

Documents detailing the number of prisoners who were selected from the satellite camps to be murdered in the gas chambers of Auschwitz do not exist. Some idea of the percentage of prisoners who were murdered can be gained, however, from studies and incomplete documents that deal with some of the camps. For example, Miroslav Karny wrote about the mortality in Monowitz:

> In the last two months of 1942, the average prisoner population of the camp was 3,000, 84 persons died (2.8 percent) every month, and 420 persons (14 percent) were transferred to the Auschwitz main camp or to Birkenau. Death or transfer reduced the prisoner population by about 16.8 percent per month. In the first half of 1943, the average prisoner population rose to 3,100, the mortality rate dropped a little (70 persons, or 2.2 percent per month), and the number of transfers increased to 18.6 percent per month. Death and transfer actually reduced the prisoner population by one-fifth every month, while the number of new arrivals caused the absolute number of prisoners to rise continually: in April to 3,200 and in June to 4,000. Given the good relations between IG Farben and the SS, it was no problem to replace dead prisoners with new ones.[35]

Almost all of the survivors recalled frequent selections in the satellite camps in their testimonies. Moshe Kubowicki wrote about selections in the Fürstengrube camp,[36] Zeev Sapir about selections in Jaworzno.[37]

Every day brought a bitter struggle for survival for the prisoners. But because they believed in the imminent collapse of the Third Reich, their efforts to survive were meaningful. The struggle for survival—from individual and mutual help to varying forms of resistance—deserve a separate study. It is important to stress the significant role that doctors and medical staffs of the infirmaries played in many of the satellite camps. These people, prisoners themselves and Jews for the most part, were in positions where they could provide some help to other prisoners, but not without taking tremendous personal risks. Here is but one example from Dov Levy:

> The doctors working in Golleschau did everything they could to help the prisoners, to take care of them, so that they could recover. There were many cases of phlegmon, which could not be cured, because of the bad physical condition of these prisoners, especially in the cases when a prisoner working in the stone pit was hit with a stone and the wound would develop into a phlegmon. The doctors in the infirmary strived to save people from being sent to Auschwitz. Everything was done to help people to recover. In many cases they succeeded, but in many others nothing could be done, and it was impossible to bring people to a condition that they could be able to work and thus be saved from deportation.[38]

Prisoners in the satellite camps, unlike those in the main camp of Auschwitz I or the death camp of Auschwitz II-Birkenau, were not isolated from the outside world. The satellite camps were usually situated in or near cities and towns. As SS guards led prisoners through the streets to their workplaces every day, thousands of townspeople could watch the exhausted, starved skeletons of men and women moving with difficulty and suffering the torments of the SS men. The prisoners also frequently came in contact with civilians in their workplaces. Sometimes they worked alongside civilians, but more frequently they were supervised by civilians, called Meisters. Almost all the civilian supervisors were German, and only in rare instances did contact with them result in help.

Reports of some survivors mention contacts with members of the local population in the camps. Dov Levy wrote about such contacts in Golleschau camp:

> Contacts with local population were very limited. Here and there the workers helped some prisoners, giving them a piece of bread, ham, or meat. The prisoners repaid with cigarettes, which they started to receive at the final period. The attitude of the population toward the prisoners was not in principle hostile. However, the negative or positive attitude did not have any influence on the conditions in the camp.[39]

Many survivors reported cruel behavior of the German "masters." For example, Shmuel Blumenfeld testified about their extremely brutal behavior in the Jawischowitz camp, where about 1,200 prisoners worked in the coal mines. On the other hand, Blumenfeld gave examples of friendly behavior by Polish miners, who sought to encourage the prisoners.[40]

On January 18, 1945, the evacuation of Auschwitz and the satellite camps began as a result of the renewed offensive of the Soviet Army in the direction of Krakow. Thus the history of Auschwitz and its satellite camps began to draw to an end. But it was not the end of suffering for the prisoners. Many were murdered during the death marches. Those who lived were taken to other concentration camps, mainly Gross-Rosen, Buchenwald, Mauthausen, and Dachau, where they experienced more months of suffering. Only a few survived.[41]

NOTES

1. Assize Court of Bremen, 27.11.1953, judgment in the criminal case against (1) Hermann Philip Heilmann, (2) Josef Kierspel, and (3) Johann Mirbeth. Docu-

ment number 3Ks 2/53, p. 75; copy in Yad Vashem Archives, file TR-10/472 (hereafter cited as Bremen).

2. Martin Broszat, "Nationalsozialistische Konzentrationslager 1933–1945," in Martin Broszat, ed., *Anatomie des SS-Staats,* vol. 2 (Freiburg im Breisgau, 1965), p. 130.

3. Nuremberg document PS-645.

4. Nuremberg document PS-682.

5. Benjamin B. Ferencz, *Less Than Slave: Jewish Forced Labor and the Quest for Compensation* (Cambridge, Mass., 1979).

6. Alfred Konieczny, "Die Zwangsarbeit der Juden in Schlesien im Rahmen der Organisation Schmelt," in *Sozialpolitik und Judenvernichtung—Gibt es eine ökonomie der Endlösung?* (Berlin, 1987), pp. 97–107.

7. Hans-Eckhardt Kannapin, *Wirtschaft unter Zwang* (Cologne, 1966), p. 58.

8. Bremen, p. 87.

9. Irena Strzelecka, "Arbeitslager Gleiwitz I," *Hefte von Auschwitz* 14 (1973), pp. 75–106.

10. Emeryka Iwaszko, "Podoboz Janinagrube," *Zeszyty Oswiecimskie* 10 (1967), pp. 59–82.

11. Franciszek Piper, "Podoboz Janinagrube," *Zeszyty Oswiecimskie* 11 (1969), p. 105.

12. Franciszek Piper, "Das Nebenlager Neu-Dachs," *Hefte von Auschwitz* 12 (1971), pp. 55–111.

13. E. Iwaszko, p. 81.

14. Tadeusz Iwaszko, "Das Nebenlager Fürstengrube," *Hefte von Auschwitz* 16 (1978), p. 33.

15. Tadeusz Iwaszko, "Das Nebenlager Guntherbrube," *Hefte von Auschwitz* 12 (1971), p. 124.

16. Irena Strzelecka, "Podoboz Hindenburg," *Zeszyty Oswiecimskie* 11 (1969), p. 123.

17. Bremen, p. 77.

18. Yad Vashem Archives 03/1762.

19. Franciszek Piper, "Podoboz Althammer," *Zeszyty Oswiecimskie* 13 (1971), p. 151.

20. Yad Vashem Archives 03/2816.

21. E. Iwaszko, p. 72.

22. Yad Vashem Archives 03/2954.

23. Ibid. 03/794.

24. Ibid. 03/3588.

25. Ibid. 03/2816.

26. Ibid. 03/1762.

27. Ibid. 03/2954.

28. Bremen, pp. 77–78.

29. Testimonies by Joel Rys, Yad Vashem Archives 03/3538, and Abraham Chmielnik, ibid. 03/3523.

30. Ibid. 03/3129.

31. Bremen, p. 83.

32. Yad Vashem Archives 03/3588.

33. Testimonies by Moshe Kubowicki, ibid. 03/1048, and Kopel Bojman, ibid. 03/3115.

34. Bremen, p. 77.

35. Miroslav Karny, "Vernichtung durch Arbeit," in *Sozialpolitik und Judenvernichtung* (see n. 6 above) p. 146.

36. Yad Vashem Archives 03/1048.

37. Ibid. 03/1762.

38. Ibid. 03/3588.

39. Ibid.

40. Ibid. 03/3129.

41. Shmuel Krakowski, "The Death Marches in the Period of the Evacuation of the Camps," in *The Nazi Concentration Camps: Proceedings of the Fourth Yad Vashem International Historical Conference* (Jerusalem, 1984), pp. 475–89.

4

The Number of Victims

FRANCISZEK PIPER

In erasing traces of the crimes perpetrated in Auschwitz-Birkenau, the Nazis destroyed documents that could serve as the basis for determining how many people died there. When Soviet soldiers liberated the camp in January 1945, they found documents that confirmed only 100,000 deaths. Yet surviving prisoners maintained that millions had perished at Auschwitz.

Faced with this disparity, officials of the Soviet Extraordinary State Commission, the organization entrusted with investigating the crimes committed at Auschwitz, conducted an in-depth study. Based on witness testimonies regarding the capacity of the camp and the length of time that its machinery for mass murder was operative, the commission concluded that no fewer than four million persons were put to death at the camp, a number later reiterated by a Polish commission also investigating the crimes at Auschwitz. The former camp commandant, Rudolf Höss, testified before the International Military Tribunal in Nuremberg that three million persons died at the camp. Four million, however, is the number recorded in Polish literature, as well as in publications of other countries.

In *The Final Solution*, one of the first books to deal with the Holocaust, published in 1953, the figure of four million was radically reevaluated. English historian Gerald Reitlinger estimated the number of victims of Auschwitz to be roughly 800,000 to 900,000, based on an analysis of the losses of Jews reported by specific countries as well as his study of extermination records. Since then, other estimates lower than the figures quoted by the Soviet and Polish commissions have been advanced, especially in Western publications. These estimates have ranged upward from one million.

The Auschwitz-Birkenau State Museum, the leading Polish institution on Auschwitz history, decided in 1990 to undertake a reassessment of the four million figure, which it was using in its own publications and had engraved on a statue that commemorates the victims at Birkenau. As a result of this reassessment, new calculations indicate that the number of victims was at least 1.1 million, about 90 percent of whom were Jews from almost every country in Europe. This figure was approved and accepted by another leading research institution investigating Nazi crimes in Poland, the Main Commission for the Investigation of Nazi Crimes.

As a result of this recent study, a significant, though not complete, agreement has been reached, one that is critical not only for the history of the Auschwitz camp but also for the historiography of Nazi genocide as a whole. But fundamental questions arise. Why had such discrepant estimates been advanced during the study of the camp? How could they have been perpetuated over such a long period? Is it possible to identify objective causes for the varying estimates? To what extent did subjective factors play a part?

The destruction by the Nazis of most Auschwitz records is the most important cause of divergent estimates.[1] In an attempt to reconstruct these records, an extensive search of archives in various European countries was conducted by the Auschwitz-Birkenau State Museum. This search turned up important records of agencies and institutions involved in mass extermination, especially data concerning deportations to Auschwitz and other camps. In many cases, these records made possible a more precise estimate of deportees from various countries and, consequently, a more accurate estimate of the number of losses. Before these records were discovered, researchers had to rely on discrepant and imprecise data from testimonies and depositions from witnesses, former prisoners, and Nazi functionaries and on court decisions and fragmentary and incomplete records of camp registries, archives, and other institutions.

Testimonies by Prisoners and SS Functionaries

The first attempts to estimate the number of victims of Auschwitz were made by prisoners who were members of the resistance movement in the camp. Their reports, which were transmitted to underground centers in Poland and other countries, revealed varying estimates of the number of deportees and the number of victims.[2] Because of the difficulty these prisoners had in gaining access to information and the inevitable distortions that occurred when the data were analyzed and transmitted, these reports are marred by serious errors, discrepancies, and contradictions.

An early resistance movement report maintained that before December 15, 1942, about 640,000 persons had perished in Auschwitz, including 520,000 Jews; the remainder were Poles and victims from other countries.[3] Subsequent research demonstrated that these figures must have been an overestimate, since they exceeded the number of deportees to the camp at the time.

Jerzy Tabeau,[4] a Pole who escaped from the camp on November 19, 1943, reported in December 1943 and January 1944 to the Polish underground in Krakow that 1.5 million Jews had been killed at Auschwitz. This figure, too, turned out to be an overestimate. Tabeau had based his estimate exclusively on his own observations and information he had received from other prisoners.

Two Jewish prisoners, Alfred Wetzler and Walter Rosenberg (Rudolf Vrba),[5] who escaped on April 7, 1944, reported on their arrival in Zilina, Slovakia, that 1,765,000 Jews had been killed in the camp from April 1942 to April 1944. Their estimate, based on their own observations and on notes taken during their two-year stay in the camp, also proved too high. Their data can be checked by analyzing specific figures. For example, their figures for the number of French and Belgian Jews killed in Auschwitz exceeded the total losses of Jews in these two countries, according to figures determined after the war.

Just two weeks before Wetzler and Rosenberg escaped, a much lower figure was cited in the *Los Angeles Times*.[6] The *Times* quoted the Ministry of Information of the Polish government-in-exile in London, which reported that "over 500,000 persons, mostly Jews, have been murdered in a concentration camp southwest of Krakow." Considering that more than a half-million people were brought to the camp (438,000 Jews from Hungary, 60,000 to 70,000 Jews from Lodz, about 13,000 Poles from Warsaw, and thousands of Jews from Slovakia and Theresienstadt) in 1944, the *Times* figure, although a slight underestimate, was closer to reality.

Despite considerable accuracy in certain details, the figures quoted by resistance sources must be considered cautiously because they lacked access to aggregate figures. Similar objections may be raised regarding figures quoted by prisoners not affiliated with any underground organizations in the camp. Even prisoners employed as scribes in camp offices had access to a limited number of records. For the most part, these records pertained to registered prisoners, not to the mass transports so critical to estimating the number of deportees and victims. The figures quoted by individual prisoners rely mostly on numbers of autopsies and on information overheard from SS men or other prisoners. The most significant fact in the prisoners' reports and communications is that mass extermination continued incessantly.

Characteristically, the *Sonderkommando*, the prisoners employed in cremating bodies, did not quote aggregate figures in their notes written during the camp's existence. They recorded only general estimates, such as "millions of people perished in the camp." For example, Zalman Gradowski, a member of the Sonderkommando,[7] wrote in a manuscript buried near the crematoria and unearthed after the war: "I have buried this under the ashes, considering it the safest place, bound to be dug up to find traces of the millions of murdered people."

In testimonies given after the war, former Sonderkommando members quoted numbers of murdered victims that varied by several million. Shlomo Dragon,[8] a Sonderkommando prisoner from December 9, 1942, to January 1945, testified in 1945, "According to my own calculations, over four million people were gassed in bunkers and the four crematoria." The same figure was used by another Sonderkommando prisoner, Henryk Tauber.[9] Similar numbers were quoted by other prisoners. Former prisoner Kazimierz Smolen,[10] who worked in the prisoner registry office, put the figure at 2.8 million. Erwin Olszowka,[11] chief clerk in the office of the camp deputy commandant, estimated the number of victims at 4.5 million.

Such estimates were advanced by SS functionaries as well. Pery Broad, who was convicted in the trial of members of the Auschwitz SS in 1963–65 at Frankfurt am Main, testified that "Auschwitz was an extermination camp, the largest such camp in history. In the course of its existence, two to three million Jews were murdered there, as well as thousands of Poles, Russians, Czechs, Yugoslavs, and others."[12]

But it is the testimony of Rudolf Höss, Auschwitz's commandant from 1940 through 1943, that draws the special attention of scholars. Höss is considered a credible witness because he also supervised camp affairs for the SS Economic-Administrative Main Office in 1944. Furthermore, he returned to Auschwitz briefly to oversee the extermination of Hungarian Jews. After he was arrested by the British on March 11, 1946, Höss testified several times before various Allied prosecuting agencies. His most important testimonies were at the Kaltenbrunner trial before the International Military Tribunal in Nuremberg and later, after he was extradited to Poland, before the Polish authorities.

On April 15, 1946, Höss's certified testimony was read during the Kaltenbrunner trial. "According to my calculations," he stated, "at least 2.5 million people were put to death, gassed, and subsequently burned there; in addition, 500,000 people died of exhaustion and illness, which gives a total of three million victims. That figure constitutes 70 to 80 percent of all Auschwitz prisoners. . . ."[13] Later, in a conversation with psychiatrist G. M. Gilbert in Nuremberg[14] and in testimonies given in Poland, Höss repudiated these figures, claiming he had received them from Adolf Eichmann, who had been head of the SS Office of Jewish Emigration. A more accurate estimation, he reported, was 1.13 million, based on his recollection of the extermination of Jews from particular countries. The figure is almost identical to the number of Jews deported to Auschwitz, as established by this author (see below).[15]

Since the Höss testimonies, researchers have accepted figures from Höss that ranged from one to three million—depending on how reliable they consider his testimonies to be. It is unclear from Höss's Nuremberg testimony whether the number he gave for those killed in the camp pertains to the period of his tenure as camp commandant or the camp's entire existence. As a result, some scholars add to Höss's figure the number of victims during 1944, mainly the 438,000 Hungarian Jews deported to Auschwitz that year.

Investigating and Prosecuting Agencies and Tribunals

As noted, the first institution to estimate the number of Auschwitz victims was the Soviet Extraordinary State Commission, which began its investigation days after the camp's liberation. Officials inspected the crematoria, gathered testimonies from former prisoners and other witnesses, surveyed the extant camp records, and heard expert opinions. The results of the investigation were published on May 8, 1945.[16]

In its calculations, the commission used the following estimates of the daily burning capacity and the number of days the crematoria were in operation: crematorium I—300 bodies, 720 days; crematorium II—3,000 bodies, 570 days; crematorium III—3,000 bodies, 540 days; crematorium IV—1,500 bodies, 510 days; crematorium V—1,500 bodies, 540 days. (Subsequent research does not deviate substantially from these figures.) By multiplying the burning capacity of each crematorium by the number of days that each was in existence, then tallying the sums, one obtains a total of 5.121 million casualties, assuming that the installations were used at four-fifths of capacity. Statistics regarding transports bound for Auschwitz indicate, however, that the installations lay idle for days at a time and that fewer deportees arrived during certain periods. Transports from France, Belgium, Holland, and Germany, for example, generally carried 1,000 persons each, approximately half the number included in other transports. When such mitigating factors are considered, one concludes that a lower figure is probably more accurate.

The Polish Commission,[17] which conducted its investigations in 1945 and 1946, came to conclusions similar to those reached by its Soviet counterpart.

The Supreme National Tribunal in Poland,[18] which tried Höss in 1947, indicted him for "taking part in the perpetration of the murder of some 300,000 people placed in the camp as officially registered prisoners; of an indeterminate number [of victims], but certainly no less than 2,500,000, mostly Jews, brought in transports to the camp from various European countries for the purpose of immediate extermination, and therefore not officially registered; and of at least 12,000 Soviet prisoners of war. . . ." The tribunal cited the death of between three and four million persons as one of the reasons for the sentence it passed on Höss.

The International Military Tribunal in Nuremberg[19] did not address the question of how many persons were killed at Auschwitz. It did state, however, that "as far as Auschwitz is concerned, the Tribunal examined as a witness the commandant of this camp from May 1940 to December 1, 1943. The witness stated that during this period in the Auschwitz camp alone, 2.5 million people had been killed, and that another half a million died of starvation and illness."

Scholarly Publications

Analysis of the number of victims is seldom encountered in scientific studies, let alone in popular or journalistic publications. Studies published in the West usually cite low estimates that refer only to the Jewish victims. (The question of extermination of prisoners of other nationalities has been treated marginally because of a lack of information about the national composition of the prisoner population.)

Estimates based on Höss's testimony vary widely: Hilberg[20] and Crankshaw[21]—one million; Poliakoff,[22] Dawidowicz,[23] Gilbert,[24] and Billig,[25]—two million; Bauer[26]—2.5 million; *Encyclopaedia Judaica*[27]—one to 2.5 million; and Weiss[28]—1.2 to 2.5 million. One exception is Kogon,[29] who put the number of victims of Auschwitz at 3.5 to 4.5 million.

Studies published in Poland, East Germany, and Czechoslovakia usually cite the assessments of the Soviet Commission (four million) or the Supreme National Tribunal in Poland (2.8 to four million). Figures in this range are also attributed to studies by Madajczyk,[30] Pawelczynska,[31] and Dunin-Wasowicz;[32] to the publications of the Auschwitz-Birkenau State Museum by K. Smolen,[33] D. Czech,[34] and F. Piper;[35] to the publications of the Main Commission for the Investigation of Nazi Crimes in Poland by Pilichowski[36] and Gumkowski;[37] and to a collective study on Nazi camps in Poland, published in Warsaw.[38]

None of these authors conducted their own studies; nor did they discuss the figures with authors who cited conflicting figures, even though the discrepancies must have aroused doubts and reservations. The authors no doubt were convinced that an accurate estimation would be next to impossible because of gaps in the source material and the unresolvable contradictions and discrepancies in the extant sources.[39] One must also consider the probable psychological resistance to reexamining the numbers. Historians might be hesitant to come up with new estimates that could never be properly substantiated. They also might fear that any change could be criticized as an attempt to minimize the crime of genocide in general and the crimes perpetrated in Auschwitz in particular. Every researcher of Auschwitz assumes a heavy responsibility in view of the massive scale of the crimes and, above all, the attempted mass extermination of Jews in the framework of the so-called *Entlösung* (final solution). The testimonies of survivors have made Auschwitz a symbol of Nazi genocide for the world. Any revision of existing assessments might be seen as diminishing this powerful symbol.[40]

Yet several factors now prompt historians to attempt to verify widely used figures, including the scientific demand for objectivity in the study of Nazi crimes. Scholars are also aware of the consequences of inconsistency, including the neo-Nazis' exploitation of such discrepancies in their attempts to whitewash Nazi criminals and to negate the character of their deeds.[41]

The turning point on this issue came with the publication in 1983 of a study by the French scholar and former Auschwitz prisoner Georges Wellers, of the Paris Center for Documentation of Contemporary Jewry, attempting to determine the number of deaths in Auschwitz.[42] Wellers concluded that 1,613,455 persons had been deported to Auschwitz (1,433,405 Jews, 146,605 Poles and others, 21,665 Gypsies, and 11,780 Soviet prisoners of war) and that 1,471,595 of them had died (1,352,980 Jews, 86,675 Poles and others, 20,255 Gypsies, and 11,685 Soviet POWs). The significance of Wellers's study lies in his decision to disregard contemporary estimates and figures quoted in witness testimonies (mostly by Höss) and instead to base his calculations on historiographical assessments of the number of persons deported from various countries to the camp and their fate. Thus Wellers refined a methodological concept proposed by Gerald Reitlinger in 1953.

Despite the significance of Wellers's pioneering effort, it is not free of methodological and substantive deficiencies. Wellers drew on a very slender base of bibliographical and source material of just 26 publications and three archival documents. That resulted in the omission of data of great importance.[43] Wellers also combined approximate figures with precise numbers, a method that cannot result in accurate totals. Furthermore, some of his estimates are based on erroneous assumptions and hypothetical and arbitrary premises.[44]

As a result of these methodological shortcomings, Wellers overestimated the number of deportees to the camp by more than 300,000 persons, chiefly because of his overestimate of the number of Polish Jews. He also failed to take into consideration the transfer of prisoners to other camps before May 18, 1944, and other events, such as releases and escapes from the camp. These omissions, along with his exclusion of all prisoners who were transferred to other camps after May 18, 1944, resulted in his underestimation of the number of survivors of Auschwitz by about 80,000. In addition, Wellers did not take into account the deportation and murder of about 15,000 Poles, Soviet prisoners of war, and Gypsies who were not registered. By overestimating the number of deportees to the camp and underestimating the number of survivors, Wellers overestimated the number of Auschwitz deaths by about 400,000.

The New Study

This author undertook the study of the number of Auschwitz victims in 1980, as part of a broader research project planned and carried out by the Auschwitz-Birkenau State Museum. The study's conclusions were presented in an extensive document, of which this essay is an abridged version, containing only the main theses, premises, and conclusions.[45]

The calculation method draws on all numerical data relating to the transports of persons deported to the camp, and to all reductions in prisoner population caused by transfers to other camps and by releases and escapes. By subtracting the latter figure from the former, one can obtain the number of persons who died in Auschwitz.

The Number Deported

Jews. Jews made up the largest group of deportees. Research findings in various countries served as the basis for a number of studies on the extermination of their Jewish nationals, including deportation of part of this group to Auschwitz. In France and Belgium, complete lists of names have been published, whereas in other countries, numerical totals have been prepared. The numbers of Jewish deportees add up to 1,100,000.

The breakdown in terms of individual countries is as follows: Hungary, 438,000;[46] Poland, 300,000;[47] France, 69,000;[48] Netherlands, 60,000;[49] Greece, 55,000;[50] Bohemia and Moravia (Theresienstadt), 46,000;[51] Slovakia, 27,000;[52] Belgium, 25,000;[53] Germany and Austria, 23,000;[54] Yugoslavia, 10,000;[55] Italy, 7,500;[56] Norway, 690;[57] concentration camps and other places, 34,000.[58] The approximate total is 1,095,190, which the author has rounded to 1,100,000.

The same total can be reached by tallying all the transports to Auschwitz as M. Gilbert listed them in his *Atlas of the Holocaust*.[59] In contrast, the total number of deported Jews included in Reitlinger's tally in *The Final Solution* adds up to 851,000.[60] Thus the estimates presented by this author differ from figures cited by Reitlinger by about 250,000, a difference attributable to Reitlinger's underestimating the number of Polish (200,000) and Hungarian (380,000) Jews deported to the camp. These two figures alone resulted in Reitlinger's underestimating the total number of Jews deported to Auschwitz by 158,000. The remaining 90,000 can be accounted for in the underestimation of deportees from other countries from several thousand to over 10,000. For example, Reitlinger underestimated the number of French Jews by 14,000 and Greek Jews by 10,000.

Wellers put the total number of Jews deported to Auschwitz at 1,433,405. This figure involved an overestimation (by about 320,000) of the number of Polish Jews deported to the camp (Wellers put it at 622,935). Wellers roughly calculated this figure by multiplying the number of transports carrying those subjected to selection as listed by D. Czech in her *Kalendarium* (119) by the average of 5,000 persons per transport. To that number (595,000) he added the known number of 27,935 Polish Jewish deportees who were deported in 27 transports but were not subjected to selection. The reason for overestimating the number of Polish Jews deported to Auschwitz was Wellers's acceptance of an exaggerated figure of 5,000 deportees per transport, reckoned by analogy to transports of Polish Jews from Warsaw to Treblinka, to two transports originating in Przemysl and Kolomyja bound for Belzec, and to the size of transports of Hungarian Jews, as well as to Auschwitz-bound transports from Bedzin and Sosnowiec.[61] Although the transports to Treblinka and Belzec did carry 5,000 (and possibly more) deportees, the Auschwitz-bound transports from Hungary and the transports that originated in Bedzin and Sosnowiec (August 1–4, 1943) were smaller, numbering about 3,000 Jews each. Wellers's error in lowering the total number of transports from Hungary (87 instead of 148)[62] and from Sosnowiec and Bedzin (four instead of nine)[63] resulted in his overestimation of the average transport by 2,000. No detailed assessments of individual transports confirm such a high average figure per transport to Auschwitz. Transport sizes varied from about 1,000 to about 3,000, an average of about 2,000 deportees per transport. Thus, for example, the timetable of transports dispatched in February 1943 from Bialystok to Auschwitz provided for 2,000 deportees per train.[64] Even the incomplete figures cited by Czech[65] and Gilbert[66] (200,000–250,000) speak in favor of rejecting Wellers's estimates.

Poles. Gaps in source material permit only an approximation of the number of Poles deported to Auschwitz. Like other non-Jewish prisoners, Poles were assigned serial numbers. Therefore Polish prisoners can be counted among the 400,000 registered prisoners (with the exception of those not included in numerical registration). By deducting from that figure 205,000 registered Jewish prisoners,[67] 21,000 registered Gypsies, and 12,000 registered Soviet prisoners of war, one arrives at 162,000 prisoners comprising Poles and other nationalities, including 151,000 prisoners (not counting Jews) within the general (ordinary) serial camp category and 11,000 prisoners assigned the EH (reeducation) serial category comprising almost exclusively Poles.[68]

On the basis of transport lists that include 105,000 prisoners in the general category (without Jews) brought in from ten countries, it can be determined that 87,447, or 83.28 percent of all transports, came from Poland. Extrapolating that percent to the total of 151,000 prisoners produces, together with the EH category, a total of 137,000 registered Poles. In addition, at least 10,000 Poles were deported and subsequently put to death without having been registered,[69] including between 3,000 and 4,500 police prisoners. Thus the total number of Poles brought to the camp is estimated at 140,000 to 150,000.

Gypsies. Available evidence indicates that about 21,000 Gypsies were registered in the camp. Their names are listed in the camp's main book (*Hauptbuch*),[70] salvaged by prisoners. Most came from Germany, Austria, and the Protectorate of Bohemia and Moravia. In addition, about 1,700 nonregistered Gypsies were killed in the camp.[71] That adds up to a total of 23,000 Gypsies deported to Auschwitz.

Soviet prisoners of war. In the years 1941–44, some 12,000 Soviet POWs were registered and assigned serial numbers.[72] Other groups of POWs, not registered, were killed upon arrival in gas chambers or executed by shooting. Testimonies, accounts, and materials of the camp resistance movement allow one to estimate that there were at least 3,000 unregistered prisoners.[73] This means that at least 15,000 Soviet POWs ended up in the camp.

Other nationalities. The remaining 25,000 registered prisoners represented other nationalities, including Belorussians, Russians, Ukrainians, Lithuanians, Czechs, French, Yugoslavs, Germans, Austrians, and Italians. They were brought in groups ranging from a few prisoners to several thousand.[74]

In summary, from 1940 to 1945, at least 1,300,000 persons were deported to Auschwitz.

The Number Killed

Given the lack of camp documents, the only way to establish how many perished is by reconciling the increases and decreases in the number of prisoners at the camp. That can be accomplished by referring to camp and resistance-movement documents, lists of Auschwitz prisoners compiled after they arrived at other concentration camps, and other scattered sources of information.

Incomplete source material precludes the possibility of calculating all the numbers of transfers, releases, and escapes. Some prisoners may have been counted twice if, for example, a transport that carried prisoners from Auschwitz to an unknown destination was counted again in a list drawn up by another concentration camp. Even when calculations are made with all due care, faultless verification is not always possible.

According to two tables of information in the Auschwitz-Birkenau State Museum,[75] some 25,000 prisoners were transported from Auschwitz-Birkenau to other camps in the years 1940–43. A considerable discrepancy exists for the years 1944 and 1945. Therefore one must accept lists published by Andrzej Strzelecki[76] that give a total of 187,820 persons, including registered prisoners and unregistered Jews from the transit camp in Birkenau. (According to Czech's *Kalendarium*, the latter category comprised about 25,000 persons.)[77]

To the number of prisoners who were transferred out of Auschwitz from 1940 to 1945 (212,820), one must add 1,500 released prisoners, 500 escapees, and 8,000 liberated inmates, for an estimated grand total of 222,820 prisoners who left the camp alive. However, many of these prisoners did not live to see the end of the war. Some perished en route to other camps, and many lost their lives in the last phase of the war. Former Auschwitz prisoners, for example, were among victims on the ship *Cap Arcona*, which was bombed one day before the end of the war.

Based on these calculations (1,300,000 deportees minus 200,000 survivors), at least 1,100,000 persons were killed or died in the camp. But if this number is regarded as a minimum estimate, what figure can we accept as a hypothetical ceiling?

Theoretically, any significant increase in the estimates can apply only to Jews, since in principle, prisoners of other nationalities were accounted for within the system of numerical registration. Even taking into account data contained in sources omitted from this analysis because of their dubious reliability, the number of unregistered Poles, Soviet POWs, and other prisoners could not have exceeded several tens of thousands.

If the aggregate losses sustained by the Jewish population are not changed, a hypothetical increase in the number of Jews killed in Auschwitz can occur only if one lowers the estimates of losses in other camps and extermination sites and adjusts the Auschwitz tally accordingly. Such revision is highly unlikely in the case of Hilberg, who estimated the global demographic losses of Jews at 5.1 million (including one million in Auschwitz). Hilberg's figures relating to other camps and extermination sites were carefully determined by checking them against various sources. Therefore they must be regarded as minimum estimates. Statistical adjustments are more likely with Gilbert's figures, which put the global losses among Jews at 5.75 million. Taking into consideration that the 650,000 difference between Hilberg's and Gilbert's figures derives, among other things, from Gilbert's estimating the losses of Russian Jews (who were not deported to Auschwitz) as 300,000 higher than Hilberg, an increase in the estimate of the

Jewish victims of Auschwitz could reach 350,000 at most. This figure is equal to the difference between Hilberg's and Gilbert's estimates (1.7 million and 2.05 million respectively for the global losses in the four main centers of extermination of Jews—Treblinka, Belzec, Chelmno, and Sobibór). If Auschwitz is "credited" with this difference, the number of Jewish victims killed in the camp would rise to about 1.35 million, with the total number of Auschwitz victims reaching about 1.5 million.

At present, these considerations remain in the realm of conjecture. Any upward revision of these estimates of deportees to Auschwitz and its victims must be verified by source materials. Some recent studies cite aggregate figures for Jewish losses that approximate and even exceed Gilbert's estimates. For example, the *Encyclopedia of the Holocaust* uses 5,596,000 as a minimum estimate and 5,860,000 as a maximum.[78] A recently published work edited by the German scholar Wolfgang Benz sets a minimum estimate of 5,290,000 and a maximum exceeding six million.[79] It is difficult to determine if such approximations should significantly affect the figures used in this study for the Jewish victims put to death immediately upon arrival in Auschwitz.

NOTES

1. A. Palarczykowa, "Wladze hitlerowskiego obozu koncentracyjnego Oswiecimiu, ich kancelaria i pozostala po nich spuscizna aktowa," *Archeion* 40 (1964), pp. 227–49.

2. H. Swiebocki, "Ujawnianie i demaskowanie zbrodni SS," in *Oswiecim, hitlerowski oboz zaglady* (Warsaw, 1987), pp. 137–45; and "Przyobozowy ruch oporu w akcji niesienia pomocy wiezniom KL Auschwitz," *Zeszyty Oswiecimskie* 19 (1988), pp. 5–152.

3. "Oboz koncentracyjny Oswiecim w swietle akt Delegatury Rzady RP na kraj," *Zeszyty Oswiecimskie*, special issue no. 1 (1968), p. 89.

4. Archives of the Auschwitz-Birkenau State Museum (ASAM), Proces zalogi (Trial of former Auschwitz functionaries conducted in Krakow before the Supreme National Tribunal of Poland), file 44, cards 24–94.

5. Ibid., card 93.

6. Quoted in M. Marmelstein, *By Bread Alone: The Story of A-4685* (Huntington Beach, Calif., 1981), p. 61 (press clipping for March 22, 1944).

7. *Amidst a Nightmare of Crime: Notes of Prisoners of Sonderkommando Found at Auschwitz* (Oswiecim, 1973), p. 75.

8. ASAM, Trial of Höss, file 11, card 113, testimony of Shlomo Dragon.

9. Ibid., card 149, testimony of Henryk Tauber.

10. Ibid., file 7, card 221, testimony of Kazimierz Smolen.

11. Ibid., file 25, card 67, testimony of Erwin Olszowka.

12. Pery Broad, "Errinnerungen," in *Auschwitz in den Augen der SS* (Katowice, 1981), p. 136.

13. *Der Nürnberger Prozess gegen die Hauptkriegsverbrecher vor dem Internationalen Militargerichtshof,* vol. 11 (Nuremberg, 1947), p. 458.

14. Höss stated in the Gilbert conversation that 1.3 million people had died in Auschwitz; see E. Crankshaw, *Die Gestapo* (Berlin, 1964), p. 194.

15. The numbers quoted by Höss add up a total that is almost identical to the minimum number of Jews deported to the camp, although certain figures have been put into question by recent research. For example: 110,000 Jews deported from France, or 90,000 from Slovakia. Rudolf Höss, "Aufzeichnungen," in *Auschwitz in den Augen der SS,* pp. 123–24.

16. ASAM, Trial of Höss, file 8, cards 28–29.

17. K. Smolen, "Auschwitz Concentration Camp," in *Selected Problems from the History of KL Auschwitz* (Oswiecim, 1979), p. 26.

18. *Wspomnienia Rudolfa Hössa komendanta obozu oswiecimskiego* (Warsaw, 1965), p. 27.

19. *Der Nürnberger Prozess gegen die Hauptkriegsverbrecher,* vol. 1, p. 282.

20. R. Hilberg, *The Destruction of the European Jews* (London, 1961), p. 572.

21. Crankshaw, p. 191.

22. L. Poliakoff, *Breviaire de la Haine* (Paris, 1951).

23. L. Dawidowicz, *The War against the Jews 1933–1945* (Aylesburg, 1979), p. 191.

24. M. Gilbert, *Atlas of the Holocaust* (London, 1982), p. 100. It should be pointed out, however, that the total number of deportees in the Auschwitz-bound transports as listed by Gilbert reached 1.1 million.

25. J. Billig, *Les camps de concentration dans l'économie du Reich hitlerien* (Paris, 1973), pp. 101, 102.

26. Y. Bauer, "Auschwitz," in *Der Mord an den Juden im Zweiten Weltkrieg* (Stuttgart, 1985), p. 173 (the author cites Polish figures). Later, in an interview given in 1989 and in his articles, Bauer quoted Georges Wellers's figures as the most reliable; see his "Danger of Distortion, Poles and Jews alike are supplying those who deny the Holocaust with the best possible arguments," in the *Jerusalem Post* international edition, September 30, 1989. However, the figure of 1.6 million advanced by Wellers as the number of deportees was initially quoted in the articles as the number of victims (1.471 million).

27. *Encyclopaedia Judaica,* vol. 3 (Jerusalem, 1974), p. 855.

28. A. Weiss, "Categories of Camps, Their Character and Role in the Execution of Final Solution of the Jewish Question," in *The Nazi Concentration Camps* (Jerusalem, 1984), p. 132.

29. E. Kogon, *Der SS Staat* (Munich, 1974), p. 157.

30. C. Madajczyk, *Polityka Trzeciej Rzeszy w okupowanej Polsce,* vol. 2 (Warsaw, 1970), pp. 293–94. The author quotes the verdict of the Supreme National Tribunal in Poland and Höss's testimony.

31. A. Pawelczynska, *Values and Violence in Auschwitz: A Sociological Analysis* (London, 1979), p. 25.

32. K. Dunin-Wasowicz, *Resistance in the Nazi Concentration Camps 1933–1945* (Warsaw, 1982), p. 44.

33. K. Smolen, *Auschwitz 1940-1945: Guide through the Museum* (Katowice, 1981), p. 19 and "Bestrafung der Verbrecher von Auschwitz," in *Auschwitz: Geschichte und Wirklichkeit des Vernichtunglagers* (Reinbek bei Hamburg, 1980), p. 211.

34. D. Czech, "Konzentrationslager Auschwitz: Abriss der Geschichte," in *Auschwitz: Geschichte und Wirklichkeit des Konzentrationslagers,* p. 42.

35. F. Piper, *Zatrudnienie wiezniow KL Auschwitz: Organizacja pracy i metody eksploatacji sily roboczej* (Oswiecim, 1981), p. 47.

36. C. Pilichowski, *Falszerstwo czy prowokacja: Odwetowcy w roli oskarzycieli* (Warsaw, 1977), pp. 178–79.

37. J. Gumkowski, *Obozy koncentracyjne i zaglady na ziemiach polskich w latach 1939–1945* (Warsaw, 1967), p. 121.

38. *Obozy hitlerowskie na ziemiach polskich 1939–1945: Informator encyklopedyczny* (Warsaw, 1979), p. 369.

39. Kazimierz Smolen, director of the State Auschwitz Museum for many years and a former Auschwitz prisoner, stated in an interview: "In my view, no one can deny the number of 4 million," *Dziennik Zachodni*, February 8, 1991.

40. The chairman of the board of the Central Council of Jews in West Germany, Heinz Galinski, and Hermann Baumann have sharply criticized the revised number of victims of the Auschwitz-Birkenau State Museum; the revised figures are close to the estimates advanced by Jewish historians (Hilberg, Wellers). See "Zynische Zahlenspiele," in *Allgemeine Jüdische Wochenzeitung*, July 26, 1990, and *Auschwitz Information*, Ausgabe, Vienna, June 1990.

41. The neo-Nazi weekly *National Zeitung*, having juxtaposed varying figures relating to the victims of Auschwitz, commented, "Jewish Historians Demolish Soviet Propaganda," no. 45, November 2, 1984.

42. G. Wellers, "Essai de détermination du nombre de morts au camp d'Auschwitz," *Le Monde Juif*, October-December 1983, pp. 127–59.

43. Wellers failed to take into account the following studies, among others: A. Strzelecki, *Ewakuacja, likwidacja i wyzolenie KL Auschwitz* (Oswiecim, 1982; lists of transports transferred and evacuated from Auschwitz); Hilberg (data pertaining to the extermination and deportation of Jews to Auschwitz from various countries); and Gilbert (transports to Auschwitz).

44. Wellers arbitrarily accepted 2.5 percent as the proportion of the gassed victims among Poles and the ratio of Poles to Jews (25 percent to 75 percent) for the 66,022 prisoners who remained in the camp on January 17, 1945. He used the resulting numbers to compute the number of Polish and Jewish survivors of Auschwitz (59,930 and 80,425, respectively).

45. An abridged version of the longer document was also published in *Yad Vashem Studies* 21 (1991). The manuscript of the complete version is in the Auschwitz-Birkenau State Museum. The first draft was completed in 1986. The author compared his findings with Wellers's figures during the conference in Krakow-Mogilany, in 1987.

46. R. L. Braham, *The Destruction of Hungarian Jewry* (New York, 1963), pp. 443, 522. The figure of 437,402 Hungarian Jews, cited by Braham, should be supplemented by two transports of Hungarian Jews from the Kistarcsa camp, on August 13, 1944 (at least 131 persons) and October 18, 1944 (152 persons). See also D. Czech, *Kalendarium der Ereignisse im Konzentrationslager Auschwitz-Birkenau 1939–1945* (Reinbek bei Hamburg, 1989), pp. 848, 911.

47. Czech, *Kalendarium der Ereignisse*, passim; Gilbert, passim.

48. S. Klarsfeld, *Memorial to the Jews Deported from France 1942–1944* (New York, 1983).

49. *Documenten van de Jodenvervolging in Nederland 1940–1944* (Amsterdam, 1965), pp. 115–20.

50. D. Czech, "Deportation und Vernichtung der Griechischen Juden im KL Auschwitz," *Hefte von Auschwitz* 11 (1970), p. 537.

51. H. G. Adler, *Theresienstadt 1941–1945* (Tübingen, 1955), pp. 50, 688–94; K. Lagus, *Josef Polak: Mesto nad mrizemi* (Prague, 1964).

52. Hilberg, pp. 458–73. See also Moreshet Archives, Giv'at Haviva, Israel, call no. D.1. 5705.

53. S. Klarsfeld, *Maxime Steinberg: Memorial de la déportation des Juifs de Belgique* (Brussels, 1982).

54. *Juden unterm Hakenkreuz: Verfolgung und Ausrottung der deutschen Juden 1933–1945* (Berlin, 1973); *Gedenkbuch: Opfern der Verfolgung der Juden under der nationalsozialistischen Gewaltherrschaft in Deutschland 1933–1945* (Koblenz, 1986); K. M. Kempner, "Die Ermordung von 35,000 berliner Juden," in *Gegenwart im Ruckblick: Festgabe für die Jüdische Gemeinde zu Berlin 25 Jahre nach dem Neubeginn* (Heidelberg, 1970), pp. 184–88.

55. J. Romano and L. Kadelburg, "The Third Reich: Initiator, Organizer and Executant of Anti-Jewish Measures and Genocide in Yugoslavia," in *The Third Reich and Yugoslavia 1933–1945* (Belgrade, 1977), pp. 684, 690; E. le Chene, "Yugoslavs in Nazi Concentration Camps," in ibid.; Czech, *Kalendarium*, pp. 280, 284, 287, 290, 488, 493.

56. *Ebrei in Italia: Deportatione, resistenza, giuntina* (Florence, 1975), table-deportatione degli Ebrei dall Italia.

57. L. Poliakoff and J. Wulf, *Das Dritte Reich und die Juden: Dokumente und Aufsätze* (Berlin-Grunewald, 1961), p. 140; *Dokumentensammlung über "Die Deportierung der Juden aus Norwegen nach Auschwitz"* (Ramat Gan, 1963), pp. 1–52; Czech, *Kalendarium*, pp. 347–427; ASAM, D-RF-3/121/transport 32.

58. Czech, *Kalendarium*, passim.

59. Gilbert, passim.

60. G. Reitlinger, *The Final Solution* (London, 1971), p. 500.

61. Wellers, pp. 147–49.

62. Wellers relied on the figure of 87 transports from Hungary, as published by Czech in her *Kalendarium*; however, not all transports are listed there. In fact, there were 148 such transports, which averages about 3,000 persons per transport (437,402 divided by 148 equals 2,955). Thus the actual number of deportees in transports from Hungary accorded with the figures projected at the Vienna conference on May 4–5, 1944. See R. Hilberg, *Sonderzüge nach Auschwitz* (Frankfurt am Main and Berlin, 1987), pp. 88–89. Hilberg lists 147 transports up to July 8, 1944.

63. This is obviously Wellers's error, since Czech, in her *Kalendarium*, lists nine transports for the period August 1–4, 1943. Since the figure of 20,000 Jews brought in from Bedzin and Sosnowiec relates to these transports, it should be divided not by four, as done by Wellers, who obtained 5,000 as average size, but by nine, which yields an average transport capacity of 2,222.

64. Hilberg, *Sonderzüge nach Auschwitz*, pp. 211–12. The figure of 2,000 as average transport capacity was also mentioned by Höss in his Nuremberg testimony ("kamen täglich zwei bis drei Zuge mit je zirka 2,000 Personen an"), *Der Nurnberger Prozess gegen die Hauptkriegsverbrecher,* vol. 11, p. 442.

65. Czech, *Kalendarium*, passim.

66. Gilbert, passim.

67. This number tallies the data relating to the RSHA transports (about 200,000 persons) as well as other transports.

68. The highest serial number in the EH (reeducation) category was assigned to an unknown prisoner who died in Czechoslovakia during the evacuation of the camp; ASAM, Mat 1207.

69. Determined mainly on the basis of records of the resistance movement and depositions by former prisoners.

70. The highest serial number entered into the Hauptbuch of the Gypsies is 10,094; ASAM, D-AuII-3/1/2. The highest number assigned to a Gypsy woman—10,888—was entered in the book of block 22B in the women's camp; ASAM, D-AuI-3/1, p. 87.

71. ASAM, Depositions, file 123, card 58, account by a former prisoner, Tadeusz Joachimowski.

72. The highest number assigned to a Soviet POW to be found in documents preserved in ASAM is 11,964 (Yakushel); ASAM, D-AuII-3a/1134. In addition, several numbers were assigned to two prisoners each. According to J. Brandhuber, this double assignation occurred also in the AU series (with a total of 177 serial numbers); see Brandhuber, "Die sowjetischen Kriegsgefangenen im Konzentrationslager Auschwitz," *Hefte von Auschwitz* 4 (1961), p. 45.

73. Brandhuber, p. 45, lists four such groups of prisoners, numbering over 1,800 persons. According to a Sonderkommando prisoner, 10 to 15 prisoners were executed weekly by shooting at the crematoria ovens in Auschwitz, and even more were shot in Birkenau. These figures warrant a conclusion that in two years, more than 1,000 POWs were put to death in this fashion. See *Amidst a Nightmare of Crime*, p. 44 (cited in n. 7 above).

74. At the present state of research, we are unable to break down this figure precisely into national categories. For example, among the 39,159 preserved camp photos, we find, in addition to Poles, Jews, and Gypsies, 4,760 photographs of Germans, 2,465 of Czechs, 1,578 of Russians (not POWs), 797 of Yugoslavs, 654 of French, 548 of Ukrainians, nine of Dutch, two of Danes, two of Romanians, two of Spaniards, and one of a Lithuanian.

75. The list, compiled by L. Krysta, comprises some 182,000 transferred prisoners; a similar list, prepared by St. Iwaszko, has 225,000. These figures require verification. ASAM, Collection, file 100.

76. Strzelecki (cited in n. 43), tables, pp. 248–318.

77. This number is an approximation, since sources do not always indicate whether a given transport comprised registered or unregistered prisoners.

78. Y. Gutman, ed., *Encyclopedia of the Holocaust*, vol. 4 (New York and London, 1990), p. 1799.

79. W. Benz, *Dimension des Volkermords: Die Zahl der jüdischen Opfer des Nationalsozialismus* (Munich, 1991).

Part *II*

Dimensions of Genocide

RAUL HILBERG'S *Destruction of the European Jews* is arguably the single most important book about the Holocaust, detailing the development and implementation of the "final solution" in which Auschwitz played a central role. Hilberg's essay here discusses the evolution of Nazi policy toward the Jews and the role of Auschwitz in the implementation of that policy. It considers Auschwitz in comparison with the other major killing centers of Treblinka, Sobibor, Belzec, Chelmno, and Majdanek, as well as with other concentration and slave-labor camps. It also explores the singularity of Auschwitz and the use of prussic acid, or Zyklon B, in its gas chambers.

Hilberg's chapter traces the evolution of Auschwitz from an ordinary concentration camp built for Poles into a lethal killing center. In the winter of 1940–41, Auschwitz was chosen by a German corporation as a plant site because of its mines, railway access, and cheap slave labor. By September 1941, Auschwitz had expanded in anticipation of the arrival of Soviet prisoners of war, and later that year Auschwitz was given a new mandate: the annihilation of the Jewish people. With this assignment came a change in the instrumentalities of death, from the first experiment with Zyklon B to the sophisticated operation of large gas chambers and crematoria, which could be used to murder hundreds of thousands of Hungarian Jews in a brief period. In typical understatement, Hilberg points out that the commandant of Auschwitz, Rudolf Höss, saw gassing as a way of sparing his men the psychological devastation other forms of murder might have caused them.

Robert-Jan van Pelt is a young architectural historian who has brought the unique tools of his profession to bear on a study of Auschwitz. Like Jean-Claude Pressac, van Pelt has explored the archives in Moscow and Oswiecim that contain the building plans for Auschwitz and the vast correspondence surrounding the erection of the crematoria. He has also worked at the archives of the United States Holocaust Research Institute, which contain microfilms of this voluminous material alongside other extensive holdings. His contribution to this volume traces the evolution of Auschwitz from model town to killing center and provides a new angle on the evolution of Auschwitz as a camp.

One sees his professional insights when discussing space allocations per prisoner. Van Pelt concludes that the definition of Soviet soldiers as *untermenschen* was translated into architectural terms in the very dimensions of the camps and their "living quarters," the space allocated in units the size of a coffin or shallow grave.

Van Pelt traces the evolution of the plans for cremation. He concludes that the plan of January 1942 reveals, in the end, a lethal environment— death by starvation, disease, hard labor—precisely the conditions present from the beginning at Birkenau, where the construction mortality rate for Soviet POWs was 240 percent per year. Yet the situation in 1944 can be explained only as the result of lethal technology—the gas chambers.

With his keen sense of detail, van Pelt documents what the late Terrence Des Pres called "excremental assault" and adds to our understanding of the Nazi assault against human dignity. Construction plans called for one wash barrack per 7,800 inmates and one laboratory hut per 7,000 prisoners. Given the design of the entrance ways and walkways, the absence of privacy, seating or water for the evacuation of the excrement, the inevitable result was, as van Pelt says with typical understatement, "secretory catastrophe." The word is bound to enter the professional literature of the *lager*.

The history of the technology of mass murder at Auschwitz from 1941 to 1944, including the exact process by which it took place, is described by Franciszek Piper. He traces the evolution of the killing process and the increasingly efficient use of prussic acid, as well as the complex technology of the Auschwitz crematoria. The first experiments with gassing were conducted in block 11, but they could not be kept secret and the gas could not be easily contained. Soon Auschwitz I had its own crematorium building screened from the camp by flowerbeds and the SS hospital. It could dispose of 340 bodies in 24 hours. A charnel house was soon converted into a gas chamber that could hold some 700 persons. By 1942 the gassing operation was moved to Birkenau (Auschwitz II). Piper details the structure of the crematoria as well as the elaborate deceptions of the SS, which included the labeling of the area and the presence of physicians and Red Cross insignias. Attention is paid to the operations of the various Sonderkommando teams. Especially interesting is Piper's description of the process of unearthing bodies from 1942 onward. In the summer of 1944, Piper notes, "the combined capacity of all the incineration installations reached the staggering number of 20,000 victims."

In a chapter that has the length and density of a historical monograph, Jean-Claude Pressac, a French student of Nazi technologies of genocide, provides a narrative of the design, construction, financing, development, and functioning of the gas chambers and crematoria at Auschwitz, adapted from his book *Les Crématoires d'Auschwitz: La machinerie du meurtre de masse*, published in Paris in 1993. Pressac relies on a largely untapped archival resource: the records of the construction bureau at the Auschwitz concentration camp, which was responsible for all building projects within the camp complex, including the construction of gas chambers and crematoria. The correspondence, fiscal accounts, and architectural drawings of the Auschwitz construction bureau enable Pressac to reconstruct in minute detail the evolution of genocidal technologies.

Robert-Jan van Pelt collaborated in the editing of Pressac's masterful essay, working with him on the translation word by word, detail by detail. He brings to Pressac's essay thorough familiarity with the documentary sources used by Pressac and his own concern for meticulously documenting the past.

Many of Pressac's conclusions are debatable; his argument that the gas chambers erected in Birkenau were not initially designed for genocide, for example, is sure to generate controversy among historians of the Holocaust. But his most valuable contribution is the story of how the technology of gassing and incineration evolved over time and was adapted to ever-changing circumstances and demands from SS headquarters in Berlin. Pressac also exposes an arrestingly mundane tale of commercial rivalry among competitors for SS-funded construction contracts at Auschwitz and other camps, of bureaucratic infighting among various branches within the SS hierarchy of power, and of the political intrigues of engineer Karl Prüfer, who sold equipment for gassing and incineration to the Auschwitz SS and, largely for reasons of personal gain, played a decisive role in developing a technology of genocide.

Andrzej Strzelecki documents the process of body disposal by describing in detail the confiscation and shipment of the murdered victims' possessions to German industries and the use that was made of their bodies. Every possible use was made of hair, fat, gold from teeth. "Respectable" corporations throughout the Reich, even the Reichsbank, received this material without inquiring from whence it came and at what cost, then requested more. A distinguished university awarded a Ph.D. for a theory on the reuse of dental gold. What Strzelecki demonstrates is dehumanization not of the victims but of their SS killers and businessmen of the Reich.

The crematoria played an important role in the Nazi implementation of genocide. At first, bodies were buried in mass graves. Soon the sheer size of the killing process made this impossible. Eventually, the SS returned to sites of mass murder to dig up and burn the bodies. Given the magnitude of murder at Auschwitz-Birkenau, the open burning of bodies was difficult; consequently the crematoria, which could dispose of the bodies in an effective and efficient manner, were introduced. Dissecting tables were nearby so that inner cavities could be opened if there was a suspicion that the victim had hidden valuables. Although everything of value within the human body was recycled, there is no evidence, despite widespread reports, that human fat was used for soap. The United States Holocaust Memorial Museum tested several bars of soap reported to be composed of human fat but no such fat was found. Nevertheless, the crematoria represent an extensive recycling of human beings who had become consumable raw material discarded in the process of manufacture. Furthermore, the disposal of bodies removed material evidence of the crime.

Michael Berenbaum

5

Auschwitz and the Final Solution

RAUL HILBERG

One place has become a symbol for the Jewish catastrophe in Europe: Auschwitz. Its preeminence is rooted in at least three of its many attributes. One is the brute fact of numbers. More Jews died there than in any other locality. Another is geographic. Auschwitz alone was truly continental in scope, drawing its victims from a wide variety of countries and regions. Finally, Auschwitz was also long-standing. After all other death camps had been shut down, it remained in operation—a solitary killing center signifying the will of Nazi Germany to annihilate the Jews in the last hours of a losing war.

Yet Auschwitz had not been created for this ultimate role. The camp's complex history reveals a succession of purposes. At the beginning, it was an ordinary concentration camp established in a region seized from Poland and incorporated into Germany. Its original inmates were, in the main, Poles who were shipped in immediately after a group of buildings, most of which had belonged to the Polish army, had been taken over to form the camp. The first commandant, Rudolf Höss, was an experienced but not high-ranking Nazi concentration camp man who had been stationed for several years in Dachau and Sachsenhausen. Nothing in these early days indicated that Auschwitz would become something more than a relatively unimposing component of Nazi SS chief Heinrich Himmler's concentration camp empire.

The initial unexceptional function of Auschwitz was enlarged and transformed in the late winter of 1940–41, when the IG Farben concern selected the area for the construction of major new plant facilities. The choice was dictated by the availability of a nearby railway junction and the existence close by of mines, as well as a tax exemption offered by the Third Reich to companies that moved into newly incorporated territories.[1] For IG Farben, and later for other firms, there was to be an additional inducement: cheap concentration camp labor. The SS, on its part, could look forward to an income from the arrangement and, more generally, to a recognition of its growing economic importance.

At the time of this ferment, Himmler visited Auschwitz and ordered the expansion of the camp to hold 30,000 prisoners. He also wanted Birkenau, a village about two miles from Auschwitz, to be added to the camp, supplying room for another 100,000 inmates.[2] Himmler's optimism, however, was somewhat premature. Mass arrests on such a scale were as yet politically infeasible, and Höss, skirting the judicial authorities, even resorted to an unorthodox agreement with the local *Landrat* whereby ethnic Germans and Poles who refused work in the free market would be incarcerated in the camp over a period of eight weeks to facilitate their "education."[3]

In September 1941, the SS anticipated an improvement of its labor situation. The German attack on the Soviet Union had netted an overflow of captured Red Army soldiers. When Himmler proposed to erect new camps for prisoners of war, the army promised him 325,000 of these men. Lublin (Majdanek) and the Birkenau portion of Auschwitz were hurriedly restyled Prisoner of War Camps of the Armed SS, and on September 27, the SS construction chief, Hans Kammler, ordered that the two camps be readied with utmost speed for 50,000 prisoners each.[4] By October 9, Kammler had arrived in Auschwitz with word that Birkenau was to be built to accommodate as many as 200,000 inmates.[5] From that moment, planning was intensified, and progressively more ambitious blueprints were produced in rapid succession. The masses of prisoners did not materialize, however. Barely 15,000 of them were marched on foot from a nearby army camp to Auschwitz. Höss had been told that these captives were the cream of the crop for hard labor, but by the end of February 1942, most of them were already dead.[6]

In the midst of the planning and scheming, during the second half of 1941, Auschwitz was given a mandate in the "final solution of the Jewish question." Over the years, the Jews of Europe had been subjected to expropriation, exploitation, and segregation. In the 1930s they had been prodded to leave. Now their emigration across spreading war zones and battlefields was not a practical possibility. At the same time the deteriorated situation of the Jews was not going to be frozen, nor was the momentum of measures cascading upon them going to be halted. The Jews would be uprooted from the cities of Western Europe and the teeming ghettos of Poland to be sent to secluded places where they were going to meet their end. Auschwitz was one of these locations.

At first glance it would seem that this conjunction of needs was fortuitous for Auschwitz in its quest for labor, and for the deportation specialists groping for an ideal terminal. Neither was the case. The final solution was not supposed to consist of prolonged stays in barracks, with labor allocations to industrial projects. It required means for rapid killing and an equally effective method for the disposal of bodies. Such devices could not be created instantaneously. Yet Auschwitz became a central feature of the evolving program. It was, in fact, a part of Jewish history from the moment when the final solution was decided.

Höss recalled that in the summer of 1941 he was summoned to Berlin by Heinrich Himmler himself. In a few spare words Himmler told him of Hitler's decision to annihilate the Jews. One of the factors in the choice of Auschwitz, said Himmler, was its location near railways. This consideration, of course, is identical to the ideas explored by IG Farben a few months earlier. But in discussing the selection, Himmler also stated why Höss was going to be in charge. At first, he said, a higher-ranking SS leader, presumably outside the concentration camp hierarchy, originally was to have been given the assignment. This possibility, he explained, was discarded to avoid a jurisdictional dispute within the SS. Höss would therefore have to carry out the mission. Details would be brought to Höss by Adolf Eichmann of the Reich Main Security Office. Underscoring the gravity of the conversation, Himmler admonished Höss to observe strict secrecy. Höss was not to mention anything even to his immediate superior, the inspector of concentration camps, Richard Glücks.[7]

Indeed, Höss was not an ordinary concentration camp commander. He had proved himself as a soldier in the First World War, when he was the youngest sergeant in the German Army, and he had acquired high Nazi credentials in the early 1920s, after his participation in the murder of a schoolteacher suspected of having betrayed a German saboteur to French occupation troops. Höss was sentenced to ten years in prison for this crime.[8] According to the SS investigation judge, Georg Konrad Morgen, Höss had a close connection with the man who later became the chief of the party Chancellery, Martin Bormann. Because of this relationship, says Morgen, the SS treated Höss like a "raw egg." Morgen even supposes that Bormann urged Hitler to give the task of solving the Jewish question to Höss.[9]

Not long after Himmler had commissioned Höss to carry out the killing operation, Eichmann came to Auschwitz, and at the end of November Höss reciprocated by attending a conference in Eichmann's office. The talk there was about railroads and arrangements for trains.[10] It is at this point that the scope of the undertaking took form. Germany ruled or exercised influence in large tracts of Europe, and everywhere in this domain the Jews were to be rooted out. Auschwitz, however, was not designated as the receiving station for all these Jews. The fact that Eichmann was the organizer of the transports to Auschwitz indicates something about the limits of the original deportation area from which the camp was going to obtain its victims. Eichmann had no functions in the newly invaded regions of the Soviet Union, where the Jews were shot, and he did not have any responsibilities in the central part of occupied Poland, known as the General Government, where the Jews were dispatched by local SS and police officials to Belzec, Sobibor, and Treblinka, all located within General Government boundaries.

Even outside these territories, Himmler did not rely entirely on Auschwitz. From the ghettos in the Wartheland, which was incorporated from Poland into the Reich, Jews were sent to Kulmhof (Chelmno), a primitive camp set up in the province. As for the Old Reich, Austria, and the Protectorate of Bohemia and Moravia, the destination did not matter as long as the Jews were moved out of this Germanic heartland.

As early as September 16, 1941, Himmler notified Gauleiter Arthur Greiser of the Wartheland that he was shipping 60,000 Jews to the city of Lodz. Because of local opposition to such a movement, the ultimate number was a shade below 20,000. But there were other final stops on the map. On October 2, 1941, Himmler proposed to Hitler the deportation of German Jews to the Lublin District of the General Government, as well as to Minsk in Byelorussia and Tallin in Estonia. By October 10, the Reich Main Security Office had revised this list, substituting Riga in Latvia for the more distant Tallin. Then a procession of trains proceeded northeast to the Baltic region during the fall and winter. About 5,000 Jews were unloaded in Kaunas (Kovno) to be shot there in November, and a larger number of deportees arrived in Riga and Minsk. Later, more Jews were routed from Germany to the Lublin District and the Warsaw ghetto. From there they were sent to die in General Government camps. The first satellite state to become a deportation country was Slovakia. Most of the Slovak transports, which began in March 1942, were also directed to the LublinDistrict.

In the meantime, Auschwitz was not ready for its new role. If one may speak of a first step, it was taken in the early days of September 1941, while Höss was away on business. About 850 inmates, including 200 who were ill and 650 who were Soviet prisoners of war, were locked into a building and gassed with prussic acid, or Zyklon B. The killing, carried out at the initiative of Höss's deputy, Karl Fritsch, was an experiment, but not necessarily with a view to the final solution. Soviet prisoners had been shot in small batches at Auschwitz, pursuant to orders for the execution of Communist party functionaries and other dangerous elements in the Red Army. Fritsch had thought of the poison, which was stocked at Auschwitz for fumigation purposes, as an alternative to shooting, and had tried to determine the proper lethal dosage. Once the gassing had taken place, however, Höss saw it as the answer to his Jewish problem. In December, another batch of Soviet prisoners was killed with Zyklon B in the mortuary of the Auschwitz crematorium. Höss observed the corpses and listened to explanations of camp physicians. The victims, he was assured, had not suffocated in agony. He concluded that death from the gas was bloodless and would spare his men a great psychological burden.[11]

The mortuary now became the first gas chamber. In addition, two farm houses in Birkenau were converted for gassings. The first was ready for use in March, but its capacity, according to a camp doctor, was limited to about 300 people.[12] The second was more spacious, but it did not become operational until the end of June.[13]

Himmler visited the camp on July 17 and 18, 1942. He watched one of the gassings. It is probably on this occasion that he remarked on the inadequacy of the camps in the General Government for the Europeanwide final solution. He told Höss that Eichmann's transports would rise from month to month, that Jews incapable of work were to be annihilated ruthlessly, and that the Gypsies too were to be killed.[14]

The crematorium in the base camp and the two huts in Birkenau were, however, the only gassing capabilities of Auschwitz until March 1943. Considering that 1942 was Jewry's most deadly year, the Jews who arrived during that time were but a small fraction of the total number of Jewish deportees, let alone the aggregate of the dead in camps, ghettos, and shooting sites. Table 1 is a breakdown of the Jews sent to the death camps up to December 31, 1942. Table 2 shows the breakdown of the Auschwitz arrival figures for the period ending in 1942 and for the first three months of 1943 by area of origin. Noteworthy in this tabulation is not only an overall total, as of March 1943, which is not more than approximately 280,000, but a subtotal of barely 150,000 representing all the countries outside the Reich, the Bohemian-Moravian Protectorate, and Poland.

In the final solution conference of January 20, 1942, the Reich Main Security Office offered the following population statistics for these countries:[15] Finland, 2,300; Norway, 1,200; Denmark, 5,600; Netherlands, 160,000; Belgium, 43,000; France (occupied), 165,000; France (unoccupied), 700,000 [*sic*]; Italy, 58,000; Croatia, 40,000; Serbia, 10,000; Albania, 200; Greece, 69,000; Bulgaria, 48,000; Romania, 342,000; Hungary, 742,000; Slovakia, 88,000. The total is 2,475,100. But the sum was inflated, principally because of the gross overestimate for unoccupied France, by about 600,000 people. Even so, a realistic assessment would have come to 1,850,000, or more than 12 times the number of Jewish victims delivered from the area to Auschwitz by the end of March 1943. There was, of course, a reason for the restricted flow of Jews from the west and from the south. In most areas within this region, the Germans had to deal with foreign sensibilities, and in some cases with foreign governments. The experience was often frustrating to the Reich Main Security Office and its partner, the Foreign Office. Deferments or exemptions were allowed for various categories of Jews, and where resistance to deportation by one of Germany's allies was adamant, an entire Jewish community was out of reach. Hungary itself protected nearly half of the Jews who might have been on Eichmann's deportation lists.

Table 1. Deportation of Jews to Auschwitz and Other Camps to December 31, 1942

	Number	*Percent*
Auschwitz	Up to 175,000	Ca. 11
Kulmhof (Chelmno)	145,301	Ca. 9
General Government camps	1,274,166	Ca. 80

For sources, see endnote 28.

Table 2. Arrival of Jews in Auschwitz from Specific Regions through March 1943

	To December 31, 1942	*January – March 1943*
France	41,951	3,998
Netherlands	38,571	9,408
Upper Silesia and Ciechanow	30,225	Ca. 1,000
Slovakia	18,748	—
Belgium	16,886	1,616
Bialystok District	Over 13,000	Over 47,000
Croatia	4,927	—
Germany and Austria	Ca. 4,000	Ca. 15,000
Theresienstadt	1,886	7,001
Concentration camps	Ca. 1,600	—
Lublin (Majdanek)	Hundreds	—
Soviet prisoners of war	Hundreds	—
Salonika	—	Ca. 10,000
General Government	—	Ca. 7,000
Wartheland	—	Ca. 1,000
Norway	532	158
Total	Up to 175,000	Near 105,000

For sources, see endnote 29.

For Auschwitz, these problems spelled out special complications. Unlike the General Government camps, which received the vast majority of their victims from territories wholly dominated by Germany, the Auschwitz administration faced an almost constant unpredictability about the volume and timing of arriving transports. Inevitably, questions had to arise about adding new buildings for gassing and cremation, and about the rate of such an expansion.

The Jews who died in the Birkenau gas buildings were buried. For some time, however, a new crematorium was on the drawing boards. On February 27, 1942, Kammler visited the camp again and ordered that the two ovens, each with three retorts, planned for this facility, be increased to five ovens, with a total of 15 retorts. The memorandum recording the visit makes clear that crematorium II was to be located in Birkenau.[16] Not specified are Kammler's reasons for the order, but Poles had been brought in on a daily basis of only dozens, seldom hundreds, and the arrival on a mass scale of Soviet prisoners was no longer a realistic expectation. The Jews, on the other hand, were supposed to come in heavy transports, and as a matter of policy were to be put to death. For the corpses, graves would do at the start, but crematoria could be used over and over.

As of the summer of 1942, four crematoria were planned for Birkenau. By then, there was also a major revision in the planning: the crematoria were to have gas chambers.[17] In July the construction of the first of these crematoria was to begin immediately, given "the situation created by the special actions."[18] Contracts were approved for the construction of all the crematoria.[19] Yet in August, a note of hesitancy was introduced. At a construction conference that month about the next crematorium, the decision was to "wait for the result of ongoing negotiations with the Reich Main Security Office [Eichmann] about the allocation of contingents,"[20] that is to say, contingents of Jews.

By the beginning of 1943, the Belzec and Kulmhof death camps were out of commission, confined to burning their accumulated bodies, while Auschwitz was still wrestling with cost considerations and technical complications in the completion of its new crematoria. For Jews already in Auschwitz, these problems did not mean a reprieve: at the end of 1942, only 1,412 were still alive in the camp.[21] Accordingly, when Himmler decided in December of that year that the industries in Auschwitz should receive additional labor forces, Gestapo chief Heinrich Müller issued a directive to draw 45,000 Jews quickly from areas completely controlled by the Reich: 30,000 from the Bialystok District, 10,000 from the Theresienstadt ghetto, and the remainder from the Netherlands and Berlin.[22] Possibly a third of these 45,000 Jews were going to be fit for labor. The rest would have to be gassed. Such numbers were still manageable in January 1943, but an additional flow in February and March presented obvious difficulties. Despite frantic efforts to open the first of the new crematoria with its built-in gassing facilities for "immediate measures," there were continual delays, and transports from afar were consequently routed over even greater distances to the General Government, as shown in table 3.

All four crematoria were operational by June 1943.[23] Birkenau now had vastly increased capabilities for killing and body disposal. Theoretically, the four units in Birkenau, together with the old crematorium in the base camp, could burn 4,736 corpses in a 24-hour working day.[24] As a practical matter, the maximum was about two-thirds of that number.[25] Still, on a yearly basis, the actual capacity after June 1943 was more than a million. Yet during the period from April 1943 to March 1944 inclusively, Auschwitz received no more than about 160,000 Jews. The transports basically constituted a continuation of the earlier deportation program: more trains from the Netherlands, Belgium, France, and Salonika, more from Theresienstadt, and more from Upper Silesia and the General Government. By the summer of 1943, the supply of deportees from Upper Silesia was almost completely exhausted, and Salonika had been drained. The core of Romania and the prewar territory of Bulgaria had to be written off as deportation countries. The labor supply in Auschwitz was so depleted that several thousand Jews were transferred to the camp from Lublin (Majdanek) in August. As Jean-Claude Pressac has pointed out, the camp had reached a stage of overcapacity.[26]

Table 3. Deportation of Jews from Three Regions to General Government Camps

	March 1943	*After March 1943*
Macedonia and Thrace (to Treblinka)	11,346	—
Netherlands (to Sobibor)	4,424	29,889
France (to Sobibor)	3,994	—

For sources, see endnote 30.

All this changed radically in the spring of 1944. The cause was the invasion by Germany of its neighbor Hungary on March 19, 1944. Within Hungary's boundaries the largest Jewish community in the Axis world had remained at liberty. Now these people could be deported forthwith. Auschwitz prepared feverishly for this haul. Railway tracks were laid to the crematoria. The second of Birkenau's 1942 gas buildings, which had not been used for a long time, was rehabilitated. Pits were dug near this facility for rapid, open-air burning. And Höss, who had been promoted in November 1943 to a post in the concentration camp management near Berlin, returned to the scene. Hungary was going to lift Auschwitz to the top. Table 4 reveals the extent of this development.

More Jews were transported to Auschwitz during the following eight months than had arrived there in the preceding two years. The Hungarian Jews were joined by Jews from Poland as the remnant ghetto of Lodz was dissolved and labor camps in the General Government were cleared. More Jews came from Theresienstadt, Slovakia, and the West. Not all of them, however, were killed right away. Germany's labor shortage had become acute, and possibly 30,000 Jews were transferred to other camps for war work. Young women far outnumbered young men among the deportees of 1944, mainly because Hungary had retained a sizable group of Jews in its army labor companies, but the sex ratio did not deter Himmler, who was willing to compromise the final solution by sending out men and women to work in industrial as well as agricultural projects. Auschwitz, however, was still much more efficient as a killing center than as an employer or labor exchange. The last roll call revealed the presence of 67,012 inmates, perhaps four-fifths of them Jews,[27] but thousands were still dying during the final days of the camp and in the course of its evacuation.

Table 4. Arrival of Jews in Auschwitz from Specific Regions, April 1943 through November 1944

	April 1943 – March 1944	*April–November 1944*
Salonika	Ca. 36,000	—
Other Greek areas	—	7,222
Italy and Rhodes	Ca. 3,400	Ca. 5,500
France	15,438	7,534
Netherlands	Ca. 11,400	Ca. 2,200
Belgium	5,386	1,695
Croatia	Ca. 2,000	—
Germany and Austria	Ca. 1,500	Ca. 2,000
Theresienstadt	10,014	25,907
Slovakia	—	7,936
Hungary	—	Ca. 426,000
Upper Silesia	Ca. 47,500	Ca. 7,000
Wartheland (mainly Lodz)	Ca. 5,000	Ca. 67,000
General Government	Ca. 14,000	Ca. 23,000
Bialystok children	1,260	—
Majdanek	Ca. 3,000	Hundreds
Bergen-Belsen	Ca. 1,700	—
Other camps	Ca. 2,000	Ca. 4,000
Total	Ca. 160,000	Over 585,000

For sources, see endnote 31.

NOTES

1. Memoranda by Fritz ter Meer (IG Farben), February 10, 1941, Nuremberg trials documents NI-11111, NI-11112, and NI-11113. Ter Meer to IG Farben Director Dencker and Ministerialrat Romer of the Economy Ministry, February 22, 1941, NI-11114. Summary of a meeting between General Governor Hans Frank and Directors Weiss and Eisfeld of IG Farben, September 11, 1941, Frank Diary, National Archives record group 238, T992, roll 4.

2. Danuta Czech, *Kalendarium der Ereignisse im Konzentrationslager Auschwitz-Birkenau 1939–1945* (Reinbek bei Hamburg, 1989), entry for March 1, 1941, p. 79.

3. Weekly report by IG Farben (Auschwitz) engineer Max Faust, covering August 17–23, NI-15254.

4. Jozef Marszalek, *Majdanek* (Reinbek bei Hamburg, 1982), pp. 27–28.

5. Czech, entry for October 8/9, 1941, p. 128n.

6. Kazimierz Smolen, *Auschwitz—Gang durch das Museum* (Katowice, 1978), p. 22.

7. Rudolf Höss, *Kommandant in Auschwitz* (Munich, 1978), pp. 157, 180–81. See also his testimony to the International Military Tribunal, in *Trial of the Major War Criminals*, vol. 11 (Nuremberg, 1947–49), p. 398. Höss does not recall the precise date of the meeting with Himmler, although his earliest statement, which is also the most confused, notes June; see his affidavit of March 14, 1946, Nuremberg trials document NO-1210. July has been considered more likely. Richard Breitmann, reviewing Himmler's traveling, specifies July 13–15 as the only time when Himmler was in Berlin that month; see his *Architect of Genocide* (New York, 1991), p. 295. Czech suggests in her *Kalendarium* entry for July 29, pp. 106–7, that in July Höss was absent from Auschwitz only on the 29th. In effect, July may therefore be ruled out altogether in favor of a somewhat later summer date.

8. Höss, pp. 36–37.

9. Affidavit by Konrad Morgen, July 13, 1946, Nuremberg trials document SS(A)-65.

10. Höss, p. 158.

11. Ibid., pp. 125–27.

12. Affidavit by Friedrich Entress, April 14, 1947, Nuremberg trials document NO-2368.

13. See Höss, pp. 158, 161.

14. Ibid., pp. 181–85.

15. Summary of the final solution conference of January 20, 1942, Nuremberg trials document NG-2586.

16. Hauptsturmführer Bischoff (Zentralbauleitung in Auschwitz) to Sturmbannführer Wirtz (Wirtschafts-Verwaltungshauptamt C III), March 30, 1942, Nuremberg trials document NO-4472.

17. Jean-Claude Pressac, *Auschwitz: Technique and Operation of the Gas Chambers* (New York, 1989), p. 98. See also Pressac's essay in this volume (chap. 7).

18. Bischoff to Wirtschafts-Verwaltungshauptamt CV, October 13, 1942, facsimile in ibid., pp. 197–99.

19. Pressac, pp. 98, 200. Höss, pp. 160–61.

20. Memorandum by Untersturmführer Ertl of the Zentralbauleitung in Auschwitz, August 21, 1942; facsimile in Pressac, pp. 204–5.

21. SS Statistician Korherr to Himmler (the first Korherr report about the final solution), March 23, 1943, Nuremberg trials document NO-5195.

22. Order by Müller, December 16, 1942, Nuremberg trials document PS-1472.

23. Bauleitung list with dates; facsimile in Pressac, p. 246.

24. Sturmbannführer Jahrling (Zentralbauleitung Auschwitz) to Kammler (Chief of Office Group C in the Wirtschafts-Verwaltungshauptamt), June 28, 1943; facsimile in ibid., p. 247.

25. Pressac, p. 244.

26. Ibid., p. 227.

27. Czech, entry for January 17, 1945, pp. 965–69. The roll call covered Auschwitz, Birkenau, and the industrial camp of Monowitz. There is a breakdown for the men in Auschwitz-Birkenau, indicating a total of 15,317, of whom 11,102, or 72.48 percent, were Jews. In Monowitz, not including satellite stations, on January 13, 1945, there were 9,806 inmates, of whom 9,054, or 92.33 percent, were Jews. Ibid., p. 960.

28. Sources for table 1. For the Auschwitz compilation, see n. 29. The figures for Kulmhof (Chelmno) and the General Government camps are taken from the first report of SS Statistician Korherr to Himmler about the final solution, March 23, 1943, Nuremberg trials document NO-5195. The General Government camps included Belzec, Sobibor, and Treblinka. Lublin (Majdanek), which received relatively few Jews, may or may not have been included in the General Government figure.

29. Sources for table 2. The figures for France, the Netherlands, Belgium, Croatia, and Norway are taken from the first and second Korherr reports, March and April 1943, Nuremberg trial documents NO-5195 and NO-5193. The combined figure to December 31, 1942, for Upper Silesia and Ciechanow is computed from the first Korherr report. The Auschwitz portion of the Slovak deportations is furnished by Bedrich Steiner (formerly with the statistical office of the Ustredna Zidov) in the trial of Adolf Eichmann in Jerusalem, English transcript, May 24, 1960, session 50, p. Wl. Transports from Germany to Auschwitz originated mainly in Berlin. See the compilation in the indictment of Berlin Gestapo officials, February 22, 1969, 1 Js 9/65, Leo Baeck Institute microfilm 239. In this document, the transport of November 29, 1942, with 1,001 Jews is listed as destined either for Auschwitz or Riga, and the transport of December 14, 1942, with 811 deportees is allocated to Riga. The prosecutor could not find survivors of either transport, and proof of their arrival in Riga is lacking. It is likely that both were directed to Auschwitz, and they are accordingly included in the figure of 4,000. Also part of the 4,000 is a transport from Vienna. See Jonny Maser, "Osterreich," in Wolfgang Benz, ed., *Dimension des Volkermords* (Munich, 1991), pp. 86–87, and the report by the Jewish Elder in Vienna, Josef Lowenherz, for 1942, Yad Vashem document O 30/3. The number in the right column for Germany is calculated from the deficit, which is 19,417, from December 31, 1942, to March 31, 1943, as noted in the Korherr reports, with allowance for transports to Theresienstadt and deaths in Germany. See the Kommission zur Erforschung der Geschichte der Frankfurter Juden, *Dokumente zur Geschichte der Frankfurter Juden 1933–1945* (Frankfurt, 1963), pp. 488–98, particularly p. 498; the indictment of the Berlin Gestapo; and Czech's *Kalendarium*. Theresienstadt data are provided by H. G. Adler, *Theresienstadt 1941–1945* (Tübingen, 1960), pp. 53–54. The remaining numbers, which are less precise, may be gleaned from Czech's *Kalendarium*. Based on projections and counts in the files of the German railroads, the size of the Bialystok

transports are assumed here to have averaged somewhat over 2,000 each. See the railroad correspondence respecting Bialystok in Archives of the U.S. Holocaust Memorial Museum, 22.03 (Belarus Central Archives), roll 2, fond 378, opis 1, folder 784.

30. Sources for table 3. The figure for Macedonia and Thrace, under Bulgarian rule, is reported by Korherr, April 1943, NO-5193. See also Frederick B. Chary, *The Bulgarian Jews and the Final Solution* (Pittsburgh, 1972), pp. 101–26. The numbers of Dutch Jews are recapitulated by Adalbert Ruckerl, *NS-Vernichtungslager* (Munich, 1979), pp. 156–57. The data for the French transports are in Serge Klarsfeld, *Memorial to the Jews Deported from France 1942–1944* (New York, 1983), pp. 396–425. The four French transports, all departing from Drancy near Paris, are listed with their Sobibor destination in the Tagesverzeichnis für Reisesonderzüge 1942/1943, German Federal Archives III (Potsdam), 43.01 Reichsverkehrsministerium alt 713.

31. Sources for table 4. The total number of Jews transported from Greek areas occupied by the Germans before the Italian surrender in September 1943 was 45,984, as computed from the detailed enumerations by Josef Nehama in Michael Molho, ed., *In Memorian—Hommage aux victimes juives des Nazi en Grèce* (Salonika, 1948), p. 184. About 10,000 of these deportees arrived at their destination by March 31, 1943, the remainder during the following months. The Greek statistics for 1944, comprising deportees from former Italian-occupied areas on the mainland and the island of Corfu, are also taken from Nehama, ibid. The Italian figures are based on data in Liliana Picciotto Fargion, *Il libro della memoria* (Milan, 1991). The French statistics are in Klarsfeld, *Memorial*. Belgian numbers are in Serge Klarsfeld, *Maxime Steinberg: Memorial de la déportation des juifs de Belgique* (Brussels and New York, 1982). Theresienstadt data are listed in Adler, *Theresienstadt*, pp. 56–59. The Slovak figure is that of Steiner in his testimony at the Eichmann trial, May 24, 1961, English transcript, session 50, p. xi. The Hungarian total comes from several sources. Ca. 3,800 Jews were reported on April 29, 1944, by German Minister Veesenmayer in Hungary as departing; facsimile in Randolph Braham, ed., *The Destruction of Hungarian Jewry* (New York, 1963), p. 363. Some 437,410 Jews were reported by Veesenmayer on June 13 and 30 and July 9 as having been deported from five zones in Greater Hungary; Nuremberg trials documents NG-5619, NG-2263, and NG-5615. An additional transport of ca. 1,700 from the internment camp of Kistarcsa was mentioned in testimony by Rudolf Kastner, Nuremberg subsequent trials (Ministries Case), English transcript, p. 36256. The total then is derived by subtracting 14,700 who were diverted to Austria for possible ransom, a number cited by the Economy Ministry in a letter to the Foreign Office, August 3, 1944, in Braham, pp. 465–66. The remaining figures are derived from Czech's *Kalendarium*. The 4,000 listed under "other camps" in the second column include inmates of Blechhammer and Gleiwitz, two camps in Upper Silesia that were annexed by Auschwitz (Monowitz).

6

A Site in Search of a Mission

ROBERT-JAN VAN PELT

Its name seems unassimilable. Before we have recovered from its harsh and repulsive beginning (*Ausch*), we are hit by its violent and sarcastic end (*witz*). The name suggests the content, which, according to Lyotard, is "the experience of language that brings speculative discourse to an end."[1] Staunch Heideggerians, seeking to justify their master's inability to confront or even name the Holocaust, have declared Auschwitz to be an unthinkable realm shrouded in silence. Many others believe that silence serves the pious memory of the victims and shows a deferential respect for the survivors. They declare Auschwitz to be an unintelligible world, a strange universe, that cannot be explained. Hochhuth called it Planet Auschwitz, a forlorn, damned, and desolate world.

Banished from the world of description, analysis, and conclusion, Auschwitz has become a myth in which the assumed universality of its impact obscures the contingencies of its beginning. I use the word *myth* in the sense that Barthes gave to it in his essay "Myth Today." Mythification, he argued, occurs when language empties a narrative of its historical contingency to fill it with an unchanging nature. "In passing from history to nature, myth acts economically: it abolishes the complexity of human acts, it gives them simplicity of essences." The result is an account of "blissful clarity" in which there are no contradictions because statements of fact are interpreted as explanations; "things appear to mean something by themselves."[2] Few events can rival the mythic power of "Auschwitz."

In this essay I aim to recover some of the historical quality of Auschwitz, which, in the words of Barthes, is the memory that it once was made.[3] A characteristic of a mythic site is that it has always been, since its significance is assigned at the beginning of creation, to be redeemed at the end of history. Auschwitz was not preordained to become the major site of the Holocaust. It acquired that role almost by accident, and even the fact that it became a site of mass murder at all was due more to the failure to achieve one goal than to the ambition to realize another. To reclaim the reality of Auschwitz, we must become attuned to the contradictions of what may be defined to have been, between 1941 and 1943, "a site in search of a mission."[4]

As Jean-Claude Pressac shows in his essay in this volume, the contingency of Auschwitz's evolution applies even to its mythic core: the crematoria. In this essay I will concentrate on another contradiction of the site that clashes with an essential aspect of the myth of Auschwitz: the idea that it was quite literally "the end of the world," a place far away from everywhere else. My choice of subject stems from personal experience. The first time I visited Auschwitz I was surprised by the juxtaposition of a center of extermination and a major town. I had seen Lanzmann's film *Shoah* and remembered its depiction of the isolation of the death camps of Treblinka and Sobibor, the silence of the forests that surrounded them. It was the same seclusion that I knew from the Dutch transit camp of Westerbork, where the weekly trains set out upon their fatal journey eastward. Growing up in Holland, I had always assumed that the secret terminus of those trains would be as deserted as their point of departure. When, 40 years later, I followed their route, I arrived in a densely populated area, with large towns, huge industries, and little camouflage. And all that development seemed more than 50 years old. I began to investigate the archives in Poland and found that not only was the camp at Auschwitz built right next to an existing town, but this very town had been designated as a center of growth by the same men who had ordered the construction of the camp. Auschwitz under the National Socialists was to become a district capital and the site of massive industrial activity. It became clear that the mythification of Auschwitz, to which I had contributed, had blinded me to a more complex reality in which seemingly opposite things—the design for utopia and the reality of dystopia—existed side by side.[5]

I aim to situate this relationship within the German mental map of Central Europe and the geography of the industrialized region of Upper Silesia. In other words, I try to understand the place of Auschwitz. I will show how that place became the focus of a Faustian project to create a German paradise amid Polish perdition. The issue of "place," the location of Auschwitz under the sky on Planet Earth, raises the issue of "space," the relation of the camp to the human body. Thus I address the architecture of Auschwitz. Architecture can be defined as the art that mediates, through place and space, between the infinite of nature (sky and earth) and the finitude of the body.[6] I explore some of the historical links between the place of Auschwitz and space in Auschwitz. Metaphorically speaking, I try to describe the stage on which was played out one of the most profound tragedies the human race has ever permitted or endured. My story ends when the curtain rises—in the month separating January 26, 1942, when Himmler informed the Inspector of Concentration Camps to expect 150,000 Jews in the concentration camps within four weeks, and February 27, 1942, when the Chief of SS Construction, SS-Oberführer (Brigadier-General) Dr. Ing. Hans Kammler, chaired a meeting in Auschwitz that led, as I infer on the basis of one hitherto undiscovered document, to the construction of the gas chambers of bunker 1.

Preserved in the archives of the Auschwitz-Birkenau State Museum is a proposal for the *Stammlager* (main camp) at Auschwitz that was drafted in the summer of 1942—a few months after the killing of Jews had started (fig. 1). The plan was drawn up by the architect Lothar Hartjenstein, who worked in the SS design office in Berlin. Not only does it show the concentration camp itself (usually designated as Auschwitz I), with its barracks, roll-call place, hospital, prison, workshops, and auxiliary structures such as the Kommandantur, the offices of the Gestapo, the barracks for the SS men, and so on, but it also shows a pleasant village for the married SS men and their families, including a hotel, shops, sports facilities, and, at the edge of the barbed-wire fence close to the prisoners' hospital, a primary school. The plan symbolizes but does not exhaust the juxtaposition of the nightmare and the dream. It does not show the enormous camp at Auschwitz-Birkenau (a mile west of the main camp), nor the town of Auschwitz itself (a mile east of the SS village). By the time Hartjenstein completed this drawing, the camp at Birkenau (also known as Auschwitz II) had become the terminus of countless transports bringing Jews from all over Europe. And the town of Auschwitz was the reason the Germans were there to start with, and why they had built the enormous camp.

Before we explore in more detail the situation in Auschwitz, we must get some sense of the mindset and ambitions of the SS men who killed in the camp by day and dreamed in the village by night. The plan seems a perfect evocation of the pride with which National Socialists regarded their ability to recognize the Manichean polarity in the world. The resulting black-white vision, suggested in the opposition camp-village, was perceived as an expression of intellectual clarity. Hence Dietrich Klagges, in his *Geschichtsunterricht als national-politische Erziehung* (History instruction as national-political education), called for a historiography that would portray history as the battle between good (German) and evil (non-German, especially the Jew).

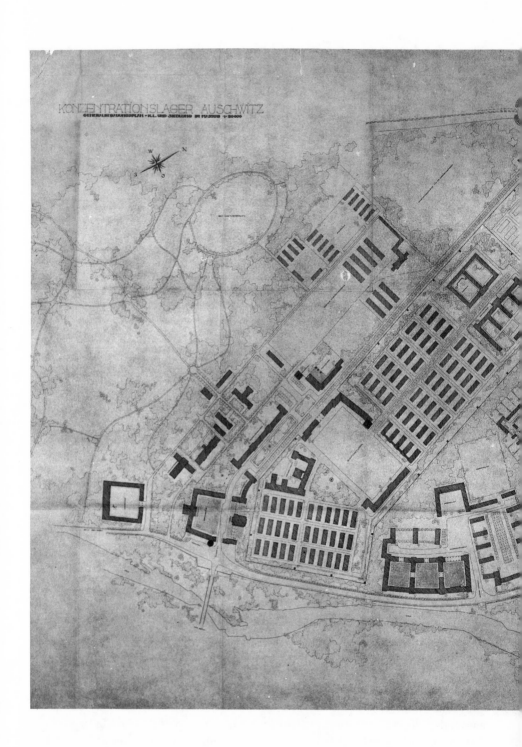

KONZENTRATIONSLAGER AUSCHWITZ

FIGURE 1. Master plan for the expansion of the main camp at Auschwitz. Architect Lothar Hartjenstein. Summer 1942. Source: Archive, Auschwitz-Birkenau State Museum.

The left side of the drawing depicts the concentration camp. Its center is the enormous roll-call place, designed to hold 30,000 inmates. Along the sides are the various administration buildings, with offices for the camp Gestapo and the Lagerführer (north and west), the prisoner reception building with the delousing installation and the laundry (southwest), and the kitchens (east). To the south of this place are the brick barracks of the original camp, built in 1916 as a labor-exchange center for Polish seasonal workers in Germany. To the north of the roll-call place are five connected workshops, 45 newly built barracks, the camp hospital, and the camp prison. On the west side of the camp are the buildings of the Kommandantur and various industries, and to the east the SS base and a *Siedlung* for the married SS men and their families. The center of town includes a hotel and shops. Along the river are the SS sports facilities. The large building at the bend of the road that goes west from the village center is a primary school. It is a stone's throw from the electrified fence of the camp.

> It is dangerously one-sided to present youth only with leaders and masters, the healthy creative forces of the nation. . . . Forces of destruction oppose in fierce combat all these constructive forces. One must constantly refer to these. . . . These include the traitors from our own race, and the racial-alien Jew, who would like to appear German, but who attempts at the same time to destroy the people and the land. They work together with the enemies from outside, those from the North and the South, from the East and the West who have always tried to oppress Germany, to conquer it, to destroy it, and to transform it into a wilderness.[7]

History was thus a protracted battle between the forces of creation and order and the powers of destruction and chaos. As we all know, this need for an aesthetic and moral symmetry that balanced the two was nowhere so present as in the death camps. It was no accident that the self-declared Nordic racial avant-garde, the men and women of the SS, were the perpetrators of the Holocaust. This dialectic seems to be present in Hartjenstein's plan. The problem, however, is that the true opposition exists only within the confines of the camp, in the actual encounter between the well-groomed, well-dressed, racially superior SS man and the filthy, rag-clad, racially inferior *Untermensch*. The village is only a contingent implication of the fact that even SS men need to relax, eat, and sleep. It has, however, no direct bearing on our understanding of the camp itself.

There is another way to interpret the bisection of the plan. This is not based on the commonplace of National Socialist racism, but on the complex of German vocation. Since the second half of the nineteenth century, Germans had been taught to believe that they, and they alone, had been the *Kulturträger* in the land that they called *Der deutsche Osten*, which roughly coincided with the territory of the present Republic of Poland. There was some justification to this claim. In the Middle Ages, in their notorious *Drang nach Osten*, Germans had brought Western technological, economic, and political know-how to the less-developed Slavs. But they had done the same for the natives from Cameroon at the turn of the century. What made the German East different from Cameroon was the fact that Germany's civilizing role in Africa had not affected the German sense of identity, while the German involvement with Poland, according to prominent scholars, had shaped the Germans' sense of themselves and their destiny. In 1934 the German anthropologist Josef Nadler identified the German "push to the east" as the event that had shaped the Germans into a *Weltvolk*, involving all the German tribes which had remained politically, culturally, and also partly linguistically independent. Hence "this space [the East] became the cradle of the idea of a common German destiny, of a common German language, of a common modern German education, of a united German state. . . . When the Germans cross the historic border river [between West and East], a new

German world epoch begins, ethnic, spiritual, and political."[8] Three years later, a popular history of this push to the east stated unequivocally:

> The German settlement of the East proves itself as the central pillar in the total make-up of the German nation. Its history mirrors German history in general with penetrating clarity. One must know it for a general understanding of the history of the German land and the German people, and, consequently, for a correct and profound appreciation of the German character.[9]

The central word here is *settlement*. The geopolitical doctrine of *Lebensraum*, which formed the foundation of Germany's infatuation with the East, implied that a nation gained nothing by conquering other nations in order to rule them for economic profit. The only purpose of colonization was settlement. To a German in the 1930s, *Der (deutsche) Osten* equaled *Siedlung*. All agreed that the ideology of settlement pervades and vitalizes the whole of German history.[10] Therefore the German East was the mythical region that held German history together. The resulting German self-definition as a nation of *Siedlers* (settlers) was attractive, as it brought together in one image the opposites of adventure and commitment, horizon and place, the future and the past, the universal and the particular. As a popular history of the German East explained:

> Energetic German people from all lineages regained in constant, peaceful *Kulturarbeit* the land in which once before Germans had lived. Quietly they anchored the German character in their new *Heimat*. As a result we can say with every justification that "that land is German!" After all it is not superficially "occupied," but truly acquired and transformed into the soil of German people and German culture.

The narrative closed with the observation that "this is also the reason that this 'Great Feat of the German Nation,' as the colonization of the East has been characterized, has survived the centuries and, taken up again after stagnation and obstruction, profoundly influences the direction of contemporary German life."[11]

The man who was chiefly responsible for transforming the ideology of resettlement into practical policy was Reichsführer-SS Heinrich Himmler. This responsibility dated from October 7, 1939, when Hitler had appointed Himmler as Reichskommissar für die Festigung deutschen Volkstums, and as such responsible for a massive program to evacuate hundreds of thousands of ethnic Germans who were scattered in the countries that had fallen within the Soviet sphere of influence as a result of the Molotov-Ribbentrop pact, and to resettle them in those parts of Poland that Germany had conquered in September 1939 and was to officially annex on October 26 of that year. Hitler had openly announced this program in his Reichstag speech a day before Himmler's appointment when he called for the establishment of a new ethnic order in the former Polish territories with an eye to the "resettlement of nationalities in such a manner that the process ultimately results in the obtaining of better dividing lines than is the case in the present."[12] From the very beginning Himmler took great pride in the new role that allowed him to become one of the master builders of the New Europe. In an illustrated editorial in *Das Schwarze Korps*, he reflected on the history and future of German settlement in the German East:

> Great times of a nation find the ultimate expression of inner force and power in its works of culture. *One* truth stands at the beginning and the end of each historic epoch: stones will talk when the people have fallen silent. Great times already speak in stone to the present.

Following this was a description of the German castles in the East, "testimony to soldier-like conquest and stubborn defense as well as symbols of high German culture." The most famous German castle, the one-time headquarters of the Teutonic Order at Marienburg, was "a memorial of the right to life and the will to persist of the whole German nation in the East."[13] For Himmler the castles had preserved Germany's claim on the German East throughout the more than five centuries between the collapse of German power in the fifteenth century and the rise of National Socialism in the present. Thus these castles urged Germans to create conditions such that a decline of German power would never happen again.

One of the reasons that Himmler had been chosen by Hitler as Reichskommissar was that he headed the ideal tool to create this New Order: the SS. As a paramilitary force it had the muscle to take responsibility for the necessary ethnic cleansing, and as the National Socialist racial and ideological avant-garde, imbued with ideas of "blood and soil," it could provide the human resource to rebuild the German East into a Nordic paradise. The ordinary SS men were left in no doubt as to their role in these territories, which was described in detail in *Der Kampf um die deutsche Ostgrenze* (The struggle for the German eastern border), a handbook for SS men published in 1941. It taught the SS men that the conquest of Poland had not brought an alien land under German control. On the contrary, it had restored to the German *Lebensraum* "what German diligence had created in the course of time." A massive program of reconstruction was to consolidate "what has been gained in the battle and make it into an eternally linked part of the Greater German space. *The German East was for centuries the German people's space of destiny. It will remain so for the following centuries.*"

This reconstruction had a demographic dimension. "The *ethnic mosaic* of the East demands a *new arrangement*, which is historically, morally, and ethically totally justified. With the *new ordering of the space of the East* there is not only the *German-Polish problem* and that caused by other ethnic minorities, but also the *Solution to the Jewish Problem* as such." The handbook went on to blame the Jews for all that was wrong in Poland. The ghettos were the source of epidemics and the breeding grounds of a criminal class. "The cooperation of Jewry and Poles produced the notorious '*Polish State of Affairs.*' What this Polish State of Affairs amounted to became clear during the Polish Campaign to even the simplest German soldier. *In the regained areas in the East a comprehensive reconstruction is taking place, with the aim to overcome this Polish State of Affairs and to bring in its place German order and German culture, lifting up the suppressed and enslaved Germans from the East, and finally linking this soil forever with the German nation.*" The handbook continued with the observation that the reconstruction was a titanic enterprise involving a radical land reform in which up to ten small, nonviable Polish farms would be combined to make one prosperous German farm. "The land will have to be rebuilt from the soil up, village by village. Whole villages will have to disappear when low-yielding fields are reforested." Traditionally the German East had suffered from the draining effect of the departure of farm laborers for industrial areas in the West. To give them a reason to stay, it was important to improve their conditions, which included their housing.

> In the same way that the unacceptable division of property demands reform, so does the unacceptable state of the *farmer's houses, stables, and barns*. The planning of a *comprehensive housing program* for the East has already been completed. This program also involves *the architectural reconstruction of the towns* in the East, which should again become as centers of a German will for reconstructing what they were in earlier days, like the German farms and villages: symbols of German life and German creation.[14]

We have some remarkable accounts that attest to Himmler's obsession with this utopian project. One of them dates from early 1940, and was written by Himmler's personal friend Henns Johst. Johst traveled with Himmler through Poland to inspect the progress of Himmler's program of ethnic cleansing, and recorded how, repeatedly during their trip,

> the Reichsführer-SS stopped the car, climbed over the furrowed ditches, walked into fields plowed over by grenade shells, took some dirt between his fingers, smelled it thoughtfully with his head bowed, crushed the crumbs of the field between his fingers, and looked then over the vast, vast space which

FIGURE 2. Reichsführer-SS Heinrich Himmler as Reichskommissar für die Festigung deutschen Volkstums. 1941. Source: German Federal Archives, Koblenz.

Heinrich Himmler (*center, with glasses*) explains to Rudolf Höss (*hands folded*) a model of a prototype farm to be built in the German East. Immediately to the right of Himmler stands Martin Bormann (*head down*), and the next to him Himmler's chief advisor on the reconstruction of the East, Professor Doktor Konrad Meyer. The setting of the gathering is an exhibition entitled "Planung und Aufbau im Osten" (Planning and Reconstruction in the East), held in Berlin in early 1941.

was full, full to the horizon, with this good, fertile earth. Thus we stood like ancient farmers and we smiled at each other with twinkling eyes. All of this was now German soil!

The two men reflected on how the German settlers would soon change the appearance of the land. Trees and hedges would be planted. Shrubs would grow, and weasels and hedgehogs, buzzards and falcons would prevent the destruction of half the harvest by mice and vermin. All of this was a great work of culture undertaken in awe of nature. They speculated on how these changes would "create protection from the wind, increase dew, and stimulate the formation of clouds, force rain and thus push a more economically viable climate further toward the East." Referring to the great resettlement programs already underway, they predicted that "under professional, rational, and scientific leadership, the Balt, Galician and Volhynian returnees will perform miracles." Johst recorded how the two men stood in the fields, held the conquered soil in their hands, and gazed "over the whole of these indifferently treated surfaces . . . populat[ing] them with villages, surrounded by rustling orchards." Almost as a kind of afterthought he jotted down, "The Western world cannot understand this pure pleasure derived from task and work, from sweat and calluses. It thinks in terms of business, of turnover, where we look forward to action!!"[15]

Neither Himmler nor Johst was concerned about the millions of Gentile and Jewish Poles who were to be deported from their farms, villages, and towns to make space for the ethnic German arrivals. On their trip through Poland, Himmler and Johst visited Upper Silesia, in the eastern region of which towns such as Auschwitz, Blachstadt, and Saybusch, regarded by Himmler as relics of German medieval colonization, had become centers of ethnic cleansing and large-scale ecological, architectural, and urban reconstruction. In a meeting in the government house of Upper Silesia, located in the town of Kattowitz, Himmler and the military and civilian authorities in the region talked openly about the policies to be enacted:

> These lecturers do not speak in commonplaces, which one can noddingly affirm without further thought. They present the hard facts, and they ask concrete questions of Heinrich Himmler in his capacity as chief of the resettlement. He takes the word and in his final answer gives these gentlemen and their offices clear and forcible directions.

Johst was enthralled:

> It is wonderful to experience how the migration of whole nations is organized here calmly and dispassionately. Hundreds of thousands of people stream into

the Reich, and are settled in the East . . . others are deported . . . and all while the nation is fighting the greatest defensive battle of its existence. Everything happens as if it is the most self-evident, the simplest issue in the world!

He added, "At such moments I almost understand the hatred of the Western world for everything German. Nothing was ever so hateful as superiority, as natural superiority, by virtue of the belief in an idea, by virtue of the achievements, and by virtue of the results."[16]

Johst was not the only one who would be astonished at the frankness with which Himmler talked publicly about the nature and impact of his policies. In his notorious speech to the SS leadership of October 4, 1943, Himmler discussed the Holocaust openly, congratulating himself and his comrades for having "carried out this heaviest of our tasks in a spirit of love for our people. And our inward being, our soul, our character has not suffered injury from it."[17] A year earlier he had discussed with equal frankness the problem of labor in the German East. Originally Himmler intended to rely on the Reich Labor Service to plant new forests, drain the marshes, build the roads, prepare the settlements, and so on. But by 1942 the whole of this service had been mobilized for the war, and had ceased to be at Himmler's disposal. Himmler could not wait until the Reich Labor Service could furnish manpower for peacetime projects. Noting that the SS had been charged with providing a stable foundation for a German future in the East, "a foundation that allows individuals who come fifty, eighty, a hundred, or two hundred years after us to cave in or to lose their heads without endangering the future of the German *Imperium*," Himmler announced the formation of an enormous army of slaves:

> If we do not create the bricks here, if we do not fill our camps with slaves—in this room I state these things precisely and clearly—with work slaves who will build our cities, our villages, and our farms, irrespective of losses, then, after a long war, we will not have the money to create settlements that will allow a truly Germanic people to live with dignity and root within one generation.[18]

Himmler's use of the word *bricks* had both a metaphorical and a literal sense. The German concentration camps, which Himmler controlled as Reichsführer-SS, had in the late 1930s taken on a key role in the German production of building materials. Originally the camps were intended as an instrument of terror to stabilize the National Socialist regime; at first they had not been used to furnish labor for productive work, as this would have competed with German business and hindered the reduction of high unemployment. By 1937, however, the camps had become largely superfluous as an instrument of terror, for the regime was now firmly estabished and enjoyed general approval. The number of inmates had dropped to 10,000, and a German future without concentration camps had become conceivable. Yet Himmler did not want to close them. First, they provided him a political power base; more important, he clearly saw the camps' economic potential in a situation of labor shortage.

Himmler began to consider the productive potential of possible concentration camp sites. Dachau was to remain where it was, but the new camps at Buchenwald and Sachsenhausen were established in places that seemed optimal. Both were to produce bricks for the local program of urban reconstruction. With an eye to providing the city of Weimar with bricks, the SS decided to locate Buchenwald on the wooded Ettersberg, five miles from the city, a site chosen because it was adjacent to large loam and clay deposits. Sachsenhausen was to serve Speer's building program in Berlin. Located twenty-five miles north of the city along the Hohenzollern canal in the town of Oranienburg, it offered good possibilities for bulk transport to the capital. Having decided on the location of these two camps, in early 1938 Himmler founded the Deutsche Erd- und Steinwerke (DESt, or German Earth and Stone Works) to set up and run the brickworks at Buchenwald, Sachsenhausen, and possibly other places, as well as to open and exploit granite quarries. The first brickyard to be opened was the one near Buchenwald, with a planned capacity of 7 million bricks per year. With a subsidy of RM 9.5 million given by Speer, DESt began construction in Oranienburg of the largest brickyard in the world, with an annual production of 150 million bricks, 10 times as many as the largest existing brickyards could yield. That same year DESt bought a defunct brickyard near Hamburg and began to plan a 40-million-brick-a-year production facility to supply the reconstruction of that city. A new concentration camp, Neuengamme, was built adjacent to the factory.

To supply Speer with granite, DESt began to operate granite quarries in 1938. The first two to be acquired were a quarry near Flossenbürg, close to the Czech border in the Upper Palatinate, and a famous granite quarry adjacent to the Upper Austrian town of Mauthausen, near Linz. Before 1914 the quarries of Mauthausen had supplied most of the granite used in Vienna, Budapest, and the smaller cities of the former Austrian-Hungarian empire.[19] The quality of the stone and the town's location along a major transport corridor had contributed to its fame. With the dissolution of the empire, Mauthausen had fallen on hard times. Little was being built, and the modern predilection for concrete over granite did not help. For the town of Mauthausen, the Anschluss of 1938 was a welcome event: in Hitler's Germany, granite was again the premier construction material for public buildings. A few days after the Anschluss, Himmler and his aide Oswald Pohl, who controlled the administration of the SS and its companies, toured the Mauthausen area with an eye to establishing a DESt branch to exploit its riches. After some negotiation, the city leased two quarries to DESt; adjacent to each, the SS began to build a camp. The same pattern applied in Flossen-bürg, and in the DESt operations in Silesia and Alsace. Quarries were identified and assessed in relation to transport and markets, then leased or purchased, and finally complemented by new camps to provide labor: in Silesia the quarries, which Speer had designated as the main supplier of Berlin, were to be serviced by Gross-Rosen; in the Alsace, by Natzweiler. In some camps the pattern was reversed. The concentration camp in Auschwitz, for example, was established adjacent to the formerly Polish town for demographic and political reasons. But within a few months of its establishment, DESt acquired a gravel and sand production facility close to the camp. In 1941 the presence of DESt in Auschwitz was one of the factors that influenced the decision by the management of IG Farben to build one of their largest plants there.

More important than the production of gravel was Auschwitz's function as a labor reserve to facilitate the reconstruction of the eastern part of Upper Silesia. For various economic and geopolitical reasons, Auschwitz had attracted the attention of the men charged by Himmler with the long-range planning of the German East. As early as July 1940, Himmler had been convinced by Professor Doktor Konrad Meyer that a speedy Germanization of the area around Auschwitz was of the highest priority.[20] Himmler's chief of staff as Reichskommissar, Ulrich Greifelt, concurred. He wrote Himmler, "It is urgent that a purely ethnic German corner be created at this point." Greifelt suggested a number of the area's communities as potential places of settlement by ethnic Germans. These included the town of Auschwitz and the village of Birkenau.[21] On Thursday, October 10, 1940, at a meeting held in Kattowitz and attended by the SS and Upper Silesia's civil servants, it was decided that part of the new province would be used for massive settlement by ethnic Germans. A map created for this meeting designated the area around Auschwitz as Siedlungszone (Zone of Settlement) 1a (fig. 3).[22] This designation implied that the given area offered few impediments to the envisioned physical and social transformation. A master plan for the future of the region should be completed by the spring of 1941.[23] Himmler became very interested in Auschwitz. As was recorded in the protocol of the founding of the IG Farben plant in Auschwitz, Himmler insisted that all Poles and Jews would be removed from the area, and that Auschwitz itself would become "a paradigm of the settlement in the East."[24]

Planning started quickly indeed. The Germans set to work on both regional and municipal designs. In December 1940 the architect Dr. Hans Stosberg accepted the task of creating a master plan for the reconstruction and enlargement of Auschwitz. After two months of work he produced a

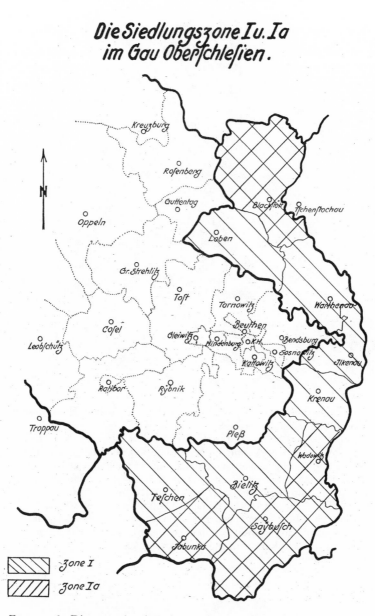

Die Siedlungszone I u. Ia
im Gau Oberschlesien.

Zone I

Zone Ia

FIGURE 3. Diagram showing the settlement zones in eastern
Upper Silesia, 1940. Source: German Federal Archives, Koblenz.

The whole eastern half of Upper Silesia is given priority in development (Zone 1). The counties in the north and south of this
zone are given extra priority. These are to become the so-called
pure German corners. Auschwitz is located close to the point
where the districts of Bielitz, Krenau, and Wadowitz meet.

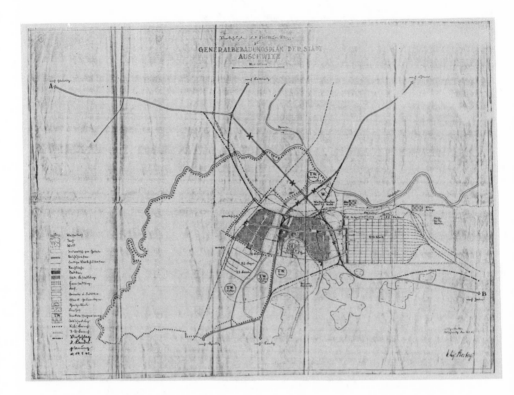

FIGURE 4. First master plan for the expansion of Auschwitz. Architect Hans Stosberg. Spring 1941. Source: Auschwitz Municipal Archive.

The Vistula runs from southwest (*left*) to east (*right*). The tributary river Przemsza comes from the north (*top*), and the Sola from the south (*bottom*). The old town of Auschwitz is located alongside the Sola. A major avenue connects the old town to the station (*west*) and the industrial area to be developed by IG Farben (*east*). South of the station are the SS barracks and the concentration camp (*K.Z. Lager*). The area defined by the dotted line is the camp's Zone of Interests. The circles with the digraph TW indicate areas where drinking water is pumped up. The chessboard-like rectangles are wastewater treatment plants. The plan shows one modification already in the location of the main road Gleiwitz-Zator. The straight section between the turnoff to Kattowitz and the town has been canceled for a new route that comes closer to the station.

preliminary design, accompanied by an explanatory document (fig. 4).[25] It noted that Auschwitz was located at the center of three major industrial areas, and that it offered good building ground and a bountiful supply of water. This was important because the Upper Silesian coal mines were located on the watershed between the Oder and the Vistula; their coal, being of relatively low grade, was intended to serve as raw material for the chemical industry, but the unavailability of water effectively prevented the development of such an industry adjacent to the mines. Auschwitz, because of the confluence of three rivers, was the closest site with the requisite water supply. Stosberg's draft assumes a city of first 35,500 and later 47,000 inhabitants. The largest single employer would be from the chemical industry, an IG Farben plant, to make artificial rubber and synthetic gasoline from coal, a complex that would employ 3,000 people who were to live in their own quarter. Eventually, both the plant and part of the IG Farben neighborhood were built. The draft continues with the railways, which would employ 1,500 people. These workers and their families were to live in a quarter close to the station. The document also mentions "SS and ancillary businesses (but not the barracks and the concentration camp inmates)." This would involve 1,500 workplaces.

Stosberg's design had a number of vexing limitations. Space was tight. It was clear that the industry was to go to the town's east. To the south and north there was a large floodplain unsuitable for any but recreational use, and the town's west was surrounded on three sides by the concentration camp's *Interessengebiet* (Zone of Interests), which was forbidden territory. In this initial report, Stosberg had thought it possible to harmonize the needs of the concentration camp for security with the needs of the town for some breathing space. But as he continued to design and as the camp continued to expand, relations between Stosberg and the SS soured. Stosberg and SS architect Hartjenstein developed mutually exclusive plans for the quarter located between the railway lines with the station, the main camp in Zasole, and the river Sola (fig. 5).[26] Stosberg's design for the civic peninsula that carved its way from the river bank into the camp's Zone of Interests was meant to provide the citizens with dignified if not festive access to the trains by means of a great boulevard that was to be the spine of New Town West, a densely built-up neighborhood for 7,500 people. Hartjenstein's proposal for the SS settlement engulfed some 50 percent of Stosberg's neighborhood, reducing it to what Stosberg termed a "torso." Furthermore, the vernacular character of the SS Garden City, with its cozy one-family homesteads surrounded by large gardens, contradicted the strongly urban character of Stosberg's plan, a note the latter considered to be appropriate for the central urban axis connecting the city's major elements: the station to the medieval *Ring* and, beyond that, the new plaza (*Parteiforum*) that was to embody

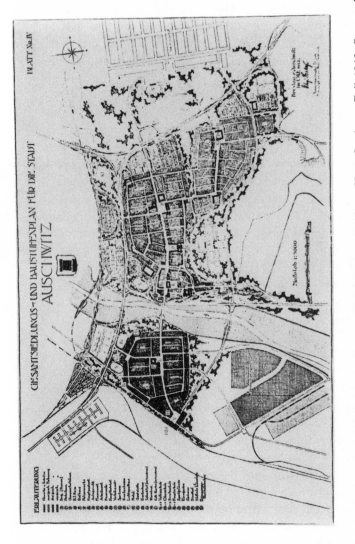

FIGURE 5. Final master plan for the expansion of Auschwitz. Architect Hans Stosberg. Fall 1942. Source: Niels Gutschow, Absteinach.

The final plan reveals some important modifications over the first. The eastern district of Auschwitz has been split into two separate units, each with its own center. The main plaza for the party headquarters has been inserted just east of the old town. The connection between the camp's Zone of Interests and the western district of Auschwitz has changed. In the 1941 proposal, Stosberg assumed that the two areas would directly touch each other, with a plaza marking the entrance into the SS headquarters and the Zone of Interests (fig. 4). Then came Hartjenstein's proposal that inserted an SS settlement between the SS barracks and the main road connecting the station to the rest of Auschwitz (fig. 1). Stosberg's final master plan, drawn up after the meeting of September 23, 1942, includes the camp and the SS barracks. The site that Hartjenstein had claimed for the settlement is now occupied by a green belt, a second road between the station and the IG Farben site, and the southern part of the western district.

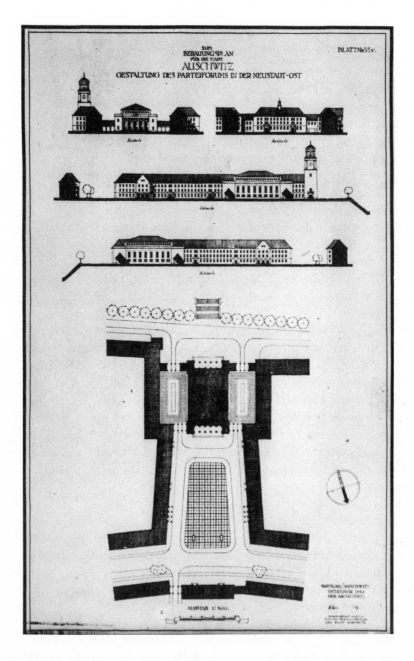

FIGURE 6. Design for the County Party Headquarters at Auschwitz, January 1943. Architect Hans Stosberg. Source: Archive, Auschwitz-Birkenau State Museum.

The plaza is located along the great avenue that connects the railway station to the IG Farben site. Between the plaza and the large sports fields that are located in the floodplain in the south is the great gathering hall, which follows the aesthetics of National Socialist monumental architecture as conceived by Adolf Hitler, developed by Ludwig Troost, and perfected by Albert Speer.

Auschwitz's new dignity as the capital of a new county (fig. 6), the eastern neighborhood, and the immense IG Farben plant that was to provide the economic justification for all these improvements.

There were really two solutions to the problem: either the SS settlement had to conform to the urban density of Stosberg's plan, providing an appropriate southern flank to the avenue mentioned above, or the SS had to move the Garden City to another site within their Zone of Interests, allowing for a new border between the city and the camp closer to the main camp. Stosberg was supported by the provincial bureaucracy. But the camp also had strong supporters, not the least of whom was Himmler. The two parties argued for almost a year, pushing the border between the city and the camp up and down between the proposed avenue and the perimeter of the camp. Ultimately the issue was settled in favor of the city: in a large meeting held in Auschwitz on Wednesday, September 23, 1942, the chief of the SS-Wirtschafts Verwaltungshauptamt (SS Economic and Administrative Department, or WVHA), SS-Obergruppenführer (General) Oswald Pohl, withdrew Hartjenstein's proposal and announced that he had ordered the architect to prepare a master plan that would move the settlement to the south side of the main camp, firmly within the camp's Zone of Interests.[27] None of these difficulties was anticipated in Stosberg's 1941 report. There he still assumed that the camp's development would not obstruct the "organic" development of the town. In view of the later use of Auschwitz-Birkenau as an extermination plant, it is ironic that Stosberg identified that area (between the station and the Vistula) as a good site for "SS industrial installations."

Stosberg continued to work on his plan, of which important relics remain. One is a double-folded New Year's greeting card that he sent in December 1941. On the front he wished his benefactors and friends "health, happiness and a good outcome for each beginning." The double middle page showed his proposal for the rehabilitation of Auschwitz's market (fig. 7), while the back contains a four-sentence meditation that firmly places Auschwitz within the National Socialist myth of the German East:

> In the year 1241 Silesian knights warded off as saviors of the Reich the Mongolian assault at Wahlstatt. In that same century Auschwitz was founded as a German town. After 600 years the Führer Adolf Hitler turns away the Bolshevik menace from Europe. This year, 1941, the construction of a new German city and the reconstruction of the old Silesian market were planned and initiated.[28]

As we will see below, the suggested relation between Hitler's attack on the Soviet Union and the reconstruction of Auschwitz did not exist only in history. It also applied to space.

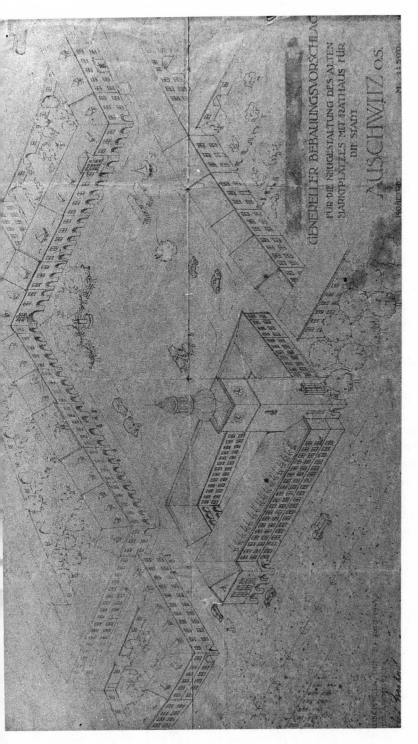

FIGURE 7. Bird's-eye view of the reconstructed marketplace of the old town of Auschwitz. Fall 1941. Architect Hans Stosberg. Source: Sławomir Staszak, Harmese.

Stosberg included a reduced version of this drawing on his greeting card. His proposal homogenizes the façades along the market through the continuing arcade. The terrace of houses on the north side of the market has become part of the town hall, with its massive tower that stands on axis with the bridge over the river Soła. As an urban marker, this tower takes the place of the demolished tower of the parish church.

The realization of Stosberg's proposal depended on the availability of labor. The SS was to oblige him. In December 1940 the commandant of the concentration camp, SS-Sturmbannführer (Major) Rudolf Höss, had offered the city of Auschwitz the use of prisoners for large-scale projects to improve the dikes along the Vistula and the Sola, and the trajectory of the two rivers.[29] Höss's offer was the direct result of his meeting with Himmler a few days earlier. During that meeting Himmler had become aware that the concentration camp in Auschwitz, established earlier that year to support ethnic cleansing in the area, could also serve a second purpose. Höss was to transform the camp into a huge agricultural experimental station, to include huge laboratories, plant cultivation departments, sections devoted to cattle breeding, and so on. As a first step it was necessary to drain the marshlands and regulate the Vistula. In 1946 Höss recalled that at that meeting Himmler "continued with his agricultural planning even down to the smallest details and stopped only when his adjutant called his attention to the fact that a very important person had been waiting for a long time to see him."[30] In this meeting Himmler decided that the experimental station was to employ most of the camp's 10,000 inmates.[31] If the concentration camp was also to provide labor for other projects, it had to expand dramatically.

On March 1, 1941, on his way to a gathering of Bukowinian Germans who were waiting in camps in and around Breslau for their final resettlement in the region just south of Auschwitz, Himmler visited Auschwitz and ordered the construction of a large prisoner-of-war camp in Birkenau. A few weeks earlier he had been informed of Hitler's decision to attack the Soviet Union in the spring, and Himmler had immediately recognized that the expected mass of Soviet prisoners of war would provide him with the labor force he needed to continue the reconstruction of the German East. As the area around Auschwitz had been assigned top priority in this project, it made sense for the region to receive the bulk of the prisoners of war who would be transferred into SS custody by the army. According to Höss, the various provincial officials present at Himmler's visit were not very happy with the prospect of 100,000 prisoners two kilometers from Auschwitz, and raised their objections with the Reichsführer-SS. "Himmler just smiled," Höss recalled in 1946, "and disposed of their objections, saying, 'Gentlemen, this project will be completed; my reasons are more important than your objections!'"[32] Even purely technical objections were not taken seriously. The wetlands of Birkenau were of crucial significance for the province's future. Most of Upper Silesia's population lived in a densely settled industrial belt occupying a plateau that formed, as we saw before, a watershed between the rivers Oder and Vistula; as a result the region lacked water, a deficiency that potentially limited future development. To redress this, the province had designated the lowland between the Vistula and the Sola as a major water reservoir for the industrial heart of Upper Silesia.[33] Provincial bureaucrats now argued that the sewage of 100,000 people would make it impossible to maintain the water, but Himmler impatiently dismissed their concerns: water management was merely a matter of technology to be solved by the experts.[34]

On Sunday, June 22, 1941, the German army surprised the Soviet Union in an early morning attack. Goebbels instructed the media to report the war in the East as the unmasking of "the greatest Jewish swindle of all times." The press was instructed to present the situation in the Soviet Union through

> an impressive juxtaposition of inhuman conditions in the Soviet Union on the one hand and the social progress, the high cultural standard and the healthy *Lebensfreude* of the working man in National Socialist Germany. A good choice of pictures, contrasting the bestialized bolshevik types with the free and open gaze of the German worker, filthy Soviet hutments with Germans workers' settlements, muddy tracks with the German Reich highways, etc., will be of particular importance in this connection.[35]

From this it was only a small step to a rhetoric pitting the European *Mensch* against the Soviet *Untermensch*, which had come to mean a Russian in the clutches of Judeo-Bolshevism.

The simple polarization of human being and subhuman was graphically depicted in *Der Untermensch*, an SS publication released simultaneously in fifteen European languages to arouse enthusiasm across the continent for the German crusade in the East. An organ for Himmler's view of history, *Der Untermensch* emphasized the centuries-old conflict between the European *Mensch* and the predecessor of the Soviet *Untermensch*, the Hun and the Mongol horseman, whom the National Socialists conflated and confused. A two-page spread depicted the Hun/Mongol nemesis of the past and the Soviet enemy of the present. Mounted Huns trampling Germanic women and children were shown on the left, while on the right were portraits of six Soviet prisoners of war. "The challenge of the *Untermensch* began with the bloody rides of [the Hun] Attila and [the Mongol] Genghis Khan," explained the text on the left. "On ugly little horses, almost grown together with the skin of their animals, the Hun hordes dashed against Europe. Their split eyes glowed with the lust to kill, and behind them they left only wilderness, murder, fire, and destruction." Turning to the pictures of the prisoners of war, the caption continued on the right-hand page, "now they are here again, the Huns, caricatures of human faces, nightmares that have become reality, a fist blow into the face of all that is good."[36]

Convinced that the war against the Soviet Union was a crusade to protect the European cradle of civilization against Asian barbarism, the leadership of the German army had decided on September 8, 1941, that rules of war as established by custom and formulated in international law did not apply to the war in the East. This decision reflected a widely felt German sentiment. More than a month before the German attack on the Soviet Union, Colonel-General Höpner, commander of Panzer Group Four, had already written that:

> The war against the Soviet Union is an essential component of the German people's struggle for existence. It is the old struggle of the Germans against the Slavs, the defense of European culture against the Muscovite-Asiatic fold, the warding off of Jewish Bolshevism. . . . Both the planning and the execution of every battle must be dictated by an iron will to bring about a merciless, total annihilation of the enemy.[37]

In early October another commander reminded his soldiers that their task was "the complete destruction" of the Soviet amy and "the eradication of the Asiatic influence on the European cultural sphere." German troops had special tasks,

> which go beyond the conventional unilateral soldierly tradition. In the East the soldier is not only a fighter according to the rules of warfare, but also a carrier of an inexorable racial conception and the avenger of all the bestialities which have been committed against the Germans and related races.[38]

In November another commander explained to his troops,

> Here in the East spiritually unbridgeable conceptions are fighting each other: German sense of honour and race, and a soldierly tradition of many centuries, against an Asiatic mode of thinking and primitive instincts, whipped up by a small number of mostly Jewish intellectuals. . . . We clearly recognize our mission to save European culture from the advancing Asiatic barbarism. We know that we have come up against an incensed and tough opponent. This battle can only end with the destruction of one or the other; a compromise is out of the question.[39]

The new attitude also affected the treatment of Soviet prisoners of war. In the notorious "Guidelines for the Treatment of Political Commissars," better known as the "Commissar Order," which was issued on June 6, 1941, the German army was forbidden to grant captured Soviet political commissars prisoner-of-war status. Instead these "bearers of the Judeo-Bolshevik world view" were to be shot after identification. The army's acceptance of the Commissar Order opened the way for more violations of international law. On June 28, 1941, the general in charge of the Prisoner of War Department of the German Army High Command concluded a draft agreement with the SS that allowed SS *Einsatzkommandos* (Special Units) to enter the prisoner-of-war camps to select and execute already imprisoned commissars, Communist functionaries of all ranks, agitators and fanatical Communists, and "all Jews."[40] This agreement came into force on July 17. The army justified it by noting that "the special situation of the Eastern campaign . . . demands special measures." Military considerations were now going to give way to the "political objective": to "protect the German nation from Bolshevik inciters."[41]

Less dramatic, but ultimately even more deadly, was the Germans' unwillingness to provide the remaining prisoners with adequate accommodations. Three major international conventions, the First Hague Convention (1899), the Second Hague Convention (1907), and the Geneva Convention (1929), had established minimal standards of prisoner maintenance. Yet because the Soviet Union had not been a signatory to the last convention, which had merely clarified certain points of the earlier ones which were already regarded as law on the basis of custom, the German high command was led to the criminal assumption that none of the conventions applied. I will discuss some of their provisions later in more detail. Suffice it to note that already in the early summer of 1941, conditions were becoming catastrophic in the camps holding Soviet prisoners of war. *Camps* is in fact a euphemism: a camp consisted of fields surrounded with barbed-wire fences. The inmates were to build themselves shelters, but no materials were provided. One of them, camp Lamsdorf in Silesia, reportedly held some 200,000 prisoners:

> The camp was simply a square area of land where most of the Russians huddled together in huts made from the earth which they had built themselves. Food distribution to the camp was irregular and totally inadequate. The prisoners cooked for themselves in fire pits in the ground.[42]

Unwilling and unable to deal with the problem, the army negotiated a transfer of Soviet prisoners with Himmler.[43] As we have seen, on Saturday, March 1, 1941, Himmler had designated Birkenau as the site for a large camp. Yet for months nothing had been done to make the camp a reality, and no money had been allocated. Himmler's decision of March 1 had been inspired by a desire to impress the leadership of IG Farben with his committment to improve the town of Auschwitz, but other and more important issues had quickly come up, and the town could wait. But in the summer of 1941 it became increasingly clear that the success of the whole enterprise to develop the area around Auschwitz depended on the willingness of highly skilled IG Farben employees to move to the area, and no one wanted to move east. By the early fall of 1941 there was a consensus among the IG Farben leadership that a rapid urban reconstruction of the town was of the highest priority.[44] Himmler now saw himself forced to deliver on the promise made on March 1, and decided in September to actually concentrate the promised labor force in Auschwitz. On September 25 the Department of Prisoners of War of the German army formally agreed to transfer up to 100,000 Russians to the SS.

When a first batch of 10,000 Soviet prisoners arrived in Birkenau in early October, there was no camp available. Yet the Germans were happy to supply the designs. In fact, they had created a new architectural office to oversee the construction of Birkenau. It was headed by Karl Bischoff (fig. 8). Bischoff had begun work in early October 1941, and a first master plan

FIGURE 8. Karl Bischoff. 1938. Source: Berlin Document Center.

FIGURE 9. Fritz Ertl. 1938. Source: Berlin Document Center.

was drawn up by his assistant, the thirty-three-year-old Bauhaus graduate Fritz Ertl (fig. 9), on October 7. The plan proposed a two-part camp for a total of 97,000 inmates. The smaller part, Bauabschnitt I (Building Sector I, abbreviated as BA I), which could hold a little under 17,000 inmates, was a quarantine camp, which made sense in regard to the bad physical condition of the arriving prisoners; the larger part, BA II, designed to hold a little over 80,000 inmates, was the regular camp. It was separated by a "neutral zone" (fig. 10). In a meeting held in mid-October the plan was modified, and the second version became the basis for the 14-page document which explains the design in detail.[45] The most important change was an increase in the camp's capacity from 97,000 to 125,000 inmates. One drawing, which shows a section of the standard hut to be built, leaves no doubt that the increase was achieved by cramming more inmates into the same space. The original drawing, signed by Bischoff on October 8, listed a capacity of 550 men (fig. 11). A week later Bischoff had crossed out "550" and replaced it with "744."[46] Nothing else had changed. Perhaps Bischoff's decision was inspired by the arrival of the first prisoners of war. "They arrived in Auschwitz after long weeks of marching with very little food supplied to them on route. During the breaks in their march they were simply led into nearby fields and told to 'graze' like cattle on everything that was edible." Having arrived, "they walked around aimlessly in a daze, or they crawled anywhere into a protected area to swallow something edible that they found. They tried to force it down their throats, or they simply, quietly found a place to die."[47] Fear of anarchy led also to another modification: the main camp (BA II) was now to be subdivided into twelve smaller, self-sufficient "camps"—an arrangement which was to persist throughout all subsequent modifications. Yet another modification was the inclusion of a rail spur to connect the camp directly to the railway junction a mile to the east. In the future, prisoners were to arrive by train (fig. 12).

Working in a hurry, Bischoff had been drafting plans without informing Berlin, and without a sense of how much money would be available. On October 25 the SS headquarters telegraphed Bischoff to remind him that he could get approval, that is, a budget, only if he submitted the plans according to the usual procedures.[48] A package was hastily created. The total budget was to be RM 8.9 million, which compares in 1993 to $36 million. In an accompanying letter Bischoff wrote that BA I was already under construction and would be finished in 14 days. It was not the last time that Bischoff proved to be far too optimistic as to the amount of construction that could be achieved in Auschwitz. The Soviet prisoners were, as Höss observed, "perfectly willing to work but were unable to accomplish anything because of their weakened condition. . . . The entire body organism was finished and could no longer function."[49] None of this affected calculations back in Berlin: the SS head office there reduced the total cost from RM 8.9 to 7.7 million, as the standard rate for labor costs did not apply because the prisoners were to build the camp themselves, and for free.

Closer study of the actual designs reveals how the Nazi identification of the Soviet soldier as an *Untermensch* was translated into architectural terms.

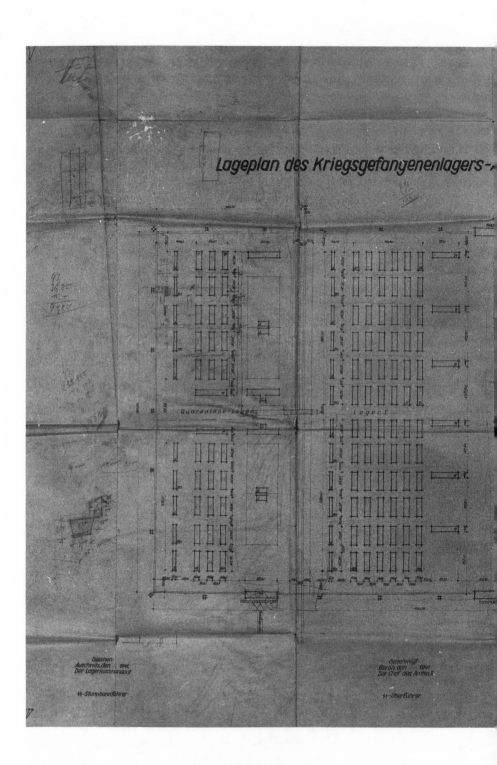

Lageplan des Kriegsgefangenenlagers-

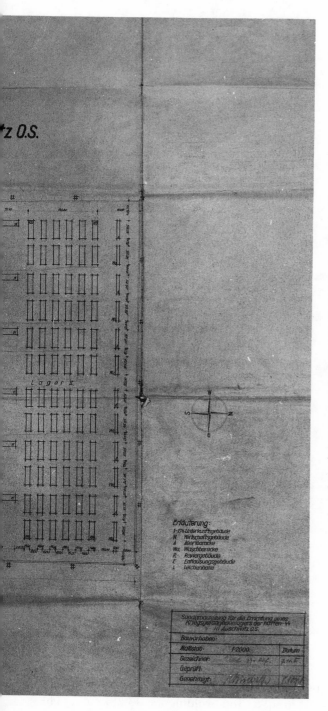

‡z O.S.

FIGURE 10. First Plan of Auschwitz-Birkenau, October 1941. Architect Fritz Ertl. Source: Archive, Auschwitz-Birkenau State Museum.

The camp is divided into two parts. To the left is the quarantine camp for 17,000 inmates. To the right, centered on an enormous *Appelplatz* (roll-call place), is the camp proper, designed to hold 80,000 inmates. Already in this first design the camp was organized on the basis of discrete units which included 12 dwelling barracks, a kitchen barrack, a wash barrack, and a latrine barrack. The plan is drawn in ink. During the meeting at which this plan was discussed, Bischoff sketched in pencil lines indicating barbed-wire fences between the units. These became a fixed part of the second design (fig. 12) and those that followed them.

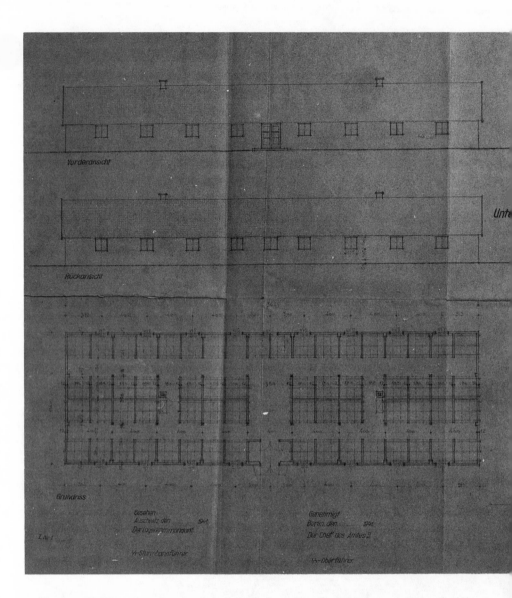

FIGURE 11. Plan, elevation, section, and detail section of a brick barrack at Auschwitz-Birkenau. October 1941. Architect Fritz Ertl. Source: Archive, Auschwitz-Birkenau State Museum.

In the designation of the drawing, the number that indicated the *Fassungsvermogen* (capacity) is inked in as roughly 550. Bischoff changed this with pencil into 744. For an interior view of this barrack, see fig. 13.

The prisoners were to be housed in 174 barracks. Each barrack was to measure 116 ft. by 36 ft., that is, 4,176 sq. ft. Total volume was 13,257 cu. ft. The barrack was subdivided into 62 bays, each of 43 sq. ft. Each bay had three "roosts." Each roost was originally supposed to hold three prisoners, but, as

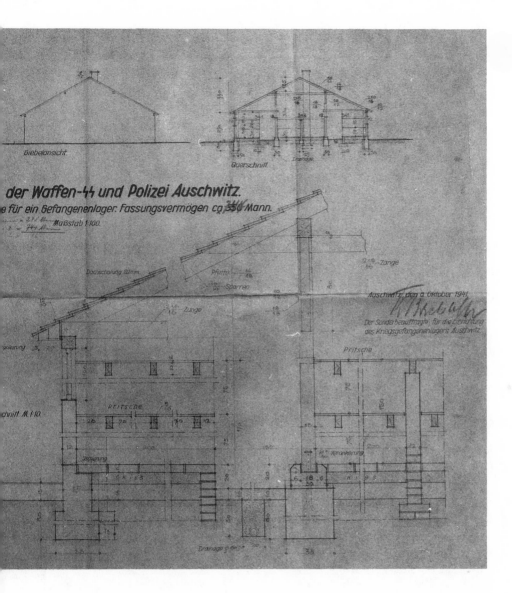

der Waffen-ss und Polizei Auschwitz.
e für ein Gefangenenlager. Fassungsvermögen ca. 350 Mann.
Maßstab 1:100.

Giebelansicht.

Querschnitt.

Auschwitz, den a. Oktober 1941.

Der Sonderbeauftragte für die Errichtung
des Kriegsgefangenenlagers Auschwitz.

we have seen, in mid-October the capacity had been increased to four. To sleep, sit, and keep his belongings, each prisoner was now provider coffin, with "private" space that amounted to 11 sq. ft., the dimensions of a large or an average volume of 53 cu. ft., the size of a shallow grave. The cost per barrack was to be RM 12,400, or RM 16.67 per inmate (fig. 13).

Inmates were being deprived of the minimum space needed to exist. Tadeusz Borowski, who was interned in Auschwitz in 1943 as prisoner

FIGURE 12. Bird's-eye view of the second design for Auschwitz-Birkenau, October 1941. Reconstruction and drawing by Robert-Jan van Pelt, Peter Gallagher, and Paul Backewich. July 1993. Source: Author's Collection.

South of the railway terminus is the quarantine camp with 2 delousing stations, 2 kitchens, 30 barracks each accommodating 744 inmates, 5 toilet barracks, and 5 washrooms. To the north of the terminus are 12 camps, each with 12 barracks, 1 kitchen, 1 toilet barrack, and 1 washroom. The quarantine section was completed as planned, the main camp expanded in size, and furthermore changed as the result of Kammler's decision to replace the brick barracks with prefabricated wooden horse stables. This drawing is one result of an as yet unfinished project to create a comprehensive computer model of the construction history of Auschwitz.

number 119,198, described the conditions in the camp as more horrendous than medieval fantasies about hell:

> If the barrack walls were suddenly to fall away, many thousands of people, packed together, squeezed tightly in their bunks, would remain suspended in mid-air. Such a sight would be more gruesome than the medieval paintings of the last Judgement. For one of the ugliest sights to a man is that of another man sleeping on his tiny portion of the bunk, of the space which he must occupy, because he has a body—a body that has been exploited to the utmost: with a number tattooed on it to save on dog tags, with just enough sleep at night to work during the day, and just enough time to eat. And just enough food so it will not die wastefully. As for actual living there is only one place for it—a piece of bunk. The rest belongs to the camp, the fatherland.[50]

FIGURE 13. Interior of barrack from Birkenau after the camp's liberation by the Red Army. Photo: S. Mucha. Spring 1945. Source: Author's Collection.

Borowski's comparison with medieval visions of hell was apt. Yet if there is a certain justification for the suffering of the medieval sinners, as they had been judged by God, nothing can justify the treatment of the inmates of

Birkenau, who were arbitrarily selected by an SS doctor. In the medieval paintings and reliefs, guilt and retribution are still related as cause and effect; in Birkenau it was the other way around. In a Kafkaesque inversion of crime and punishment, it penalized people first and then made them guilty. Anyone forced to live in those barracks would become a good object for a photo essay exploring the life and appearance of the *Untermensch*.

The extraordinarily small space allocated to each inmate and the high mortality rate within the huts meant that inmates would often die during the night, and the others would have no way to remove the corpse. Primo Levi, who experienced this in January 1945, reflected on the implications of this forced intimacy between the living and the dead.

> It is man who kills, man who creates or suffers injustice; it is no longer man who, having lost all restraint, shares his bed with a corpse. Whoever waits for his neighbour to die in order to take his piece of bread is, albeit guiltless, further from the model of thinking man than the most primitive pygmy or the most vicious sadist. Part of our existence lies in the feelings of those near to us. This is why the experience of someone who has lived for days during which man was merely a thing in the eyes of man is non-human.[51]

Confronted with such a world, we, outsiders, can only react like the Soviet soldiers who liberated the camp the next day. Levi described how they stood at the barbed wire, looking at the emaciated prisoners and the corpses. "They did not greet us, nor did they smile; they seemed oppressed not only by compassion but by a confused restraint, which sealed their lips and bound their eyes to the funereal scene." It was not that they were horrified: these were veterans who fought themselves west from Stalingrad to Auschwitz. These hardened soldiers were not horrified, but ashamed—ashamed of being human:

> It was that shame we knew so well, the shame that drowned us after the selections, and every time we had to watch, or submit to, some outrage: the shame the Germans did not know, that the just man experiences at another man's suffering; the feeling of guilt that such a crime should exist, that it should have been introduced irrevocably into the world of things that exist.[52]

The design, which postulated a living space so tiny that it was fit for a coffin and not a human being, showed a blatant disregard for international law protecting prisoners of war. According to article seven of the 1899 Hague Convention of 1899, "Prisoners of war shall be treated as regards food, quarters, and clothing, on the same footing as the troops of the government which has captured them."[53] This principle was reaffirmed in a second convention in 1907. The German General Staff acknowledged its validity. Their sole clarification of article seven was that the prisoners were to be treated like German soldiers, "not worse but also not better."[54] The 1929 Geneva Convention sought to establish the standard soldier with whom a prisoner should be compared. Article ten of this convention set forth two criteria. First, prisoners were to be lodged "in buildings or in barracks affording all possible guarantees of hygiene and healthfulness. The quarters must be fully protected from dampness, sufficiently heated and lighted. All precautions must be taken against danger of fire." This statement was open to interpretation. It assumed a compromise between generally accepted standards of comfort and healthiness and limitations on the means of the detaining power to meet them. Second, a more objective standard was given: "With regard to dormitories—the total surface, minimum cubic amount of air, arrangement and material of bedding—the conditions shall be the same as for the troops at base camps of the detaining power."[55] The designation "base camps" indicated that it was not the accommodations of the soldiers in the trenches that were to be taken as a standard, but those of the soldiers at rest or in training in the rear. As prisoner-of-war camps were supposed to be in the rear, in practice this meant that the accommodations of the prisoners and their guards were to be comparable. That this was not the case in Birkenau is demonstrated by a photo illustrating the guards' quarters (fig. 14). For a bedroom for nine guards, the official guidelines stipulated 3,600 cu ft., or 400 cu ft. per person. That is eight times as much space allocated for the sleeping accommodations alone, to which are added dining halls, recreation rooms, and so on.[56]

This should suffice. Yet a perverse curiosity makes us compare the accommodations of the prisoner-of-war camp at Birkenau with the official SS standards for concentration camp barracks. On the same day that Bischoff began work in Birkenau, his immediate superior Kammler issued a standard plan for the housing of concentration camp inmates (fig. 15).[57] A comparison of the two plans reveals how the Germans viewed the Soviet *Untermensch* in comparison with European concentration camp inmates. To allow for a fair comparison, we must note that the concentration camp barrack includes a washroom and toilets. When those are taken out, there remains 6,515 sq. ft. for 200 prisoners. At a height of 9 ft. this is 58,650 cu. ft., or 293 cu. ft. per inmate. That is almost sixfold the space allocated to the Soviet *Untermensch*. To prevent any misconception: if we compare the 293 cu. ft. allocated to the hypothetical concentration camp inmate with the 400 cu. ft. allocated to a guard (see previous paragraph), we must bear in mind that the latter number referred only to the guard's sleeping accommodations, while the 293 cu. ft. is the total living space of the concentration camp inmate. To continue the comparison: the huts in Birkenau provided 181 sq. ft. of window surface for 744 prisoners, or 0.25 sq. ft. per inmate. The standard concentration camp

FIGURE 14. Guards' dormitory in Auschwitz-Birkenau. Photo: Kamann. 1943. Source: Archive, Auschwitz-Birkenau State Museum.

barrack provided 18 times as much light. The dismal comparison can be applied to every aspect of the design. In Ertl's second design for Birkenau the toilets and washrooms were housed in 16 wash barracks and 18 latrines; that is 1 wash barrack per 7,800 inmates and 1 latrine hut per 7,000 inmates. Each hut had a surface of 1,745 sq. ft., for a little more than 0.2 sq. ft. per inmate. The standard concentration camp hut provides 4.9 sq. ft. of wash space per inmate, almost 20 times as much. Toilet space in the concentration camp was less generous at only 2.5 sq. ft. per inmate—but still more than 12 times that allocated to the Soviet *Untermensch*.

The design of the wash barracks and the privies is paradoxically "symbolic" of the fundamentally a-symbolic situation of Birkenau. Article thirteen of the Geneva Convention required belligerents "to take all sanitary measures necessary to assure the cleanliness and healthfulness of camps and prevent epidemics." Prisoners were to have "at their disposal, day and night, installations conforming to sanitary rules and constantly maintained in a state of cleanliness." They were also to "be furnished a sufficient quantity of water for the care of their own bodily cleanliness."[58] This explicit concern for

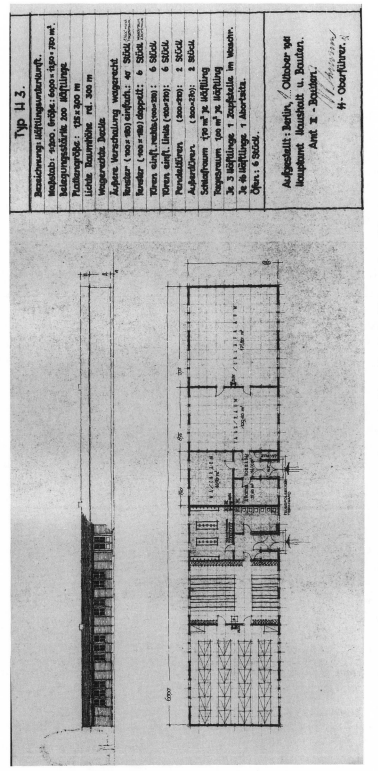

FIGURE 15. Barrack Type *Häftlinge* 3 (Prisoners 3). Fall 1941. Source: Archive, Auschwitz-Birkenau State Museum. This sheet is one of 25 types issued by Hans Kammler in the fall of 1941 to standardize concentration camp design. One barrack was to house a total of 200 inmates in two sections. Each section contained a day room, a dormitory, a washroom, and a toilet room. Cf. the barracks designed for Birkenau (figs. 11 and 13).

the cleanliness of the prisoners was engendered by the fear of lice, the most common host of the typhus virus. Lack of water, lack of soap, and insufficient changes of clothing allow lice to gain a foothold on the human body, and so may expose the prisoner population to a typhus epidemic. Yet there is also another reason. It has to do with the fundamentally symbolic nature of the consciousness of the self that makes us unable to live with our own excrement. Julia Kristeva labeled excrement as the confusing "abject" that is neither subject (me) nor object (that), "but not nothing either. A 'Something' that I do not recognize as a thing. A weight of meaninglessness, about which there is nothing insignificant, and which crushes me."[59] Excrement, so she believes, links us directly to the child's separation from the mother, and with that to the origin of a person's sense of identity. Describing defilement as the oldest and most universal symbol of evil, Paul Ricoeur has come to the same conclusion. Confronted with the excremental states of dirt, decay, and rot, we feel "a threat which, beyond the threat of suffering and death, aims at a diminution of existence, a loss of the personal core of one's being."[60]

In a masterly essay on life in the death camps, the late Terrence Des Pres examined what he labeled as the camp's "excremental assault" on the inmates. The camp's filth, he argued, was the result of a deliberate policy to destroy the last vestiges of the prisoners' sense of self-worth. It was not enough just to kill the prisoners. They had to be totally broken first. Only when the inmates were completely crushed would the SS "reach the orgasmic peak of their potential domination. . . . Spiritual destruction became an end in itself, quite apart from the requirements of mass murder"[61] Des Pres is incorrect that the defilement was the result of the SS's desire to exercise total power. The root cause was an inadequacy of design, a lack of willingness on the part of bureaucrats far away from the camps to allocate more than a minimum of material and financial resources for the camp's construction, and an assumption about the camp's use (about which more below) which did not materialize. Yet intended or not, the result was the same: with the latrines submerged in excrement, with very little water to be had at very few points, and with mud all around, what remained was an inmate population without the means to preserve any outward sign of human dignity. As Des Pres asked, "How much self-esteem can one maintain, how readily can one respond to the needs of another, if both stink, if both are caked with mud and feces?"[62] This excremental assault led to the collapse between symbol and reality that I discussed with regard to the 53 cu. ft. allocated to each prisoner. In the extreme conditions of the camp, Des Pres reflected, the division between "concrete existence" and "symbolic modes of being" disappeared. With that "body and spirit become the ground of each other, each bearing the other's need, the other's sorrow, and each responds directly to the other's total condition."[63] The result was a situation in which "meaning no longer exists above and beyond the world; it re-enters concrete experience, becomes immanent and invests each act and each moment with urgent depth."[64]

This, then, brings us back to the designs. Were they simply incompetent, given the situation? First of all there is the spatial arrangement: the "privy" that was meant to serve 7,000 inmates was a shed with one concrete open sewer, 118 feet long and 3 feet wide, without seats and with one long beam as a back support (fig. 16). The design was adapted from a model latrine designed for winter quarters for large units that had been published in a leaflet

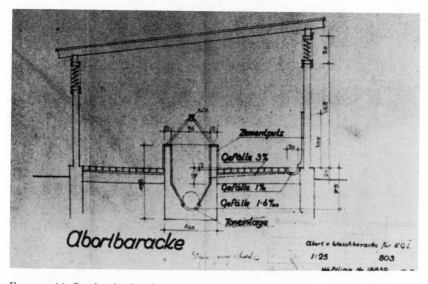

FIGURE 16. Section latrine for Auschwitz-Birkenau. Fall 1941. Source: Archive, Auschwitz-Birkenau State Museum.

The latrine is nothing more than an open sewer enclosed by a shed. This design was built with a few modifications. The shed roof was ultimately replaced by a shallow hip roof.

on wartime emergency construction (fig. 17).[65] Like the model latrine, the camp latrine pit could be accessed from walkways at both sides. Neither in Auschwitz nor in the model on which it was based were the walkways connected; but in Auschwitz this proved catastrophic, as each of the walkways was 118 ft. long. Access was provided by doors at each of the building's short sides. Imagine 7,000 inmates at sunrise, suffering from diarrhea or dysentery, trying to enter, find an unoccupied place, defecate, manage not to fall into the sewer, and get out in the 10 or so minutes allocated by the camp's regulations to such necessities. Assuming that 150 inmates could find a place at one time, and also assuming that all 7,000 inmates were to move their bowels in the

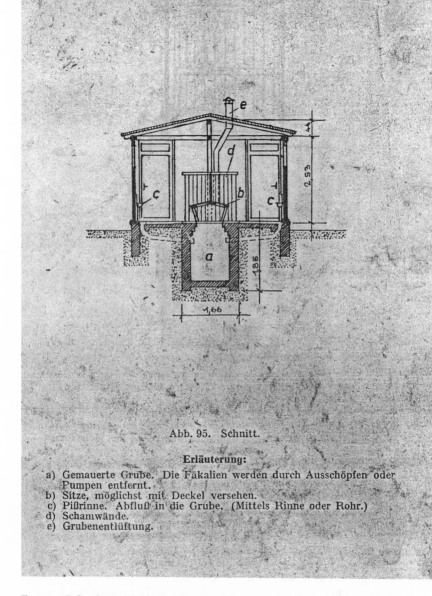

Abb. 95. Schnitt.

Erläuterung:

a) Gemauerte Grube. Die Fäkalien werden durch Ausschöpfen oder Pumpen entfernt.
b) Sitze, möglichst mit Deckel versehen.
c) Pißrinne. Abfluß in die Grube. (Mittels Rinne oder Rohr.)
d) Schamwände.
e) Grubenentlüftung.

FIGURE 17. Section model latrine for the winter quarters of large units. 1940. Source: Archive, Auschwitz-Birkenau State Museum.

morning, it would require 46 successive "seatings," with all the traffic jams involved. Had the design provided a series of doors on the long sides, like the old English commuter trains used to have, it would have accelerated matters significantly; but the basic problem would have remained. One sewer, supplied with an anemic supply of water and with a drop of only 1.6 percent, could never flush the discharge of 7,000 people in such a short time. The result was a secretory catastrophe. Added to that are a few omissions in the Auschwitz version that made the whole experience considerably more unpleasant. First, there were no seats. The support was based on the minimal design of the field latrine, to be used only at the front. Second, the "shame walls" were removed, which might have provided at least some physical privacy for those who had to defecate next to each other. Finally, the separate air extraction for the pit was omitted (which was superfluous anyway, as the pit in the Auschwitz model was open), which meant an insufferable stench. Gisella Perl, who was forced to use these latrines after BA I had become the women's camp of Birkenau, gives us a succinct description of the situation.

> There was one latrine for thirty to thirty-two thousand women and we were permitted to use it only at certain hours of the day. We stood in line to get in to this tiny building, knee-deep in human excrement. As we all suffered from dysentery, we could rarely wait until our turn came, and soiled our ragged clothes, which never came off our bodies, thus adding to the horror of our existence by the terrible smell which surrounded us like a cloud.

Added to this was the indignity of the arrangement itself. "The latrine consisted of a deep ditch with planks thrown across it at certain intervals. We squatted on these planks like birds perched on a telegraph wire, so close together that we could not help soiling one another."[66]

No explanation can justify or even qualify the horror of the latrines, or for that matter of the 53 cu. ft. of living space allocated to each prisoner. We have seen how the design decisions were framed by a general ideology that assigned the Soviet prisoner of war the lowly status of *Untermensch*. But there was also another reason why Ertl and Bischoff thought that they could get away with less than the absolute minimum, a reason explained in one document discussing the intended capacity of the wastewater treatment plant of Birkenau. Originally the camp had been planned as a base for crews of slave workers who were to be employed in melioration and construction activities in the surrounding area. As it was to be largely empty during the day, the architects reasoned that even when the camp was filled to capacity, it would be possible to run it with only 66 percent of the minimum of sanitary facilities, for prisoners could be serviced by locally dug field latrines at their place of work.[67] That reasoning was mistaken, for it entirely neglected the question of peak use in the early morning and evening, when all the prisoners had to use the facilities simultaneously.

This mistake made the lives of the inmates insufferable. Remarkable enough, it also created huge problems for the SS. As we have seen, as early as March 1, 1941, provincial officials had noted that the camp's sewage was going to create problems. Himmler had dismissed their concerns then, and he dismissed them again later. Bischoff, characterized by an SS psychologist as servile toward his superiors, difficult with his colleagues, and tyrannical to his subordinates, was not going to make trouble about it.[68] Facing serious shortages in material and manpower, the architect callously reasoned that the camp was temporary, that the inmates were going to be working out of it during the day: why not dump the sewage directly into the Vistula? In the first brief for the camp, he had projected three sewers to take the wastewater from the camp to an open channel which connected to the Vistula. No screens, sedimentation basins, or other cleansing units were planned.[69] The total budget was RM 250,000, that is, 2.8 percent of a budget of almost RM 9 million.[70]

But even this minimal arrangement was not realized. Bischoff blamed a lack of prisoners to dig the trenches.[71] The inmates were not Bischoff's only headache. The local and provincial planners created trouble from the moment they received Bischoff's proposals for approval. In early February 1942 the provincial chief of construction, Wittmer, predicted that sewage would leak from the open channels into the surrounding area and argued that a flood, which was a distinct possibility in the lowland around Birkenau, would lead to severe pollution.[72] Provincial planner Dr. Gerhard Ziegler concluded that enough was enough, and that it was time to remind Himmler of his responsibilities. In a letter of February 18, 1942, he wrote the Reichsführer-SS, "When I gave my permission some time ago to create a concentration camp, I made it clear that a camp of this enormous size, located in such an extraordinarily well-located place for industry (close to coal, at a major road and railway junction, and at the confluence of three rivers), would be expected to accept many conditions in the interest of other parties or for the common good." He noted that Höss had always understood this, and that therefore there had been no problems until then.[73]

Ziegler's letter alarmed the SS headquarters: despite appearances, the SS was not all-powerful, and while they certainly had total control over what happened within their camps once they were built, they also had to adhere to normal planning procedures and, if necessary, inspections while the camps were under construction. Ziegler had the power to stop the expansion of Auschwitz. Hence the SS main office instructed Bischoff to draw up a new plan for the camp's wastewater management which would satisfy the province. Within a week it was completed. For a total expenditure of RM 424,000, Auschwitz-Birkenau would receive a seven-branch sewer within the camp which was to have a total length of one mile (RM 52,000), three sedimentation basins (RM 205,500), a separate drainage system of pipes which connected to a collection pipe for a total length of nine miles (RM 117,000), and finally, a 0.7-mile-long open channel to discharge the effluent into the Vistula (RM 49,500).[74]

But paper is patient, and not much was done. Spring came, and then summer, and the camp continued to expand. More and more sewage flowed untreated into the Vistula, and relations between the town, the province, and the camp steadily worsened Finally, on September 23, 1942, the parties met to settle their differences. It was the same meeting in which the SS yielded on the issue of Hartjenstein's Garden City: with sewage spilling into the rivers, Oswald Pohl needed to give in somewhere—especially as he lacked the resources to install a system capable of dealing with the waste that the camp produced. When the sewage came up as the last point of the agenda, Pohl chose to humbug his way through the issue. The municipal and provincial bureaucrats, who had just won an important victory with regard to the relocation of the SS settlement, allowed him to get away with it. All agreed that the matter needed the special attention of Himmler, and that they would hold a special meeting in the near future devoted solely to resolving the sewage problem.[75]

Thus began a period in which the creation of various provisional and more sophisticated sewage-treatment plants became a major obsession in the Auschwitz Zentralbauleitung (Central Construction Office). Designs became more intricate and technologically advanced, but work on the ground progressed only slowly. Only in July 1943 was Bischoff able to complete the first provisional sedimentation basin, just south of the recently completed crematorium II (fig. 18). This was to service BA I of Auschwitz-Birkenau, which had been completed a year earlier. The basin was located adjacent to the crematorium on the windward side of the camp, significantly contributing to the all-pervasive excremental stench. Progress on the provisional treatment facilities of BA II, north of crematorium III, was slow, as there were no guards to oversee the prisoners who were to dig the channels.[76] When Pohl visited the camp on August 17, 1943, the completion of the sewage plants was the central topic of discussion. Bischoff explained that one of the difficulties in constructing the system was the lack of guards to oversee the prisoners: the treatment facilities had been planned outside the camp's barbed-wire fence, and the channels which had to be dug ran for a total of more than three miles through lightly guarded terrain. The massive deployment of prisoners needed to complete the project that year would be possible only if the camp could provide a steady and predictable supply of guards. Knowing that Bischoff was hysterical on the issue of prisoner labor, Pohl decided to see the site for himself.[77] He must have urged

FIGURE 18. Sedimentation basin of BA I, Auschwitz-Birkenau. Summer 1943. Source: Archive, Auschwitz-Birkenau State Museum.

North of the sedimentation basin we see crematorium II with its blackened chimney and, in the far distance, the barracks of BA II.

the camp to heed Bischoff's request, because for a few weeks a lot of work was done. But by mid-September the supply of guards started to dry up, and progress was halted.

Bischoff's inability to complete the sewers because of the shortage of guards points up what was perhaps the greatest fallacy of Himmler's original proposal to use slave labor to build up the German East. Himmler had been inspired by two precedents: the Reich Labor Service and the Soviet Gulag. The Reich Labor Service, which had become mandatory on June 26, 1935, was established to do exactly the kind of work that Himmler expected from slave labor. By 1937 its ambitions had extended to one-fifth of Germany.[78] The organization was involved in the reclamation of marshes, the draining and irrigation of underdeveloped land, the concentration of fragmented farm properties, the protection of lowlands by dikes, and the reclamation of land from the sea. But the men of the Labor Service worked with minimal supervision. They did not need guards. They took pride in their work. And the hundreds of thousands of prisoners within the Soviet Gulag worked most often in desolate areas in which an escape from the camp meant certain death in the wilderness. Himmler, however, had to deploy his slave labor (fig. 19) in a highly developed environment and, as the war continued,

FIGURE 19. Jewish slave labor from Mauthausen as depicted in *Das Schwarze Korps* (June 26, 1941). Source: Sterling Memorial Library, Yale University.

Few visual references to the fate of concentration camp inmates can be found in contemporary German literature. One of these is the short visual essay "Usefully Employed," published in June 1941. The text reads as follows: "The pictures on this page are not the result of years of intensive collection activity. Neither were they taken in a wax museum or a cabinet of abnormalities. And they are not a record of Germany's now-long-past housecleaning of Jewish criminals. These illustrations merely depict Dutch labor leaders. Having committed terrible crimes, they are now employed in strict work conditions for the public good, and this time against their will. They must have thought not too long ago that their 'future business' would be quite different."

with an increasing shortage of manpower to guard them. Birkenau's original purpose had been unattainable from its inception.

This brings us, then, to the camp's transformation from a prisoner-of-war camp into a concentration camp for Jews. From the moment of their arrival, the Soviet prisoners of war, who were supposed to build their own accommodations, had died more rapidly than the SS expected. Höss recalled that "the situation became really terrible during the muddy period in the winter of 1941–42. They could bear the cold, but not the dampness and wearing clothes which were always wet. This together with the primitive, half-finished, hastily thrown-together barracks at the start of Camp Birkenau caused the death rate to steadily climb."[79] Snow began to fall at the end of November. Höss sent a report to Berlin indicating a catastrophic situation. In response Kammler phoned Bischoff on December 3, demanding a full report within 24 hours. Bischoff's statement introduced the bad news with some statistics meant to impress upon Kammler how much work had been done: in a little over one month 140,000 cu. ft. of earth had been moved, 1,600 concrete foundations had been poured, and 86,000 cu. ft. of brickwork had been erected, using 1.1 million bricks. Furthermore, 600 concrete posts had been erected for the fence, and 100,000 stretching ft. of barbed wire had been put into place. The bad news was that only 2 of the huts in BA I had been completed, 12 had been provisionally closed, 7 were so far advanced that work could begin on the girders, and the walls of 9 were under construction.[80]

A major reason for the slow progress was that the Russians had not been supplied with building materials. Bischoff's original brief, drafted in October, mentioned that "the barracks will be for the greatest part built from brick, as there is no wood available, and the material will be partly derived from the demolition of the hamlet of Birkenau."[81] Thus the first batch of Soviet prisoners of war were told to cannibalize the village in the same way the Germans had driven them to cannibalize each other—as Höss later admitted when recalling this early period in the history of the camp.

> Cases of cannibalism happened quite often in Birkenau. Once I found the body of a Russian lying between two piles of bricks. The body had been ripped open with a dull instrument. The liver was missing. They beat each other to death just to get something to eat. . . . During the levelling of the land and the trench-digging in the first section of Birkenau [BA I], the men discovered several corpses of Russians apparently beaten to death and partially eaten. . . . [The Soviets] had become animals who looked for only one thing, food.[82]

Not only did the SS overseers not provide any materials to the sub-humans, but they did not even give them tools with which to cannibalize the houses in Birkenau. The houses were to be pulled down with bare hands, and the barracks built likewise. This contributed to the high mortality during construction. In the month of October, 1,255 Soviets died; in November, 3,726; in December, 1,912; and in January, 1,017. By the end of January almost 8,000 of the 10,000 men had died, which translates into a mortality rate of 240 percent per year. One more month would suffice to kill the remaining 2,000.

In the second week of October, shortly after he had begun work on Birkenau, Bischoff realized that the existing crematorium of the concentration camp (later to be known as crematorium I) would not be able to service the prisoner-of-war camp. It had been designed a year earlier to service an inmate population of 10,000. Bischoff summoned Kurt Prüfer of the Erfurt firm of Topf and Sons, which had supplied the incinerators of crematorium I.[83] In his important contribution to this volume, Pressac describes in great detail the events that both preceded and followed this visit. In the following pages I aim to add some observations to his discussion, and to introduce one piece of evidence that he did not utilize. For illustrations of the plans, I refer to those that accompany Pressac's essay.

Prüfer arrived in Auschwitz on Tuesday, October 21, and joined Bischoff in a two-day design charette.[84] As Pressac described, Prüfer's firm had been able to corner the concentration camp market for incinerators by offering stripped-down versions of civilian furnaces. The Topf model lacked the cumbersome economizer, which saved fuel but was very expensive to construct. A further savings had been obtained by grouping two muffles (the space that held the coffin or the body) in one furnace—a practice that was legally forbidden in civilian incinerators, as it removed from the cremation process the sense of "privacy" appropriate to the occasion. In the concentration camp environment such niceties did not matter; Prüfer had realized this early on and used his insight to double the furnace's capacity for the same price. Prüfer suggested to Bischoff that he could create another 50 percent increase in capacity through a combination of three incineration muffles in a single furnace. As to the location of the crematorium, the men decided that it made sense to build it in the main camp: Birkenau promised to be only a temporary camp, and it would be a waste of money to build a relatively expensive structure such as a crematorium (the whole building Bischoff budgeted for RM 650,000)[85] on a site that was going to revert to farming a few years later.[86]

After his return to Erfurt, Prüfer worked on the design of the furnaces and the firm's accountants settled price. Prüfer was able to bring down the price of each triple-muffle furnace to RM 6,378, or RM 31,890 for the five furnaces.[87] That is an investment of RM 0.25 per inmate. Also of interest is that Prüfer assumed that one muffle per 8,300 inmates would suffice. These numbers provide a basis for comparison and, consequently, judgment. Unlike German prisons, concentration camps relied exclusively from the outset on crematoria for disposal of the dead: the quick incineration of remains was a straightforward way to efface any evidence of corporal punishment, torture, or murder. Until 1939, concentration camps used the crematorium of the nearest town. Yet as early as 1937, when the SS had begun a complete overhaul of the concentration camp system which was to lead to the construction of brand new camps in Dachau, Buchenwald, and Sachsenhausen (to service the south, the center, and the north of Germany),[88] the feasibility of in-house cremation had been raised. One likely reason was the fact that the incineration of corpses in public crematoria had become subject to strict regulation by a law of May 15, 1934, and a number of administrative measures adopted in June of that year.[89] Designed to safeguard the rights of the family of the deceased and the identity of the ashes, the new law required the managers of public crematoria to enforce certain minimum standards of corpse disposal that far exceeded the needs of the SS and also, if necessary, to raise uncomfortable questions. As Pressac has shown, the SS leadership in Munich decided in May 1937 to include a crematorium within the new camp under construction at Dachau. It was to be a small building, equipped with a single-muffle furnace. After shopping around, the camp authorities decided on an incinerator produced by a local firm. The price was RM 9,250.[90] As the camp was to have a capacity of 6,240 inmates, there was an initial investment of RM 1.48 per person. Yet nothing was done for two years.

In the spring of 1939 the issue of the crematoria took on new urgency. The total inmate population in the three camps had risen from 24,000 to 60,000 as a result of the arrests that followed the Austrian Anschluss in the spring of 1938, the so-called *Reichskristallnacht* of November 9, 1938, and the December annexation of the Czech Sudetenland. Dr. Grawitz, the chief SS doctor, feared that the overcrowding in the camps would lead to an epidemic and, as a result, increased mortality.[91] Also, the regime in the camps had become harsher. As we have seen, the concentration camps had become since 1937 important producers of building materials. Contrary to intuition, conditions in the camps did not improve as the labor potential of the inmates became important. In fact, the opposite happened. Forced labor, which originally had been assigned a pedagogic purpose (hence *Arbeit macht Frei*, or "Work Sets Free"), now became slave labor. Eugen Kogon described DESt's tile yards and clay pits as places where the nature of the work was enough "to finish off anyone in short order." The quarries were even worse. Despite the original intention to exploit these places efficiently from an economic point of view, they became veritable death traps for the prisoners. This should not surprise us: even when performed by civilians protected by union regulations, the quarrying of stone is dangerous. In the words of Mauthausen's biographer Gordon Horwitz, "Much difficult labour is involved in blasting, hammering, picking, and hauling blocks of stone."

> One needs a rugged constitution for outdoor activity, keen eyes with which to work the rock, and healthy feet to remain standing long hours. During the labour, stone dust may rain down upon the work site, and strong lungs are required to withstand it. In working the rock, fingers have a way of being overlooked; hands are bloodied in handling sharp edges; bones may snap or a body flatten in a fall from great heights.[92]

The concentration camp inmates were poorly prepared for the work in the quarries. They were in a bad constitution to begin with, ill equipped, without protective gear, and subjected to constant harassment by the guards. Kogon observed that "work in the quarries was always hard, especially dragging the lorries uphill—if any one aspect can be singled out at all."

> Every night saw its procession of dead and injured, trundled into camp on wheelbarrows and stretchers—oftentimes there were two or three dozen. The mistreatment was indescribable—stonings, beatings, "accidents," deliberate hurlings into the pit, shootings, and every imaginable form of torture. Thousands fell victim. A favourite method of disposing of death candidates was to have them *push* empty (or even loaded) lorries up the steep slope. Even two men were altogether unequal to such a task. Inevitably they were crushed under the back-sliding weight and the blows of their tormentors.[93]

Both the overcrowding and the increased violence within the camps focused attention on the problem of corpse disposal. As Pressac described, Topf offered to supply Dachau with a stripped-down mobile furnace with two oil-fired forced-draft muffles with a capacity of two corpses per hour and a price tag of RM 8,750.[94] As by now the assumed capacity of the camp had been doubled (by assigning twice as many inmates to the relatively spacious barracks), the capacity remained one muffle per 6,240 inmates. Yet the investment had dropped from RM 1.48 to RM 0.70 per inmate.

These kinds of figures were a perfect introduction to the other camps, and Topf also got the job of providing Buchenwald with a crematorium. There the camp authorities had first raised the need to install an in-house incinerator in June of 1938, when the camp went through a period of very rapid growth.[95] Topf got the Buchenwald contract on the basis of a fixed version of the mobile Dachau model which, at a base price of RM 7,753, was even cheaper than that model. Added to the base price, however, was an extra RM 1,250 for a reinforced draft in the chimney.[96] The result was one muffle per 5,000 inmates and an investment of RM 0.90 per inmate. In 1940

Prüfer also was given the job of building a double-muffle incinerator in the new concentration camp at Auschwitz for RM 9,000. That is one muffle per 5,000 inmates and an expense of RM 0.90 per inmate. Yet this furnace was 50 percent more powerful than the Dachau model of 1939.[97] Taking this into account, we can say that it counts as a three-muffle oven of the old model. Hence I will designate its capacity as that of three "units," that is, one unit per 3,333 inmates. A second double-muffle (three-unit) furnace was soon added alongside the first.[98] The total was now four muffles (six units) for a camp of 10,000; that is one unit per 1,666 inmates. Total investment for incinerators was now RM 1.67 per inmate.

If we compare these numbers with the figures for the Birkenau crematorium, it becomes apparent that, assuming that the camp was indeed going to be completed and filled to capacity, the sequence of five three-muffle furnaces was *not* an excessive proposition. In other words, neither Bischoff nor Prüfer anticipated in October 1941 the very high mortality rate of the prisoners of war that actually occurred. With a capacity of 15 muffles or 22.5 units for 125,000 inmates, we come to 1 unit per 5,555 inmates, that is, less than a third of the capacity of Auschwitz I, and very much in line with Dachau and Buchenwald. At an investment of RM 0.25 per inmate, it cost one-sixth that of the main camp. These figures suggest that the mortality rate for the Soviet prisoners of war was expected to be the same as that for concentration camp inmates in the Reich, and less than that for the Polish inmates in the concentration camp on the other side of the tracks. Figures that would point to a more sinister scenario, such as Pressac's assertion that Prüfer initially calculated that the crematorium would be capable of burning 1,440 bodies in 24 hours (and, consequently, that it could theoretically incinerate the remains of all 125,000 in three or four months), must be considered either in the context of the fact that the furnaces in the main camp were estimated at a total output of 140 bodies in 24 hours, that is, two and a half months to burn the remains of the officially designated 10,000 inmates, or as an error or at least a disregard for scholarly convention on Pressac's part. In my own research I have encountered only one document that states the number of 1,440: the letter that Bischoff sent to Kammler on June 28, 1943.[99] Either I missed an important source that Pressac found but failed to properly annotate, or he creatively projected the numbers of June 1943 back into the discussions of October 1941. Whatever may prove to be the case, the conclusion must be that the mortality rate of the Soviet *Untermenschen* was not expected to be higher than that of the "typical" concentration camp inmates.

A last point that seems to support this conclusion is that as the mortality rate of the prisoners of war began to rise, the plans for the camp were changed. In December 1941 Bischoff ordered the creation of a new master plan, which was completed in the first week of January 1942 (fig. 20). Two of

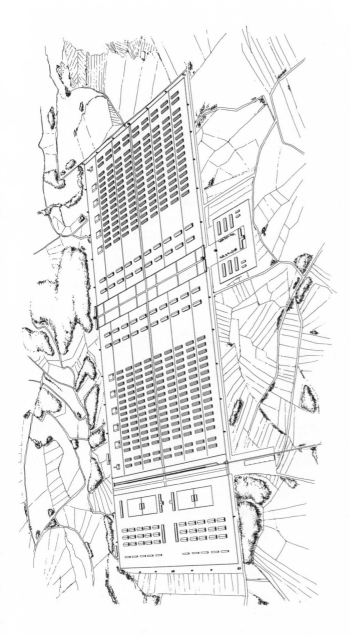

FIGURE 20. Bird's-eye view of the third design for Auschwitz-Birkenau, January 1942. Reconstruction and drawing by Robert-Jan van Pelt, Peter Gallagher, and Paul Backewich. July 1993. Source: Author's Collection.

South of the railway terminus is the quarantine camp with 2 delousing stations, 2 kitchens, 30 barracks each accommodating 744 inmates, 5 toilet barracks, and 5 washrooms. To the north of the terminus are 10 camps, 8 of which have 28 wooden horse stable barracks, 2 kitchen barracks, 2 storage barracks, 2 wooden toilet barracks, and 2 wooden washroom barracks, and 2 camps are half the usual size. To the west of the living section of the camp is a strip with 10 morgues, and 2 back-up crematoria. Both of these crematoria were canceled by Kammler on February 27, 1942. This drawing is one result of an as yet unfinished project to create a comprehensive computer model of the construction history of Auschwitz.

the most striking elements of this plan relate directly to the catastrophic conditions. First, it changed the barracks in BA II and BA III from the original brick to the prefabricated wooden huts that had been designed as horse stables for the Army. As these could be erected with a minimum of labor, it implied a significant reduction in the mortality that had occurred with the construction of the brick barracks. Furthermore, at the western edge of BA II and BA III a new zone was designated which was to include two auxiliary crematoria and 10 corpse cellars. The plan was approved on January 6, 1942, and a few weeks later Prüfer returned to Auschwitz to discuss the incinerators to be used. The engineer proposed to equip each with a simplified version of his triple-muffle furnace. Without a compressed air blower, and using only a small amount of iron, they were to cost RM 7,326 each.[100] As these were to be built in addition to the large crematorium to be constructed in the main camp, the investment in incinerating capacity had risen to a total of RM 46,542, or RM 0.37 per inmate. With a capacity of 31.5 units, the unit-per-inmate ratio had risen from 1:5,555 to 1:4,000.

These numbers seem more evolutionary than revolutionary, yet there is another difference from the original plans that gives the whole picture, at least at first sight, a more sinister aspect: the 10 enormous corpse cellars. In the crematorium already under design, the total volume of the two major morgues (a small third one was used only "for administrative purposes") was a little over 50,000 cu. ft. Its capacity was 420 corpses, or roughly 1 corpse per 300 inmates.[101] In comparison, Sachsenhausen had a morgue capacity of 1 corpse per 50 inmates. The plan of January 6 added another 250,000 cu. ft., to arrive at Sachsenhausen's capacity of 1 corpse per 50 inmates. In short, this sixfold amplification was meant only to bring the morgue capacity of the camp in line with that found in other concentration camps, and does not yet suggest the industrialized murder that was provisionally initiated in the spring of 1942. The large morgues point to a high contingent mortality, with relatively long periods to incinerate the corpses afterwards. It is significant in this context to note that two and half years later, as extermination peaked in the so-called Hungarian action, the camp had an incineration ratio which was, at 1:1160, 4.5 times that projected in October 1941 (based on an actual capacity of 80,000 inmates and an official incinerating capacity of 46 muffles, that is, 69 units), while it had virtually no morgue capacity. It pointed to a different kind of death. If the plan of January 1942 suggests the anticipation of a sudden rise in mortality as the result of epidemics, with periods of relatively low mortality in between, then the situation in 1944 suggests a steady and high mortality as a result of murder, controlled through selection. The plan of January 1942 reveals, in the end, a lethal environment, while the situation of 1944 must be explained as a result of lethal technology.

Yet 6 of the 10 morgues and the two small crematoria were taken out of the design seven weeks later. Kammler visited the camp on Thursday, February 27, 1942. In a letter written to Topf a week later, Bischoff related that Kammler had decided during that trip that the back-up incinerators were to be canceled, "and that the five triple-muffle furnaces, ordered by the letter of October 22, 1941, correspondence register no. 215/41/Ho, must be constructed in the prisoner of war camp."[102] In other words, the crematorium that had been intended for the main camp was now to be built in Birkenau.

Jean-Claude Pressac attaches no significance to Kammler's decision to move the crematorium from the main camp to Birkenau either in his important 1989 book *Auschwitz: Technique and Operation of the Gaschambers* or in his contribution to this volume.[103] Danuta Czech mentioned neither Kammler's visit nor his decision in her monumental chronology of the history of Auschwitz and Birkenau.[104] I, however, believe that the decision to move the crematorium may be interpreted as the counterpart of an otherwise unrecorded decision to transform a red house belonging to the Polish peasant Wiechuja, located at the northwest edge of the terrain reserved for the prisoner-of-war camp, into the extermination installation known as Bunker I—the place where the history of the Holocaust merged with the history of Auschwitz-Birkenau.

What do we know about the origins of Bunker I? First of all, it was not the first place in Auschwitz where Jews were gassed. Most likely the first transport to be liquidated arrived on February 15. These were Jews from the Upper Silesian town of Beuthen. In his reminiscences, written shortly after the war while he was in British detention, SS-Unterscharführer Pery Broad described how shortly before the arrival of this transport, the SS closed all the roads and the offices that had a view of crematorium I.

> Then a sad procession walked along the streets of the camp. It had started at the railway siding, located between the garrison storehouse and the German Armaments Factory (the siding branched off from the main railway line, which led to the camp). There, at the ramp, cattle vans were being unloaded, and people who had arrived in them were slowly marching towards their unknown destination. All of them had large, yellow Jewish stars on their miserable clothes. Their worn faces showed that they had suffered many a hardship. The majority were elderly people.[105]

They were led to crematorium I, and killed. As Broad noted, it was not an ideal situation from a management perspective. Using crematorium I as a killing station for a large transport interrupted the life of the camp.

This, then, makes the visit of Kammler twelve days after the first gassing in crematorium I so important. We know that Kammler discussed the problem of incineration, and it is highly likely that the issue of the recent gassings in crematorium I came up in the conversation. Kammler must have suggested that the killings be moved to Birkenau. Allowing for two or three weeks to select and transform a house into a simple extermination facility, one would expect that the first killings could take place in Birkenau in the third week of March. Indeed, the historians at the Auschwitz-Birkenau State Museum have determined March 20 as the date that Bunker I was put into operation.[106]

Pressac has consistently disagreed with those historians. In his 1989 book he provides a long analysis of Bunker I, but does not date it in this section.[107] In his discussion of crematoria II and III he gives a date for Bunker I of January 1942, but does not provide documentation or a discussion of the evidence to support this date.[108] It is clear that he followed here one passage in Höss's memoir on the implementation of the Final Solution in Auschwitz, in which he stated that the killing of Jews probably started either in September 1941, "or perhaps not until January 1942."[109] In his contribution to this volume, Pressac changed his mind. "In May, Höss selected a little farmhouse (the 'little red house') on the edge of the birch forest at Birkenau to be the new gas chamber." In his autobiography Höss indeed stated that Bunker I came into operation in the spring, and not in the winter of 1942.[110] Pressac, however, does not justify his change of mind except by invoking the fact that crematorium I had become unavailable because of a technical breakdown. Hence I view at least this part of his otherwise very useful account with certain reservations.

Given the problems with the gassings in crematorium I as observed by Broad, and the generally accepted date of March 20 as the beginning of gassings in Bunker I, it is more than likely either that Kammler decided on his visit of February 27 to move the killing operation to Birkenau, or that he was confronted with Höss's decision to do so, and that he responded by canceling the two back-up incinerators and building the large crematorium (II) instead, to provide as close as possible to the killing site all the incineration capacity needed to eliminate the remains of the victims.

One hitherto unknown document, preserved in the portions of the archive of the Auschwitz Zentralbauleitung confiscated by the Red Army, graphically suggests the connection between the decision to build crematorium II in Birkenau and Bunker I. In a reworked version of the plan of January 6, discussed above, the two back-up incinerators have been deleted, and crematorium II has been assigned the place of the canceled incinerator at the northwest corner of Birkenau—immediately adjacent to Bunker I (fig. 21).[111] This intended juxtaposition of a bunker and an incineration facility was not untypical. In August 1942 Prüfer suggested that two extra crematoria (IV and V) be built "next to the 'Bathing Facilities for Special Actions'"[112]—that is, next to Bunker II.

If this juxtaposition in space does indeed indicate a causal connection, why did Kammler not decide to remove only the southern back-up incinerator, leaving the northern one to deal with the "output" of Bunker I? I believe that there are two important reasons. First of all, the two stripped-down three-muffle incinerators would not have had sufficient capacity. Even a most generous calculation could not push the capacity of such an incinerator beyond 24 corpses per hour. More important, however, was the question of time. In the October meeting, Prüfer and Bischoff had agreed that Topf would supply all the parts for the furnaces of the new crematorium in three months.[113] On the basis of this agreement, Kammler and Bischoff must have assumed that the five triple-muffle furnaces, ordered almost four months earlier, would soon be available, while the stripped-down version, which had not even been designed yet, would take longer, especially in view of the increasingly difficult rationing situation. Also, the designs for the

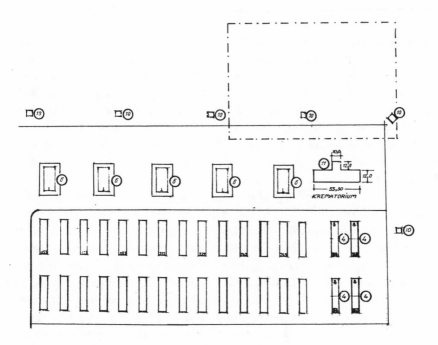

FIGURE 21. Part of a modified version of the third design for Auschwitz-Birkenau. March 1942. Source: Central Archives of Russia, Moscow.

In this version of the design of January 6, 1942, both back-up incinerators have been deleted, and crematorium II has replaced the incinerator in the northwest corner of the camp. Bunker I, which was torn down in 1943, must have stood somewhere in the area defined by the broken line (added by author). The number 4 indicates wash and toilet barracks, 6 indicates morgues, 10 indicates guard towers, and the building marked 11 is crematorium II.

crematorium that was to house the five incinerators had been both completed and approved. At least on paper, everything was ready for construction of the crematorium agreed upon in October.

This leaves the vexing problem of the ratio between incineration capacity and the size of the camp. To interpret Kammler's visit as the key event in the transformation of Birkenau into an extermination site raises the paradox that the decision to begin mass murder coincided with the decision to reduce the incineration capacity of the camp from 1:4,000 to 1:5,555. But this reduction is only apparent, because in February 1942 it had begun to seem that Birkenau was going to have no inmates at all, and hence the entire projected incineration capacity could be applied to the mass murder of the Jews.

As we have seen, Auschwitz-Birkenau was conceived as a large camp for Soviet prisoners of war who were to be employed in the reconstruction of the town of Auschwitz. This was a civilian project, even if initiated and overseen by the SS. In September 1941, when Himmler negotiated the transfer of up to 100,000 prisoners of war from the army to the SS, the generals were happy to be rid of the prisoners. But by the time the first Russians arrived in Auschwitz, perceptions about the usefulness of these men had begun to change. It became increasingly clear that Operation Barbarossa had failed as a Blitzkrieg, and that Germany must mobilize all of its resources to continue the war. With more men being called up in the army, and more demands being made on German industry—especially the armaments industry—labor had become a commodity in short supply. Even the Soviet prisoners of war became a resource too precious to be wasted. On October 31, 1941, Hitler decided that Soviet prisoners of war should be put to work in the armaments industry. In November, Reich Marshal Hermann Göring gained control as Plenipotentiary for the Four Year Plan over all prisoners of war, charging the Labor Allocation Division of the Office of the Plenipotentiary with creating and executing a policy to exploit their labor potential. The Labor Allocation Division began with a census to establish needs and resources, and issued a decree on January 8, 1942, which assigned all prisoners of war to the armaments industry, and to a selected number of other activities such as agriculture, forestry, and mining. It also stipulated that no prisoners of war could be employed for building construction.[114]

The decree of January 8 brought an effective end to Himmler's plan to collect a large Russian labor force in Birkenau. Beginning in January there were some 3,000 Soviet prisoners of war left in Auschwitz, and the SS was to get no more. On January 8, 1942, Auschwitz-Birkenau became quite literally a site in search of a mission.

Part of the original mission could still be accomplished by replacing Soviets with Jews. In December 1941, Kammler had indicated the interchangeability of the two groups when he designated both Soviet prisoners of war and Jews as potential slave laborers for the building brigades. Initiated to ensure continuation of the SS building program, the program to establish building brigades was a kind of rear-guard action meant to guarantee a future supply of prisoners of war to the SS. The brigades did not materialize that year, but Kammler's suggestion that Soviet prisoners of war and Jews were somehow interchangeable stuck. It influenced SS-Obergruppenführer Heydrich's language in the Wannsee conference, when he stated that "under appropriate leadership, the Jews should be put to work in a suitable way within the framework of the final solution. In large labor columns, with separation of the sexes, the able-bodied Jews will be made to build roads as they are led into territories [i.e., the East]."[115] Roads, and not model towns: Roads are essential to conduct a war; model towns are not.

Of course, Heydrich did not intend for roads to be the only product of Jewish labor. It was equally important that the workers would die. Heydrich did not state what would happen to those who could not work, but it was clear that they were to be killed right away. He was, however, quite explicit about the fate of those who would survive the hardships of forced labor. "Since the ultimate survivors will undoubtedly constitute the most resistant group, they must be treated accordingly [that is, eliminated], since this natural elite, if released, must be viewed as the potential germ cell of a new Jewish order."[116]

Six days after the Wannsee conference, Himmler sent a telegram to Inspector of Concentration Camps Glücks:

> As no Russian prisoners of war can be expected in the near future, I am sending to the camps a large number of Jews who have emigrated from Germany. Will you therefore make preparations to receive within the next four weeks 100,000 Jews and up to 50,000 Jewesses in the concentration camps. The concentration camps will be faced with great economic tasks in the coming weeks. SS-Gruppenführer Pohl will inform you in detail.[117]

Three weeks later a first transport of Jews arrived in Auschwitz. Mainly old people, they were brought to the main camp, and gassed in crematorium I.

A month after Himmler's letter, and seven weeks after Göring had brought an end to Himmler's dream of constructing his utopia with Soviet prisoners of war, Kammler arrived in Auschwitz. Let us consider the situation that presented itself to him. The ultimate end of the SS presence in Auschwitz had not changed. The town and its surroundings were to become a model of German settlement in the East. The construction of the IG Farben plant continued as planned. The reconstruction and expansion of the town of Auschwitz, however, had to wait until the defeat of the

Soviet Union. When this occurred, it was likely that the decree that the Labor Allocation Division of the Office of the Plenipotentiary had issued on January 8 would be annulled, and that the SS would receive its complement of Soviet prisoners of war and other prisoners. In October 1941 they had been ill prepared to receive them. Thus it was better to continue construction of Auschwitz-Birkenau in anticipation of the resumption of construction activity in the town. This included the building of a crematorium.

In view of the decisions made in the last part of January, it made sense to bring Jews to Birkenau. The able-bodied could be put to work to continue construction of the camp, while those who could not work could be liquidated in accordance with the practice that had commenced 12 days earlier. As the killing in the main camp generated too many practical problems, it was logical to move the extermination to Birkenau. One crematorium with five triple-muffle furnaces would suffice to handle the mortality of both the camp and the transports, as the number of Jews to be put to work in the construction of Birkenau was to remain far below the planned capacity of 100,000.

In other words, the role of Auschwitz in the final solution of the Jewish problem was to be temporary. Of course, the whole program to exterminate Europe's Jews was by definition one of limited duration. The other camps that acquired a dominant role in the Holocaust—Belzec, Sobibor, and Treblinka—were indeed makeshift constructions to be pulled down after a year or two. In Auschwitz the extermination of the Jews was meant to be a

FIGURE 22. Hans Kammler. 1935. Source: Berlin Document Center.

transient phenomenon in the history of the camp. Hence, throughout 1942 and 1943, Bischoff continued to plan for the camp that was to exist after the conclusion of the Holocaust.

That other future never materialized. Thus the name Auschwitz became synonymous with the Holocaust, and not with Himmler's model town.

NOTES

1. Jean-François Lyotard, as quoted in Gillian Rose, "Architecture after Auschwitz," *Assemblage* 21 (September 1993), p. 63.
2. Roland Barthes, *Mythologies*, trans. Annette Lavers (London, 1972), p. 143.
3. Ibid.
4. This characterization of Auschwitz was offered by Raul Hilberg in his address at the opening conference of the United States Holocaust Research Institute, December 5, 1993.
5. Robert-Jan van Pelt and Carroll William Westfall, *Architectural Principles in the Age of Historicism* (New Haven and London, 1991).
6. Hans van der Laan, *Architectonic Space*, trans. Richard Padovan (Leiden, 1983).
7. Dietrich Klagges, *Geschichtsunterricht als nationalpolitische Erziehung* (Frankfurt am Main, 1937), p. 199.
8. Josef Nadler, *Das stammhafte Gefüge des deutschen Volkes* (Munich, 1934), pp. 110f.
9. Rudolf Kötzschke and Wolfgang Ebert, *Geschichte der ostdeutsche Kolonisation* (Leipzig, 1937), p. 19.
10. Ibid., p. 9.
11. Ibid., p. 10.
12. As quoted in Adolf Hitler, *My New Order*, ed. Raoul de Roussy de Sales (New York, 1941), pp. 737f.
13. Heinrich Himmler, "Deutsche Burgen im Osten," *Das Schwarze Korps* 7 (January 23, 1941), p. 4.
14. SS-Hauptamt-Schulungsamt, *Der Kampf um die deutsche Ostgrenze* (Berlin, 1941), pp. 41ff.
15. Hanns Johst, *Ruf des Reiches—Echo des Volkes: Eine Ostfahrt* (Munich, 1940), pp. 86ff.
16. Ibid., pp. 126f.
17. Quoted in Lucy S. Dawidowicz, ed., *A Holocaust Reader* (New York, 1976), p. 134.
18. "Der Reichsführer-SS vor den Oberabschnittsführern und Hauptamtschefs im Haus der Flieger in Berlin am 9. Juni 1942," ms., German Federal Archives, Koblenz, Coll. NS 19, no. 4009, p. 18.
19. See Gordon J. Horwitz, *In the Shadow of Death: Living outside the Gates of Mauthausen* (New York, 1990), pp. 23ff.
20. Letter, Konrad Meyer to Gerhard Ziegler, July 5, 1940, German Federal Archives, Koblenz, Coll. R 49, no. 902.

21. Ulrich Greifelt, "Vermerk [Siedlungszone I]," August 8, 1940, ms., German Federal Archives, Koblenz, Coll. R 49, no. 902, pp. 2, 9–10.

22. "Vermerk über eine Sitzung am 10.10.40 in Kattowitz," October 14, 1940, ms., German Federal Archives, Koblenz, Coll. R 49, no. 902.

23. Letter, Konrad Meyer to Fritz Arlt, December 12, 1940, German Federal Archives, Koblenz, Coll. R 49, no. 902.

24. "Zur Gründung des Werkes Auschwitz; Niederschrift über die Gründungssitzung am 7. April 1941 in Kattowitz," ms., Central Archives of Russia, Moscow, Coll. 502/5, no. 6, p. 40 (9) (United States Holocaust Research Institute Archives, microfilm RG-11.001M.03, reel 71).

25. Hans Stosberg, "Auschwitz: Erläuterung zur Raumordnungsskizze," ms., Provincial Archive, Katowice, Coll. Landesplanung Gau Oberschlesien, no. 467, pp. 198–206.

26. "Vermerk betr. Ortsplanung Auschwitz," September 14, 1942, ms., Provincial Archive, Katowice, Coll. Landesplanung Gau Oberschlesien, no. 467, pp. 103–5.

27. "Vermerk betr.: KL-Auschwitz, Eisenbahn-, Siedlungs-, Grenz- u. Wasserfragen," ms., Provincial Archive, Katowice, Coll. Landesplanung Gau Oberschlesien, no. 467, pp. 96–99.

28. Stosberg, "Zum Jahreswechsel 1941–1942," ms., Provincial Archive, Katowice, Coll. Landesplanung Gau Oberschlesien, no. 467, pp. 148–51.

29. Letter, Regierungsbaurat Derpa to the mayor of Auschwitz, January 3, 1941, Central Archives of Russia, Moscow, Coll. 502/1, no. 76, p. 53 (United States Holocaust Research Institute Archives, microfilm RG-11.001M.03, reel 23).

30. Rudolf Höss, *Death Dealer: The Memoirs of the SS Kommandant at Auschwitz*, trans. Andrew Pollinger, ed. Steven Paskuly (Buffalo, 1992), pp. 283f.

31. "Anhang zum Aktenvermerk vom 29. März 1941. Betreff: Arbeitseinsatz fuur das neuerstehende Buna-Werk Auschwitz," ms., Central Archives of Russia, Moscow, Coll. 502/1, no. 280 (United States Holocaust Research Institute Archives, microfilm RG-11.001M.03, reel 38).

32. Höss, *Memoirs*, p. 285.

33. Letter, Gerhard Ziegler to Himmler, February 18, 1942, Provincial Archive, Katowice, Coll. Landesplanung Gau Oberschlesien, no. 467, p. 130.

34. Höss, *Memoirs*, p. 285.

35. Minutes of the ministerial conference held at the Ministry of Propaganda, Berlin, on July 5, 1941. As quoted in Willi A. Boelcke, ed., *The Secret Conferences of Dr. Goebbels: The Nazi Propaganda War 1939–1943*, trans. Ewald Osers (New York, 1970), pp. 177f.

36. Reichsführer SS, *Der Untermensch* (Berlin, 1942), pp. 4f.

37. As quoted in Omer Bartov, *Hitler's Army: Soldiers, Nazis and War in the Third Reich* (New York and Oxford, 1991), p. 129.

38. Ibid.

39. Ibid., pp. 130f.

40. Christian Streit, "The German Army and the Politics of Genocide," in Gerhard Hirschfeld, ed., *The Policies of Genocide: Jews and Soviet Prisoners of War in Nazi Germany* (London, 1986), p. 4.

41. As quoted in Jürgen Förster, "The German Army and the Ideological War against the Soviet Union," in Hirschfeld, *The Policies of Genocide*, p. 20.

42. Höss, *Memoirs*, p. 132.

43. Christian Streit, *Keine Kamaraden: Die Wehrmacht und die sowjetischen Kriegsgefangenen 1941–1945* (Stuttgart, 1978), pp. 217ff.

44. Letter, Ambros and Dürrfeld to the Generalbevollmächtigten für Sonderfragen der chemischen Erzeugung Prof. Dr. Krauch, 25 October 1941, Central Archives of Russia, Moscow, Coll. 502/5, no. 6 (United States Holocaust Research Institute Archives, microfilm RG-11.001M.03, reel 71).

45. Karl Bischoff, "Erläuterungsbericht zum Vorentwurf für den Neubau des Kriegsgefangenenlagers der Waffen-SS, Auschwitz O/S," ms., Central Archives of Russia, Moscow, Coll. 502/1, no. 232 (United States Holocaust Research Institute Archives, microfilm RG-11.001M.03, reel 35).

46. Archive, Auschwitz-Birkenau State Museum, neg. 21493/1.

47. Höss, *Memoirs,* p. 133.

48. Telegram, SS-Hauptstürmführer Sesemann to the Architectural Office of the Waffen SS, Auschwitz, October 25, 1941, Central Archives of Russia, Moscow, Coll. 502/1, no. 215 (United States Holocaust Research Institute Archives, microfilm RG-11.001M.03, reel 34).

49. Höss, *Memoirs,* pp. 132f.

50. Tadeusz Borowski, *This Way for the Gas, Ladies and Gentlemen,* trans. Barbara Vedder (New York, 1976), pp. 130f.

51. Primo Levi, *If This Is a Man?,* trans. Stuart Woolf (New York, 1959), pp. 204f.

52. Primo Levi, *The Reawakening,* trans. Stuart Woolf (Boston and Toronto, 1965), p. 12.

53. Carnegie Endowment for International Peace, Division of International Law, pamphlet 5: *The Hague Conventions of 1899 (II) and 1907 (IV) Respecting the Laws and Customs of War on Land* (Washington, D.C., 1915), pp. 10f.

54. Christian Meurer, *Das Kriegsrecht der Haager Konferenz* (Munich, 1907), p. 125.

55. U.S. Congress, Senate, *Treaties, Conventions, International Acts, Protocols and Agreements between the United States of America and Other Powers (1923–1937),* 75th Congress, 3d sess., 1938, S. Doc. 134, p. 5231.

56. My source is a folder with 25 standard plans for barracks to be used in a typical concentration camp. These plans were issued by the SS-HHB/II (Bauten) in the fall of 1941 to regulate concentration camp design. The plan I chose for my calculation is *Truppenunterkunft B.* Archive, Auschwitz-Birkenau State Museum, Coll. BW, no. 3/3a, file 3/5.

57. Type H3: *Häftlingsunterkunft,* Archive, Auschwitz-Birkenau State Museum, Coll. BW, no. 3/3a, file 3/5.

58. U.S. Congress, Senate, *Treaties, Conventions, International Acts, Protocols and Agreements between the United States of America and Other Powers (1923–1937),* 75th Congress, 3d sess., 1938, S. Doc. 134, p. 5230.

59. Julia Kristeva, *Powers of Horror: An Essay on Abjection,* trans. Leon S. Roudiez (New York, 1982), p. 2.

60. Paul Ricoeur, *The Symbolism of Evil,* trans. Emerson Buchanan (New York, 1967), p. 41.

61. Terrence Des Pres, *The Survivor: An Anatomy of Life in the Death Camps* (New York, 1976), p. 60.

62. Ibid.

63. Ibid., p. 65.

64. Ibid, p. 69.

65. *Behelfsmässiges Bauen im Kriege,* Part I: "Shelter"; Section J: "Sanitation"; Chapter I: "Latrines." Archive, Auschwitz-Birkenau State Museum, Coll. BW, no. 6a, file 6a + 7a/2.

66. Gisella Perl, *I Was a Doctor in Auschwitz* (New York, 1948), p. 33.

67. "Vorentwurf für den Ausbau der Kläranlage II im K.G.L. Auschwitz," ms., Archive, Auschwitz-Birkenau State Museum, Coll. BW, no. 18, file 18/70, p. 3.

68. "Beurteilung," November 14, 1944; ms., Berlin Document Center, Coll. SSO, file Bischoff, Karl, 9.8.97.

69. "Erläuterungsbericht zum Vorentwurf für den Neubau des Kriegsgefangenenlagers der Waffen-SS, Auschwitz O/S," ms., Central Archives of Russia, Moscow, Coll. 502/1, no. 232, p. 5 (United States Holocaust Research Institute Archives, microfilm RG-11.001M.03, reel 35).

70. "Kostenvoranschlag für den Vorentwurf über den Neubau des Kriegsgefangenenlagers der Waffen-SS, Auschwitz O/S," ms., Central Archives of Russia, Moscow, Coll. 502/1, no. 232, p. 4 (United States Holocaust Research Institute Archives, microfilm RG-11.001M.03, reel 35).

71. "Baubericht über den Stand der Bauarbeiten für das Bauvorhaben Kriegsgefangenenlager der Waffen-SS Auschwitz, 10 Dezember 1941," ms., Central Archives of Russia, Moscow, Coll. 502/1, no. 219, p. 3 (United States Holocaust Research Institute Archives, microfilm RG-11.001M.03, reel 34).

72. Letter, Wittmer to Ziegler, February 7, 1942, Provincial Archive, Katowice, Coll. Landesplanung Gau Oberschlesien, no. 467, pp. 137–39.

73. Ibid., p. 132.

74. "Kostenüberschlag für das Bauvorhaben: Kriegsgefangenenlager der Waffen-SS in Auschwitz O/S, 25.2.1942," and "Baubeschreibung Kriegsgefangenenlager der Waffen-SS in Auschwitz, Kanalisation und Kläranlagen," mss., Central Archives of Russia, Moscow, Coll. 502/1, no. 235, pp. 8, 19 (United States Holocaust Research Institute Archives, microfilm RG-11.001M.03, reel 35).

75. "Vermerk betr.: KL-Auschwitz, Eisenbahn-, Siedlungs-, Grenz- u. Wasserfragen," ms., Provincial Archive, Katowice, Coll. Landesplanung Gau Oberschlesien, no. 467, pp. 3f.

76. Letter, Bischoff to Kammler, July 26, 1943, Archive, Auschwitz-Birkenau State Museum, Coll. BW, no. 1/5, file 1/17.

77. "Aktenvermerk betr.: besuch des Hauptamtschef . . . Pohl in Auschwitz, 17. August 1943," ms., Central Archives of Russia, Moscow, Coll. 502/1, no. 233 (United States Holocaust Research Institute Archives, microfilm RG-11.001M.03, reel 35).

78. Will Decker, "Der deutsche Arbeitsdienst: Ziele, Leistungen und Organisation des Reichsarbeitsdienst," in *Wehrhaftes Volk: der organisatorische Aufbau Teil III*, ed. Paul Meier-Bennechenstein, vol. 3 of *Das Dritte Reich im Aufbau* (Berlin, 1939), pp. 487f.

79. Höss, *Memoirs*, p. 133.

80. Letter, Bischoff to Kammler, December 4, 1941, Central Archives of Russia, Moscow, Coll. 502/1, no. 219, pp. 26–28 (United States Holocaust Research Institute Archives, microfilm RG-11.001M.03, reel 34).

81. Ms., Central Archives of Russia, Moscow, Coll. 502/1, no. 232, p. 3 (United States Holocaust Research Institute Archives, microfilm RG-11.001M.03, reel 35).

82. Höss, *Memoirs*, pp. 133f.

83. Telegram, Bauleitung, October 11, 1941, Central Archives of Russia, Moscow, Coll. 502/1, no. 313 (United States Holocaust Research Institute Archives, microfilm RG-11.001M.03, reel 41).

84. Letter, Topf, October 14, 1941, Central Archives of Russia, Moscow, Coll.

502/1, no. 313 (United States Holocaust Research Institute Archives, microfilm RG-11.001M.03, reel 41).

85. "Erläuterungsbericht zum Vorentwurf für den Neubau des Kriegsgefangenenlagers der Waffen-SS, Auschwitz O/S," ms., Central Archives of Russia, Moscow, Coll. 502/1, no. 232, p. 6 (United States Holocaust Research Institute Archives, microfilm RG-11.001M.03, reel 35).

86. Plan of the Main Camp at Auschwitz, February 19, 1942, Archive, Auschwitz-Birkenau State Museum, neg. 20931/4.

87. Bill, Topf, January 27, 1943, Central Archives of Russia, Moscow, Coll. 502/1, no. 327 (United States Holocaust Research Institute Archives, microfilm RG-11.001M.03, reel 42).

88. See Martin Broszat, "The Concentration Camps 1933–45," in Helmut Krausnick, Hans Buchheim, Martin Broszat, and Hans-Adolf Jacobsen, *Anatomy of the SS State*, trans. Richard Barry, Marian Jackson, and Dorothy Long (New York, 1968), pp. 445f.

89. *Reichsgesetzblatt* I, 1383.

90. Pressac, "Constructing the Machinery of Mass Murder," n. 4.

91. Broszat, "The Concentration Camps 1933–45," p. 458.

92. Horwitz, *In the Shadow of Death*, p. 24.

93. Eugen Kogon, *The Theory and Practice of Hell: The German Concentration Camps and the System behind Them*, trans. Heinz Norden (New York, 1950), pp. 97, 93.

94. Pressac, "Constructing the Machinery of Mass Murder," n. 5.

95. Ibid., n. 7.

96. Ibid., n. 8.

97. Ibid., n. 14.

98. Offer, Topf, November 13, 1940, Central Archives of Russia, Moscow, Coll. 502/1, no. 312 (United States Holocaust Research Institute Archives, microfilm RG-11.001M.03, reel 41).

99. Letter, Bischoff to Kammler, June 28, 1943, Central Archives of Russia, Moscow, Coll. 502/1, no. 314 (United States Holocaust Research Institute Archives, microfilm RG-11.001M.03, reel 41).

100. "Kostenanschlag auf Lieferung von 2 Stück Dreimuffel-Einäscherungs-Öfen," ms., Central Archives of Russia, Moscow, Coll. 502/1, no. 313 (United States Holocaust Research Institute Archives, microfilm RG-11.001M.03, reel 41).

101. Plan of morgue, Sachsenhausen, November 1940, German Federal Archives, Koblenz, Coll. NS 3, no. 377.

102. Letter, Bischoff to Topf, March 5, 1942, Archive, Auschwitz-Birkenau State Museum, Coll. BW, file 30/25, p. 1; see also letter, Bischoff to Wirtz, March 30, 1942, Archive, Auschwitz-Birkenau State Museum, Coll. BW, file 30/34, p. 37. These letters are published in Jean-Claude Pressac, *Auschwitz: Technique and Operation of the Gaschambers* (New York, 1989), pp. 191, 193.

103. Pressac, *Auschwitz*, p. 184.

104. Danuta Czech, *Kalendarium der Ereignisse im Konzentrationslager Auschwitz-Birkenau 1939–1945*, trans. Jochen August et al. (Reinbek, 1989), p. 178.

105. Pery Broad, "Reminiscences," in Rudolf Höss, Pery Broad, and Johann Paul Kremer, *KL Auschwitz Seen by the SS*, trans. Krystyna Michalik (Warsaw, 1991), pp. 128f.

106. Czech, *Kalendarium*, p. 186.

107. Pressac, *Auschwitz*, pp. 161ff.

108. Ibid., p. 184.

109. Höss, *Memoirs*, p. 31.

110. Ibid., p. 157.

111. Reworked version of plan of Birkenau of January 6, 1942; no date, but probably produced just after February 27, 1942; Central Archives of Russia, Moscow, Coll. 502/2, no. 95 (United States Holocaust Research Institute Archives, microfilm RG-11.001M.03, reel 63).

112. "Aktenvermerk Betr.: Anwesenheit von Obering. Prüfer der Fa. Topf u. Söhne Erfurt, bezüglich Ausbau der Einäscherungsanlagen im K.G.L. Auschwitz," August 21, 1942, ms., Central Archives of Russia, Moscow, Coll. 502/1, no. 313 (United States Holocaust Research Institute Archives, microfilm RG-11.001M.03, reel 41).

113. Letter, Bischoff to Topf, October 22, 1941, Central Archives of Russia, Moscow, Coll. 502/1, no. 313 (United States Holocaust Research Institute Archives, microfilm RG-11.001M.03, reel 41).

114. See Streit, *Keine Kamaraden*, p. 209.

115. As quoted in Jochen von Lang, ed., *Eichmann Interrogated: Transcripts from the Archives of the Israeli Police*, trans. Ralph Manheim (London, 1983), p. 91.

116. Ibid.

117. As quoted in Broszat, "The Concentration Camps 1933–45," p. 483.

7

Gas Chambers and Crematoria

FRANCISZEK PIPER

In the wake of SS chief Heinrich Himmler's decision in the summer of 1941 that Auschwitz was to play a part in the plan to annihilate European Jews,[1] a new method of mass killing in gas chambers was introduced. When Himmler notified camp commandant Rudolf Höss of his decision, he described the gas chambers enigmatically as "installations."[2] It was the chief of the Reich Main Security Office's Jewish Department, Adolf Eichmann, who spelled out the details of the proposed installations to Höss. In keeping with Himmler's announcement, Eichmann arrived at Auschwitz shortly thereafter.[3] He explained to Höss the workings of the static gas chambers in euthanasia stations[4] and the mobile chambers installed in automobiles.[5] He commented, however, that neither type was suitable for the mass-scale extermination that was planned for Auschwitz.

The type of gas to be used remained an open question. Owing to difficulties in transportation and utilization, carbon monoxide in cylinder containers as used in euthanasia stations was deemed unsuitable. Eichmann, whose position and official contacts offered him greater access to relevant firms and institutions, promised to locate a gas suitable for the task. Ultimately, Zyklon B (prussic acid), hitherto used for disinfection, turned out to be available locally.

The first experiments with prussic acid as a killing agent took place in late summer 1941 in the basement of block 11 (until August 1941, it had been designated as number 13). The first and best-known mass killing operation during this period was the murder of some 600 Soviet prisoners of war and about 250 sick prisoners on September 3–5.[6] A situation report covering the period from August 15 to September 15 was compiled by the prisoner underground:

> The camp has been the scene of a hideous crime when on the night of September 5–6, about 600 Soviet prisoners, including political officers of the army, were crammed into a bunker together with some 200 Poles. After the bunker had been sealed they were poisoned by gas, their bodies brought to the crematorium and incinerated.[7]

For many reasons the cellars of block 11 proved unsuitable for the task of mass gassings. A complicated maze of corridors and cells hampered the removal of bodies and the airing of the bunker, which, according to the commandant, should take two days.[8] Not only did the equipment and personnel have to be moved out while gassing was in progress, but it also proved exceedingly difficult to keep the entire proceeding secret. The block itself was located on the grounds of Auschwitz I, the main camp, near the buildings where prisoners were held. Although no one was allowed to leave the buildings during gassings, prisoners could watch the operation surreptitiously, witnessing both the marching of the victims to the site and the removal of the bodies. For these reasons the gassing procedure was relocated to the camp crematorium.

Crematorium I

The so-called old crematorium in Auschwitz,[9] later designated as crematorium I, was initially designed for burning the bodies of prisoners who died a natural death or were killed or executed. The crematorium also was used to incinerate the bodies of prisoners from Birkenau and the satellite camps. Construction began in early July 1940, when a building that had served as a depot before the war was remodeled. The crematorium was put into operation in September 1940.[10] Until that time, the bodies of dead prisoners were shipped off to Gliwice and incinerated in the municipal crematorium.

The extant plan, dated September 25, 1941, shows that the crematorium building was 26.57 meters long, 14.61 m wide, and about 3 m high. It had one entrance on the northwest side and included a furnace room with three two-retort furnaces and a charnel house that was 78.2 sq m (17 m in length and 4.6 m in width).[11] The concrete roof was flat. The building had earth embankments on three sides with openings for the window of the coke plant (through which coke was thrown inside). There were two windows in the furnace room that were probably used to lower the temperature inside the building. An external chimney was connected to the furnaces by underground flues. The entrance to the building was camouflaged by a concrete-slab wall several meters high that enclosed a courtyard. Two massive gates, made of wooden beams, led to the courtyard. In front of the entrance were meticulously kept flowerbeds. The crematorium was screened from view from the camp by a one-story building that housed the SS hospital. The east and north sides were screened by the barracks of the political department and camp workshops. According to official German figures, the "capacity" of the expanded crematorium was 340 bodies in 24 hours.[12] Crematorium I operated until July 1942, with an interlude at the turn of 1941–42 for the construction of a third furnace.

With the launching of new large crematoria in Birkenau (March–June 1943), incineration of bodies in the old crematorium was discontinued, and the bodies of prisoners who died in the main camp and the satellite camps were shipped to Birkenau for cremation. The prisoner personnel who serviced crematorium I were also transferred to Birkenau on July 19, 1943.[13] After that time, the crematorium building was used to store cinerary urns and medicines. In 1944, it was converted into an air-raid shelter for SS personnel from the nearby hospital.[14]

Following the experimental gassing of the Soviet prisoners of war and sick prisoners in block 11, the room that had served as the mortuary was converted to a gas chamber.[15] The conversion included sealing the doors that led to the washing room and the furnace room, and boring openings in the ceiling through which Zyklon B was to be poured.[16] Later, a ventilator was installed to air the premises, which facilitated the removal of the bodies.[17]

Filip Müller, a member of the *Sonderkommando*, the prisoners who serviced the crematoria, testified that the chamber could hold over 700 people. Former camp commandant Höss and former prisoners testified that even more prisoners could be crammed inside.[18]

The victims consigned to gassing in crematorium I usually were brought into the camp in late evening or early morning by train or in cars that pulled up at the entrance. In the former case, the victims disembarked at a loading ramp that adjoined the camp and were marched to their destination.

In his memoirs, Höss described the first gassing of a transport of Soviet prisoners of war in the chamber.

> I have a clearer recollection of the gassing of 900 Russians that took place shortly afterwards in the old crematorium, since the use of block 11 for this purpose caused too much trouble. While the transport was detraining, holes were pierced in the earth and concrete ceiling of the mortuary. The Russians were ordered to undress in an anteroom; they then quietly entered the mortuary, for they had been told they were to be deloused. The whole transport exactly

filled the mortuary to capacity. The doors were then sealed and the gas shaken down through the holes in the roof. I do not know how long this killing took. For a little while a humming sound could be heard. When the powder was thrown in, there were cries of "Gas!" then a great bellowing, and the trapped prisoners hurled themselves against both doors. But the doors held. They were opened several hours later, so that the place might be aired.[19]

After that, the chamber was used to gas several hundred Soviet POWs at a time,[20] as well as numerous transports of Jews who were killed wholesale, including entire families regardless of sex or age.[21] One camp functionary, Pery Broad, who witnessed the mass murders, recalled that

a sad procession walked along the streets of the camp. It had started at the railway siding . . . branching out from the main railway line, which led to the camp. . . . Suspecting nothing the column marched in, five persons abreast, and came to a halt in the yard. They numbered from 400 to 500 people. The SS man, somewhat nervous, waited for the last man to enter the yard. At that moment he quickly shut the gate and bolted it. Grabner and Hossler were standing on the roof of the crematorium. Grabner spoke to the Jews who awaited their fate, suspecting nothing: "You will now bathe and undergo disinfection; we don't want any epidemics in the camp. Then you will go to your barracks and get some hot soup. You will be assigned to jobs according to your professional qualifications. Now undress and put your clothes in front of you on the ground." The first lines entered the mortuary through the anteroom. . . . As soon as the last person had entered, the SS guards disappeared without much ado. Suddenly the door was closed; it had been gas-proofed with rubber and reinforced with iron fittings. Those inside heard the heavy bolts being secured. A deadly, paralyzing terror gripped the victims. They started to beat on the door, hammering it with their fists in helpless rage and despair.[22]

The gas chamber attached to crematorium I operated until fall 1942. The last victims were several hundred prisoners of the Sonderkommando in Birkenau who were employed in the killing operations. They were gassed in early December 1942.[23] Their murder was but one of a series of mass murders of Sonderkommando prisoners, doomed as witnesses and executors of Nazi crimes. One of the handful of Sonderkommando prisoners who survived the successive hecatombs, Müller, serviced crematorium I from May 1942 to July 1943. He concluded on the basis of personal observation that several tens of thousands of Jews from Upper Silesia, Slovakia, France, Holland, Yugoslavia, and the ghettos of Theresienstadt, Ciechanow, and Grodno perished there.[24]

Bunkers—Provisional Gas Chambers

In the first months of 1942,[25] the gassing operation was extended to nearby Birkenau owing to the small capacity of the gas chamber and ovens in Auschwitz and the difficulties in camouflaging the proceedings. The move signaled the implementation of the Nazi plan to exterminate European Jews and coincided with the arrival of the first Jewish transports. Construction of the new camp had been under way since October 1941.

Initially the victims were gassed in one gas chamber. By mid-1942,[26] the mass murders took place in two provisional gas chambers that were installed in the cottages of two peasants, Harmata and Wichaj, who had been evicted earlier.

The building in which the first gas chamber was installed, called bunker 1 by the SS men, had been earmarked for that purpose the previous year, when Eichmann first visited Auschwitz. It was an unplastered brick building with a tile roof (which explains its nickname, the "little red house"). It measured 15 m long and 6.3 m wide.[27] As part of the remodeling, its windows were bricked up. Only small openings remained, which could be closed with flaps sealed at the edges with felt. The number of inner rooms was reduced from four to two. Each had only one door with a sign "Zur Desinfektion" (To Disinfection). The doors were made of wooden beams and sealed at the edges with felt. There were no peepholes. The doors could be shut by tightening two bolts that doubled as door handles. The interior walls of the two rooms were painted white, and the floors were strewn with sawdust. The building was surrounded by fruit trees. Nearby stood a barn and two barracks that were constructed during the conversion work.[28]

Bunker 2 was brought into operation several months later. It was housed in a brick building that was thatched and plastered (and therefore nicknamed by the prisoners the "little white house"). It was bigger than the first building, measuring 17.07 m by 8.34 m.[29] Like the first building, its windows were bricked up, with only small openings covered with wooden flaps. It had four rooms of different sizes, each with its own entrance and exit. The doors were the same as the doors in bunker 1. As part of the conversion work the wooden ceiling was replaced with concrete.

The new gas chambers were the sites of systematic and unceasing murder of Jews who were brought in mass transports from various German-occupied European countries. On the loading ramp, in the process called "selections," some of the men and women were picked for work in the camp. But the majority of the prisoners, including all the elderly, the children, and many women, were consigned for immediate extermination.

According to Shlomo Dragon, who serviced the bunker from December 1942 to the spring of 1943, signs were posted on the gas chamber doors. On the outside of the entrance, which was visible when the door was closed, a sign read "Hochspannung—Lebensgefahr" (High Tension—Lethal Danger). It served as a precaution against accidentally opening the chamber filled with dead bodies and gas. On the interior side, which was visible when the door was open (the side the victims saw as they entered) was the sign "Zum Baden" (To the Baths). On the exit door, behind which lay the rail tracks and pits for burning dead bodies, was affixed the sign "Zur Desinfektion."[30]

Bunkers 1 and 2 were surrounded on all sides by woods. Three barracks that served as dressing rooms were nearby. Mass graves, screened from view by hedges, were located several dozen to several hundred meters from both gas chambers. They were later replaced by incinerating pits. Small trolleys or flat-bed trucks that rolled on narrow-gauge tracks transported the corpses from the gas chambers to the pits.[31]

Train transports that carried the victims were unloaded at the ramp of the freight railway station situated 2.5 km from the bunkers. When transports arrived at night, the victims were hauled in trucks to the killing site. During the day, trucks were only used to transport victims who were unable to walk the distance on their own. The able-bodied were marched past the barracks of the Birkenau camp then under construction and across the meadows, where building sector 3 was later erected. The SS men who escorted the victims sometimes engaged them in innocent conversation aimed at putting the victims off guard. The marching column was accompanied by a car with the emblem of the Red Cross. The car carried the poison gas under SS guard. It also carried an SS doctor with medicines and an oxygen bottle for use in an emergency, such as the accidental poisoning of SS men taking part in the gassing.

Upon arrival, the victims were told that before taking up residence in the camp they had to go to the bath and undergo delousing. They were also told to remember the spot where they left their effects. They were told to undress, either in the barracks or outside behind hedges. From there, under a rain of blows and attack dogs, they were chased into the gas chamber. Those who could not be accommodated were shot, or in instances where there were a large number of people, they were held naked in the barracks until the gas chamber was emptied.

Once the chamber was full (according to Höss, bunker 1 could hold 800 people[32] and bunker 2 about 1,200[33]), the gas-proof doors were screwed shut and the trained SS disinfectors wearing gas masks discharged the contents of Zyklon B cans into each bunker room through vents in the side walls. All the victims were dead within several minutes.

One of the SS doctors who oversaw the gassing procedure, Johann

Kremer, testified after the war that after the gas had been poured in, "Shouting and screaming of the victims could be heard through that opening and it was clear that they fought for their lives (*Lebenskampf*). These shouts lasted a short while. I should think it was several minutes, though I cannot give a precise estimate."[34] In addition to extending emergency medical assistance to the disinfectors, the SS doctors were there to ascertain that the victims were dead.

The gas chamber was opened a half hour after the gas was administered to ensure there were no survivors. When the pace of incoming transports slowed, the bodies of victims who were gassed at night or late in the evening remained in the bunkers under SS guard until morning. Only then were the doors opened, the premises aired, and the Sonderkommando prisoners brought in to remove the bodies.

The Sonderkommando prisoners worked in several teams. Those servicing the gas chamber wore gas masks. Their task was to remove the bodies to the yard, where gold teeth were extracted, jewelry recovered, and women's hair cut. Another team loaded the corpses onto the narrow-gauge trolleys and transported them to deep pits, where they were placed in layers and covered with chlorinated lime and soil. Since the entire area was floodlit, the work could be carried out day and night. Each time the bunkers were emptied, Sonderkommando prisoners whitewashed the walls and washed the floors.[35]

During Himmler's second inspection visit to Auschwitz on July 17, 1942, he witnessed the entire procedure of liquidation of one transport—from unloading the train cars to gassing (in bunker 2) and removing the bodies.[36] It cannot be ruled out that his observations resulted in the decision to cremate the bodies instead of burying them. In fact, shortly after Himmler's visit, Standartenführer Paul Blobel of Eichmann's office arrived at Auschwitz with orders to exhume all the buried bodies, burn them, and scatter the ashes to prevent the possible reconstruction of the number of victims.

Consequently, as early as September 1942, unearthing of the mass graves at Birkenau commenced. The bodies that had been buried because the main Auschwitz crematorium could not accommodate them at the time were cremated. The fires were stoked with oil refuse and methanol. At the same time, the bodies of the more recently gassed victims were also being incinerated. First they were burned on timber pyres with 2,000 bodies each. Later they were burned in pits along with the bodies that had been buried there earlier. Alternate layers of bodies and timber were placed in a pit 30 m long, 7 m wide, and 3 m deep. The four corners were doused with flammable liquid. One of the SS men would then throw a burning comb or a rag soaked in oil on the pyre to set it on fire. Body fat that drained off in special cavities was used to stoke the fire. By late November 1942, all the mass graves, containing over 100,000 corpses, had been emptied.[37]

In the spring of 1943, with the launching of new gas chambers and crematoria, the two bunkers were shut down. Shortly thereafter, bunker 1 and the nearby barracks were dismantled. The incineration pits were filled in with earth and leveled. The same work was performed on the pits and barracks of bunker 2, but the bunker itself was left intact. It was brought into operation again in May 1944 during the extermination of Hungarian Jews.[38] At that time several incineration pits were reexcavated and new barracks for undressing were constructed.

The bunker was operative until the fall of 1944. It was dismantled when the gassing was discontinued that November. The ashes from the incineration pits were removed, and the entire terrain was leveled.[39]

Crematoria II, III, IV, and V—Construction and Operation

Himmler inspected Auschwitz on March 1, 1941, and ordered that a POW camp be built. Acting on his orders, Department II of the Main Budget and Construction Office drew up a preliminary plan[40] for the construction of a camp nearby at Birkenau for 125,000 prisoners.[41]

Among other projects, the plan provided for the construction of a crematorium capable of incinerating 1,440 bodies in 24 hours. It was projected to consist of five three-retort ovens for burning bodies, one oven for burning refuse, and one underground mortuary.[42] The site was to be in the main camp at Auschwitz.

In consideration of the ongoing preparations for the extermination of Jews, it was decided to adapt the installation for mass killing by constructing a gas chamber next to it, in an underground facility also designated as a mortuary. The second room was to serve as a "dressing room."[43] Both were to be ventilated mechanically.

An order placed with the firm Topf and Sons of Erfurt on October 22, 1941, stressed the urgency of the entire undertaking, demanding fast delivery: two weeks for technical drawings of the foundations and three months for parts of the ovens (fireclay elements, metal castings, pipes, ventilators).[44] However, before the construction work began, Heinz Kammler, chief of group C of the SS Economic-Administrative Main Office and one of the closest associates of Himmler, arrived at Auschwitz on February 27, 1942, and ordered that the five-oven crematorium projected for Auschwitz be constructed at Birkenau.[45]

The oldest preserved technical drawings of the crematorium that was built at Birkenau are dated January 15, 1942. They were made by SS-Unterscharführer Ulmer of Zentralbauleitung (the Central Construction Administration), checked by SS-Untersturmführer Walter Dejaco of the same office, and approved by the office head, SS-Sturmbannführer Karl Bischoff (drawing nos. 936, 937, 938).[46] More detailed drawings and plans followed in short order.

With the completion of the first stage of planning on July 1, 1942, the Zentralbauleitung offered two construction firms, Huta Hoch- und Tiefbau AG and Schlesische Industriehaus Lenz und CO AG in Kattowitz, which had been cooperating with the camp for some time, to undertake the construction of the crematorium building (number II).[47] Ovens and other equipment were to be installed by Topf and Sons. On July 13, 1942, Huta responded to the proposal by submitting its offer along with a cost estimate totaling 133,756.65 marks.[48] Lenz, however, replied that owing to manpower shortages it could not undertake the project. Under these conditions, the Zentralbauleitung instructed Huta to undertake the construction of the crematorium forthwith in line with the submitted offer.[49]

Shortly thereafter, orders were placed with Huta for the construction of three more crematoria, designated on technical plans by the numbers III, IV, and V. Again the ovens and other equipment were to be installed by Topf and Sons. In September 1942, the Zentralbauleitung placed an order with the same firm for five ovens and three installations of mechanical draft for crematorium III, and in October for ventilation for the "dressing room" and the gas chamber. In both cases Topf and Sons confirmed receipt of the orders, thanked the SS authorities for commissioning them to do the work, and expressed satisfaction at the degree of cooperation hitherto.[50]

In addition to plans and technical drawings, Topf and Sons supplied many items to Birkenau: fireclay and metal parts for 12 crematoria ovens (ten three-retorts and two eight-retorts), two ovens for refuse burning, engines, ventilators for chimney drafts, engines and ventilators for gas chambers and "dressing rooms," two electrical elevators for removing corpses from the gas chamber to the oven room, and a number of stretchers for sliding bodies into the retorts.[51] The letter from the Zentralbauleitung, dated February 26, 1943, indicates that the firm also was to supply ten gas testers (*Gasprüfer*) for crematorium II. No specific information about this equipment is available.

Despite the hectic pace of work, which went on day and night, the approved deadlines for launching the crematoria failed to be met.[52] The camp administration did not take delivery of the crematoria and gas chambers until the spring and summer of 1943: crematorium IV on March 22, crematorium II on March 31, crematorium V on April 4, and crematorium III on June 25 (or 26).[53]

A letter from the Zentralbauleitung to group C of June 28, 1943,[54] indicates that the capacity for a 24-hour period was estimated at 340 bodies for crematorium I; 1,440 each for crematoria II and III; and 768 each for crematoria IV and V. Thus the five crematoria could incinerate 4,765 bodies each day. This estimate coincided with the guidelines established in 1941 concerning the capacity of a five-retort crematorium for prisoners of war, according to which two bodies could be incinerated in one retort within 30 minutes. The next month, however, crematorium I was shut down, reducing the capacity to 4,415.

In their efforts to increase the burning capacity of the ovens, the camp authorities recommended that the incineration time be reduced to 20 minutes and the number of bodies be increased to three, depending on the size of the body.[55] As a result, the capacity of the crematoria almost doubled, reaching about 8,000 bodies in 24 hours, according to the statement of a Sonderkommando prisoner, Feinsilber.

Situated behind the fences surrounding the Birkenau barracks, the crematoria constituted a separate complex of installations of mass extermination. Crematoria II and III had their own barbed-wire fences. Two gates led to the crematorium II compound and one gate to crematorium III. Trees and bushes planted all around functioned as a natural screen, or "greenbelt" (*Grüngürtel*), that hid them from view by unauthorized persons—above all the prisoners who lived in adjoining barracks. A common fence enclosed crematoria IV and V. The latter was also screened from view by a tall hedge concealing the bodies that were burned outside.[56]

Crematoria II and III were constructed according to nearly identical, symmetrically printed plans. They consisted of three principal parts, two of which were underground—the "dressing room," with an area of 392.45 sq m (49.49 x 7.93), and the gas chamber, 210 sq m (30 x 7). The "dressing room" was 2.3 m high, the gas chamber, 2.4 m high.[57] The third part, the furnace room, was 337.2 sq m (30 x 11.24) and was on the ground floor.

The two underground rooms, designated on camp charts as mortuaries (*Leichenkeller*), were windowless and had to be lit artificially. The ceiling, which was made of reinforced concrete and covered with grass turf, was supported by concrete posts arrayed in a straight line and linked by a bearing beam. According to the original plan, the "undressing room" was to be nearly twice as large as the gas chamber to enable the victims to undress in relatively uncramped conditions. Both the gas chamber and the "dressing room" were mechanically ventilated. The power was supplied by generators in the attic of the crematorium. The outlet of the ventilation shafts was situated above the roof of the crematorium.[58]

Wooden benches were placed along the walls of the "dressing room." Above them were numbered wooden clothes hooks. A narrow passage, about 5 m long, connected the "dressing room" with the gas chamber. The passage ended with a spacious anteroom with an entrance to the gas chamber. The entrance door, 1.92 m high and 1 m wide, was made of two layers of planks with a proofing sheet between them. The edges of the door and the door frame were padded with felt. A circular peephole, made of two glass plates 8 mm thick and air-proofed with rubber gaskets, was mounted in the door at eye level. After several incidents in which the victims trapped inside broke the glass, the peephole was covered with a semicircular grille on the gas-chamber side. Later the hole was covered with a sheet of iron. The doors were shut by means of iron bolts, which also served as door handles, and secured with screws. The inside walls of the gas chamber were plastered and whitewashed. Electrical installations and lamps were located on both sides of the bearing beam, and perforated plates mounted on wooden blocks were installed beneath the ceiling in imitation of showers. Ventilation shafts were situated where the walls met the ceiling and the floor. The vent of the upper (intake) shaft was covered with perforated sheet iron, whereas the vent of the lower (extraction) shaft was covered with a metal grille.[59]

Zyklon B was distributed in the gas chamber through four introduction columns custom-made in the metalwork shops of the camp. They were shaped like pillars and made of two wire grids with a movable core. Cross sections of the pillars, 3 m high, formed a square, each side measuring 70 cm. Fastened to the floor, they passed through openings in the ceiling, ending outside as little chimneys closed with a concrete cover equipped with two handles. The external grid (made of wire 3 mm thick) formed interstices measuring 45 mm x 45 mm, and was fastened to cube-shaped metal scantlings (cross section 50 mm x 10 mm). Interstices of the external grid—150 mm apart from the internal grid and similarly fastened—were smaller (25 mm x 25 mm). The two grids served as a screen for the movable core that could be introduced through the opening in the ceiling. The core consisted of a tin prism measuring 150 mm x 150 mm at the cross section. The bottom of the core was flat, and the top was a cone. A wire mesh with interstices of one sq mm extended from the base of the core to the base of the cone, and was fastened to a post 25 mm away. The entire length of the core was covered with tin. When Zyklon B pellets fell onto the cone, they spread uniformly throughout the core and stopped in its lower part. After the gas evaporated, the entire core was removed from the gas chamber and the used pellets of diatomite were poured out.[60]

Photographs taken by Allied aircraft in 1944 indicate that the gas introduction columns of crematorium II were arrayed in a straight line, roughly along the longitudinal axis of the gas chamber, whereas in crematorium III they were spaced in pairs on both sides of the axis. This placement was meant to ensure rapid and uniform spread of the poison inside the chamber.

At the end of 1943, each of the gas chambers in both crematoria was divided by a wall, and the passage linking them was closed by a door identical to the entrance door. After that time, smaller transports were led into the back room.[61]

The underground part of the building contained two other rooms in addition to the undressing room and the gas chamber. One was used to store hair, spectacles, and other effects of the murdered victims. The second served as a convenient storage room for Zyklon B pellets. The shaft of the elevator that was used to transport corpses to the furnace room was equipped with doors and adjoined the anteroom. Initially the elevator consisted of a provisional platform (*Platoaufzug*) that measured 2.76 m in length and 1.43 m in width.

Crematorium II had a second entrance to the anteroom, situated in the angle formed by the undressing room and the gas chamber. In addition to the stairway it housed a special concrete chute (*Rutsche*) through which corpses brought for cremation from the camp were lowered straight down to the elevator shaft.[62]

The furnace room occupied the largest interior space on the ground floor of the crematorium. It housed five furnaces, each with three retorts (about 2 m long, 80 cm wide, and 1 m high) that were used to push the bodies into the furnace. There were two generators of coke gas on the opposite side. The fumes were funneled to a single chimney through flues under the floor. Initially the furnaces of crematorium II were equipped with a forced-draft installation. The draft was produced by three intake ventilators situated between the furnaces and the chimney. Within a short time, however, they burned out. Similar ventilators were not installed in the remaining crematoria.[63]

To the left of the entrance to crematorium II was a room described in the plans as a dissecting room (*Sezierraum*). It was in this room that prisoner-physician Miklos Nyiszli conducted dissections of bodies of twins for SS Dr. Josef Mengele. According to Dr. Nyiszli, a similar room in crematorium III housed a melting pot to melt gold teeth.[64]

In addition, crematoria II and III were equipped with special furnaces for incinerating less-valuable articles, such as personal papers, women's purses, books, and toys, that were found in the luggage of the murdered victims. Incriminating camp documents were also incinerated there, particularly in the last stage of the camp's existence. The furnaces, designated as "garbage incinerators" (*Müllverbrennungsofen*) in the technical plans, were housed in an outbuilding that adjoined the crematorium chimney. The disinfected hair of gassed women was dried in the attic. And in the summer of 1944, Sonderkommando prisoners who serviced the crematoria resided in the attics of crematoria II and III.[65]

Crematoria IV and V were similar to the other two in that they consisted of three basic components: dressing room, gas chamber, and furnace room. But the components were arranged differently. To cut costs, both the gas chamber and the dressing room were on the ground floor instead of underground.[66] The entire structure measured 67.5 m in length and 12.87 m in width (not counting an outbuilding that served as the coke storage room). Near the crematorium entrance were lodgings of Sonderkommando prisoners and a kitchen. To the left of these structures sat three gas chambers: one with an area of 98.19 sq m (11.69 x 8.40); the second 95.34 sq m (12.35 x 7.72), and the third 43.25 sq m (11.69 x 3.70). The combined area of the three gas chambers was 236.78 sq m.[67] Sometime later, the smaller chamber was further divided into two, and gas-proof doors, nearly identical to those in the gas bunkers, were constructed.

In addition to the interior doors, the two largest gas chambers had doors that led directly outside. The doors were used to air the premises and to remove the corpses for cremation in incineration pits. Instead of windows, the exterior walls of the gas chambers had openings 30 cm wide and 40 cm high, which were covered with gas-proof flaps. The preserved original plans indicate that the first chamber had three such openings, the second two, and the remaining smallest chambers one each. Plans provided for the construction of a waste-disposal system in the two largest chambers, as well as heating furnaces to facilitate quicker evaporation of the Zyklon B gas pellets. Although signs reading "Zum Desinfektion" were posted in the chambers, neither automatic ventilators nor dummy showers were installed. The part of the crematorium building that housed the gas chamber was lower and looked like an outbuilding.[68]

A spacious dressing room, covering 245.02 sq m (19.84 x 12.35), lay to the right of the crematorium entrance. Initially, no windows were planned, but preserved photographs taken during the construction phase indicate that ultimately small openings, similar to those in the gas chamber walls, were made in the exterior walls. It cannot be ruled out that this modification was made with a view to the possibility of using the dressing room as a gas chamber in the event that there was an accumulation of transports. Behind the dressing room was an anteroom with a crematorium chimney and further down another room that housed one eight-retort furnace with four coke hearths. Fumes were evacuated through two chimneys by natural draft. Adjoining this room was the office of the crematoria chief, the sanitation office, and the coking plant.[69]

The extermination process and cremation of the corpses in crematoria II and III went as follows. After selection for death, the Jews who could walk were marched from the loading ramp to the crematorium. The weak, the invalid, and the sick were transported on trucks. In the crematorium yard, the SS men told the prisoners that they would undergo a disinfection that consisted of delousing and bathing. The victims were led down the staircase to the dressing room in the basement, where they could see the signs (in German) "To the Baths" and "To Disinfection." Similar signs were posted on a portable board in the native language of the victims.

On the way to the gas chamber some victims were issued a piece of soap and a towel. As a rule, the women and children went in first, followed by the men. Each group was led inside the chamber behind a cordon of SS men that edged toward the door as the chamber filled. With the refractory ones spurred on by blows and dogs, about 2,000 persons on average were crammed inside.

When the chamber was full or the entire transport was inside and the personnel had left (two SS noncommissioned officers always stayed until the end), the doors were shut, the bolts were slid into place, and the screws were tightened. On order of the supervising SS doctor (the job was assigned to, among others, Josef Mengele, Hans König, and Hans Thilo), the SS disinfectors (Scheinmetz, among others) opened the Zyklon B cans and poured their contents into the vents down the induction shafts inside the chamber.

Within several minutes, 20 at most, all the victims were dead. The time required for the gas to take effect depended on various factors that affected the evaporation of the gas: temperature, humidity, the congestion inside the chamber. Whenever the outside air temperature was higher than the inside temperature, the cool air was extracted by ventilators from the chamber before the gas pellets were poured inside. To speed up the evaporation of the poison gas in winter, iron baskets filled with red-hot coke were brought inside. Some unsuccessful attempts were made to heat the chamber interior with heat from the chimney flues.

Höss, who personally observed the killing in the gas chambers, described the process:

> It could be observed through the peephole in the door that those who were standing nearest to the induction vents were killed at once. It can be said that about one-third died straightaway. The remainder staggered about and began to scream and struggle for air. The screaming, however, soon changed to the death rattle and in a few minutes all lay still.[70]

About a half hour after the induction of the gas, the ventilation was turned on, the door was opened, and Sonderkommando prisoners wearing gas masks began dragging the corpses out of the chamber. In cases of great congestion, many of the dead were found half-squatting, their skin colored pink with occasional red or green spots. Some foamed at the mouth, others bled from the ears.

In the gas chamber's anteroom, the bodies were relieved of spectacles and artificial limbs, and the women's hair was cut off. Thereupon the corpses were loaded on the elevator platform and lifted to the ground floor. Some of the corpses were dragged directly to the oven area. Others were moved to the corpse storage room opposite the elevator, which also served as a site of executions by shooting. Just before incineration, Sonderkommando prisoners removed jewelry, which they tossed into a special numbered crate.

Teeth with metal fillings, crowns, and bridges made of gold or other precious metals were extracted from the mouths of the gassed victims and deposited in a crate marked "Zahnstation" (dental station). Sonderkommando prisoners who were dentists by occupation performed this task under SS supervision. The only ones whose mouths were not inspected were children. If in the course of the sporadic inspections it was established that not all gold teeth had been extracted, occasionally the Sonderkommando prisoner guilty of neglect was punished by being thrown alive into the furnace.

It took about four hours to empty the gas chamber. Initially the corpses were delivered to the furnaces on small trolleys that ran on rails, as was done in the main camp. The trolleys also served to load the corpses into the furnace retorts. This arrangement, however, did not last long. On the initiative of the *Kapo* August Bruck, special corpse stretchers, which could be rolled into the retorts, were introduced. To facilitate the loading, the corpse stretchers were lubricated with soapy water. Methods of loading the corpses varied; each team servicing the furnaces had its own technique. For example, H. Tauber's team would put two corpses into one retort two times, then add as many children's corpses as possible to the second load.

It took about 20 minutes to cremate three corpses in one retort. However, in their efforts to reduce the number of loadings, prisoners cremated four to five corpses at one time and extended the cremation time to about 25 to 30 minutes. When the time was up, the next load would be put into the retort, regardless of the degree of incineration of the preceding load. The incompletely incinerated bones fell through the grille into the ash pit, were ground with wooden mortars along with the ashes, then poured into pits near the crematorium. Next they were removed from the pits and poured into the Vistula River or nearby ponds. Sometimes they were used to prepare compost; other times they were used directly to fertilize the fields of the camp farms.

About 2,500 corpses could be cremated in 24 hours in each of crematoria II and III. This rate exceeded the crematoria capacity as calculated by Topf and Sons (1,440) by 43 percent. (Topf assumed that two corpses could be cremated in a half hour.) The excessive overloading caused breakdowns of the furnaces, ventilators, and chimneys.[71]

In the killing process at crematoria IV and V, the prisoners were also brought in cars or were marched to the crematoria, then led to the dressing room. There one of the SS men—the Kommandoführer—would stand on a bench in front of them and explain that the healthy would go to work and the sick and the women and children would remain in the barracks. But first, they would go to the bath.

After undressing, the prisoners were led through the anteroom to the gas chamber. When the chamber was full, the SS guards shut the doors, and one of them, wearing a gas mask, climbed a ladder or a chair. When the SS doctor on duty gave a sign, the SS man would pour Zyklon B pellets into the opening. In the summer of 1944, Mengele served most often as the duty doctor in crematoria IV and V, and Kommandoführer Scheinmetz, who supervised the Sonderkommando work in crematorium V, poured the pellets.

Half an hour later, on orders of the same SS doctor, the gas chamber doors were opened, and the Sonderkommando prisoners, who had been locked up in the coke plant during the gassing, went to work. Wearing gas masks, they dragged the corpses to the hallway, where the women's hair was cut. Next the corpses were transported to the dressing room and stacked in layers. The gas chambers had to be emptied as quickly as possible to make room for the next transport. When it was not possible to remove all the corpses from the dressing room before the next transport arrived, the doomed prisoners undressed outside, behind the hedge that screened crematorium V and the incineration pits from the road.

Yehuda Backon, a survivor who later became a painter in Jerusalem, arrived at Birkenau from the Theresienstadt ghetto when he was 14 years old, in 1943. He came into contact with Sonderkommando prisoners while he was at Birkenau and later testified in the Eichmann trial.

Presiding judge: Describe the drawing [made close to the time of liberation, and accepted as an exhibit by the court].

Answer: Here is crematorium number 2, the modern one. Numbers 1 and 2 were identical. Numbers 3 and 4 were somewhat less modern. Lodgings of the Sonderkommando men, forced to live there, were at the top.

Presiding judge: Inside the building?

A: In the fall of 1944 they had to live inside the crematorium, here on top, while some were put up in the gas chambers of crematoria nos. 3 and 4.

Presiding judge: In the attic?

A: In crematoria 1 and 2, and in crematoria 3 and 4, they lived right inside the gas chambers.

Presiding judge: It had windows, as shown in your drawing?

A: These were "corridors" of the prisoners. Windows were in the lower part, this was the place where the corpses were burned, and the place where they undressed. In crematoria 1 and 2, the gas chambers were underground. People descended several stairs, then had to undress. I recall that Sonderkommando men related, they wanted to tell everything, and I told them that perhaps I would be able to tell the story. So they told me everything in detail. When a transport arrived, they had to climb down. Outside were signs "Baths" and "Sauna." Then they were brought to *Entkleidungskammer* [dressing room]. To the side there were benches and clothes hooks with numbers. Sometimes men and women entered separately, and on other occasions, when time was short, they entered together. They had to undress and the SS man told them: "Remember your clothes hook number, put the clothes in one pile so that you'll get them back on the other side." People asked for water, as they were very thirsty after a long journey in sealed train cars. They were told: "Well, hurry up, coffee is waiting for you in the camp, and it's getting cold," and other such reassuring remarks, to calm them. Naked, they had to move on, on the left-hand side, to the gas chambers. In crematoria 1 and 2 there were two rooms of the gas chambers next to the Entkleidungskammer. In addition, there was another structure called *Rutschbahn* [chute] for people with artificial limbs who could not walk on their own, with a slide which brought them straight to the dressing rooms close to the gas chambers. In crematoria 1 and 2 there was a very long room divided into two, because sometimes there were not enough people, and to save the gas, they were brought only inside one part of the room.[72]

The corpses stacked up in the dressing room were removed to a narrow room, where Sonderkommando prisoners extracted dentures, crowns, bridges, etc., made of gold and precious metals; removed jewelry that had not been taken during the undressing; and brought the corpses to the cremation furnaces.

Servicing the furnaces and the cremation process in crematoria IV and V did not differ significantly from the practices followed in the two other crematoria. According to the Zentralbauleitung letter, given the normal pace of cremation (half an hour for two corpses in one retort), each crematorium could incinerate 768 corpses in 24 hours. However, Sonderkommando prisoners testified that up to 1,500 corpses were burned in 24 hours (three to five within 20 to 30 minutes).

Furnace overload caused frequent breakdowns. For example, in the initial stages of the extermination of Hungarian Jews, crematorium V had to be shut down due to a breakdown of the chimneys. As a result, some bodies were incinerated in crematorium IV. The remainder were burned at the rate of about 5,000 corpses in 24 hours in the incineration pits near the crematoria. The same number were incinerated in the pits of bunker 2, which was reactivated in the spring of 1944.

Thus in the summer of 1944, the combined capacity of all the incineration installations reached the staggering number of 20,000 victims. A few months later, in light of Germany's deteriorating situation on the war fronts, and possibly in connection with negotiations launched on Himmler's instructions, gassing of prisoners was discontinued. The last victims to undergo selection was a transport from Theresienstadt, which arrived at Auschwitz on October 30, 1944. The next transport, from Sered, which arrived on November 3, 1944, was registered in the camp in its entirety.[73]

Three weeks later, on November 25, 1944, Himmler ordered the demolition of the Auschwitz gas chambers and crematoria. The same day, work began on dismantling the installations of crematorium II at Birkenau. After the furnace, the chimneys, the roof, and all the installations in the walls of the crematorium building were taken apart, openings were made for dynamite charges to blow up the entire structure. In connection with the halt in the influx of mass transports, a quarantine camp for male prisoners (BIIa) was liquidated on November 3.[74]

Among others, 70 Sonderkommando prisoners worked to liquidate the installations of mass murder. In addition, two special women's labor squads were formed. On December 1, 1944, a special group, initially comprising 100 women prisoners, began dismantling crematorium III. On December 5, 50 more women were incorporated into the squad. At the same time, another squad of 50 women was formed. Its task was to remove the ashes from the incineration pits, fill them in, and cover them with turf.[75]

About the same time, work was completed on dismantling the remains of crematorium IV, which had been burned during a Sonderkommando revolt, and on bunker 2 and the nearby barracks that had served as dressing rooms.[76]

On January 20, 1945, an SS detachment that had been dispatched to Auschwitz shot about 200 Jewish women prisoners and ordered another group of prisoners to move crates with dynamite to crematoria II and III. Both buildings were blown up the same day. Crematorium V, the last to remain in operation, as late as January, was blown up on January 26, 1945, one day before the liberation of the camp.

There was no time to remove the ruins of the destroyed installations, so the Nazis were only partially successful in obliterating the traces of their crimes. The walls and floors and the underground dressing rooms and gas chambers of crematoria II and III remained relatively intact. The rails built into the floor of the furnace room are clearly visible, and parts of the walls also have been preserved. Some of the furnace parts of crematorium V have been preserved. The furnaces of the other crematoria were dismantled and removed before the buildings were blown up. Assorted metal furnace parts were found on the grounds of the camp farmsteads (bunkers 1 and 2).

Crematorium VI

In late 1942 and early 1943, the colossal scale of the mass exterminations which the Nazis were carrying out led them to doubt whether the crematoria then under construction could handle the ever-increasing number of bodies. The advisability of constructing a new crematorium with much greater capacity, designated as crematorium VI, was discussed.

Information on this issue remains scanty, since only two documents have been preserved. A letter dated February 12, 1943, from Bischoff, head of the Zentralbauleitung, to commandant Höss[77] indicates that Bischoff discussed the matter with engineer Kurt Prüfer, a representative of Topf and Sons, during the latter's visit to Auschwitz on January 29, 1943.[78] As a result of the meeting, the Zentralbauleitung instructed the firm to produce a preliminary technical sketch of the proposed crematorium. The plan was delivered to the Zentralbauleitung in the first half of February 1943. At the same time, Topf informed the Zentralbauleitung in a letter of February 5[79] that the preliminary cost estimate would soon be ready. The firm also asked for a formal invoice, should the preliminary offer be accepted.

The speed with which Topf and Sons reacted to the initiatives of the Zentralbauleitung indicates that the project was by no means news to the firm. In fact, it cannot be ruled out that the firm was the prime mover behind the initiative. At any rate, the firm eagerly offered its services to the SS.

In Bischoff's letter, he asked Höss to help group D of the Economic-Administrative Main Office submit a work order to group C in the event the project was approved. He also pointed out that in order to begin construction of crematorium VI, the firm would need an additional labor force of 150 prisoner bricklayers and 200 prisoners for auxiliary jobs. Neither Höss's reply to the query nor the sketch that Bischoff sent has been preserved. On the basis of the contents of the two letters, one gets only an impression of how the projected crematorium was to be constructed and how it would function. In any event, crematorium VI was never built.

Three designations were used to describe the crematorium in the letters: open incineration site (*offene Verbrennungstatte*), open incineration chamber (*offene Verbrennungskammer*), and large ring cremation furnace (*grosser Ringeinäscherungsofen*) measuring 48.77 m by 3.76 m. The Polish investigating magistrate, Jan Sehn, concluded that the crematorium was to be based on the principle of cremating corpses in pits by combining their large capacity with the economy of incineration in crematoria.[80]

The project was brought up again in 1944 in connection with Eichmann's forecasts of new transports due to arrive in late 1944 and early 1945. According to Höss's testimony, work on the construction of large crematoria was about to begin. He described them as projected to be built "in the shape of a huge brickworks with a ring furnace." The installation was to be built underground. But due to lack of time, not even technical documentation was drawn up.[81]

More than one million persons were murdered in the gas chambers of Auschwitz-Birkenau. Murder on such a large scale could not have been accomplished without the installations described in this essay. Preserved camp records and witness accounts, some of which were used in this study, allow one to reconstruct with relative precision the technical aspects of the process of mass murder.[82]

NOTES

1. Rudolf Höss, *Commandant of Auschwitz* (London, 1961), p. 206.
2. According to Raul Hilberg, Himmler took the decision to use gas chambers in the east and in the killing centers on the advice of the chief physician of the SS, Dr. Grawitz; see Hilberg, *The Destruction of the European Jews* (Chicago, 1961), p. 562.
3. Höss, p. 206.
4. *Ibid.*, p. 207.
5. These automobiles were sealed vans into which exhaust fumes were piped. This particular killing method was invented by Oberdienstleiter Victor Brack of the main party Chancellery of Adolf Hitler. In September 1941, the Einsatzkommando, headed by Standartenführer Paul Blobel, used such vans in the Ukraine. From December 1941 on, similar mobile gas chambers operated in the death camp at Chelmno on Ner and in Semlina, Serbia. See Hilberg, p. 561; Gerald Reitlinger, The Final Solution (London, 1971), pp. 145–46; Artur Eisenbach, *The Nazis Policy of Extermination of Jews* (in Polish) (Warsaw, 1961), p. 274.
6. Danuta Czech, *Kalendarium der Ereignisse im Konzentrationslager Auschwitz-Birkenau 1939–1945* (Reinbek bei Hamburg, 1989), pp. 116–19. Among testimonies touching on this issue that were given during the trial of Höss and members of the Auschwitz personnel, particularly noteworthy are testimonies of former prisoners who on orders of the SS took part in various activities in connection with preparing rooms in block 11, selection of the sick, and removal of corpses (Marian Dybus, Wladyslaw Fejkiel, Wladyslaw Tondos, Bogdan Glinski, Marian Przeda): Archives of the Auschwitz-Birkenau State Museum (ASAM), collection Trial of Höss, vol. 4, card 156, vol. 27, card 107, vol. 4, card 176, vol. 27, cards 72–73; collection Trial of Auschwitz personnel, vol. 54, cards 211, 134. See also collection Statements, vol. 32, cards 81–86, vol. 67, card 57, accounts by Konrad Szweda and Adam Szczerbowski. See also a study by Stanislaw Klodzinski, "The First Gassing of Prisoners and POWs in the Auschwitz Camp" (in Polish), in *Przeglad Lekarski-Oswiecim* (1972), p. 80, where the author discusses and summarizes findings of a questionnaire dealing with this event, administered by him to several hundred subjects.
7. "The Auschwitz Concentration Camp in Light of the Documents of Delegatura (Representation) of the Republic of Poland in the Country" (in Polish), *Ze-*

szyty Oswiecimskie, special issue no. 1 (1968), pp. 13–14. Other references are on pp. 11 and 14. See also materials of the camp underground, ASAM, collection Underground materials, vol. 5b, card 363.

8. Höss, p. 209.

9. ASAM, Trial of Höss, vol. 11, card 23.

10. The date has been established by this author on the basis of an entry in the personal file of prisoner Waclaw Lipka. The entry says that from September 1940 on, the latter worked as a stoker in the crematorium.

11. Jean-Claude Pressac, *Auschwitz: Technique and Operation of the Gas Chambers* (New York, 1989), pp. 151, 159. See also chap. 7 in this volume.

12. ASAM, collection Bauleitung, BW 30/42/card 2, letter from the Zentralbauleitung to Kammler, June 28, 1943. The Polish Commission for the Investigation of Nazi Crimes determined that the capacity of crematorium I was 350 corpses in 14 hours; ASAM, PH, vol. 11, card 24.

13. *Amidst a Nightmare of Crime: Notes of Prisoners of Sonderkommando Found at Auschwitz* (Oswiecim, 1973), p. 47; testimony of Jankowski-Feinsilber, ASAM, Mauthausen files, entries in employment files of prisoners Jozef Ilczuk and Waclaw Lipka.

14. Jan Sehn, *Concentration Camp Oswiecim-Brzesinka* (Warsaw, 1957), p. 152. Plan no. 4287, "Ausbau des Alten Krematorium: Luftschutzbunker für SS-Revier mit einem Operationsraum," dated September 21, 1944, ASAM, collection Bauleitung; Pressac, p. 156.

15. According to D. Czech, this occurred as early as September 1941; see *KL Auschwitz, as Seen by the SS: Höss, Broad, Kremer* (Oswiecim, 1978), p. 45, n. 45. According to former prisoner Badenitz, gassing in crematorium I commenced in September 1941; ASAM, Trial of Höss, vol. 16, card 89. According to former SS man Stark, the chamber was brought into operation in the fall of 1941.

16. The openings were made by prisoner Sulkowski; ASAM, collection Statements, vol. 74, card 74. When crematorium I was converted into an air-raid shelter, the openings were bricked up. The surviving fragments allowed the reconstruction of four openings after the war. Broad and Müller claimed that there were six such openings. See ibid., vol. 96, card 60, account by former prisoner Adam Zlobnicki; Filip Müller, *Eyewitness Auschwitz: Three Years in the Gas Chambers* (New York, 1979), p. 38; KL Auschwitz, p. 157 (Broad).

17. Prisoner Michal Kula was employed in installing the ventilator; ASAM, Trial of Höss, vol. 25, cards 17–18.

18. Former prisoner Koczorowski, who had access to the plans of crematorium I, testified that the gas chamber was designated as a mortuary (*Leichenhalle*) for 600 persons; ibid., vol. 4, card 32. According to Filip Müller, over 700 persons could be accommodated inside. Höss spoke about 900 Soviet POWs crammed inside, whereas former prisoner Halgas stated that groups of 1,000 people were gassed there; see Müller, p. 44; Höss, p. 164.

19. Höss, p. 164.

20. Former prisoner Kula witnessed the chasing of 300 prisoners to the crematorium; ASAM, Trial of Höss, vol. 25, cards 17–18; testimony of M. Kula, collection Statements, vol. 98, card 239. According to Halgas, at least 5,000 to 6,000 Soviet POWs were gassed in the mortuary of crematorium I; ibid., account by former prisoner Kazimier Halgas.

21. Ibid., vol. 4, card 21, testimony of former prisoner J. Krokowski.

22. *KL Auschwitz,* pp. 173–74 (Broad).

23. Czech, *Kalendarium*, p. 349, quotes the figure of 300 prisoners, whereas Jankowski-Feinsilber (*Amidst a Nightmare*, pp. 45–46) mentions 390.

24. Müller, p. 51. According to Pressac, p. 132, no more than 10,000 persons were gassed in this chamber. Broad resorts to generalities: "One transport after another disappeared in the Auschwitz crematorium every day. More and more victims kept coming in," *KL Auschwitz*, p. 175 (Broad). On the part played by crematorium I in the machinery of extermination, see also Georges Wellers, "The Existence of Gas Chambers," in *The Holocaust and the Neo-Nazi Mythomania* (New York, 1978), p. 110.

25. Insufficient source material does not allow us to determine the exact date of bringing bunker 1 into operation. According to Czech (*Kalendarium*, p. 161), it became operative in early spring 1942. This is confirmed by Höss, p. 209.

26. According to Czech, *Kalendarium*, p. 239, bunker 2 was launched on June 30, 1942; according to Höss, p. 211, it was in the summer of 1942. In any event, launching of bunker 2 took place before the inspection visit of Himmler on July 17–18, 1942.

27. Measurements on the basis of cadastral survey. We may conclude that the total area of the building was 93.5 sq m. Assuming that the walls covered approximately 10 sq m, we estimate that the area of both interior rooms was about 83 m; ASAM, negative no. 21416/7.

28. Ibid., collection Statements, vol. 70, card 51, vol. 113, cards 77–78, accounts of Franciszek Gulba and Jozefa Wisinska; Trial of Höss, vol. 11, cards 105–17, vol. 24, card 217, testimony of Shlomo Dragon; Höss, p. 211; *KL Auschwitz*, pp. 175–81 (Broad).

29. The total area of the building was 142.36 sq m. The combined area of the four interior rooms was 105 sq m. These figures were computed on the basis of the findings of the survey of the foundations, July 29, 1985; ASAM, call no. DP-Z.Bau 2044/Bw 2/5/53.

30. Ibid., Trial of Höss, vol. 11, cards 103–5, testimony of Shlomo Dragon.

31. Ibid., card 105, vol. 24, card 220, testimony of Shlomo Dragon and Wilhelm Wohlfarth; Höss, p. 210; *KL Auschwitz*, pp. 175–81 (Broad).

32. Höss, p. 208. Given the density of 10 persons per one sq m, bunker 1 could accommodate about 830 persons.

33. Following Dragon, Sehn estimated the combined capacity of the two bunkers at 2,000 persons. However, in view of the size of both buildings, this appears to be an overestimate. The capacity of 1,200 given by Höss is corroborated by, among others, an entry in Johann Kremer's diary dated October 12, 1942, concerning the gassing in bunker 2 of the entire transport from the Netherlands (of the total of 1,703 victims in this transport—Kremer quotes the figure of 1,600—1,251 were sent to the gas chamber); *KL Auschwitz*, p. 222; Höss, p. 211. Assuming the density of 10 persons per sq m, the chamber could contain 1,050 persons.

34. *KL Auschwitz*, pp. 212–13.

35. ASAM, Trial of Höss, vol. 4, card 74; vol. 11, cards 30, 103–6; vol. 17, card 142; vol. 21, cards 4–5; vol. 28, cards 45–47, testimonies of Reinhold Puchala, Shlomo Dragon, Wlodzimierz Bilan, Rudolf Höss, Arnost Rosin, as well as conclusions of the commission investigating the Nazi crimes in Auschwitz; see also ibid., Trial of the Auschwitz personnel, vol. 44, cards 240–46, vol. 55, card 240, testimonies of Erich Merbach and Marian Przad.

36. Höss, p. 21.

37. Höss wrote that this took place late in the summer of 1942. That year, similar operations of liquidation of mass graves were carried out in the killing centers at

Chelmno, Treblinka, Sobibor, and Belzec. In every one of these locations, the practice of burying the bodies was replaced by cremation outdoors. See Höss, p. 211; ASAM, Trial of Höss, vol. 11, card 100, testimony of Michal Kula.

38. At that time, this chamber also was referred to as bunker 5, *KL Auschwitz*, p. 184 (Broad); Höss, p. 216; ASAM, Trial of Höss, vol. 6, card 35, testimony of Otton Wolken; vol. 4, card 73, testimony of Jozef Plaskura.

39. In 1965, Hydrokop, a chemical mining technical enterprise based in Krakow, was commissioned by the Auschwitz-Birkenau State Museum to carry out geological tests at Birkenau aimed at determining the locations of incineration pits and pyres. Specialists of Hydrokop bored 303 holes up to 3 m deep. Traces of human ashes, bones, and hair turned up in 42 sites. Documentation of all the holes and the diagrams of their distribution are preserved in the Conservation Department of the museum.

40. The exact dates of the drafting of the project and of its original version are not known. We have only an annotation to the preliminary version, dated Auschwitz, October 31, 1941 (*Erläuterungsbericht zur Vorentwurf*), ASAM, microfilm 1034, cards 1–17.

41. This figure is quoted in ibid., cards 4, 7.

42. When annotations to the preliminary project were drafted, i.e., by late October 1941, the conception of the purpose and outfitting of this crematorium had lost its relevance. The Bauleitung's letter of commission, dated October 22, 1941, which was sent to the furnace builder, Topf and Sons, indicates that not one but two underground mortuaries were planned for construction near the crematorium. See ASAM collection Bauleitung, BW 30/34, card 116.

43. In a Bauleitung letter of March 6, 1943, mortuary 2 was referred to as "undressing room" (*Auskleideraum*). In another letter, one of the underground mortuaries was designated as "gas cellar" (*Vergasungskeller*); ASAM, Trial of Höss, vol. 11, card 9; microfilm 1060, card 100. Höss, p. 215, confirms that the underground spaces at crematoria II and III served as undressing rooms and gas chambers and were outfitted with an automatic ventilation system.

44. ASAM, collection Bauleitung, BW 30/34, card 116.

45. Ibid., BW 30/25, Bischoff to Topf and Sons, March 5, 1942, BW 30/34, card 37, Bischoff to Amt C III, March 30, 1942; BW 30/34, card 35, Amt C III to Topf and Sons. In a letter to Zentralbauleitung of March 2, 1942, Oswald Pohl approved the construction in 1942 of a crematorium at Birkenau; see *Trials of War Criminals before the Nuremberg Military Tribunals*, vol. 5 (Washington, D.C., 1950), pp. 612–13, Nuremberg Document NO-4464.

46. Ibid., collection Zentralbauleitung, BW 30/4–6.

47. Ibid., call no. D.-Z.bau/6.

48. Ibid., collection Zentralbauleitung, BW 30/26, cards 1–20, the Huta firm to Zentralbauleitung, July 13, 1942. The sum of 133,741.65 marks is mentioned therein; later this figure was revised; ASAM, call no. D.-Z.bau/6, inventory no. 29754.

49. On July 29, 1942, Zentralbauleitung acknowledged in writing receipt of the offer; ibid., collection Zentralbauleitung, BW 30/26.

50. Ibid., collection Bauleitung, BW 30/34, card 114, Topf and Sons to Zentralbauleitung, September 30, 1942; BW 30/34, card 113, Topf and Sons to Zentralbauleitung, October 31, 1942. On August 20, 1942, Zentralbauleitung offered to the Köhler firm of Myslowice to submit tender for bricklaying work in the construction of chimneys to crematoria IV and V. Tenders were to be opened on August 30, 1942; BW 30/26, cards 52–53.

51. Ibid., collection Zentralbauleitung, BW 30/34, card 48, Zentralbauleitung to Topf and Sons, cable of February 26, 1943.

52. Ibid., collection Bauleitung, BW 30/34, cards 1–101, Prüfer to Zentralbauleitung, January 29, 1943, report on the results of inspection of the construction of crematoria in Birkenau. Crematorium II was scheduled to be brought into operation on February 15, 1943; crematorium III, on April 17, 1943; crematorium IV, on February 28, 1943. The date of launching of crematorium V was made contingent on the weather.

53. Ibid., BW 1, file 73 (unnumbered pages), document entitled "Aufstellung der Bereits übergebenen Bauwerke die Standortverwaltung." June 25, 1943, was mentioned as the date of delivery of crematorium III, whereas in the letter from Zentralbauleitung to Kammler, dated June 28, 1943, the date was June 26; ibid., BW 30/42, card 2.

54. Ibid., BW 30/42, card 2.

55. Höss, p. 224, confirms the existence of this practice. In contrast, Tauber maintains that Sonderkommando prisoners were under orders to load no more than three corpses every half hour. If we accept Höss's contention that the cremation of one load of corpses lasted 20 minutes and every second load consisted of two corpses only, the number of corpses incinerated in crematoria II and III would reach 2,700 in each and in crematoria IV and V 1,440 in each, yielding a total of 8,280. Höss, however, wrote that 2,000 corpses each were cremated in crematoria II and III and 1,500 each in crematoria IV and V, giving the total of 7,000 corpses cremated in 24 hours. See ASAM, Trial of Höss, vol. 11, card 135, testimony of Tauber; Höss, pp. 215, 216.

56. ASAM, Trial of Höss, vol. 11, card 67; Nuremberg Document NO-4463; Zentralbauleitung to Ceasar, November 6, 1943, concerning the supply of 1,600 tree and bush seedlings for a hedge, which would screen crematoria II and III from view ("Grüngürtel als naturlicher Abschluss zum Lager"); collection Statements, vol. 113, card 5, account of former prisoner Alter Fajnzylberg alias Feinsilber; Trial of Höss, vol. 11, card 65a, an official note drafted in connection with Pohl's visit to Auschwitz on June 16, 1944. Pohl approved, among other things, the planting of a second hedge around the crematoria and camouflaging them by means of rough mats ("Die Tarnung durch Rohmatte"); see *KL Auschwitz*, documentary photographs, no. 166.

57. Measurements quoted from plan no. 933, dated January 19, 1942; ASAM, collection Bauleitung, BW 30/2. See also Trial of Höss, vol. 11, card 36, protocol.

58. The ventilation system does not figure in the undressing room plans. Its installation is indicated in the preserved correspondence dealing with construction of the crematoria; Pressac, pp. 355–78.

59. ASAM, Trial of Höss, vol. 2, card 100; vol. 11, cards 128–30; vol. 21, card 6, testimony of Michal Kula; Protocol, testimonies of H. Tauber and R. Höss; collection Statements, vol. 49, card 81, testimony of former prisoner Szwemberg, who worked in laying electric installations in the gas chambers.

60. Ibid., Trial of Höss, vol. 2, cards 99–101; vol. 11, cards 116, 130; vol. 25, card 33, testimony of former prisoner Michal Kula, employed at metalwork shop where the wire-grid shafts were manufactured; see also testimony of Shlomo Dragon and H. Tauber.

61. Ibid., vol. 11, cards 128–30, testimony of H. Tauber; collection Statements, vol. 94, card 33, testimony of Wladyslaw Girsa.

62. Ibid., Trial of Höss, vol. 11, cards 36–37; Survey protocol, vol. 11, card 128, testimony of H. Tauber.

63. Ibid., cards 32, 133; Protocol, testimony of H. Tauber.

64. Miklos Nyiszli, *Auschwitz: A Doctor's Eyewitness Account* (New York, 1960), p. 72.

65. ASAM, Trial of Höss, vol. 11, cards 34, 133; Survey protocol, testimony of H. Tauber; Nyiszli, p. 43.

66. Höss, p. 217.

67. ASAM, Trial of Höss, vol. 11, card 40; Survey protocol.

68. The description is based on accounts by two former Sonderkommando prisoners employed in crematoria IV and V, Shlomo Dragon and Alter Feinsilber; on conclusions of the Polish prosecuting bodies; and on plans, photographs, and the preserved foundations. Ibid., cards 40, 108; Survey protocol, testimony of Shlomo Dragon; collection Statements, vol. 113, cards 4–5, testimony of former prisoner Alter Fajnzylberg alias Feinsilber.

69. Ibid.

70. Höss, pp. 223, 224. ASAM, Trial of Höss, vol. 11, cards 45–46, 136–37; vol. 21, card 7. Survey protocol, testimony of H. Tauber; testimony of Höss, March 14, 1946; Nyiszli, pp. 50–51.

71. ASAM, Trial of Höss, vol. 11, cards 47, 131–39; vol. 45, card 128; Survey protocol; testimony of former prisoners H. Tauber and K. Markus. According to Tauber, 2,500 corpses were incinerated in crematoria II and III each, whereas Höss, pp. 215–16, gives a lower estimate of 2,000.

72. Trial of Eichmann, testimonies (in Hebrew), vol. 2 (Jerusalem, 1963), pp. 114–15.

73. According to H. G. Adler, gassings in Auschwitz were discontinued on November 2, 1944; Adler, *Theresienstadt 1941–1945* (Tübingen, 1955), p. 694.

74. According to the testimony of the leader of the Hungarian Zionists, Rezso Kastner, a copy of the order to demolish gas chambers and crematoria, shown to him by Himmler's associate Kurt Becher, bore the date November 25, 1944. This date is borne out by an annotation in a manuscript by an anonymous author, a prisoner and Sonderkommando, to the effect that dismantling of crematorium II commenced on November 25. In contrast, Adler, p. 694, accepts the date of November 26. See also Ota Kraus and Erich Kulka, *Die Todesfabrik* (Berlin 1957), p. 229; R. L. Braham, *The Destruction of Hungarian Jewry* (New York, 1963), pp. 919, 920; testimony given by Kastner in London on September 13, 1945, ASAM, call no. D-AuII-3/1, card 8, Quarantane-Liste; ibid., Trial of Höss, vol. 22, card 81, indictment.

75. Czech, *Kalendarium*, pp. 940, 941, 952. Until December 12, 1944, the size of the labor squad of women prisoners employed in dismantling of crematorium III remained unchanged.

76. An anonymous author wrote in notes found after the liberation of the camp: "Dismantling of the walls of crematorium IV commenced on October 14, 1944. The job is done by prisoners of Sonderkommando. Today, November 25, they began dismantling crematorium II, and crematorium III is next. Interestingly, the first to be dismantled is the ventilation motor and pipes, which are sent to other camps—some to Mauthausen, others to Gross-Rosen. Since this is used to gas human beings on a large scale—no such mechanisms existed at all in crematoria IV and V—one is led to believe that identical sites for exterminating Jews will be established on the grounds of those camps," *Amidst a Nightmare*, pp. 120–22. The transfer of the ventilation system from Auschwitz to Mauthausen is confirmed by Hans Marsalek, although we have no information about elements of the cremation furnaces themselves. In his study of the Gross-Rosen camp, Mieczyslaw Moldawa wrote that the furnaces got bogged down at some point en route and did not reach the camp. See Marsalek, *Die*

Geschichte des Konzentrationslager Mauthausen: Dokumentation (Vienna, 1974), p. 162; Moldawa, *Gross-Rosen: A Concentration Camp in Silesia* (in Polish) (Warsaw, 1979), p. 33; Andrzej Strzelecki, *Evacuation, Liquidation, and Liberation of KL Auschwitz* (in Polish) (Oswiecim, 1982) pp. 125–26, 135–36, 202.

77. ASAM, collection Bauleitung, BW 30/34, card 80. See also ibid., Trial of Höss, vol. 11, card 58; facsimile of the document in Ota Kraus and Erich Kulka, *Night and Fog* (in Czech) (Prague, 1958), pp. 112–13.

78. At that time, Prüfer inspected the construction site of crematoria at Birkenau and later drafted a report on the progress of work; ASAM, collection Bauleitung, BW 30/34, card 101.

79. Ibid., BW 30/34, card 94; see also Trial of Höss, vol. 11, card 7.

80. Sehn, p. 140.

81. ASAM, Trial of Höss, vol. 26, card 170, testimony Höss.

82. One attempt undertaken by neo-Nazi apologists in the late 1980s to cast doubt on the existence of installations of mass murder is the so-called Leuchter Report. Its main argument, allegedly refuting the fact that prussic acid was used in gas chambers, is that the amounts of prussic acid compounds found on the walls of the gas chambers were negligible compared to those found in disinfection chambers. The author of this report completely ignores the facts explaining these differences: in gas chambers, the amount of prussic acid used was reduced to the minimum needed to kill the victims; the time during which different gas chambers were in use; the state in which various installations were preserved (with the exception of the gas chamber of crematorium I, used sporadically for one year, ruins of the remaining chambers were exposed to changing weather throughout the postwar period).

8

The Machinery of Mass Murder at Auschwitz

JEAN-CLAUDE PRESSAC WITH ROBERT-JAN VAN PELT

The Design, Construction, Use, Modifications, and Destruction of the Crematoria and Gas Chambers of the Auschwitz / Birkenau Concentration Camps

This essay presents the history of the instruments of extermination employed by the Germans against Jews and others at Auschwitz-Birkenau. It is based on ten years' study of the archives of the architectural and construction office of the Nazi Schutzstaffel (SS), which built the camps at Auschwitz. Two-thirds of these archives survive in Moscow. Taken by the Soviet Army in 1945, they were unavailable for study until the demise of the Soviet Union. The rest remain at Auschwitz, as part of the holdings of the Auschwitz-Birkenau State Museum.

In the year that the Berlin Wall fell (1989), Jean-Claude Pressac published a book that presented the history of the construction of the gas chambers and crematoria at Auschwitz as it could be reconstructed on the basis of material in Oswiecim (Poland), the Federal Archives in Koblenz (Germany), the State Archives in Weimar (then the German Democratic Republic), and the Yad Vashem Archives (Israel).[1] Study of the material in the Central Archives of the Soviet Union (now Russia), which became available in 1991, has led to this revision of some of the author's earlier conclusions.

In 1928, two engineers from Hamburg, Hans Volckmann and Karl Ludwig, applied for a patent for a new kind of incinerating furnace to be used for cremation.[2] Until then, a standard incineration furnace had a core that consisted of a crucible, or muffle, which took in the coffin, and a burner. Added to this core was an economizer, which retrieved heat from the combustion gasses to channel it through a complex heat exchanger back into the crucible. The economizer made it possible to shut off the burner at an early stage of the incineration process and continue it with the energy already absorbed into the furnace. Yet there was one problem: though the economizer saved on fuel, it was expensive to construct. The complex system of overlapping circuits sometimes took up as much as two-thirds of the total mass of the furnace. Volckmann and Ludwig aimed to slash the prevailing prices by replacing the cumbersome economizer with a cheaper system based on the introduction of compressed cold air into the crucible.

The patent did not bring the expected riches, and by the end of 1934, Volckmann and Ludwig's system had disappeared from the German market. But another company was able to capitalize on the idea. Kurt Prüfer (figure 1), an engineer in the small department of crematorium construction of the reputable Erfurt firm of Topf and Sons, famous for its industrial blast furnaces, adapted Volckmann and Ludwig's idea, and in 1935, Topf installed in various German crematoria seven gas-heated furnaces without an economizer that used compressed air instead.[3]

FIGURE 1. Kurt Prüfer, engineer for Topf and Sons, builders of furnaces for the crematoria at Auschwitz-Birkenau. State Archives Weimar, file 2/555a.

Topf's crematorium furnaces had acquired a good reputation when, in 1937, a new market opened. In May, the SS leadership in Munich decided to build a crematorium in the concentration camp at Dachau and invited bids for a furnace. Until that year, Nazi concentration camps had used the crematoria of the nearest towns to incinerate the remains of prisoners who died in the camps. Yet at times that created inopportune publicity; also, the mortality rate in the camps sometimes exceeded the limited capacity of the civilian crematoria.

A response to the SS invitation came from Walter Müller of Allach, a firm that had a proven record with the Munich SS, as it had built the central heating system for the local SS barracks and the SS training camp at Dachau. Müller proposed to construct a single-muffle furnace without an economizer and with a compressed-air device (figure 2). The cost would be 9,250 reichsmarks (RM), which in 1937 equaled $3,700 and today translates to roughly $37,000.

FIGURE 2. Walter Müller's proposal for a single-muffle furnace with a marble neo-Grecian pediment, for use in the crematorium at Dachau. Archives of the Memorial Place, Dachau, file 943.

Müller claimed that there was a direct relation between increased use and increased economy. If the cold furnace required 175 kilograms (kg) of coke to start up a new incineration, it needed only 100 kg if it had been used the day before; a second and third incineration on the same day would not require any extra fuel, thanks to the compressed air; and those that followed would call for only small amounts of extra energy.[4] Yet Müller's furnace was not built. A massive reorganization of the camps received a higher priority, and the idea of equipping Dachau and the other camps with their own crematoria was temporarily dropped.

In spring 1939, the issue of the crematoria acquired new urgency. By that time, a new office in Berlin had taken control of SS construction activities in the concentration camps. This Central SS Office of Budget and Building (SS-Hauptamt Haushalt und Bauten, or SS-HHB), with the resources to finance and service the building and operation of crematoria, awarded Topf and Sons the Dachau contract because Prüfer realized that a concentration camp didn't need an indestructible civilian furnace embellished with a marble neo-Grecian pediment, as Müller had proposed. Instead, Prüfer proposed a stripped-down mobile furnace with two incinerating muffles, a fuel oil burner, a system to blow compressed air into the muffles, and forced draft. Its estimated yield was two corpses an hour.[5] The SS-HHB accepted this simple, efficient model, which at 8,750 RM (1992: $35,000) was modestly priced.[6]

The furnace was in operation at Dachau by the end of 1939, when Prüfer received an order from the Buchenwald concentration camp. Camp authorities there had first raised the need to install a crematorium in June 1938.[7] Close to Erfurt, Buchenwald now became Prüfer's preserve, the testing ground for two of his furnace models.

The first model (figure 3) was a fixed version of the mobile model at Dachau. Its base price, 7,753 RM (1992: $31,000), was cheaper than the furnace at Dachau. The discount was possible because its construction on the spot in Buchenwald made it possible to use prisoner labor, which the SS furnished at no cost to the company. The SS also provided certain materials, such as cement, lime, sand, and bricks, at no charge. Added to the base price, however, was an extra 1,250 RM (1992: $6,000) for a reinforced draft in the chimney.[8]

By the time Topf began construction of the Dachau furnace, Poland had been carved up between Germany and the Soviet Union. Germany not only recovered its pre-1919 eastern territories but also annexed additional land that before the First World War had belonged to Russian and Austrian Poland. This strip of land included the town of Oswiecim, or Auschwitz, as the Germans knew it. The town of 12,000 inhabitants was located at an important railway junction, allowing easy communication with Berlin, Warsaw, Lwow (Lemberg), and Vienna. And in its suburb of Zasole stood 22 sturdy Polish army barracks, deserted since the end of hostilities.

In early 1940, the SS decided to install in the former army base a camp for quarantining 10,000 Polish prisoners. The camp was to have its own incinerating furnace. The SS-HHB requested Topf to submit estimates for a mobile, double-muffle oil-heated furnace at Auschwitz and for one at the concentration camp of Flossenburg. In March, the SS-HHB gave Topf the order to produce the two furnaces for 9,000 RM (1992: $36,000) each.[9]

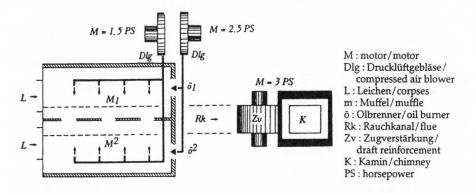

FIGURE 3. Diagram of the Topf and Sons fixed, double-muffle oil-heated furnace, installed at Buchenwald. Unless otherwise noted, all diagrams were prepared from drawings © Jean-Claude Pressac.

The new contract must have pleased Prüfer, and not only because of the 2 percent commission he received on the profit of each order.[10] With Topf furnaces in Dachau, Buchenwald, Flossenburg, and Auschwitz, he was on his way to acquiring a monopoly in what could only be an expanding market. His only obstacle was the Kori firm, which, because of its good contacts with some high-ranking SS men in Berlin, had received a contract to install two units of its mobile, single-muffle oil-burning furnace in the Sachsenhausen concentration camp (figure 4). The success of these furnaces led to other orders as well. In the end, Kori constructed a dozen of them in various concentration camps; five, more or less well preserved, still exist in Poland.

On May 10, 1940, German armed forces attacked the Low Countries and France, and gasoline, petroleum, and fuel oil were rationed in Germany. Because all the furnaces in the concentration camps had oil burners, it was likely that the crematoria would now face shortages. Kori was better prepared than Topf to face the new situation. Only a month earlier, the firm had negotiated the sale of a fixed, single-muffle furnace with a coke burner to the Mauthausen concentration camp. It had become operational on May 5, and soon it was the only camp furnace able to function. Topf had not foreseen the fuel shortage and found itself barraged by complaints from Dachau and Buchenwald, as their furnaces had fallen idle.[11] Topf also began

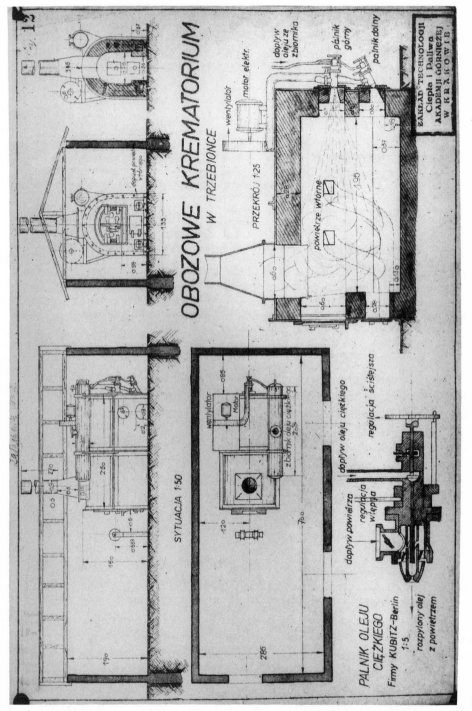

FIGURE 4. Plan for the Kori firm's mobile, single-muffle oil-burning furnace, installed at Sachsenhausen. Archives of the Auschwitz-Birkenau State Museum, negative 6671.

to worry that the SS-HHB would cancel the orders for Flossenburg and Auschwitz.

At the end of May, the Auschwitz Neubauleitung (New Construction Administration) communicated to Topf that the mobile furnace it had on order should use coke.[12] Prüfer decided not to tamper with the mobile model, which could not be so easily adapted, but instead to redesign the fixed, double-muffle furnace supplied earlier to Buchenwald (figure 5). Both Auschwitz and Flossenburg went along with the modification, which added two external coke burners on both sides of the underground flue that linked the furnace to the smokestack.[13]

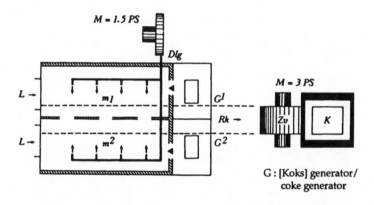

FIGURE 5. Diagram of the Topf fixed, double-muffle Buchenwald furnace, modified for coke heating. Key same as for figure 3; G—coke generator.

As Prüfer was remodeling the Buchenwald furnace, the Auschwitz Neubauleitung began on June 28 to adapt an old powder magazine on the former army base into a shell for the new crematorium. Wilhelm Koch and another overseer from Topf arrived at the site on July 5. They decided to rotate the furnace 90 degrees in relation to the underground flue in order to obtain the most efficient use of the available space. Twenty days later, the furnace was installed at Auschwitz (figure 6).

Equipped with an electric forced-draft fan capable of removing 4,000 cubic meters (cu m) of smoke an hour and fitted with an electric blower to inject blasts of cold air into the crucibles, the furnace was 50 percent more powerful than the Dachau model of 1939.[14] Fritz Sander and Paul Erdmann, Prüfer's superiors at Topf, estimated an output of 30 to 36 bodies in 10 hours, or about 70 bodies for a 20-hour cycle.[15] The furnace required three hours of maintenance a day. Yet the furnace could not yet be tested. The Bauleitung had not completed the 10-m smokestack. Only on August 15 was everything ready, and a first cremation was carried out satisfactorily in what came to be known as Auschwitz's crematorium I.

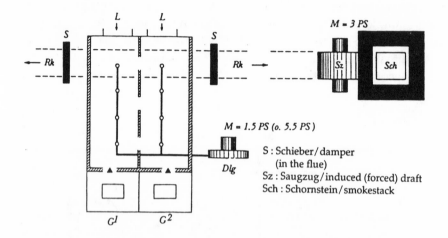

FIGURE 6. Diagram of the Topf fixed, double-muffle furnace, of the Auschwitz type and coke-heated. Blowoff: 4,000 cu m of smoke an hour.

Further incinerations followed without causing any problems, and thus the recently appointed head of the Auschwitz Neubauleitung, SS-Sergeant Schlachter, informed the SS-HHB after a month of trials that the crematorium functioned flawlessly. Schlachter had another reason to be pleased with Topf. Despite the radical change in the furnace model, which had raised the actual cost of the furnace by a little over 25 percent, the firm had decided not to renegotiate the original price.[16] Patriotically absorbing the extra cost and allowing the quality of the furnace to speak for itself, Topf paved the road for future commissions.

Topf did not provide Flossenburg with the new model furnace it had installed in Auschwitz. Although the firm had already completed the construction in Erfurt of the mobile, double-muffle furnace with oil burners originally agreed upon, at the beginning of July, Topf was informed that this furnace, with supplementary coke burners, should be installed in a subcamp of Mauthausen at Gusen.[17] Smaller than the Buchenwald model, the furnace for Gusen did not allow for the addition of the coke burners at the back. Therefore Topf added the units on the sides, doubling the width of the unit.

Prüfer was pleased that he had gained a foothold in Mauthausen, which hitherto had been in the Kori sphere of influence. At the end of October, he traveled to Mauthausen to meet the chief of the Bauleitung, SS Adjutant Büchner. They discussed the construction of one more furnace for Gusen and another for the projected prison infirmary at Mauthausen.[18] Noting that the Auschwitz Neubauleitung had asked Topf to build a second furnace along the same lines as the first,[19] Prüfer sold Büchner an Auschwitz-type fixed, double-muffle furnace to be installed at Gusen. Büchner did not yet want to commit himself on the one for the prison infirmary, as he did not know whether the mortality rate warranted a single- or double-muffle furnace (in the end he settled for the double-muffle model).[20]

In December 1940, August Willing traveled from Topf and Sons to Gusen to install the mobile furnace.[21] On his way he stopped in Dachau to add two lateral coke burners (figure 7) to its existing mobile furnace.[22] By February 4, 1941, Willing had completed the Dachau and Gusen jobs. Both camps had to pay an extra 2,000 RM for the modification from oil to coke.[23] Yet the furnaces worked well. At an estimated capacity of two corpses an hour, the Gusen furnace (figure 8) was less powerful than the Auschwitz model.[24] Still, it worked more than satisfactorily, especially when, in November 1941, it cleared a backlog of 600 cadavers in one continuous 12-day operation.

In Auschwitz, preparations were under way for the construction of a second double-muffle furnace at the crematorium, for which Topf had quoted the same price as for the first (7,753 RM), yet which did not include a forced-draft ventilator. That was not an oversight; Prüfer assumed that the already-installed ventilator would suffice for two furnaces.[25] On November 19, 1940, Prüfer was in Auschwitz to decide on the exact site for the second furnace. He was accompanied by Schlachter's deputy, Walter Urbanczyk, who until the next October was effectively in charge of crematorium construction. They decided to build the second furnace alongside the first.[26]

Prüfer suggested that Urbanczyk call on another Topf employee, Karl Schultze, to see if concentration of two furnaces in one tight and unventilated space would create difficulties in the adjacent autopsy room and morgue. Urbanczyk followed up on the suggestion, and Schultze submitted within a few days a proposal for a limited ventilation system to extract air from the autopsy room and morgue (figure 9).[27] The Neubauleitung asked Schultze to modify the 1,784 RM proposal because it did not service the furnace room.[28]

At the beginning of January 1941, the first furnace in the crematorium at Auschwitz broke down, giving new urgency to the construction of the second furnace.[29] On January 17, a railway car left Erfurt with parts to repair the damaged furnace and material for the construction of the second one.

FIGURE 7. The Topf mobile furnace at Dachau, with two lateral coke burners added by August Willing. Collection of Jean-Claude Pressac.

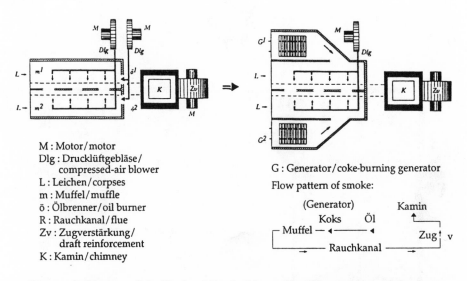

M : Motor / motor
Dlg : Drucklüftgebläse /
    compressed-air blower
L : Leichen / corpses
m : Muffel / muffle
ö : Ölbrenner / oil burner
R : Rauchkanal / flue
Zv : Zugverstärkung /
    draft reinforcement
K : Kamin / chimney

G : Generator / coke-burning generator

Flow pattern of smoke:

FIGURE 8. Diagram of the Topf mobile, double-muffle oil-heated furnace, first installed at Dachau, then modified for coke heating and set up at Gusen (Mauthausen).

Work began on January 20 and was finished a month later.[30] Topf, however, had failed to send a modified design for the ventilation of the crematorium, and as its construction had become urgent, Schlachter turned to the firm of Friedrich Boos, which was about to install central heating in the SS guards' quarters. Having the requisite material and technology for the ventilation system, Boos constructed it between February 23 and March 1.[31] SS Corporal Pery Broad of the Political Department (Gestapo) described it as "a large curved pipe rising from the roof [of the crematorium], which gave off a monotonous sound . . . a ventilator suction device designed to purify the air in the incineration chamber [and the morgue] . . . in the ceiling of the morgue [was located] . . . the ventilator." A Neubauleitung blueprint which we have examined confirms Broad's remarks.[32]

Schultze meantime tackled the problem of ventilating the autopsy room and morgue in the crematorium building. These were still ventilated together by grilled suction sleeves dropping from two collecting pipes (one for each room). These pipes ran into an angle of the ceiling and led to a blower that was coupled to the evacuation smokestack and dispensed 6,000 cu m an hour. This system cost 1,727 RM, 54 RM less than for the first device because the pipes were not as long, owing to the modifications made by Schultze. The furnace hall (320 cu m) was ventilated separately by a vertical pipe with four grilled openings (two per furnace) leading to a number 300

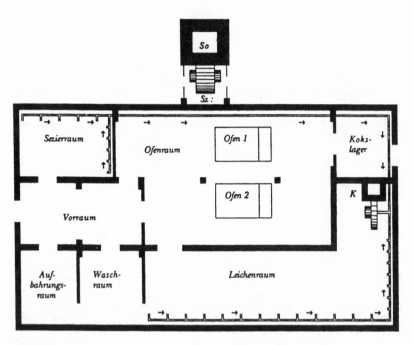

Sezierraum/autopsy room
    (10 air exchangers)
Vorraum/vestibule
Aufbahrungsraum/laying-out room
    (for bodies)
Waschraum/washroom
Leichenraum/morgue (20 air exchangers)
So : Schornstein/smokestack

Sz : Saugzug/induced (forced) air
Ofenraum/furnace room
Kokslager/coke room
Gebläse/blower
K : Kamin/chimney

FIGURE 9. Organization of crematorium I at Auschwitz, showing the probable first arrangement of its air extraction system, designed by Karl Schultze and dated December 9, 1940, on the basis of Topf blueprint D. 57,999, dated November 30, 1940. Blowoff: 6,000 cu m an hour; 1.5-hp motor.

blower with a .75-horsepower (hp) motor, dispersing 3,000 cu m of air an hour. This, too, was linked to the evacuation smokestack and cost 757 RM (figure 10).

For the warm air, Schultze required only a coefficient of 10 cu m an hour per cu m to be deaerated. Topf justified this separate circulation to prevent the warm air from entering the morgue.[33] Schultze's concept was simple: instead of completely recasting the project, he added a second one to the first so as to meet the new specifications demanded of him. Such reliance on previous studies would become the rule during the working out of ventilation systems for later crematoria of Birkenau. On February 15, the Neubauleitung rejected this proposal, insisting that the air suctioned in must no longer

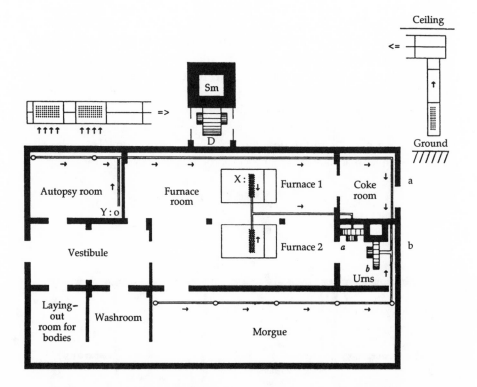

FIGURE 10. Presumed organization of the air extraction system of crematorium I at Auschwitz in the second design by Karl Schultze, dated February 3, 1941. Blowoff at a: 3,000 cu m an hour; .75-hp motor. Blowoff at b: 6,000 cu m an hour; 1.5-hp motor. Sm—smokestack; D—forced draft; X—suction pipe on top of furnace (frontal view); Y—suction sleeve linked to a collecting pipe (O) (frontal view).

pass through a separate smokestack but must go into the smokestack evacuating smoke from the furnaces.[34]

On February 24, a third project was sketched out (figure 11).[35] The deaeration of the morgue was left unchanged, with five vertical suction devices attached to a horizontal collecting pipe, going all the way to the smokestack of the furnaces. The ventilation of the autopsy room was replaced by air intake grilles in the form of shutters. A pipe with four openings ran above the furnaces. The three collecting pipes met in the furnace room, and their effluent was swept into a number 550 blower with a 3-hp motor, dispersing 8,300 cu m of air an hour, spewing into the smokestack from the furnaces. Materials for this device would cost 1,884 RM, and its assembly 596 RM. This proposal was accepted on March 15 by Urbanczyk, who then asked Topf to manufacture and deliver it in the shortest time possible. The firm estimated it would take up to six months, or until August 15.[36]

The first visit to Auschwitz, on March 1, 1941, of SS chief Heinrich Himmler was a watershed in the history of the camp. Himmler decided to enlarge the camp to hold 30,000 prisoners and to create at nearby Birkenau a camp for 100,000 prisoners of war. Furthermore, he decided to provide IG Farben-industrie with 10,000 prisoners for building an industrial zone dedicated to the production of methanol and synthetic rubber, to increase agricultural activity within the camp zone, and to develop the camp's workshops. Himmler also announced that an armaments plant would be installed close to the camp.

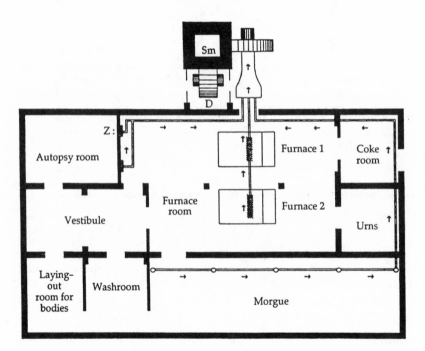

FIGURE 11. Organization of the air extraction system of crematorium I at Auschwitz in the third design by Karl Schultze, dated February 24, 1941. Blowoff: 8,300 cu m an hour; 3-hp motor. Z—air intake grille in the form of shutters, placed vertically.

The 100,000 prisoners of war were to be used as a labor force for the creation of a "colony" (*Siedlung*) at Auschwitz. In this vast scheme for the total Germanization of the city and its surroundings, Auschwitz was to be a pilot project and the seedbed for other German colonies in the east. For a year and a half, an architect from Breslau worked on the planning of this city.[37] Only the Nazi defeat at Stalingrad on January 31, 1943, put an end to his labors.

Himmler's plans did not affect ongoing activities at the Auschwitz crematorium. The second furnace proved unsatisfactory for lack of proper draft. After unsatisfactory communications with Topf,[38] Schlachter decided to address the problem himself. Increasing the height of the smokestack to 20 m got the draft going again.

Another and ultimately more pernicious problem was a situation stemming from the close presence of SS-Untersturmführer Maximilian Grabner, head of the Political Department of the camp. Grabner used a hut right behind the crematorium for his Gestapo interrogations and the morgue as his place of execution. When both furnaces were going, which happened almost every day, they released so much heat that the ventilation system, which was supposed to extract air from the morgue, actually sent hot air into it from the furnace room. The only way to prevent this was to disconnect the morgue from the ventilation system—with unwanted consequences in the hot summer air. Grabner denounced this "scandal" to the Bauleitung and asked that it equip the morgue with two ventilators, one to bring fresh air in (to aerate, *belüften*) and one to take stale air out (to deaerate, or *entlüften*) and discharge it in conformity with the earlier plans through the smokestack.[39]

The continuous incinerations had done more than just disturb Grabner's comfort. They had also cracked the smokestack. All cremation was stopped between June 23 and 28 to hoop the chimney with iron bands.[40]

At Topf in Erfurt, the crematorium's ventilation system was almost ready, and work on the Mauthausen order was progressing smoothly. Yet on August 18, a letter arrived from the new construction chief at Mauthausen, SS-Obersturmführer Naumann, canceling the order for the Gusen furnace. Naumann also refused to pay for anything except the fireproof material that had already been delivered. Prüfer angrily accepted the cancellation of the Gusen furnace, hoping that the order for the other furnace would not be affected.[41] Within two weeks, Prüfer had been able to turn the Gusen furnace into a furnace for Auschwitz. On September 16, Urbanczyk ordered a third double-muffle furnace to be installed in the crematorium autopsy room, and Prüfer believed that the Gusen furnace would do just fine.[42] The only person at Topf who resented the new order was Schultze; he now had to change the crematorium's ventilation system for the third time (figure 12).

On September 24, Naumann contacted Topf again because the original Gusen furnace had broken down. Willing, who had set up this furnace, returned to Gusen and worked on it from October 11 to November 10. Then Prüfer sought to exploit the renewed relationship with Mauthausen. He plotted so successfully with his connections in the SS-HHB that on October 16, Naumann got a telephone call from Berlin. An SS adjutant named Heider ordered him to put in an immediate order with Topf for an Auschwitz-type double-muffle furnace. Naumann respectfully obeyed but then launched a secret campaign against Topf to sabotage this compulsory contract. As a result, it took more than a year for all the parts for the two furnaces to be assembled. And this was only in Gusen, since Mauthausen refused to stock Topf's material. When, in January 1943, Topf inquired when its overseers could come to build the furnaces, Naumann responded that no such installation was being planned.[43]

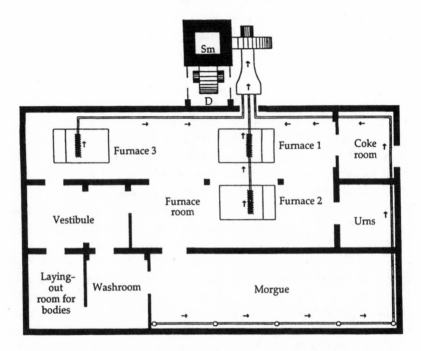

FIGURE 12. Presumed organization of the final air extraction system of crematorium I at Auschwitz in the fourth design by Karl Schultze, end of September 1941. Blowoff: 8,300 cu m an hour; 3-hp motor.

In Auschwitz, preparations began for the construction of the prisoner-of-war camp (*Kriegsgefangenenlager,* or KGL) that Himmler had ordered set up at Birkenau. On October 1, 1941, the chief of buildings of the SS-HHB, SS-Oberführer Hans Kammler, appointed SS-Hauptsturmführer Karl Bischoff to head a special office to oversee construction of the camp (Sonderbauleitung für die Errichtung eines KGL). Bischoff was on the job as of that day.

Bischoff had been a member of the Luftwaffe since 1935 and had worked as a warrant officer in northern France and Belgium, setting up airfields from which attacks were launched against England. In that time he became acquainted with Kammler, who also worked for the air force. After the Battle of Britain, Bischoff was left with little to do, and Kammler, who had moved to the SS, suggested that Bischoff make a similar move. He offered him officer rank and independence as the chief architect of an enormous prisoner-of-war camp.[44]

Bischoff accepted the offer, but not before negotiating the privilege of appointing his own man as head of the crucial design section of the Bauleitung. He had in mind the Austrian architect Walter Dejaco, who had worked for a short time under Schlachter and was employed in fall 1941 at the SS-HHB. After Kammler agreed, Bischoff traveled to Auschwitz and went to work. Dejaco was to follow on October 24, but Bischoff did not await the arrival of his new chief designer.

Within one week after Bischoff took control, his office produced the first plan for a camp of 125,000 inmates. It proposed a large enclosure divided into three sectors: one for quarantining prisoners and two for lodging them. A second plan, drawn up on October 14, introduced a railway spur between the quarantine camp and the rest.[45]

As he was developing the design, Bischoff realized that his camp, which was expecting to handle 100,000 prisoners of war, could not rely on the crematorium in the main camp, which was designed to service 10,000 inmates. Hence on October 11, he telegraphed Topf to dispatch Prüfer to Auschwitz.[46] Prufer arrived ten days later, and he and Bischoff closeted themselves for the next two days.[47] The two men liked one another; both were veterans of the Great War, professional builders, energetic and hard-working, and beholden for their careers to nobody but themselves.

Prüfer convinced Bischoff to create the necessary incineration capacity at the POW facility by grouping three incinerating crucibles in a single furnace and lining the necessary number of furnaces next to each other. That would make it possible to create a large incineration capacity in one relatively compact building. The triple-muffle furnace seemed a natural evolution of Topf's double-muffle model, and the arrangement combined efficiency with economy (figure 13). Prüfer did not yet dare to suggest a quadruple-muffle model.·

Assuming one crucible for 8,000 prisoners, Prüfer calculated that 15 crucibles would suffice. That translated into five furnaces of three crucibles each, linked to a common smokestack. Prüfer calculated that each crucible could handle two bodies every 30 minutes and that the installation as a whole therefore would be capable of burning 60 bodies an hour, or 1,440 bodies in 24 hours. Running day and night, the new crematorium theoretically could incinerate all the inmates of the projected camp in three or four months.

The building was not to be at Birkenau but in Auschwitz's main camp, behind the existing crematorium, across from the administration building.[48] Prüfer sketched a plan for a crematorium measuring 55 to 60 m by 12 m (175 feet by 37 feet).[49] Its center was to be a large furnace room. Adjacent to it were to be a storage room for coke, rooms for washing and laying out corpses

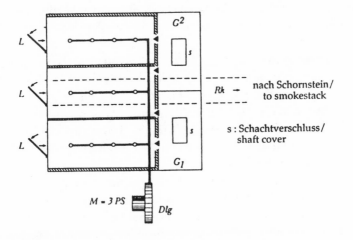

FIGURE 13. Diagram of the Topf triple-muffle furnace, as set up at Buchenwald (2 units) and Auschwitz-Birkenau (10 units). Rk—flue.

that had been selected for dissection, and an autopsy room, replacing the autopsy room of the existing crematorium, which would be displaced by the third furnace. A central projecting wing was to house a furnace for burning refuse, two ventilators to create a forced draft, and a double smokestack. The basement was to have two vast morgues. One morgue was to store "fresh" bodies; the other was for corpses about to be incinerated. An elevator was to connect the morgues to the furnace and autopsy rooms.[50] Prüfer and Bischoff decided that Schultze was to design the ventilation system to extract air from the furnace hall, the autopsy room, and the two morgues below.[51] In conformity with the arrangement in the existing crematorium, one of the morgues was also to receive a system to bring in fresh air.

Dejaco arrived in Auschwitz just as Prüfer was about to leave, and he was given the job of elaborating the engineer's sketches into a design. He produced two drawings: a plan of the ground floor and an elevation (figure 14). In the plan, he indicated the dimensions of the morgues below: the "B. Keller" (*Belüfteterkeller,* or aerated cellar) was to measure 7 m by 30 m, and the "L. Keller" (*Leichenkeller,* or morgue) 8 m by 60 m. An architect who worked in Berlin for the SS-HHB, Werkmann, was also asked to apply himself to the problem. His crematorium improved on Prüfer's initial sketch: it was more monumental in elevation and more practical in plan (figures 15 and 16). For example, Werkmann included a chute to facilitate the transport of corpses from an entrance on the ground floor to the morgues in the basement. He did not fix the length of the morgues, both of which he designated

"L. Keller." In all respects more accomplished than Dejaco's design, Werkmann's proposal was accepted and signed by Kammler and sent to Auschwitz on November 20.

In Erfurt, meanwhile, Topf worked on the design of the furnaces for the new crematorium. As the size of the crucibles in the triple-muffle furnace was larger than those in the double-muffle furnaces, the firm decided to increase from two to three the number of ventilators to create a forced draft. It also decided to increase their total extractive power from 20,000 to 120,000 cu m an hour. One of the brothers who owned the firm, Ernst-Wolfgang Topf, assured the Sonderbauleitung that "the installation being built would be appropriate and well-designed."[52]

Financial calculations suggested that Auschwitz was going to get a bargain: each triple-muffle furnace was to cost a mere 6,378 RM (1992: $25,400) and the furnace for refuse only 4,474 RM (1992: $18,000). The project as a whole came to 51,237 RM (1992: $205,000). This price included the building of underground smoke ducts leading to the smokestack but not the common smokestack with three ducts.[53] Nor did it include the cost of ventilation, which was an extra 7,795 RM (1992: $31,000).

Schultze assigned an hourly extraction capacity of 10 cu m for each cu m in each room to be ventilated. To achieve this, he proposed for the 483-cu-m B. Keller, which was to be both aerated and deaerated, a double system run by two 2-hp blowers, which could bring 4,800 cu m of fresh air into the room each hour and extract 4,000 cu m of air from the room. The L. Keller, which was double the size of the B. Keller, was to be deaerated only and was to receive a ventilation system with a 5.5-hp blower capable of extracting 10,000 cu m of air an hour. A similar system was to be installed in the furnace room, which had roughly the same volume as the L. Keller. The rooms that served for dissections totaled 300 cu m and were to be equipped with a system capable of extracting 3,000 cu m of air an hour.[54] Around this time, the older of the two proprietors of the firm, Ludwig Topf, was called up to serve the Fatherland as an ordinary soldier in a construction battalion. The firm's personnel resented this, because the bachelor Ludwig was more easygoing than his aggressive, pretentious, and harsh younger brother (who was married and therefore exempt). Prüfer asked Bischoff's support to gain Ludwig's exemption, permanently if possible. He justified the extraordinary request with the fabrication that Ludwig had been instrumental in developing the triple-muffle furnace and the new crematorium could not be completed without his supervision. Bischoff pulled some strings, and in December, Ludwig got his leave.[55] Once back in Erfurt, he managed to get out of all his military obligations. But he was now beholden to Bischoff.

Prüfer by now had acquired acquired a reputation at the SS-HHB as a "magician" of cremation. In mid-November 1941, the head of technical

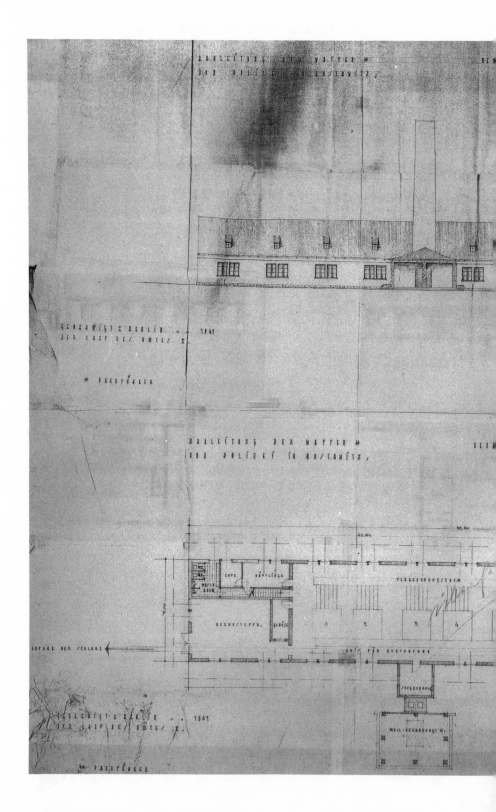

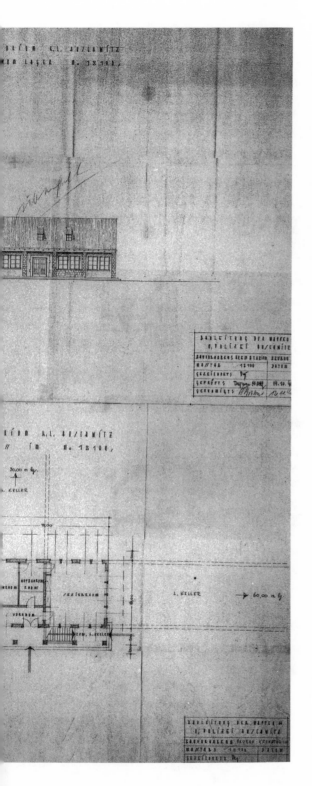

FIGURE 14. Drawings by Austrian architect and SS-Untersturmführer Walter Dejaco for proposed crematorium at Auschwitz, dated October 24, 1941. Plan of the ground floor (below) and elevation. Central State Special Archives, Moscow, files 502-2-146 and 502-1-285.

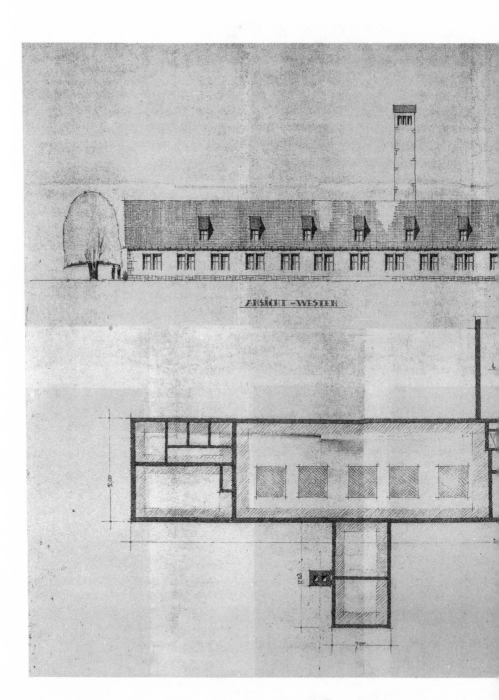

FIGURE 15. SS architect Werkmann's drawings for proposed crematorium at Auschwitz, dated November 1941. Plan of the basement (below) and elevations. Central State Special Archives, Moscow, file 502-2-146.

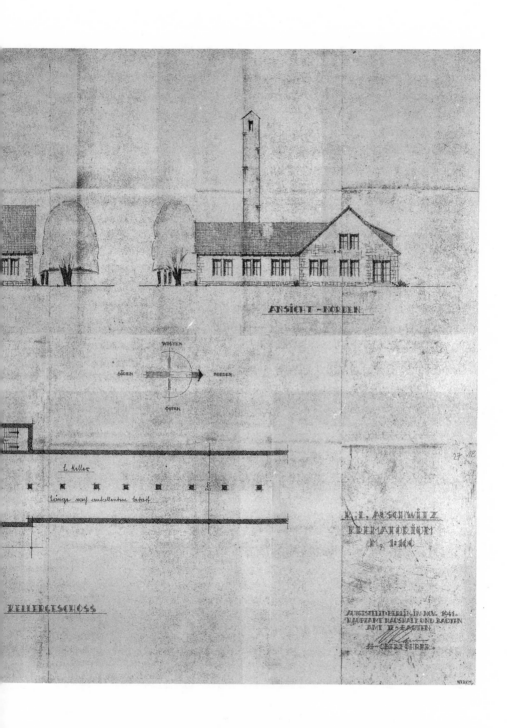

ANSICHT - NORDEN

WESTEN

SÜDEN · NORDEN

OSTEN

1. Keller

Länge nach anfallendem Bedarf

K.L. AUSCHWITZ
KREMATORIUM
M. 1:100

AUFGESTELLT BERLIN IM NOV. 1941.
BAUFIRMA HAUSHALT UND BAUTEN
AMT II BAUTEN

SS-OBERFÜHRER

KELLERGESCHOSS

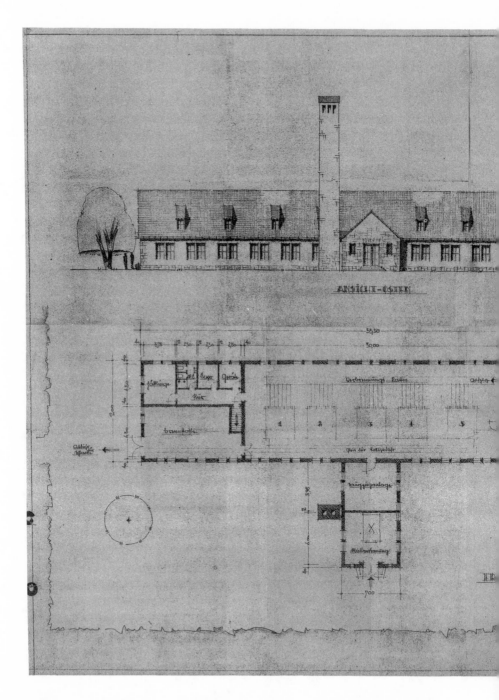

FIGURE 16. SS architect Werkmann's drawings for proposed crematorium at Auschwitz, dated November 1941. Plan of the ground floor (below) and elevations. Central State Special Archives, Moscow, file 502-2-146.

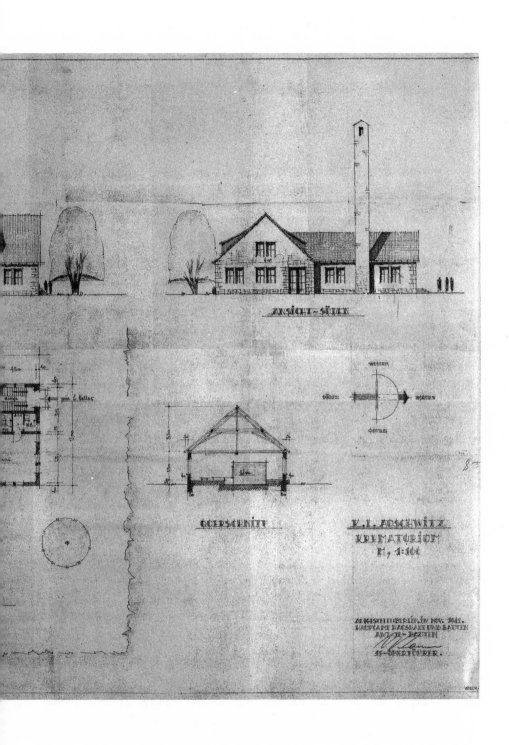

ANSICHT - SÜDEN

QUERSCHNITT

K. L. AUSCHWITZ
KREMATORIUM
M. 1:100

AUGESTELLT BERLIN, IM NOV. 1941.
HAUPTAMT HAUSHALT UND BAUTEN
AMT II - BAUTEN
SS-OBERFÜHRER.

operations of the SS-HHB building department, SS-Stürmbannfuhrer Wirtz, invited Prüfer to Berlin. The topic of discussion was the installation of a "crematorium site" at Mogilev, in Russia.[56] Prüfer had just come to the conclusion that it was technically possible to increase the number of crucibles from three to four per furnace, and he suggested to Wirtz that a double furnace with four muffles would do fine as a basic element (figure 17). Two elements were to provide one unit with eight crucibles.

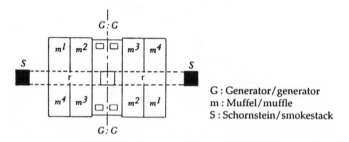

FIGURE 17. Diagram of the Topf quadri-muffle furnace.

G : Generator/generator
m : Muffel/muffle
S : Schornstein/smokestack

Compared with the Auschwitz furnace, the Mogilev version was simple. To be heated with wood, it had neither doors for closing the burner generators nor internal thermal insulation. It was also cheap. One unit with eight muffles cost only 13,800 RM (1992: $55,200), that is, 1,725 RM per crucible (compared with 2,126 RM per crucible in the three-muffle version and 5,000 per crucible in the two-muffle version already installed in Auschwitz). The SS-HHB wanted to build four units, a total of 32 crucibles, and came to an agreement with Topf on December 4. The total job was worth 55,200 RM (1992: $220,000).[57]

As usual, the SS was in a hurry, and Wirtz requested Prüfer to leave for Mogilev within a week after signing the contract. He was to inspect the site and accompany the transport of the fireproof materials for the furnaces. On December 19, Topf asked for payment of half the price of the contract, or 27,600 RM (it was paid in May 1942). On December 30, one four-muffle element was delivered to Mogilev. Yet nothing more happened in Mogilev, despite another payment of 15,000 RM to Topf.[58]

Amid all the excitement of the Mogilev contract, Topf also had to look after the installation of the third furnace for crematorium I at Auschwitz. On November 20, an overseer named A. Mahr had begun laying the foundations for the furnace. He worked for three weeks[59] but could not continue because the Collmener Schamottenwerke of Colditz in Saxony had not delivered the fireclay to Topf. Mahr returned to Erfurt.

Shortly after Mahr's departure, the first lethal gassing was carried out with

Zyklon B at Auschwitz in the cellars of block 11. Zyklon B, a hydrocyanic acid (prussic acid) pesticide, was made by the Degesch company of Frankfurt am Main and supplied through a wholesaler, Tesch and Stabenow of Hamburg. It was available in metal containers of four sizes (200 g, 500 g, 1 kg, and 1.5 kg), which also included an inert, porous medium and an irritant designed to alert the unprotected user to the presence of the odorless gas. Under most conditions, the pesticide was not dangerous, as the prussic acid would only vaporize at a temperature of 27 degrees Celsius.[60] Zyklon B had first been introduced at Auschwitz in July 1940, when it was used to fumigate the former Polish barracks, which were to house the camp's SS guards. It had remained a staple fumigant through 1940 and 1941.[61]

In December 1941, Zyklon B was administered for the first time not to vermin but to 250 "incurable" concentration camp inmates and 600 Soviet prisoners of war.[62] According to Höss (who was away at the time), death was immediate. Others claimed that some victims were still alive two days later and that it was necessary to introduce a second batch of poison. The killers were experimenting; they did not know yet how much Zyklon B was lethal for how many people, and they did not fully realize that hydrogen cyanide vaporizes only at 27 degrees Celsius. The basement of block 11 had not been heated. Cremation of the 850 victims also presented an unexpected problem: the intensive operation caused the second furnace to deteriorate.[63]

When the experiment was over, it had become clear that the cellars of block 11 were less than ideal as gas chambers because of lack of ventilation. Also, the distance from block 11 to the crematorium was too great—the killers did not want to move 850 corpses through the main street of the camp. The morgue of the crematorium recommended itself as a more efficient gas chamber. It had a mechanical ventilation system that could extract the poison gas, and being a one-story structure, it provided an easy means of introducing Zyklon B into the room through three square stacks to be created on the roof.[64]

The new gas chamber in the morgue at crematorium I operated probably intermittently from January 1942 until May, when it had to be shut down for construction of the third furnace. By that time it had also become clear that the crematorium did not provide the "privacy" necessary for the gassings, and shortly before Topf's men moved in to construct the new furnace, the decision was made to transfer the gassings to Birkenau.

In the winter of 1941–42, Birkenau became more and more integrated with the main camp. On December 1, the building office of the main camp and Bischoff's Sonderbauleitung KGL merged into a new organization, the Zentralbauleitung der Waffen SS und Polizei, Auschwitz O/S (Central Building Authority of the Waffen SS and the Police, Auschwitz, Upper Silesia), headed by Bischoff. From mid-January to the beginning of February

1942, this office produced eight blueprints for the new POW crematorium (called series 900), based on Werkmann's design of the preceding November.[65] Dejaco made small changes to Werkmann's design, relocating the smokestack and adding a third room in the basement for crematorium operations. This room, labeled morgue 3, was to receive the corpses for registration. The projected location of the crematorium, in the main camp, remained unchanged.[66]

At the end of January 1942, Prüfer returned to Auschwitz to plan the building of the third furnace for crematorium I and, probably in response to Bischoff's wish, to discuss the possibility of constructing a backup incineration facility in Birkenau in addition to a new crematorium. Prüfer now proposed a crematorium with two stripped-down versions of his triple-muffle furnace, without a compressed-air blower and using only a small amount of iron in their structure. Placed around a central smokestack, the furnaces were to cost 14,652 RM (1992: $58,600) (figures 18 and 19).[67]

But then Kammler, who had become head of the building department of the powerful successor to the SS-HHB, the SS Wirtschafts-Verwaltungshauptamt (SS-WVHA, or Economic-Administrative Main Office), annulled the project during his visit of February 27.[68] He suggested that it made more sense to build the new crematorium at Birkenau. Topf was not happy; yet it was prepared to forgo any further claim if the SS took care of the 1,769.36 RM (1992: $7,500) which the firm had invested in studying the aborted project.[69] The company was paid, but it would come to regret taking the money.

In mid-March, Bischoff received new calculations from Schultze. After reviewing the original numbers, he had decided that it was better to increase the total capacity of the ventilation system of the new crematorium, now to be built at Birkenau, from 32,600 cu m of air an hour to 45,000 an hour. The room most affected by this was the B. Keller, which was to receive a system capable of aerating and deaerating 8,000 instead of 4,800 cu m an hour, that is, a 66-percent increase. Bischoff accepted Schultze's new proposal on April 2. He asked Topf to bring the designation on the firm's blueprints into line with the ones drawn up in the camp.[70] This meant that B. Keller became L. Keller 1 and L. Keller became L. Keller 2. The Topf design was modified accordingly and returned to Auschwitz on May 8.[71]

On April 30, a railroad car arrived in Auschwitz from Erfurt loaded with 11 tons of material, which included two-thirds of the metal parts and all the compressed-air blowers for the five triple-muffle furnaces to be built in the new crematorium in Birkenau, the iron fittings needed for the third double-muffle furnace of crematorium I, and all the deaeration equipment.[72] Most of the car's contents were stockpiled. Only the iron fittings for the third double-muffle furnace were of immediate use.

At the same time, Prüfer was supervising the construction at Buchenwald

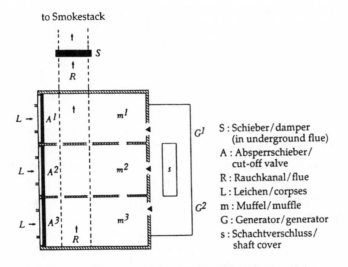

FIGURE 18. Diagram of the Topf stripped-down triple-muffle furnace for the incineration system of the proposed crematorium at Auschwitz.

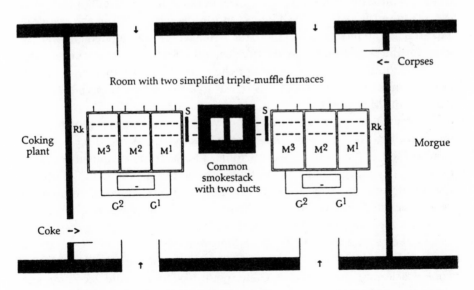

FIGURE 19. Probable layout of the proposed back-up crematorium at Birkenau, with two simplified triple-muffle furnaces.

of the first of two triple-muffle furnaces. He hoped that early completion would provide him with concrete data before setting up five similar furnaces in Birkenau. At the end of May, the furnace was completed except for the compressed-air blower. On May 29, Topf asked Bischoff to lend Buchenwald one of the stockpiled blowers for its three-muffle furnaces and a 3-hp motor.[73] We do not know if Auschwitz went along with this or if Topf had to remake the missing parts. Whatever happened, the first Buchenwald furnace was not operational until August 23 and the second on October 3. After 12 and six weeks of operation, Prüfer revised his original estimate for Auschwitz. Extrapolating the Buchenwald data for Auschwitz, Prüfer concluded that the five furnaces of the new crematorium in Birkenau could incinerate 800 corpses in 24 hours.[74] That was sharply lower than the original figure of 1,440 mentioned a year earlier.

In May, Höss selected a little farmhouse (the "little red house") on the edge of the birch forest at Birkenau to be the new gas chamber. It was to replace the morgue in the first crematorium, which was undergoing repairs. The house, measuring 60–80 sq m, consisted of two rooms into which 500 persons could be crammed. The doors were made airtight, the windows were walled up, and small openings were installed for the insertion of Zyklon B into the rooms. No mechanical ventilation was installed to extract the gas from the two rooms. The executions were to occur in the evening; and after all the prisoners had died, the doors were to be opened and remain open for the whole night. By daybreak it would be possible to remove the bodies without danger and transport them to burial pits dug in the birch forest. Bunker 1, as the execution site was to be known, entered into service that month (May 1942).

The crematorium in the main camp was in the meantime repaired and modified. On May 30, everything seemed ready, but as the three furnaces were started up, something went wrong. The hooping of the smokestack broke off, deep cracks appeared in the masonry, and the men of the Political Department began to fear that the smokestack would collapse on their offices. Bischoff ordered an investigation, and on the basis of the report, Kammler approved a complete overhaul.[75]

A local expert, engineer Robert Köhler from Myslowitz, recommended a new smokestack 25 to 30 m high. Grabner howled, demanding that the smokestack not exceed 10 m.[76] Köhler realized that he could accommodate Grabner's wishes by connecting the 10-m smokestack to a 20-m underground flue, creating a "virtual" chimney height of 30 m. Yet there was no room to do this. Bischoff asked a second opinion from Topf. The firm responded that 15 m would suffice. Then Köhler added a 12-m connecting flue to Topf's smokestack and obtained a draft 27 m long.[77] Work began on June 12.

To this point, Auschwitz had played a completely marginal role in the killing of Jews. The cumulative evidence of documents in the archive of the Zentralbauleitung proves that the adaptation of the camp for genocidal purposes only started in June 1942. This conclusion contradicts Auschwitz commandant Rudolf Höss's statement, made in 1946, that Himmler had informed him that Birkenau would be used as a killing center in the summer of 1941. The evidence that we have studied suggests that Höss retrospectively confused 1941 with 1942. Himmler must have summoned Höss to Berlin at the beginning of June 1942 to inform him about the future use of the camp. One condition that justified the choice of Auschwitz applied both in 1941 and 1942: the camp's excellent rail connections. But another factor of prime importance had arisen only since the end of 1941: an extraordinary crematorium capable of incinerating 1,440 (or was it only 800?) corpses a day. It was the combination of these two circumstances that made Auschwitz attractive to Himmler.

The mass murders were to begin on July 1. That created a problem: the crematorium existed only in plan. Since May 17, a single detachment of 100 prisoners had been digging foundations, but that was all.[78] Furthermore, bunker 1 could not be used for continuous gassing, since it had no mechanical ventilation to speedily extract the gas. In addition, the camp was short of materials. Yet such considerations were mere cavils for Himmler, and he trusted that Höss would be able to find a solution.

Not far from bunker 1 was another farmhouse, whitewashed and, with a surface of 105 sq m, slightly larger than the "little red house." Höss decided to transform it into a gas chamber following the pattern of bunker 1. The place could hold 800 persons.

Bischoff was called in to advise on the ventilation. He recalled an article by Dr. G. Peters, director of Degesch, the manufacturer of Zyklon B,[79] which described a delousing system using Zyklon B with eight little gas chambers of 10 cu m each, set up side by side. Each cell had two gas-tight doors (made of metal or wood), one serving to take in personal effects on the dirty side and the other to remove them on the clean side. There was a radiator for heating and interior circular ventilation which assured, first, the regular passage of the agent over the goods to be deloused and second, when the 60- to 90-minute treatment was over, efficient deaeration. Peters's article had already served as a source of inspiration when, in December 1941, Dejaco had proposed to install in the future reception building at Auschwitz a delousing system with 19 similar gas chambers (set up in two rows). Degesch had proposed that the delousing chambers ought to be 50 cu m each.

It was easy to install a modified form of the parallel rooms with doors at both sides in the little farmhouse. Yet the radiators to provide circular aeration posed a problem. This system had to be set up by Boos, and the delivery process would be subject to long delays.[80] It was decided to drop this idea and limit the modification to the installation of four small parallel gas chambers of 50 cu m each. As the gas chambers were oriented to the prevailing wind direction (north-south in Birkenau), it was thought that natural ventilation would suffice. The method for introducing the poison gas was copied from bunker 1. One or two 500-g boxes of Zyklon B per cell would cause rapid death. The "little white house," or bunker 2, was operational by the end of June 1942.

Nature competed with man to create mass death in Auschwitz. SS doctors were confronted in May with a massive outbreak of typhoid fever as the result of untreated water. By the end of June, SS officers and employees of the camps' 17 civilian firms were forbidden to drink the camp's water. Mineral water was provided free. To make matters worse, typhus broke out. The camp doctors were surprised. They thought that prophylactic measures (quarantining, shearing of hair) and hygiene (local disinfection of hair, showers) applied to the prisoners upon arrival would prevent the introduction of the plague into the camp by eradicating the agent of the disease, lice.

The trouble came from persons who had not been subjected to the delousing treatment, the free or civilian workers, who were in everyday contact with the prisoners. By the middle of 1942, the new arrangements in the Auschwitz region (the concentration camp complex and the Siedlung) had brought in civilian companies employing a thousand civilian workers. They were lodged as circumstances permitted. While the staff and the bosses of the work sites resided in houses or apartments requisitioned from the town of Auschwitz, the bulk of the workers were quartered in wooden barracks adjacent to the camps. On July 1, the first case of typhus occurred in the workers' barracks, followed within two days by three new cases.[81]

The death rate of the prisoners soared. From May to December 1940, an estimated 220 died each month. From January to July 1941, this number tripled. From August to December 1941, it reached 1,000; by July 1942, it had passed 4,000.[82] The unsanitary situation was obviously getting out of control. The typhus had to be prevented from spreading to the surrounding region. On July 10, a partial quarantine was declared.

But if the exits from the camp were blocked, its entrances were open. Convoys of Jews had begun to arrive. On July 4, the first selection of prisoners was applied to a convoy of Slovakian Jews, and those judged unfit for work were immediately gassed. Within a week this procedure had become routine.

Visitors who received a better welcome were Himmler and Kammler, who arrived in the camp on July 17 to inspect the progress of the Siedlung and the IG Farben complex. Bischoff briefed his superiors with maps, blueprints, and scale models. The presentation was followed by a visit to the camp's various agricultural and industrial operations and Birkenau. In the afternoon, Himmler was present at the selection of a convoy of Dutch Jews and the gassing of the unfit in bunker 2. Then he went to the IG Farben work site in Monowitz. A grand reception brought the day to a close.

The next day, Himmler inspected the main camp. He saw the three double-muffle Topf furnaces and the crematorium's new smokestack under construction. After a few other excursions, Himmler ordered Höss to speed up the work, to raise the camp's population capability from 100,000 to 200,000, and to get rid of the repugnant pits full of corpses behind the bunkers. Höss also received a promotion, to the rank of lieutenant colonel in the SS.[83] Himmler never returned.

Höss had succeeded in hiding from Himmler the deplorable unsanitary conditions in the camp, and the typhus epidemic continued its ravages. Within a week after Himmler's departure, the situation became catastrophic. On July 23, the camp was placed under total quarantine. Everything had to be deloused immediately: personal effects, barracks, buildings, and workshops. Tons of Zyklon B were needed to save the camp. The only way to get large quantities rapidly was through the WVHA's intervention. Not willing to admit that they had fooled Himmler, the Auschwitz SS explained that the epidemic had broken out only after his departure. On July 22, Berlin authorized a truck to fetch two-and-a-half tons of the product. A week later, a second truck was sent on its way. Yet even that did not suffice.

Around August 20, the epidemic was still raging, but the stockpile of Zyklon B had disappeared. The Auschwitz hierarchy was loath to request more prussic acid, as it implied they had been incapable of bringing the situation under control. Then someone got the idea to justify the purchase of further quantities of Zyklon B by referring to the gassing of Jews. The higher-ups of the WVHA knew that Jews were killed with the insecticide, yet they did not know how much poison was used in the operation. In fact, only 4 kg of prussic acid was enough to kill a transport of 1,000 persons. Inflating by more than 3,000 percent the quantities needed to do the job in the gas chambers allowed the SS to siphon off more than 95 percent for delousing. The trick worked. On August 26 and September 14, massive new purchases of Zyklon B were approved for "special treatment" and "special actions," terms that referred to the liquidation of unfit Jews at Birkenau.[84]

All of this happened while the camp had no crematorium to clean up after the killers. As a result of setting up the third furnace and building the new smokestack, the crematorium had been unusable for three months, and the effects of its stoppage had been especially noticeable once the typhus epidemic began multiplying the corpses. (In his memoirs, Höss dates this stoppage to the winter of 1941–42.)[85] Thus 10,000 bodies that ought to have been incinerated had been buried in pits in the birch forest at Birkenau along with the bodies of the unfit Jews who had been gassed. Once started up again after completion of the new smokestack on August 8, the three double-muffle furnaces operated at their maximum capacity (200 to 250 incinerations a day). That caused new damage to the smokestack on August 13. It became clear that this first crematorium was nearing the end of its career.

Even two months earlier, as more and more Jews were being killed on arrival, completion of the new crematorium had become a matter of highest urgency. On June 18, a railway car had left Erfurt with five tons of material, comprising the missing parts of the five triple-muffle furnaces, the furnace for refuse, and the three blowers for the forced draft. The 1.5-hp motors followed on August 6.[86]

At the beginning of July, the Zentralbauleitung invited a tender for the construction of the crematorium's shell from the two firms involved in construction in Birkenau, Huta and Lenz & Company. Lenz refused on account of a shortage of personnel.[87] On July 13, Huta accepted the proposal to handle the construction of the building for 133,756.65 RM (1992: $535,000).[88] The firm agreed to begin work on Monday, August 10.

In a report filed three months later with the WVHA, the Auschwitz Zentralbauleitung indicated that it had been necessary to set about building the new crematorium immediately owing to the situation created by the "special actions."[89] This statement formally confirms the essential role played by the new crematorium in the choice of Auschwitz as the site for the annihilation of Jews. Originally envisaged as a normal instrument of sanitation for a prisoner-of-war camp, this crematorium had taken on new importance thanks to the combination of Prüfer's commercial convictions, professional passions, creative genius, and cordial ties with Bischoff.

Slowly the men in the WVHA had begun to associate the "final solution of the Jewish problem" with the capacity of the new crematorium—or crematoria, as Bischoff had begun to consider the construction of a second crematorium in Birkenau. Himmler had ordered that the camp should accommodate 200,000 inmates, and the Zentralbauleitung had completed a design for the enlarged camp at the end of July. The corollary to this increase in population was an extra crematorium. For the sake of architectural balance, Bischoff decided to erect the two buildings side by side, each the mirror image of the other (figure 20). The number of incinerating crucibles was raised to 30, or one for every 6,670 prisoners. Yet perhaps even that would not be enough, as convoy after convoy poured in.

Prüfer arrived in Auschwitz on August 18 to take stock. A day later, camp authorities approved the construction of two more crematoria above and beyond the one under construction (originally intended for POWs) and the second one that had been planned to cope with the expansion of the camp. Prüfer picked up more than 80,000 RM (1992: $320,000) in new contracts.[90]

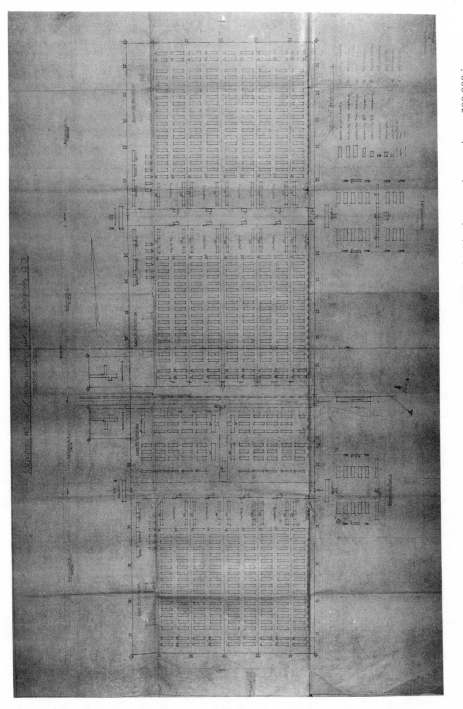

FIGURE 20. Plan for Birkenau, drawn up in response to Himmler's order in 1942 to double the camp's capacity to 200,000 inmates. Archives of the Auschwitz-Birkenau State Museum, file BW 2/10.

Preparatory studies cleared Prüfer's path. Bischoff had already decided on a second crematorium with 15 crucibles alongside the first. He also had considered building an incinerator alongside bunkers 1 and 2 to absorb their "production," which, according to Himmler's order, must no longer be buried but burned. With so many crematoria under consideration, Bischoff introduced a new nomenclature. The existing crematorium in Auschwitz was to be called crematorium I; crematoria II through V were to be built in Birkenau. Added to this array were four other crematoria to be built eventually in Birkenau. Crematoria II and III were to be equipped with five three-muffle furnaces, and crematoria IV and V were to have two stripped-down three-muffle furnaces each. Crematorium IV was to be erected next to bunker 2, and crematorium V next to bunker 1. (Another designation, based on the building project, defined crematorium II as BW [Bauwerk] 30, crematorium III as BW 30a, crematorium IV as BW 30b, and crematorium V as BW 30c.)

Prüfer now considered the technical aspects of crematoria IV and V. The stripped-down triple-muffle furnace, which he had proposed for the first Birkenau crematorium earlier that year, had not been further developed. Pressed for an instant solution, Prüfer recalled the proposed Mogilev double furnaces with four muffles. As the series was already in production, the Erfurt factory could rapidly manufacture others. Bischoff approved Prüfer's idea and had blueprints drawn up on August 14.[91] They showed only the layout of the double furnace with its two smokestacks; the diagram of the morgue remained incomplete (figure 21).

On the morning of August 19, Prüfer went to the Auschwitz Bauhof, the warehouse where materials were stockpiled, to see whether all the metal parts of the five triple-muffle furnaces had been received and were in good condition. He found, among the 11 tons of materials sent from Erfurt on April 16, most of the metal elements destined for the second double-muffle furnace in Mauthausen. They had remained in storage at Erfurt because of SS Lieutenant Naumann's obstinate dilatory tactics. Prüfer decided to exploit the mistake to his own advantage.

After lunch, Prüfer attended a meeting with the smokestack expert Robert Köhler at the Bauleitung chaired by SS Second Lieutenant Fritz Ertl (Bischoff had been called to Berlin). They decided to begin construction of the five furnaces for crematorium II as soon as Martin Holick, who had just started up the first triple-muffle furnace at Buchenwald, was on hand. Köhler would line the furnaces and build the underground flues and the common smokestack with three ducts.

Prüfer proposed fitting crematoria IV and V with the four-muffle double furnaces that had been readied for delivery to Mogilev. He noted that the SS-WVHA had been informed and was negotiating a transfer with the Bauleitung of Russland-Mitte. Köhler was to be responsible for the four smokestacks.[92] To be on the safe side, the Zentralbauleitung asked Köhler to make an estimate for the improvised crematorium with stripped-down triple-muffle furnaces. Bischoff still had doubts regarding the adoption of the Mogilev scheme, especially because Prüfer could not immediately provide the four overseers necessary for the simultaneous construction of the furnaces in the four crematoria.

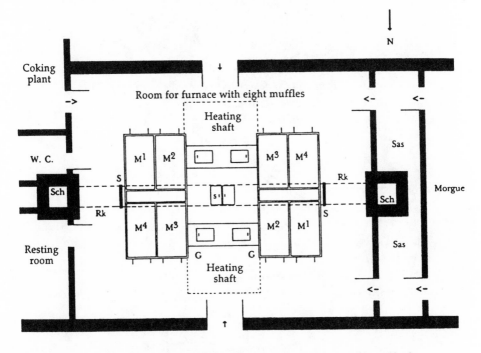

FIGURE 21. Diagram of the incineration system, with a double quadri-muffle furnace, for crematorium IV in Birkenau. W.C.—toilet; Sas—sluice and storage.

It was clear to all participants in this meeting that crematoria IV and V were to be involved in mass murder. Ertl, in his report on the meeting, designated bunkers 1 and 2, located in the Sperrgebiet at Birkenau, as "bath installations for special action" (figure 22). Köhler took personal responsibility at the meeting for committing his own firm to these "special works." Prüfer did not have full power to commit his company to such a deal, so he acted on his own. Yet he knew that his superiors would back him, since Ludwig Topf owed his demobilization to the SS.

The final item on the agenda was crematorium III, the reversed counterpart of crematorium II (figure 20). It was to be constructed last, because the opening of its work site depended entirely on negotiations under way with

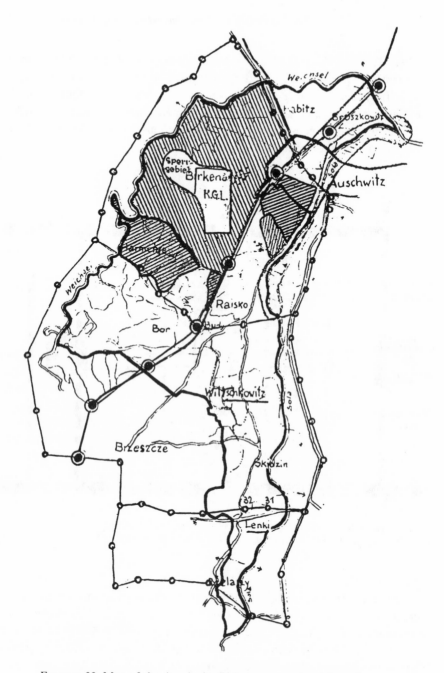

FIGURE 22. Map of the Auschwitz-Birkenau area, dated June 2, 1943, showing the Sperrgebiet, where the killing chambers designated as bunkers 1 and 2 (the "little red" and "little white" houses) were located. Central State Special Archives, Moscow, file 502-1-88.

the SS-RSHA (the Reichsicherheitshauptamt, or Reich Main Security Office) to get the release of the needed iron. At that point, Prüfer pointed out the mistaken delivery he had noticed that morning and suggested, given the urgency of the situation, immediately setting up the Mauthausen double-muffle furnace at Auschwitz.

The next day, SS Corporal Josef Janisch accompanied Prüfer and Köhler to Birkenau to show them around the work site of crematorium II. Before heading back to Erfurt, Prüfer asked for a handwritten confirmation of either the order for the four simplified triple-muffle furnaces or the Mogilev furnaces for crematoria IV and V.[93] Ertl settled matters on August 24 after consultation with the WVHA (but not with Bischoff, who could not be reached).[94] The double-muffle furnace would return to Mauthausen, and the two four-muffle double furnaces from the Mogilev contract would be built at Birkenau. When Bischoff returned from Berlin, he raked Ertl over the coals for acting on his own. He was especially angry about Ertl's decision to ship the Mauthausen furnace back to Erfurt.[95]

Despite the availability of thousands of prisoners, the Auschwitz Zentralbauleitung was unable to carry out the construction of the Birkenau crematoria all by itself. While its members were capable of running fairly simple work sites (building wooden barracks or residential houses), they needed outside help for more technical projects. Both for preliminary studies done by civil engineers from the specialized firms they called on and for actual construction, which was directed by several work-site foremen sent there by the company in question, outside help was crucial. To manage relations, Bischoff assigned to each specific project a second lieutenant specialist called at first SS-Fachführer, then Sonderführer. The Sonderführer would deal with the civilian firm, oversee the execution of the works in progress, and see to it that the job was finished promptly.

Eleven civilian companies were involved with the construction of the new crematoria in Birkenau. Topf was to build the furnaces and install the ventilation systems. The Köhler company from Myslowitz was to set up the smokestacks. The Huta firm from Kattowitz, which was already working on the shell of crematorium II, began those of crematoria IV and V before agreeing to build all of crematorium III. One of Huta's subcontractors, the Vedag company from Breslau, waterproofed the cellars of crematoria II and III. The drainage of crematorium II, which had been started by the Continentale Wasserwerks-Gesellschaft (Ltd.) of Berlin, was continued by the Karl Falck company from Gleiwitz and the Triton firm from Kattowitz. The latter two subsequently handled the drainage of crematoria III, IV, and V. The Konrad Segnitz company from Beuthen planned the roofing of the four buildings and manufactured the parts, but it was the Industrie-Bau-A.G. that put them in. Riedel and Son from Bielitz replaced Huta in building the shell of crematoria IV and V, which it also finished. The Kluge company from Gleiwitz helped Topf build the furnaces for crematoria IV and V. Each work site employed 100 to 150 persons, of whom two-thirds were prisoners and one-third civilians, all directed by overseers from the companies concerned.

Huta finished the floor and walls of the two underground morgues of crematorium II at the end of August. But they still had to be asphalted to protect them from water. Huta asked Vedag to take care of this. Vedag accepted, but as asphalt was rationed and the company didn't have enough in stock for the job, it had to ask for quotas to be removed from the necessary amount. Vedag applied according to normal procedure, which meant at best a long wait and at worst a refusal. Seeing the application drag on, Bischoff pulled strings at the WVHA, and the desired asphalt was released at the end of October.[96] As a result, the morgues of crematoria II and III were sealed tight just before the winter rise of the groundwater.

One problem Topf faced that fall was to modify the double four-muffle furnace (also called an eight-muffle furnace) which had been designed for Mogilev to burn wood rather than coke. Furthermore, it needed internal insulating and doors for closing the generators. These items added a total of 3,258 RM per unit.[97] On September 8, the constitutive elements (iron fittings and fireclay) of two complete eight-muffle furnaces, weighing 12 tons, left Erfurt by rail. The train arrived in Auschwitz on September 16.[98] The material was checked and signed for by two overseers from Topf, Martin Holick and Wilhelm Koch, who had just begun work on the foundations of the five furnaces of crematorium II.

Remarkably, neither Bischoff nor Prüfer had yet broached the question of the price of the furnaces. At the end of October, the Bauleitung finally asked what the price was, including the cost of anchoring the furnace to the ground. Topf telegraphed that an eight-muffle furnace cost 13,800 RM.[99] The final estimate, taking into consideration that some of the labor was to be done by the metal shop of the SS-owned Deutsche Ausrüstungswerke (German Equipment Works, or DAW) in Auschwitz, reduced the sum to 12,972 RM.[100]

On the morning of September 23, the head of the WVHA, SS-Gruppenführer Oswald Pohl, suddenly appeared in Auschwitz to find out where all the tons of Zyklon B were going.[101] Pohl went first to the Zentralbauleitung, had the overall layout of the camp explained to him, and got a description of the buildings that had been completed, those under construction (including the four crematoria in Birkenau), and the ones still on the drawing board. When he asked about the Zyklon B, he was told that the product was for the simultaneous destruction of lice and Jews. Pohl had no further questions on that topic. To prevent typhoid and malaria, he recommended speeding up construction of a large water-purification plant.

Yet the immediate concerns of the Zentralbauleitung were of a slightly different nature. On September 25, Bischoff ordered from Topf the incineration equipment for crematorium III. It was identical to that of crematorium II, except that it had no furnace for waste disposal.[102] Despite the agreement reached at the end of August to build crematorium III last, Bischoff decided that it would now take priority over crematorium V.[103]

The approach of the Silesian winter made it more and more difficult to use bunkers 1 and 2. The temperature outside kept falling, and the prussic acid ceased to vaporize properly. At the end of October 1942, the Zentralbauleitung began to consider transfer of the gassing from bunkers 1 and 2 to a room in a crematorium. It urgently requested Topf to send all the blueprints of the projected ventilation systems.[104] Within a week, it received the overall blueprints for installing the aeration and ventilation systems in crematoria II and III and the definitive blueprint for the ventilation system of crematorium I, which had arrived in April and had never been installed.

It was decided to transform morgue 1 of crematorium II into a gas chamber. One indication that such a decision was taken is a "leak"—that is, any mention in a document (writing, blueprint, photograph) of an abnormal use of the crematoria that could not be explained except by the massive gassing of human beings—that occurred on November 27, when one of Bischoff's assistants, Wolter, called Topf to ask for a master metalworker to install the ventilation systems in the morgues of crematorium II. His colleague Janisch, who was formally in charge of the site, canceled the request. Wolter drew up a note to inform Bischoff what had happened. In this note he designated the corpse cellar in crematorium II as "special cellar" (*Sonderkeller*).[105] That was not the only slip. Every document in a 120-item inventory of material needed for the completion of Birkenau, undertaken between December 10 and 18, was captioned "Re: Kriegsgefangenenlager Auschwitz (Durchführung der Sonderbehandlung)," or "Concerning: Prisoner-of-War Camp Auschwitz (Carrying Out of Special Treatment)," which referred to the killing operations.[106]

Another leak occurred when Dejaco set out to adapt the crematoria to their genocidal function. The ground floor, with the hall of furnaces and its service rooms, did not need modification, but the basement had to be changed to accommodate the new function. The building that was under construction provided for a chute at the center of a staircase to transfer corpses more easily from the surface to the two underground morgues, whereas victims to be gassed could walk down to the morgue that was now destined to serve as the gas chamber. The corpse chute no longer served any purpose and had to go.

On December 19, Dejaco sketched a new configuration of the basement that provided for a staircase for the victims (drawing 2003).[107] According to the captions in the blueprint, the staircase became the only access to the morgues—which implied, strictly speaking, that the dead would have to walk down the staircase. The blueprint arrived too late at work sites 30 and 30a; the concrete for the chutes had already been poured. Later, when the SS decided to add to the gas chamber a clothes room (Leichenkeller 2) with its own stairway, the part where the chute projected into the vestibule interfered with the passage of the victims. The top of the chute was demolished, and its outlet was masked by a wooden partition.

Dejaco faced greater problems than the simple one of locating stairs and chutes. By November, the SS had become accustomed to the operational procedure of bunkers 1 and 2, in which the victims undressed in the barracks-stables, were gassed in the bunkers, and their bodies dumped in pits, and it made sense to apply it to the crematoria. Yet the builders ran up against problems with layout and compatibility. For crematoria II and III, the choice of Leichenkeller 1 (ventilated) as a gas chamber was obvious. The SS also planned to use the two remaining morgues as gas chambers, wrongly imagining that the high yield anticipated for the five triple-muffle furnaces would allow a staggered operation. In this configuration, an outside undressing room was indispensable. It was to open directly onto the service stairway connecting the two halls by way of the central vestibule. Moreover, it proved necessary to improve the ventilation of Leichenkeller 2 (which was only deaerated) by adding an aeration system to bring air into the room. After the furnaces had been tested and their output better estimated, it became clear that they could not handle the "yield" of two gas chambers. Consequently, Leichenkeller 2 became an undressing room. In this configuration, deaeration no longer served any purpose (except to ventilate the body odors of the victims, which could just as easily be done by a natural air current).

Leichenkeller I proved in the end to be too large for a gas chamber. At the end of 1943, in order to "regularize" the operation of crematoria II and III, the camp administration divided their gas chambers in two, allowing no more than 100 sq m for the killing of 1,000 new arrivals (unfit for work) in 24 hours.[108]

The first sketch of crematoria IV and V, dating from August 1942, showed only the incinerating section.[109] In mid-October, the Konrad Segnitz company, which was in charge of the roof, drew it up in its definitive dimensions. The furnace hall was extended by a vast morgue that measured 48 by 12 m (576 sq m), which indicated that it was being used as the "end of the chain." The undressing and gassing of the victims was still taking place in bunker 2, but the corpses were to be deposited in the morgue of crematorium IV to be incinerated there.[110]

Then the SS tried to put a gas chamber (heated with a stove) at the center of the building, which would have resulted in the disposition of victims from clothes room to gas chamber to "storage" to sluice to the hall with the eight-muffle furnace. Since no mechanical ventilation had been planned for crematoria IV and V, deaerating a gas chamber there by natural means carried with it too many risks of accidental poisoning. It was decided to locate the gas chamber as far away from the incinerators as possible. A modification of the first arrangement placed it at the opposite end of the furnace hall, which led to the disposition of victims from gas chamber to morgue to sluice to the hall with the eight-muffle furnace. The problem with this arrangement was that there was no undressing room. Building a barracks-stable outside made up for that.

Crematoria IV and V had an incinerating yield much smaller than that of II and III, and so their gas chambers had to be more modest. The SS combined its need for low-capacity gas chambers (100 sq m) for "treating" small groups of victims with the idea of staggered operations, and thus on January 11, 1943 it established the definitive blueprint for the killing procedure at crematorium IV.[111]

As we have seen, this concept required the construction of an external undressing room. Yet, to save money, it was decided that in good weather the victims could undress outdoors (as they did in the summer of 1944). In the winter, the central hall doubled as undressing room and morgue. The victims came in, undressed, then walked naked into the two gas chambers. After being killed, they were dragged back into the central hall and laid there before being incinerated. The procedure did not make much sense from a functional point of view, especially when compared with the rational arrangement of the new crematorium at Dachau, in which victims could walk through the entrance into a heated clothes room to undress, then walk into a heated and deaerated gas chamber ("shower room") for killing; their bodies could then be taken to the morgue and on to the furnace hall. The gas chamber at Dachau could be placed in the center because it was fitted with a system of mechanical deaeration. Fortunately, it was never put into service.

Designing gas chambers and incineration furnaces and getting them built are two different things. Even in Auschwitz there were limits to what the SS could get done. Typhus, which had been largely suppressed, nevertheless affected the progress of work in an unexpected way. In November, conditions within Auschwitz began to concern people living in the surrounding area. They knew about the typhus in the camp and were worried about its spread beyond the barbed-wire fence.

During an informational meeting in the town of Bielitz on November 17, the regional councillor pointed out two cases of typhus. One Polish woman from Auschwitz had fallen ill, and her infection could be traced back to the camp through her 16-year-old son, a civilian worker with the Karl Falck company. Another woman from Przecischau had died of typhus on November 3. Her husband was a free worker in the construction of the concentration camp. The regional councillor blamed the SS for not preventing contact between civilian workers and contagious prisoners. He urgently requested that the quarantine be rigorously observed.[112] On December 4, a plenary meeting took place at Auschwitz between the regional councillor, the physician of the concentration camp garrison, SS-Hauptsturmführer Eduard Wirths, and various regional, municipal, political, military, and sanitation officials. Three additional cases of typhus had been discovered that could be traced back to the camp. Wirths refused to accept blame. As far as he was concerned, the quarantine had been strictly enforced, and hence the contagion was not the fault of the SS. The mayor of Auschwitz pointed out that he had seen SS men and civilians from the camp (recognizable by their green armbands) rubbing shoulders with civilians from the outside at the Auschwitz train station. That led to the crucial point of the discussion: the end-of-year leave for the civilian workers. It was decided that the leave would begin on December 25, and that those affected would be carefully deloused and isolated for three weeks before their departure.[113]

The men of the 32 companies involved were angry when they heard that the quarantine had been prolonged for another 21 days. They became even more furious when, on December 10, a civilian worker at the lodging camp shared by Huta and Lenz came down with the disease. Observing the 21-day rule meant that no one could leave before December 31. That was the straw that broke the camel's back: the civilians, who had been locked up in Auschwitz for five months, had had enough and began to leave the work sites on December 17 and 18.[114] On December 18, after an ineffective intervention by the camp Gestapo and after discussions with company executives, the camp leadership capitulated and granted its 1,000 civilian workers a leave from December 23, 1942, to January 4, 1943.[115]

The leave further delayed completion of the crematoria. In a report to Kammler, Ertl communicated on orders of Bischoff that crematorium II would be ready on January 31, crematorium IV on February 28, and crematorium III on March 31.[116] That meant an average delay of two months. No date was set for crematorium V. Informed about the new target dates, Kammler insisted that they be met and asked for a weekly report, to be transmitted by radio, on the progress of the work.[117] Invoking a directive from Himmler, Höss's adjutant refused to allow such transmissions, and in the end the reports were sent by mail.[118]

Bischoff pulled out all the stops to finish crematorium II by January 31.[119] He informed Topf that it had to deliver the materials needed according to the original schedule, so that crematoria II and III could be finished by January 31 and crematoria IV and V by March 31. Prüfer was asked to come to Auschwitz to coordinate everything.

Prüfer's arrival was preceded by that of Heinrich Messing, who left Erfurt by train on January 4, arrived at Auschwitz at dawn the next day, and was immediately taken to crematorium II, where he worked for 10 hours setting up the forced-draft system for the chimney. Thereafter Messing worked, regularly and without resting, 11 hours a day every day of the week except Sunday (when he had to work for only eight hours). The three forced drafts for crematorium II were in place by January 26.[120] Yet the crematorium was still not complete: the compressed-air blowers, which controlled the speed of incineration, had not been installed. Messing began setting them up on January 26 and finished the job on February 7.

On January 29, work sites 30, 30a, 30b, and 30c were inspected by Bischoff, Kirschneck, and Prüfer. SS-Untersturmführer Kirschneck drew up a detailed report on the status of the work sites. Prüfer, taking his inspiration from Kirschneck's report, wrote up his own version, which was sent to Kammler. Although crematorium II was not operational, Prüfer declared it almost ready and promised it would be fully operational by February 15. Upon receiving the report, Kammler promoted Bischoff to the rank of SS-Sturmbannführer. In Kammler's letter of February 29, another leak occurred when he designated Leichenkeller 1 in crematorium II as a *"Vergasungskeller"* (gassing cellar).[121]

Bischoff, grateful to Prüfer for covering him with Kammler, rewarded the engineer with an order for four hot-air chambers to delouse personal effects in the "Zentral-Sauna" for the outrageous price of 39,122 RM. In so doing, he passed over an equivalent installation proposed by Kori for only 5,000 RM.[122] Furthermore, he ordered from Topf a furnace for burning refuse in crematorium III (5,791 RM),[123] a temporary elevator with 1,500 kg of portative force for crematorium III (968 RM), and two permanent elevators for crematoria II and III (9,371 RM each).[124]

The order for the elevators reflected Bischoff's failure to find them in Upper Silesia. Huta had been able to find only one second-hand goods elevator to connect the gas chambers to the furnace room. It was installed at the beginning of February in crematorium II. The task of finding a temporary elevator for crematorium III and permanent ones which would not break down under the expected heavy work load was given to Topf, as it was assumed that it would be easier to find them in Thuringia. Indeed, Prüfer quickly found what Bischoff needed. A firm in Erfurt, Gustav Linse, provided a goods elevator with 750 kg of portative power, which could be raised to 1,500 kg by doubling the cables (figure 23).

Prüfer also received an order for a new crematorium (VI), which was to be basically a pit for outdoor incineration (25,148 RM).[125] Thus Prüfer had been able to exploit his position and Bischoff's difficulties for a grand total of 90,000 RM (1992: $360,000) worth of contracts, not counting the extra labor costs.

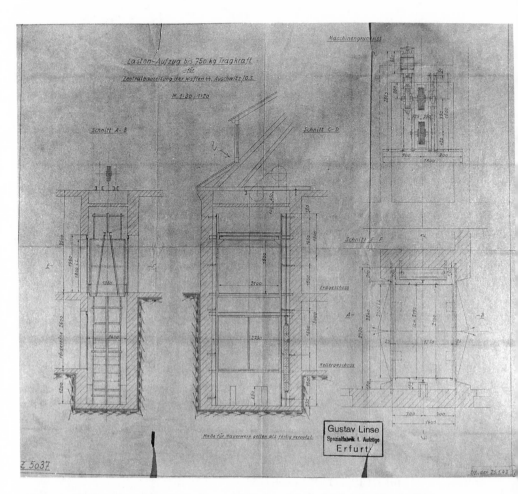

FIGURE 23. Drawing of goods elevator supplied to Auschwitz by the Gustav Linse firm of Erfurt and installed in crematorium III. Archives of the Auschwitz-Birkenau State Museum, file BW 37/4, no. 723.

At that point, Topf and the Zentralbauleitung were on such close terms that the latter asked Prüfer to come and spend two or three days a week supervising the work sites. Apparently Prüfer did not go along with this but instead sent Martin Holick and Arnold Seyffarth to Auschwitz in early February. Prüfer also promised to send a second master metalworker to finish the installation of the ventilation systems, but the man never arrived. Progress on the construction of the ventilation system for crematorium II had halted because of the failure of various subcontractors to honor their obligations. That led to a postponement of the installation of the aeration and deaeration systems for the gas chamber (morgue 1), originally planned for February 8. The missing parts finally arrived in Auschwitz on February 11. This three-day stoppage irritated Bischoff, and he complained to Kammler. He was particularly unhappy because Topf's last shipment did not include the motor for deaerating Leichenkeller 2.

Letters and telegrams exchanged on February 11 and 12 between the Zentralbauleitung and Topf mention a wooden blower for Leichenkeller 1.[126] This reference confirms the use of the morgue as a gas chamber: Bischoff and Prüfer thought that the extraction of air mixed with concentrated prussic acid (20 g per cu m) required a noncorroding ventilator (figure 24).

16123

FIGURE 24. Noncorroding wooden ventilator. From Bruno Eck, *Ventilatoren*, 3rd edition (Berlin: Springer-Verlag, 1957), p. 388; the first edition was published in 1937.

Other new elements of equipment needed for crematorium II were detectors for measuring traces of prussic acid. Prüfer's and Schultze's superiors at Topf and Sons, Sander and Erdmann, were informed of this singular request. Sander contacted several companies seeking the detectors. The Zentralbauleitung urged in a telegram of February 26 the immediate shipment of the gas detectors to Auschwitz, as the gas chamber could not be completed without them.[127]

Another point of concern was the power of the ventilation system in the gas chamber. It had been designed to provide high aeration and low deaeration, which fitted its use as a morgue. As a gas chamber, it should work the other way around. Sander and Prüfer wrote to the Zentralbauleitung on March 2 (see figure 25 for the German original):

> Re: Crematorium (II). We acknowledge receipt of your telegram stating: "Immediate shipment of 10 gas detectors as agreed. Estimate to be furnished later." Concerning this matter, we can tell you that for two weeks now we have been making inquiries of five different firms about the apparatus you want indicating the traces of prussic acid [*Anzeigegeräte für Blausaüre-Reste*]. We have received negative responses from 3 firms and we are still awaiting answers from the other 2. When we receive further information on this subject, we will let you know immediately so that we can put you in touch with the firm making this apparatus. Heil Hitler!

The Bauleitung received this letter, which amounts to another leak of the existence of a lethal gas chamber in crematorium II, on March 5.

Another last-minute problem arose because of defective arrangement of the three forced drafts around the smokestack. Transfer of heat from the smokestack to the ventilation system was to increase the temperature in all the rooms serviced by the system. Prüfer had pointed out this drawback on February 19 and had suggested channeling the excess heat to morgue 1—a suggestion that clearly reveals that the morgue, which must by definition remain cool, had become a gas chamber.[128] Heating the morgue would ensure more rapid diffusion of Zyklon B. The plan was immediately accepted by the SS, and on February 22, Topf sent to Auschwitz a cast-iron blower with an extractive power of 9,000 to 10,000 cu m an hour, priced at 522 RM (1992: $2,100).[129]

A relatively minor item that had not yet been made was a metal connecting pipe, in the shape of a trident, to be placed in the loft between the ceilings of the rooms with forced draft and the blower, which fed into the smokestack used to evacuate the gas from the gas chamber. A sliding damper in the smokestack allowed control of the flow of air. Closed and with activated blower, the flow of hot air would go to the gas chamber and

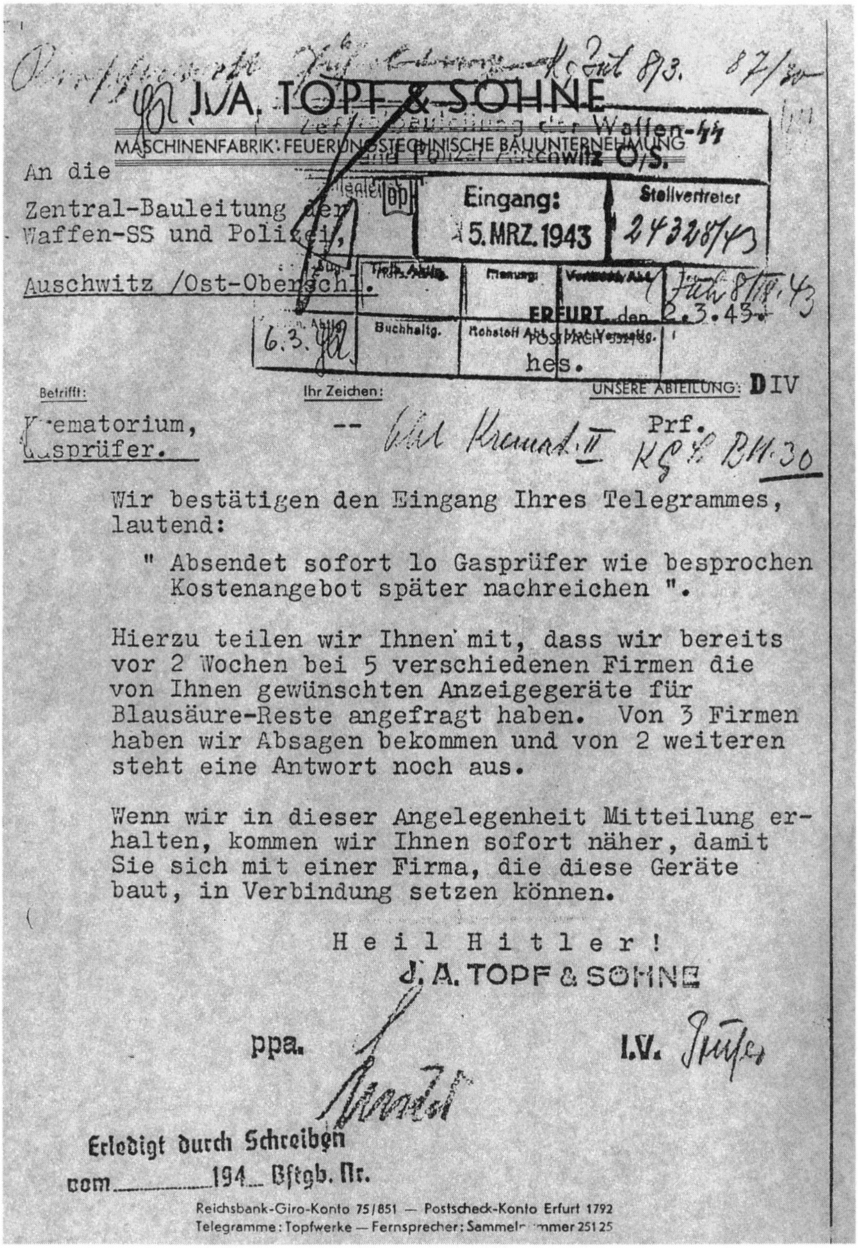

J.A. TOPF & SÖHNE
MASCHINENFABRIK · FEUERUNGSTECHNISCHE BAUUNTERNEHMUNG

An die
Zentral-Bauleitung der
Waffen-SS und Polizei,
Auschwitz /Ost-Oberschl.

Eingang: 5. MRZ. 1943

ERFURT, den 2.3.43
POSTFACH
hes.

Betrifft: Krematorium, Gasprüfer.

Ihr Zeichen: --

UNSERE ABTEILUNG: D IV
Prf.

Wir bestätigen den Eingang Ihres Telegrammes, lautend:

" Absendet sofort lo Gasprüfer wie besprochen Kostenangebot später nachreichen ".

Hierzu teilen wir Ihnen mit, dass wir bereits vor 2 Wochen bei 5 verschiedenen Firmen die von Ihnen gewünschten Anzeigegeräte für Blausäure-Reste angefragt haben. Von 3 Firmen haben wir Absagen bekommen und von 2 weiteren steht eine Antwort noch aus.

Wenn wir in dieser Angelegenheit Mitteilung erhalten, kommen wir Ihnen sofort näher, damit Sie sich mit einer Firma, die diese Geräte baut, in Verbindung setzen können.

Heil Hitler!
J. A. TOPF & SÖHNE

ppa. I.V.

Erledigt durch Schreiben
vom ________ 194__ Bstgb. Nr.

Reichsbank-Giro-Konto 75/851 — Postscheck-Konto Erfurt 1792
Telegramme: Topfwerke — Fernsprecher: Sammelnummer 25125

FIGURE 25. Letter from Sander and Prufer of Topf and Sons to Zentralbauleitung, dated March 2, 1943, concerning ventilation system for the gas chamber in crematorium II, under construction in Birkenau. See text for English translation. Central State Special Archives, Moscow, file 502-1-313.

preheat it. Open, it would allow for the extraction of the toxic gas. The order for the connecting pipe was officially approved on March 6 at a price of 1,070 RM. It was to be manufactured within the week.

Schultze went to Auschwitz on March 1, and Prüfer joined him on March 4.[130] That day the five triple-muffle furnaces in crematorium II were tried out for the first time in the presence of Prüfer, Schultze, SS men from the Bauleitung and the Political Department, and high-ranking SS men from Berlin. For this purpose, fifty corpses of overweight men had been selected in bunker 2 and transported to crematorium II, where they were put into the furnaces. The incineration lasted, according to the rough estimate of Henryk Tauber, a stoker from the Sonderkommando, 45 minutes. The officials, who timed the incineration with watches in hand, noted that it took longer than planned. After this trial, Prüfer judged that the furnaces were not dry enough and recommended that they be heated for a week without being used.[131]

On March 10, Schultze and Messing tested the aeration and deaeration systems of the gas chamber in crematorium II. Apparently the installation was still not quite right, because Messing continued to work on it on March 11 and 13.[132] Then, on the evening of Saturday, March 13, the ventilation system was declared operational.

That same night, 1,492 women, children, and old people, selected from a convoy of 2,000 Jews from the Krakow ghetto, were killed in the new crematorium.[133] Six kilos of Zyklon B were poured into the stacks that opened into the four grillework columns implanted between the pillars that supported the ceiling.[134] Within five minutes, all the victims had succumbed. The aeration (8,000 cu m an hour) and the deaeration system (same strength) were then started up and, after 15 to 20 minutes, the atmosphere, which had been practically renewed every three to four minutes, was sufficiently pure so that members of the Sonderkommando could enter the stiflingly hot gas chamber. During this first gassing, the Sonderkommandos wore gas masks as a precaution. The bodies were untangled and dragged to the goods elevator. Hair was clipped, gold teeth pulled out, wedding rings and jewels removed. Once hoisted into the furnace hall, the bodies were dragged onto a broad moistened gutter right in front of the muffles and pushed into the furnaces. Incineration of the 1,492 "pieces" lasted for two days.

Although the gas chambers of crematorium II had been put into operation, it was not yet completed. After liquidation of the Jews from Krakow, crematorium II remained inactive until March 20, when 2,191 Greek Jews from Salonika were gassed.[135] As their bodies were being incinerated, a fire broke out on the level of the forced drafts, which had overheated. Prüfer and Schultze, hurriedly summoned to the scene, surveyed the damage on March 24. On March 25, they decided to remove the forced draft and thus abandoned the possibility of preheating the gas chamber. They also decided to replace the wooden blower for the deaeration system of the gas chamber with a metal one, as the danger of corrosion had been exaggerated.[136] Through March, Messing continued to work on the ventilation system of the undressing rooms, which was not finished until March 31. That day the undressing barrack was pulled down, and the future victims entered the undressing room by a stairway opened up at its western end.

Crematorium II was finally delivered on March 31 at a cost of 554,500 RM (1992: $2,215,000).[137] The memorandum acknowledging receipt of the building indicated that morgue 1 was equipped with a gas-tight door, four "wire netting inserting devices" (*Drahtnetzeinschiebvorrichtung*, i.e., grillework columns for pouring Zyklon B into the gas chamber), and four "wooden lids" (*Holzblenden*). The deaeration system of morgue 2, which was of no interest once it became an undressing room, was not equipped with a motor. Hence the system was useless.

In early April, crematorium II functioned without any problems. One day, however, it was noticed that the sliding dampers were malfunctioning. A more thorough investigation revealed that the internal lining was collapsing and that the underground connecting flues were not in much better shape. The Zentralbauleitung telephoned Prüfer and asked him what to do. The engineer promised to send new blueprints for the smokestack and went off on a business trip to the Rhineland, as he felt that it was not really Topf's problem: his firm had not built the smokestack. When the blueprints failed to arrive, the Bauleitung sent telegram after telegram to demand them. It also requested a study of whether heat released by the refuse furnace in crematorium III could be used to warm the water for 100 showers. On April 15, Prüfer returned to Erfurt and promised to leave for Auschwitz two days later. He got there on April 19,[138] calmed down the SS, promised blueprints for a new smokestack, and noted with feigned sadness that the guarantee of crematorium IV's furnace had expired and that he could no longer repair a furnace built with second-class materials. He nonetheless estimated that its gas chambers were still usable, provided they were ventilated mechanically; he pocketed an order for two deaeration systems for crematoria IV and V, amounting to 2,510 RM,[139] and returned to Erfurt on April 20.

Crematorium II was stopped on May 22 or 23, and the Köhler company began to clear away the rubbish from the smokestack. This job was completed on May 29,[140] yet Köhler could not begin the repairs because Prüfer's blueprints still had not arrived. They did not arrive until a month later, at the end of a bittersweet correspondence between the Zentralbauleitung, Topf, and Köhler, in which each side cast blame on the other for the damages and delays.

The delays in the completion of crematorium II in March had made crematorium IV the first to be officially handed over to the camp administration, on March 22. It had cost 203,000 RM (1992: $810,000).[141] Again there are leaks that inform us about the use of the building. On February 28, an overseer from Riedel and Son, whose crew was finishing the interior of the west section, had to put in "windows" of solid wood with the chinks filled up. In his daily report, he wrote, "Putting in gas-tight windows." On March 2, when he had to asphalt the ground of the area where the gas-tight windows had been put in, he wrote at the end of the day: "Ground to be asphalted in gas chamber."[142]

The first gassing in crematorium IV did not go well. An SS man, wearing a face mask, had to climb a little ladder to get to a "window," then open it with one hand and pour in the Zyklon B with the other. This acrobatic routine had to be repeated six times. When the gas-tight doors were opened to evacuate the gas, it was noticed that the natural aeration was ineffective; a door had to be cut immediately into the north corridor to get an air current flowing.[143]

The double four-muffle furnace in crematorium IV functioned well for only a short time. It soon began to show problems because Prüfer, in his haste to lower its price, had oversimplified it. After only two weeks of intensive operation, the furnace split open. Koch filled in the cracks with fireproof rammed earth, but they reappeared. By mid-May the furnace was again out of service, and crematorium IV ceased to be used, once and for all.

Prüfer blamed the mediocre quality of the materials, yet he knew that he himself was responsible. In fact, Prüfer had known that the furnace was going to produce problems for more than a month before its inauguration. In February, Prüfer had been informed that the Mogilev prototype had developed cracks due to the overly centralized structure of the furnace. In the component unit of this model furnace, two muffles and a generator (figure 26), the muffle (M1) between the generator and the central duct for evacuating smoke got considerably hotter than the other muffle (M2), which was farther away from the generator. The thermal distortion gave rise to tensions in the fireclay, which eventually broke and split open.

Unable to do anything about the furnace in crematorium IV, Prüfer decided to modify the furnace in crematorium V. He redesigned its structure, regrouping the muffles and surrounding them with two ducts placed around the edge (figure 27). This new arrangement "thickened" and "reinforced" the furnace.[144] But Prüfer was unable to remedy the principal cause of the cracks, the lateral generator. Crematorium V was delivered on April 4, although the gas-tight doors of its gas chambers were not put in until April 16–17.[145]

Work progressed in the meantime on crematorium III. At the beginning of May, Messing fitted its gas chamber. There was great urgency to complete it, as the incinerating capacity of the concentration camp had plum-

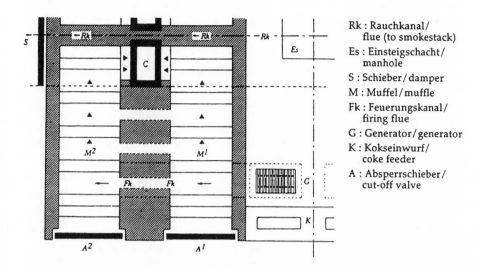

Rk : Rauchkanal/
flue (to smokestack)

Es : Einsteigschacht/
manhole

S : Schieber/damper

M : Muffel/muffle

Fk : Feuerungskanal/
firing flue

G : Generator/generator

K : Kokseinwurf/
coke feeder

A : Absperrschieber/
cut-off valve

FIGURE 26. Diagram of a component unit of the eight-muffle furnace, initial type, for crematorium IV at Birkenau. C—central duct for evacuating smoke, connecting the two muffles to the underground smoke flue.

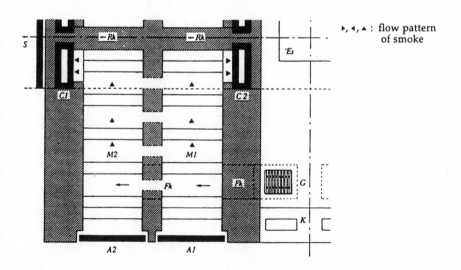

▶, ◀, ▲ : flow pattern
of smoke

FIGURE 27. Diagram of component unit of the eight-muffle furnace, reinforced type, for crematorium V at Birkenau. C1 and C2 are peripheral ducts for evacuating smoke, linking the two muffles to the underground smoke flue.

meted drastically with crematorium IV out of service and II stopped. Only crematorium I in the main camp and V, which had a fragile furnace that might quit at any moment if pressed too hard, were in operation. Crematorium III was finally delivered on June 24.[146] The detailed invoice mentions that its morgue 1 contained a gas-tight door and 14 (false) showers, two features incompatible with its function as a morgue.[147] As in crematorium II, no motor was put in for deaerating morgue 2 (the undressing room, labeled as such twice by Messing).

Within a week, crematorium II had been brought back into operation, and the Zentralbauleitung submitted a report to the WVHA showing the camp's daily incinerating output, calculated by taking as a "unit" 70 to 100 kg of animal remains. There seems to be a large discrepancy between these official figures and the potential output: 340 kg versus 250 kg for crematorium I; 1,400 kg versus 1,000 kg for crematoria II and III; and 768 kg versus 500 kg for crematoria IV and V. (Real output, of course, was considerably less, since all the crematoria were not in use.) Nevertheless the figures were valid in a way: the time it took to incinerate two children weighing 10 kg each and a woman weighing 50 kg was equal to that for a man weighing 70 kg. This introduces a multiplying factor varying from one to three and makes all the statistics of crematorium output a matter of chance. The estimated yield of crematoria IV and V had been calculated on the basis of crematorium II, assuming that each muffle had the same capacity as one in crematoria II and III.

But the estimate was more than optimistic. At the end of June, crematorium IV was out of service and crematorium II was stopped. At the end of July, crematorium I was neutralized at the request of the Political Department. As for crematorium V, it would not be used after September because crematoria II (repaired) and III would thereafter suffice to "treat" the daily flow of convoys of Jews.

The Köhler company began on June 22 the overhaul of the internal fixtures of the smokestack in crematorium II. The work lasted a month.[148] Then the Zentralbauleitung asked Topf to repair the underground smoke ducts, which were still under warranty. The Zentralbauleitung installed new dampers, built by the metalwork shop of the DAW. This work continued until the end of August. After three months of stoppage, crematorium II was started up again in September.

Who would pay for the extra expenses remained unresolved. The question was debated on September 10 and 11. The Zentralbauleitung considered Topf responsible for the damage, wrongly believing that the 1,769.36 RM paid for the study of the crematorium with two simplified triple-muffle furnaces (a project thrust aside by Kammler in 1942) represented the price of the blueprints and statistical calculations done for Köhler's smokestack for crematorium II. Topf accused Köhler of having used inadequate materials, which Köhler vehemently denied. Topf had supplied Köhler with the blueprints for new fittings; yet, as Topf had not been able to monitor the proper execution of its plans, it considered itself free of all responsibility. Only Köhler had the courage to raise the real issue: that the damage to the smokestack had been caused by overuse of crematorium II. Since no one could agree, the Zentralbauleitung divided the expenses incurred into three parts, which came to 4,863.90 RM, and each side had to pay a share of 1,621.90 RM.[149]

Relations between Topf and the Zentralbauleitung sharply deteriorated after September. Both parties felt uncomfortable with the other. The Bauleitung criticized Topf for the failure of the furnace in crematorium IV and for the trouble with the smokestack of crematorium II, and Topf was beginning to realize what a quagmire it had gotten into. As the military situation of the Axis was getting very shaky, certain Topf officials began to consider what the future of the firm might be after an Allied victory. They realized that the outlook was bleak.

Above all, Topf realized that working with the SS had been no sinecure. First of all, the SS had picked over the smallest bill. Then it had paid slowly. On August 20, 1943, the Zentralbauleitung owed Topf almost 90,000 RM.[150] Dozens of follow-up letters were sometimes necessary before the company could get what it was owed. Finally, the SS had been capricious and inconsistent, making Topf wrack its brains for days on end over a project that the SS would then abandon without explanation, such as, for example, crematorium VI, which never saw the light of day, and the preheating of morgue 1 in crematoria II and III, and the 100 showers in crematorium III, which never got past the drawing board. Or else it ordered installations that, once built, it had no further need of, such as the ventilation system in crematorium I.

The last chapter in relations between Topf and Auschwitz occurred in 1944. Planning the imminent arrival of Hungarian Jews, the new head of the Bauleitung, SS-Obersturmführer Werner Jothann, wanted to ensure that crematoria II and III were in top order; he also hoped to reactivate crematoria IV and V, which had not been used since September 1943. He asked Topf to install permanent elevators in crematoria II and III and to set up deaeration systems for the gas chambers in crematoria IV and V to allow for massive gassings. After enormous difficulties and direct intervention from the WVHA with the Reich Ministry for Arms and Munitions, the two elevators were delivered to Auschwitz in May 1944.[151] But time was running out to set them up. Installation of the deaeration system in crematorium V, the parts of which had been in the warehouse since January, was done in May.[152] For the two gas chambers and the corridor, which represented a volume of 480 cu m, almost equal to that of morgue 1 in both crematoria II and III,

Schultze had planned a deaeration system of the same power: a number 450 blower with a 3.5-hp motor extracting 8,000 cu m an hour (figure 28).[153] A second ventilation system was not set up.

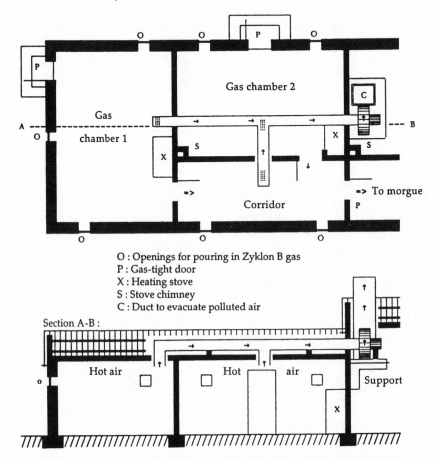

FIGURE 28. Diagram of air extraction system of the gas chambers of crematorium V at Birkenau, designed by Karl Schultze in June 1943 and set up in May 1944. Layout above, section view below. Blowoff: 8,000 cu m an hour; 3.5-hp motor.

The massacre of Hungarian Jews in May and June 1944 was carried out principally in crematoria II, III, and V. The furnace of crematorium V was rapidly overwhelmed, and pits were dug alongside its gas chambers to incinerate the victims in the open air. Also, bunker 2 was reactivated for the occasion to handle small groups, whose bodies were burned in an incineration pit measuring 30 sq m.[154] Toward the end of the summer, when Zyklon B began to run short, victims were flung headlong into the burning pits of crematorium V and bunker 2.

As thousands of women, children, and old people disappeared into the flames, the Zentralbauleitung and Topf were settling their accounts. The Zentralbauleitung had paid practically all its outstanding bills during the last trimester of 1943 and at the beginning of February 1944. But it wanted Topf to pay for the jobs it had commissioned the metalwork shop of the DAW to do and for various little things that Topf needed on the work sites and that the Zentralbauleitung had procured. For example, the cost of a cylinder of oxygen, lent for two months, amounted to 2.10 RM; borrowed motor oil came to 8.25 RM. Topf challenged these bills, which totaled 9,000 RM. The total then was reduced to 7,500.

The touchiest question remained the matter of the two eight-muffle furnaces. The Bauleitung of Russland-Mitte had ordered the four furnaces for Mogilev from Topf for 55,520 RM and had paid, in two installments, a total of 42,600 RM. The Auschwitz Zentralbauleitung had ordered two furnaces for 27,600 RM and had paid one installment of 10,000 RM. Topf believed that it had sold six furnaces at 13,800 RM apiece, while the two furnaces at Birkenau had been subtracted from the delivery to Mogilev. The two Bauleitungen owed Topf a balance not of 30,200 RM (for six furnaces) but of 2,600 RM (for four furnaces), which the Auschwitz Bauleitung agreed to take care of. In reality, Topf had built in toto two furnaces in Birkenau and half of one in Mogilev, or 34,500 RM worth, and ought to have returned 18,000 RM that it had unfairly pocketed. By accepting a supplementary credit of 2,600 RM, it made a nice 20,700 RM (1992: $83,000) profit on that operation, which compensated for its disputes with the Auschwitz SS.[155] The dupe in this farce was the Bauleitung of Russland-Mitte.

On October 7, 1944, members of the Sonderkommando at Birkenau revolted. Crematorium IV, where most of them were lodged, was set on fire. The insurrection was put down violently by the SS. The building was then torn down, and the metal elements from the stoves were retrieved and stored in the Bauhof.[156]

At the end of November, on a verbal order from Himmler, the gassings were halted. A demolition commando, formed at the beginning of December, then dismantled crematoria II and III. Crematorium V continued to be used, but henceforth in a "normal" fashion, for the incineration of persons who died "naturally."

By mid-January 1945, nothing was left of crematoria II and III but their asphalted carcasses. The camp complex was evacuated on January 18. At noon on January 20, the SS blew up the resistant structures of crematoria II and III. Crematorium V, still intact, was dynamited at 1:00 A.M. on January 22, and on January 27, Soviet soldiers arrived at the snow-covered rubble of the four structures.

The United States Third Army liberated Buchenwald less than three months later, on April 11. On the 12th, Eisenhower visited that camp. The two triple-muffle furnaces of the Buchenwald crematorium ensured Topf's immediate celebrity. The Third Reich surrendered on May 8. On May 30, after a botched investigation, the U.S. Military Police arrested Prüfer.[157] Ludwig Topf committed suicide on the night of May 30-31[158]—needlessly, as it turned out, since on June 13, Prüfer was set free, even managing to come away with an order for a furnace from the Americans. The U.S. investigators, failing to search the company's home offices, did not understand Topf's role in setting up the gas chambers at Auschwitz.

From June 14 to 21, Ernst-Wolfgang Topf and Prüfer apparently destroyed all the contracts the firm had signed with the SS at Auschwitz.[159] As the U.S. army was withdrawing from Erfurt, which was to be part of the Soviet zone, the younger Topf brother moved west with the Americans on June 21, carrying no wealth with him other than technical and industrial documents.[160]

On July 3, the Soviets occupied Erfurt. On October 11, Gustav Braun, Topf's director of development, was questioned by the Soviet military about Prüfer and the Topf brothers.[161] On March 4, 1946, the Soviets arrested Braun (who had become temporary director), Sander, Prüfer, and Schultze.[162] Erdmann escaped internment because he was registered in a communist union.[163] Braun was condemned to 25 years in the Gulag but was freed in 1955.[164] The fate of Prüfer is unknown, but he and the other two engineers probably met the same fate as Braun. Unlike the Americans, the Soviets immediately discerned Prüfer's role in the construction of Auschwitz.[165]

Ernst-Wolfgang Topf tried to rebuild his company in Wiesbaden in 1949, but his financial means were reduced, the attempt fell short, and the Wiesbaden branch was dissolved in 1963.[166] He was never troubled by the law, despite the blunder of his only engineer, Martin Klettner, who in 1950 shamelessly submitted a patent application for an incinerating furnace. That naturally caused a stir, and was the inspiration for the play *Patent Pending* by Wim van Leer, produced in London in 1963.[167]

Bischoff led a quiet postwar life and died in 1950. Only two members of the Zentralbauleitung, Walter Dejaco and Fritz Ertl, went before a tribunal. Dejaco had personally monitored all the blueprints as head of the blueprint section. Ertl was indicted because he had presided over the infamous meeting with Prüfer and Köhler at Auschwitz on August 19, 1942, when Bischoff was in Berlin, and had countersigned a few blueprints for the new crematorium. The trial of the two "architects of the crematoria" in Vienna in January 1972 ended with the release of both.

NOTES

The following archives were used in the preparation of this study: Central State Special Archives of Russia (Moscow); October Revolution Archives (Moscow/October Revolution); State Archives Weimar (Weimar); State Archives Katowice (Katowice); Archive of the Memorial Buchenwald (Buchenwald); Archive of the Memorial Place Dachau (Dachau); Archive Auschwitz-Birkenau State Museum (Oswiecim); Archive Yad Vashem, Jerusalem (Jerusalem); Berlin Document Center (Berlin); Federal Archives Koblenz (Koblenz); Chamber of Commerce and Industry, Wiesbaden (Wiesbaden); Centre de Documentation Juive Contemporaine, Paris (Paris); Central Committee for the Investigation of Hitlerite Crimes in Poland, Warsaw (Warsaw); National Institute for Industrial Protection, Compiegne (Compiegne); Landesgericht für Strafsachen, Vienna (Vienna).

1. Jean-Claude Pressac, *Auschwitz: Technique and Operation of the Gas Chambers,* trans. Peter Moss (New York, 1989).

2. Compiegne, 24d/1/506,627.

3. Weimar, dossier Prüfer 2/555a, letter of Topf to Leisse, April 14, 1936.

4. Dachau, files 943 and 2111.

5. Koblenz, letter Topf November 1, 1940. NS 4 Ma/54.

6. Weimar, 2/555a, order 39/D/1218.

7. Koblenz, letter June 18, 1939. NS 3/18–3.

8. Paris, CXXXVIII-129; Koblenz, NS 3/18–3.

9. Weimar, 2/555a, order 40/D/263 and 264.

10. Weimar, 2/555a, letter Topf to Prüfer April 13, 1933.

11. Koblenz, letter Topf July 25, 1940. NS 4 Ma/54.

12. Moscow, 502–1–327. Letter Topf May 31 and June 11, 1940.

13. Weimar, 2/555a, order 40/D/664 and 665.

14. Moscow, 502–1–214, weekly reports of July 5, 12, 20, 26, and August 17, 1940; Moscow, 502–1–327, letters Topf May 31 and June 11, 1940, and letter Bauleitung September 16, 1940; Koblenz, NS 4 Ma/54, letter Topf January 6, 1941.

15. Weimar, LK 6451, letter Topf July 14, 1941.

16. Moscow, 502–1–327, letters Topf September 18, 23, and 30, 1940.

17. Koblenz, NS 4 Ma/54, letter Bauleitung Mauthausen, July 5, 1940.

18. Koblenz, NS 4 Ma/54, letters Topf November 1 and 11, 1940; Weimar, 2/555a, order 41/D/80.

19. Moscow, 502–1–312, letter Bauleitung Auschwitz November 7, 1940; Koblenz, NS 4 Ma/54, letter Topf November 23, 1940.

20. Koblenz, NS 4 Ma/54, letter Bauleitung Mauthausen, May 8, 1941.

21. Koblenz, NS 4 Ma/54, summary of work of Willing from December 26, 1940, to January 1, 1941.

22. Koblenz NS 4 Ma/54, note by Willing to Dachau.

23. Koblenz, NS 4 Ma/54, bill Topf February 5, 1941.

24. Koblenz, NS 4 Ma/54, letter Topf November 1, 1940.

25. Moscow, 502–1–327, letter Topf November 13, 1940.

26. Moscow, 502–1–312, plan Topf D 57.999 November 30, 1940.

27. Moscow, 502–1–312, letter Topf December 9, 1940.

28. Moscow, 502–1–327, letter Bauleitung January 21, 1941.

29. Moscow, 502–1–312, telegram Bauleitung January 13, 1941; 502–1–327, letter Bauleitung January 21, 1941.

30. Moscow, 502–1–214, weekly reports of Schlachter February 1, 10, 17 and 22, 1941.

31. Moscow, 502–1–214, weekly reports of Schlachter October 4, 14, and 28, 1940, which mention Boos; 502–1–214, weekly report Schlachter, March 1, 1941.

32. Statement of Broad published in *Auschwitz in den Augen der SS* (Katowice, 1981).

33. Moscow, 502–1–312, letter Topf February 3, 1941.

34. Moscow, 502–1–312, letter Bauleitung February 15, 1941.

35. Moscow, 502–1–327, letter Topf February 24, 1941.

36. Moscow, 502–1–327, letter Bauleitung March 15, 1941, and letter Topf February 24, 1941.

37. Katowice, Pl Go/S, 467.

38. Moscow, 502–1–312, letter and telegram Bauleitung April 2, 1941; letter Topf April 2, 1941.

39. Moscow, 502–1–312, letter Grabner June 7, 1941.

40. Moscow, 502–1–214, weekly report of June 28, 1941.

41. Koblenz, NS 4 Ma/54, letters of August 18, 21, 25, 28 and September 4, 1941.

42. Moscow, 502–1–312, telegram Bauleitung September 16, 1941; 502–2–23, letter Topf September 25, 1941; Oswiecim, negatives 20818/1 and 21033/1 of plan D 59.042 of September 25, 1941.

43. Koblenz, NS 4 Ma/54, correspondence between Bauleitung Mauthausen and Topf between September 24, 1941, and August 28, 1943.

44. Berlin, SSO, autobiography Karl Bischoff.

45. Oswiecim, BW 2/1 (old), negative 21135/1.

46. Moscow, 502–1–313, telegram Bauleitung October 11, 1941.

47. Moscow, 502–1–313, letter Topf October 14, 1941.

48. Oswiecim, negative 20931/4, plan of the main camp at Auschwitz, February 19, 1942.

49. Oswiecim, negative 1034/7.

50. Moscow, 502–1–313 and Oswiecim, BW 30/27 and BW 30/34.

51. Moscow, 502–1–312, letter Topf October 31, 1941.

52. Moscow, 502–1–313, letter Topf November 4, 1941.

53. Moscow, 502–1–327, bill Topf January 27, 1943.

54. Moscow, 502–1–327, letter Topf November 4, 1941.

55. Moscow, 502–1–314, letter Bischoff November 12, 1941, letter Prüfer November 21, 1941, and undated telegram.

56. Moscow, 502–1–314, letter Prüfer November 21, 1941; 502–1–327, letter Wirtz December 4, 1941.

57. Moscow, 502–1–313, letter Topf August 31, 1942.

58. Moscow, 502–1–314, letter SS Bauinspektion June 24, 1943; 502–1–327, letter Bauleitung July 2, 1943, letter Topf July 7, 1943.

59. Oswiecim, BW 11/1, letter Bauleitung January 5, 1942; letter Topf January 9, 1942; Moscow, 502–1–312, letter Topf November 24, 1941, letters Bauleitung November 27, 1941, December 8, 1941, January 5, 1942.

60. Degesch, *Zyklon for Pest Control* (Frankfurt am Main, 1972).

61. Moscow, 502–1–214, weekly report of July 12, 1940.

62. I reject Danuta Czech's dating of the first gassing in September 1941 in favor of one based on Jan Sehn's statement that the first gassing of Soviet prisoners took place after the month-long visit of a Gestapo team in November 1941. Sehn's

account seems reliable, especially as he describes how the basement of block 11 needed two days of ventilation before it could be entered. See Danuta Czech, *Kalendarium der Ereignisse im Konzentrationslager Auschwitz-Birkenau 1939–1945* (Reinbek bei Hamburg, 1989), 117 and 119; Jan Sehn, *Concentration Camp Oswiecim-Brzezinka* (Warsaw, 1957), p. 105.

63. Moscow, 502–1–312, letter Grabner January 31, 1942.

64. Warsaw, photo taken by Stanislav Luczko, no. 5149.

65. Oswiecim, BW 30/1 to BW 30/7 (plans 932–38 and 980).

66. Oswiecim, plan 933.

67. Moscow, 502–1–313 and Oswiecim, BW 30/34, 31ff.

68. Oswiecim, BW 30/25, 1.

69. Moscow, 502–1–313, 314, letter Bauleitung March 39, 1942; Oswiecim, BW 30/34, 115.

70. Moscow, 502–1–312, letter Bauleitung April 2, 1942; Oswiecim, BW 11/1, 12.

71. Moscow, 502–1–312, letter Topf May 8, 1942.

72. Moscow, 502–1–312, bill of lading, April 16, 1942.

73. Moscow, 502–1–312, letter Topf June 6, 1942.

74. Weimar, 2/555a, letter Prüfer November 15, 1942.

75. Moscow, 502–1–312 and 313, report by Pollock May 30, 1942, telegram Kammler June 2, 1942.

76. Moscow, 502–1–312, letter Robert Köhler June 5, 1942.

77. Moscow, 502–1–312, telegram Kirschneck June 5, 1942, telegram Topf June 6, 1942; 502–2–146, plan Topf D. 59,463.

78. Oswiecim, box BW 1/2, file BW 1/16, 172, box BW 1/6, file BW 1/31, 1–4.

79. Moscow, 502–1–322; G. Peters and E. Wuestinger, "Entlausung mit Zyklon-Blausaeure in Kreislauf-Begasungskamern," in *Zeitschrift für hygienische Zoologie und schaedlingsbekaempfung,* 10–11 (1940).

80. Moscow, 502–1–331, plans Boos 16.591 and 16.600.

81. Moscow, 502–1–322, report Dienstelle Arbeitseinsatz, July 2, 1942; letter public health office Bielitz, July 3, 1942.

82. Moscow, 502–4–2 to 502–4–47, the 46 death books of Auschwitz.

83. Czech, pp. 250f.

84. Pressac, p. 188.

85. Rudolf Höss, *Death Dealer: The Memoir of the SS Kommandant at Auschwitz,* ed. Steven Paskuly, trans. Andrew Pollinger (Buffalo, N.Y., 1992), p. 32.

86. Moscow, 502–1–313, bill of lading June 18, 1942; 502–1–327, bill of lading August 6, 1942.

87. Moscow/October Revolution, 7021–108–32, 45–7, letter Bauleitung October 13, 1942.

88. Oswiecim, BW 30/30, 23; BW 30/26, 22.

89. Moscow/October Revolution, 7021–108–32, 46.

90. Weimar, 2/555a, contracts 41 D 2435 (27,600 RM), 42/1422/3 (3,258 RM), 42/1454/1 (53,702 RM).

91. Oswiecim, BW 30b–30c/22.

92. Moscow, 502–1–313.

93. Moscow, 502–1–313 and Oswiecim, BW 30/27, which include Ertl's minutes of the meeting.

94. Ibid.

95. Jerusalem, TR 10/1119 (vol. 8a). Vienna, 20 Vr 3806/64, ON 484, Ertl's in-

terrogation of January 21, 1972, concerning the minutes of the meeting of August 19 and 20.

96. Moscow, 502–1–313, letter Bischoff October 9, 1942.

97. Moscow, 502–1–312, letter Bauleitung September 15; 502–1–313, letter Topf September 22, 1942.

98. Moscow, 502–1–313, bill of lading September 8, 1942.

99. Moscow, 502–1–313, telegram and letter Topf October 27, 1942.

100. Moscow, 502–1–313, estimate Topf November 16, 1942.

101. Johann Paul Kremer, *KL Auschwitz as Seen by the SS* (Oswiecim, Panstwowe Muzeum), pp. 104, 218.

102. Moscow, 502–1–327, bill Topf May 27, 1943.

103. Oswiecim, BW 30/27, 17.

104. Oswiecim, BW 30/34, 96.

105. Moscow, note by Wolter November 27, 1942.

106. Oswiecim, BW 1/19.

107. Oswiecim, BW 30/12.

108. See Pressac, pp. 481ff.

109. Oswiecim, BW 30b–30c/22.

110. Oswiecim, BW 30b–30c/24.

111. Oswiecim, BW 30b–30c/23.

112. Moscow, 502–1–322, letter city councillor of Bielitz November 17, 1942.

113. Moscow, 502–1–322, letters Wirths December 4 and December 15, 1942.

114. Oswiecim, BW 30/37, 86.

115. Moscow, 502–1–322, letter Bischoff December 18, 1942.

116. Oswiecim, BW 30/27, 17.

117. Moscow, 502–1–313, letter Kammler January 11, 1943.

118. Moscow, 502–1–313, letter Bischoff January 23, 1943.

119. Oswiecim, BW 30/30, 6 and Moscow, 502–1–313, letter Mulka January 29, 1943.

120. See Pressac, p. 370.

121. Oswiecim, BW 30/34, 100–106; Moscow/October Revolution, 7021–108–32, 51ff.

122. Moscow, 502–2–27, estimate Topf February 5, 1943; 502–1–332, letter Kori February 2, 1943.

123. Moscow, 502–1–327, bill Topf August 23, 1943.

124. Moscow, 502–1–327, reminder notice Topf April 16, 1943.

125. Reimund Schnabel, *Macht ohne Moral* (Frankfurt am Main, 1957), p. 351. The location of the original order is not known.

126. Oswiecim, BW 30/34, 84; BW 30/27, 29.

127. Oswiecim, BW 30/34, 48.

128. Oswiecim, BW 30/25, 7.

129. Moscow, 502–1–311, bill Topf May 24, 1943.

130. Oswiecim, BW 30/34, 55.

131. See Pressac, pp. 481ff.

132. Oswiecim, BW 30/41, 28.

133. Czech, p. 440.

134. Moscow, 502–2–54, 8.

135. Czech, p. 445.

136. Oswiecim, BW 30/25, 8.

137. Moscow, 502–2–54, transfer March 31, 1943; 502–1–281, letter WVHA June 23, 1944.

138. That day Prüfer signed for a blueprint made in the Zentralbauleitung.

139. Moscow, 502–2–26, letter Topf June 9, 1943.

140. Moscow, 502–2–26, letter Topf June 9, 1943; 502–1–313, letter Köhler May 21, 1943.

141. Moscow, 502–2–54, transfer agreement March 19/22, 1943; 502–1–281, letter WVHA June 24, 1944; also Oswiecim, BW 30/43, 31f.

142. Oswiecim, BW 30/28, 73, 68.

143. *Auschwitz Album* (New York, 1980), photo 112.

144. Deduction based on the roughly 50 cm difference in spacing between the axes of the two crucibles of the basic element of the eight-muffle furnace placed in crematoria IV and V. The measurements were taken from the remains of the furnace in the ruins of crematorium V in Birkenau, and from photo Oswiecim negative 888.

145. Oswiecim, BW 30/25, 14; BW 30/26, 27.

146. Moscow, 502–2–54, transfer June 24, 1943.

147. Moscow, 502–2–54, 87.

148. Oswiecim, BW 30/34, 17.

149. Oswiecim, BW 30/25, 11f.

150. Moscow, 502–1–313, letter Topf August 20, 1943.

151. Oswiecim, BW 30/34, 18; Moscow, 502–1–313 telegram Bauleitung May 12, 1944; 502–1–327, letter Betzinger June 15, 1944.

152. Moscow, 502–1–327, letter Betzinger June 13, 1944.

153. Moscow, 502–1–327, bill Topf December 23, 1943.

154. Moscow/October Revolution, Russian plan of bunker 2, scale 1:1000 of March 3, 1945.

155. Moscow, 502–1–314, letter Bauleitung Russland-Mitte June 2, 1943, notes Jährling January 31, February 21, 1944.

156. Oswiecim, photo negative 888.

157. Weimar, 2/555a, note June 18, 1945.

158. Weimar, 211, 3; LK 4651, letter February 7, 1946.

159. Study of the personnel file of Prüfer shows that it lacks all contracts negotiated after March 1941.

160. Buchenwald, 64–0–2, letter Topf September 25, 1945; Wiesbaden, dossier Topf, letter January 6, 1948.

161. Weimar, 2/555, report Gustav Braun October 11, 1945.

162. Weimar, 2/555 (Prüfer) and 2/381 (Braun), notes of April 26, 1946 of Machemehl, secretary of the firm.

163. Weimar, 2/938 and 2/938a, personnel file Erdmann.

164. Moscow, internment file 236334, Braun.

165. Cf. Pravda, no. 109, May 7, 1945; French translation in *Forfaits hitleriens* (Geneva and Paris, 1945), p. 309.

166. Wiesbaden, dossier Topf, ordinance of March 19, 1963.

167. Compiegne, German patent, 24/d/1, no. 861.731.

9

The Plunder of Victims and Their Corpses

ANDRZEJ STRZELECKI

The widely reported systematic plunder of victims in concentration camps is often cited as evidence of particular Nazi cruelty. Clothes, money, food, medicine, gold teeth, even hair were taken from the victims and recycled for use by Germans. The gathering of these properties also posed a significant temptation for members of the Schutzstaffel (SS) to violate their discipline and avail themselves of the loot. Few scholars have considered the decision to plunder the victims in terms of its psychological functions, its economic implications, or the far-reaching ramifications for our understanding of what is often regarded as a minor side effect of the destruction process. This essay examines the evolution of plunder at Auschwitz-Birkenau as it relates both to the destruction process and to its impact on the economy of German-occupied Europe.

During the early years of the Second World War, prisoners in Auschwitz were the target of systematic but limited plunder. In 1942, however, when annihilation replaced incarceration as Nazi policy toward Jewish prisoners, all Jewish possessions were thoroughly plundered. Prisoners were usually forced to remove all their clothing as part of the extermination operations. Nakedness served two important functions: it terrorized and psychologically subdued the victims, and it facilitated the plunder of their personal belongings.

Department IV (Administration and Economy) of the SS was responsible for confiscating the property of extermination victims in Auschwitz. Lieutenant SS Max Meyer was the first manager of the department. He was succeeded by Captain SS Rudolf Wagner, who ran the department until July

1942; Major SS Willi Mazi Josef Johann Burger, who ran it until April 1943; and Lieutenant Colonel SS Karl Ernst Möckel, who ran it until the camp was closed. In July 1943, Department IV also began serving as the administrative office of the Auschwitz SS garrison (SS-Standortverwaltung Auschwitz). The branch of camp administration most extensively involved in confiscation was called Administration of Inmate Property (Gefangeneneigentumsverwaltung; Haftlingseigentumsverwaltung). Obersturmführer SS Theodor Kratzer headed this branch.

The SS administration was in charge of plundering in all concentration camps and killing centers with the exception of Chelmno. After February 1942, the Economic-Administrative Main Office of the SS (SS-WVHA) ran the operation.[1] The SS shared management responsibilities for the looted goods with the Ministry of Economy of the Reich, the Finance Ministry, and other Nazi government agencies. Once confiscated, all goods became the property of the Third Reich.

During the first two years of Auschwitz, when transports were carrying mostly non-Jewish prisoners, personal belongings were rarely confiscated. As prisoners checked in and changed into regulation camp fatigues, SS men made them put their personal belongings in designated areas. The SS men collected food, carry-on luggage, gold wedding rings, watches, jewelry, clothes, shoes, and other items. All goods were deposited in camp storerooms and turned over to relatives in the event of a prisoner's death. When prisoners perished in the camps, their clothing, shoes, and valuables were officially designated as "effects of the deceased" (*Nachlass verstorbener Haftlinge*). But these effects automatically became the property of the Reich if the authorities could not reach the prisoners' relatives or if the relatives failed to reply to official notifications. As the war continued and inmate populations swelled to include prisoners from countries overrun by the Wehrmacht, confiscation of property gradually increased.

From 1941 to 1944, the Reich Main Security Office (RSHA) of the SS and the Reich Interior Ministry[2] issued instructions that gradually allowed the Auschwitz camp command and other camps to limit the transfer of belongings to the families of murdered prisoners. As early as April 1941, the Reich issued specific instructions concerning the appropriation of valuables left behind by deceased Jewish prisoners. Later directives officially sanctioned the confiscation of all property of deceased prisoners—Jews, Poles, Soviet nationals (with the exception of the Ostarbeiter), French citizens sent to the camps as part of the "night and fog" operation, and Gypsies.

German currency was deposited in special bank accounts belonging to the D departments of the SS-WVHA (the controlling agencies of the camps). Foreign currency and valuables were sent to the Reichsbank via the SS-

WVHA. Clothes and shoes were issued to released prisoners, remade into prison fatigues, or recycled in the textile industry. When looted goods were shipped to the Reichsbank, special steps were taken to ensure that they contained no inscriptions, annotations, or stamps that would reveal that they came from a camp.

By the end of March 1944, Auschwitz and 15 other camps had dispatched special couriers to deliver more than 20 sealed packages to the D departments of the SS-WVHA. The packages contained currency and valuables appropriated on behalf of the Third Reich from the deceased prisoners over a period of several months. Two packages were sent from the Auschwitz camp that month. One contained money, including 124,940 zloty, 20,415 rubles, 1,858 Romanian lei, 828 Belgian francs, and 567 Czechoslovak kroner. The other package contained, among other things, more than 1.5 kg (3.3 pounds) of gold; about 4.5 kg (9.9 pounds) of silver, probably in the form of ingots cast from gold and silver objects of little-known origin; some silver coins; 1.8 g of diamonds; 6.4 g of pearls; 69.6 g of coral; and 65.5 g of various precious and semiprecious stones.[3]

Auschwitz storerooms served as depots for money, clothing, shoes, and other personal items that belonged to Jewish prisoners who were declared security risks to the Third Reich. In the early years of the war, the treatment of these Jewish prisoners was similar to that extended to non-Jewish prisoners. But the belongings of Jews deported to Auschwitz for immediate annihilation were confiscated without delay. After 1942, the property of Jews who were part of the labor force was also confiscated immediately.

Plunder was an integral part of Nazi policy toward Jews even before the outbreak of the war. Jews were ousted from business and public life in Germany, Austria, and Czechoslovakia. Economic enterprises belonging to Jews were confiscated during the war. Jews were dismissed from their professions and barred from civil service. In some countries, plundered Jewish property was split between the Reich and local authorities. As Jews were deported, the Reich took over their apartments and buildings. In ghettos and transit camps, plunder took the form of forcible "contributions." Jews left behind most of their movable property, which the Nazis and their local collaborators subsequently appropriated.

The last plundering phase took place in the killing centers. Jews arriving at Auschwitz and the other death camps were scrupulously deprived of their personal belongings and material property. The plunder was clearly and precisely codified in secret Nazi directives. But to preserve a semblance of legality, the Nazis always used guarded phrasing in their public directives concerning Jewish property. The Nazi control apparatus classified such activities as top secret. For this reason, SS authorities in charge of the concentration camps and other killing centers used special euphemisms in their instructions and other official documents to designate the looted Jewish property. They used such terms as "property of resettled Jews" (*Besitz der umgesiedelten Juden*), "acquired Jewish personal property" (*die anfallenden jüdischen Effekten*), and "property of Jewish thieves and fences" (*das jüdische Hehler- u. Diebesgut*). Often the Nazis used more specific terms. "Textile junk from resettlement of Jews" (*Textil-Altmaterial aus der Judenaussiedlung*) referred to used or secondhand textile products that could be recycled. Other materials were labeled "rags from among unusable civilian articles from particular operations in Auschwitz and other camps" *(Lumpen von den nicht brauchbaren Zivilsachen aus den einzelnen Aktionen von Auschwitz und anderen Lagern).*

The killing of Jews and plundering of their property in the General Government in Poland was carried out as part of a larger plan code-named "Operation Reinhard."[4] Despoliation of Jewish property at Auschwitz was carried out under the same code name.

The Nazis used a campaign of deception to deport Jews from the ghettos and various transit camps to Auschwitz and other centers of mass extermination. This campaign involved luring victims with the prospect of resettlement in new areas. Deceived by the ploy, Jews took the belongings they deemed useful for living in an unknown place for an unspecified period of time.

In keeping with Nazi instructions, Jews usually arrived at Auschwitz with luggage weighing no more than 66 to 110 pounds. They brought clothes; food; personal belongings; assorted household articles, such as sleeping blankets, sheets, pots, and rugs; and professional tools and other necessities. For example, physicians usually arrived with their medical instruments and drugs. Because the Jewish deportees believed they were being resettled, many of them inscribed their names, addresses, and even their dates of birth on their luggage to facilitate finding their belongings when they reached their destination. They did this either voluntarily or under instructions from Nazi authorities. As a rule, the victims were prohibited from taking valuables and large amounts of money with them.[5] However, many disregarded these prohibitions and hid valuables in their luggage, clothing, shoes, and food.

Most prisoners brought enough food for two or three days to the trains. Separate freight cars carried a two-week supply of food for the transport. According to testimony by former prisoner Kazimierz Smolen (camp number 1327), officials at camp headquarters notified the department in charge of the extermination of the Jewish population (Department IV B4 of the Reich Main Security Office) of the food that was arriving at the camp. Camp officials also notified the department about the number of new arrivals and the number of persons who were to be subjected to "special treatment," that is, selection and killing in the gas chambers.[6]

In May 1944, SS personnel at Auschwitz began taking delivery of Jewish transports at a specially built spur of track at the freight depot called the "Jewish ramp" (*Judenrampe*). Later, transports took prisoners directly to a ramp inside the Birkenau camp. It was on these ramps that the newly arrived Jewish prisoners went through the first phase of looting. Jews obeyed orders issued by the SS men in a rushed atmosphere. They were instructed to leave all heavy or bulky luggage either in the train cars or at designated spots on the ramp. Only hand luggage was allowed beyond the ramp. Those refusing to comply with the orders were usually beaten or shot.

Prisoners assigned to the labor squad at the ramp, known officially as *Aufraumungskommando an der Rampe*, quickly unloaded the belongings that the prisoners left behind and cleaned up the refuse.[7] They performed their work as the victims were dispatched to the gas chambers. With help from other prisoners, the members of the labor squad hauled the items into trucks to be transported to the camp storage depots. The unloading ramp was also the workplace of the "commando of food pickers" (*Essenwarensammlerkommando an der Rampe*). Their job was to rummage through the looted property for food and to transfer it to the food warehouses.

Before entering the gas chambers, the Jewish prisoners were forced to leave their clothes, shoes, and other possessions outside or in special changing rooms. Led to believe that they were going to bathe, the prisoners were not aware that they were to be looted and murdered. As soon as they entered the gas chamber, their belongings were immediately sorted and shipped to the camp storerooms. The task of sorting and loading the loot was assigned to *Sonderkommando* prisoners, who serviced the gas chambers and crematoria. Money and other valuables found among the victims' clothes were heaped in piles at places designated by the supervising SS men. When large amounts of valuables accumulated, they were transferred to the storerooms.

Initially, all the prisoners' clothes and hand luggage was stored in a warehouse (block 26) in the main Auschwitz camp. However, by mid-1942, there was so much looted property that the camp authorities started using six barracks near the main camp for storage. Before long, these barracks also were too small to house the incoming loot. To accommodate the goods, camp officials created an extensive network of storage depots where goods could be prepared for shipment or for use at the camp. These storage facilities were officially called "storerooms of movables" (*Effektenkammern* or *Effektenlager*). They were similar to the storerooms where the clothes and personal belongings of the camp prisoners were kept. Prisoner labor squads working in the storerooms were known in the official camp terminology as "order kommandos" (*Aufräumungskommando*).

The camp prisoners came to refer to the property that was looted from the victims as "Canada." They associated the sheer amount of the loot and its mind-boggling value with the riches symbolized by Canada. In time, some members of the camp personnel and the management also adopted the term.

"Canada" storage facilities occupied several dozen barracks and other buildings. The most important among them were Canada I (Effektenlager I) and Canada II (Effektenlager II). Both were situated in the BIIg sector of the Birkenau camp. Canada I comprised six storage barracks near the main camp. The complex was in the vicinity of the Deutsche Ausrüstungswerke (DAW) plant and warehouses that held construction materials.[8] An adapted apartment building situated near the barracks housed the disinfection chamber (*Entwesungskammer*) that was used to fumigate clothing. The barracks and the building that housed the gas chamber were fenced off with barbed wire. SS personnel manned guard towers along the fence at all times.

Until December 1943, the storerooms of Canada I functioned as the central facility for sorting material looted from Jews and preparing it for future use. From 1942 through 1943, between 1,000 and 1,600 male and female prisoners worked there in two shifts. Canada I was run by a succession of SS men: Richard Wiegleb, Georg Hocker, and Emanuel Glumbik.

Canada II started operating in December 1943.[9] It comprised 30 barracks, most of which served as the main storage and sorting facilities for plundered Jewish goods until the liquidation of Auschwitz. The remaining barracks contained clothes and hand luggage that belonged to prisoners incarcerated in the camp. They also housed offices and living quarters for some of the prisoner personnel who worked there. The clothing disinfection facility was in an adjacent building.

Canada II quickly became larger than Canada I. On July 22, 1944, a total of 590 men worked in Canada II. At that time, only 210 men worked in the old storerooms of Canada I. On October 2, 1944, Canada II employed 815 women prisoners, whereas 250 women worked in Canada I. With the increase in the number of transports rolling into the camp, the labor force working in the storerooms of Canada II swelled to between 1,500 and 2,000 men and women prisoners. SS men Georg Hocker and Werner Hahn, among others, managed the storage complex.

In 1942, the SS began sorting and storing leather goods in the buildings of the former Auschwitz tannery. Some of the shoes, empty suitcases, and other leather goods were used as raw material in nearby workshops (*Bekleidungswerkstätten Lederfabrik*). Erich Gronke, a German, managed the storerooms and workshops on behalf of the camp administration. Between 500 and 800 prisoners worked there.

Clothes and underwear were processed in ancillary sorting plants from 1942 through 1943. These plants included a wooden barrack (block no. 6;

later known as block no. 35) in the vicinity of crematorium II in Birkenau and the "camp extension" (*Lagererweiterung*) in the main camp. Approximately 300 prisoners worked in the wooden barrack. Unterscharführer SS Gerhard Effinger was head of the plant in BIa. SS man Hans Wagner managed the plant in BIb. The camp extension comprised five brick blocks that were put into operation in the spring of 1944. They were used to store suitcases, baskets, clothes, phylacteries, shoes, spectacles, paint brushes, rugs, sewing machines, and other items.

A storeroom for food was next to the prisoners' kitchen (*Häftlingsmagazin-Lebensmittelnmagazin*) in the main camp. Under the direction of Unterscharführer SS Franz Schebeck, food was issued to prisoners in the main camp and other sections, including the subsidiary camps. Food looted from the victims was brought to the storeroom, where it was inspected in an area known as Schebeck Canada. Most of the valuable items, such as liquor, canned goods, cocoa, and chocolate, were diverted to the SS storage facility in the basement of the camp headquarters.

After the killing operations moved into high gear, the amount of looted goods sent to Canada I and II was so huge it had to be temporarily stored outside near the storerooms. Vast piles of clothes, suitcases, and parcels would lie there for weeks before being searched. Then they would be unpacked in great haste. Valuables were thrown into special boxes with locked lids and openings through which the goods were deposited. Separate sites were assigned for money, food, drugs, and utensils. Clothes, which had been fumigated earlier,[10] were carefully inspected for hidden precious objects. Stars of David sewn onto the clothing were removed. Then the clothes, underwear, sheets, quilts, and blankets were packed away for shipment. Other assorted plundered goods, such as shoes and suitcases, were scrupulously searched for hidden money (especially hard currency) and other valuables. Every day, hundreds of pairs of shoes were torn apart in the tannery in the search. Once the looted goods were sorted, they were stored in special rooms to await shipment out of Auschwitz or to be used in the camp itself.

The camp prisoners regarded the labor squads that worked in Canada (Aufräumungskommandos) as better commandos than were the members of other labor squads. Male and female prisoners working in Canada had incomparably better chances to obtain illegally—in camp slang, to "organize"—food, clothing, and other highly valued articles. To increase their chances of survival, they often took advantage of available opportunities to steal needed goods. For this reason, the SS guards who worked in the Canada warehouses were especially vigilant when overseeing prisoners who were sorting and searching the looted property for hidden money and valuables. Prisoners caught "organizing" were usually harshly punished. On some occasions, offenders were shot on the spot. After work, and sometimes even during working hours, the prisoners were subjected to thorough, brutal personal searches. Such searches were particularly painful for women.[11]

Among surviving Nazi documents are reports that indicate that the looted property was funneled from Auschwitz through an extensive distribution network that served many individuals and various economic branches of the Third Reich. The SS-WVHA issued one of the most important instructions concerning distribution of the looted material on September 26, 1942. It was addressed to the heads of the administrative departments of Auschwitz and Majdanek.[12] The decree established rules for the distribution and utilization of plundered Jewish goods.

The camp administrations were ordered to make cash payments in German banknotes to an SS-WVHA account in the Reichsbank in Berlin and to ship hard currency, valuables, and precious metals directly to the SS-WVHA. Economic branches of the SS subordinate to the SS-WVHA, a special SS agency in charge of resettlement of ethnic Germans (Volksdeutsche Mittelstelle, or VoMi), and the Ministry of Economy of the Reich were empowered to take delivery of the plundered goods. Most usable textiles, leather products, household utensils, and other assorted items were diverted for the use of resettled Germans and SS camp personnel. Some clothes and shoes were set aside for prisoners. The Reich Ministry of Economy was named as the recipient of damaged property that could be used as raw material in industrial plants. It was assumed that the institutions, enterprises, and organizations benefiting from the loot would remit fair sums (corresponding, in principle, to their average value), or, alternatively, payments were to be agreed upon in the future. These payments would enrich the Nazi treasury.

On October 14, 1942, with the Christmas holiday approaching, Reichsführer-SS Heinrich Himmler, undoubtedly acting in the context of these earlier instructions, directed SS-WVHA chief Oswald Pohl and VoMi chief Werner Lorenz to supply more than 230,000 resettled Volksdeutsche and Germans, including 45,000 German settlers in the Zytomierz region in the Ukraine, with goods from the Auschwitz and Majdanek storerooms. Himmler ordered that each resettled German should be given clothes, a coat, headgear, and other necessities. Needy families were to be supplied with blankets, sheets, and quilts.[13]

Despite occasional mechanical difficulties, 824 train cars loaded with textiles and leather goods departed from Auschwitz and Majdanek in February 1943. The goods they carried were gathered in the course of the "resettlement of Jews" *(aus der Judenumsiedlung)*. In other words, they were plundered from Jewish victims. The Ministry of Economy of the Reich took delivery of 569 cars loaded predominantly with damaged, unusable clothes and other "tatters and rags" (*Lumpen*) suitable for industrial processing as raw materials. VoMi took delivery of 211 train cars containing hundreds of thousands of pieces of clothing, bed linens, tablecloths, towels, and other assorted items. Usable textile items also were given to German settlers. The remaining 44 cars, loaded with clothes and shoes, were directed to other concentration camps, to the headquarters of several paramilitary organizations, and to the chemical works of IG Farbenindustrie in Auschwitz-Monowitz (Dwory). SS-WVHA chief Pohl quoted all these figures in a special report submitted to Himmler on February 6, 1943.[14] According to Rudolf Höss, the commandant of Auschwitz, as many as 20 train cars per day were loaded with confiscated property at the Auschwitz railroad ramps.

Department DII of the SS-WVHA confirmed delivery of successive shipments of watches, watch cases, watch bracelets, fountain pens, mechanical pencils, and other unspecified utensils in a letter sent on January 24, 1944, to the Auschwitz management. On this occasion, the addressees were told how to deliver further shipments.[15] According to testimony given in January 1947 by Karl Sommer, a former official of DII department, his office regularly took delivery of watches confiscated in Auschwitz and Majdanek in keeping with a special directive from Pohl. Confiscated watches were subsequently shipped to a watchmaker's workshop on the grounds of the Sachsenhausen concentration camp that Pohl established especially for that purpose.[16]

SS officials wrote instructions, reports, and official letters concerning the property of victims of extermination operations in May, August, September, November, and December 1943 and July and August 1944.[17] These writings, which the SS-WVHA sent out in September 1942 along with the instructions detailed above, reveal the extent of the SS processing operation.

A broad assortment of utensils plundered from the murdered victims in Auschwitz and other killing centers were amassed, evaluated, cleaned, and repaired in special workshops that the SS-WVHA controlled. In addition to watches, fountain pens, and mechanical pencils, items included safety razors, scissors, and pocket flashlights. Wristwatches and fountain pens were first allocated to soldiers of front-line SS divisions, Luftwaffe pilots, and submarine crews. Safety razors and blades were delivered to SS infirmaries and sold in SS mess halls. Scissors, depending on their design, were sent to SS barbershops, among other places. In July 1944, 2,500 watches were allocated to Berlin residents who suffered damage during air bombardments.

It is known from clarifications and recollections of former Auschwitz camp personnel that the volume of looted money and valuables (mostly jewelry and wristwatches made of precious metals) streaming into the collection centers was so large that the SS functionaries were permanently occupied with inspecting, sorting, and counting it. Every few weeks the precious loot was shipped out of Auschwitz on trucks in sealed crates. The trucks traveled under armed SS escort to the SS center.

Recollections of SS personnel vary. Möckel, who directed the administration of the Auschwitz SS garrison and headed the camp administration, stated that 15 to 20 suitcases (*Handkoffer*) of valuables were delivered to the SS-WVHA every three months. In contrast, Wlodzimierz Bilan, director of Canada I and a functionary of the camp Gestapo (Politische Abteilung), claimed that every month at least two 1,000-kg crates of valuables were shipped from Auschwitz to Berlin.[18]

In accordance with an agreement reached in mid-1942 between Himmler and Economy Minister Walter Funk, money and valuables flowing from Auschwitz and other killing centers to the SS center were regularly transferred to the Reichsbank in Berlin. Captain SS Melmer of Department A of the SS-WVHA indirectly supervised the shipments. Parts of the shipments delivered to the bank, such as hard currency and ingots cast from precious metals, were immediately added to the Reichsbank resources. Institutions subordinate to or in collaboration with the Reichsbank appropriated some jewelry and gems. Other jewelry, gems, and share holdings went to Berliner Pfandleiheanstalt. The profits went to the state treasury (Reichshauptkassen), where they were put into a special account of the Finance Ministry code-named "Max Heiliger." Some of the looted valuables were sold in Switzerland, among other places.

The financial needs of the SS were not overlooked. Both the Reichsbank and the Gold Discount Bank aerated special loan funds similar to the "Max Heiliger" account that were based on profits from the looted valuables. Called *Reinhardtfonds*, they were designed as accounts from which the SS could borrow money to finance its economic enterprises.

After the war, Albert Thoms, a former senior bank official, clarified the Reichsbank's role in the appropriation of property of victims of the Nazi extermination policy. He claimed to have witnessed the Reichsbank receive shipments from the Auschwitz concentration camp. Höss and Möckel also pointed to the Reichsbank as a recipient of valuables looted in Auschwitz. Möckel even mentioned SS functionary Melmer as a liaison between the SS-WVHA and the Reichsbank.[19]

Many German organizations, institutions, and economic enterprises received textiles, leather products, and assorted utensils confiscated from Auschwitz victims. Nazi documents are not the sole source of this information. Barbara Adamkiewicz, a forced-labor worker, claimed in her 1976 memoirs that in the winter of 1942–43, she was employed in the Bertohld Steinkopf plant in Kiel recycling large amounts of clothing shipped there from Auschwitz and from other camps. Her task was to cut the fabric into pieces measuring 40 by 40 cm; they were used to clean German industrial machinery. Jozef Kubiscik, a resident of Chelmno, near Auschwitz, testified in 1960 that the local Bata factory (under German management during the war) received large numbers of shoes from Auschwitz and the General Government in Poland.[20]

Looted clothing also was shipped in bulk from Auschwitz to other concentration camps. After the clothes were inspected and processed at camp workshops, they were issued to new prisoners in lieu of the regulation striped fatigues. Leather goods were turned into footwear for prisoners.

Looted goods were used in many, often ingenious ways in the concentration camps. For example, prisoner Henryk Kwiatkowski testified that "sacks and assorted rags" from Canada I were used to clean machinery in the camp dairy. Aleksander Nowosielski, a prisoner in the Neuengamme concentration camp, recalled that in the winter of 1944-45, an attempt was made to replace coal with clothing from Auschwitz as fuel for the generating station of the brick works (*Klinkerwerk*). Accounts by former prisoners Mieczyslaw Gadomski and Mieczyslaw Kazimierz Wendowski reveal that assorted goods, such as bars of soap, toothpaste, and even white shoe polish, taken from the Auschwitz victims were turned into soap in special soap workshops.[21]

Large quantities of looted medicines and medical implements were transferred en masse from the camp storerooms to medical establishments and first aid clinics serving SS men and their families. Prime-quality foods and beverages such as bottles of vintage wine were presented to SS notables who visited Auschwitz or were consumed in the dining rooms that served the camp personnel. Poor-quality food was diverted to the kitchen that served the prisoners. Even baby carriages were among the looted property of the Auschwitz victims. Large numbers of them were stored in the Canada warehouses. Former prisoner Wanda Szaynok testified that she witnessed an enormous number of carriages being transported from the camp to the Auschwitz train station. It took more than an hour for a column of carriages, five abreast, to pass.[22]

Camp personnel and other Third Reich nationals used to submit applications to the camp administration asking for allocation or resale of various property (clothes, baby carriages, and household utensils) looted from the Jewish victims. The administration often responded positively to their requests.[23]

Himmler ordered all Auschwitz camp personnel to abide by the "principle of holiness of property" (*Grundsatz über die Heiligkeit des Eigentums*). Camp personnel were forbidden to appropriate for themselves any goods that were considered state property—goods that belonged to the SS or other Nazi organizations or private citizens of the Third Reich. Notwithstanding the SS pledge, camp commandants Höss and Arthur Liebehenschel repeatedly noted in their orders instances of willful and illicit appropriation by SS men of all kinds of looted goods. These references were accompanied by instructions aimed at counteracting these practices.[24] On May 22, 1944, coinciding with the mass extermination of Hungarian Jews, members of the camp staff were required to sign personal pledges to refrain from arbitrary appropriation of Jewish property and to keep the extermination activities secret. The passage dealing with Jewish property read: "I am aware and today I have been instructed to this effect that I shall be punished by death should I make an attempt to appropriate any Jewish property."[25]

SS authorities did not hesitate to inflict severe punishment on rank-and-file camp personnel found guilty of willful appropriation of the property of murdered victims. One example is an SS court sentence against SS-Unterscharführer Franz Wunsch on July 18, 1944.[26] Wunsch served as overseer of prisoners working in the Canada warehouses. He appropriated some small articles, including leather gloves, 50 cigarettes, two hunting knives, and a pocket flashlight, with a total value of $14 (30 marks). He was sentenced to five weeks of arrest with strict regime. The fact that he had not appropriated any valuables was quoted as a mitigating circumstance.

The riches plundered from extermination victims cast a strong spell over the SS men serving in Auschwitz. Many were overcome with a feverish desire to lay their hands on as much loot, especially valuables, as possible. One camp personnel member who siphoned off items was a physician and doctor of philosophy, First Lieutenant SS Johann Paul Kremer. Entries in his diary reveal that he repeatedly sent out parcels containing items of great value that he appropriated from the Canada warehouses.[27]

Some members of the Auschwitz camp management, including Höss and the chief of the Political Department (the Gestapo), SS-Unterscharführer Maximilian Grabner, also illicitly seized confiscated goods. For example, Höss's wife, Hedwig, with her husband's tacit approval, frequently visited the camp storerooms and other facilities to collect high-quality food and other goods. For this she either paid nothing or left a nominal payment. SS-Unterscharführer Franz Schebeck, head of the food depot, and SS-Oberscharführer Engelbrecht, who controlled the camp canteens, also helped replenish the Höss household's supplies of wine, canned fish, and cigarettes. Erich Gronke, head of the warehouses and workshops at the former Auschwitz tannery, owed Höss for his release from the camp and for his position as a civilian functionary in the camp administration. As repayment, Gronke did not spare any effort to supply the Höss family with leather goods, such as shoes, women's bags, leather armchairs, and other articles.[28]

In the second half of 1943, a special commission headed by SS Major Konrad Morgen, a doctor of law, acting on behalf of the SS judiciary, launched a special inquest concerning embezzlement and theft by SS men at Auschwitz.[29] Grabner was among those indicted. Searches of the living quarters of a number of SS men uncovered large quantities of valuables and other illicitly appropriated articles. The objects were stored as material exhibits in a barrack attached to crematorium I that belonged to the Political Department. On the night of December 7, 1943, all the articles went up in flames in a fire that broke out from undetermined causes. In all likelihood, the fire was set by SS men with a vested interest in destroying the evidence that would have been used against them. In October 1944, Grabner was put on trial before an SS court in Weimar. The court proposed a 12-year prison sentence for his offenses in Auschwitz, including the arbitrary killing of non-Jewish prisoners. Shortly thereafter, the trial was postponed.

Surviving Nazi documents do not contain data that would enable a rough or even partial estimate of the value of the property that the Nazis looted from the victims of Auschwitz. It appears, however, that the cash value reached at least several hundred million German marks.[30]

The Nazis fully exploited concentration camp and death camp inmates, even in death. Practices went far beyond the plunder of prisoners' personal property or their use as slave laborers. Jews who were killed on arrival at Auschwitz were treated as raw material, their hair, bones, and teeth made of precious metals sold to enrich the Third Reich.

In 1940, Victor Scholz published a doctoral dissertation, "On the Possibilities of Recycling Gold from the Mouths of the Dead," with the approval of the Medical Department and Stomatology Institute of Breslau University. His discussion of removing dental gold from the dead was far from theoretical. The SS soon took steps to implement his teaching.

On September 23, 1940, Himmler ordered the removal of dental gold (*Zahngold*) from the mouths of prisoners who died in concentration camps. According to Höss, Adolf Eichmann, chief of the RSHA department in charge of liquidating the Jewish population, relayed Himmler's order to remove gold teeth from Jews killed in gas ovens.[31]

The pace of destruction in death camps such as Treblinka and Sobibor and extermination centers in concentration camps such as Auschwitz and Majdanek yielded large quantities of precious metals beginning in 1942. A postwar study by the Main Commission for the Investigation of German Crimes in Poland, which surveyed over 2,900 reports on the removal of false teeth,[32] concluded that 16,325 teeth made of gold and alloys of precious metals had been removed from 2,904 Auschwitz prisoners between May and December 1942. By early 1944, members of the prisoner underground in Auschwitz estimated that the SS had amassed 10 to 12 kg (22 to 26.4 pounds) of gold a month. According to a secret report smuggled out of the camp at the start of the extermination of Hungarian Jews in May 1944, the SS took delivery of 40 kg (80 pounds) of gold and "white metal" (probably platinum).[33]

On admission to Auschwitz, all prisoners' dental work was examined, and annotations were recorded in their records. The presence of false teeth was noted, as was their removal when the prisoner died. The extraction of precious metals from dead prisoners was first carried out by SS dentists, assisted by prisoners. By 1943, the work was done in camp sick bays, morgues, and crematoria by imprisoned dentists known as gold workers (*Goldarbeiter*) or by the Sonderkommandos who worked at the gas chambers and crematoria. Under the close supervision of the SS, the metal teeth were extracted with dental pincers, chisels, or crowbars. In the summer of 1944, at the peak of extermination, at least 40 prisoners were employed at this labor. The teeth were soaked in muriatic acid to remove scraps of muscle tissue and bone, then the gold was melted and cast into ingots weighing from 0.5 to 1 kg (1.1 to 2.2 pounds) or into disks of 140 g (4.9 ounces).

In May 1942, annotations on a technical drawing made in connection with planning for new gas chambers and crematoria in Birkenau (crematoria II and III) provided for a gold workshop (*Goldarb*).[34] The planners envisioned a facility for melting the gold and platinum teeth and recasting the metal into ingots. The facility was established at crematorium III in Birkenau in 1943. Only prisoners were employed in this facility. Former Sonderkommando prisoners Miklos Nyisli and Filip Müller described its operation in their memoirs.[35]

Dental gold was sent to the main SS administration, which turned it over to the SS Sanitation Office.[36] This agency allocated the gold to dentists treating SS men and their families. By October 8, 1942, the Sanitation Office had accumulated 50 kg (110.25 pounds) of gold, according to a report to Himmler, an amount sufficient to satisfy the SS dental service for five years. As a result, the SS channeled the gold from Auschwitz and other extermination camps to the Reichsbank.[37] The first shipments of dental gold reached the bank in November 1942, according to a statement in 1949 by an employee of the Reichsbank. The Reichsbank received increasing quantities of dental gold and other precious metals during the final years of the war.[38] But not all precious metals were shipped to the SS dental service or the Reichsbank. As much as 30 percent, according to one underground report, slipped through Nazi control. In many cases, this "illegal" gold found its way into the hands of the SS camp personnel. Also, the teeth were sometimes "appropriated" by other prisoners, undoubtedly to use as payment for food.

Prisoners, men and women alike, usually had their hair shaved off on arrival. Hair removal made escape more difficult and helped in maintaining sanitary conditions. The hair was not reused at first, but on August 6, 1942, the SS-WVHA ordered camp authorities to gather hair that was at least 2 cm (.78 inch) in length. Camp commandants were informed that "human hairs will be processed into felt to be used in industry, and thread will be spun out of them." In particular, "the combed-out and cut-off women's hair will be used to make socks for submarine crews and to manufacture felt stockings for railroad workers." The commandants were required to submit monthly reports on the amount of hair collected.[39]

In instructions issued on January 4 and 11, 1943, the administrative authorities of 11 concentration camps were directed to deliver the hair to the following German firms: Alex Zink Filzfabrik AG in Roth, near Nuremberg; Paul Reinmann in Mieroszow, in the Sudeten (Freidland Bez. Breslau); and Färberei Forst AG, in Forst on the Luzycka Nysa (Neisse) River. One kg (2.2 pounds) of hair was worth 0.50 Reichsmark (RM; about $1.09).[40]

In 1942, more than 160 kg (352 pounds) of hair was cut from the heads of prisoners in Majdanek. Between January 1943 and March 1944, 730 kg (1,606 pounds) of hair was shipped from Majdanek to Forst. Copies of reports sent to the SS-WVHA, official letters, and accounts remain of the correspondence between the Majdanek camp administration and the firms of Paul Reinmann and Farberei Forst AG.[41] No analogous documentation from Auschwitz has been discovered. In all probability, these records would have detailed larger quantities of hair than Majdanek.

In addition to the hair of prisoners, the Nazis also utilized the hair of Jewish women murdered immediately upon arrival in death camps. In Belzec, Sobibor, and Treblinka, women had their hair cut just before entering the gas chambers, whereas in Auschwitz, the hair was cut from the heads of women already gassed. According to Höss, the order to cut the hair of dead Jewish women was issued by Himmler when the first transports carrying Jews began rolling toward the camp.[42]

A report dated February 6, 1943, by SS-WVHA chief Pohl, noted that more than 800 trainloads of material goods yielded from the Jews of Auschwitz and Majdanek included 3,000 kg (6,600 pounds) of women's hair.[43] This hair was used in a broad range of industrial products. According to reports by former prisoners Kazimierz Gwizdek, Filip Müller, Kazimierz Szwemberg, and Henryk Tauber, the hair was stored in crematoria lofts where it could be dried by heat from the ovens and chimneys before it was shipped.[44] A detachment of prisoners, the *Reinkommando*, was assigned the task of cleaning the hair in one loft.[45] In 1961, former prisoner Karol Bienias described this job:

> We cleaned the women's hair of pins and other objects, then combed it with our hands and packed it into sacks for shipment. We loaded one shipment of 1,500 kg [3,300 pounds] of hair at the train station in Auschwitz. Faulty sorting was punished by flogging.[46]

When Soviet troops entered Auschwitz in 1945, they discovered 293 sacks of human hair weighing on average 20 kg (44 pounds) each, and 12 sacks weighing on average 88 kg (193.6 pounds) each—some seven tons in all. Apparently the SS ran out of time to ship them out for industrial processing. The sacks bore inscriptions indicating their weight and were marked "KL

Au" (Konzentrationlager Auschwitz), revealing their origin. Assuming that one person's hair weighs an average of 40 to 50 g (1.4 to 1.8 ounces), Soviet experts determined that the hair belonged to about 140,000 Auschwitz victims.[47] The storeroom with human hair was filmed as part of investigative work conducted by a Soviet commission.

In 1945, an examination by the Institute of Judicial Expertise in Krakow of a sample of hair found in Auschwitz revealed the presence of compounds of prussic acid, the basic component of the Zyklon B gas used in the gas chambers of Auschwitz. Traces of the acid were also discovered in metal objects found in the hair, such as pins, clasps, and gold-plated spectacle holders.[48]

Hair from Auschwitz was shipped to the industrial firm Teppichfabrik G. Schoffler AG, situated relatively close to Auschwitz at Kietrz (Katscher) in the Opole region. After the liberation of Keitrz, at least 1,950 kg (4,290 pounds) of what appeared to be human hair was discovered in the factory. Analysis of the hair in August 1946 confirmed it to be human. The Institute of Judicial Expertise determined in March 1947 that the hair contained traces of prussic acid.[49] Several rolls of haircloth fabric found in the Kietrz works were sent to the Auschwitz-Birkenau State Museum in 1947. The Institute of Forensic Medicine in Krakow later confirmed that the fabric was made of human hair.[50] Another firm that processed human hair was Bremer Wollkammerei in Bremen-Blumenthal, a company that operates today under a different name. In all likelihood, at least part of the firm's raw material originated in Auschwitz.[51]

There is no doubt that hair from the victims of Auschwitz and other camps was used to manufacture felt, yarn (threads), fabric (haircloth), stockings, and socks. Testimonies, memoirs, research analyses, and some court rulings indicate that human hair was used in the ignition mechanism of bombs with delayed ignitions, ropes and cords (on ships), and mattresses and clothing.[52]

Ashes and bones from the bodies incinerated in Auschwitz crematoria were crushed with wooden mortars, then buried in pits or sunk in the Sola and Vistula rivers or in ponds near Birkenau. The ashes and bones were also used as fill in the terrain and bogs and as fertilizer for fields belonging to the camp. Camp authorities sought to scatter the remains as broadly as possible to prevent their being used as evidence of the crimes committed in the camp.[53]

The fat that dripped from the bodies burned in pits or on pyres was collected in ditches dug for that purpose near the incineration sites, then used as fuel for the fires that burned the bodies. This practice was especially common on rainy days. From time to time, the bodies of new arrivals were thrown into the crematoria with the bodies of emaciated veteran prisoners so that body fat from the healthier new arrivals made the burning process

more efficient. There is no evidence that human fat was used to manufacture soap, or that human skin was treated to make lampshades, book-
bindings, purses, or similar objects in Auschwitz.

Human bodies were also used for experiments conducted by SS doctors.
For example, Friedrich Entress carried out autopsies on the bodies of
prisoners who died as a result of medical experiments. Other physicians, including Carl Clauberg, Johann Paul Kremer, and Josef Mengele, autopsied
the bodies of prisoners killed for the purpose of examining their internal
organs. Eighty Auschwitz prisoners were killed in the Natzweiler-Stuthoff
concentration camp in 1943 so that their bodies could be preserved in the
Anatomy Institute of the Reich University in Strasburg for eventual inclusion in a collection of human skeletons.

All told, the Nazis extracted approximately 60 tons of hair and six tons of
dental gold from the bodies of victims in Auschwitz, according to Professor
Roman Dawidowski, cited in the April 1947 trial of Höss. But these figures
are rough estimates calculated on the assumption that the victims of the
Auschwitz camp numbered about four million—a figure that is now known
to be a gross overestimate.[54] As yet, no new estimates have been made.

The highest echelons of the SS once estimated the profit generated by
the average concentration camp prisoner.[55] Based on an average prisoner life
expectancy of nine months, the profit totaled 1,431 RM (about $654) per
prisoner after deducting costs of upkeep. The value of money, valuables,
clothing, personal belongings, and teeth of precious metals reached 200 RM
($91) after the costs of burning the body had been deducted. Thus,
according to calculations made by Nazis themselves, the total average profit
from one prisoner, not including the value of the victim's bones, totaled
1,631 RM ($745).

NOTES

This essay is an abridged version of an unpublished study written in the 1980s as
part of research conducted by the Auschwitz-Birkenau State Museum. In addition to
Nazi documents, to publications relevant to the subject by Jan Sehn, Artur Eisenbach, Raul Hilberg, Stanislaw Klonzinski, and others, and to memoirs of former
prisoners Filip Müller and Miklos Nyiszli, the sources for this study include accounts
and reminiscences found in the archives of the museum in the following collections:
Proces Hössa (Höss Trial); Proces czlonkow zalogi SS obozu oswiecimskiego (Trial of
members of the SS personnel of the Auschwitz camp); Oswiadczenia (Statements);
Wspomnienia (Memoirs).

1. Raul Hilberg, *Die Vernichtung der europäischer Juden: Die Gesamtgeschichte des
Holocaust* (Berlin, 1982), pp. 643, 650.

2. Archives of the Auschwitz-Birkenau State Museum (ASAM), Trial of Pohl, file Pd. 5, cards 177, 178, 181, 191, 200, 201; file Pd. 22, card 77; Trial of Höss, file 12, cards 164, 179–84, 189–97; Trial of the Auschwitz camp personnel, file 37, cards 123, 124.

3. Ibid., collection marked call no. D-RF-3/RSHA/177 (photocopies of reports and lists related to the parcels mentioned).

4. The code name Aktion Reinhard Reinhard, which described deportations from ghettos and mass murders of Jews by the SS, was adopted by the SS to commemorate the chief of the Reich Main Security Office, Obergruppenführer Reinhard Heydrich, assassinated in June 1942 by the Czech resistance. The fact that the code name Aktion Reinhard served also to camouflage the plunder of Jewish property is attested by, among other things, an order issued by chief of SS-WVHA Oswald Pohl on December 9, 1943 (see Nuremberg document NO-725), which dealt with the channeling of funds yielded by Jewish loot. Among the addressees of Pohl's order was the administration of the Auschwitz camp and SS functionaires responsible for the outcome of Aktion Reinhard in the General Government. Signature of the order included the word "Reinh.," an abbreviation of the code name.

5. German Jews were allowed to take along 100 marks per person.

6. Testimony by former prisoner Kazimierz Smolen, who worked in the reception office of the Auschwitz camp Gestapo; ASAM, Trial of Höss, file 7, card 121.

7. "Aufraumungskommando an der Rampe" appears as one of the prisoner squads in "rolls of employed prisoners in KL Auschwitz II (Birkenau)," call no. D-AuII-3a/1–47, preserved in ASAM. Photographs documenting the shipping of plundered property out of Auschwitz are found in *L'Album d'Auschwitz* (Paris, 1983), pp. 147–49.

8. Buildings comprising Canada I, the loot amassed within its bounds, and the work of prisoners sorting it are documented in photographs in *L'Album d'Auschwitz*, pp. 144–45, 156–61.

9. See *L'Album d'Auschwitz*, pp. 146, 150–55.

10. Furs and sheepskin coats were fumigated exclusively in gas chambers designed especially for this purpose; for example, in a gas chamber operating in Canada I.

11. The best-known account of work conditions in the storerooms and warehouses is found in the memoirs of Kitty Hart, *Return to Auschwitz* (London, 1981), the remarkable story of a girl who survived the Holocaust.

12. Nuremberg document NO-724.

13. Ibid., NO-606 (NO-5395).

14. Ibid., NO-1257. In addition to two orders and one report presented here, numerous other Nazi documents have been preserved which concern utilization of the plundered textile and leather wares.

15. Ibid., NO-4468.

16. Comment by K. Sommer, ASAM, Trial of Pohl, file Pd 1, card 79, 80. Cf. "Autobiography of Höss," in *KL Auschwitz, as Seen by the SS* (New York, 1984), p. 131.

17. Nuremberg documents NO-2003, NO-2749, NO-2751, NO-2753-2755, and others.

18. ASAM, Comment by Wlodzimierz Bilan. Trial of Höss, file 17, card 148; comments by the following former SS functionaries: Georg Höcker, Karl Heinrich Hykes, Karl Ernst Möckel, Karl Morle, and Heinrich Neumann; see also testimony by former prisoner Marian Przada. Trial of the Auschwitz camp personnel, file 52, cards 153, 194, 197, 198, 213, 220, 221, 227–33, 241, 242, file 55, card 241. We have

in our possession a document containing an order for a five-ton truck and a passenger car to depart from Auschwitz for Oranienburg and return for the purpose of transporting the "movables" (*Effektentransport*). The order was signed on September 27, 1944, by the director of the camp administration, Obersturmbannführer Möckel (ASAM, Trial of the Auschwitz camp personnel, file 38, cards 130, 131). There is no question that part of this transport consisted of plundered valuables.

19. Comment by Albert Thoms, May 8, 1946; see Nuremberg document PS-3951. Comment by Karl Ernst Möckel, ASAM, Trial of the Auschwitz camp personnel, file 52, card 198, 220; "Autobiography of Höss," p. 131. Cf. Hilberg, pp. 647–50.

20. Account by J. Kubiscik, ASAM, Statements collection, file 12, cards 40–43; Barbara Adamkiewicz, "Nie chcialam zasilic niemieckiej rasy," in *Z litera "P": Polacy na robotach przymusowych w hitlerowskiej Rzeszy 1939–1945* (Poznan, 1976), pp. 53, 54.

21. Accounts by former prisoners M. Gadomski, H. Kwiatkowski, and K. Wendowski, ASAM, Statements collection, file 17, card 57, file 39, cards 4–9, file 65, card 57; Aleksander Nowosielski, "In the Neuengamme Camp: Dr. Zygmunt Szafranski," in *Przeglad Lekarski-Oswiecim*, vol. 34 (Krakow, 1977), p. 209.

22. ASAM, Trial of Höss, file 5, card 133.

23. Ibid., Trial of the Auschwitz camp personnel, file 37, cards 121, 122 (copy of the order).

24. Ibid., Order of the commander of the camp personnel (Sturmbann-Befehl), no. 85/43, dated May 25, 1943, and orders issued by command of the camp garrison (Stadortbefehle), no. 31/43, dated August 6, 1943; no. 51/43, dated November 16, 1943.

25. Ibid., personal files of SS men, for example, of Ludwig Damm, Alfred Fischer, and Otto Klauss.

26. Ibid., personal files of F. Wunsch; see also Trial of the Auschwitz camp personnel, file 37, cards 199–203.

27. "Diary of Johann Paul Kremer," in *KL Auschwitz*, pp. 222, 224, 231.

28. See, for example, testimony by former prisoner Stanislaw Dubiak in *KL Auschwitz*, pp. 287–92; Jerzy Rawicz, *Dzien powszedni ludobojcy* (Working day of a genocidalist) (Warsaw, 1973), pp. 102–12, 116, 128–30.

29. Testimony by Konrad Morgen, ASAM, Statements collection file 72, cards 53, 60–68; Hermann Langbein, *Menschen in Auschwitz* (Vienna, 1972), pp. 339–41, 373–75; *KL Auschwitz*, pp. 197, 303.

30. Cf. ASAM, Trial of Höss, file 22, card 74 (information supplied by one of the SS men on the Auschwitz camp staff); "Oboz koncentracyjny Oswiecim w swietle akt Delegatury Rzadu RP no Kraj," in *Zeszyty Oswiecimskie*, special issue no. 1 (1968), p. 52.

31. "Autobiography of Höss," in: *KL Auschwitz*, p. 115.

32. ASAM, personal cards of prisoners marked, for example, with camp serial numbers 133691, 134249, and 138791; protocol of the inspection of reports concerning extraction of teeth, Höss trial, vol. 3, k. 84–86.

33. ASAM, materials on resistance, vol. 7, k. 446, 485.

34. Technical drawing no. 1311, dated May 14, 1942, ASAM, collection Bauleitung, call no. Bauwerk (BW) 30/11. Cf. crematoria plans of December 19, 1942 (no. 2003), and March 19, 1943 (no. 2197). Ibid., call no. BW 30/12, 14. Cf. protocol of investigations conducted by members of the Main Commission for the Investigation of German (Nazi) Crimes in Poland in the years 1945-46 on the grounds of the former Auschwitz camp. ASAM, Höss trial, vol. 11, k. 36, 54, 55.

35. Miklos Nyiszli, *Auschwitz: A Doctor's Eyewitness Account* (New York, 1960), pp. 72–76; Filip Müller, *Sonderbehandlung: Drei Jahre in den Krematorien und Gaskammern* (Munich, 1979), pp. 106, 107. Cf. an essay by a former prisoner, David Olere, "The Gold Melters," in *Spiritual Resistance: Art from Concentration Camps 1940–1945* (New York, 1981), p. 149.

36. ASAM, Collection of directives of SS-WVHA, call number D-RF-9/WVHA/8/2, vol. 3, k. 277.

37. Nuremberg document NO-2305.

38. ASAM, Pohl Trial, vol. Pd 18 k. 104 (Pohl's testimony), vol. Pd 22 k. 38, 41, 42 (Pohl's testimony), vol. Pd 28 k. 56 (Thoms's testimony).

39. Nuremberg document SU-511.

40. Edward Dziadosz, "Trade Relations between the Majdanek Concentration Camp and the Paul Reinman Firm" (in Polish) in *Zeszyty Majdanka*, 1967, no. 2, pp. 176 (instruction of January 4, 1943, Nuremberg document 3680-PS), 177 (directive of November 3, 1943).

41. Dziadosz, pp. 173–204.

42. "Autobiography of Höss," p. 115. Cf. testimony by Höss, February 14, 1947, ASAM, call no. IZ-13/71 k. 13.

43. Nuremberg document NO-1257.

44. ASAM, Höss trial, vol. 11, k. 55, 133 (testimony by H. Tauber); Statements collection, vol. 49, k. 83 (K. Szwemberg's testimony); Memoirs collection, vol. 66, k. 20–23 (memoir by K. Gwizdek). Müller, p. 103.

45. Müller, pp. 103, 104; Zalman Gradowski, *In hare fin gehinom: A dokument fin Oyschwitzer Zonderkommando 1944* (Jerusalem, 1978), information in the chapter "Working in the Kommando."

46. ASAM, Statements collection, vol. 21, k. 83.

47. Protocol of an inspection of the recovered hair, conducted by Soviet experts (photocopies). ASAM, collection, call no. IZ-1/5, vol. 56 G, k. 29–34. Presence of a large number of combs, pins, ribbons, and similar objects in the hair found in the camp, in conjunction with explanations provided by former prisoner members of Sonderkommando, was construed by Soviet experts as warranting the conclusion that the hair was cut from heads of bodies of persons murdered in Auschwitz.

48. Protocol of investigations conducted in 1945–46 on the grounds of the Auschwitz camp by members of the Main Commission for the Investigation of German Crimes in Poland, and an opinion of the Institute of Judicial Expertise in Krakow, December 15, 1945, concerning the analysis of human hair found in Auschwitz. ASAM, Höss Trial, vol. 11, k. 30, 72–76.

49. Correspondence and expert opinions regarding hair preserved in Kietrz is to be found in the archival collections of the Institute of National Memory, Poland. In ASAM, see photocopies of parts of this documentation, call no. IZ-13/71; microfilms 24 and 1183. See also testimonies of employees of the Kietrz works, Julian Krischke and Henryk Linkwitz, May 1946, ASAM, Statements collection, vol. 125, k. 32, 33.

50. Expert opinion of the Institute of Forensic Medicine of the Jagiellonian University, November 9, 1949, ASAM, Materials collection, vol. 122, call no. Mat/1030.

51. Christoph U. Schminck-Gustavus, *Hungern für Hitler: Errinnerungen polnischer Zwangsarbeiter im Deutschen Reich 1940–1945* (Reinbek bei Hamburg, 1984), pp. 53–54, 97–99, 105, 112, 114–15.

52. We may assume that former prisoners of Nazi camps who mentioned in their testimonies and memoirs various methods of utilization of human hair as raw industrial material referred to overheard (first- or secondhand) conversations between SS

men on this subject. There is no doubt that some SS men were quite familiar with this subject. See, for instance, an excerpt from testimony by the former commandant of the Treblinka death camp, Franz Stangel, in Adalbert Ruckerl, *Nationalsozialistische Vernichtungslager im spiegel deutscher Strafprocesse: Belzec, Sobibor, Treblinka, Chelmno,* (Munich, 1977), p. 223.

53. Concerning the use of human ashes as fertilizer, see, for example, ASAM, "Report of a Polish major or reminiscences of a former prisoner, Dr. Jerzy Tabeau, composed in 1943–44, shortly after his escape from KL Auschwitz" (in Polish), Resistance movement materials, vol. 5, k. 232; memoirs by a former prisoner, Wanda Urbanska, Memoirs collection, vol. 72, k. 45. See also Tonka Starcevic, "The Sowing of Ashes" (in Polish), in: *Testimonies of Yugoslavs from Nazi Camps and Prisons* (Warsaw, 1975), p. 31. According to testimonies of former prisoners, human ashes also were used in construction and repairs of camp roads, for sprinkling paths passing along living quarters of the camp staff, and for thermal insulation in various construction sites within the camp.

54. ASAM, Höss trial, vol. 32, k. 32. Based on an expert opinion of Dawidowski, references to 6,000 kg of gold and 60 tons of hair appeared in publications dealing with Auschwitz. See, for example, O. Kraus and E. Kulka, *Die Todesfabrik* (Berlin, 1957), p. 125.

55. Eugen Kogon, *Der SS Staat: Das System der deutschen Konzentrationslager,* (Frankfurt am Main, 1946), pp. 296, 297; R. Schnabel, *Macht ohne Moral* (Frankfurt am Main, 1957), p. 203; Yves Ternon and Socrate Helman, *History of the SS Medicine, or the Myth of Biological Racism* (in Polish) (Warsaw, 1973), p. 245. It is not known whether the quoted calculation has been preserved as the original document.

Part *III*

The Perpetrators

MANY NAZI VICTIMS, in their testimonies, memoirs, and writings, claim that the killers were different from ordinary human beings. And psychologists, sociologists, historians, and political scientists have been fascinated by the question of who the killers were. Hannah Arendt provoked considerable controversy in the 1960s with her portrayal of Adolf Eichmann and the banality of evil. Arendt depicted him as a master bureaucrat whose deeds were neither demonic nor sadistic but essentially ordinary, simple, and banal. Christopher Browning has probed the ordinary men of Germany's battalion 101 who became mass murderers when they were assigned the task of shooting Jews daily. Some psychologists, such as Stanley Milgram, have seen the key to understanding the killers in their penchant for obedience, while others, such as Robert Jay Lifton, have sought to understand the psychology of the killers as doubling, the creation of an Auschwitz self to coexist with the non-Auschwitz self.

In two chapters, Aleksander Lasik depicts the perpetrators. His first chapter is a careful examination of Auschwitz camp personnel records that yield some general characteristics about the 6,800 SS men and 200 women who served in the camps. The structure of power was hierarchical. Discipline was maintained by a strict regime of reward and punishment as well as surveillance. By no means were staff members all youthful. Most were born just before or after the First World War and almost half were in their late twenties to mid-thirties. They generally came from a low occupational status with few skills. White-collar workers were not well represented. Yet professional men—doctors and lawyers—fulfilled their professional tasks. Germans and Austrians occupied the higher status jobs. *Volksdeutsch* (ethnic Germans) were often subject to relative discrimination. And when a shortage of personnel forced a reconfiguration of staff, volunteers from occupied territories replaced the SS personnel. Few requested reassignment. Most performed their unpleasant task with the certain knowledge that assignment to the collapsing and deadly Soviet front was an even less desirable alternative. At Auschwitz, the first to "undergo the dehumanization program," Lasik writes, "were the SS men." Their deeds reveal how deeply successful was the process.

Lasik then describes in his second chapter the rise and fall and rise again of Rudolf Höss, the commandant of Auschwitz when Zyklon B and the crematoria were developed and again later during its most lethal stage. Painting less a psychological than a sociohistorical portrait, Lasik explores the making of a mass murderer by depicting Höss's origins, ambitions, frustrations, achievements, and postwar confessions. As a young man, Höss abandoned his family's plans for him to become a priest. He dropped out of school and joined the army in the fervor of the First World War, becoming a decorated soldier. He joined the Nazi party in its earliest years after being mesmerized by Hitler. Upon joining, he renounced his membership in the Roman Catholic Church. As an early Nazi, Höss participated in and was convicted for an assassination and served several years in prison.

As the Nazis came to power, Höss joined the SS and was assigned to Dachau, where he began his concentration camp career. He was a good administrator and rose slowly up the ranks of command. His big break came in 1940, when he was assigned to a commission to recommend use of Auschwitz. He exploited the opportunity and became the first commandant of Auschwitz in 1940, impressing Himmler with his personal dedication to him and with his administrative talents. Höss sought to set a personal example of mental fitness. As commandant, he presided over the rapid expansion of the camp and development of all the instrumentalities of death. He almost became a victim of his success when widespread reports of corruption of camp personnel, tempted by the booty of the "final solution," led to the discharge of 700 men. Höss accepted personal responsibility and was reassigned in 1943. Thanks to bureaucratic maneuvering, he continued in a high position in the concentration camp headquarters and later returned to Auschwitz in time to preside over the annihilation of Hungarian Jews and the dismantling of the camps. Captured after the war, he did not deny his deed. He stood trial, provided much needed information, wrote a biography, and was as generally solicitous of his captors as he had been of his Nazi superiors. His final punishment: death by hanging in gallows erected adjacent to the gas chamber in Auschwitz I. While in jail, he wrote his memoirs, which are an important document for our understanding of the concentration camp phenomenon in general and Auschwitz in particular.

Robert Jay Lifton and Amy Hackett have placed Nazi medical practices at Auschwitz in a larger context as the last stage in the Nazi policy of eugenic purification through medicine. They depict Auschwitz in continuity with earlier sterilization practices and the euthanasia program that had begun in 1938 and moved into a higher gear with Hitler's order backdated to September 1, 1939. This order initiated the systematic murder of mentally retarded, emotionally disturbed, and physically infirm Germans who were an embarrassment to the myth of Aryan supremacy. The ultimate stage of this process of "therapy through mass murder" was reached at Auschwitz and other death camps when doctors presided at the *selektion* ramp in Birkenau. Medical experimentation was but a small part of the medicalized killings. Lifton and Hackett distinguish between the ideological experiments and the pseudoscientific research undertaken by individual Nazi doctors at Auschwitz. They portray individual researchers and the projects they undertook. They also describe the dilemma of the prisoner physicians who often sought to use their special status to preserve the lives of those who could be saved. As the authors put it, healing and killing at Auschwitz were inextricably linked.

Helena Kubica describes the range of important criminal medical experiments carried out in Auschwitz. These experiments included Carl Clauberg's mass sterilizations in Birkenau (using chemical irritants) and Horst Schumann's x-ray sterilizations. Kubica describes in detail Mengele's experiments on twins, the physiology and pathology of dwarfs, the phenomenon of differential coloring of irises, and the causes and treatment of gangrene among Gypsy prisoners. Starvation-inducement experiments by Johann Paul Kremer are also described, as well as the testing of new drugs on behalf of IG Farben and experiments in the treatment of typhus and tuberculosis. "How did it happen," Kubica asks, "that a promising scientist specializing in genetics, a zealous disciple of eugenics, . . . could send thousands to their deaths, and kill scores of children in the name of science?" Kubica proceeds to answer the question with precision, detailing the biography of Mengele, his scientific interest, and his bureaucratic battles. She also describes his escape to South America, where he eluded capture.

Michael Berenbaum

10

Historical-Sociological Profile of the Auschwitz SS

ALEKSANDER LASIK

Contemporary historiography has considerably expanded our knowledge about the perpetrators of the crimes committed by the Nazi Third Reich. A great deal is known about those who planned the Holocaust. But there are still gaps in our knowledge about those who constituted the last link in the enterprise of genocide in the death camps: the ones who pushed the victims into the gas chambers, shut the doors, poured Zyklon B gas capsules into the gas chambers, then sorted, counted, weighed, and assessed the loot that contributed to the Nazi state's economic strength. They were the ones who formed the framework of what is often referred to as the SS state (*SS Staat*). They were, among others, the personnel of the Nazi concentration and death camps, who at the end of the war numbered several tens of thousands. This essay deals with this particular group. Specifically, it examines one subgroup—the SS men and women who ran the largest Nazi camp, Konzentrationlager (KL) Auschwitz.

Thanks to the extant papers of SS staff members, such as personnel records and data, army cards, and similar documents, one is able to undertake a sociological analysis of this group of functionaries and to shed light on the factors that united them as a social group. An empirical sociological account cannot answer how it was possible in the 20th century in a country with formidable humanistic traditions to recruit such a large group of criminals from among people whose psychological-social profile did not deviate much from the average. Such an analysis may convince us, however, that under certain political conditions it is possible to turn average persons into criminals.

The Auschwitz Camp and Its Organization

The Auschwitz concentration camp was established by Reichsführer-SS Heinrich Himmler's order on April 27, 1940.[1] Like all state concentration camps,[2] it was placed organizationally and structurally under the SS Main Office (Hauptamt). In the police hierarchy, however, it was subordinate to the Reich Main Security Office (Reichssicherheitshauptamt). Recruitment of SS men to the Auschwitz camp and specific personnel policies were under the jurisdiction of the SS Main Leadership Office (Führungshauptamt). Economically, Auschwitz belonged to the SS Main Office of Budget and Construction (Hauptabteilung Haushalt und Bauten).

Beginning in February 1942, Auschwitz came under the newly established SS Economic-Administrative Main Office (Wirtschafts-Verwaltungshauptamt, or WVHA). Part of this organization's group D—Concentration Camps (Amtsgruppe D SS-WVHA)—was a unit that coordinated the entire network of camps, the Inspectorate for Concentration Camps (Der Inspekteur des Konzentrationslager), headed by SS-Gruppenführer Richard Glücks.[3]

To better understand the SS personnel at Auschwitz, it is necessary to consider some basic principles and the modus operandi of the concentration camps. All Nazi concentration camps had the same organizational structure, which, broadly speaking, consisted of three components—camp administration, guard forces, and branches or units of the main SS offices.

Camp administration comprised five departments, or *Abteilungen*, marked identically in every camp with Roman numerals. (From 1942 on, there were seven departments.)

The first (Abteilung I) was the Headquarters (Kommandantur) Department, headed by a deputy camp commandant known as the adjutant for SS personnel affairs. This department included the camp communication center, the car pool, and the legal and personnel office.

The second was the Political Department (Abteilung II–Politische Abteilung), which constituted an outpost of the political police (the Gestapo) and the criminal police (the Kripo) within the camp. The Political Department's jurisdiction included registration of prisoners, intake procedures and release of prisoners from the camp, and documentation of dead prisoners. These tasks were assigned to specific subdepartments—receptions and releases, registration, and the registry. The second area of activity of the Political Department was police work. Those functions were assigned to several agencies—the monitoring service, which prepared prisoner identification papers; the investigations and interrogations department; and the department that dealt with surveillance of the prisoners.

Department III–Camp Administration (Abteilung III–Schutzhaftlagerführung) was responsible for the prisoner's quarters and for order and discipline in the camp. Its chief, the Schutzhaftlagerführer, also served as permanent deputy commandant and as the commandant's chief assistant for prisoner affairs. In 1942, the autonomous Department IIIa was created within this department. Designated Abteilung IIIa–Arbeitseinsatz, it assumed responsibility for the organization of prisoner labor, accounting, and the formation of labor squads.

The structure of Department IV–Administration-Economy (Abteilung IV–Verwaltung), was somewhat more complicated. It was responsible for supplies, clothing, the camp laundries and baths, the printing office, and, from 1942 on, the technical aspects of the camp operation. It managed the property of prisoners (both registered prisoners and those consigned to immediate destruction). Confiscated property was amassed in huge depots, and its cash value was accounted for to the central SS authorities after the death of the victims.

Department V–Camp Physician (Abteilung V–Standortarzt) was responsible for sanitation in the camp. Serving under the chief physician in Auschwitz were the camp doctors (Lagerärzte), the doctors of SS units (SS-Truppenärzte) and their assistants—SS medics (Sanitätsdienstgarde-SDG), the director of the dental clinic (Zahnstation), the director of the camp pharmacy (Lagerapotheke), and SS personnel.

Department VI (Abteilung VI–Fürsorge, Schulung, und Truppenbetreuung) was responsible for the care and training of the SS units. It operated as a separate entity and, from 1942 on, was responsible for the schooling and the cultural life of the camp SS personnel.[4]

The guard forces were organized along military lines. The guard battalion (SS-Totenkopfsturmbann) comprised company-size units (SS-Totenkopf-wach-Kompanie), platoons (Zug), and squads (Gruppe). A typical guard company was 200 strong. The number of such companies varied from a few to more than a dozen, depending on the size of the camp at the time.

The guard forces were integrated into the organizational structure of the entire Auschwitz camp complex. In addition to their primary tasks of ensuring complete isolation of camp grounds from the outside world and preventing prisoners from escaping, guard companies served as a reserve personnel pool for various agencies of the camp administration. It was a sizable pool, considering that guards constituted about 75 percent of camp personnel.[5]

In addition to the two main groups of camp personnel, there were other units that operated in Auschwitz. They included the Construction Administration, which came directly under the "Silesia" Construction Inspectorate; the Waffen SS Institute of Hygiene in Rajsko, a branch of the Main Waffen SS Institute in Berlin; Supply Depots of SS Formations (SS-Truppen-Wirtschafts-Lager); German Equipment Works (Deutsche Ausrüstungswerke); and, among others, a branch of the German Foodstuffs Works (Deutsche Lebensmittel GmbH). Before 1942, these groups were not under the direct control of the camp commandant. Only in that year were commandants appointed to head all SS agencies operating in their camps.[6]

Evolution of the SS Personnel

The order that established the Auschwitz concentration camp marked the beginning of the recruitment of SS personnel for the camp. At the outset, SS officers and noncommissioned officers were dispatched from various SS camps and central agencies to set up the camp's basic administrative and economic operations. At the same time, the Auschwitz guard battalion began to take shape.

In 1940, total SS staff members in Auschwitz did not exceed 500. In 1941, the figure rose to 700. By June 1942, the number of SS personnel had grown to 2,000, undoubtedly because of the expansion of the Auschwitz complex and the commencement of the mass extermination of Jews in the framework of the "final solution." In April 1944, there were 2,950 SS staff members in the camp. In August of that year, they numbered 3,342, in part due to the liquidation of the Majdanek camp one month earlier and the ensuing transfer of some prisoners and SS personnel.[7] On January 15, 1945, one day before the camp evacuation, the number of SS personnel reached its peak of 4,481 SS men and 71 SS women supervisors (SS-Aufseherinnen).[8]

Through the entire Auschwitz death enterprise, a total of 6,800 SS men and about 200 SS women supervisors served in the camp. That means that during the years 1940–45, when the average strength was about 3,000, the ranks of Auschwitz SS personnel were completely restaffed.[9] For this sociological analysis, however, all those who ever served at Auschwitz will be considered.

The SS Camp Hierarchy

Every SS person on the camp staff was subordinate to at least two superiors, regardless of his or her position in the camp hierarchy of authority. For example, a rank-and-file guard would be under a squad commander who would assign practical duties. In turn, this squad commander would be under a platoon commander who reported to a company commander, and so forth, up to the camp commandant. Similar principles applied to officials of the camp administration. For example, a mail censor would be directly subordinate to the camp post office director who, in turn, would be responsible to the commandant's adjutant who was subordinate to the commandant.

There were other controls as well. While on duty, a guard would be supervised by an inspection officer as well as by the mobile patrols of the headquarters (the Streifendienst) who made unannounced security checks in the camp. Officials of the camp administration, who constituted the Headquarters Staff (Kommandantur-Stab) and therefore were released from guard duty, were supervised by their direct superiors as well as a noncommissioned staff officer (SS-Stabsscharführer), a position that existed in Departments I, IV, and V. Every staff member on the camp grounds (*Lagerbereich*) was also subject to sudden, unannounced inspections by the mobile patrols.[10]

Department II was responsible for monitoring the conduct of the camp personnel. It was the political agency entrusted with wide powers, including the power to arrest any member of the camp staff anywhere, anytime.[11]

The Documentary Materials

The personnel papers of the SS staff at Auschwitz constitute a basic source of information. The documents can be divided into three categories: (1) original German documents, such as personnel files, questionnaires, forms, and other papers such as transfers, releases, and work histories; (2) documents drawn up for the SS personnel in detention centers in the western occupation zones of Germany after the war; and (3) court records of trials of SS personnel after the war.[12]

These documents include 6,161 files of SS personnel, which contain various kinds of information that is useful as raw data for sociological analysis. These files cover about 85 percent of all SS personnel who served in the camp. Due to the multifaceted character of the data, not all sociological characteristics can be presented equally here, but their veracity cannot be doubted.

Age of SS Personnel

Dates of birth were treated as sociological information. They are available in 3,447, or 56 percent, of the SS personnel files. Thus the ages are known for over half of the group under discussion, a factor that bears significantly on the objectivity of this analysis. The availability of these data made it possible to construct a demographic chart (table 1).

The age difference between the youngest and the oldest members of the camp staff was 49 years. The largest age groups were those born in 1907–13 and 1919–24. The drop in the number born between 1914 and 1918 reflects

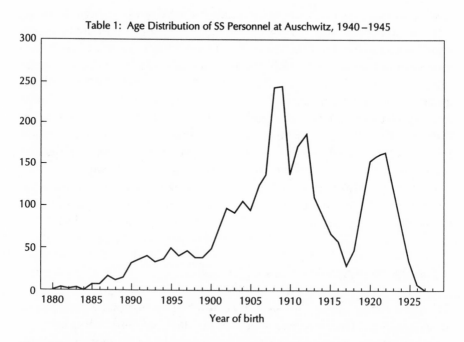

Table 1: Age Distribution of SS Personnel at Auschwitz, 1940–1945

Note: The gap between 1914 and 1920 reflects the effect on birth-rates of World War I.
Source: Aleksander Lasik

a decrease in the birth rate and an increase in the death rate among Germans during the First World War.

The static nature of this table precludes an analysis of the change in age groups of the SS camp staff for each year that the camp was in existence. That is unfortunate because such an analysis could include qualitative conclusions about the personnel policies of the SS Main Leadership Office with respect to job assignments for the camp staff for each year of the war.

Cross tabulation of the age groups of SS personnel with the dates of their tours of duty in the Auschwitz camp yields the following information. In 1940, the largest age group comprised those born in 1907–12. This group constituted 49.7 percent of all SS personnel who served in the camp that year. In 1941, those born in 1904–12 constituted the largest group of personnel (47.1 percent). In 1942, the age groups of those born in 1902–13 constituted 43.8 percent and those born in 1919–24 constituted 30.7 percent. In 1943, the age groups of those born in 1908–11 constituted 30.1 percent. In 1944, the distribution of age groups was the most diverse, with those born in 1891–97 making up 24.4 percent of all SS camp personnel. During that same year, those born in 1900–1901, 1904, 1906–9, and 1913–15 added up to 28.1 percent of SS staff personnel.

These figures indicate that in 1940–41, the Auschwitz SS force remained relatively stable as far as age was concerned. From 1942 on, younger SS personnel were assigned to duty in the camp. In 1943, the younger SS personnel were withdrawn from Auschwitz, clearly because of the situation on the war front. In 1943, the proportion of older age groups increased due to, among other reasons, the assignment to Auschwitz of soldiers of the Wehrmacht and Country Defense (Landes Schutzen) who were unfit for front-line duty.

This analysis does not include 1945 because that was the year that Auschwitz was evacuated and because most of the SS personnel assigned there at that time were from the Debica garrison and the Plaszow concentration camp, among others, and served in the camp only during evacuation.

Studies by Zofia Leszczynska and Miroslaw Glinski[13] focus on SS personnel in the camps of Majdanek and Stutthof. These studies indicate that demographically, the personnel policies of the central SS authorities in these camps were similar to the policies in Auschwitz. In 1944, when Stutthof, Majdanek, and Auschwitz were in operation, the average ages of their SS staffs were 36.1, 36.7, and 36.1, respectively.

Occupation and Education

Personnel papers reveal the former occupations of 1,209 SS personnel who were assigned to Auschwitz. This number represents 19.6 percent of the total population under consideration. As with the dates of birth, the authenticity of the occupational information cannot be doubted.

Analysis of the data indicates that the majority of SS personnel— approximately two-thirds of the group under study—were of low occupational status. In most cases, they came from occupations that required few skills, such as farmers, factory workers, artisans (cobblers, tailors, barbers), waiters, and salaried drivers. The next largest group, accounting for about one-fifth of the SS personnel, comprised clerical workers and merchants. The least represented were skilled white-collar workers, such as teachers, engineers, and physicians.

The occupational distribution of the Auschwitz SS personnel was closely related to the personnel requirements of the camp. Persons with few qualifications were assigned to guard duty. Professionals were assigned to the camp administration. Professional drivers and lawyers were assigned to Department I (the car pool and the legal department). Department IV (Administration-Economy) recruited cooks and restaurateurs to work in food supply, cobblers and tailors to work in clothing supply, jewelers and bank workers to handle prisoner and victim property, and electricians and plumbers to work in the camp's technical services.

Personnel policy guided the staffing of the other administrative posts in the camp, with the obvious exception of SS doctors who worked in medical services. For example, the staff of the camp Gestapo branch, Department II (Political), comprised the management sent by the Katowice police (Polizei-leitstelle Kattowitz) and other functionaries selected from the guard forces. One of the most important criteria with regard to the latter was a command of foreign languages—an important asset as far as investigations and interrogations of prisoners were concerned.[14]

Most of the employees of Department III (Camp Administration) were chosen for duty on the basis of criteria unrelated to their occupational skills. The head of the prisoner block could be anyone who was sufficiently brutal and devoid of humanitarian impulses when it came to relations with the prisoners. On the other hand, labor squad leaders (Kommandoführer) in Department IIIa were selected on the basis of their occupational skills because they were called on to lead specialized squads of gardeners, electricians, and car mechanics. The remaining SS personnel were selected without regard for their civilian occupational qualifications.

An interesting situation existed in Department V (Camp Physician). In addition to SS doctors, the department employed auxiliary personnel made up of SS medics who represented a gamut of professions, most of which had nothing to do with medicine. Among them were cobblers, tailors, and farmers who were given a six-week training course in Oranienburg. In truth, no proven medical skills were required, since most of these workers were assigned tasks similar to those of block leaders. The only difference was that they worked in prisoner hospitals. In operations of mass murder—pouring Zyklon B gas into the gas chambers—all they had to know was the safety rules pertaining to poisonous gases.[15] Department VI did not play a significant role in the camp, and its SS functionaries appear to have been assigned there at random.

Education levels appear to be closely related to the civilian occupations of the SS personnel. Unfortunately, only a handful of the available personnel papers reveal information about the types of schools that the Auschwitz SS staff completed. Therefore, only an indirect analysis is possible. Assuming that farmers, workers, and drivers probably had no more than a primary education, one may deduce that nearly three-quarters (73 percent) of the SS personnel had an elementary education. Slightly more than one-fifth (21.5 percent) of the group (merchants and clerks) had a secondary education, and only 5.5 percent of them (physicians, teachers, and engineers) had a higher education.

Comparison of these data with the occupational and educational cross section of German society as a whole, as revealed in various statistical yearbooks, leads to the conclusion that the SS camp force was not exceptional in its occupational structure or in its levels of education. The camp staff was very much like the society from which it was drawn.

Religious Denominations

The personnel papers of the Auschwitz SS afford information about religious beliefs in two ways. First, beginning in 1937, the SS leadership initiated an unpublicized policy of pressuring its members to leave the religious organizations to which they belonged. From that time on, the term *gottgläubig*, which designated atheism, began to appear as the answer to the question in personnel papers about religious persuasion.[16] Second, a special form was introduced at about the same time, on which the SS personnel pledged to accept a lack of religious denomination. Copies of the forms were included in the files of the SS personnel, and were kept in the appropriate branches of the main SS authority.[17] Nothing is known about the religious practices of the camp personnel who did not renounce their religious beliefs. It is known, however, that there were no chapels in the camp.

Information about religious persuasion, including the gottgläubig category, covers 9 percent of the population under study. More detailed analysis reveals five declared denominations as well as the category "absence of denomination." These data are displayed in table 2, where the SS staff members are further divided into nonmembers and members of the National Socialist (Nazi) Party. Its members especially were pressured to leave their congregations. Data in the table confirm the theory that members of the Nazi party were more likely than nonparty members to leave their churches and that the gottgläubig category was larger than either the Catholic or the Evangelical categories.

Nationalities before 1938

Analysis of the nationalities of the SS personnel who served in the camp and the proportion of them who were Volksdeutsche (citizens of occupied or allied countries of German and Austrian origins) contributes significantly to an understanding of this social group. One important consideration is that in 1938, on the basis of the Munich Agreement, the so-called Sudeten area, with its population of ethnic Germans, was incorporated into Germany. Until that time, these ethnic Germans had been Czechoslovak nationals. It also should be emphasized that Nazi doctrine did not treat Austria as an autonomous state but rather as an integral part of the German Reich. In line

Table 2. Religious Persuasion and Party Membership of Auschwitz SS Staff, 1940–45

Declared Religious Denomination	Nazi Party Member		Nonparty Member		Total
	No.	%	No.	%	%
Catholic	20	3.6	217	39.0	42.6
Evangelical	41	7.4	162	29.1	36.5
Greek-Catholic	—	—	2	0.4	0.4
Adventist	—	—	1	0.2	0.2
Methodist	—	—	1	0.2	0.2
Gottgläubig	64	11.5	48	9.6	20.1
Total	125	22.5	431	77.5	100.0

with this doctrine, the phrase "former Austrian" never appears in personnel papers of SS men under the heading "nationality" (*Staatsangehörigkeit*).

In addition to Czechoslovak nationals from the Sudeten area and later from the Protectorate of Bohemia and Moravia, Volksdeutsche from other countries joined the ranks of SS personnel in the camps. This influx can be attributed to two factors: successive occupation of new territories by the Third Reich and agreements signed by Nazi Germany with the governments of Hungary, Yugoslavia, Romania, and Slovakia that repatriated persons of German origin in territories under the legal control of the Nazi state.[18] Thus in 1940, the ranks of the Auschwitz SS camp staff included nationals of the Czech-Slovak state (Germans from the Sudeten) and the Polish state (from various regions, but mostly from Silesia). In subsequent years, Volksdeutsche nationals arrived from other countries. Their numbers and proportions among the SS staff are presented in table 3.

One interesting regularity revealed by table 3 is that from 1940 to 1943 the proportion of personnel of German origin (who had been considered nationals of other countries until 1938) actually grew at the expense of the proportion of the Reichsdeutsche and Austrians. This was the case even though Reichsdeutsche and Austrians never composed less than half of the camp personnel. In this context, the numbers for 1944 should be viewed in the larger context of personnel shifts, especially the arrival at Auschwitz of SS personnel from agencies, institutions, and concentration camps situated east of Auschwitz that were being liquidated as the front lines advanced westward. In 1944 and 1945, SS personnel documents no longer provided information on former nationality.

Table 3. Pre-1938 Nationalities of SS Staff at Auschwitz, 1940–45

Nationality before 1938	1940 Cases	%	1941 Cases	%	1942 Cases	%	1943 Cases	%	1944 Cases	%	1945 Cases	%
Austrian and German	132	84.6	296	71.8	416	62.1	415	52.1	530	56.1	419	58.1
Czechoslovak:												
–Slovakia	—	—	2	0.5	4	0.6	34	4.3	35	3.7	23	3.2
–Sudeten	9	5.8	19	4.6	25	3.7	25	3.1	23	2.4	18	2.5
Estonian	—	—	1	0.2	1	0.2	1	0.2	2	0.2	2	0.3
Yugoslav	—	—	—	—	74	11.0	118	14.8	129	13.7	92	12.8
Lithuanian	—	—	23	5.6	26	3.9	29	3.6	25	2.7	18	2.5
Latvian	—	—	—	—	—	—	—	—	1	0.1	1	0.1
Polish	15	9.6	35	8.6	58	8.7	52	6.5	63	6.6	56	7.8
Rumanian	—	—	36	8.7	48	7.1	84	10.6	101	10.7	73	10.1
Hungarian	—	—	—	—	18	2.7	38	4.8	36	3.8	19	2.6
Total	156	100	412	100	670	100	796	100	945	100	721	100

Sources: own research.

A question arises. Did the steadily growing influx of Volksdeutsche into the ranks of the Auschwitz SS affect key posts or the camp hierarchy of power? Qualitative analysis of the data indicates that the incoming Volksdeutsche did not assume important positions. They were relatively discriminated against when compared with the Reichsdeutsche and the Austrians, to whom "affirmative action" personnel policies applied. Only the least important offices were reserved for the Volksdeutsche, such as posts in various branches of Department IV—administration and economy (supplies, clothing, and technical services). The Volksdeutsche were also disproportionately represented as chiefs of prisoner blocks, the lowest rung of power in Department III. The majority of the Volksdeutsche were assigned to guard duty. This can be attributed to the mechanisms of promotion in the camp hierarchy of power. For the most part, Volksdeutsche were transferred to Auschwitz immediately upon their recruitment into ranks of the SS, which meant that they lacked knowledge about the way the camp functioned and about the formal and less formal mechanisms of promotion. Most SS personnel who reached senior positions did so after years of service and a steady climb up the organizational ladder.[19] In the struggle of Volksdeutsche for power inside the camp, they were also hampered by the fact that many of them knew little German. That is evident from the handwritten personal histories in their personnel files.

Official Ranks

In addition to the hierarchy of offices in the camp, the SS staff had an official ranking system similar to other military organizations. The system was based on the traditions of the Freikorps, which were active in Germany after the First World War.[20] It had three corps: rank and file, noncommissioned officers, and officers (including generals). The ratio of these categories in Auschwitz was rank and file, 69.7 percent; noncommissioned officers, 26.1 percent; and officers, 4.2 percent.

Promotion in the SS was guided by several principles. Among the rank and file, where the highest rank was that of SS-Rottenführer, promotion was discretionary. The necessary condition to attain the rank of noncommissioned officer (from SS-Unterscharführer to SS-Sturmscharführer) was to complete a noncommissioned officer's course (Unterführerlehrgang) in the camp or to pass a special course such as the one for SS men serving in the camp administration, which was organized in SS training centers outside Auschwitz.

Officer ranks (from SS-Untersturmführer to SS-Obersturmbannführer) were awarded after training in the SS officer school in Braunschweig or Bad Tölz (SS-Junkerschulen). Another option was the SS Higher Technical School in Vienna (Technische Hochschule SS Wien). In rare instances, officer ranks were awarded to SS men who had joined the organization in the 1920s, and who had low serial numbers (the *Alte-Garde*).[21]

Another promotion route was open to the Reichswehr or Wehrmacht servicemen who held military ranks above private. In line with the agreements between the army and Waffen SS, servicemen who transferred to Waffen SS were automatically awarded the equivalent of their military ranks.[22] This policy did not apply to the Volksdeutsche who held military ranks in armies other than German or Austrian. However, previous army service was sometimes taken into consideration in selecting candidates for the SS noncommissioned officer courses.

Force Fluctuations

As mentioned, a total of about 7,000 SS personnel served at Auschwitz during its existence. Since there were on average about 3,000 SS personnel at the camp at any one time, this meant that each position at the camp had to be filled at least twice. This proved to be a difficult task. As early as 1942, searches were under way for suitable personnel reserves, so that any number of SS personnel serving in the camps could be sent for front-line duty. The men were increasingly replaced by women, who assumed three categories of jobs: SS supervisors in camps for women, radio operators and stenographers, and nurses in the SS hospitals serving camp personnel.

At the same time, companies of dog leaders (SS Hundestaffel) were being formed to compensate for the depleted strength of the guard forces.[23] In another move, SS authorities began replacing personnel with volunteers from Ukraine, Lithuania, and Latvia.

SS Personnel Arriving at Auschwitz

The process of selecting the SS camp staff began when the Auschwitz concentration camp was established. In 1940, the SS men assigned to guard duty at Auschwitz arrived mainly from the Dachau, Buchenwald, and Sachsenhausen camps. In 1941, SS personnel began to arrive from various frontline SS formations (including those whose injuries rendered them unfit for front-line duty). Most were from the Sixth Mountain Division Nord. But it was only in 1942 that the number of points of origin of the incoming SS personnel increased significantly, due in all probability to the expansion of the camp and its tasks.

At that time the recruitment effort focused on those who had been incorporated into the SS by the replenishment offices, which operated at each SS Higher Sector (Erganzungstellen bei dem SS-Oberabschnitte). Many came from the replenishment office of the XIII SS-Oberabschnitte Southeast in Vienna, where there were large numbers of Volksdeutsche from Hungary, Yugoslavia, and Romania. Others came to Auschwitz from the Gross-Rosen, Neuengamme, and Mauthausen-Gusen concentration camps, and from the Second SS Armored Division Das Reich. In 1943, the Auschwitz SS force was boosted by recruits from various SS training camps, especially from Debica (SS-Truppen-Übungsplatz Debica). In 1944, a large number of SS personnel were sent to Auschwitz from the Majdanek and Plaszow concentration camps, which had been evacuated. The recruitment effort also encompassed Wehrmacht servicemen, who constituted 38.7 percent of all the new arrivals.

SS Personnel Leaving Auschwitz

Parallel with the influx of new recruits was the movement of personnel out of the Auschwitz camp. Beginning in 1941, this movement assumed significant dimensions as large numbers of SS men were transferred to the Sixth Mountain Division Nord. In 1942, the number of those leaving the camp increased. In addition to the Nord Division, considerable numbers were transferred to the Fifth SS Armored Division Viking and to the Gross-Rosen and

Neuengamme camps. In 1943, the pattern of departures remained largely unchanged with regard to numbers and destinations. In 1944, the situation changed when the Stutthof camp attracted many Auschwitz veterans. The largest numbers, however, were transferred to two SS training camps: Beneszow in Czechoslovakia (SS-Truppen-Übungsplatz "Bohmen" Beneschau), and Lieberose (SS-Truppen-Übungsplatz "Kurmark" Lieberose).

During the final liquidation of the Auschwitz camp in 1945, very few SS camp personnel were transferred to combat formations because in the preceding years practically all members of the Auschwitz SS staff who were fit for combat duty had been transferred to Waffen SS. Most SS staff members were transferred to other concentration camps, especially camps that served as destination points for evacuated prisoners—Buchenwald, Sachsenhausen, Gross-Rosen, Mittelbau-Dora, Mauthausen-Gusen, Neuengamme, Flossenburg, and Dachau. These transfers marked the end of the Auschwitz camp and its SS personnel. The superiors of the central SS authorities held the Auschwitz staff in high regard. Many of the SS men who held prominent positions at Auschwitz assumed similar responsibilities in other camps—including the Lagerführer (adjutant to the camp commandant) and the chief of administrative agencies.

Effectiveness

Considered as a social group, the Auschwitz SS personnel were highly heterogeneous. Before 1938, members differed from each other in a number of ways—age, occupation, education, religion, nationality. Fluctuations in membership indicate that the group also exhibited a low degree of cohesiveness. In light of this information, it is interesting to consider the factors that enabled such a highly diversified collectivity to function so effectively in the Nazi murder apparatus. The underlying causes undoubtedly derived from many factors, but two elements played the most significant roles—the internal regime of the group and the conditions that strengthened individual motivation to accomplish specific tasks.

The cornerstone of the internal regime of the SS staff was the strict hierarchical structure of power in the camp, where every superior evoked fear in his subordinates. That led to frequent abuses of power, especially when one considers that camp regulations were often phrased imprecisely. Violations of identical or similar regulations often resulted in different punishments for different SS personnel. Punishments included arrest, transfer to another camp, expulsion to an SS penal company, or trial by the SS court. Any punishment impeded ambitious individuals from advancing their careers. There is also evidence that informal discrimination against the Volksdeutsche took place. This discrimination was a fertile ground for feelings of frustration, which in some cases was vented on the prisoners. Superiors as well as servicemen held toughness in high regard.

The second important instrument of coercion was the surveillance branch of Department II. This branch not only infiltrated the prisoner population but also closely monitored any contacts between the SS personnel and the prisoners. Of special concern were transactions of gold, food, alcohol, and other commodities and any humane treatment of prisoners in violation of regulations. There is no doubt that the SS camp authorities were aware of the mood that prevailed among their subordinates. It appears, however, that the relations that existed among members of the SS personnel were deemed desirable, and consequently were tacitly approved. In this case, the principle of divide and rule proved workable.

Camp authorities also used rewards to produce desired behavior. Like punishments, rewards were meted out selectively. They included commendations, promotions, bonuses for shooting prisoners at the death wall, and extra food or alcohol rations for participating in mass extermination operations.

Psychologically, many SS men considered their tour of duty in the camp as an opportunity to avoid being sent to the front. At the same time, it offered them opportunities to get rich quickly by plundering the property of victims murdered in the gas chambers. Camp authorities were aware of this and tolerated such "irregularities" to varying degrees, especially since they also took active roles in the plundering. But in time, corruption and embezzlement reached such alarming proportions that Himmler was forced to set up a special commission of SS judges. On the basis of the commission's recommendations, several hundred SS men were arrested, including the director of the political department in Auschwitz, SS-Untersturmführer Max Grabner, who by virtue of the powers invested in his agency was supposed to uphold the legal system.[24]

For power-hungry individuals who were often harassed by their direct superiors, duty in the camp provided an opportunity to compensate for feelings of inferiority. SS men were practically free to beat, brutalize, and murder prisoners. Superiors exhibited tolerant attitudes in such cases despite formal regulations that prohibited such actions. The price that the SS men had to pay to avoid punishment and to be eligible for rewards was the same for every member of the force. They had to renounce their moral principles and actively participate in the mass murder of prisoners. Almost without exception, the members of the SS force agreed to pay that price.

Despite the fear of punishment and the hopes for rewards, there were alternatives to brutality available to the SS men. They could submit requests to be relieved from duty in the camp or to be completely relieved from duty in the SS. (In 1940–42, the authorities granted many such requests.) SS men could extend limited assistance to the prisoners, or express disinterested but favorable attitudes toward them. That some SS men chose these alternatives is attested by court records of trials against them after the war; these records show that they were acquitted on the basis of witness testimonies of former prisoners.

No extant camp document contains any evidence of punishment inflicted on an SS man for refusing to take part in the Holocaust. That people were willing to murder thousands of others does, however, testify to the destructive and efficient functioning of the camp ideology and a regime that aimed to dehumanize some prisoners. But the first to undergo the dehumanization process, and on a much larger scale, were the SS personnel who served there.

NOTES

1. D. Czech, "Konzentrationlager Auschwitz: Zarys historyczny," in: *Oswiecim: Hitlerowski oboz masowej zaglady* (Warsaw, 1987), p. 15.

2. The designation "state concentration camp" (*Staatliches Konzentrationlager*) was apparently used for the first time by the chief of the Bavarian Political Police (Bayerische Politische Polizei), later chief of the Reich Main Security Office, SS-Obergruppenführer Reinhard Heydrich, to distinguish the camps controlled by the SS (before the so-called "Rohm putsch") from "wild" detention centers designed for opponents of the brown regime. See H. G. Richardi, "Schule der Gewalt: Das KL Dachau also Modell für den Aufbau des KZ-Sytems," in *Verfolgung, Ausbeutung, Vernichtung: Die Lebens- und arbeitsbedingungen der Häftlinge in deutschen Konzentrationslagern 1933–1945* (Hannover, 1985), p. 37.

3. A. Lasik, "Ewolucja kadrowa formacji SS 'Totenkopf,' a udzial Volksdeutschow polskich w zalodze obozu koncentracyjnego w Oswiecimiu" (Evolution of the cadres of the SS formation 'Totenkopf' and Polish Volksdeutsche on the staff of the Auschwitz concentration camp), *Przeglad Zachodni*, 1989, no. 4, p. 106.

4. See study by A. Lasik, "Zaloga SS w obozie koncentracyjnym w Oswiecimiu w latach 1940–1945: Analiza historyczno-socjologiczna," in files of the library of the A. Mickiewicz University in Poznan.

5. Ibid.

6. F. Piper, *Zatrudnienie wiezniow KL Auschwitz: Organizacja pracy i metody exploatacji sily roboczej* (Oswiecim, 1981), p. 84.

7. T. Iwaszko, "Ucieczki wiezniow z obozu koncentracyjnego w Oswiecimiu," in *Zeszvtv Oswiecimskie*, 1963, no. 7, p. 20.

8. Archives of the Main Commission for the Investigation of Nazi Crimes in Poland (AMC), microfilm collection, call no. M-891, frame 51.

9. Estimates were reached by this author, who has in his possession a card index of members of the SS camp personnel. This card index is continuously updated with every available piece of information from various archival sources.

10. See n. 4 above.

11. See n. 4 above.

12. After the war, over 600 former members of the SS staff were formally charged and prosecuted in Poland. Court records are in AMC.

13. Z. Leszczynska, "Struktora osobowa wladz obozu koncentracyjnego na Majdanku," in *Zeszyty Majdanka*, vol. 2 (Lublin, 1967), pp. 22–91; M. Glinski, "Zaloga obozu koncentracyjnego Stutthof (September 1, 1939–May 9, 1945)," in *Stutthof Zeszyty Museum*, 1984, no. 5, pp. 187–216; no. 6/1gB5, pp. 97–120; 1987, no. 7, pp. 202–34, Wroclaw Warsaw-Krakow-Gdansk-Lodz.

14. See n. 4 above.

15. See n. 4 above.

16. H. Höhne, *Der Orden unter dem Totenkopf: Die Geschichte der SS* (Hamburg, 1966), p. 472.

17. See, for example, Bundesarchiv Koblenz (BA), call no. NS.4 (Hi)12.

18. Copies of some of these agreements are to be found in Federal Koblenz Archives; see BA, call no. NS.7/91.

19. See comparison of careers of a number of SS men from Dachau, in *Konzentrationslager Dachau 1933–1945* (Dachau, 1978), pp. 78–79.

20. R. Majewski, Waffen-SS, *Mity i Rzeczywistosc* (Wroclaw-Krakow-Gdansk, 1977), p. 2as.

21. One SS man promoted in this fashion in Auschwitz was Schutzhaftlagerführer Hans Aumeier; see *Autobiografia Rudolfa Hossa, komendanta obozu oswiecimskiego* (Warsaw, 1989), p. 207.

22. Majewski; *Autobiografia Rudolfa Hossa*, p. 350.

23. *Autobiografia Rudolfa Hossa*, pp. 139–40.

24. This commission was headed by the SS judge, SS-Sturmbannführer Konrad Morgen. The commission's work resulted in the dismissal from their posts of commandants of concentration camps at Sachsenhausen, Hertogenbosch, and Flossenburg, among others. Höhne, p. 403.

11

Rudolf Höss: Manager of Crime

ALEKSANDER LASIK

More than any other Nazi concentration camp commandant, Rudolf Höss has been sharply etched in history. The man who founded and commanded Auschwitz appears in the index of virtually every book dealing with the fate of European Jews during the Second World War. His personality has been studied by psychologists and sociologists, and his autobiography has served as the basis for a novel.[1]

Who was this man? How did he reconcile his love for family and fondness for animals with his involvement in the construction and operation of a death factory, the greatest graveyard in the world? While historians find it interesting, even necessary, to speculate on the factors that shaped Höss's life, it is the examination of facts within a broader social-historical perspective that permits an objective and accurate evaluation of the individual's true role in history.

Rudolf Franz Ferdinand Höss[2] was born on November 25, 1900, in Baden-Baden in southwest Germany. His father, Franz Xaver Höss, was a successful merchant's clerk, his mother, Pauline Höss, née Speck, a housewife. The oldest of three children, Rudolf was the only son. He spent his first six years in Baden-Baden, a provincial town well known as a health resort. Thanks to the financial independence of his father, Rudolf's boyhood was relatively carefree and prosperous. In his autobiography, written 40 years later in a Polish prison,[3] Höss recalled with nostalgia an idyllic childhood when his horse was his loyal companion.

His home resembled others in the German middle class with its intermingling of elements of nationalism and a measure of extreme Catholic piety. In

1906 or 1907, the Höss family moved to the nearby town of Mannheim, where Rudolf was taught for two years by a private tutor and then enrolled in elementary school. On Rudolf's graduation, his father signed him up at a humanities school in the hope that his son would become a priest. Shortly afterward, on the eve of the outbreak of the First World War, Rudolf's father died.

In those prewar years, the atmosphere in Germany was suffused with a nationalist euphoria that peaked when Germany entered the war. It engulfed young Rudolf, who, as he wrote in his autobiography, was raised in the cult of the uniform and military tradition. Höss abandoned plans to become a priest, and in late July 1916, dropped out of school to join the army. Although too young for conscription, Höss succeeded in joining the 21st Reserve Squadron of the Second Baden Dragoon Regiment.

After four weeks of military training at the reserve cavalry squadron at Bruchsal/Baden, his subunit was incorporated into the Asia Corps and assigned to fight alongside the Turkish Sixth Army. In the course of combat, Höss was wounded three times, and he received the Iron Cross Second Class. Although still underage, Höss assumed command of his own cavalry unit in the spring of 1918 and shortly thereafter received the Iron Cross First Class. By that time Germany and its allies had, for all practical purposes, lost the war. Haunted by the specter of prison, Höss returned to Germany on his own.

Höss's mother had died during his absence and he found himself at odds with the remaining family members because of his unwillingness to become a priest. He joined the East Prussian Free Corps (Freikorps), a military unit led by Lieutenant Gerhard Rossbach that operated independently of the regular German army (the Reichswehr). Höss took part in the suppression of disturbances in Latvia and in quelling workers who were staging a revolt in the Ruhr in 1920. Shortly thereafter, the Freikorps Rossbach was disbanded, then reorganized and deployed to suppress an uprising of ethnic Poles who opposed the League of Nations plan for the Polish-German border in Upper Silesia. For his exploits in these battles, Höss was awarded the Baltic Cross and the Cross of the Silesian Eagle.[4] In 1922, the Freikorps was finally dissolved, although its traditions endured.[5]

That November, Höss attended a reunion of Freikorps Rossbach veterans in Munich, where he saw Adolf Hitler speak for the first time. Höss was so impressed that he immediately joined the Nazi party. His very low party serial number, 3,240, indicating his early membership in the party, became a badge of honor. When Höss joined the party, he renounced his membership in the Roman Catholic Church.[6]

Due to Germany's failure to pay war reparations, France and Belgium entered and occupied the Upper Rhine region in January 1923. Extremist

German circles responded by organizing acts of sabotage. Leading the groups of saboteurs was Albert Leo Schlageter, who was eventually arrested by the French after former Freikorpsman Walter Kadow denounced the groups' actions. In reprisal, Höss, in concert with two others, murdered Kadow on the estate that belonged to Martin Bormann, Hitler's future secretary.[7] Kadow's assassination is the only known case of Höss's direct participation in a "criminal" act.

On March 15, 1923, Höss was sentenced to ten years in prison by the State Tribunal for the Protection of the Republic. Since the crime was classified as politically motivated rather than common murder, Höss was allowed to maintain his party membership and assume the glory of a veteran Nazi fighter.[8] His prison sentence prevented him from taking part in the Munich putsch on November 9, 1923, which might have changed the direction of his career in the Nazi regime.[9]

In his autobiography, Höss recalled that his prison experience helped prepare him for his future responsibilities in concentration camps. He was released from prison following amnesty in 1929, having served half of his sentence (five years). Upon release, he opted for life as a farmer despite offers from those who had appreciated his determination and devotion to the Nazi cause. He maintained party ties by becoming a member of an agrarian organization affiliated with the Nazi party. It was in this group, the League of Artamans, that he met his future wife, Hedwig Hansel, whom he married on August 7, 1929.

Hitler took power on January 30, 1933, and began the task of realizing his vision of a National Socialist (Nazi) state. In the aftermath of the February Reichstag fire, a concentration camp, Dachau, was set up near Munich on March 23 and another was established several days later at Oranienburg, near Berlin. The two main opposition parties, the Communist and the Social Democrat, were declared illegal. The Nazi party leadership made a broad appeal to all devoted activists and Nazi sympathizers who had not yet assumed a post in the party or in the state apparatus, both of which were undergoing purges at every level.

Höss decided to abandon farming and return to the uniform he revered. On September 20, 1933, he applied to the Allgemeine SS, part of the Nazi storm troops, the SA. The SS became autonomous in July 1934, following its contribution to the suppression of the so-called "Röhm putsch."[10] That same month, the SS took over all the concentration camps within the SA's jurisdiction. From then on, the "black order" campaigned to consolidate an independent power base, which became known as "SS Staat."

Initially a soldier in the second battalion of the Fifth SS Regiment, Höss was transferred in June 1934 to the tenth battalion of the Ninth Allgemeine SS Regiment. The turning point of his career came when he signed a 12-

year professional contract with this organization. That same day Höss joined the SS guard battalion (SS-Wachtgruppe) at Dachau, serving under Camp Inspector (and future SS-Gruppenführer) Theodor Eicke.[11] Eicke created the regime of camp discipline adopted throughout the camp system.

The future Auschwitz commandant trained for several weeks at Dachau, then assumed guard duties, like all SS beginners. He waited more than a year for his first promotion, on March 1, 1935, then was transferred to Department IIa[12] as a prison block leader, or Blockführer. In addition to maintaining order and discipline, Höss assisted in punishing prisoners by flogging them, a policy sanctioned by Eicke as a legitimate penalty. Little is known about Höss's attitudes and conduct during this period.[13] It appears that he did not stand out from other henchmen; nor does his name appear in reminiscences of prisoners incarcerated in Dachau during his tenure.

Höss waited almost three years for his next promotion. On April 1, 1936, he was promoted to SS noncommissioned report officer (SS-Rapportführer). In his new position he commanded all the Blockführers, and acted as right hand to the camp manager (Schutzhaftlagerführer).

Political changes in the Third Reich brought changes to the state concentration camps. Smaller camps were replaced by larger ones that could house several tens of thousands of prisoners. In 1937, two large camps, Sachsenhausen and Buchenwald, were set up to replace smaller ones. The exception was Dachau, which continued to operate. As the SS expanded and consolidated the economic foundations of its power, it relied increasingly on the free labor of prisoners, who were treated as raw material for its operations.[14]

Reorganization of the camp system affected Höss, who was transferred to Sachsenhausen as SS Rapportführer on August 1, 1938. Höss had gained sufficient seniority and experience at Dachau, which served as the camp administration training facility in the 1930s, so his abilities were put to use at Sachsenhausen, where a new team of administrative officials was being assembled. Höss quickly gained recognition. Having advanced to the post of commandant adjutant after the outbreak of the war, he assumed the duties of commandant deputy for prisoner affairs, the Shutzhaftlagerführer. He also moved up the ranks of the SS. A first private in April 1934, he was named first corporal in November 1934, platoon leader in April 1935, sergeant in July 1935, first sergeant in March 1936, second lieutenant in September 1936, first lieutenant in September 1938, and captain in November 1938. Höss won his epaulets without completing the required education or graduating from SS officer school.[15]

The outbreak of war with Poland on September 1, 1939, meant new opportunities for SS members and for those who worked in the SS concentration camp system. Once a large concentration camp was established at Mauthausen in Austria, the SS began searching for potential sites in Poland to incarcerate ideological and political opponents of the Third Reich. Of particular interest were areas of Poland that were incorporated into the Reich at the time and of Silesia, where German troops had begun mass arrests and murders of Poles and Polish Jews.

As mass roundups continued and overcrowding of the provisional detention centers reached unmanageable proportions, SS policymakers decided to establish a large concentration camp in Silesia. In January 1940, a commission headed by the Schutzhaftlagerführer from Sachsenhausen, SS-Obersturmführer Walter Eisfeld, was dispatched to a site at Auschwitz and other locations. At Auschwitz, the commission evaluated the feasibility of establishing a new camp on the grounds of a former Polish army barracks. Eisfeld advised against the proposed location, but the Auschwitz camp was established by the winter of 1940.

Höss assumed duties of camp director at Sachsenhausen. He had not been recruited into the Waffen SS formations that Eicke was assembling in Dachau in September 1939 because of a directive issued by SS chief Heinrich Himmler excluding senior camp officials from front-line duty. Himmler was concerned that senior officials might be captured and forced to inform the enemy about the camp system.

Höss was appointed to head a commission to decide how to use the Polish army barracks at Auschwitz. His recommendations prompted Himmler to issue an order on April 27, 1940, that established KL Auschwitz to house about 10,000 prisoners. Eisfeld and Höss differed on the use of Auschwitz due to one issue—the task of setting up a new camp. After Eisfeld inspected the terrain and evaluated the difficulties involved, he decided not to accept the position of Auschwitz commandant. Höss, on the other hand, seized the opportunity to display his organizational talents. Thus Höss's personal ambition apparently played a key role in the choice of Auschwitz as a concentration camp site.

Höss was appointed commandant of the new camp on May 1, 1940. He tackled the tasks at hand with a passion. In addition to converting the old army barracks, he established a camp agricultural farm and created appropriate conditions to establish SS-owned firms in the camp.[16] When Himmler first visited Auschwitz on March 1, 1941, he was impressed with Höss's successes. Himmler instructed Höss to expand the Stammlager (main camp) to hold the 30,000 prisoners expected to arrive in the course of the anticipated war with the Soviet Union. In addition, Himmler ordered that a camp for 100,000 prisoners of war be set up in nearby Brzezinka (KL Auschwitz-Birkenau) and that a labor force of 10,000 prisoners be placed at the disposal of IG Farbenindustrie to construct a chemical works. Höss, who must have conceived of this colossal task as his own special mission, lost no time in getting to work.[17]

Hitler, however, scaled back Himmler's grand plans for Auschwitz in 1941. Instead, Auschwitz was assigned a special role in the plan to liquidate European Jews, euphemistically termed the "final solution of the Jewish question" (*Endlösung der Judenfrage*). Thus Höss launched the multifaceted preparations necessary for the ghastly mission of the camp. In his autobiography, Höss maintained that he first learned of the plan and the designation of Auschwitz as the hub of the Holocaust in the summer of 1941. Accordingly, he modified his plans for Birkenau and began setting up installations of mass extermination.

In the search to find a way to quickly and effectively kill masses of people, an experiment was conducted at Auschwitz on September 3, 1941, using the gas prussic (hydrocyanic) acid, known commercially as Zyklon B. Six hundred Soviet POWs and 250 camp prisoners were gassed in the cellars of block 11. Höss's postwar claim that the gassing took place in his absence is questionable; at any rate, as camp commandant he must have issued the order to authorize an operation of that scale. He must have been satisfied with the results of the test. The death of several hundred persons did not seem to trouble his conscience. He had again proved that he could be counted on to carry out any task assigned to him.

With the site of the Holocaust finally designated and a suitable number of trained SS personnel, equipment, and chemicals ready, Reinhard Heydrich, chief of the Reich Main Security Office (RSHA) and SS-Obergruppenführer, convened a coordinating conference at Wannsee, near Berlin. The conference was held on January 20 to coordinate the RSHA's actions with other administrative agencies of the Third Reich.[18] The wheels of the Holocaust had already started to roll and did not stop until November 1944.

Shortly after the Wannsee Conference, the first transports of Jews from Silesia rolled into Auschwitz. The deportees were killed with Zyklon B in a specially refitted charnel house attached to crematorium I in the main camp. The number of persons consigned to death soon reached such proportions that Höss issued an order to convert two old peasant houses in the village of Brzezinka into gas chambers. These additions proved insufficient, as it became clear that the chief technical obstacle was not the gassing but the disposal of the bodies by incineration. Consequently, plans were made to construct four large units, each combining a crematorium with a gas chamber. During construction in late July and early August 1942, surplus bodies were incinerated on special outdoor pyres.

In Höss's mind, his duties went beyond monitoring and supervising the death factory: the commandant should set a personal example of mental fitness for the SS personnel directly involved in the mass murders. In many accounts, prisoners referred to Höss's stony, expressionless face, which seemed to betray no emotion whatsoever. In his reminiscences, Höss attempted to justify his demeanor, although any feelings of pity he mustered for the prisoners must have emerged in prison rather than on the Birkenau off-loading platform.

Höss's diligence in constructing the death factory, in overseeing its efficient functioning, and in presenting an example of an unimpeachable psychological fortitude to his SS subordinates proved unequal, however, to a phenomenon that reached alarming proportions in the death camps—corruption of camp personnel. Reports of corruption that reached the SS main command centers in 1942 forced Reichsführer-SS Himmler to take action. In 1943, Himmler ordered the formation of a special commission of SS judges, headed by SS-Sturmbannführer Major Dr. Konrad Morgen, to investigate abuses in the camps. As a result of the commission's work, more than 700 SS men from various camps were either discharged from active service or put under arrest. Some were put on trial before SS courts or sent to the front. Others were hospitalized in psychiatric wards.[19]

In Auschwitz, the Morgen commission uncovered the existence of massive corruption, willful killing of prisoners, and a special fund, called Schwarze Kasse, through which monies were funneled for officer corps banquets. Despite the destruction of key evidence in a barracks fire set by "unknown perpetrators," a number of SS men were put under arrest for criminal activity and abuse. The most senior victim of the purge at Auschwitz was the chief of the camp Gestapo, SS-Untersturmführer Maximilian Grabner, who was responsible for preventing such abuse. The second in importance was camp henchman and Rapportführer Gerhard Palitzsch, a protégé of Höss's who held the rank of technical sergeant.

Höss did not mention the affair in his autobiography. In all likelihood, he was not personally involved. But in the aftermath of the scandal, for which he bore formal responsibility, Höss could no longer serve as camp commandant. His previous accomplishments saved him from being arrested or otherwise called to account. In Auschwitz, he had been promoted to major in January 1941 and lieutenant-colonel in July 1942 and decorated with high orders usually awarded to front-line combatants, the War Service Cross Second Class with Swords in April 1941 and the War Service Cross First Class with Swords in April 1943.

On November 11, 1943, Höss was transferred and appointed chief of Department DI—Central Office within the SS Economic-Administrative Main Office (WVHA). He assumed his new post in January 1944, replacing SS-Obersturmbannführer Arthur Liebehenschel, who was appointed to replace Höss as commandant of the Auschwitz camp.[20] In this new position, Höss enjoyed much broader powers and authority than he had at Auschwitz. In the organizational hierarchy of the camp administration, he was deputy to the inspector for concentration camps, a post held by SS-Gruppenführer

Richard Glücks.[21] Höss coordinated all undertakings within the entire camp system, had the right to control the activities of camp commandants, and could submit proposals for personnel changes in the camps. In this regard, the corruption affair in Auschwitz had a happy ending for Höss. His new appointment was not an exile but a promotion, as he affirmed in his autobiography. At his new headquarters in Oranienburg, Höss acquired detailed knowledge of the entire camp system—its size, administrative methods, and decision-making mechanisms. As Auschwitz camp commandant he had been in charge of one part of the system and unable to assess it as a whole.

As manager of crime, Höss's was concerned mainly to improve the camp machinery of death. But he was either not good at office duties or took no interest in them. He missed commanding the action and the crime apparatus. This interest led him back to Auschwitz. After Adolf Eichmann ordered the deportation of several hundred thousand Jews from Hungary to Auschwitz in mid-1944, Höss arranged for his successor at Auschwitz, Liebehenschel, to be appointed commandant of the Lublin-Majdanek camp,[22] and then returned to Auschwitz, where he assumed command of the SS garrison for several months. The commandants of all the Auschwitz camps (KL Auschwitz I, II, and III) now answered directly and formally to him. He personally coordinated the destruction of the Hungarian Jews, code-named "Aktion Höss." He also managed the liquidation of sector BIIe in Birkenau in August 1944, which had been inhabited by Gypsies since February 1943. Shortly thereafter, Höss returned to Oranienburg.

The Third Reich was collapsing, and with it, the camp system, although the camps continued to execute prisoners. Höss faced the urgent task of preparing the evacuation of the camps, which were perilously close to the front lines in Western and Eastern Europe. Again Höss turned his attention to Auschwitz, then under the command of SS-Sturmbannführer Richard Bär.[23] Many died in the mass chaos as victims evacuated the camps on foot. Even those who managed to reach their destinations found no relief. In some places, such as Bergen-Belsen, the desperate prisoners went through nightmarish ordeals that included incidents of cannibalism.

For political reasons, Himmler did not give the order to liquidate all camp prisoners. When the order finally came, the former Auschwitz commandant lacked any means to carry it out, although he probably would have done so without hesitation or scruples.

In May 1945, Höss set out for Flensburg, Himmler's last headquarters. He traveled with SS-Gruppenführer Glücks and the chief of Department DII-Prisoner Labor at SS-WVHA, SS-Standartenführer Gerhard Maurer. At Flensburg, Himmler learned of Hitler's political testament stripping him of all state positions and expelling him from the Nazi party. It is no surprise that Höss's last meeting with his SS superior, with whom he had become

close over the years, left Höss very disappointed. He was especially dis-
heartened by the suggestion that SS men disguise themselves as Wehrmacht soldiers to await the outbreak of the Third World War.[24] While he
may have been indignant at the suggestion, Höss nonetheless treated it as
an order. He obtained the official papers of a boatswain of the Kriegsmarine
and went into hiding on Sylt Island, where he was captured by the British.
His identity unknown to his captors, Höss declared he had been a farmer in
civilian life and was allowed to go. He assumed the identity of "Fritz Lang"
and worked as a farmer for some time.

As a result of intensive searches by the British Field Security Police, Höss
was captured and his identity revealed nine months after the end of the war,
on March 11, 1946. He did not follow in the footsteps of his mentor and
leader, Himmler, who committed suicide. He was imprisoned in former
army barracks at Heide, then was transferred to the main British center for
interrogations of the most wanted war criminals, at Minden. Later he was
subpoenaed as a witness for the defense of the Reich Central Security chief,
SS-Obergruppenführer Ernst Kaltenbrunner,[25] and was taken to Nuremberg,
where the chief Nazi criminals were tried before the International Military
Tribunal.

But the plans of Kaltenbrunner's defense counsel ran aground. Höss was
outspoken in his testimony. Impassively, he gave precise answers to questions by the judges, the prosecution, and the defense counsel. He corrected
figures when he knew them and statements that he judged to be untrue.
According to the transcript of his interrogation on April 4, 1946, he claimed
that "the total of 2,500,000 victims were incinerated in Auschwitz, with at
least 500,000 more who died of illness and exhaustion." He later claimed
that he received these figures from Eichmann. Höss neither protected
anyone nor evaded his own responsibility. His stance came as a surprise to
many, especially those who viewed him as a bloodthirsty beast. Instead, he
viewed his crimes in terms of the technical obstacles and challenges with
which he had to cope. Höss stated that he led the killings in Auschwitz on
express orders of Reichsführer Himmler.

On May 25, 1946, at the request of the Polish government, Höss was extradited, and he arrived in Poland for the last time. The Supreme National
Tribunal had been formed to try the major Nazi criminals who operated in
the Polish state from 1939 through 1945.[26] The proceedings against the
former commandant, which opened on March 11, 1947, in Warsaw, aroused
considerable international interest. The indictment drafted by the prosecution contained two main charges: belonging to a criminal organization, the
SS, and the Nazi party, and acting as commandant of the Auschwitz camp
from May 1, 1940, to October 1943, as chief of Department DI of SS-WVHA
from December 1943 to May 1945, and as commander of the Auschwitz gar-

rison from June 1944 to September 1944, during which times he was involved in taking the lives of 300,000 prisoners, four million citizens (mostly Jews), and 12,000 Soviet prisoners of war. The second charge also included moral and mental abuse of prisoners and overseeing the plunder of property and valuables that involved profanation of the dead by removing dental work made of precious metals and alloys.[27]

Experts, former prisoners, and members of the Auschwitz camp personnel who also had been extradited to Poland took the stand during the proceedings. Höss behaved as he had at the Nuremberg trial. He replied briefly, precisely, and impassively to every question posed to him. He did not deny the charges nor behave provocatively. Just as he had applied himself consistently and impassively to the task of building the ghastly death factory a few years earlier, he explained details without emotion. He did not display servility or attempt to draw a lighter sentence by admitting guilt. He never indicated that he entertained any illusions about his sentence. His last words restated his responsibility for all that had happened in Auschwitz. He did not appeal for leniency. He only asked for permission to send a farewell letter to his family and to return his wedding ring to his wife. The proceedings concluded on March 29.

The sentence of death was passed on April 2. While the sentence and its grounds were read out, Höss stood stiffly at attention with a stony face that betrayed no emotion. After he was sentenced, he made a statement thanking his defense counsel for the effort invested in his case, and declared that he would not ask for clemency. The next day, Höss was sent under reinforced escort to the Wadowice prison, from which he was moved to Auschwitz for execution. On the morning of April 16, 1947, several dozen yards from his former villa near crematorium I in the main camp, Höss was hanged. At ten minutes past eight o'clock, the court doctor pronounced him dead.

Höss became a symbol of Nazi crimes against nationals of many European countries, and of European Jews in particular. For a variety of reasons, Höss eclipsed his superiors in the popular historical memory of the Holocaust. First, he had never concealed his identity, so he was well known to the prisoners, many of whom recalled him in their memoirs and testimonies. Second, he wrote an autobiography while in the Polish prison which makes fascinating reading despite its subjective and one-sided character. His story was published in several editions and translated into several languages. Third, in contrast to many other Nazi defendants, his behavior during the proceedings against him revealed a man capable of assuming responsibility for his deeds without begging for his life or trying to save it by lying or shifting the blame to others. He was what he appeared to be: no ideological fanatic but obedient and devoted to the slogans of German nationalism and a fairly gifted organizer and bureaucrat. Had his life taken a different turn—

had he become a factory director, for example, he undoubtedly would have applied himself to his assigned tasks with equal diligence.

NOTES

1. *Death Is My Profession*, by Robert Merle.

2. In scholarly literature and in belles lettres, we come across two spellings of his name: "Höss" and "Hoss." He signed his name "Ho."

3. All personal details in this article were gleaned from the Polish edition of Höss's memoirs, *Autobiografia Rudolfa Hossa, komendanta obozu oswiecimskiego* (Warsaw, 1989).

4. Information on Höss's whereabouts at different times, his promotions, and his decorations is to be found in his personal papers preserved in the Auschwitz-Birkenau State Museum; see collection "Assorted Höss documents," call no. D.Au.I-1/5–D.Au.I-1/19a.

5. The SS kept alive Freikorps traditions by retaining, for example, their ranks and badges of rank.

6. Every NSDAP (Nazi party) member received a party serial number according to the date of acceptance. Thus the number indicated one's seniority in NSDAP, which in some cases was an important consideration in promotions. At the same time, the party and later also the SS authorities insisted that new members renounce their membership in religious congregations, although such a step was not mandatory. Once the new member signed the appropriate declaration, the religious denomination in his personal records was designated "gottgläubig," a euphemism for atheism.

7. J. Rawicz, *Dzien powszedni ludobojcy* (Warsaw, 1973), p. 30.

8. In Nazi parlance, *Alte Garde* and *Alte Kämpfer* referred to persons who joined the party or the SS at an early stage.

9. Participants in the Munich putsch later advanced to high positions in the Third Reich. Among them were Hermann Göring, Rudolf Hess (Hitler's deputy for party affairs), Hans Frank, Heinrich Himmler, Wilhelm Frick, Julius Streicher, and Ernst Röhm. To commemorate this event, the Nazis even introduced the so-called Blood Order (*Blutorden*), the highest honorable distinction in the Third Reich.

10. SS comprised three separate organizational structures. Until 1934, the so-called General SS (Allgemeine-SS) constituted the broad base of the organization; later it performed the functions of a paramilitary organization. In July 1934, Reserve or Special Troops came into being, which in 1940 spun off Waffen SS and the SS Guard Forces, later transformed into SS-Totenkpfverbande consisting of guards and administrators of concentration camps. Both Allgemeine SS and Waffen SS had their own systems of rank; those of Waffen SS were recognized as analogous to parallel ranks in the Wehrmacht and vice versa.

11. Theodor Eicke was born on October 17, 1892. His Nazi party card carried the serial number 114,901 and his SS number was 2,921. Eicke created the concentration camp system. Initially he served as commandant of Dachau and Esterwegen and later became inspector for concentration camps. The prisoner book of regulations, which he conceived in Esterwegen, remained binding, with few modifi-

cations, until the end of the war. Shortly before the outbreak of the war, he was commissioned by Himmler to assemble SS front-line divisions at Dachau, consisting of guards on duty in concentration camps. Eicke was appointed their commander. He was killed near Kharkov in March 1943.

12. At that time, the designation "IIa" described a department within the organizational camp structure in charge of "order and discipline" in the camps. In 1937, it became Department III—camp management (Abteilung III-Schutzhaftlagerführer).

13. Höss as Blockführer in Dachau does not appear in any accounts, nor in memoirs by prisoners or members of the SS camp personnel.

14. Over time, a number of SS enterprises came into existence: German Wood Works (DAW), German Earth and Stone Works (GmbH), German Food Works (GmbH), and others.

15. Routinely, to qualify for advancement an SS member was required to complete one of two SS officer schools (SS-Junkerschule Braunschweig or SS-Junkerschule Bad Tolz) or the special SS Technical Academy in Vienna (SS-Technische Hochschule). Exceptions were occasionally made for the "old guard combatants" whose contributions to the Nazi movement sometimes earned them officer's epaulettes without having to attend special SS officer schools.

16. The following firms operated in Auschwitz: Deutsche Ausrustungs-werke, Deutsche Lebensmittel GmbH, Deutsche Erd- und Steinwerke GmbH, Deutsche Versuchsanstalt für Ernährung und Verpflegung GmbH, and Golleschauer Portland-Zement AG. All of them were owned by the SS.

17. D. Czech, "Konzentrationslager Auschwitz. Zarys historyczny," in *Oswiecim: Hitlerowski oboz masowej zaglady* (Warsaw, 1987), p. 19.

18. Within the internal organizational system of the SS, the Reich Main Security Office (RSHA) dealt with arrests and isolating the Jewish population, as well as transports to the death camps. In this sense, the RSHA acted as a "forwarding agent." The SS Economic-Administrative Main Office was in charge of killing the victims, plundering their property, and conveying it to the Reichsbank and other Nazi institutions.

19. Rawicz, passim.

20. Arthur Liebehenschel was born on November 25, 1901, in Posen. He was a treasury official by occupation, a member of the Nazi party with serial number 932,760, and a member of the SS with serial number 39,254. In 1934, he served as adjutant to the commandant of the Lichtburg concentration camp, and in 1936 he was transferred to the Inspectorate for Concentration Camps. After the establishment in February 1942 of SS-WVHA, which incorporated the Inspectorate for Concentration Camps, Liebehenschel was appointed chief of Department DI-Central Office, in charge of prisoner affairs, equipment, and arms for camp personnel and personnel training. In the aftermath of the corruption affair uncovered in the camps, he was appointed commandant of Auschwitz. From May 8, 1944, to July 22, 1944, he served as commandant of Lublin-Majdanek. He was subsequently transferred to Trieste and placed under the high SS and police leader, SS-Gruppenführer Odilo Globocnik. Extradited to Poland after the war, he was sentenced to death by the Supreme National Tribunal in the trial of 40 former members of the Auschwitz camp personnel, and executed.

21. SS-Gruppenführer Richard Glücks was born on April 22, 1889. His serial numbers were 214,855 in the Nazi party and 58,703 in the SS. He served as staff officer in the Inspectorate for Concentration Camps in 1936. He replaced Eicke as inspector for concentration camps. After the war, he was recorded as missing.

22. It is probable that before assuming the Auschwitz post, Höss arranged for Liebehenschel's transfer because he did not want to create a situation in which his erstwhile superior would be subordinated to him.

23. SS-Sturmbannführer Richard Bär was born on September 9, 1911. His serial numbers were 454,991 in the Nazi party and 44,225 in the SS. His service in the camp system commenced in 1933 in Dachau. In 1939, he was assigned to the division that was assembled by Eicke. After he was wounded, he was recalled from combat duty and assigned to the chief of SS-WVHA, SS-Obergruppenführer Oswald Pohl, as his adjutant. He was subsequently transferred to Auschwitz, and after the liquidation of the camp he assumed the post of commandant of the Mittelbau-Dora concentration camp. He remained in hiding until December 1960. After his arrest, he died in July 1963 during preparations for his trial in Frankfurt am Main.

24. As the war drew to a close, Himmler often made such pronouncements. Moreover, he told SS-Obergruppenführer Hans-Adolf Prutzman to create an underground sabotage organization, Wehrwolf, whose members were later to engage actively in military operations.

25. Kaltenbrunner's defense counsel must have hoped to shift the entire responsibility for the Holocaust to SS-WVHA. See also n. 18.

26. The following defendants were tried by the Supreme National Tribunal in Poland: Gauleiter Arthur Grieser and Gauleiter Albert Forster; commandant of the Plaszow concentration camp Amon Goeth and Rudolf Höss; deputy and "administration chief" in the General Government, Josef Buhler; 40 members of the SS camp personnel; functionaries of SS and the police in the General Government, Ludwig Fischer, Ludwig Leist, Josef Misinger, and Max Daume.

27. The sentence and its whys and wherefores are to be found in T. Cyprian and J. Sawicki, *Siedem Wyrokow Trybunalu Narodowego* (Poznan, 1962), pp. 92–136.

12

Nazi Doctors

ROBERT JAY LIFTON AND AMY HACKETT

Nazi medical behavior in Auschwitz must be viewed as an end point of a gradual but steady process of attempts at eugenic purification through medicine. The first step was taken in June 1933 with a sterilization law that identified several hereditary illnesses whose bearers threatened the health of the German *Volk*. They included congenital feeblemindedness, schizophrenia, manic-depressive insanity, epilepsy, Huntington's chorea, hereditary blindness and deafness, grave bodily malformation, and hereditary alcoholism. Special "hereditary health courts" were created to decide on candidates for surgical sterilization. Later experiments at Auschwitz sought more efficient means of mass sterilization than those available in 1933.

"Euthanasia" was the next stage in Nazi racial molding. It began in 1938 with children as victims. No doubt responding to both the logic of Nazi ideology and the human difficulties of rearing children with physical and mental deformities, several parents petitioned the regime to grant their own children mercy killings. The "child euthanasia" program got under way when, in late 1938 or early 1939, Germany's Führer Adolf Hitler ordered Karl Brandt, his personal physician and close confidant, to investigate one such case in Leipzig. On returning to Berlin, Brandt was authorized by Hitler to formalize a program with the aid of Philip Bouhler, chief of Hitler's Chancellery. Hitler himself chose not to be publicly identified with the project. Killings first took place on pediatric wards, with injections; later, starvation became the more widespread method in special homelike facilities.

"Euthanasia" was expanded from children to adults through the "Führer decree" of October 1939, pursuant to discussions among Hitler, Leonardo

Conti, health secretary in the Interior Ministry, and Reich Chancellery head Hans Lammers. In this group, Hitler revealed his intent to eliminate, not just sterilize, the "life unworthy of life" of those with severe mental illnesses. The decree made Bouhler and Brandt responsible for extending the authority of selected physicians to give a "mercy death" to such patients. It was issued in October but backdated to September 1 to relate to the outbreak of war, for it was perceived as a matter of national defense, made the more urgent in light of the inevitable wartime losses of Germany's finest blood.

The program became known as T4, for the Tiergarten 4 address of its camouflage organization, the "Reich Work Group of Sanatoriums and Nursing Homes" in the Berlin Chancellery. The killings were carried out in special facilities throughout the Reich. Staffed by physicians, these facilities employed gas chambers disguised as showers in a foreshadowing of the death camps. The physicians both evaluated and chose those patients who would be killed and supervised the gassing, again in a rehearsal for Auschwitz.

The final transition to the mass exterminations carried out at death camps such as Auschwitz was the "14f13" program, so called because of the bureaucratic designation of its file. It began in early 1941, when T4 leader Bouhler allowed SS chief Heinrich Himmler to use T4 personnel and facilities to rid the concentration camps of "excess" prisoners, notably those with severe mental and physical illnesses. This program is sometimes known as "prisoner euthanasia," or Operation Invalid. T4 psychiatrists visited the camps, using evaluation forms which were much skimpier than the pretentious ones employed by T4 doctors. In another use of camouflage, inmates selected for death were told they would be sent to rest homes. While the 14f13 examinations were always perfunctory, in the case of Jews, collective diagnoses and participation in the implementation of the "final solution" soon came into use.

The 14f13 project itself provided two crucial bridges, one ideological and the other institutional, between earlier concepts and policies and unrestrained genocide. The ideological bridge linked the killing of those deemed physiologically unworthy of life with the elimination, under doctors' directions, of virtually anyone the regime on ideological assumptions thought undesirable or useless. The institutional bridge linked T4 to the concentration camps, which had sprouted up all over Reich territory since 1933. The camps, which initially had held mainly political enemies, became sites for medical-eugenic killing. Importantly, the 14f13 program borrowed the term *Sonderbehandlung*—special treatment or handling—from the Gestapo, which had used it for extralegal executions. The term, with its melding of bureaucratic and medical overtones, perfectly caught the essence of Nazi medicalization of killing.

In Auschwitz, Nazi doctors presided over the murder of most of the one million victims of that camp. Doctors performed selections of prisoners—for labor or for death—both on the ramp among arriving Jewish transports and in the camps among prisoners and on the medical blocks. Doctors supervised the killings in the gas chambers and decided when the victims were dead. Doctors consulted actively on how best to keep selections running smoothly, on how many people to permit to remain alive to fill the slave labor requirements of the IG Farben enterprise at Auschwitz, and on how to burn the enormous numbers of bodies that strained the facilities of the crematoria.

In sum, we may say that doctors were given much of the responsibility for the murderous ecology of Auschwitz—the choosing of victims, the carrying through of the physical and psychological mechanics of killing, and the balancing of killing and work functions in the camp. While doctors by no means ran Auschwitz, they did participate in the system and lend it a perverse medical aura. As one survivor who closely observed the process put the matter, "Auschwitz was like a medical operation," and "the killing program was led by doctors from beginning to end." We may say that the doctor standing at the ramp represented a kind of omega point, a mythical gatekeeper, between the worlds of the dead and the living, a final common pathway of the Nazi vision of therapy via mass murder.

Medical experimentation, then, was a small part of the extensive and systematic medicalized killing that was basic to the Nazi enterprise as perfected at Auschwitz. As tangible medical crimes, however, such experiments achieved considerable prominence at the Nuremberg Doctors' Trial in 1946–47. Indeed, their blending of ordinary science and extreme ideology make them emblematic of science under Germany's National Socialist regime. The considerable curiosity and notoriety aroused by research they carried out has to do with ethical questions that reach beyond Nazi doctors, and particularly with the radical Nazi reversal of healing and killing.

Nazi medical experiments fell into two basic categories: those sponsored by the regime for a specific ideological or military purpose, and those reflecting the allegedly scientific interest of a particular doctor. For example, the extensive sterilization and castration experiments conducted at Auschwitz by doctors Carl Clauberg and Horst Schumann received official encouragement as direct expressions of racial theory and policy. The military's concern about epidemics among the troops and civilian personnel in the East led to experiments with typhus contagion, which took place at Auschwitz and more extensively at other camps. On the other hand, Auschwitz's chief SS doctor, Eduard Wirths, had a prior interest in the study of precancerous conditions of the cervix; the camp provided him (and his gynecologist brother) with abundant subjects for research in this area. But the categories could overlap, as in the case of Josef Mengele's research on twins, which grew out of his specific scientific interests but was also congruent with Nazi ideology.

Uniting all these experiments was this basic fact about Auschwitz: There were no limits, either to the supply of subjects or to what could be done with them. Indeed, so plentiful was the supply that Auschwitz exported them. For example, it sent children to Neuengamme near Hamburg for tuberculosis experiments and shipped prepared specimens to the anatomical "museum" of Dr. August Hirt in Strasbourg.

The most important center for experimentation at Auschwitz was block 10. Although located in the men's camp, it housed mostly women prisoners. The block was a topic for rumor and speculation, including tales of doctors artificially inseminating women with monsters and a museum of body parts. Its windows were kept closed and shuttered or boarded to cut off communication with the outside world. One woman prisoner doctor who spent a year there described it as a "horror place" resembling both hell and a mental institution. Outside was the courtyard of block 11, where prisoners were executed.

The "guinea pigs" of block 10, all Jewish, came from throughout occupied Europe. They were usually selected directly from transports according to the needs of the Nazi physician experimenter. Some wanted married women, others young girls, still others a mixture of all categories. Overall, conditions in block 10, as in other research units, were superior to those experienced by most Auschwitz prisoners; the life expectancy of research subjects no doubt exceeded—especially for women—that of the average Jew arriving on a transport. Still, inmates suffered from hunger and constant uncertainty about their future in light of the Auschwitz principle that anything was permitted. In particular, they feared transfer to Birkenau. In block 10 they might at least have a hope that "maybe they will still let us live after this."[1] Thus, ironically, although locked up at night "like animals in a cage," according to one such inmate, they "felt freer."[2]

Block 10 was divided into separate research areas: those of the sterilizers Clauberg and Schumann, that of Dr. Wirths and his brother Helmut, and a special area for studies conducted by the local facility of the Hygienic Institute, an SS public health bureau with branches at several camps. (The institute's responsibility at Auschwitz included the maintenance and supply of Zyklon B because of its ostensible use for "pest control.") Block 10 also housed some 20 prostitutes, its only regular non-Jewish residents, who were available to elite prisoners as a work incentive and prophylactic against homosexual practices.

Widely known as "Clauberg's block," block 10 was created for his research on cheap and effective means of mass sterilization. In addition to patient wards, his empire included an elaborate x-ray apparatus and four special experimental rooms, including a darkroom. Although he held the reserve SS rank Gruppenführer, equivalent to lieutenant general, Clauberg was a civilian, an esteemed professor from the University of Kiel, who rented facilities, research subjects, and prisoner doctors from the SS. He came to Auschwitz because of Himmler's interest in his work. He set up shop first in Birkenau in December 1942, then moved to block 10 in April 1943.

But experiments took place throughout the camp. In block 41 at Birkenau, for example, three noted German professors conducted surgery that entailed the exposure of leg muscles and the test application of medications. Medical students performed experimental surgery on a female hospital block, which offered the opportunity to practice whatever procedure suited their particular interests. (Sometimes a prisoner with a relevant medical condition was selected; sometimes the choice was arbitrary.) With no ethical considerations at issue, a more opportunistic surgical laboratory than Auschwitz could hardly be imagined. Beyond convenience, a doctor could rationalize his experimentation with the thought that since his patient was ultimately condemned to death in any case, he could truly do no harm.

A male experimental block was created within block 28 in the medical area of the main camp. With the help of an advanced medical student, relatively healthy Jewish inmates had toxic substances, some petroleum-based, rubbed into their arms and legs. It was hoped that the resulting infections and abscesses would provide information useful in detecting ruses by malingerers trying to avoid military service. Other experiments that produced liver damage are thought to have reflected Himmler's interest in medical problems suffered by the troops. Block 28 primarily reflected military concerns but probably involved the "scientific curiosity" of individual scientists. Its advanced photographic equipment made it especially desirable for aspiring researchers.[3]

The ubiquity of medical research at Auschwitz was exemplified by Josef Mengele. His reputation of being everywhere in Auschwitz began at the ramp, where his frequent presence led inmate doctor Olga Lengyel to call him "far and away the chief provider for the gas chamber and the crematory ovens."[4] Though Mengele apparently took his turn like other doctors in this duty, which the Nazis identified as a matter of the Volk's health, he was often present at other times to promote collection of the twins his research demanded. (Moreover, the zealous enthusiasm with which he carried out his "ramp duty" made him more visible than other doctors.) Mengele created an elaborate and far-flung research structure. Besides the unit used by all SS doctors, he had three offices in the men's, women's, and Gypsy camps, mainly for his work with twins. Special blocks for twin children were established in medical units, sometimes shared with other research subjects, such as dwarfs or inmates with other abnormalities. Mengele also had an inner sanctum in Birkenau, where he was the chief doctor: a room with comfortable armchairs, three microscopes, and a well-stocked library, adjacent to which was a special dissection room for the main prisoner pathologist, Dr. Miklos Nyiszli. Equipped with a "dissecting table of polished marble," a basin, three porcelain sinks, and windows with screens to keep out flies and mosquitoes, it was, in Nyiszli's words, "the exact replica of any large city's institute of pathology."[5]

The subject of medical experimentation at Auschwitz requires some detailed attention to the particular projects, their methodology and intent. Clauberg's sterilization experiments, as noted, clearly fit the National Socialist ideological agenda and were directly sponsored by the regime. Clauberg represented the established scientist with Nazi convictions. He developed the hormonal preparations Progynon and Prolutin, which are still used to treat infertility, as well as the Clauberg test for measuring the action of progesterone. He joined the party in 1933. Clauberg came to Himmler's attention through his treatment of infertility in the wife of a high-ranking SS officer. Thus, whereas the Nazis often favored youth and inexperience for the "euthanasia" program and reliable Nazi credentials for Auschwitz, Clauberg was chosen both for his Nazi standing and his scientific qualifications.

At his initial meeting with Himmler in 1940, Clauberg told the Reichsführer of his intention to establish a research institute for reproductive biology, to investigate both the causes and treatment of infertility and the development of a nonsurgical means of sterilization. In a series of conversations and letters, the two men elaborated their common interests. Himmler promised financial support, and Clauberg began looking into possible techniques. Himmler initially intended that the doctor be set up in Ravensbrück, a camp appropriate to his need for female subjects. But, backed by Ernst Robert Grawitz, chief SS physician, Clauberg convinced him that Auschwitz would be more practical because of its proximity to his own clinical facilities in Königshütte.

Clauberg proposed that the institute be named after Himmler—the "Research Institute of the Reichsführer SS for Biological Propagation." In approving the project and specifying his practical expectations from such research, Himmler expressed his interest in finding out "how long it would take to sterilize a thousand Jewesses."[6]

Clauberg's sterilization method was the injection of a caustic substance into a woman's cervix in order to obstruct the fallopian tubes. His subjects were married women between the ages of 20 and 40, preferably those who had proven their fertility by bearing children. After injecting them with an opaque liquid, he then x-rayed them to exclude prior blockage or impairment. Clauberg was secretive about the substances he used, probably to protect any "discoveries" from competing researchers. Most likely the preferred substance was formalin, sometimes injected with novocaine in a formula apparently developed with the assistance of Dr. Johannes Goebel, chief chemist with the Schering pharmaceutical firm. The course of treatment took place in stages over a few months, during which the caustic substances would create adhesions which ultimately obstructed the tubes, thus preventing fertilization. According to camp commandant Rudolf Höss, Clauberg intended that after a year he would test his method by matching the women with selected male inmates. The course of the war thwarted this trial.[7]

Despite his high-ranking sponsors, Clauberg's progress was slow, hindered by delays in acquiring radiological equipment and by personal conflicts with other doctors that were exacerbated by his own arrogant and difficult personality. The promises made to Himmler about the efficacy of his method had probably been excessive. But Clauberg was so dedicated to his research that as Soviet troops approached Auschwitz, he fled to Ravensbrück and even arranged that some of his subjects be sent there. But three months later he was forced to flee again, and in June 1945 he was captured by the Soviets. Convicted of war crimes, he was imprisoned, then repatriated after Stalin's death. In 1955, he resumed the practice of medicine in the Federal Republic of Germany, proudly advertising his experience with "positive eugenics" and sterilization techniques. His license was finally revoked, and he died under mysterious circumstances while awaiting trial in 1957.[8]

Clauberg's archrival and fellow researcher on sterilization at Auschwitz was Horst Schumann, who had joined the SA and Nazi party in 1930, three years before the seizure of power. Thus he was more of a Nazi medical "old fighter" than the more renowned Clauberg. Schumann favored wearing a Luftwaffe uniform, while Clauberg was very much the white-coated scientist. Schumann came to Auschwitz after assignments at the "euthanasia" facilities at Grafeneck and Sonnenstein and then in the related 14f13 program in the camps. His qualifications for the Auschwitz experiments with x-ray sterilization, which Himmler played a crucial role in formulating, were highly political.

Himmler was already expressing his interest in x-ray sterilizations in memos exchanged in early 1941 with Victor Brack, the Chancellery bureaucrat active in the "euthanasia" and death camp projects. Brack conceived of an assembly line in which the victim, while innocently filling in forms for a few minutes, would be irradiated by an official seated behind a counter: "With a two-valve installation about 150–200 persons could then be sterilized per day, and therefore with 20 such installations as many as 3,000–4,000 persons per day."[9] The demand for such programs was fed as German military penetration into the Soviet Union incorporated ever more Jews into the Reich, some of whom were "fit" for slave labor but should be prevented from propagating. Schumann was chosen for this task, and by late 1942 he was experimenting with x-rays in the women's hospital on block 30 in Birkenau, in a large room with two extensive x-ray apparatuses and a shielded booth for himself.

Schumann's experimental subjects—relatively healthy men and women in their late teens or early twenties—were lined up in a waiting room and brought in one by one. Women were placed between plates which covered their abdomen and back, while men were positioned with penis and scrotum on a plate. The "treatment" lasted several minutes. Many of the women received substantial burns, which became infected or led to peritonitis. Following x-rays, the victims often underwent castration surgery. Women had their ovaries removed, which carried a further risk of infection, so that laboratory examinations could determine whether the x-rays had effectively destroyed tissue. These rough operations were usually performed by prisoner doctor Wladislaw Dering, who ultimately perfected his technique to attain a proficiency of 10 within two hours. The victimized women were given a spinal anesthetic but were awake during the surgery. The men, after their exposure to x-rays, had their sperm collected through the brutal massage of their prostates with pieces of wood inserted into the rectum. This was followed by surgery to remove one or both testes for examination. Dering performed these operations as well. These x-ray castrations were performed mainly on Jews but also on one group of Polish men, who were probably given an even higher dosage, which caused their genitals to rot away. When they did not respond to ointments, they were ultimately gassed. While statistics are uncertain, the best estimate is that some 1,000 prisoners, male and female, underwent these x-ray procedures and that some 200 were subjected to further surgical removal of sex organs.[10]

Schumann contrived a second x-ray project at Auschwitz. It involved treatment of a fungal condition of the face caused by the common use of a shaving brush. Although treatable with existing medicines, the problem inspired Schumann to try his x-ray machines, which, caused severe skin eruptions and infections, impairment of salivary and tear duct functions, and in some cases facial paralysis. These complications caused a number of men to be gassed.[11]

Schumann was also sufficiently involved with his work that when Auschwitz closed down, he too moved his research to Ravensbrück, where he briefly experimented on Gypsy girls.

The awful toll of these experiments on their victims was clear. Yet in the insane world of Auschwitz, such cruel experiments could be life-saving, particularly if one's case was medically interesting and if one did not become so debilitated as to be consigned to the gas chambers. Surviving victims were often left with permanent mutilation.

One set of experiments conducted at block 10's Hygienic Institute may have been constructed with the intention of saving lives. They involved the possible relationship between dental infections and rheumatic and other physical symptoms, which was to be tested through injection of vaccines made from dental material. This procedure produced large inflammations on the upper thighs, creating an impression of a procedure more dangerous than in fact was the case. Dental x-rays were then taken to confirm tooth infections in the people from whom the vaccines had been made. Some of these people were the wives and relatives of male prisoners working in the Hygienic Institute, who were rescued from Clauberg's more dangerous unit. The subterfuge further involved a fictional declaration of the patient's death and her being smuggled out to a work camp. The physician who contrived this scheme (called "Dr. B." in one account) derived satisfaction from foiling the despised Clauberg and helping prisoners with whom he was friendly. Moreover, he claimed to have been genuinely interested in experiments for which he otherwise would not have found the subjects so generously provided by Auschwitz's infinite reserves.

The Hygienic Institute, which had facilities on block 10 as well as in Raisko, a town on the outskirts of Auschwitz, provided a haven of sorts for its physicians. Conditions were relatively pleasant, there were no selections to be made, and they were assigned real medical work dealing with bacteriological and hematological problems. The block 10 unit also did considerable makework in the form of extensive blood and urine analyses and other procedures. Yet harmful experiments were carried out under the institute's aegis.

Bruno Weber, the institute's chief, injected inmates with various blood groups to study the resultant harmful agglutination of blood cells. Furthermore, blood for experiments or transfusions was often collected from weakened inmates and sometimes through the carotid artery, causing fatal blood loss. Such procedures were sometimes carried out by SS staff with no medical training. The Hygienic Institute used human, rather than animal, muscle for its culture media. Animal meat was simply dearer in such an environment, even as Auschwitz substituted human guinea pigs for lab animals. Weber carried out further experiments on chemical means to extract confessions in a conscious attempt to compete with Soviet expertise in this area. Such techniques were particularly desired to extract information from Poles regarding underground activities. This work with barbiturates and morphine derivatives resulted in at least two deaths.[12]

The institute was also the site for phenol killings, used for relatively small groups, such as debilitated prisoners in hospital wards and political prisoners, especially in the early period at Auschwitz. Phenol injections were the most medicalized form of killing at Auschwitz. Thus even the Hygienic Institute, practitioner of perhaps the most "normal" medicine at the camp, was indelibly compromised by the atmosphere. Healing and killing at Auschwitz were inextricably connected.

Chief camp physician Wirths was the sponsor and facilitator for a number of experiments bordering on "normal" medicine which enjoyed approval in Berlin. These included experiments with contagious diseases that, of course, might threaten the health of troops. The camps provided ideal conditions for the spread and study of such diseases. Especially noteworthy in this regard was SS Captain Dr. Helmuth Vetter, an employee of the Bayer group WII of IG Farben, who ran trials on sulfa and other medications at both Auschwitz and Mauthausen. Vetter drew other SS doctors, including Wirths, into his research. Wirths himself pursued typhus trials which caused the death of several Jewish inmates who had been artificially injected with the disease.[13] Vetter represented the Nazi research functionary and the connection with German industry, for which Auschwitz was the ideal testing site, since concern for the trial subjects imposed no limits on research protocol.

Auschwitz provided a grotesque research arena for another SS doctor who had a longstanding interest in the medical aspects of starvation. Johann Paul Kremer came to Auschwitz as an anatomy professor at the University of Münster, the only university professor to serve as an SS camp doctor. He selected "specimens" to be placed on a dissection table, where statements were taken regarding weight loss. As an SS orderly injected phenol into the person's heart, the doctor stood by with jars ready for organs that would be studied for the effects of starvation. On his own, Kremer assembled samples for later research that he hoped to carry on in his own laboratory after the war.[14] Kremer is particularly interesting as an example of the limits that Nazism could place on research. The professor had earlier run afoul of the German medical establishment over several of his pet theories. The most revealing involved Kremer's belief in the inheritance of traumatically acquired deformities, a theory too absurd for even the passionate hereditary commitments of Nazified German medicine.

Auschwitz's value for the study of starvation led to one significant piece of research, which was conducted by prisoner doctors. To get the approval of Dr. Hans Wilhelm König, they couched their intent in terms of studying weight loss "from a medical point of view." Although König may well have envisioned the possibility of publishing the results under his own name in a German medical journal, probably without much attention to the context of the experiments, their ultimate publication documented the physiological effects of dietary deprivations in a way that implicated the Auschwitz context.[15]

Wirths most directly and extremely lived out the Auschwitz healing-killing conflict and paradox. He had a reputation as a dedicated physician, and those inmates to whom he was closest characterized him as conscientious and decent. Yet he was the one who established Auschwitz's system of selections and medicalized killing and then supervised this process during the two years of heaviest mass murder. But prisoners' views depended on their particular vantage points, and some were extremely critical of his experimental work.

Wirths's primary research, as noted, arose from his own longstanding medical interest in precancerous growths of the cervix. By inserting a colposcope, a new instrument at the time, through the vagina, Wirths viewed the cervix first in its natural state and then after the application of certain substances (notably acetic acid and an iodized compound). The protocol called for surgical removal of the cervix in cases where changes were observed (even questionable cases). The excised cervix was then sent to Wirths's brother's lab in Hamburg-Altona, where it was studied for precancerous growths. The brother, Helmut, did some of this surgery himself and also held demonstrations in the camp. Some inmates considered Helmut to be the initiator of this research.[16]

The Wirths brothers' surgery, if arising from genuine research interests and not directly related to Nazi ideology, was nonetheless far from harmless. The colposcope was unreliable, a biopsy could have been used rather than total cervix removal, and the poor physical conditions of Auschwitz inmates fostered such complications as infections and hemorrhages, some of which were directly fatal while others were sufficiently debilitating as to cause patients to be selected for death. As noted, Wirths's involvement in typhus experiments resulted in some fatalities; it was particularly criticized on ethical grounds by Hermann Langbein, the inmate secretary who otherwise defended Wirths.[17]

The physician who came to be known as "Dr. Auschwitz" for his seeming embodiment of medical evil in the camp was not immediately notorious after the war. Josef Mengele was not among the accused at the Nuremberg doctors' trial, and only in the 1950s, when he was already in South American exile, did he begin to assume his fiendish stature. By the time Rolf Hochhuth wrote his play *The Deputy* (1964), the figure of Mengele clearly stood behind "the Doctor" who was intended to represent Absolute Evil.

Mengele joined the SA in 1934 and the party and SS in 1937, and thus was not a medical "old fighter" like the older Schumann. His medical studies included work in physical anthropology and genetics at the Frankfurt University Institute for Hereditary Biology and Racial Hygiene, specializing in various forms of hereditary abnormality under the mentorship of Professor Otmar von Verschuer. Thus his scientific interests blended with his ideological fervor in promoting the Nazi biomedical vision of genetic purification. Wounded in action in the East, Mengele was declared medically unfit for combat. When he arrived in Auschwitz on May 30, 1943, he held a captain's rank and was the camp's most decorated doctor. He chose the assignment for its research opportunities, and indeed his mentor Verschuer obtained support for his student's work from the German Research Society.

This support, authorized by Himmler, was to underwrite work on albuminous matter and eye color. The research was to be carried out through anthropological examinations and blood tests, which were to be sent back to Frankfurt.

Mengele carried out his research with the energy of a fanatic, particularly his studies of twins, which had apparently begun while he was working under Verschuer and which tied into his interest in the mechanisms of heredity, especially in relation to race. It was his interest in twins that had particularly commended Auschwitz to him. What it lacked in data on generations of families it made up for in the availability of a relatively rare commodity, identical twins.

Mengele created an elaborate research empire, with tentacles throughout the camp. Twins had special status wherever they were housed, with a separate numbering sequence and "ZW" (for *Zwilling* i.e., "twin") often incorporated into their tatoo. They were frequently allowed to keep their clothing and even their hair, which of course was one of those hereditary characteristics to be marked. They were often housed in special blocks, especially, in the case of children, within medical units, sometimes together with other "interesting" subjects, such as dwarfs or inmates with congenital abnormalities. An older child or adult twin, known as a "twin father" (*Zwillingsvater*) was put in charge as block chief. With the influx of Hungarian Jews in 1944, Mengele ultimately presided over some 250 twins in Birkenau, mainly children but some adolescents, and about 100 more in the men's camp; their ages ranged from three to 70 years. Mothers of young female twins were sometimes allowed to stay on their block but could be sent back to the regular camp, usually to their death, at any time.

Identical twins were, of course, Mengele's most ideal and valuable subject. They were regularly forced to sit together nude for hours while every part of their bodies was measured and compared, from the width of their ears or nose to their bone structure. Mengele was helped by a woman prisoner anthropologist who before the war had been involved in such measurings, a research interest which was widespread in the anthropological community. Twins might be measured as often as twice a week for five months or so. An enormous amount of blood was drawn in these sessions, an estimated 10 cc each time.

Like other research subjects at Auschwitz, Mengele's twins lived in a bizarre atmosphere that combined sanctuary and terror in totally arbitrary proportions. In the words of one twin, "A single thing kept us alive . . . his experiments." Some twins were given desirable jobs and could move about with relative freedom. They received rewards for their cooperation, notably such Auschwitz "delicacies" as white bread and macaroni, in part to compensate for the blood drawn. But Mengele's role as protector was inseparably tied to his role as potential destroyer. A child almost had to be a twin to survive. One inmate estimated a mortality rate among twins of 15 percent, low in the context of Auschwitz.

Because of their valued status as research subjects, twins were typically murdered by means of the best "medical" procedure rather than being simply sent to the gas chambers, their corpses then lost to the anonymity of the crematoria. Rather, they were murdered with injections, usually of phenol or chloroform, into the heart, usually to be dissected immediately. Not only did Auschwitz provide a number of twin sets for study, but they could be observed under regulated conditions, indeed even made to "die together . . . and in good health."[18] On at least one occasion, a set of twins was killed just to resolve a dispute over a diagnosis between Mengele and other doctors. (He had been wrong, as it turned out.)

Mengele's method in studying twins was more or less standard for research in physical anthropology at that time, as was his zeal to measure everything. But his claim to scientific rigor was rendered absurd by his ideological fanaticism and the murderous corruptions of the environment. More than a few siblings were able to masquerade as twins, and fraternal twins pretended to be identical twins. Yet Mengele intended to use his research for the *Habilitation* that would give him academic legitimacy and credentials. Indeed, Mengele seemed to have felt that it would be a crime against science not to use his unique opportunity at Auschwitz. Beyond his passion for measuring, there was a prevailing belief at Auschwitz that Mengele's ultimate purpose was to seek the cause of multiple births, with an aim of more quickly repopulating Germany, even though he showed little interest in the mothers of twins. In any case, he almost certainly intended to use his findings in the overall Nazi mission to create genetically superior individuals, twins or otherwise.

Mengele's further interests in abnormal births included dwarfs. (He was delighted when Auschwitz brought him one whole family.) Scouting incoming transports for twins with the order *Zwillinge heraus!* (Twins forward!), he also looked for individuals with physical abnormalities who might be used for interesting postmortems. Their measurements were taken, they were shot by an SS noncom, and their bodies dissected. Sometimes their cleaned bones were sent to Verschuer's second research institute in Berlin-Dahlem.

Mengele also sought to further his scientific reputation with research on noma, a topic which may have been suggested to him by a prisoner physician. This gangrenous condition of the face and mouth can be caused by extreme debilitation. It was especially prevalent in the Gypsy camp, where hygienic conditions were particularly deplorable. Yet Mengele seems to have been less interested in environmental causes than in some genetic or racial source. Those suffering from noma might then be treated or killed for a postmortem study.

Eye color is a classic index for reputable genetic research. Yet Mengele's work with this hereditary characteristic was especially strange. He regularly sent the eyes of Gypsies to Berlin-Dahlem, where eye color was being studied. Particular interest was paid to heterochromia of the iris, manifested when one individual has eyes of two different colors. But Mengele also embarked on the bizarre project of changing eye color in an "Aryan" direction, paying particular attention to boys who had brown eyes despite their blond hair. Mengele tried injecting methylene blue in the eyes of his subjects. This produced pain and even death in one case, but had no permanent effect.[19]

Mengele's attempt to produce blue-eyed blonds in conformity with Nazi racial stereotypes would seem to belie his interest in heredity (he might as well have experimented with hair coloring for brunettes with blue eyes). Yet they exemplified his basic scientific pattern, which he shared with the prototypes of Nazi science: results should substantiate prejudices, while data or ideas that ran contrary to preconceptions were to be ignored. Blonds *should* have blue eyes. Mengele's efforts to find "proof" for his theories were accordingly often strained. A prisoner artist who worked with him reported his not surprising discovery that Gypsies' ostensibly blue eyes had "little brown freckles . . . so . . . they are not pure Aryan blue eyes." A prisoner doctor, referring to Mengele's experiments regarding the relative susceptibility of twins to poison, noted that this was "a crazy idea of a man who understood nothing about real scientific problems but . . . had the possibility . . . to experiment . . . without any control or restrictions." Eventually, Mengele fled Auschwitz for the Berlin-Dahlem institute, purportedly to report on his work.

Like other SS doctors at Auschwitz, Mengele made use of prisoner doctors (as well as other inmate professionals, notably the anthropologist with experience in measuring). Most were Jewish, and they were used primarily to diagnose and sometimes treat research subjects. But the experienced pathologist Nyiszli carried out the dissections that were central to Mengele's research. Mengele went so far as to set up a series of colloquia with prisoner doctors, some imported from other camps. As noted earlier, the prisoner doctors at Auschwitz included many distinguished physicians. Most were vastly superior in skills and knowledge to the SS doctors, the youngest of whom, in particular, had had their medical training compromised by the extraordinary circumstances of the Nazi disruption and purging of medical faculties, and then the war itself.

Prisoner doctors were subjected to terrible moral dilemmas about "becoming part of the system," as one put it. Most wished to avoid having any part in selections on the medical wards but at the same time sought to convince the Nazi doctors performing them not to send to the gas chamber patients who had a chance to survive. Prisoner doctors also had to balance professional engagement in their medical work with compromising their professionalism and falsifying diagnoses and laboratory results if by doing so they could save prisoners' lives.

Since diagnoses of such diseases as tuberculosis might mean immediate death, most prisoner physicians subscribed to a code that enjoined against such diagnoses where possible. This constrained ethos of avoiding harm seems to have prevailed at Auschwitz. In a related case, Professor Berthold Epstein, a distinguished Czech Jewish pediatrician, received an offer from Mengele that initially offended his sense of honor. In return for an "extension of his life," Epstein would help with research which would be published under the Nazi doctor's name. His colleagues persuaded Epstein to allow realism to overcome honor and then to use his situation to aid other inmates. Epstein proposed research on noma, which became one of Mengele's pet projects.[20] The subsequent "noma office" provided a haven of sorts to 45 to 70 children, most of them Gypsies, some of whom were successfully treated only to be killed when the Gypsy camp was liquidated.

By late 1942, SS doctors and the Auschwitz command realized their interest in keeping prison physicians alive and permitting them to function medically. The great majority of them managed, by means of medical commitment and ingenuity, to remain healers in an otherwise murderous environment.

An exception was Wladislaw Dering. A Polish doctor imprisoned for his underground activities, he was an example of an inmate who became deeply involved in experimental procedures, notably the removal of ovaries and testes in Schumann's x-ray sterilization research. Indeed Leon Uris's novel *Exodus* included him along with Nazi doctors in a litany of Auschwitz medical criminals. He initiated a libel case in London, which he won on a technicality. During its course, however, he was confronted by survivors he had victimized by his surgery, and the award of "one ha'penny" constituted a severe moral condemnation.[21] He moved from terror to servility, and finally to identification with the SS doctors and their medicalized power over life and death.

It was the Nazi doctors themselves, however, who were most implicated in Nazi mass murder and brutal experimentation in Auschwitz. There probably has never been an episode in history in which doctors have been as guilty of abrogating their healing function.

NOTES

1. Adelaide Hautval, "Survey of the Experiments Performed in the Women's Camps at Auschwitz and Ravensbrück" (unpublished testimony), and personal communication.

2. Unpublished testimony from Mme. Kleinova, M.D. (Prague), regarding her stay on block 10.

3. Hermann Langbein, *Menschen in Auschwitz* (Vienna, 1972), p. 389, and *Der Auschwitz-Prozess: Eine Dokumentation* (Frankfurt am Main, 1965), vol. 2, p. 578; Jan Olbrycht, "The Nazi Health Office Actively Participated with the SS Administration in Auschwitz," *Anthology* 1 (Warsaw, 1971–72), no 1, pp. 187–88.

4. Olga Lengyel, *Five Chimneys: The Story of Auschwitz* (Chicago, 1947), p. 144.

5. Miklos Nyiszli, *Auschwitz: A Doctor's Eyewitness Account* (New York, 1960), pp. 39–40.

6. Rudolf Brandt to Clauberg, 10 July 1942 (NO-213), *Nuremberg Medical Case*, vol. 1, p. 729.

7. Langbein, *Menschen*, p. 386; Jan Sehn, "Carl Claubergs verbrecherische Unfruchtbarmachungs-Versuche an Haftlings-Frauen in den Nazi-Konzentrationslagern," *Hefte von Auschwitz* 2 (1959), pp. 3–31.

8. Philippe Aziz, *Doctors of Death*, vol. 2 (Geneva, 1976), pp. 236–41; Sehn, pp. 14, 26–27.

9. Brack to Himmler, 28 March 1941 (NO-203), *Nuremberg Medical Case*, vol. 1, p. 720.

10. Stanislaw Klodzinski, "'Sterilization' and Castration with the Help of X-Rays in the Concentration Camps: The Crimes of Horst Schumann," *Anthology*, 1, no. 2, pp. 59–63.

11. Désiree Haffner (original MS.).

12. Olbrycht, pp. 188–89; Langbein, *Auschwitz-Prozess* vol. 2, pp. 676–77; Bernd Naumann, *Auschwitz: A Report on the Proceedings against Robert Karl Ludwig Mulka and Others before the Court at Frankfurt* (New York, 1966), p. 155.

13. Stanislaw Klodzinski, "Criminal Pharmacological Experiments on Inmates of the Concentration Camp in Auschwitz," *Anthology* 1, no. 2, pp. 15–43; Lengyel, pp. 4, 175.

14. Jan Sehn, "The Case of the Auschwitz SS Physician J. P. Kremer," *Anthology* 1, no. 1, pp. 211–14, 233; "Kremers Tagebuch," *Hefte von Auschwitz* 13 (1971), pp. 42–70.

15. Georges Wellers and Robert Waitz, "Recherches sur la dénutrition prolongée dans les camps de déportation," *Revue Canadienne de Biologie* 6 (1947).

16. Langbein, *Menschen*, pp. 426–28.

17. Ibid., pp. 428–30

18. Nyiszli, p. 59.

19. Langbein, *Menschen*, p. 383.

20. Yad Vashem Archives, Jerusalem, 2039 (Dr. Aharon Beilin).

21. Langbein, *Menschen*, pp. 255–57; Mavis M. Hill and L. Norman Williams, *Auschwitz in England: A Record of a Libel Action* (New York, 1965).

13

The Crimes of Josef Mengele

HELENA KUBICA

In numerous studies, Dr. Josef Mengele, the Auschwitz "Angel of Death" and for many years one of the most wanted Nazi war criminals, has been portrayed as a unique case among the German physicians who abetted the Nazi enterprise. His contribution to the crime of genocide is often attributed to singular personality traits.

How could Mengele, a promising scientist specializing in genetics, a zealous disciple of eugenics, who took the Hippocratic Oath that embodies medicine's fundamental principle, *primum non nocere* (first of all, do no harm), send thousands to their death, even kill scores of children, in the name of science? In our attempt to answer this question, we must consider the ideological and institutional context in which he worked.

Mengele's career and his involvement in criminal medical practices are inextricably bound with his interest in genetics, which played a special part in Nazi ideology. The scientific basis for the theory of superiority of the Germanic race came in the form of eugenics, a term conceived in the mid–19th century by Sir Francis Galton, an English professor. Galton claimed that the inherited traits of an individual, and therefore of humanity as a whole, could be perfected for the benefit of society and humankind. This objective could be achieved by identifying and then improving positive inherited traits while suppressing negative ones, especially hereditary diseases. Accomplishing these aims would involve such endeavors as premarital counseling, family planning, combating alcoholism and venereal diseases, improving hygiene in workplaces, cultivating mental health, and encouraging physical activity.

Initially, eugenics met with its greatest support in Great Britain, the United States, and Canada. In Germany, public interest in eugenics did not emerge strongly until after Hitler's rise to power, when it assumed the radically different and notorious form of racial genetics. In the hands of the Nazis, eugenics provided a scientific foundation for removing and killing persons suffering from mental illness or incurable disease, as well as compulsory sterilization of those suspected of carrying hereditary diseases, an operation code-named T4.

The Institute of Heredity and Racial Hygiene at the Frankfurt University, headed by Professor Otmar Freiherer von Verschauer, served as the academic center of racial genetics.[1] There, scientific research was combined with clinical practice. In 1937, Mengele, then a promising young scientist, joined the staff.

Born on March 16, 1911, in Gunzburg, Bavaria, Mengele was the eldest of three sons of Karl Mengele, manufacturer of agricultural machinery. The family was Catholic. Since Karl Mengele was not a Nazi sympathizer, it is unlikely the family home affected Josef's political views. Karl Mengele's dream was that his sons would take over the family business, but Josef, whose interests were in music and natural sciences, wanted to become a doctor. Refined and intelligent, the young man became a popular figure in his hometown. He wrote amateur plays staged as part of charity fund drives. Yet in 1931, at the age of 20, Mengele seemed to abandon his artistic and humanistic inclinations by joining Stahlhelm, a paramilitary organization.[2]

During his study of philosophy at the Munich University and medicine at the Frankfurt am Main University, Mengele learned of racial genetics and quickly became a zealous proponent of its tenets. In 1935, he successfully defended his dissertation, "Racial-Morphological Study of Lower Jaw in Four Racial Groups," which earned him a Ph.D. degree from the Munich University. Two years later, the Frankfurt am Main University awarded him a doctor of medicine degree based on his dissertation, "Genealogical Studies of Cases of Lip-Palate Cleft."

Interested in Mengele's work in racial genetics, Professor von Verschauer hired the young researcher as his assistant. Mengele's interest in twins dates from his early collaboration with von Verschauer, who pursued research on twins as "the most efficient method to ascertain inherited human traits, particularly diseases."[3]

At the time he became von Verschauer's assistant, Mengele was closely involved in the Nazi movement. Stahlhelm had been incorporated into the Sturmabteilung (SA), or storm troopers, in 1934. In 1937, he was accepted into the Nazi party (card number 5574974), and in May 1938, joined the ranks of the SS. In 1939 Mengele married Irene Schoenbein, who in 1944 bore him his only son, Rolf.

War interrupted the progress of the career of the young scientist. He had three months' training in 1938 with a unit of mountain riflemen, the Gebigsjaeger, then in June 1940 was called up by the Wehrmacht. After serving one month, Mengele was transferred at his request to Waffen SS, where he served in a reserve medical battalion from August 1 to November 4, 1940. He was next assigned to the Genealogical Section of the Race and Resettlement Office, which loaned him as an expert to the Reichskommissariat for the Strengthening of Germanhood in Pozen, where his task was to evaluate the suitability of uprooted residents for Germanization.[4]

In January 1942, Mengele joined the medical corps of the Waffen SS Viking division as a medical officer. He was initially stationed in France, then experienced battlefield conditions in the Soviet Union, where he became a battalion medical officer and was promoted to SS-Hauptsturmführer (SS captain). For saving two soldiers from a burning tank under enemy fire, he was awarded the Iron Cross First Class. In addition, he received the Black Badge for the Wounded and the Medal for the Care of the German People.[5]

In the summer of 1942, Mengele was seriously wounded in fighting on the Don River and pronounced unfit for front-line service. That enabled him to resume his scientific work, especially as in November 1942 his advocate and mentor, von Verschauer, was appointed director of the Kaiser Wilhelm Institute for Anthropology, Heredity, and Eugenics. With Verschauer's encouragement, Mengele asked his superiors at the Office of the Chief SS and Police Physician in Berlin to post him to concentration camps.[6] His request was approved, and on May 30, 1943, Mengele reported to the largest concentration camp and the center of mass killing, Auschwitz-Birkenau.

The chief physician of the Auschwitz garrison, SS-Standortzarzt Dr. Eduard Wirths, appointed Mengele chief physician of the Gypsy family camp (BIIe), established in February 1943 on the grounds of the Birkenau camp. In this capacity, he worked in hospitals and outpatient clinics in other sectors of the Birkenau camp. Thus for all practical purposes his authority as SS doctor extended over the entire Birkenau camp. From October or November 1944, following liquidation of the Gypsy camp, he served as chief physician of the hospital for male prisoners in Birkenau (sector BIIf). In December 1944 he was transferred to the SS infirmary in Birkenau.

Mengele seized the broad opportunities offered by the concentration camp, and on instructions from the Institute for Anthropological and Biological-Racial Research (Institute for Rassenbiologische und Antropologische Forschungen) at the Kaiser Wilhelm Institute in Berlin-Dahlem, he began anthropological studies of various racial groups, mainly Gypsies, and of twins, especially monozygotic, or identical, twins. This research was to supply scientific support for the Nazi thesis that the Nordic race was innately superior by demonstrating the absolute primacy of heredity over environment.[7] His other interests in the context of research on twins included the physiology and pathology of dwarfism, the phenomenon of different coloring of irises (heterochromia iridis), and children born with other abnormalities.

In the summer of 1943, the Gypsy family camp at Birkenau was struck by a disease hitherto unknown among prisoners. Called water cancer (noma faciei, gangrene of the cheek), it primarily attacked children and young people. Mengele decided to study its causes and treatment methods. On his instructions, in November 1943, prisoners afflicted with noma were placed in a separate barrack, 22, in the compound of the Gypsy camp hospital.[8] Also on his instructions, some children afflicted with the disease were put to death and their bodies transported to the SS Institute of Hygiene at Rajsk for histopathological study. The institute prepared specimens of selected body organs and preserved heads of the children in formaldehyde jars, which were delivered to the SS Medical Academy in Graz, among other places.[9]

Mengele placed barrack 22 under the supervision of Dr. Bertold Epstein, a world-famous pediatrician, professor at Prague University, and a Czech Jew. Epstein was transferred from the Buna satellite camp to the Gypsy camp in August 1943 especially for this purpose. A dermatologist, Dr. Rudolf Vitek (Weiskopf in the camp), also a Czech Jew, was assigned as Mengele's helper and assistant. On Mengele's orders and under his direct supervision, they studied the course and origins of the disease and worked to develop a treatment. In addition, they analyzed the results of research undertaken by their boss, including studies of noma, twins, and hereditary abnormalities.[10] Research on noma was pursued from the fall of 1943 to June 1944, when the Gypsy camp hospital was disbanded prior to the final liquidation of the camp.

Mengele began his experiments in the Gypsy camp with twins. He was gentle with the children under his care, made sure they received enough food, even gave them toys and sweets taken from Jewish children consigned to extermination in the gas chambers. Children repaid him with trust and called him "good uncle."[11]

Mengele ordered the establishment of a kindergarten in barracks 29 and 31 for children who served as subjects of his experiments (who occupied barrack 31), and all Gypsy children under age six. Several hundred children stayed in the kindergarten from 8:00 A.M. to 2:00 P.M., cared for by several women prisoners, including Helena Hanemann, a German married to a Gypsy, imprisoned with their five children; two Polish women; and an Estonian Jew, Vera Luke. The kindergarten barracks were in better condition than others; their whitewashed walls were decorated with color paintings featuring scenes from fairy tales. The backyard of barrack 31 was fenced as a playground, complete with sandbox, merry-go-round, swings, and exercise equipment.

For a short while, the kindergarten children received better food: milk, butter, white bread, meat soup, even jam and chocolate. While the quality and quantity of food varied according to the age of the children, this type of nourishment was unheard of in other sectors of the camp. Not all food reached the kindergarten; some was stolen in depots by SS men and later by the kindergarten staff. Although these special food privileges were eventually revoked, the Gypsy children continued to receive better food than their counterparts in other barracks.

Initially, prisoners working in the kindergarten block were astonished by Mengele's actions; with time, however, they realized that the facility was constructed for propaganda purposes, for the benefit of top-ranking SS and civilian officials who often visited the Gypsy camp and the kindergarten, took photographs, and filmed the children at play.[12] The truth turned out to be grim: the famed kindergarten served as a pool of living experimental material for Mengele. Children selected for the experiments were periodically brought from barrack 31 to a special laboratory housed in the sauna building behind barrack 32 on the grounds of the Gypsy camp.[13]

Unfortunately, no documents have been found to show how many Gypsy twins passed through Mengele's laboratory. One document mentions 17 pairs of Gypsy monozygotic twins of both sexes.[14] According to testimonies of former prisoners, on August 2, 1944, the day of the final liquidation of the Gypsy camp, 12 pairs of twins survived. In all likelihood, Mengele personally shot them in the anteroom of a crematorium at Birkenau and ordered the dissection of their bodies.[15]

With the establishment in September 1943 of a family camp for Jews from the Terezin ghetto in sector BIIb,[16] Mengele became interested in the children staying there. Occasionally, he selected twins with their mothers for experiments. Beginning in the middle of May 1944, experimental subjects were also picked during selections on the unloading ramp from among Jewish transports consigned for annihilation in gas chambers. In an account by a former prisoner we find this testimony: when the convoys arrived, soldiers scouted the ranks lined up before the boxcars, hunting for twins and dwarfs. Mothers, hoping for special treatment for their twin children, readily gave them up to the scout. Adult twins, knowing that they were of interest from a scientific point of view, voluntarily presented themselves, in the hope of better treatment; so did dwarfs.[17]

From May 1944, some of the Jewish twins were placed in the women's camp hospital (sector BIa), in barracks 22. In July 1944, they were transferred to barracks 1 (a new numeration system was introduced in the second half of 1944). This group comprised girls aged two to 16 and boys aged seven and eight. Mothers with twins under two were left in barracks 22. Older boys, adult men, dwarfs, and handicapped males were incarcerated in barracks 15 on the grounds of the male camp hospital at Birkenau (sector BIIf). In July 1944, with the liquidation of the so-called family camp for Jews, twin girls were incorporated into a group of twins in the women's camp and twin boys transferred to barracks 15 in the male camp hospital.[18]

The number of twins in these barracks remains unknown. Elzbieta Warszawska, a prisoner who worked as a nurse in barracks 1, testified that about 350 pairs of twins of both sexes, aged two to 16, lived there. While they were of various nationalities, most were Jewish children from Hungarian and Czech (Terezin) transports, along with some Jewish children from German and Italian transports.

Another woman prisoner who worked in the same barracks testified that there were about 200 children, most of them aged two to 16, including six under age three.[19] In the archives of the Auschwitz-Birkenau State Museum is a document listing personal data and copies of findings of anthropological research on 296 Jewish women prisoners from Greece, Hungary, the Netherlands, France, and Italy, on whom Mengele conducted experiments. The list includes 111 pairs of Jewish Hungarian twins of both sexes who lived in the women's camp.[20]

According to one survivor of Mengele's experiments on twins, about 107 pairs of male twins, aged four to 60, were incarcerated in barrack 15, sector BIIf.

> The youngest twin in our group was "Pepichko" from Czechoslovakia, who was four or five years old [Josef Kleinmann, born on April 14, 1940, camp serial no. A-2459]. There was also Rene, a few years older [Rene Gutmann, born on December 21, 1937, camp serial no. 169,091]. Most of them were 12 to 15 years old. There were also Jewish triplets from Germany, aged about 60. In our block, we also had a family of dwarfs, consisting of two men and five women. The men stayed with us. I don't know where the women stayed; it's possible they were together with female twins.[21]

Another document preserved in the museum is a hand-made copy of a list of male adult and children twins from Jewish transports, who arrived at the camp in 1943 and 1944 from the Terezin ghetto and Hungary. It contains 125 names, including names of 52 boys under age 14.[22]

Living conditions in the barracks designated for twins both in the women's camp and the men's camp did not differ significantly from the conditions in other prisoner barracks. There were three-tiered bunk beds without sheets or pillows. The barracks for twins, however, were less congested: two to four prisoners, depending on age, slept on one bunk. Diet was also similar: black bread, margarine, and black coffee for supper and soup for lunch. The diet of twins in the women's camp was supplemented in the morning by milk soup, white bread, and jam or a small piece of sausage on Sundays and holidays.[23]

Regardless of age, twins in the women's and men's camp were not required to work. They remained exclusively at Mengele's disposal, which protected them from selections carried out among Jewish prisoners and from maltreatment by other prisoners and SS men.

According to accounts of prisoners assigned official duties in blocks for twins, and of twins themselves, individual pairs of twins were subjected to various examinations by Mengele in preparation for experiments. Broadly speaking, there were four types of examinations: anthropometric, morphological, x-ray, and psychiatric evaluation.[24]

In the anthropological exam, each body part was precisely measured; twins were measured together and results compared. Documentation includes descriptions of such details as shape of the mouth, nose, and auricle, color of the eyes, and coloring of the skin in various parts of the body. Mengele conducted the measurements personally, using the latest Swiss precision measuring instruments, assisted by Martyna Puzyna, a Polish prisoner and a doctor of anthropology. According to Puzyna's account, she conducted measurements of about 250 pairs of twins beginning in May 1944, when she became Mengele's assistant.[25] Initially, the research was conducted in Mengele's laboratory, on the grounds of the sauna in the Gypsy camp. In November 1944, the laboratory was moved to barracks 15, on the premises of the men's hospital (sector BIIf).

During measurements, which often lasted several hours, the twins stood naked in an unheated room, which was particularly exhausting for small children. Mengele often personally photographed the objects of his interest or entrusted this task to the photographic workshop (*Erkennungsdienst*) in the main camp, Auschwitz I. In addition to Puzyna, he employed Janina Prazmowska, a Polish prisoner, as a typist, and Dinah Gottlieb, a Czech Jew, as a painter. The latter made comparative drawings of individual body parts of twins, dwarfs, and other experimental subjects. After the war, she related that Dr. Mengele did not like color photography: "He wanted a natural paint copy of all possible colors and shades of the skin. I painted in the same room in which he performed his experiments."[26]

Morphological, x-ray, and surgical examinations, as well as sight, hearing, and dental checks, were conducted by men and women doctor-prisoners, specialists in a relevant branch of medicine, at the hospital for male prisoners and in the outpatient clinic of the women's camp. Sometimes twins were examined in block 10 in the main camp. X-ray, dental, and ophthalmological examination rooms were set up in block 15 in the hospital for male prisoners. In the course of dental examinations, plaster casts of the jaws of twins were made. During ophthalmological examinations, drops of a liquid unknown to the prisoners were put into their eyes, which resulted in suppuration; in extreme cases, children suffered partial loss of sight.[27]

Up to 20 cubic centimeters of blood was collected from each pair of twins. Blood, urine, stool, and saliva samples were sent for analysis to the lab of the Hygiene Institute. Archives of the Auschwitz-Birkenau State Museum contain numerous requests for analysis bearing Mengele's signature. The institute operated a number of laboratories: biological, pathological anatomy, bacteriological, chemical, and serological. All analyses were performed by prisoners, often specialists with international reputations, including Dr. Vaclav Tomasek, a professor of bacteriology at the University of Brno.

Frequent collection of large amounts of blood from malnourished children often resulted in anemia. Former prisoner Hani Schick, a mother of twins who was subjected to experiments together with her children, testified that on July 4, 1944, on Mengele's instructions, blood samples were collected from her children in such quantities that the procedure ended in the death of both son and daughter.[28]

As part of morphological research, Mengele performed blood transfusions between twins, observing their reactions. Since these experiments were not preceded by blood cross-matching, they often led to serious complications. Furthermore, he performed a procedure known as pneumocerebrum to permit analysis of the cerebral-spinal fluid.[29] There is also evidence that Mengele performed ghastly experiments on children for no medical purpose. Vera Alexandar, a Jewish prisoner posted to the barracks for twins in the Gypsy camp, testified:

> One day Mengele brought chocolate and special clothes. The next day an SS man, on Mengele's instructions, took away two children, who happened to be my favorites: Guido and Nino, aged about four. Two, perhaps three days later the SS man brought them back in a frightening condition. They had been sewn together like Siamese twins. The hunchbacked child was tied to the second one on the back and wrists. Mengele had sewn their veins together. The wounds were filthy and they festered. There was a powerful stench of gangrene. The children screamed all night long. Somehow their mother managed to get hold of morphine and put an end to their suffering.[30]

Moshe Ofer (Moshe Bleier in the camp), imprisoned with his twin brother, Tibi, at the age of 12, gave an account of his encounter with Mengele.

> He visited us as a good uncle, bringing us chocolate. Before applying the scalpel or the syringe, he would say: "Don't be afraid, nothing is going to happen to you." He made incisions in our testicles, injected chemical substances, performed surgery on Tibi's spine. After the experiments he would bring us gifts. Even today I can see him entering through the door and am paralyzed with

fear. In the course of later experiments, he had pins inserted into our heads. The puncture scars are still visible. One day he took Tibi away. My brother was gone for several days. When he was brought back, his head was all dressed in bandages. He died in my arms.[31]

The documentation of Mengele's research, including photographs, drawings, accounts, and analysis, was preserved in special files, one for each person subjected to experiments.

The last stage of Mengele's research was the analysis of body parts during dissection. Victims were killed by intracardiac phenol injection, either by Mengele personally or on his instruction. Initially the dissecting room was located in the Gypsy camp, and dissections were performed by Dr. Jancu Vexler, a Jewish prisoner from France or Belgium. Later the facility was moved to a building outside barracks 12 of the men's hospital. In 1944, Mengele ordered the outfitting of a special laboratory and dissecting room with the most modern equipment in the compounds of crematorium II in Birkenau.

It was there that, in late June 1944, Mengele employed Miklos Nyiszli, a Hungarian Jew (camp serial no. A-8450), an anatomist and pathologist by profession, to conduct dissections of prisoners, comparative analyses of selected internal organs, and analyses of the findings. He assigned a number of other prisoner physicians as Nyiszli's assistants: Dr. Denes Gorog, an anthropologist; Dr. Jozef Korner of Nice; and Adolf Fischer, dissection assistant from the Institute of Anatomy in Prague. Organs extracted during dissections were preserved as anatomical specimens and sent to the Institute of Anthropological and Biological-Race Research at Berlin-Dahlem.[32] Here is Nyiszli's account:

In accordance with orders received [from Mengele], I returned the corpses to the prisoners whose duty it was to burn them. They performed their job without delay. I had to keep any organs of possible scientific interest, so that Dr. Mengele could examine them. Those which might interest the Anthropological Institute at Berlin-Dahlem were preserved in alcohol. These parts were specially packed to be sent through the mail. Stamped "War Material—Urgent," they were given top priority in transit. In the course of my work at the crematorium, I dispatched an impressive number of such packages. I received, in reply, either precise scientific observations or instructions. In order to classify this correspondence, I had to set up special files. The directors of the Berlin-Dahlem institute always warmly thanked Dr. Mengele for this rare and precious material.[33]

In addition to twins, Mengele evinced special interest in the phenomenon of differential coloring of the eyes, the so-called heterochromia (heterochromia iridis). Evidence of this interest is found in a report drafted by von Verschauer on the research work of the institute and submitted on March 20, 1944, to the German Research Council. It covered two research projects: specific proteins (Specifische Eiweisskorper) and eye color (Augenfarbe). Von Verschauer wrote: "My assistant, doctor of philosophy and medicine Mengele, joined this research department as collaborator. He was posted to the Auschwitz concentration camp as a camp physician [Lagerarzt] in the rank of Hauptsturmführer. With the permission of the Reichsführer SS, anthropological studies of different racial groups are pursued there, and blood samples are dispatched to my lab for further analysis."[34] Mengele was the supplier of research material in the form of eyeballs preserved in formaldehyde solution. The material was used for scientific purposes at the institute by von Verschauer's assistant, Dr. Karin Magnussen.

Nyiszli recalled that on Mengele's instructions, he often put in formaldehyde solution the different-colored eyeballs extracted from prisoners' bodies. That was confirmed by Marck Berkowitz, a prisoner in the twins' camp at age 12 who was employed by Mengele as a messenger. Berkowitz had to fetch these macabre specimens from the dissecting room to Mengele. Dr. Jancu Vekler testified after the war that "in September 1943 I arrived at the Birkenau Gypsy camp. There I saw a wooden table with eyeballs laying on it. All of them were tagged with numbers and little notes. They were pale yellow, pale blue, green, and violet."[35]

It appears that these experiments were related to attempts to change eye color by injecting unknown chemical substances into children's eyes; this procedure was performed on twins, as well as on other Jewish and non-Jewish (Polish, Russian) children selected from children's blocks in the women's camp in Birkenau. Both infants and older children were subjected to these experiments. Side effects included strong reddening of the eyes, swelling and suppuration, and occasional partial or total loss of sight. There were some cases of death among infants.[36]

Testimonies and accounts by former prisoners indicate that Mengele was also interested in dwarfs and persons with innate abnormalities and treated them as he did other objects of scientific interest. Having placed them in separate blocks, he photographed them, carried out anthropological measurements, x-rayed them, collected their blood samples, then killed them or ordered other SS men to do so. He mailed specially prepared skeletons of the murdered dwarfs and handicapped persons to the Anthropological Institute at the Kaiser Wilhelm Institue for their collection.[37]

One of Mengele's chief duties was participation in selections of Jewish transports on the unloading ramp, in addition to selections of prisoners within the camp. The selections provided him with a constant supply of research material, as well as prisoner specialists, mostly physicians, whom he pressed into service, using their knowledge to pursue his interests. Another duty, supervising medical care of prisoners and exercising responsibility for health conditions in the camp, helped further his objectives, as it provided him with unlimited access to specialist and analytical laboratories and the authority to set up and outfit his own laboratories.

In attending to his criminal duties, Mengele showed uncommon meticulousness, especially as far as selections were concerned. Many other SS doctors considered making selections as the most stressful of all their official duties in the camp. In an interview with the *New York Times* printed on May 5, 1975, Dr. Ella Lingens, a former doctor-prisoner from Austria, described Mengele's attitude to selections: "Some [SS doctors] like Werner Rhoede, who hated his work, and Hans Koenig, who was deeply disgusted by the job, had to get drunk before they appeared on the ramp. Only two doctors performed the selections without stimulants of any kind: Dr. Josef Mengele and Dr. Fritz Klein. Dr. Mengele was particularly cynical and cold."[38]

Mengele dispatched thousands of people to the gas chambers. He became agitated and excited only at the sight of victims who could provide him with an interesting "test case." Like other SS doctors, he never examined, or even touched, sick prisoners during rounds or during selections in the sick bay. He evinced no interest whatsoever in their health, concerning himself exclusively with the hospital charts, which had to be meticulously kept by the prisoner medical staff. The condition of every prisoner-patient had to be recorded every three days. Mengele was concerned solely with the formal aspect of medical care.

During selections he was ruthless, sometimes even cynical. When, for example, he noticed a prisoner with an 18-month-old baby in his arms during his inspection of the men's quarantine camp, he immediately dispatched the prisoner to the gas chamber, even though the man was healthy and physically fit. On another occasion, when inspecting the women's sick bay, his attention was drawn to a certain woman prisoner. Mengele had her disease chart brought to him and noticed that her temperature had been unusually high. He said to her, "Well, you've been on the other side already, how are things over there?" When the patient shrugged her shoulders, he told her, "You'll know soon enough."[39]

In performing selections among Jewish children, Mengele took into consideration not only their health and fitness but also their height. Lazer Greis, then 13, gave an account of one such selection: "On October 2, 1944, the selection was carried out by the second Lagerarzt, Dr. Mengele. He used a special yardstick mounted not far from the camp fence, vis-à-vis our block. I don't know how high the bar was placed. We had to pass under it one by one. Those who could pass even though their head touched the bar were ordered by Dr. Mengele to get into the block."[40]

Mengele's superiors—particularly the chief physician of the camp and the SS garrison, the SS Standortarzt, a post occupied beginning in September 1942 by SS Hauptsturmführer Eduard Wirths—held him in very high regard. Wirths was pleased by a radical new method Mengele applied in late 1943 to combat a typhus epidemic in the women's camp. In an application submitted in February 1944 to the SS top echelons, Wirths praised his subordinate's innovation in requesting that Mengele be awarded the War Cross of Merit, or War Service Medal.[41]

Mengele's method of combating typhus was described by the Austrian physician Lingens. Noting that about 7,000 of some 20,000 half-starved women were seriously ill, Lingens said that Mengele

> sent one entire Jewish block of 600 women to the gas chamber and cleared the block. He then had it disinfected from top to bottom. Then he put bathtubs between this block and the next, and the women from the next block came out to be disinfected and then transferred to the clean block. Here they were given a clean new nightshirt. The next block was cleaned in this way and so on until all the blocks were disinfected. End of typhus![42]

Thus the disinfection cost the lives of the first 600 women. The same technique was used later by Mengele in other camp sectors to combat a scarlet fever epidemic among Hungarian Jews in camp BIIc and measles epidemics in the Jewish children's block (BIIa) and the Gypsy family camp. In these cases, however, all sick prisoners were dispatched to the gas chamber.[43]

Under the pretext of combating a spotted fever epidemic, the camp of Jewish prisoners from Terezin was liquidated in July 1944. Mengele personally supervised the gassing of about 4,000 women, children, and men. Two months earlier, in May 1944, he supported the decision to liquidate the Gypsy camp, then dispatched 2,857 Gypsies to the gas chambers on August 2, 1944.

Wirths's recommendation was approved and Mengele was awarded the War Cross of Merit Second Class with Swords. In an official assessment of his subordinate, drafted on August 19, 1944, Wirths wrote:

> During his employment as physician at the concentration camp Auschwitz, he put his knowledge to practical and theoretical use while combating serious epidemics. With prudence, perseverance, and energy, he has carried out all tasks given to him, often under very difficult conditions, to the complete satisfaction of his superiors and has shown himself able to cope with every situation. Furthermore, he, as an anthropologist, has most zealously used his little off-time duty to educate himself further and, utilizing the scientific material at his disposal due to his official position, has made a valuable contribution in his work to anthropological science. Therefore, his performance can be called outstand-

ing. While conscientiously applying himself to his official duties in combating a severe typhoid epidemic, he was infected himself with scarlet fever. On the basis of his extraordinary achievements, he was awarded War Cross of Merit Second Class with Swords. In addition to his proficiency in medicine, Dr. Mengele is also very knowledgeable in anthropology. He appears entirely suitable for every other employment, also for employment in the next higher rank.[44]

In recognition of his involvement in the Nazi cause, Mengele was promoted in 1944 to the post of First Physician of Auschwitz II-Birkenau.[45]

Mengele's career was cut short by the successful Soviet offensive. Well aware that the war was lost and that capture by Allied troops meant a death sentence, he decided to run and hide. Unlike most other SS men, he didn't have his blood type tattooed under his armpit, so he stood a good chance of eluding capture. On January 18, 1945, Mengele departed from the camp, taking with him the documents containing the results of his research. Together with other doctors, he fled to the Gross-Rosen concentration camp,[46] and from there, dressed in a Wehrmacht officer's uniform, to Czechoslovakia. On May 2, he joined a motorized German field hospital, 2/591, where he met Dr. Hans Otto Kahler, his friend from front-line service.

Together with his new unit, he crossed the frontier from Czechoslovakia into Saxony and some time later found himself in a no-man's land separating U.S. and Soviet forces. He remained there until June 15, when U.S. forces entered the area and took some 10,000 German prisoners. Mengele was not among them. However, his luck did not last long. He was captured and brought to a U.S. prison camp in the town of Weiden. In July, he was transferred to the prison camp at Ingolstadt, Bavaria.[47] Although Mengele's name was known to his captors in both camps, he was not identified as a principal war criminal, since the special units of U.S. military intelligence hunting down war criminals did not visit these two camps.

One day he succeeded in escaping from the camp. Helped by friends, he managed to find shelter under the name of Fritz Hollman on the farm of Georg and Maria Fischer, where he worked as a farmhand. In 1946, he met his wife, Irene, who informed him that he had been wanted by the U.S. military since 1945. He also learned that Irene was living with another man and wanted a divorce.

Allied military tribunals began conducting trials of Nazi criminals, including the "criminals in white coats," the doctors who had used concentration camp prisoners as guinea pigs in their experiments. The tribunals did not hesitate to impose the highest penalty. Mengele was among the most wanted Nazi criminals, after Adolf Eichmann and Martin Borman.[48]

In the summer of 1949, with financial help from his family and support from the "Edelweiss Group," an organization of former Nazi officers operating in Tyrol, Mengele was furnished with a blank International Red Cross travel document. He entered the name of Helmut Gregor, born August 11, 1911, in Tyrol, technician by profession. The document bore the number 100501. Using the "monastery route" across Italy, Mengele headed for Argentina, where scores of former Nazis had found shelter, thanks to the policy of President Juan Perón. Once in Buenos Aires, Mengele exchanged his Red Cross travel document for identity paper number 394048, which he used until 1957 while working as a physician.[49]

During this period he felt safe. The Cold War in Europe had dampened the momentum for prosecuting war criminals. West Germany had assumed responsibility for prosecuting Nazi war criminals in accord with standard German legal procedures, and that resulted in a protracted process of gathering evidence. The recently established State of Israel was beset by myriad problems other than hunting Nazis who had murdered millions of Jews.

Mengele felt so safe in 1956 that he traveled to Switzerland, where he met his son Rolf. In 1958 he became co-owner of a pharmaceutical firm, Fadro Farm, under his real name; he paid one million pesos for his share.[50] The firm prospered, making Mengele a rich man and a prominent member of a strong German expatriate community in Buenos Aires. In 1958, the widow of his brother Karl arrived from Gunzburg and married Mengele on July 25 in Uruguay.

But Mengele's luck was running out. Bowing to the pressure of world opinion, the German judiciary launched preparations for trials of war criminals, including former members of the Auschwitz personnel. The preliminary investigation conducted by prosecutors in Freiburg yielded so much incriminating evidence that the court issued a warrant for the arrest of Mengele in July 1959 and formally applied to the Argentine authorities for his extradition. In January 1964, the Hessen administrative court stripped Mengele of his medical diploma in absentia.

In the spring of 1960, Mengele moved to Paraguay, where Hans Rudl, a neo-Nazi, former Luftwaffe ace pilot, and personal friend of the country's dictator, Alfredo Stroessner, helped him to obtain Paraguayan citizenship. On May 11, 1960, agents of the Israeli Mossad abducted Adolf Eichmann, mastermind of the Nazi annihilation of the Jews. The Israelis planned to abduct Mengele as well, but he managed to elude his pursuers and disappear. After Eichmann's trial, the Israelis made two more attempts to capture the Nazi doctor, but in view of international complications in the aftermath of Eichmann's abduction, Israeli Prime Minister David Ben-Gurion apparently did not approve further operations of this kind.[51]

In Paraguay, Mengele met Wolfgang Gerhard, an immigrant from Austria, a former Hitler Jugend functionary. Gerhard found accommodation for Mengele at the estate of Gitta and Geza Stammer, who owned a small farm 250 kilometers northwest of São Paulo. Mengele used the alias of Peter Hochbichler. Shortly thereafter, he became their business partner and together they bought a farm not far from São Paulo. However, Mengele turned out to be difficult to get along with. A plenipotentiary of the Mengele company arrived from Gunzburg and pacified the Stammers by buying a larger farm for them not far from the city of Caieiras.

Gerhard also introduced Mengele to Wolfram Bossert, an Austrian immigrant with extreme right-wing views. They liked each other and met quite often. Bossert recorded some of their meetings. His notes make it clear that Mengele did not show any remorse over his past. Unable to find a common ground with the Stammers, Mengele left them and moved into a small house on the outskirts of São Paulo (Estrada Alvarenga 5555). Bossert continued to visit him, and even photographed him doing household chores.[52]

Mengele no longer felt safe. A reward of three million dollars was offered for his capture, prosecutors in Frankfurt were looking for him, and the Israeli secret police and other Nazi hunters were after him. He was also wanted by the Brazilian police. Gerhard responded to his imploring letters and came to São Paulo from Austria, where he lived taking care of his family. He gave Mengele his identity card, and from then on the Nazi doctor lived under the name of Wolfgang Gerhard.

On January 24, 1979, Bossert and his wife went to Bertioga for a holiday. On February 7, Mengele joined them, and on the same day, while swimming in the ocean, he died of a stroke. He was buried as Wolfgang Gerhard at the Embu cemetery, 25 miles from São Paulo. The Bosserts informed Mengele's family through Hans Sedlmeier, an executive in the Mengele company. However, neither the Mengeles nor the Bosserts were keen to make Josef Mengele's death public. The former did not want to disclose their connection with him, and the Bosserts were loath to be brought to account for sheltering a war criminal.

The search for Mengele went on, although its object was dead. In 1981, the court in Freiburg issued a new arrest warrant and requested his extradition from Paraguayan authorities. In reply, the government of Paraguay said that Mengele had been stripped of citizenship in 1980 because he had not been present in the country since 1960.

In 1984, the victims of Mengele's macabre experiments founded an organization called CANDLES (Children of Auschwitz Nazi Deadly Lab Experiments Survivors) whose goal was to gather evidence of Mengele's crimes, inform public opinion about them, and ultimately bring him to trial.[53] On their initiative, a mock trial of Mengele was staged in 1985 in Jerusalem.[54]

Several months later, in May 1985, the Freiburg prosecution learned that Hans Sedlmeier had told a German university professor that he had maintained contact with a major war criminal hiding in South America. Acting on this clue, the Germans put Sedlmeier under surveillance and later raided his apartment. The search yielded an unexpected and rich bounty in the form of Sedlmeier's correspondence with Mengele, as well as photographs he had taken in Brazil.[55] The name and role of the Bosserts as Mengele's protectors emerged. During a search of their apartment, documents belonging to Mengele were discovered. Under questioning, the Bosserts revealed details of the last years of the Nazi criminal's life and the location of his grave.

On June 6, 1985, the body of "Wolfgang Gerhard" was exhumed at the Embu cemetery in the presence of officials of the German and Brazilian criminal police and prosecution, as well as experts from the United States and Israel. The exhumed remains were then analyzed with sophisticated forensic methods. On the basis of anthropometric measurements, comparison of the exhumed body's dentition with Mengele's dental chart of 1938, the match between signs of injury on the body and data on a motorcycle accident in 1943,[56] and skull damage corresponding to the injuries suffered by Mengele on the eastern front, it was concluded that the body exhumed from the Embu cemetery was that of Josef Mengele.[57] The only missing factor was matching the fingerprints of "Wolfgang Gerhard" with those of Mengele, a circumstance cited by some to cast doubt on Mengele's death.[58]

In the course of the lengthy search for Mengele, the "Angel of Death" became the subject of considerable media attention as an archcriminal who for years eluded the police of many countries. But in the last years of his life, Mengele, an old and sick man, lived in constant fear of capture. Only one detail of the archcriminal characterization was true: Mengele never expressed any regrets over his crimes. A final investigation revealed that Mengele had met with his son Rolf for a final time in São Paulo in 1977. In an interview in August 1985 with Gerald L. Posner and John Ware, authors of *Mengele: The Complete Story,* Rolf revealed that his father had broached the subject of his activities in Auschwitz-Birkenau. Mengele absolved himself by maintaining that he had not made decisions in Auschwitz and did not feel personally responsible for what had taken place there. According to Mengele, he had sought to help the prisoners but had few opportunities to do so. When he had a chance, he could help only a few. He claimed that his main task was to classify the new arrivals as either fit or unfit for work. Although he went to great lengths to classify as many as possible as fit for work, Mengele told Rolf, he could not do so in every case, since many of the new arrivals were already half-dead. Nonetheless, he maintained that he saved thousands of people. Mengele also emphasized that he had not been in charge of extermination and therefore could not be held accountable for it. Neither had he been involved in killing or harming twins, but had tried to save their lives. Mengele asked Rolf not to believe what was written about him in the press.[59]

Mengele thus fit the mold of the overwhelming majority of Nazi criminals; dissimulation, hypocrisy, and lack of critical reflection on his past characterized one of the most notorious villains of the Nazi Reich.

NOTES

1. "The Professional Origins of Dr. Mengele," *Canadian Medical Association Journal*, 133 (1985), no. 11, pp. 1169–72.

2. "Da habe für 20 Jahre Arbeit," *Der Spiegel*, April 22, 1985.

3. Stahlhelm (Bund der Frontsoldaten), was a paramilitary, nationalist, reactionary organization of combatants, veterans of the First World War, established in November 1918 by F. Seldte, later minister of labor in the Third Reich. Financed by German bourgeoisie, its purpose was to combat revolutionary elements among the workers. In 1919–23, it took part in Freikorps battles. From 1924 it accepted noncombatants into its ranks. In 1933 it became part of the SS.

4. "Professional Origins," pp. 1169–72.

5. Zdenek Zofka, "Der KL-Zrzt Josef Mengele zur Typologie Lines NS-Verbrechers," *Vierteliahrshefte für ZeitReschichte 34 Jahrgang (2 Heft)*, (Munich, 1986), p. 254.

6. Gerald L. Posner and John Ware, *Mengele: The Complete Story*, (New York, 1986), p. 17.

7. Zofka, p. 254.

8. Yves Ternon and Socrate Helman, *Histoire de la médicine SS ou le mythe du racisme biologique* (Tournai, 1970). According to Dr. Miklos Nyiszli, the purpose of the pseudoscientific experiments of Mengele was to discover the secret of twin conception. This, in turn, was "to advance one step in the search to unlock the secret of multiplying the race of superior beings destined to rule." See Nyiszli, *Auschwitz: A Doctor's Eyewitness Account* (London, 1964), p. 54.

9. On the Gypsy family camp hospital and the incidence of gangrene of the cheek there, see T. Szymanski, D. Szymanska, and T. Smieszko, "The Gypsy Family Camp Hospital in Auschwitz-Birkenau" (in Polish), *Przeglad Lekarski* (Medical Review), 1985, pp. 90–99; T. Szymanski, "Cases of Noma (Gangrene of the Cheek) in the Gypsy Family Camp at Auschwitz-Birkenau" (in Polish), *Przeglad Lekarski*, 1962, pp. 68–70.

10. Archives of the Auschwitz-Birkenau State Museum (ASAM), collection Höss Trial, vol. 7, cards 9–14, testimony of former prisoner Mieczyslaw Kieta, who worked at the SS Institute of Hygiene at Rajsk. A collection of documents pertaining to the SS Institute of Hygiene contains a request signed by Dr. Mengele for a histological examination of a head from the body of a 12-year-old boy; ASAM, collection Institute of Hygiene/62, file 41, card 69. A former prisoner, Dr. Jan Cespiva, a Czech who worked as a physician in the Gypsy camp hospital, testified that "noma broke out. Whole chunks of flesh would come off [the affected areas], lower jaw was also affected. I never saw such severe cases of gangrene of the cheek. Specimen of heads of diseased children were prepared for the SS Academy at Graz. I know about it because we wrote the addresses. The heads were preserved in formaldehyde and the bodies stored in crematorium III." Recollections of Dr. Jan Cespiva recorded by Vlasta Klav-

diva on September 11, 1963, in Vlasta Klavdiva, "Czech Gypsies in Auschwitz-Birkenau 1942–1944" (in Polish), ASAM, collection Studies, vol. 51, p. 114.

11. Danuta Czech, "The Camp Hospital for Men in Auschwitz II" (in Polish), *Zeszyty Oswiecimskie*, no. 15, p. 44, n. 91.

12. ASAM, collection Affidavits, vol. 87, cards 82, 97–98, accounts of former women prisoners Ludwika Wierzbicka and Danuta Szymanska (Markowska in the camp).

13. Klavdiva, p. 120.

14. Accounts of former prisoners Wierzbicka and Szymanska, cards 100, 87, 97a.

15. ASAM, files of Zahnstation KL Au 1, call no. D-Au 1–5/4, inventory no. 154368, p. 52.

16. See the essay by Nili Keren in this volume (chap. 17).

17. Nyiszli, p. 52.

18. ASAM, collection Affidavits, vol. 70, card 7; vol. 71, card 35; vol 74, card 225ff.; vol. 95, card 48, accounts by former prisoners Edwin Opoczynski, Waclaw Dlugoborski, Anna Lipka, Hani Schick.

19. Supplementary account, recorded on February 12, 1988, by former prisoner Elzbieta Piekut-Warszawska (manuscript in the possession of this author), and account by former prisoner Anna Lipka, a room attendant in barrack 11 for twins, ASAM, collection Affidavits, vol. 74, card 225.

20. ASAM, collection Materials of the Camp Underground Organization, call no. D-RO/22–77, vol. 30 (originals), vol. 16 (photocopies). The copies were made illicitly in the camp by former prisoner Martyna Puzyna (Puzynina), who worked as Dr. Mengele's assistant. In the middle of 1944 she handed them over to prisoner Antonina Piatkowska together with other documents, such as the clinical-psychiatric guidelines for examination of three pairs of male twins and results of a lung x-ray examination of woman prisoner no. A-5544, a twin. These documents, together with 27 photographs (obtained in the middle of 1944 in the men's camp at Birkenau) of women and children experimented upon by Mengele, were smuggled out of the camp by Piatkowska in October 1944. See A. Piatkowska, *Reminiscences from Auschwitz* (in Polish) (Krakow, 1977), pp. 123–30.

21. ASAM, collection Affidavits, vol. 125, card 121, account by former prisoner Otto Klein (camp serial no. A-5332).

22. ASAM, call no. D-Au 1–3/26, inv. no. 148855, miscellaneous. It consists of a list of names, accompanied by camp serial numbers of male prisoners, a gift to the archives by former prisoner Robert Weitz, April 13, 1965. No information is available on the circumstances under which it was compiled. Comparison of some of the names in it to the names appearing in other documents containing partial lists of twins allows us to conclude that it constitutes an incomplete list of boys and adult men who from July 1944 were present in barrack 11 in the men's camp hospital (section BIIf).

23. ASAM, collection Reminiscences, vol. 129, cards 74ff., reminiscences of former prisoner E. Piekut-Warszawska and her supplementary account. They are corroborated by accounts by former prisoners Otto Klein and Andreas Lorinci (twins) and by Apolonia Kilian-Wolska (a nurse in the barracks for twins), ASAM, collection Affidavits, vol. 125, cards 123, 146. Affidavit by A. Kilian-Wolska in the possession of this author. A somewhat different account of nourishment of the twins was given by former prisoner Anna Lipka: "The children were fed three meals a day. Their food was better than that of other children in the camp. They were given skimmed milk once, even twice, a week. Sometimes they received larger portions of

sausage. For children under six years we used to bring dairy food which included, among other things, macaroni. Children aged six to 12 were given a different kind of food, and children over 12 yet another kind. Thus we used to bring three kinds of food to the block." ASAM, collection Affidavits, vol. 74, card 226. Alfred Fiderkiewicz, a former prisoner who worked as a physician in section BIIf agrees; in his reminiscences, he mentions that twins were better fed than other prisoners; see A. Fiderkiewicz, *Birkenau: Memoirs from the Camp* (in Polish) (Warsaw, 1956).

24. Concerning experiments on the twins, see reminiscences of E. Piekut-Warszawska in *Przeglad Lekarski*, 1967, no. 1, p. 204.

25. Interview with Martyna Puzyna in Great Britain, June 1985; see Posner and Ware, pp. 36–37.

26. ASAM, collection Affidavits, vol. 102, card 74, testimony of former prisoner Dina Gottlieb (now Babbitt). Several watercolor portraits of Gypsy men and women done by Dina in the camp have been preserved in the collections of the Auschwitz-Birkenau State Museum.

27. Former prisoner Maria Hanel-Halska stated that Mengele employed her in examining the twins' dentition. She worked at HKB-Zahn-station. Prior to the liquidation of the camp, she handed over to Mengele a descriptive study of the subject, accompanied by tooth models. Tadeusz Snieszko, who worked as a physician in the Gypsy camp, was also compelled to take measurements of the twins and to collect and analyze their blood samples, ASAM, collection Affidavits, vol. 91, p. 24, vol. 15, p. 52. See also testimony of former prisoner Alfred Galewski, ASAM, collection Höss Trial, vol. 2/1, p. 23. Concerning eyedrops, see testimony of Olga Klimenko (ASAM, collection Affidavits, vol. 53, card 72); Otto Klein (as above, p. 123); memoirs of E. Piekut-Warszawska (as above. pp. 79–80).

28. Affidavit by former prisoner Schick, card 50.

29. ASAM, collection Höss Trial, vol. 2/1, card 10. Testimony of former prisoner Maria Stoppelman, who from July 1944 worked in the laboratory of the women's camp hospital in Birkenau, ASAM, collection Höss Trial, vol. 2/1, card 10.

30. Testimonies of former prisoners Vera Alexandar and Moshe Ofer before the Jerusalem tribunal which tried Mengele in absentia (February 1985), recorded by collaborator of Sternn. Helen Davis; "Schreie die nie verhallen," *Der Stern*, 1985, no. 18. See also Posner and Ware, p. 37.

31. See n. 30.

32. Szymanski, Szymanska, and Sneiszko, p. 97; Nyiszli, p. 86.

33. Nyiszli, pp. 56–57.

34. These projects were submitted earlier under the general heading "Auschwitz-Projekt" by von Verschauer for approval to the German Research Council, which was to sponsor it, since the Kaiser Wilhelm Gesselschaft did not command sufficient resources to finance the research. Both projects were approved by the German Research Council on September 7, 1943. See Benno Müller-Hill, *Tödliche Wissenschaft: Die Aussonderung von Juden, Zigeunern und Geisteskranken* (Hamburg, 1984), pp. 72–74; see also Zofka, p. 258.

35. Testimony of Jancu Vexler before Judge Horst von Glasenapp, March 13, 1973; Posner and Ware, p. 25.

36. Account by former woman prisoner Klimenko, card 72; former prisoner Henryk Szymanski, ASAM, collection Affidavits, vol. 32, card 98; testimony of former prisoner Ivanova Vera Pavlova, ASAM, collection Files of the Soviet Commission for the Investigation of Nazi Crimes in Auschwitz, call no. IZ/1/1, vol. 3, card 78/458.

37. Nyiszli, pp. 56–57; ASAM, collection Files of the Soviet Commission for the Investigation of Nazi Crimes in Auschwitz, call no. 1Z/1/1, vol. 3, cards 136–39. Unfortunately, the number of dwarfs of both sexes subjected to experiments by Dr. Mengele remains unknown. The only evidence is an employment roster of women prisoners from Birkenau, dated December 5, 1944, which contains notations on 16 women dwarfs who were transferred that day from the men's camp hospital (BIIf) to the women's camp; by December 8 only five women dwarfs remained in the camp. It is possible that the remaining 11 women dwarfs died or were killed, since on the same day 11 women were listed as dead; ASAM, call no. D-AuII-3a/66b.

38. Posner and Ware, pp. 26–27.

39. ASAM, collection Höss Trial, vol. 6. card 13, vol. 2, cards 9–14, testimonies of former prisoners Otto Wolken and Maria Stoppelman.

40. ASAM, collection Höss Trial, vol. 117, cards 7–8, testimony of former prisoner Lazar Greis.

41. Berlin Document Center file on Josef Mengele: Beurteilung des Standortarztes (Assessment of the CS District Doctor), in Posner and Ware, p. 26. The SS top echelons considered work in concentration camps as front-line service for which the SS functionaries could be awarded special decorations. One such award was the War Cross of Merit First or Second Class, ASAM, collection Studies, vol. 94b, p. 694, chap. 7, n. 3 (MS. of Aleksander Lasik's Ph.D. dissertation).

42. Interview with former woman prisoner Ella Lingens, March 14, 1984, in Posner and Ware, p. 25.

43. In putting into practice his radical method of fighting epidemics, Dr. Mengele was implementing a secret order of Himmler, which recommended that "doctors should liquidate in a discreet fashion the sick Gypsies, especially children." See Rudolf Höss, *Commandant of Auschwitz* (London, 1961), p. 133.

44. ASAM, Mengele file, Berlin Document Center, microfiche 1613/33 (assessment of SS-Hauptsturmführer Dr. Josef Mengele, SS-Lagerarzt in KL Birkenau, by SS-Standortarzt Eduard Wirths, August 19, 1944).

45. Requests for sending samples of substances collected from prisoners to the SS Institute of Hygiene at Rajsk were signed by Mengele in his capacity as first physician of Auschwitz II; ASAM, collection SS Hygiene Institute/62, 64, files 41, 43, cards 69, 183.

46. Posner and Ware, p. 351, n. 1; see also Leon Landau, *Accuse* (in Polish) (Warsaw, 1963), p. 103.

47. Posner and Ware, pp. 60–64.

48. Alan Levy, *Wanted: Nazi Criminals at Large* (New York, 1962), p. 62.

49. Erich Widemann, "Sechs Milionen, da kann ich nur lachen" and "Da have ich fur 20 Jahre Arbeit," *Der Spiegel*, 1985, no. 17, pp. 28ff.

50. Posner and Ware, pp. 114–15.

51. Widemann, "Sechs Milionen," p. 32; *Jerusalem Post*, February 6, 1985.

52. "Wie ein Soldat," *Der Spiegel*, 1985, no. 26.

53. Materials of the CANDLES organization are on file in the Auschwitz-Birkenau State Museum.

54. *Jerusalem Post*, February 1, 1985; see also n. 30.

55. Stanislaw Sterkowicz, "The Great Escape" (in Polish), *Tygodnik Kulturalny*, 1988, no. 16, p. 7.

56. ASAM, collection Kommendantur-Befehl, no. 26/43; Berlin Document Center, file on Dr. J. Mengele, microfiche 1613/100, 101.

57. "Medical Team Resolves 40-Year Mengele Riddle," *Science,* 1986, nos. 1–2, p. 75; Wilmes Robert G. Teixeira, "The Mengele Report," *American Journal of Forensic Medicine and Pathology* 4 (1985), no. 6, pp. 279–83.

58. Claudio Gatti, "The Ghost of the Henchman" (in Polish, translation of article in *Europeo*), *Glos Wielkopolski,* 1989, nos. 171–72.

59. Inge Byhan, "So entkam mein Vater, " *Bunte,* 1985, no. 26, pp. 17–33; see also Posner and Ware, p. 30. Mengele made a similar protestation of his innocence as early as 1960, in reply to the indictment of the Frankfurt prosecution. He sent his statement from Asunción to his family in Gunzburg through the Mengele company executive Hans Sedlmeier. Mengele claimed that "I never personally killed, wounded, or inflicted bodily harm against anyone." Wiedemann, "Sechs Milionen," p. 50.

Aerial view of the Auschwitz-Birkenau complex, photographed by the Allies, June 26, 1944. The captions were added after the war. Credit: National Archives, Washington, D.C.

Aerial view of Auschwitz I (Main Camp), photographed by the Allies, August 25, 1944. The captions were added after the war. Credit: National Archives, Washington, D.C.

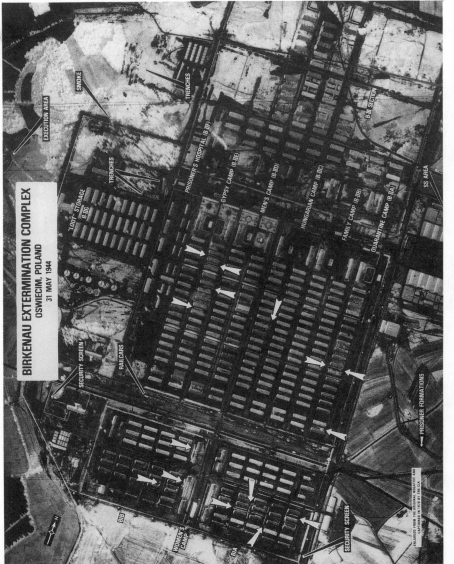

BIRKENAU EXTERMINATION COMPLEX
OSWIECIM, POLAND
31 MAY 1944

EXECUTION AREA

SMOKE

TRENCHES

TRENCHES

PRISONER'S HOSPITAL (B IIF)

GYPSY CAMP (B IIE)

MEN'S CAMP (B IID)

HUNGARIAN CAMP (B IIC)

FAMILY CAMP (B IIB)

QUARANTINE CAMP (B IIA)

SS AREA

B III SECTION

"LOOT" STORAGE
B IIG

SECURITY SCREEN

RAILCARS

B IB

WOMEN'S CAMP

B IA

SECURITY SCREEN

PRISONER FORMATIONS

ENLARGED FROM THE ORIGINAL NEGATIVE AND CAPTIONED IN 1978 BY THE CIA

N

Aerial view of the Birkenau extermination complex, photographed by the Allies, May 31, 1944. The captions were added after the war. Arrow points to prisoner formations. Credit: National Archives, Washington, D.C.

Konzentrationslager Auschwitz
Abteilung II.

Z u g ä n g e   a m   29.Juni 1941:

Haft Art	Häftl. Nr.	N a m e	Vorname	Geb.Dat.	Geb.Ort	Beruf
Staatspolizeileitstelle W i e n:						
Schutzh.P.	17397	Sanojca	Witold	19. 1.22	Stanislawow	Gymn.Schüler
"	17398	Millak	Andreas	18.12.19	Warschau	Gymn.Schüler
Schutzh.Jud.	17399	Sas	Johann	4. 5.13	Krakau	Arzt
Schutzh.P.	17400	Stolarczuk	Josef	16. 3.16	Lemberg	Elektromech.
"	17401	Krall	Josef	14. 1.10	Wartoglowiec,Baumeister	
" Prot.	17402	Hicka	Josef	1. 2.22	Zlin	Bäcker
Schutzh.P.	17403	Schoedon	Erich	19. 2.13	Schlesiengrube,Beamter	
Staatspolizeistelle L i n z:						
Schutzh.P.	17404	Machelak	Josef	7. 3.08	Sieszchow	Landarbeiter
Staatspolizeileitstelle P r a g.						
Schutzh.Prot.	17405	Komarek	Ernst	29.10.85	Nadslow	Staatsbeamte
Staatspolizeistelle Zichenau/Plock:						
Schutzh.P.	17406	Pietrowski	Johann	30. 6.04	Tschenstochau,Schloßer	
"	17407	Rosciszewski	Stefan	22. 1.94	Bromierzyk	Kraftfahrer
"	17408	Pierschela	Adam	15.11.01	Krakau	Buchhalter
"	17409	Grecki	Heinrich	28.11.79	Siedlec,	Fabriksleiter
"	17410	Switalski	Kasimir	2. 1.14	Klodawa	Buchhalter
"	17411	Kaminski	Ludwig	7. 6.15	Plock	Tischler
"	17412	Ruszczak	Valerian	14. 4.85	Radzymin	Sanitäter
"	17413	Kowalewski	Konstantin	18. 2.80	Plock	Gastwirt
"	17414	Drynski	Apolinarius	22.9.95	Plock	Gem.-Beamter
"	17415	Woyno	Georg	23. 4.96	Warschau,Bauingenieur	
"	17416	Beczkiewicz	Johann	12. 5.92	Milewko	Schuster
Staatspolizeileitstelle D a n z i g:						
Schutzh.P.	17417	Gottwald	Johann	24.12.93	Thorn	Bautechnike
"	17418	Kwasigroch	Alfons	19. 5.06	Wilhelmsruh,Postbeamter	
Staatspolizeistelle Bromberg:						
Schutzh.P.	17419	Zaganowski	Johann	7. 8.21	Gondys	Landarbeiter
Staatspolizeileitstelle P o s e n:						
Schutzh.P.	17420	Marczewski	Kasimir	28.12.99	Hohensalza	Gerichts-Angestellter
"	17421	Koscielniak	Josef	24.12.17	Misfeld	Fabrikarbeit
Staatspolizeistelle Schneidemühl:						
Schutzh.D.	17422	Parschik	Leo	19.10.10	Gesorgen	Landarbeiter

A document listing prisoners deported to Auschwitz, dated June 29, 1941. The entries are categorized by the place of and reason for arrest. The column marked "Haft Art" gives political, racial, or religious affiliations. Credit: Auschwitz-Birkenau State Museum, Oswiecim.

ft Art	Häftl. Nr.	N a m e	Vorname	Geb.Dat.	Geb.-Ort	Beruf

Staatspolizeistelle Hohensalza:

| ichutzh.D. | 17423 | Krieger | Artur | 9. 7.16 | Gnesen | Landarbeiter |

Staatspolizeistelle Litzmannstadt:

chutzh.P.	17424	Laguna	Stanislaus	5. 1.o5	Pinsk	Drogist
"	17425	Kubiak	Josef	1o. 1.92	Goliszew	Landwirt
"	17426	Zietkiewicz	Stefan	26. 7.o5	Litzmannstadt,Schloßer
"	17427	Marczak	Josef	24.12.89	Rozworsyn	Bauer
"	17428	Treffenfeld	Zenon	24. 1.19	Litzmannstadt,Hilfsschloß
"	17429	Mamonski	Johann	5. 6.76	Lubianka	Maurer
"	17430	Adamczyk	Franz	4. 5.o4	Litzmannstadt,Lehrer
"	17431	Piskula	Franz	17. 2.o2	Dobroslaw	Landarbeiter
"	17432	Wojciechowski	Franz	13. 1.o5	Sobotka	Landarbeiter

Überstellt aus KL.-D a c h a u:

| chutzh.P. | 17433 | Kasprzak | Peter | 11. 9.22 | Litzmannstadt,Arbeiter |
| " | 17434 | Kasprzak | Josef | 18. 1.2o | Litzmannstadt,Arbeiter |

Kriminalpolizeistelle Königsberg:

H./BV.-D.	17435	Kohn	Franz	6.12.14	Brandenburg,Arbeiter
"	17436	Logan	Gustav	19. 7.98	Lengern	Kammerjäger
"	17437	Gruhn	Walter	8. 6.14	Königsberg Artist
"	17438	Borutta	Rudolf	13.11.97	Aweyden	Landarbeiter
"	17439	Grigoteit	Hugo	4. 5.o3	Ellernbruch,Brenner
"	17440	Bernhard	Walter	14. 2.1o	Königsberg Kutscher
H./§ 175-D	17441	Klefeldt	Leo	18. 1.38	Bischofsburg,Büroangest.

Kriminalpolizeileitstelle Breslau:

| H./§ 175-D | 17442 | Krause | Hermann | 28. 9.91 | Tannenberg,Landarbeiter |

Kriminalpolizeistelle T i l s i t:

| H/Aso.-D. | 17443 | Lieweris | Erich | 16. 3.12 | Memel | Anstreicher |

Kriminalpolizeileitstelle Danzig:

| H./BV. - D | 17444 | Tesch | Otto | 15.1o.96 | Elbing | Former |

....
ᛋᛋ-Unterscharführer

Konzentrationslager Auschwitz ... Nr. 62017

Name und Vorname: Schwarz, Moritz, Israel
geb. 4.9.1912 in Matészalka Kr. ddn. Ungarn
Wohnort: Brüsselles, Rue de Capucinus Nr. 6
Beruf: Schneider   Rel.: mos.
Staatsangehörigk.: Ungarn   Stand: verh.
Name der Eltern: Josef u. Serem geb. Klein   Rasse: jud
Wohnort: b. gest in Matészalka
Name der Ehefrau: Esthe geb. Soliman   Rasse: jud
Wohnort: K. L. Au.   R. Ang. Keine
Kinder: Keine   Altsitzer Bruder der Familie oder der Eltern:
Vorbildung: 6 kl. Volksschule
Militärdienst: /   von — bis   /
Kriegsdienst: /   von — bis   /
Grösse: 170   Nase: spitz. geb.   Haare: d. braun.   Gestalt: schlank
Mund: normal   Bart: Keinen   Gesicht: längl.   Ohren: a. abst.
Sprache: deutsch, ungar.   Augen: braun   Zähne: 6 fehlen
Ansteckende Krankheit oder Gebrechen: Keine
Besondere Kennzeichen: Keine
Rentenempfänger: nein

Verhaftet am: 17.8.1942   wo: Brüsselles
1. Mal eingeliefert: 27.8.1942   2. Mal eingeliefert:
Einweisende Dienststelle: RSHA
Grund:
Parteiangehörigkeit: keine   von — bis
Welche Funktionen: keine
Mitglied v. Unterorganisationen: nein
Kriminelle Vorstrafen: ang. keine
Politische Vorstrafen: ang. keine

Ich bin darauf hingewiesen worden, dass meine Bestrafung wegen intellektueller Urkundenfälschung erfolgt, wenn sich die obigen Angaben als falsch erweisen sollten.

V.u.R.   Der Lagerkommandant KL.-Au.
i. A.

Moritz Schwarz
4.9.1913.

Prisoner registration at Auschwitz for Moritz Israel Schwarz. Arrested August 17, 1942, in Brussels, he arrived at Auschwitz August 27, 1942. A Hungarian citizen, he was a tailor by profession and was missing six teeth. His fate is unknown. Credit: Museum of Contemporary History, Budapest.

Mug shot of Jerzy Guminski, born March 20, 1923. He and his mother, Zofia, worked for the Polish underground. In 1940 they were denounced by collaborators and imprisoned in Pawiak. On March 6, 1942, Jerzy Guminski was transported to Auschwitz, where he was shot August 14, 1942. His mother was transported to Ravensbrück; she survived the war. Credit: Wanda Lysikiewicz/Auschwitz-Birkenau State Museum, Oswiecim.

Prisoners of Auschwitz IV at forced labor in the Siemens factory. Credit: Fédération Nationale des Déportés et Internés Résistants et Patriotes, Paris.

At Auschwitz, an orchestra made up of inmates performed during the departure and return of work battalions. This photograph, taken from a window of block 24, was used as evidence in the trial of Rudolf Höss. Credit: Auschwitz-Birkenau State Museum, Oswiecim.

SS Reichsführer Heinrich Himmler, inspecting a construction site at the Auschwitz complex, listens to an explanation by Bauleiter Faust. Camp commandant Rudolf Höss is second from right. July 17–18, 1942. Credit: Main Commission for the Investigation of Nazi War Crimes, Warsaw.

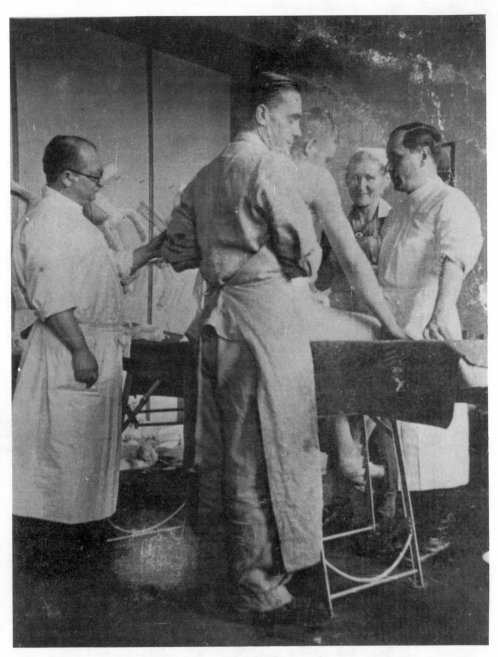

The medical staff of the operating room at Auschwitz. At far left is Dr. Carl Clauberg, who worked in Block 10 of Auschwitz I. Clauberg conducted experiments using nonsurgical methods of sterilization on female prisoners. Credit: Main Commission for the Investigation of Nazi War Crimes, Warsaw.

Gypsy (Roma) boys who were victims of Dr. Mengele's medical experiments at Auschwitz. Credit: Fédération Nationale des Déportés et Internés Résistants et Patriotes, Paris.

Prisoners pour concrete for the ceiling of the underground undressing hall of crematorium II at Auschwitz-Birkenau, 1943. Credit: Yad Vashem, Jerusalem.

Inmates working on the construction of the reception building at Auschwitz during the winter of 1944. Credit: Auschwitz-Birkenau State Museum, Oswiecim.

Arrival and selection of Hungarian Jews at Auschwitz, 1944. Credit: Yad Vashem, Jerusalem.

Arrival and selection of Hungarian Jews at Auschwitz, 1944. Credit: Yad Vashem, Jerusalem.

Suitcases belonging to victims at Auschwitz, 1945. Credit: National Archives, Washington, D.C. Credit: National Archives, Washington, D.C.

A prisoner at Auschwitz in his bunk, 1944. Credit: Fédération Nationale des Déportés et Internés Résistants et Patriotes, Paris.

Clandestine photo of women being driven to the gas chambers at Auschwitz, 1944. Credit: Auschwitz-Birkenau State Museum, Oswiecim.

Clandestine photo of the cremation of corpses at Auschwitz, 1944. When the crematoria were not working or were insufficient, bodies were burned in communal ditches. Credit: Auschwitz-Birkenau State Museum, Oswiecim.

Electrified barbed-wire fence behind block 11 at Auschwitz I, 1945. The sign in the foreground says "Danger, high voltage." Credit: Auschwitz-Birkenau State Museum, Oswiecim.

The main entrance to Auschwitz II-Birkenau, January 1945. Credit: Bund Archive.

Liberated prisoners in Auschwitz, 1945. Credit: Central State Archives of the October Revolution, Minsk.

Women's barracks after the liberation of Auschwitz, January 1945. Credit: Central State Archives of the October Revolution, Minsk.

Rudolf Franz Höss, commandant of the Auschwitz death camp, at the time of his trial, 1946. Credit: Suddeutscher Verlag Bilderdienst, Munich.

Part *IV*

The Inmates

DANUTA CZECH explores the way in which the limited SS staff at Auschwitz controlled the massive camp. They employed a system of inmate-run administration, cleverly exploiting national, ethnic, religious, and social divisions of the camp. Germans were at the top of the pyramid, Jews at the bottom. Kapos, or inmate foremen, were used extensively, and they had nearly unlimited sway over their subordinates. Criminals with unstable personalities easily did the Nazis' bidding. Mastery of the German language was helpful, even at times essential. Veteran prisoners, such as the early Polish prisoners, were able to sustain themselves with the survival skills they developed.

Czech writes of unusual assignments at Auschwitz, like the orchestras that were formed, and of the "Canada" commandos, who sorted plundered inmate property adjacent to the crematoria. She depicts the desperate plight of the *Sonderkommando*, who stoked the ovens and emptied the gas chambers. And she describes the *muselmänner*, the walking dead, those who yielded to despair. Czech also offers significant insight into the way language was manipulated with euphemisms so that the reality of camp life was obscured for both the perpetrator and the victim and into the system of rewards and punishments, which allowed the masters, so few in number, to dominate.

Irena Strzelecka details the evolution of the hospital system at Auschwitz and Birkenau. At first the hospitals were regarded by prisoners as places of shelter from the horrors of the camp, or at least as places to die peacefully. With the expansion of Auschwitz and the influx of Jewish prisoners, the hospitals soon became exclusively places to die. The process was assisted by deadly injections. Strzelecka vividly depicts the sewage problems in the hospitals, where prisoners afflicted with dysentery left feces all over the floor and "prisoners' bodies reeked."

As demand for slave labor increased, the SS tried to reduce the high mortality rate in the camp among non-Jewish prisoners. Prisoner-doctors, who had previously served only as nurses, were now employed as physicians, and Polish political prisoners, rather than German personnel, administered more of the hospitals. Prisoner personnel sought to improve conditions and to establish contact with the underground. Survival chances for Polish patients and gradually for other prisoners improved.

In a second chapter, Strzelecka describes the experience of women in Auschwitz. Jewish women comprised at least half of those murdered and non-Jewish women constituted 30 percent of those incarcerated. Yet when one thinks of Auschwitz, one envisions male prisoners. Originally established to alleviate the congestion at Ravensbrück, the women's camp at Auschwitz expanded as the functions of Auschwitz changed. By August 1942, it was transferred to Birkenau, expanding again twice in 1943 and once more in 1944.

Strzelecka portrays the special indignities associated with the registration process, in which women were tattooed and shaven, their private parts were invaded, and they were robbed of their name and their identity. Pregnant women were subjected to abortions; infants born in the camps were drowned in buckets or injected with poison until they died. Jewish women who arrived with young children were almost certain to be selected for the gas chambers along with their offspring. Women were also assigned as house aides and governesses and as musicians to entertain the SS. Women worked as sorters in the "Canada" barracks, where they inventoried and distributed the confiscated booty. They were also essential to supplying the underground with the ammunition used to blow up the crematoria at Birkenau.

Helena Kubica writes of the most vulnerable of the Nazis' victims—children. As a matter of routine at Auschwitz, she tell us, "the children were put to death in the gas chambers upon arrival." Jewish children were murdered as part of the implementation of the "final solution." Gypsy children survived with their parents in the Gypsy family camp until it too was eliminated in August 1944. The Jewish children of Theresienstadt were in family camps until July 1944, when it was "liquidated." Kubica reviews with precision the list of deportees. She counts the victims one by one to determine the number of children under age 16 who were murdered at Auschwitz. Precision of detail does not mask the murderers' passion. She also alludes to Dr. Josef Mengele's special experiments with children. He studied the effects of starvation, pursuing his medical research in the presence of the dead and the dying.

Nili Keren describes the six months of life granted to the children from Theresienstadt who arrived at Auschwitz. Through documents, oral histories, and memoirs, she probes the experiences of these children to whom the Nazis, for their own purpose, gave a brief respite en route to the gas chamber. The children were kept alive to continue the Nazi ruse that arrival at Auschwitz was actually resettlement in the East. Keren describes the unique role of an adult, Freddy Hirsch, who created a "social-educational-treatment facility" for children under 14. Remarkably, they painted pictures, wrote poems, and read books even in the midst of this death camp. Teachers even worried about their moral education. The family camp at Birkenau lasted only ten months. Keren writes: "Having fulfilled its mission, it was liquidated."

Yehuda Bauer explores the fate of Gypsies among those targeted by the Nazis for death. Distrusted and despised, Gypsies were regarded as asocial and "unworthy of life" in the Nazis' minds. Like Jews, they were placed in the gas chambers and their men, women, and children burned. Gypsy children were also subject to medical experimentation. There was a significant number of Gypsies at Auschwitz, and through diaries, memoirs, and eyewitness accounts as well as German documentation, Bauer compares their fate with the fate of other non-Jewish victims of Auschwitz as well as with the

Jews. He also details the cultural expressions of the Gypsies in Auschwitz.

Randolph L. Braham's chapter portrays the fate of Hungarian Jews, the last group to be deported to Auschwitz in large numbers. They arrived in the late spring and early summer of 1944. What is most remarkable about the Hungarian experience is the year of deportation. In 1944, Auschwitz had been in existence for four years, and for more than two years it had been gassing Jewish inmates upon arrival. Of equal importance is the speed with which the Nazis accomplished their goals. Beginning in March 1944 with ghettoization, the Hungarian deportations were complete by the summer. What took place over three or four years in Poland and two years in France and the Soviet Union occurred in less than three months in Hungary. In Auschwitz, Braham writes, "the machinery of destruction was ready to assume the regular, effective, and continuous assembly-line operation at a scale and a speed never before employed." Twelve to fourteen thousand Hungarian Jews arrived daily, and perhaps 90 percent of them were selected for death upon arrival.

Leo Eitinger, a prisoner-physician at Auschwitz—he was the doctor who operated on Elie Wiesel's leg as portrayed in Weisel's *Night*—has long been regarded as a leading scholar of the psychology of concentration camps. Eitinger writes here on the psychological structure of Auschwitz camp life and its impact on both perpetrator and victim. He uses the experience of shock as the psychological model by which to describe the response of inmates to their environment and their gradual orientation to the atmosphere of Auschwitz. He describes the psychological structure of prison life and the role of the kapos, the *muselmänner,* and the block elders, as well as the hierarchy of relationships among the killers. He also explores the psychological mechanisms that made survival possible (though by no means assured). Eitinger deals with the daily experiences of the inmates, the hourly struggle to survive, the determination to bear witness, the quest for meaning, and the impact of daily degradation and structured dehumanization on the individual psyche. As a leading authority on the postwar experience of survivors, Eitinger has studied survivors in Norway and Israel and details the results of his research. He describes the scars that survivors bore after liberation and their attempts to cope with its aftermath by bearing up and bearing witness.

Michael Berenbaum

14

The Auschwitz Prisoner Administration

DANUTA CZECH

The Nazi Schutzstaffel (SS) was experienced in operating concentration camps by the time it established Auschwitz in 1940. At Dachau, the first German concentration camp, set up in March 1933, camp commander Theodor Eicke created the system that he would later transfer to all other camps when he became the inspector of the concentration camp system. According to the National Socialist "Führer principle," Eicke also instituted a hierarchy of inmates to create the so-called inmate-run administration.

After the Second World War began, an increasing number of prisoners from defeated nations were sent to the camps. The German prisoners usually ranked highest in the inmate hierarchy. Thirty German inmates who had proved themselves reliable at Sachsenhausen were transferred to Auschwitz just before the first transport of 728 Poles arrived on June 14, 1940.

Under National Socialism, virtually every inmate of a concentration camp was forced to work. Prisoners were grouped in work commandos headed by SS personnel who reported directly to the camp director. Serving under the SS leader was an inmate commando leader, called a *Kapo*. Head kapos were sometimes put in charge of large work commandos, and there were also "underkapos" and *vorarbeiters* in charge of partial commando units. The SS leaders chose kapos whom they considered most willing to carry out SS orders. Toward this end, the SS gave the kapos practically unlimited power over the inmates—including beatings. If an inmate died, no questions were asked of the kapo responsible; the kapo was only required to report the death and to keep track of the number of inmates.

The camp director also chose inmates to supervise the blocks where the inmates lived. This "block eldest" (*Blockälteste*) was responsible for maintaining order and seeing that all commands were followed satisfactorily. Like the kapos, block eldests could use any methods they chose to carry out SS orders. Inmates under them had no means of complaint.

Following the inmate hierarchy, the block eldests reported to a "camp eldest" (*Lagerälteste*), also an inmate, who in turn reported to the SS-Rapportführer.

These inmate functionaries were identified with armbands and enjoyed a number of privileges that fostered rivalry among the prisoners. In fact, as soon as an inmate became a kapo, he or she no longer slept in the same place as the other inmates. Reichsführer-SS Heinrich Himmler described the ruthless efficiency of the kapo:

> His job is to see that the work gets done . . . thus he has to push his men. As soon as we are no longer satisfied with him, he is no longer a kapo, and returns to the other inmates. He knows that they will beat him to death his first night back. . . . Since we don't have enough Germans here, we use others—of course a French kapo for Poles, a Polish kapo for Russians; we play one nation against another.

The camp administration preferred to use prisoners with criminal records as functionaries. They wore green triangles next to their prisoner number. (Political prisoners wore red triangles. Jews, no matter what their nationality, wore "Jewish stars" on their pants and shirts—a yellow triangle under a red triangle forming the Star of David.) Many of the "greens," as they were called in the camps, had unstable personalities and were accustomed to being objects of scorn—in prison and between jail terms. The SS gave them a great deal of power, and inmates flattered them to get on their good side. While this no doubt influenced many functionaries, it would be a mistake to overgeneralize. Some greens were well-meaning, just as there were political prisoners who grossly abused their power.

Under this intentionally created inmate hierarchy, Germans were at the top; Jews, no matter their nationality, were at the bottom. Inmates of different nationalities were also ranked—Slavs toward the bottom, Russians below the Slavs.

As important to the Nazis as "racial" classification was a prisoner's ability to speak German. All orders were given in German, and prisoners had to obey them immediately to avoid beatings. Whoever did not master the language or at least learn the basic phrases used in camp had no chance of advancing in the inmate hierarchy, and less chance of survival.

Poles enjoyed special standing at Auschwitz. Since they were the first to arrive at the camp, they comprised the majority of prisoners during the first two years—until spring 1942. Those best able to adjust to the harsh conditions that prevailed during the early days of Auschwitz and those who spoke German managed to attain important positions in the camp—along with the German inmates.

The Polish prisoners were mostly young intellectuals and students who formed an influential and "camp-wise" group just below the top layer of the camp hierarchy. Many of them were assigned as assistants to the block eldests and kapos and worked to maintain order in the barracks.

Poles also served as block clerks, keeping accurate files on the inmates. They worked in the central office, where inmates' records were kept; work assignments were made; the daily roll call was prepared; transfers, deaths, and illnesses were registered; and an accurate prisoner count was maintained.

As Auschwitz grew, the tasks of the central office became more complex, and the SS found it increasingly difficult to maintain accurate records. As a result, the SS relied more and more on inmate clerks. Of course, the SS could transfer or get rid of a clerk, but to transfer all the clerks out of the central office at one time would have led to a partial collapse of the administrative bureaucracy. The inmate clerks were aware of that and did their best to complicate the office's bureaucratic procedures.

As the war progressed, the central administration of all concentration camps insisted on more work commandos for the war industry—in the sub-camps, the main camp, and Birkenau. In several of these industries, inmates were forced to carry out extremely difficult tasks. A beating inflicted by a kapo might increase the amount of shoveling done by a prisoner, for example, but beatings could not improve output in factory work. Kapos who understood industrial production processes were needed in the factories.

IG Farbenindustrie was the largest firm involved in the war effort to request and use slave labor. The company built its Bunawerk plant six kilometers east of Auschwitz, near Monowitz. A number of adjacent coal mines also used slave labor.

Toward the end of March 1942, women were sent to Auschwitz. An SS doctor selected those who could be put to work and those who were to be sent directly to the gas chamber. To house the prisoners able to work, a women's camp had to be established. Initially, a part of the main camp was used for the women. In August 1942, women were moved to a new camp in Birkenau. Like the males, female prisoners were made block eldests, kapos, and assistant kapos. Many of the positions were assumed by Slovak women, who were among the first Jewish women transferred from the Ravensbrück women's concentration camp.

The women learned, as did the men, that the system of giving inmate functionaries unlimited power over their fellow inmates had its limits. All armband wearers had to follow SS orders and make sure the inmates they supervised carried out all orders according to the exact administration instructions. Only within tightly defined boundaries could inmate functionaries act at their own discretion—either to gain benefits for themselves or to ease the burden on their fellow inmates. However, as the inmate population grew, it became increasingly difficult for the SS to oversee the camp, and inmate functionaries gained greater inner camp power.

With the percentage of Jewish inmates increasing during the last phase of the camp, the administration had no choice in Birkenau but to assign Jews to supervisory functions. Such assignments were most frequent in the subcamps, which almost exclusively housed Jewish prisoners. One Jewish inmate even served as camp eldest in a war-industry subcamp.

A peculiarity existed in the Political Department—as the camp's Gestapo was called—where German-speaking Jewish women were employed as secretaries. They enjoyed better living conditions than the other inmates because the SS saw to it that inmates with whom they had daily contact had more hygienic surroundings. The SS did not, after all, want to contract any of the diseases that were rampant in the camp. It is assumed that the SS preferred using Jewish women as secretaries because they mastered languages and would never see freedom again, and thus would not be able to divulge any secrets. Some secretaries, however, survived the evacuation of Auschwitz in January 1945—perhaps because the SS acted impulsively or because they were reluctant to murder inmates with whom they had daily contact and saw as distinct from the anonymous gray masses.

The SS used inmates who were more qualified than their own clerical staff as secretaries in other offices as well. The secretaries were exploited when the opportunity existed, either as sources of information or—especially toward the end of the war—as a means of influencing the camp population.

The SS established medical barracks in all concentration camps, including Auschwitz. These were directed by an SS camp doctor and his subordinate SDGs (an SS abbreviation of *Sanitätsdienstgrade*). The hierarchy within the medical barracks resembled that of the camp. The inmates at the top were camp eldests. Block eldests were responsible for the units, but nurses cared for the sick. While Jewish doctors were not used in the medical barracks of other concentration camps, the SS doctor in Auschwitz did use Jewish inmate doctors at a later stage. As of September 1943, Polish doctors even became camp eldests of the HKB, as the medical barracks were known.

Inmates feared the HKB, where the SS made practically no medication available. When an ill inmate was sent there—which could not be avoided if he failed to make it to his forced labor assignment—he was first examined by an inmate doctor. Then he would spend the night in the medical barracks and be reexamined the following morning.

The SS doctor decided whether the inmate was to remain in the medical barracks or be taken to block 20—the punishment block—and be administered a deadly phenol injection in the heart. The degree of illness was not the only factor in this decision. If the inmate seemed incapable of returning to work soon, he was taken to block 20. According to recollections of the block clerk, 90 to 95 percent of those taken to block 20 and killed with injections were Jews.

In the main camp, such actions took place until the spring of 1943. A far greater number were killed in Birkenau, especially when contagious diseases were rampant in Auschwitz. The deaths of those wearing Auschwitz prisoner identification numbers, thus not counting those inmates who were declared unfit to work and were sent to the gas chambers immediately upon arrival, were accounted for in the HKB office. The numbers were smuggled out of the camp. The highest number of such deaths was in February 1943, when 25.5 percent of all Auschwitz inmates died or were put to death. Seven inmate secretaries were kept busy day and night registering the deaths that month.

The high mortality rate and the backlog of clerical accounting enabled those who remained alive to get more food. Not all deaths could be registered on the very day they occurred. And as long as a death was not registered, the inmate kitchen would still bring a ration of food to the HKB. The inmates working in the office tried to delay registering deaths for a day or two. The extra food rations could then be divided among the workers in the medical barracks—the HKB commando.

The medical unit also differed in another way from the other commandos. While the inmates of other commandos were preoccupied with avoiding beatings and hard labor, the inmates who worked in the HKB were preoccupied with caring for the sick. As long as they were not morally broken, they were constantly reminded of their duty to assist their ill fellow inmates as much as possible.

Other work commandos had different concerns. Beginning in 1941, there was an orchestra in the main Auschwitz camp. Soon orchestras were put together in Birkenau and several subcamps as well. The Auschwitz orchestra was situated next to the camp gates and played during the inmates' exit after morning roll call. The music improved the commandos' march and made it easier for the SS to count the inmates. Some Polish inmates in the orchestra were famous musicians. Later, the orchestra had to play for the SS and at Sunday concerts in front of the commandant's villa. The musicians worked during the day in the camp kitchen, so they could easily be summoned, for example, when the SS wanted them to perform for visitors. The orchestra members wore clean white suits and were better nourished because they worked in the kitchen.

The orchestra rehearsed in a large room adjacent to the central office in block 24, next to the camp gates. Some prisoners could hear the orchestra practice; they could hear best if they crouched on the floor against the wall. Such moments helped the prisoners forget their surroundings. "Those short hours kept me from drowning in the day-to-day existence within a death camp," an inmate wrote later.

The head of the protective-custody men's camp in Birkenau was anxious to establish an orchestra as well, and insisted on the transfer of a few Polish musicians from the main camp's orchestra to Birkenau. They were transferred in the summer of 1942. Since there were not enough Polish musicians, Jews, who were not allowed to participate in the main camp's orchestra, were used in Birkenau. Two French musicians who were made to wear the Star of David in Birkenau gave a detailed account of the orchestra's development: "Our glorious music room became a place of pilgrimage for the SS as well as [a reason] for the camp's prominence. We play cheerful melodies almost nightly in our bloc. The SS likes to celebrate birthdays with lots of pomp."

In retrospect, the women's orchestra of the Birkenau women's camp was the most famous. The head of the camp, Maria Wendel, adored music. When she learned that Alma Rose, a famous musician and the daughter of a first violinist of the Vienna Philharmonic, was in the camp, she made her leader of a women's orchestra even though she was Jewish. Legends have grown up around Alma Rose's extraordinary personality. Many recall the repertoire of classical music. The orchestra's performances were not limited to the comings and goings of the work commandos. According to one account, "It had to play at all official occasions—for the camp commander's speeches, for transports, and for hangings. It also served as the entertainment for the SS and the inmates in the medical barracks." When Rose conducted, "she was in another world." Many recalled one specific episode. Once, while conducting a concert, Rose stopped the orchestra and asked for quiet because female SS guards in the audience were laughing and talking. They followed this Jewish inmate's admonition without question. Rose's death also is surrounded by legend. She died a few weeks after the inmates of the Terezin family camp in Birkenau were gassed. Some believe that she poisoned herself because her friends were killed; others suspect that she was murdered by jealous inmate functionaries.

The "Canada" commando was another work group that differed significantly from the others. It was established when Auschwitz became an extermination camp. Jews deported to Auschwitz, upon arrival, had to hand over their belongings under the false impression that they were merely being relocated. Guarded by the SS, an inmate commando gathered all the belongings, searched them for hidden valuables, and sorted the items. The inmates called the barracks where the loot was stored "Canada," their term for unimaginable riches. Everyone in the camp adopted the expression.

In all concentration camps, the SS profiteered from the camp inmates. But no corruption compared to the possibilities that existed in the mountains of possessions taken from arriving deportees. Anyone with access to Canada could avail himself of items before they were sorted, registered, and searched for hidden valuables. Some security measures were employed. The members of the Canada commando were searched upon returning to camp, and only the few SS who served as overseers could enter the closed area. But temptation was great, and theft was rampant. Anyone interested in "organizing"—a camp euphemism for stealing—had to rely on others. The SS had to rely on inmates and vice versa. Anyone clever enough to pay off possible witnesses could amass considerable wealth. Trading with witnesses—and bribing and murdering them—were all part of Canada. A few prisoners with access to Canada gained a better standard of living than the average inmate. Some would not touch camp food, some wore clean clothes every day, and some even managed to get around the barbed wire fence that separated men from women in Birkenau. The SS could be bribed. A work commando leader could be paid off with a shoe box full of watches. "Organizing" became a term closely linked with Auschwitz and Canada.

Camp Commandant Rudolf Höss complained, "The gold of the Jews became the camp's undoing." He added that even the strictest control could not put a stop to the activity. He remained silent about his own profiteering. But when he was transferred from Auschwitz to the central command of all concentration camps in Oranienburg, near Berlin, two railroad cars and an uncounted number of boxes were needed for his belongings.

The Canada barracks stood next to the crematoria. A former inmate who worked in Canada as a young girl described how inmates who were able to steal items from the heaps of riches found themselves "surely in one of the most bizarre situations of the whole world—all around us the screams of the dying, annihilation, smoking chimneys that blackened and polluted the air with the soot and smell of burnt corpses." The concept of value became grotesque. In the women's camp, for example, a diamond ring bought some water. Years later, an SS man cynically observed, "One man's death is another's bread." A death camp saw extremes whose coexistence was unthinkable anywhere else. Death, however, was for the masses, while bread from Canada was for the very few.

In contrast to those who managed to gain access to Canada were the great majority of others—the human shadows known as "muselmen." Anyone who knew Auschwitz also knew the muselman. Many have tried in retrospect to render a description of him. Jean Amery put it this way: "The muselman had no conception of good or bad, of admirable or mean, of spiritual or material. He was an unsteady corpse, a bundle of physical functions on its last breath." Primo Levi wrote: "He suffers from chronic hunger, unknown to free men, that is omnipresent in our bodies." He added that "camp itself is hunger. We are hunger, living hunger."

On top of the shock of arrival, the separation from loved ones at selection, and the eventual awareness that they had been killed in the gas chambers, new inmates had to take up the ruthless fight for survival. Courage and hope were shattered, respect for human life trampled. The question "Will I survive this?" found no room in the shadow of the crematoria and was replaced by "How will I die?" Nonetheless, there were fights for second servings of camp soup, for water, for better resting places, for pieces of blanket, in short for the most basic things.

The observant Polish doctor Wladyslaw Fejkiel described the symptoms of starvation: "The eyes became dim, the face took on an indifferent, empty, and sad expression . . . smaller and larger edemas appeared, first on the eyelids and feet. On top of the swellings was the diarrhea. Observing such a group, one felt one was looking at a group of praying Arabs." Fejkiel thus adopted the term *Muselmänner*, or *muselmen* ("Moslems"). During the evacuation of Auschwitz, Otto Wolken, an Austrian doctor assigned to work in the quarantine section of the HKB, was able to save data that describe the condition of muselmen—a prisoner 156 centimeters (five feet) tall weighed 28 kilograms (62 pounds); another was 167 cm (five feet, five inches) tall with a weight of 34.5 kg (76 pounds).

The inmate doctor Aron Bejlin observed that someone about to die from starvation starts talking of food incessantly. When soup spilled from a bucket being carried out of the kitchen, inmates would lick the soup mixed with dirt off the ground. Potato peelings were consumed. Max Mannheimer, who survived being a muselman, remembers: "I eat the potatoes with their skin. I keep a close eye on those strong enough to peel their potatoes. I beg for the peelings. I greedily devour them. I'm ashamed—and I never lose track of those who peel their potatoes."

Albert Menasche wrote later: "Our preoccupation was to avoid beatings and more importantly to find sustenance. Our biggest wish was to put an end to the miserable hunger." A woman survivor admitted that some inmates stole bread from the dying in the medical barracks and consumed it even when it was covered with excrement. Gisela Perl, an inmate doctor, recalled, "I always had most to do after food distribution. I had to bandage bloody heads, treat broken ribs, and clean wounds. This work of mine was really quite hopeless, for the same would start all over again the next day." Tadeusz Borowski, an inmate of Auschwitz and Polish writer, quite graphically described the atmosphere of Auschwitz: "You're truly hungry when another person strikes you as edible."

Vilo Jurkovic presented the picture of a muselman, "This person of skin and bones, barely capable of moving, lacking will and strength, with a discharge running from his nose onto his mouth and chin, this dirty being dressed in rags, often with lice, usually with severe diarrhea and an accordingly dirty uniform, with fallen in or bulging eyes, was a true picture of misery, of weakness, hopelessness, and horror." Benedkit Kautsky added, "This dirty, beastly, lazy individual clearly became a target for all kinds of jabs and jokes." Jurkovic explained further why a muselman often was held in disdain and disgust rather than pitied. "The inmates were terrified of muselmen because they never knew when they themselves would meet the same fate and become a sure candidate for the gas chamber or another form of death."

When a muselman died while working in a labor commando away from the camp, the survivors' response might have been, "His suffering is finally over. But now we have to carry him back to the camp." Primo Levi added this about the muselman's character, this psychologically broken being overshadowed by the crematorium, this being carved out by chronic hunger:

> The muselmen, the lost ones, form the nerve of the camp: they make up the anonymous, constantly renewable and always identical mass of silently marching and overworked nonhumans, they have lost all godly spark, they are so empty that they barely suffer anymore. One hesitates to call them living beings, one hesitates to call their death, of which they are not afraid, death, because they are too tired to grab it.
>
> I remember their faceless presence; I could use this familiar image to sum up the entire suffering of our age: a broken man, chin down and crooked shoulders, whose face and eyes show no trace of thinking.

Extermination camps also created another group of people, those who were forced to work in the crematoria and gas chambers—the unfortunate people assigned to *Sonderkommando* (special commando) work. The SS needed code words when they spoke about mass extermination of those "not worthy of living." They referred to mass extermination and transports designated for selection as "special treatment" (*Sonderbehandlung* often abbreviated as SB). Thus also the term *Sonderkommando*.

Four large crematoria with built-in gas chambers were active in Auschwitz-Birkenau in spring 1943. A Sonderkommando unit worked at each. There were precedents. The SS had already formed Sonderkommandos. Zyklon B had already been used to kill inmates in the main camp's crematorium (which was later referred to as the old crematorium, or crematorium I), as well as in the refitted farmhouses (blocks 1 and 2) in Birkenau, where inmates had been forced to work. With the exception of a few Polish and German kapos, the Sonderkommandos were Jews. Nineteen Russians, who had previously worked in a Sonderkommando at Majdanek, were assigned to a Sonderkommando in April 1944. That spring marked the beginning of the "Hungarian Action," the deportation of Hungarian Jews to Auschwitz. It was then that the mass killing reached its peak and the number of inmates working as Sonderkommandos grew to 1,000.

As deported Jews stepped out of the railcars and onto the ramp at Auschwitz, the SS usually looked for strong young men. Those picked were not sent into the camp but were dispatched to one of the crematoria's Sonderkommandos. As far as can be determined in retrospect, the Sonderkommandos at that time were composed mainly of Hungarian Jews, then Greek, Polish, French, and Czech Jews. They were forced to carry the corpses from the gas chambers to the ovens or to the pyres if the capacity of the ovens had been exceeded. First they had to cut the hair off the female corpses, then examine all corpses for gold teeth, rings, and earrings. The hair was used to make insulation material; the gold was delivered monthly to the Reich's bank in Berlin.

Upon the completion of the massive extermination actions, most of the inmates who worked as Sonderkommandos were gassed. The exceptions were the specialists, such as those who knew how to work the ovens. But some Sonderkommando members survived as well, especially those who were serving during evacuation in January 1945. Those Sonderkommandos who were still alive were transferred to the Mauthausen concentration camp along with other inmates. In the process, some were able to escape from the transport. Others were able to save themselves from execution in Mauthausen by changing the Auschwitz prisoner number tattooed on their lower left arms. They could not be located by the newly assigned Mauthausen prisoner numbers. They had planned ahead, and had presented false names at registration.

Not every survivor is ready to speak. And the silence they have chosen must be respected. Yet a few did feel strong enough to tell their stories. There were also others in contact with members of the isolated Sonderkommandos, who reported on what happened. But most important, some Sonderkommando members buried pieces of testimony that were later discovered. Much credit has to go to Henryk Porebski. As an electrician who oversaw the crematoria's installations, he learned of the buried reports and later insisted that searches be conducted to find the documents.

The most important report, that of Zalman Lewenthal, was discovered in October 1962, partially damaged and illegible. His words teach more about the Sonderkommandos:

No one can imagine the events that occurred, because it is unimaginable to exactly recount our experiences. . . . However, we—the small group of gray people—will present the historian with quite a task, as well as the psychologist interested in learning of man's mental condition while practicing such terrible, dirty work. Who knows whether these researchers will ever get to the truth, whether anyone will ever be able to.

One of the few Sonderkommando survivors remembers that Lewenthal, originally from Ciechanow, Poland, was assigned to the Sonderkommando in December 1942. He was between 25 and 27 years old, "exceptionally hardworking and decent."

One must treat with respect the few existing pieces of information on those assigned to Sonderkommando. No comparisons can be drawn to other groups. One must accept Lewenthal's memory of the first days at the gas chambers:

> We ran frightened by the clubs of the SS men who were guarding us. We had forgotten ourselves so much that none of us was aware of what he was doing, how he was doing it, and what was happening to him. We had lost ourselves to the point that we were like dead. Spurred on, we ran like machines without knowing where, without knowing what we were doing or for what reason. No one looked at anyone. I know that none of us was completely conscious. . . . Soon the work was completed. All the corpses had been brought out of the gas chamber to the pyre where those gassed yesterday and the day before were already burning. The tragedy started after work. All believed in a tormenting dream.

The SS tolerated inmate commando members who took food and alcohol from the belongings the victims left in the changing room before being ushered into the gas chambers. Lewenthal also wrote: "I must be truthful; some in this group completely lost their wits and were a real embarrassment to us." One must realize that everyone's "subconsciousness is controlled by the desire to live, the attempt to live and survive," as Lewenthal described. There are hundreds of excuses why one wants to survive. "And the truth is that one wants to live no matter what the cost."

Yet excuse is hardly the proper term for a Sonderkommando member's account that was also buried near a crematorium and found soon after the liberation of Auschwitz. Hungarian Jews asked the Sonderkommando members whether they were being led to their deaths. When told that they were, they told the man, "You must revenge our bloodshed, you must live, we understand you." Before another gassing, a young Polish woman turned to members of the Sonderkommando in the changing room: "Remember that you have the holy duty of revenge for us innocent. Tell your brothers, your people, how we met our death with knowledge and pride." They then sang the Hatikva, the Jewish national anthem. How often Sonderkommando members must have heard such things, how often they must have wanted to make known the stories of those who unknowingly went to the gas chambers, even when they, too, would not survive. Hence the buried accounts.

Even though the Sonderkommandos were isolated, some inmates of Birkenau were able to make occasional contact with them. The women's camp adjoined the crematoria. Seweryna Szmaglewska recorded her impressions: "They were a sad example of human misdirection within the burning jungle of Birkenau. On the other hand, members of this same Sonderkommando dared approach the barbed wires to bring the Jews a last farewell from their loved ones prior to entering the crematoria. Sometimes they brought souvenirs, photographs, or letters as a last sign of life."

Others describe the "tense, insane faces" and recall how none of them resembled human beings, but were robotlike. Yet others attest that Sonderkommando members contributed important material for the women's camp's medical barracks. Stanislaw Kaminski, who had been on a Jewish transport from Bialystock to Auschwitz and became a Sonderkommando kapo, frequently smuggled gold and medications to the resistance movement of the Auschwitz main camp.

Krystyna Zywulska once asked a Sonderkommando member how he managed to work there day after day. He answered, "Do you think I'm doing this of my own free will? What should I have done? Sure, I could have run into the barbed wire as other comrades have done. But I want to survive! Maybe a miracle will happen. And then I want to take revenge—I—a direct witness of their crimes. You get used to this work if it doesn't drive you crazy. Do you think that the tasks of those working in munitions factories are much nobler? Or of the girls sorting items in Canada to be sent to Germany? We're all following their orders." And he finished, "You think that those working in Sonderkommandos are monsters? I'm telling you, they're like the rest, just much more unhappy."

Jehuda Bacon was a 14-year-old member of a truck commando who had to retrieve ashes from the crematoria to spread onto the icy paths during the winter. He saw horrible events there, but also got to know Kalman Furman, who was always friendly to the teens and ready to help. Bacon remembers the "Aryan" kapo Jozef Ilczuk—a teacher who allowed children, upon completion of their work, to warm themselves in an empty gas chamber.

On July 22, 1944, approximately 400 Jews who had been deported from Corfu and had been in the men's camp more than three weeks were assigned to the Sonderkommando. They were by then well aware of what was required in the crematorium. They refused to work and subsequently were all gassed.

Only little is known about the attempts of Sonderkommando members to escape or to resist. It is known, however, that the SS murdered anyone involved in such attempts. That one Sonderkommando nonetheless was able to stage a revolt is proof of man's instinct to defend himself and his ability to retain his dignity even under the worst conditions imaginable. Many who wrote about attempts to escape or resist or survived to tell about them describe the Jewish kapo Kaminski as the driving force behind them. Kaminski, apparently betrayed, was murdered by the SS before he could participate in the revolt.

One must consider Zalman Lewenthal's words when daring to put oneself in the shoes of those forced by the SS to perform such unimaginable work: "The whole truth holds much more tragedy and much more horror."

Theodor Eicke, the commander of Dachau, the first concentration camp, created the system of collective punishments designed to abolish a prisoner's sense of self worth and to pit prisoners against each other. The underlying idea was to direct the prisoners' anger at other prisoners rather than at those inflicting the punishment (the SS). Beatings and other forms of corporal punishment were given not only to hurt but also to humiliate. As inspector of all concentration camps, Eicke instituted this system in all the camps. In addition, some camps, including Auschwitz, imposed individual forms of punishment.

Next to withholding food and standing at roll call for hours, "sport" was the most common collective punishment. Jump up and down, roll over, run, and variations of these and other commands, combined with the threat of being beaten if the commands were not followed quickly, were supposed to have two consequences. The overworked, exhausted, and chronically undernourished prisoners were supposed to vent their anger on those whose actions had brought on the collective punishment. The inmates were also expected to seek revenge on those who were exempted from punishment.

Inmate functionaries were included in this system. At one time, the head of the protective-custody camp felt that discipline was lagging and that the prisoners' marches to and from work as well as their obligatory singing were too weak. He ordered all kapos to present themselves. All were given five blows to their buttocks, and told to see to it that the marching and singing improved. Some of the kapos energetically carried out such orders.

The SS resorted most often to the dreaded "25 blows." This punishment could be administered immediately and without any special prior formalities, but it could also be the official verdict issued by the head of the protective-custody camp. In that case, the punishment was usually administered between the main camp's block 10 and bunker block 11. Sometimes the prisoner, who had to lie across a stool, received double blows.

After the woman's camp was erected at the end of March 1942, women were chosen at "selections" for slave labor. Himmler, while inspecting Auschwitz, wanted to watch the beating of a female inmate, and observed it with great interest. "He personally wanted to be the one to grant permission to administer corporal punishment on women," Höss recalled.

The "standing bunker" was an Auschwitz specialty. The Political Department ran the main camp's block 11. No inmates lived in the block, which was always locked. Its basement served as a prison. In addition to 28 cells, the basement held the standing bunker, the collective name for four cells, each smaller than a square meter. A prisoner ordered to the standing bunker had to crawl through a small opening near the floor. The cell was dark with only one air hole. The condemned was locked into the standing bunker, where he could not lie down, for a number of nights, while having to march to work during the day. When several inmates were imprisoned in one of the standing bunkers, the already restricted space became even tighter. A prisoner could be sentenced to several nights in the standing bunker if he had relieved himself behind a building or had picked fruit from a tree near his workplace.

Prisoners were also locked in the bunker without a hearing if caught engaging in illegal activities. In the fall of 1943, a young Jew from Warsaw, about 15 years old, was locked in the bunker without a hearing for drinking from an SS man's water bottle while his commando was working outdoors in the heat. During the next bunker selection, he was led out and shot against the black wall. In Auschwitz, Jews always received the heaviest punishment. The boy had known what was in store for him.

A German kapo with a green triangle was sent to the bunker for allegedly having sexual relations with a young boy he had brought into his commando. The boy, a Gypsy, was held in another cell. When no SS personnel were present in the bunker, the German kapo called out words of encouragement to the boy's cell. The boy was shot and the kapo freed, though sterilized. That was typical when an inmate functionary—usually a German and a green—was accused of having sexual relations with a young boy (usually a Pole or a Russian). In June 1943, a brothel was set up in block 24 for the use of "Aryan" inmate functionaries only.

A collective punishment, often administered to women, was to force prisoners onto their knees while raising their hands. Sometimes the condemned also had to hold stones in their hands while kneeling. An equally feared punishment was to be sent to the penal commando. The penal commando was set up in August 1940, and approximately 6,000 inmates were condemned there. The inmates were beaten, given smaller meals, and made to perform the most difficult physical labor. They were kept rigidly isolated from the other inmates.

A penal commando for women, Budy, was set up in a subcamp. It was disbanded after a terrible massacre of the women in October 1942.

The penal commando was transferred in May 1942 to Birkenau, where the prisoners had to work on a drainage ditch. The fact that prisoners marching back to the camp after work usually returned with a wagon full of corpses—the day's victims—clearly indicates the conditions that prevailed.

Every concentration camp commander wanted to avoid escapes, because successful escapes had to be reported to headquarters. There were many more escapes from Auschwitz than from other camps because conditions were much worse there and because, unlike most other camps, Auschwitz was not located in an area surrounded by Germans. During an inspection, Himmler told Höss that "Auschwitz's escape plague must stop!" As a result, Höss used all means available to him to prevent escapes. When an escapee was caught, he was brought back to the camp and hung during roll call before all the inmates. If an escapee was shot while fleeing, his corpse was hung—visible to all—next to the camp gates. A sign warned that anyone who attempted an escape would meet the same fate. Since most escapes occurred among work commandos outside the camp, the kapos in charge were also punished. For that reason, some kapos insisted that all inmates of the commando line up to be counted on a regular basis.

The first successful escape was by a Pole, who fled on July 6, 1940. As punishment, all inmates were forced to line up for 20 hours in the inspections square. An even worse punishment was meted out after another Pole fled on April 23, 1941. Ten inmates from the escapee's block were summoned and locked into a cell of the bunker with no food or drink. Marian Batko, a physics professor from Chorzow, came forward in place of the young escapee. All ten were dead by May 26.

The same penalty was meted out after another Pole's escape. Fifteen inmates were summoned from block 14 and led into a dark cell in the bunker. Maximilian Kolbe, a Franciscan priest, came forward in place of the escapee, Franciszek Gajowniczek. All 15 perished in that cell. Kolbe was made a saint because of his sacrifice.

A few escapes were highly significant for the information they brought to the outside world. One such escape was made by two Slovakian Jews, Alfred Wetzler and Rudolf Vrba, on April 7, 1944. Once free, they provided testimony about Auschwitz-Birkenau, including sketches, numbers, and details of the extermination process. The information eventually reached Hungary and the free world.

Later, other scare tactics were applied. After three Poles escaped in May 1943 from the commando that performed outdoor surveys, 12 Polish inmates from their commando were hung in the inspection grounds. The corpses were left there for some time to serve as a deterrent. This reprisal was Höss's idea, approved by Himmler. After another Pole escaped, his parents were brought to the camp. Dressed in prisoner uniforms, they were made to sit on stools by the road for all prisoners to see when they marched back to the camp from work. A sign above them stated that their punishment had been ordered by Höss and that it would be repeated if there was another escape.

When Arthur Liebehenschel replaced Höss as commandant in November 1943, such retaliations stopped. From then on, escapees who were caught were not killed but transferred to another concentration camp. Still, some attempted escapees were murdered, especially those from subcamps or prisoners who made extraordinary escape attempts, such as the Pole Edward Galinski and the Jewish women's camp messenger, Mala Zimetbaum. Liebehenschel also had the standing bunker torn down.

In addition to its use as a punishment area, block 11 was used as a holding place for inmates about whom the Political Department had suspicions. The SS had an army of inmate informants, and when they sensed the beginning of a conspiracy, they interrogated and all too frequently tortured prisoners. The most feared torture was the "swing." An inmate who survived the swing described it at the trial of SS Officer Wilhelm Boger, conducted in Frankfurt from 1963 until 1965: "Boger had me taken to the Political Department barracks and handcuffed me. My hands were placed below my knees so that a pole could be pushed between by arms and knee joints. The pole was lifted and I was hung from the so-called swing. Boger told me to count along with the 60 blows I was about to receive. If I lost count, it would start over from the beginning. Boger pushed the swing while I was being beaten." Finally, unconscious, he was taken down from the swing. "I was on the floor when I woke up to find myself being kicked by boots."

Another method of torture was described at the Boger trial. An inmate was brought to a room of the Political Department after having been beaten and forced to stand for hours in the aisle, his face to the wall. "'I know when you had your last meal. Now I'll give you some food,' I was told. Plates of herring salad stood on the table. The herring was so salty, that I ended up vomiting." The inmate was forced to finish all the food, including his own vomit. When questioned about these descriptions during the trial, Boger called them "full of gaps and not completely true."

A bunker log kept from January 9, 1941, to February 1, 1944, remained intact. Of 2,137 inmates who were brought to the bunker during this time, 821 were murdered there. More than half of those brought were Jews. Poles comprised the second-largest group (422); Germans and Austrians were next (175), then Russians (74). The percentage of Jews killed in the bunker was high; hardly a Jew left the bunker alive.

15

Hospitals

IRENA STRZELECKA

The medical service run by the Nazi Schutzstaffel (SS) in Auschwitz pursued two mutually exclusive goals. Its assigned task was to provide medical care for the entire camp, but especially for SS personnel; yet it was also responsible for eliminating weak and emaciated prisoners and those infected with contagious diseases. The latter task of extermination, which contradicted all medical doctrines and principles, was assigned to the camp hospitals.

The SS Medical System

With the establishment of Auschwitz in 1940, SS authorities followed the example of earlier concentration camps by incorporating into its administrative structure the so-called Department V in charge of the camp medical service. The first heads of this department, Auschwitz SS garrison doctors Max Fpiersch and Siegfried Schwel, were under the Sanitation Office of the Camp Inspectorate. Their successors, Oskar Dienstbach, Kurt Uhlenbrock, and Eduard Wirths, were subordinated to the chief physician of concentration camps, who also held the post of head of Department DIII in charge of camp sanitation and hygiene in the SS Economic-Administrative Main Office, or SS-WVHA (into which the Camp Inspectorate was incorporated in March 1942). Exercising overall control over hygienic conditions in the camp and administering the elaborate medical service apparatus, they also cooperated closely with Auschwitz commandants.

The camp medical service consisted of the following personnel: doctors of SS troops who were responsible for medical treatment of SS personnel, SS camp doctors who administered camp hospitals designed for prisoners, SS dentists in charge of dental services to SS men and supervising dental clinics for the prisoners, SS head of the camp pharmacy, and SS disinfection officers who carried out fumigation and delousing within the compounds.

The SS physicians responsible for medical care of prisoners played a special role in the camp apparatus. Actively involved in extermination operations and in selections of Jews brought in for annihilation, they all but renounced their medical obligations toward the prisoners, maintaining a facade of medical treatment. In administering the camp hospitals for prisoner patients, they used SS medics who had undergone some training. Their duties were confined to management and administrative tasks and supervision of prisoner-doctors and nurses, as well as other members of the prisoner hospital staff. The prisoner who exercised broadest authority in a camp hospital, both in administrative and medical matters, was the so-called camp sick bay elder, or camp dispensary elder. The elder represented the camp prisoner personnel before the SS doctors.

Like hospitals at other concentration camps of the Third Reich, the hospitals in Auschwitz enjoyed an autonomy of sorts. They were administered by a separate management and were usually set apart from other camp installations and facilities, constituting a sort of enclave in the camp.

The Hospital Network

The infirmary established in June 1940 in the building of the prewar Polish Tobacco Monopoly served as the nucleus of an extensive network of hospitals which operated in Auschwitz during the five years of its existence. Its first patients were prisoners subjected to heavy beating or those in a state of exhaustion brought about by savage punishment—often lasting for days on end—organized by SS men in the form of physical exercises (the so-called "sport activities").

In July 1940, prisoners were transferred successively from the Tobacco Monopoly building to the former army barracks located nearby. The last to be transferred were prisoners from the infirmary and the supervising staff. They were put in block 16, then a one-story building (designated 21 after the expansion of the camp). In addition to a consulting room for the SS doctor and wards for prisoner patients, an outpatient clinic, a dental clinic, and a registry were added. With the steady influx of prisoner transports and the increased number of sick prisoners, the hospital was again expanded by adding two adjoining blocks. At the peak of its expansion, the hospital occupied four blocks in Auschwitz (19, 20, 21, and 28), and, temporarily, block 9. It was divided into four wards: internal diseases, infectious diseases, surgery, and the Schonungsblock, designed for convalescents, in which Jewish prisoners not fit for work underwent selection and were dispatched to the gas chambers.

In the expanded Auschwitz camp, this hospital was outside the administrative hierarchy. It housed the Main Hospital Administration (HKB Schreistube).[1] In one of the rooms in block 20, sick prisoners were murdered by intracardiac phenol injections.

From March to August 1942, about 17,000 women prisoners, 90 percent of them Jews, lived in ten assigned blocks within the main Auschwitz camp; one block (3) was designated as a hospital.

Several hospitals for prisoners were established in Birkenau during its expansion. The first was created in May 1942 in the newly established camp for male prisoners in the BIb sector.[2] Initially, barracks 7 and 8 served as hospital blocks for this camp; in late 1942, barrack 12 was incorporated into the hospital. Barrack 7 was known by prisoners as the "death block." Up to April 1943, it was used for dumping the most seriously ill prisoners and those in a state of extreme exhaustion, who had been selected from barracks and labor squads. In the outpatient department located in barrack 8, prisoners were killed with phenol injections into the heart.

In July 1943, prisoner patients hitherto residing in the hospital barracks of sector BIb were transferred to the newly established hospital camp for men (sector BIIf, designated officially as Haftlingskrankenbau, Lager BIIf).[3] Jewish prisoners deemed incurably ill, who had been selected by SS doctors in Birkenau and the satellite camps of Auschwitz, were placed in barracks 12 and in a room of barracks 16. Usually they were gassed on Sabbath Eve and on Jewish holidays.

The next camp hospital was established in Birkenau in connection with the transfer there in the middle of August 1942 of some 13,000 women prisoners who had resided in Auschwitz. They were placed in sector BIa; the sick among them were put in barracks 22, 23, 24, 25 and 26. During 1943, due to the steadily growing number of sick prisoners, the hospital for women was expanded by adding more barracks. Following the transfer of prisoners from sector BIb to sector BIId in July 1943 and the incorporation of the camp for men into the women's camp, the camp hospital occupied nearly all wooden barracks of sector BIa. Barracks 25, nicknamed by women prisoners "death block," which formally belonged to the camp hospital, served as a dumping ground for seriously ill and extremely exhausted women prisoners, mainly Jewish, selected in the camp hospital and labor squads, and doomed to death in the gas chambers. In this barrack, as well as in the outpatient clinic located in the nearby barrack 28, women prisoners were killed by intracardiac phenol injections.

In 1943–44, smaller hospitals were created in the Gypsy family camp (BIIe),[4] the family camp for Jews from Theresienstadt (BIIb), and the quarantine camp (BIId). Organizationally they were within the jurisdiction of the administration of the camp hospital for male prisoners (BIIf).

Branches of the camp medical service were also established in satellite camps. In larger satellite camps, these were small hospitals, and in smaller ones, infirmaries. Up to November 1943 they were administered by SS doctors either in the main camp or in Birkenau. The largest was the facility established in October 1942 in the Monowitz (Buna) camp, which supplied prisoner manpower to the local chemical works of IG Farbenindustrie.[5]

Following the reorganization of the Auschwitz camp in November 1943 and the creation of Auschwitz III, the administration of hospitals and infirmaries in satellite camps supplying manpower to industrial enterprises (mostly in the industrial region of Upper Silesia), was taken over by chief physician of that camp, with headquarters in Monowitz. SS camp doctors in charge of the hospital in Monowitz made periodic inspections of satellite camps belonging to Auschwitz III, selecting the most seriously ill prisoners for transfer to Birkenau where they died in the overcrowded hospital barracks or were killed in gas chambers. The selected prisoners were often transported out of satellite camps together with the bodies of their fellow inmates who had died earlier.

Development of the Hospitals

Phase I (1940–41)

The first camp hospital created in the Auschwitz main camp was viewed by prisoners as a shelter from the horrors of camp existence, or, eventually, as a place to die peacefully. However, with the sharp increase in the mortality rate among hospitalized prisoners in the winter of 1941–42, boosted in the spring of 1942 by the raging typhus epidemic, the camp hospital came to be regarded exclusively as a place to die. With the commencement of selections carried out by SS doctors and the condemning of sick prisoners to death by phenol injection or in the gas chamber, the hospital became a scourge, earning the nickname "waiting room for the crematorium." Even seriously ill prisoners went to great lengths to avoid hospitalization.

Until the spring of 1942, prisoner-doctors were employed in Auschwitz hospitals exclusively as nurses. The most important positions within the so-called prisoner self-government were held by criminal prisoners, mostly Germans. Survival being their sole concern, they displayed indifference, often hostility, toward the patients. They harassed the few Polish prisoners employed in the hospital in menial jobs. High mortality rate, frequent selections, and brutal treatment of prisoners who attended to the needs of the patients were widespread also in other camp hospitals created in 1942. Prisoners who succeeded in being discharged from the hospital during this period usually owed their existence to their innate endurance. Medical care administered in the hospital was so insubstantial that it could not have assisted their recuperation.

Phase II (1942–43)

As the German war economy's demand for manpower grew, fed by the labor of concentration camp prisoners, the SS attempted to bring down the high mortality rate in the camps. The SS authorities assigned the camp hospitals some responsibility for enabling prisoners to recover enough strength to return to the labor force. In the spring of 1942, SS authorities allowed the employment of prisoner-doctors in the camp hospital system. A year later, women prisoners were also allowed to work in this capacity. This step, however, did not lead to the administering of medical care on a level commensurate with the basic principles of medical practice. The hospitals simply tolerated illegal efforts by prisoner doctors and nurses to help patients, as well as efforts by other medical personnel to upgrade medical equipment and improve organizational aspects of the camp hospital system. Improvement of conditions in the hospitals was slow, and until the liquidation of the camp, never reached the level of accepted standards of medical care.

In April 1943, Himmler issued an order to discontinue selections in the camp hospitals and the practice of killing sick prisoners with poor prognosis for fast recovery. Mentally ill prisoners were not covered by these guidelines.[6] However, selections and killing of sick Jewish prisoners continued.

In 1942–44, political prisoners, mostly Poles, gradually replaced German criminal prisoners in various positions in the camp hospital system, and they largely monopolized auxiliary jobs. Taking advantage of their dominant position, these prisoners endeavored to help specific patients, especially Poles. Acting mostly underground, they managed to bring sanitary conditions to a tolerable level in a number of hospitals. Thanks to their contacts with various camp underground organizations inside and outside the camp, illegal shipments of otherwise unavailable medical drugs began reaching the hospitals. A considerable quantity of medicine was procured ("organized" in camp slang) by prisoners working in the depots of commando Canada storing and sorting property plundered from the Jewish victims of mass murder. As a result, many prisoners considered at least some camp hospitals as places where professional medical help could be had.

In the second phase of its existence, the camp hospital system discharged its medical responsibilities only to those prisoners whose condition promised fast recovery and return to work. For more seriously ill Jewish prisoners, it continued to function as an instrument of extermination.

Outpatient Clinics

All larger camp hospitals operated outpatient clinics which doubled as reception rooms. Every day, following the morning and evening roll call, they were besieged by prisoners seeking emergency medical attention or hospitalization. Unconscious prisoners and those unable to stand were also brought in. The demand for services peaked in the fall-winter season. As a rule, the number of prisoners accepted for hospitalization equaled the number of those who died in the hospital that day. Beginning in the middle of 1941, SS camp doctors selected only the most emaciated and haggard-looking from among prisoners seeking help in the outpatient clinics; they were subsequently killed with intracardiac phenol injection or, beginning in 1942, in the Birkenau gas chambers.

In the first stage of their existence in Auschwitz, the outpatient clinics and hospitals were extremely poorly supplied with medical instruments and drugs. Consequently, the medical care they could administer often was symbolic rather than substantive.

Various bodily injuries, abscesses, and frostbite were dressed with paper bandages. Persons suffering from diarrhea caused by starvation were treated with a charcoal tablet or albutannin. These and other medicines were issued in small quantities to all prisoners whose illnesses required hospitalization but who could not be accepted due to lack of room.

Supplies of medical drugs and implements in the outpatient clinics improved in 1943–44. During office hours, prisoner-doctors and nurses were loaned to the outpatient clinics from other hospital departments. As a result, in the final stage of the camp's existence, prisoners could generally count on some medical help or advice. More often than before, they were met with a kind attitude by the staff, who encouraged them to continue their struggle for survival.

In the first years, the decision to hospitalize a prisoner rested with the camp director or the reporting officer. The preliminary reporting to the doctor took place after the evening roll call. Prisoners calling in sick were required to report on the double, practically at a run, naked (regardless of the weather), and briefly present their ailments. Seriously ill prisoners, often in their last throes, were often subjected to beatings and harassments. They were usually accused of laziness and malingering, received mocking advice (those suffering from diarrhea were told "not to eat so much"), kicked, and sent back. Under these circumstances, many prisoners chose not to reveal their ailments.

However, the procedure could not be avoided by prisoners who could no longer work in labor squads, especially those with visible injuries, such as broken arms or legs or prominent swelling symptomatic of a disease induced by starvation. Prisoners admitted to the camp hospital by the SS doctor were issued hospital fatigues (often shirts only) and referred to wards depending on the nature of their illness. Those deemed close to death were put on the lower-tier bunks near the exit. Prior to the introduction of tattooing, patients had their camp serial numbers inscribed with indelible pencil on their chests; this procedure facilitated the identification of dead prisoners.

With time, the admission procedure became much simplified. Prisoners could seek admission after either the morning or the evening roll call. More often, the SS doctors delegated the responsibility for admitting sick prisoners to their deputies, SS medics, who in turn deputized prisoner-doctors working in outpatient clinics.

Due to the invariably high morbidity among prisoners and general exhaustion, hospitalization was much sought after, although efforts to seek admission were often ineffective. Many of those not admitted died later in the blocks, at work, or during roll calls.

Living Conditions in Hospitals

Conditions in the camp hospitals in the first years of their existence amounted to a mockery of all accepted standards of patient care. Most prisoner patients were in a state of extreme emaciation, often unconscious, or close to death. Packed in overcrowded rooms, their shirts soiled to the point of grayness, often naked, they lay on paper pallets filled with straw which had long since been ground to dust, or wood shavings. One soiled threadbare blanket often served as a cover for two, even three prisoners. Shirts, blankets, and the straw mattresses were saturated with excrement, urine, and pus.

For a long time, Auschwitz hospitals lacked a sewage and water system. Prisoners relieved themselves into buckets, which, due to inadequate supply, were overflowing, so that the area around them was wet and slippery with human waste. Many prisoners suffering from the so-called *Durchfall* (starvation-induced diarrhea), had to evacuate their bowels scores of times a day; unable to reach the bucket in time, they soiled passages in between the bunks, while the weakest among them relieved themselves where they were. Unwashed for weeks, the sick prisoners' bodies reeked. The distinct, overpowering Durchfall stench was permanently in evidence, both in the primitive hospital barracks in Birkenau, where living conditions and overall neglect were particularly noxious, and in the rooms of hospital blocks in the main camps, despite constant airing and washing of floors several times a day. Similar conditions prevailed in rooms where patients were suffering from frostbite and phlegmon.

Hospital rooms were infested with fleas and lice. In Birkenau, the hospitals swarmed with rats. At night they gnawed at the bodies of dead prisoners, even attacking the unconscious and weakest patients. Until the last days of Auschwitz's existence, sick prisoners were allocated starvation food rations. All prisoners, especially those ill with typhus and running high fever, were tormented by thirst.

Shortage of water was particularly acute in the women's camp at Birkenau, with truly catastrophic consequences for sanitary conditions. Initially the hospitalized women prisoners were not separated according to type of illness, so that patients with different diseases lay together on the same bunk, often with the bodies of dead prisoners.

In 1943–44, living conditions in the Auschwitz hospitals, as in the camp as a whole, generally improved. Lifting the ban on incoming food parcels for non-Jewish prisoners improved the food supply of some patients. Prisoners who worked in camp kitchens made efforts to supply the hospitals with additional food. Members of the hospital staff, assembled from suitable prisoners, devoted considerable attention to the disinfection of hospital rooms and to maintaining a reasonable level of cleanliness. Convalescent prisoners helped with the assorted cleaning jobs; prisoners from other labor squads also helped, displaying considerable resourcefulness in supplying the hospitals with sanitation and medical equipment, which they procured illegally from various camp depots, mainly those of Canada. However, their efforts to improve the living conditions of the sick prisoners did not bear fruit everywhere. The most marked improvement in all aspects of living conditions took place in the hospital in the satellite camp at Monowitz; the least improvement was experienced by patients in hospitals at Birkenau.

Methods and Scope of Medical Treatment

The large numbers of sick prisoners even in the first months of the camp's existence and the steadily climbing morbidity is directly attributable to the living conditions prevailing in the camp. Incessant brutal treatment of prisoners resulted in broken bones, extensive ecchymosis, phlegmons of buttocks (caused by floggings), and ulcers and abscesses formed by gunshot wounds. In winter, late fall, and early spring, the poorly clothed and shod prisoners suffered from colds, pneumonia, pleurisy, and inflammation of the urinary tract, as well as frostbite, which often led to necrosis of extremities. Catastrophic sanitary conditions and hygiene resulted in numerous skin disorders. Vitamin deficiency caused extensive ulcerations and abscesses.

The years 1941–43, particularly 1942, entered the annals of Auschwitz as a period of epidemics, especially spotted fever. Many prisoners suffered from tuberculosis. Starvation disease was the distinct illness of the camp. Its symptoms included diarrhea (often with blood), edema of the legs, impaired eyesight and hearing, loss of memory, nervous breakdown, and, above all, extreme emaciation. Most prisoners suffered from several illnesses simultaneously.

With few exceptions, the attitude of SS doctors toward prisoner patients was uniformly hostile, or indifferent at best. During selections in the camp hospitals, they displayed ruthlessness, and the pleas of sick prisoners to spare their lives left them unmoved. As hospital managers, they were interested in administration. Their preoccupation was the preparation of documentation that created the appearance of proper treatment of prisoner patients. They drafted periodic reports designed both for their superiors at Department DIII of SS-WVHA and for the camp commandant. They also affixed their signatures to many documents manufactured by the hospital administrative offices which attributed to fictitious causes the death of prisoners killed by intracardiac phenol injections and by gas.

SS doctors carried out irregular inspections of certain hospital rooms. In the course of these haphazard rounds, they neither examined the patients nor evinced any interest in them. Instead they checked medical charts with a view to discharging prisoners who, in their view, had overstayed their welcome. Such doctors and medics, like other representatives of the camp officialdom, evoked fear and terror among prisoners; their appearance in the camp hospitals was associated with the threat of death.

Prisoner patients could expect medical treatment only from some prisoner-doctors and nurses. In the first years of Auschwitz, the handful of prisoner-doctors and nurses employed in the hospitals could do practically nothing to relieve the suffering of their fellow prisoners, many of whom lingered on their deathbed. They had very limited quantities of inferior drugs. They were terrorized by the criminal prisoners who formed the core of the "prisoner self-government" which ruled the hospitals at that time. They could only dress physical injuries and carry out minor and provisory surgical interventions.

In December 1941, the SS doctor, Untersturmführer Friedrich Entress sought to study surgery by organizing a small surgery room in block 21 of the main camp. Later, prisoner-doctors took advantage of contacts with prisoners employed at camp depots (mainly those of Canada) to equip the surgery room with some necessary instruments. Other branches and wards of the camp hospital system were equipped in a similar fashion.

The only means available to the prisoner-doctors and nurses to treat often serious skin infections were boric ointment and dermatol powder. In the first years of the camp, patients with internal disorders encountered the worst situations. With limited quantities of inferior drugs available, nursing was usually the only treatment prisoner-doctors could provide. More often than not, the only "medicine" they could dispense to the dying prisoners was words of encouragement and consolation.

As the camp hospital system grew, sprouting new wards and special services that included x-ray rooms and analytical labs and employing more prisoner-doctors (mainly Poles and Jews), among whom were prominent specialists in various branches of medicine, real treatment of sick prisoners became a possibility in some hospitals. However, efforts at improvement were systematically frustrated by the continuing practice of SS doctors of selecting the most seriously ill prisoners for death in gas chambers. In their efforts to protect as many seriously ill and emaciated prisoners as possible, prisoner-doctors and nurses occasionally hid them from the SS doctors, placing them on the top tier of bunks, where their physical condition was at least partially concealed. Some patients were temporarily discharged from hospitals in advance of imminent selections. More often, seriously ill prisoners were held in the hospital beyond the time limit set by the camp authorities by transferring them from one hospital ward to another, or, in most cases, by readmitting them shortly after discharge. Taking advantage of oversights of SS doctors and medics, prisoner-doctors falsified medical records of such patients, presenting them as having a good chance of quick recovery.

The rudimentarily preserved hospital records, many deliberately falsified, do not provide even an approximate number of prisoners who died in the hospitals. Available documents, as well as accounts, recollections, and testimonies of former prisoners, indicate that the prisoners who died in hospitals, together with those selected by SS doctors to die by phenol injections and in the gas chambers, probably constituted the greater part of all prisoners incarcerated in various camps of Auschwitz. One source, which offers a relatively sharp picture of mortality in the Auschwitz main camp, is the registration book of the camp hospital mortuary located in block 28. In addition to the serial numbers of dead prisoners, it gives the location of their death, i.e., the number of the block in which they died. In one example, entries covering the period from October 7, 1942, to July 31, 1943, reveal that during the peak of the typhus epidemic in August 1942, about 1,700 of the 2,500 prisoners who died did so in a camp hospital, most in the infectious diseases block 20.[7]

A permanent feature of the camp scene was the numerous piles of bodies of male and female prisoners amassed temporarily at various locations, mostly in washing rooms in hospital and living blocks, as well as in various outdoor sites. Masses of bodies were most visible in Birkenau, especially on the grounds of the hospitals. At any hour, prisoners encountered piles of naked bodies swarming with rats gnawing at the scraps of muscle tissue.

Killing of Prisoners

Liquidation of sick prisoners with poor prognosis for quick recovery, as well as those brought to a state of extreme emaciation, was carried out in the concentration camps as part of the euthanasia program for persons deemed expendable, implemented according to a decree by Hitler on September 1, 1939.[8]

The first instance of selection of prisoners in the Auschwitz camp in the context of the euthanasia program occurred on July 28, 1941. A special medical commission which arrived at the camp that day carried out a selection among the 575 handicapped, chronically ill, and elderly prisoners, mostly in the hospital. They were shipped to a mental asylum in Sonnenstein and killed by means of carbon monoxide. The next month, SS doctors attempted to kill seriously ill prisoners with intravenous injections of concentrated perhydrol, ether, oxidized water, gasoline, opium, and phenol. The doctors soon concluded that intracardiac phenol injection was the most effective means of disposing of prisoners.

In the main camp, prisoners were put to death in a room in block 20. Prisoners who had been selected for death were led into the room naked in the order of their serial numbers. The injection (8 to 15 grams of phenol in 10 to 15 milligrams of concentrated water solution), administered by a long puncturing needle into the heart, caused death in seconds. Victims, some still alive, were dragged into a washing room nearby, then transported to the crematorium in the evening. Prisoners also were killed with phenol injections in hospitals at Birkenau, as well as in some satellite camps of Auschwitz, such as Golleschau. In August, September, November, and December 1942 alone, 2,467 prisoners were killed in this fashion.[9]

The use of phenol injections coincided with the first SS attempts to experiment with the efficacy of the gas Zyklon B as a killing agent. On September 3, 1941, in the basement of block 11 (the so-called death block) in the Auschwitz main camp, more than 250 sick prisoners selected from hospital blocks, together with about 600 Soviet prisoners of war, were killed with Zyklon B. Once camp authorities recognized Zyklon B as a particularly useful means of extermination, they started using it in 1942 to kill prisoners deemed unfit for work, mainly patients in camp hospitals. The first large-scale liquidation of sick prisoners by means of Zyklon B was carried out on August 29, 1942. On instructions from the newly appointed SS garrison physician Kurt Uhlenbrock, who sought to stamp out the raging typhus epidemic, SS physicians selected 746 typhus patients and convalescents from hospital blocks (mainly from the contagious diseases block 20). The victims were loaded on trucks and transported to the gas chambers of Birkenau.

Until October 1944, SS physicians periodically carried out selections in camp hospitals, as well as in the camp itself, choosing from several dozen to several thousand sick prisoners with poor prognoses for gassing. From August 1943 on, only Jews were subject to selections. On August 29, 1943, SS doctors carried out the first and largest selection in the camp for male prisoners at Birkenau (sector BIId). About 4,000 Jews unfit for work were selected. On October 8, 1943, Yom Kippur eve, several thousand Jewish prisoners from both the men's and the women's camps and from the camp hospital were selected for death. One of the last selections was carried out in the camp hospital for male prisoners in Birkenau (BIIf) on October 16, 1944. Six hundred Jews lost their lives in the gas chambers that day.[10] From November 1, 1942, to December 31, 1944, following selections carried out by SS doctors in the hospital for prisoners in Monowitz (Auschwitz III), some 8,000 prisoners, mainly Jews, were transferred to Birkenau and Auschwitz. Most of them perished in the gas chambers.[11]

The victims selected for death were assembled in barracks to await their fate. On some occasions, especially in 1944, waiting on "death row" lasted several days due to overcrowding of the gas chambers with Jews from the constantly arriving transports. Prisoners condemned to death received particularly brutal treatment. In the last moments of their lives, the sick prisoners were subjected to savage beatings and kicking by SS men and prisoners on official duty who transported them to the gas chambers. Those who tried to resist were dragged by their arms and legs, while unconscious victims were simply thrown into the truck beds. Prisoners' pleas to spare their lives had no effect on the executioners.

Among the SS doctors who carried out selections of prisoners were Friedrich Entress, Erwin von Helmersen, Heinz Thilo, Edmund König, Josef Mengele, Brunmo Kitt, Horst Fischer, Fritz Klein, Helmut Vetter, Seigfried Schwela, and Eduard Wirths. Camp hospital administrative offices issued death certificates complete with false disease histories and causes of death of prisoners killed with intracardiac phenol injections.[12]

By acting in accordance with Nazi authorities, the SS doctors in Auschwitz broke the Hippocratic Oath in their conduct toward the prisoners by taking an active part in the mass murder of Jews, by condemning to death the most ill and physically ravaged prisoner patients, and by carrying out inhumane medical experiments on prisoners and performing other activities in violation of the basic principles of their occupation. In supporting the mass extermination carried out in the camps, they went down in history as criminal doctors. Prisoner-doctors (the overwhelming majority of whom were Poles and Jews), on the other hand, made great efforts to counteract the role of camp hospitals in the extermination. In this work they were supported by other prisoners among hospital personnel. Hospital work was one of the few jobs in the camp which prisoners performed with dedication and commitment.

NOTES

This essay is an abbreviated version of a study prepared by the author for the Auschwitz-Birkenau State Museum. In addition to preserved Nazi documents and reports of the Auschwitz underground movement, it draws on numerous accounts, recollections, and testimonies of former prisoners preserved in the archives of the museum. Among historiographical studies used by this author, the following deserve special mention: Alexander Mitscherlich and Fred Mielke, eds., *Medizin ohne Menschlichkeit: Dokumente des Nurnberger Arztprozessess*, (Frankfurt am Main, 1960); Yves Ternon and Socrate Helman, *Histoire de la médicine SS ou le mythe du racisme biologique* (Tournai, 1970); Reimund Schnabel, *Macht ohne Moral: Eine Dokumentation über SS* (Frankfurt am Main, 1957); Jan Mikulski, *Nazi Medicine in the Service of the Third Reich* (in Polish) (Warsaw, 1981); Rudolf Kudlin, *Arzte im Nationalsozialismus* (Cologne, 1985); Robert Jay Lifton, *The Nazi Doctors: Medical Killing and the Psychology of Genocide* (New York, 1986). The impressive research which appeared in the pages of the journal *Przeglad Lekarski—Oswiecim* (Auschwitz Medical Review), published since 1961 by the Krakow branch of the Polish Medical Society, also deserves special attention in this context. Over the past 30 years, it has published a host of articles on camp hospitals in Auschwitz and biographical studies of prisoner-doctors who died in the camp as well as of those who rendered a special service to the cause of saving fellow prisoners from death. See also *Hamburger Dokumente: Die Auschwitz Hefte, Texte der polnischen Zeitschrift "Przeglad Lekarski" über historische, psychische und medicinishe Spekte des Lebens und Sterbens in Auschwitz*, Hrsg. Vom Hamburger Institute für Sozialforschung (Weinheim and Basel, 1987), 2 vols.

1. Numerous studies of the Haftlingskrankenbau in the Auschwitz main camp appeared in *Przeglad Lekarski*. Among their authors are Wladyslaw Fejkiel, Jan Olbrycht, Stanislaw Klodzinski, Tadeusz Paczula, Jan Zielina, Tadeusz Orzeszko, Kazimierz Halgas. See also *Hamburger Dokumente*.

2. Irena Strzelecka, "The First Camp Hospital in Birkenau" (in Polish), *Przeglad Lekarski*, 1984, pp. 88–93.

3. Danuta Czech, "The Role of the Camp Hospital for Male Prisoners in Auschwitz II" (in Polish), *Zeszyty Oswiecimskie*, 1974, no. 15, pp. 5–105.

4. Tadeusz Szymanski, Danuta Szymanska, and Tadeusz Snieszko, "On the Hospital in the Gypsy Family Camp in Auschwitz-Birkenau" (in Polish), *Przeglad Lekarski*, 1965, pp. 90–99.

5. Beginning in November 1943, the satellite camp at Monowitz functioned as headquarters for the satellite camps of Auschwitz which supplied prisoner manpower for industrial enterprises. All these camps became a single administrative unit designated KL Auschwitz III. On hospitals and infirmaries in the Auschwitz satellite camps, see monographs in *Zeszyty Oswiecimskie*, nos. 9-18 (*Hefte von Auschwitz* in the German version). See also Antoni Makowski, "Organization, Development, and Functioning of the Monowitz Prisoner Hospital (KL Auschwitz III)" (in Polish), *Zeszyty Oswiecimskie*, 1974, no. 15, pp. 107–70.

6. Archives of the Auschwitz-Birkenau State Museum, collection Sammlung v. Erlassen, D-RF-9, WVHA, 8/1, card 28. See also Czech, pp. 37–38.

7. Archives of the Auschwitz-Birkenau State Museum, records of the mortuary of the Auschwitz main camp hospital (*Leichenhallebuch*), call no. D-AuI/5/I-4.

8. Yves Ternon and Helman Socrate, *Extermination of the Mentally Ill in the Third Reich, from Nazi Theoreticians to SS Practitioners* (in Polish; trans. from French) (Warsaw, 1974); *Aktion T4 1939-1945: Die "Euthanasie"—Zentrale in der Tiergartenstrasse 4* (Berlin, 1987); *Dokumente zur "Euthanasie"* (Frankfurt am Main, 1985).

9. The figure of 2,467 prisoners killed was calculated on the basis of an analysis of entries in the camp mortuary book, drawing also on materials documenting activities of the prisoner underground in the camp. Cf. Czech, p. 18.

10. Danuta Czech, *Kalendarium der Ereignisse im Konzentrationslager Auschwitz-Birkenau 1939–1945* (Hamburg, 1989), entries dated as listed.

11. Makowski, p. 131.

12. In his expert opinion given in the trial of Höss, former prisoner Dr. Jan Olbrycht evaluated the documents produced by administrative offices of Auschwitz hospitals: "Had Nazism not been defeated, an impartial observer studying medical histories of Auschwitz prisoners and the protocols of their medical treatment might have come to the conclusion that sanitation, hygiene, and medical procedures in Auschwitz were exemplary and that medical care given to prisoners conformed to the latest guidelines of medical science and craft. The autopsy reports of individual registered prisoners provide a good example of deliberate falsifying of camp documents, and thus should serve as a warning to young researchers to adopt a critical approach to this category of documents and exercise the utmost caution in using them as a basis for analytical conclusions." Archives of the Auschwitz-Birkenau State Museum, collection Trial of Höss, vol. 59, card 81.

16

Women

IRENA STRZELECKA

Jewish women and children probably constituted more than half of all the victims murdered in the gas chambers of Auschwitz. Together with women of other nationalities, they made up about 30 percent of all prisoners registered in the camp.

The need to establish a special section for women prisoners at Auschwitz arose in connection with the Nazi policy—adopted in 1942—of intensifying the exploitation of prisoner labor. In addition to transports of Jews consigned for wholesale extermination, Auschwitz became the destination of transports of Jewish men and women, some of whom had already been selected at points of departure (railroad stations) as fit for work.

The first transport of this kind, originating in Poprad, Slovakia, and carrying 999 Jewish women, reached Auschwitz on March 26, 1942. From July 1942 on, Jewish transports were routinely subjected to selections upon arrival. Jewish prisoners, both men and women, who were deemed able to provide labor became prisoners of Auschwitz.

In creating a special camp for women in Auschwitz, Nazi authorities undoubtedly sought, among other things, to relieve the congestion in the concentration camp for women established at Ravensbrück in 1939 and in other prisons. In addition to the transport of Jewish women from Slovakia, another group of 999 German women from Ravensbrück reached Auschwitz that day, and several days later the first groups of Polish women from prisons in Krakow and Tarnow arrived.

Since large numbers of women prisoners could be put to work in Auschwitz as part of the in-camp labor squads as well as in agriculture and cattle raising, the SS could reassign larger contingents of male prisoners. They were put to work at further expansion of the camp, as well as on behalf of firms working for the German armaments industry.

From March to mid-August 1942, Auschwitz-bound transports of women were placed in the main camp, in blocks marked 1 to 10, separated from the men in camp by a wall of iron sheets and concrete posts. During this period, a total of about 17,000 women prisoners, most of them Jews, arrived at Auschwitz. A large number of them (probably about 5,000) perished before the transfer of women to the camp at Birkenau.

In view of the growing number of transports and the increasing congestion in the blocks, camp authorities decided in mid-August 1942 to transfer women prisoners to Birkenau, specifically to the grounds of sector BIa, whose construction had meanwhile been completed. Women prisoners occupied 30 barracks (15 made of bricks and 15 others of timber, horse-stable style), and in 1943 five more wooden barracks were added between the row of brick barracks and the barracks housing washing rooms and lavatories.

In July 1943, the women's camp was expanded further by annexing to it sector BIb, which since March 1942 had been occupied by male prisoners. Both these sectors of the Birkenau camp functioned as concentration camps for women until November 1944. The layout and construction of the two camps were nearly identical. Apart from brick and wooden barracks serving as living quarters for the women prisoners, each had one kitchen, one potato-peeling barrack, one bath (the so-called sauna), and five barracks containing washing rooms and lavatories. In addition, the brick barracks, located in the BIb sector at the farthest edge of the complex of wooden barracks (in vicinity of crematorium II), housed the clothing depot (*Effektenkammer*), while the food depot was located next to the brick barrack designated as number 1.

After sector BIb had been annexed to the women's camp, the only women prisoners to remain in sector BIa were those employed outside the camp, as well as women in quarantine prior to incarceration, sick women, and those employed in the in-camp labor squads.

On October 1, 1944, a new women's camp was created on the grounds of the extension of the main camp; at about the same time, about 1,500 women prisoners, including workers of the Union armaments factory, were put up in blocks 22 and 23 of Auschwitz I, fenced off from the other men's blocks by electrified barbed wire.

In 1943 and 1944, some 11,000 Gypsy women lived in the family camps (BIIe), located outside the main women's camp (consisting of sectors BIa and BIb), which also housed several thousand Jewish women prisoners from Theresienstadt (sector BIIb). Most of the Gypsy women perished, either during their stay in these camps or in the Birkenau gas chambers.

In June 1944, as the extermination of Hungarian Jews proceeded, transit camps, meant to absorb Jewish transports arriving at Auschwitz, were set up in Birkenau. That was necessary due to the colossal scale of the operation, which resulted in the SS lagging behind in conducting selections. In addition, since the sheer number of victims exceeded the killing capacity of the gas chambers, Jewish women from Hungary and from the liquidated ghettos were held in the BIIc sector and in the uncompleted third construction sector of the Birkenau camp, nicknamed "Mexico."

Since they had not undergone registration, the women technically were not prisoners of Auschwitz, and their fate was yet to be decided. For most of them, these camps were "waiting rooms for the gas." Some were deported to camps in the German interior and put to work in local armaments factories; others became de facto prisoners of Auschwitz. In the summer of 1944, the average population of camps BIIc and BIII at Birkenau reached 30,000 women.

When evacuation transports from Majdanek (Lublin concentration camp) and transports of Polish deportees from Warsaw (via the camp at Pruszkow), then engulfed by an uprising, started rolling into Auschwitz, the newly arrived women were accommodated in the specially designated barracks belonging to the quarantine camp for men (BIIa).

The Camp Authorities

Until July 1942, the women's camp, on the grounds of the main camp, was technically within the jurisdiction of the headquarters of the Ravensbrück concentration camp; thereafter it was placed under the Auschwitz commandant, Rudolf Höss. The women's camp at Birkenau was under the direct jurisdiction of the Auschwitz commandant's office until November 1943. Following the division of the Auschwitz camp that month into three camps (Auschwitz I, main camp; Auschwitz II, Birkenau; and Auschwitz III, satellite camps at industrial enterprises), the Auschwitz headquarters administered the women's camp through successive commandants of Auschwitz II: Fritz Hartjenstein (until May 8, 1944) and Josef Kramer (until November 25, 1944).

The first female superintendent of the women's camp, when it was still located on the grounds of the main camp and shortly after its transfer to Birkenau, was Johanna Langefeld, who had arrived at Auschwitz on March 26, 1942, in the first transport of German women prisoners from Ravensbrück. She was recalled in October 1942 in connection with organizational shortcomings and replaced by Maria Mandel. A zealous functionary, Mandel treated prisoners with uncommon cruelty. In November 1944, Elisabeth Volkenrath became superintendent of the women's camp.

Höss, who was singularly unimpressed by the organizational skills of the German women taskmasters, introduced a parallel chain of authority in the women's camp, consisting of the camp director, a noncommissioned reporting officer, and labor squad leaders. Thus, in addition to the superintendent, the women's camp was ruled by two successive camp directors: Paul Müller and Franz Hössler. Anton Taube served as reporting officer; at different periods this post was also held by a woman: Margot Drexler, Therese Brandl, Irma Grese, Elisabeth Ruppert, Elisabeth Saretzki, and Gertrude Zlotos. Kurt Müller, in charge of employment of women prisoners, was succeeded by Richard Perschel. A parallel post was held by SS women supervisors, including, among others, Elisabeth Hasse. This double chain of command was not replicated on lower rungs of the hierarchy.

Among the SS supervisors, Mandel, Taube, Drexler, and Hasse distinguished themselves in their savage treatment of women prisoners. Their brutality was shocking even by Auschwitz standards; they also took part in selections, and often initiated them.

The "prisoner positions" staff—in some ways an extension of the SS long hand—was dominated by criminal prisoners and asocial German women brought to Auschwitz in the first transport from Ravensbrück. Höss described them:

> "Green" women prisoners [criminal elements] were one of a kind. In my opinion the worst among Ravensbrück prisoners were selected for duty in Auschwitz. In their meanness, coarseness, and baseness they had no equal among criminal prisoners. Most of them were prostitutes, with a long sentencing record, some of them truly repulsive. It was virtually certain that such beasts would ill-treat the women prisoners under them, but it could not be avoided. During his visit to Auschwitz in 1942, the Reichsführer-SS considered them suitable as kapos for Jewesses. Not counting deaths resulting from infectious diseases, not many of them died. Mental torment was completely alien to them.[1]

As new transports arrived, non-German prisoners, including Polish and Jewish women, were also assigned official duties. Motivated by the desire to insinuate themselves into the good graces of the SS or the fear of losing their positions and the benefits they entailed and, above all, by the will to survive, some of these prisoners applied themselves with great zeal to their duties, equaling the SS men and women supervisors in their capacity for cruelty and killing. Stanislawa Starostka, a Polish political prisoner, chose this option, and in her capacity as block leader, as well as the elder of the women's camp, proved to be ruthless and cruel toward her fellow prisoners. But among prisoners with official duties, there were also women who often risked their lives in trying to take advantage of the opportunities offered by their position or place of work to help their fellows in misery. Women prisoners who survived the camp recalled them with gratitude.

Prisoners

The transport that arrived at Auschwitz from Ravensbrück on March 26, 1942, comprised political prisoners, Jehovah's Witnesses, criminals, and women defined by the Nazis as asocial. The latter formed the largest group, and camp authorities assigned them various duties. With the creation in 1942 of an experimental plant-growing station at Rajsko, in which research was conducted on a rubber-yielding plant called coke-sagiz, a group of Polish women biologists, chemists, and horticulturists was brought from Ravensbrück on May 12 and June 20 and put to work doing scientific research.

Beginning in late June 1942, numerous transports carrying Jewish women from France (camps at Drancy, Beaune la Rolande, Pithiviers, and Angers St. Land) started rolling into Auschwitz. Until the transfer of the women's camp to Birkenau, they constituted the second-largest group at Auschwitz next to the Jewish Slovak women.

In December 1942 and February 1943, about 700 Polish women were deported to Auschwitz; together with their families, they had been expelled from the Zamojsk region, designated as one of the first areas of German colonization in the East. In August and September 1944, some 5,000 Polish women and girls arrived at the camp in transports carrying civilians arrested in Warsaw after the outbreak of the general Polish uprising in the city.

Beginning in July 1942, Jewish transports arriving at the camp were subjected to regular selections. SS doctors selected newly arrived Jews they considered unfit for work, primarily the sick and elderly. Among women, the pregnant and those with small children fell into this category. One of the first groups to undergo selection was a transport of Jews from Slovakia, which arrived at Auschwitz on July 4, 1942; after the selection, 108 women were placed in the camp. In the following months and years, until the discontinuation of mass exterminations of Jews in late October 1944, tens of thousands of Jewish women from Poland and from countries occupied by the Third Reich ended up in the women's camp at Auschwitz.

Former prisoners vividly recall transports of Jewish Greek women who arrived at the Birkenau women's camp, mostly in the spring of 1943. Uprooted from their sunny homeland and separated from their loved ones, who subsequently died in the gas chambers, they could not adapt themselves to the camp conditions and rapidly succumbed to various diseases.

During the existence of the women's camp in Auschwitz, a total of some 131,000 women prisoners were registered: about 28,000 in 1942, some

56,000 in 1943, and roughly 47,000 in 1944. Of this number, about 90,000 women were assigned serial numbers in the general category of Auschwitz prisoners, which, up to May 1944, also included Jewish women; some 30,000 were registered in the A series, introduced for Jewish prisoners in the middle of May 1944; in the period of mass transports of Hungarian Jews, about 11,000 were assigned Z serial numbers (introduced for Gypsy women); and some 2,000 women were registered in the E category reserved for prisoners needing "corrective education." Jewish women who survived selections constituted the overwhelming majority (82,000) of women prisoners registered in the camp, followed by Polish women (about 31,000) and Gypsies. Most of the remaining 6,000 registered women prisoners were from the Soviet Union and Germany.

Female political prisoners imprisoned on the basis of a Nazi decree promulgated on February 29, 1933, which introduced so-called protective custody, were required to wear a red triangle on their clothes. Up to the middle of 1944, Jewish women brought in transports wore six-pointed stars formed by two triangles one yellow, the other red. Later, they were further distinguished from other prisoners by a yellow stripe placed underneath the red triangle.

Small groups of women inmates comprised criminal prisoners (identified by a green triangle); asocial elements, in which the Nazis included Gypsy women (black triangles); the Bible scholars, or Jehovah's Witnesses (violet triangles), and corrective-education prisoners (identified by the letter E sewn on their camp fatigues underneath the serial number). Women prisoners in the latter category were placed in the camp for corrective education for six weeks as a punishment for such offenses as unauthorized absence from work or escape from forced labor. Since they had to undergo all the rigors of camp life, many of them died before release.

Beginning in February 1943, due to overcrowding of the Myslowice prison, so-called police prisoners were incarcerated in the main Auschwitz camp (initially on the first floor of block 2 and later on the ground floor of block 11, the "death block") until the completion of their interrogation. Following brief trials before the Police Summary Court, most of them were shot at the death wall. After the transfer of the women's camp to Birkenau, its Jewish prisoners began to be marked by serial camp numbers assigned to them during registration, tattooed on the left forearm. Beginning in spring 1943, all the remaining categories of women prisoners were tattooed with the exception of German women, corrective-education prisoners, and police prisoners. Nor was tattooing used on Polish women prisoners deported from Warsaw during the uprising in 1944 or Jewish women from Hungary and liquidated ghettos who were placed in sectors BIIc and BIII of Birkenau. Some categories of prisoners were tattooed with additional markings placed in front of the serial number; some Jewish women were identified with a triangle, and beginning in mid-1944 with the letter A, whereas Gypsy women were tattooed with the letter Z.

Surviving camp records, primarily employment rosters of women prisoners, as well as reports of the camp underground resistance organization, enable estimates to be made of the size of the prisoner population of the women's camp at different times. Thus, for example, it numbered 8,232 prisoners on December 1, 1942; 18,659 on April 30, 1943; 27,053 on January 20, 1944; 39,234 (plus about 30,000 unregistered Jewish women living in the so-called placement camps) on August 22, 1944; 43,462 (including Jewish women from the placement camps as well as 3,785 in the women's camp in Auschwitz itself) on October 3, 1944; and 12,695 in the Birkenau camp, 6,015 in the women's camp in Auschwitz, and 2,036 women prisoners in satellite camps located next to industrial enterprises on December 30, 1944.

At the last roll call, on January 17, 1945, 10,381 women prisoners reported in the Birkenau women's camp, 6,196 in the Auschwitz women's camp, and 2,095 in the satellite camps.

Living Conditions

Arriving women had their first taste of the gruesome realities of the camp at the unloading of their transport: screams and curses of the SS men, brutal pushing and shoving, blows with rifle butts, barking dogs. Frightened out of their wits by this "welcome," the newly arrived prisoners were driven like cattle to the bath on the camp grounds or to one of the barracks nearby. Often they waited for long hours before being subjected to the registration procedure.

As long as women prisoners remained incarcerated on the grounds of the Auschwitz main camp, registration was carried out in the wooden barracks located between block 1 and block 2. After the transfer of the women's camp to Birkenau, it took place in the brick bath barrack, and beginning in December 1943, also in the newly constructed building, dubbed "Sauna," located next to the barracks complex of the Canada commando, near crematoria IV and V.

First, the newly arrived prisoners (nicknamed Zugang) were relieved of their clothing and all personal articles, including valuables. In searching for the latter, some women, mainly Jews, were subjected to gynecological examinations. Then the camp barbers shaved all the hair on their bodies, using tools long since dulled by extended use.

After the bath, which took place in indescribable congestion under streams of boiling hot or freezing water and sometimes included disinfection by means of hot steam, the prisoners were issued the regulation striped camp fatigues, often crawling with lice and soiled by blood and excrement. In 1943 and 1944, these clothes were replaced by used civilian clothing marked on the back by painted red stripes, as well as wooden sabots or worn-out shoes yielded by sorting in the depots of Canada.

Female Slovak Jews, who arrived at Auschwitz in the spring of 1942, were issued the tattered uniforms of Soviet prisoners of war murdered earlier in the camp. In addition, their hair was cut—a procedure not previously applied to non-Jewish women prisoners. While undergoing this ritual of degradation, the newly arrived women were targets of humiliating and mocking remarks dispensed freely by the SS men on the scene and veteran women prisoners in official capacities on the bath staff. Emerging from the bath clothed in the camp garb, their heads shaved, the victims were often so changed in appearance that their companions could not recognize them.

Registration involved being assigned a serial number and tattoo. Up to 1943, three photographs were taken: a front-face and two profiles (with the exception of Jewish women brought in transports). After registration, the women were usually quarantined in specially designated barracks. During the quarantine in the Birkenau camp, they were held for days on end at the "visa"—a vast, empty square bordered on one side by the barracks with washing rooms and lavatories and on the other by the camp perimeter fence. They sat there on the hard ground or in mud, depending on the weather, always hungry and thirsty.

In the sudden encounter with the hate-filled atmosphere of the camp, normal values collapsed and every feminine and human impulse was ruthlessly suppressed, resulting in severe shock. The experience was so shattering that some women who could not imagine how they could survive the first stage of their ordeal in the camp either became totally apathetic or decided to commit suicide. Most often, Jewish girls, barely in their teens, threw themselves on the electrified fence. Thus they put an end to the hopelessness, loneliness, and despair that overcame them as they stood among thousands of women, having been recently brutally separated during selection from their parents and siblings, who had gone to their deaths in the gas chambers. Suicides took place also in a number of the satellite camps of Auschwitz.

Thus, for example, several days after the forced-labor camp in Gliwice had been taken over by the Auschwitz concentration camp and its prisoners tattooed with serial numbers, two young Jewish girls from Poland—Bela Londer, 18, from Sosnowiec, and Melania Borenstein, in her teens—took their own lives. Having learned they had just become Auschwitz prisoners, the two girls jumped out of the fourth floor of the factory hall.

Those who lasted through the quarantine period entered the horror of camp existence. In the main camp, women prisoners occupied blocks numbered 1 to 10. With the arrival of fresh transports, the basements and attics of these blocks also began filling with prisoners. At first, they slept on mattresses on the concrete floor, since no bunks were supplied. Any prisoner who went to the lavatory stepped on her sleeping fellow inmates.

In Birkenau, women prisoners lived in brick barracks and wooden barracks built as horse stables. Congestion there varied, depending on fluctuations in the prisoner population. During periods of overflow, women prisoners slept even in the narrow passages between the bunks. Built hastily on a swamped terrain without any insulation, the barracks lacked ceilings, and their occupants walked on dirt floors, which raised clouds of dust in the summer and turned into a muddy puddle during rainy season due to leaky roofs.

In the summer, they suffered oppressive heat and stench, whereas in winter they shivered with moisture and cold, since two iron stoves in each barrack burned only sporadically due to difficulties in procuring firewood or coal. The barracks were not lit, and two buckets put inside during the nights doubled as sanitary facilities. In addition to the ubiquitous fleas and lice, the women were plagued by rats, which descended on the bodies of dead prisoners, often attacking the weak and the sick as well.

Most horrendous was the situation of women prisoners in the first months after the transfer of the camp to Birkenau. In her memoirs published shortly after the war, former prisoner Seweryna Szmaglewska gave this account:

> In the summer of 1942, Birkenau was a swamp fenced off by electrified wire. No roads whatsoever, no paths in between the blocks. Inside dark holes, as if in layered cages, dimly lit by the candles burning here and there, the emaciated apparitions bent double, blue with cold, leaning over a bundle of soiled rags, their shaven heads sunken in between the shoulders, their bony fingers busy catching insects and squashinq them on the bunk's edge—this is what barracks looked like in 1942.[2]

Lack of water and catastrophic sanitary conditions were the main cause of the spread of infectious diseases, primarily typhus and typhoid, resulting in an extremely high mortality rate. Nearly all the women suffered from severe diarrhea, which led to total exhaustion, emaciation, and death. Dead bodies were everywhere, and within a short period nearly entire transports perished due to the dreadful living conditions in the camp. Thus of 28,000 prisoners brought to the camp in 1942, barely 5,400 remained alive at the end of the year. In 1943, some 28,000 women prisoners died in Birkenau; the highest monthly death rate was recorded in December—about 9,000 women.

To introduce a modicum of order, improve sanitary conditions, and organize a hospital (in view of some deaths among SS personnel and members of their families), the chief task of a group of doctors and medics assigned to Birkenau in 1942 was to separate live prisoners from dead.

Gradually, with the tacit agreement of the SS women supervisors, skilled prisoners, who now and then appeared at the Birkenau camp as part of various labor squads, paved the barracks' dirt floors with bricks or covered them with a layer of concrete. They also installed electric lighting, and in 1944, they started working on installing washrooms and bathrooms in some barracks. The latter, however, were not completed before the liquidation of the camp.

In 1943, primitive latrines were replaced by five barracks containing lavatories and washing rooms. When available, these facilities were packed with women. Those suffering acute diarrhea had to stand in line several times, since prisoners caught relieving themselves in other places were subject to severe punishment.

Every day, before marching off to work, each woman prisoner received about half a liter of herbal extract or grain coffee; during the short lunch break, the standard ration was about a liter of soup made of potatoes or rotting vegetables with a tiny amount of margarine; and after the evening roll call the prisoners had to make do with a daily ration of about 300 grams of bread each, a tiny piece of spoiled cheese, marmalade, or sausage of the lowest quality. Beginning in late September 1942, women prisoners were allowed to receive food parcels from their families. The contents and size of the parcels were subject to fewer and fewer restrictions as the time passed. However, Jewish women were banned from receiving such parcels, and they were the first to succumb to diseases induced by starvation.

As with other camp routines, rationing of food was accompanied by all manner of harassment, especially beating. Women prisoners appointed by the camp authorities (mainly block and room leaders) appropriated part of the bread and margarine allocated to prisoners, and stole the contents of food parcels sent from home.

Two daily roll calls were a source of undescribable torment to the women prisoners. Due to constant difficulties posed by the process of counting the prisoners, morning roll calls would start as early as 4:00. (When the women's camp was still in the Auschwitz main camp, they even started at 3:00.) Evening roll calls often lasted long into the night. In Birkenau, some exhausted women would collapse and drown in the mud, and special prisoner squads would then be dispatched to search for their bodies as the roll call was in progress. Some roll calls were particularly gruesome. Former prisoner Ludwika Wierzbicka recalled one such event:

> One roll call I remember very well. Despite repeated counting and recovery of
> several bodies of dead prisoners, the numbers refused to tally. Finally it turned

out that one woman, a Czech, had hid in the block. She was so exhausted and her spirit so broken that she no longer cared what would happen to her. She was pulled out of her hiding place and dragged in front of the block. SS man Taube beat her. The beating was so savage that I can still hear the sound of blows. Paralyzed with fear we stood ramrod straight in rows.[3]

Jewish women prisoners lived in constant fear of selections carried out periodically in the camp infirmary, during roll calls, or during return from work, and occasionally in the bath. The largest selection in the Auschwitz main camp took place in connection with the transfer of women prisoners to Birkenau. A considerable number of the women in the camp hospital (block 3), together with a group of elderly women from the camp, were dispatched to the gas chambers rather than being moved.

In the Birkenau camp, initially selections were usually carried out during return from work and in the course of the general roll calls. As women passed through the camp gate, the SS women supervisors, accompanied by Anton Taube, who stood at the gate, used sticks to remove from the column sick and weak prisoners, as well as those who had the bad luck to stumble or fall.

In the camp infirmary, selections were carried out by SS doctors: Franz Bodmann (in the main Auschwitz camp), Bruno Kitt, Werner Rohde, Josef Mengele, Hans Wilhelm König, Fritz Klein, and Rudolf Horstmann. They displayed ruthlessness and hostility toward the sick Jewish women. Cries for mercy produced no effect whatsoever.

Practically all former prisoners who lived to see the liberation speak about selections in their testimonies, accounts, or memoirs. One such description is found, for example, in memoirs of the former Jewish prisoner from Warsaw Halina Birnbaum:

> One day, having returned to the block from the night shift dizzy with fatigue, we lay down on hard mattresses, using our wet boots as headrests. Suddenly we heard the piercing sounds of whistles coming from all directions, accompanied by the inhuman screams of the room leaders: "Get up for roll call! All Jewesses report for roll call!" Room leaders tore blankets off the sleeping women, hitting them with fists, screaming curses. . . . Special roll call for Jewesses only, who remained in the barracks during day shift—there couldn't be any doubt what this meant. Frightened and tense, we looked at each other. Which one would survive the selection and return to the block? . . . Marching five abreast, we came to the vast empty square in front of the baths. On Nazi order, stripped naked, all of us lined up in a single file. Hundreds of women from different countries and cities, speaking different languages, tall and short, fat and thin, healthy with smooth skin and the sick, covered with boils, bruises, and lacerations. . . . Facing us, presided the eerie SS tribunal; the short baton held by Mengele passed the final sentence: to the left—death, to the right—life, on borrowed time in the Auschwitz slaughterhouse. . . . The line of naked bodies kept moving toward

the baths; Dr. Mengele, accompanied by Taube, selected his victims with deliberation. Women who had just been granted a reprieve entered the baths and shortly afterward returned to the block. Those sentenced to the ovens, crowded on the left-hand side of the square, pushed by the kapo; their numbers were taken down so that they might be stricken off the list of the living.[4]

If the gas chambers were occupied, the condemned prisoners were placed in barrack 25 (called the "death block" by the prisoners), which stood apart from the rest of the camp. It had barred windows and a single, constantly guarded gate that led to its courtyard surrounded on all sides by a brick wall. Sobs and groans of women awaiting death could be heard from there; they pushed their hands through the bars, begging for water. Descriptions of block 25 and the process of removing the Jewish women prisoners to the gas chambers are found in numerous memoirs of former prisoners. Seweryna Szmaglewska wrote:

As general roll call was taking place on the field adjoining the camp, the gate to block 25 was thrown open. Trucks pulled up and the back wall of their beds was lowered. Wandering figures, hobbling on their legs, their eyes dim, emerged from the gate. They had been awaiting this moment for several torment-filled days. Obediently, like mannequins, they climbed onto the trucks and sat pressed to each other. Perhaps there, in the crematorium, in the last moment of their lives, they would revolt, but then it would be in vain. The crematorium walls are solid, the iron stronger than human will. The SS man shut the doors, and the convoy of trucks pulled away, passing the field where a general roll call was taking place. Faces of the victims in the trucks were plainly visible. Now and then someone's hand rose in the air in the gesture of last farewell, and to the women standing in the field it seemed like a disquieting call to follow in their footsteps.

This gruesome convoy shuttled several times from the camp gate to the crematorium until block 25 had been completely emptied of its residents. The last batch comprised only the weakest women, who could not even stand on their feet. They were thrown into the trucks like so many timber logs, one on top of another, until the truck was full. As the trucks drove at top speed, the inert bodies on top rocked with every jolt; the emaciated legs and arms rose and fell in unison, waving above the columns of women standing at attention, above the road traveled for the last time.[5]

Zalman Lewenthal, a prisoner killed in the Sonderkommando revolt in October 1944, wrote notes (unearthed in 1962 in the vicinity of the ruins of crematorium III) which included an extensive description of the unloading of Jewish women condemned to death at the crematorium and recounted their stories of selections and incarceration in block 25.

It was early in 1944. A cold, dry, lashing wind was blowing. The ground was frozen solid. The first truck, loaded to capacity with naked women and young girls, pulled up at crematorium III. They did not stand pressed tightly against one another, as usual; they had been so emaciated that they just lay inertly one on top of another, in a state of extreme exhaustion. They moaned and groaned. The truck stopped, the canvas was lifted, and the human mass was thrown out, the way one dumps gravel on the ground. Those lying at the edge fell onto the hard surface, hitting their heads, which drained them of whatever strength they had left in their bodies, so that they just lay there, motionless. The remaining [women] kept falling on top, pressing them with their weight. Groans were . . . heard. Those thrown out of the trucks last tried to extricate themselves from the pile of bodies, stood shakily, trying to walk. . . . Trucks kept pulling up, the human load was thrown out, and when everyone had finally arrived, all of them were driven like cattle in the direction of the gas bunker. One heard frightful screams of despair and loud sobbing . . . terrible . . . they expressed immense pain . . . different muffled voices merged into one . . . and kept rising up from underground so long that finally a "Red Cross" automobile pulled up . . . and put an end to their pain and despair.[6]

As a result of selections, thousands of Jewish women prisoners perished in the camp. On October 1, 2, and 3, 1942, about 6,000 died; in February and March 1943, about 6,500. On August 21, 1943, there were 498, including many Jewish women from Greece,[7] and in December 1943, over 4,000. One of the last selections was carried out in the women's camp at Birkenau in November 1944 in connection with the transfer of the camp to sector BII.

The morbidity and mortality rate, high as it was, was pushed even higher by general delousing, performed periodically regardless of weather conditions or season. In the course of such operations, women prisoners were forced to leave their barracks, deliver their fatigues for delousing, then wait for long hours in front of the bath barracks for personal delousing (similar to what they had undergone during registration). After the bath, their hair was cut and hair-covered parts of their bodies were disinfected; then they waited, naked, for permission to reenter the barracks, which meanwhile had also been disinfected, and for the return of their clothes, usually still soiled, crawling with lice, and wet.

Pregnant women prisoners were doomed from the beginning. Until the middle of 1943, they were killed with phenol injections in the hospital. A number of women well advanced in their pregnancy were subjected to forced abortions as part of medical experiments. If birth occurred, the newly born infants were either drowned in buckets of water or killed with phenol injections. Children of women deported to the camp in late 1943 from Minsk and Witebsk were taken from their parents; those that fitted the Nazi racial criteria were sent to Germany via camps in Potulice and Konstancin for Germanization. In February and March 1943, about 120 sons of Polish women from the Zamojsk region and of Polish Jewish women were killed with phenol injections in block 20. In addition, two Nazi doctors, Carl Clauberg and Horst Schumann, subjected several hundred Jewish women prisoners from various countries to criminal sterilization experiments.

As if that were not enough, all kinds of punishments were inflicted on women prisoners. Brutal treatment and beatings were administered to these women daily as punishment for large or small offenses (illegal food, possession of additional clothing, family photographs, cooking food in the barracks, slow pace of work, etc.). Their taskmasters also tormented them with punitive roll calls, during which they had to kneel, holding bricks aloft in their hands; penal labor; special cells that contained enough room for standing only; camp arrest in the basement of block 11 in the main camp; flogging; and assignment to the penal squad.

Punishment by flogging was demonstrated to Himmler on his inspection visit to the camp in July 1942. One of those punished on this occasion was Liza Kraus, who had tried to "organize" (procure illegally) several potatoes. After his inspection, the Reichsführer-SS reserved to himself the right to permit flogging as punishment administered against women.

The women's penal squad was created in the middle of June 1942 in the village of Budy following the first prisoner escape, by Janina Nowak, who had worked in the labor squad raking hay on the banks of the Sola River. Women in this squad cleaned and dredged fish ponds. One of the commanders of the penal squad was an SS man named Mokrus. His savagery toward the women prisoners earned his squad the camp nickname "Mokrus circus." One particularly tragic incident in the women's penal squad occurred in early October 1942 when, under the pretext of suppressing an alleged revolt, German women prisoners acting in an official capacity killed about 90 French Jewish women with poles and axes.

Women prisoners worked in an atmosphere of constant danger and terror. From the spring of 1942 on, large numbers of them were put to work in the agricultural establishments serving the camp in growing grain, vegetables, and flowers; fish, poultry, rabbit, and cattle breeding; and in forestry, clearing the ground of stumps of cut trees. In 1943, about 2,400 women worked in agriculture. Several hundred women (between 400 and 1,000 in 1943) worked in all kinds of auxiliary jobs in connection with the expansion of the camp: leveling houses emptied of their Polish inhabitants in the areas adjoining the camp, road construction, digging ditches, leveling ground in advance of construction of new buildings, transporting construction materials.

The largest number of women prisoners (about half of those employed on average) worked in labor squads servicing the camp and the SS: in kitchens, food and clothes depots, camp equipment, the Canada commando (sorting the belongings plundered from the Jewish victims of immediate extermination), and the auxiliary depots, including packinghouses, mess rooms, baths, the camp infirmary, offices of the Political Department, the Labor Department, camp headquarters, administration and camp expansion offices; in clothing shops (mending prisoner fatigues and the clothes of Jewish victims); and in servicing the transportation wagons. Women prisoners were also on the block staff, serving as translators and messengers.

In October 1943, women prisoners started working for the armaments firm Weichsel Union Metallwerke, which manufactured fuses for artillery shells. For one year, they had to walk to their place of work from Birkenau, and on October 1, 1944 they were moved to the women's camp established on the grounds of the extension of the main camp. By December 31, 1943, the Union employed 506 women (in two shifts), and in the following year, 1,088.

More than 1,000 women prisoners were placed in agricultural and cattle-breeding satellite camps created near Auschwitz, and over 2,000 more in similar camps in Silesia and Czechoslovakia.

Taking into account the conditions in the camp, no work performed by women prisoners was easy, nor free of harassment and brutal treatment or fear. Not all jobs, however, were equal. Particularly strenuous and exhausting was the work in camp expansion, in removing rubble, dredging and cleaning fish ponds, and a wide range of agricultural and transport jobs. Women employed in leveling houses in the town of Auschwitz and its environs often perished under avalanches of rubble.

Those who worked in the fields were harnessed to ploughshares in lieu of horses requisitioned by the army. When dredging fish ponds in all weather conditions, they waded in water often up to their necks. Women working in the out-of-camp labor squads often had to walk several kilometers to their places of work. On the way to and from work, as well as during work itself, the SS men often set dogs on the prisoners, kicked and hit them with rifle butts, even killed them. As a rule, women from the newly arrived transports were assigned to these labor squads; those unable to get transferred to other work died within a short period.

The "under the roof" jobs, especially those which offered opportunities to "organize" all kinds of material goods, above all food, offered better chances to survive the camp. Women prisoners dreamed about and went to extraordinary lengths to secure such jobs. One especially "good" job was reserved for the plant-breeding squad in Rajsk. Its prisoners, women with university degrees in agriculture and biological sciences (including graduates of the Sorbonne), were engaged in research on the possibilities of growing the rubber-yielding plant coke-sagiz. Due to the importance the Nazi authorities attached to this work, these prisoners received good treatment. However, even there several of them died.

Some jobs exacted a heavy mental price. Women, mostly Jewish, working in the depots of Canada knew what fate had befallen the recent owners of the plundered Jewish property amassed there. From their hiding places, they often watched processions of doomed Jews. Some had the misfortune of discovering articles that belonged to members of their families among the belongings of the murdered victims. Every day, women prisoners, mostly Slovak Jews, employed in the offices of the Auschwitz Gestapo branch (Political Department) came across written documents attesting to mass murder. They knew that as "carriers of the secret" their fate had been sealed. Women fertilizing fields with human ashes and filling in ponds with the same "material" were constantly aware that these were the remains of their fellow prisoners.

As the population of women prisoners increased, a considerable proportion of them remained idle. In some months in 1943, as revealed by employment rosters, only one-half, sometimes even one-third, of all women prisoners in the camp were employed. Camp living conditions rendered many women unfit for work, and the camp authorities did not have enough jobs for all the women, despite shortages of personnel. Thus, for example, of the total of 29,513 women present in the camp on December 31, 1943, only 7,777 worked and 13,470 were unemployed, whereas 8,266 women prisoners were unfit for work due to illness.

Sick women tried to get help from the camp infirmary, but only a handful saved their lives in this fashion despite the dedication of the medical and nurse staff, made up of prisoners. Subordinated to the objectives of mass murder, the infirmary became the last stage of camp existence for these women, the location of death or the place where they were sentenced to death in the course of selections performed by SS doctors.

Underground Activities

In view of the conditions prevailing in the camp, struggle for survival became the most important manifestation of resistance. It was waged with a variety of weapons: extending help to newly arrived prisoners; pointing out the most dangerous SS men, SS women supervisors, and prisoners assigned official duties; offering words of encouragement and consolation; offering an additional slice of bread or a spoonful of soup; telling "good lies," such as spreading optimistic reports; spreading rumors about the imminent liberation of the camp; concealing the facts of death of loved ones from prisoners so as to keep their hopes high, strengthen their resolve to survive, and prevent mental breakdown.

Every word of support and good will, every warm and sincere holding of hand, every smile was of incalculable importance to the haunted and despairing women, often lost and lonely among thousands of prisoners, since they restored their faith in human beings and urged them to carry on relentlessly with the struggle to survive. In every national group there were women who treated helping others as their holy duty. Thus many recipients of food parcels distributed their contents to those who could not or did not receive any. Prisoners who could "organize" anything did so constantly, with their needy neighbors in mind. Prisoners assigned to official duties played a vital part in self-help activities; since they enjoyed more opportunities than prisoners working in the camp offices, especially the employment department, they were especially important in this respect. It was they who took advantage of their positions to assign, for example, official duties to prisoners judged as courageous enough to help their fellow inmates. They tried to include endangered prisoners in outgoing transports or to strike off from the transport lists names of prisoners for whom leaving the camp was not advantageous (for example, women who worked in "good" labor squads, which increased their odds of survival).

Male prisoners who had access to the women's camp while working in artisan labor squads extended assistance to its inmates, mostly Polish women. They managed to supply some of them with medicine, food, and eagerly awaited information about husbands and sons in the men's camp. Occasionally, they even succeeded in arranging meetings beween women prisoners and their loved ones.

In barracks whose block elders could be trusted, women prisoners held meetings for prayer, discussion of current topics, or simply spending some time together in an attempt to forget, at least for a while, the surrounding reality. In the company of friends, they celebrated national anniversaries and holidays in the hope that the next ones would be celebrated after liberation.

Apart from activities of self-help, which often proved decisive for a prisoner's survival, other acts of resistance also took place in the women's camp. Before the transfer of the women's camp from Auschwitz to Birkenau, its prisoners witnessed the tragic one-person act of revolt by a young Slovak Jew whose name remains unknown, who called on them to cease working for the Germans. She was shot by an SS man and died in the infirmary.

More than 40 women prisoners made escape attempts; 16 failed. The best known was the tragic escape attempt by a Jewish girl of Polish origins, Mala Zimetbaum, who arrived at Auschwitz from Belgium together with Edward Galinski, a prisoner from the first transport, who worked in the plumbers' commando. They escaped on June 24, 1944, and for two weeks the remaining prisoners entertained hopes the two had succeeded. However, Zimetbaum and Galinski were apprehended during an attempt to cross the Slovak border, and brought back to the camp. After harsh interrogation, they were sentenced to death by hanging. Shortly before the scheduled execution, Mala managed to cut her veins and, in full view of women prisoners assembled to witness the execution, slapped the face of the SS man who was to escort her to the gallows. Under these circumstances, she was killed in the crematorium. Instead of terrorizing the prisoners, the planned public execution only succeeded in evoking their admiration for the extraordinary courage of the victim and fueled the hatred for the henchmen. Mala became a legend and symbol of heroism.

Four Jewish women—Regina Sapirsztein, Alla Gartner, Ester Weissblum, and Rosa Robota—who made fuses for artillery shells for the Union armaments company did not hestitate to supply explosives with which Sonderkommando prisoners planned to blow up the crematoria during their revolt. For their deed, the four women paid the highest price: on January 6, 1945, a few days before the evacuation of the camp, they were hanged in front of a roll call.

Seeking to document the Nazi crimes, two Polish women prisoners, Monika Galica and Antonina Piatkowska, used the book of death records to compile a list of some 7,000 Polish women prisoners who had perished in the camp between August 1942 and January 1945. Martyna Puzyna, employed as a physician-anthropologist in one of Mengele's laboratories, copied personal data and results of anthropometric measurements of 296 Jewish women, including 111 Jewish twins from Hungary. Krystyna Horczak, Vera Foltynova, and Valeria Valova, who worked in the SS-Bauleitung labor squad, stole diagrams of crematoria and gas chambers. Women prisoners employed in the camp registry office composed daily reports on the size of the prisoner population by nationality. All these documents were smuggled out of the camp through underground channels and are now at the Auschwitz-Birkenau State Museum.

The horror of the camp existence was conveyed in the poems of Krystyna Zywulska and paintings of Janina Tollik, created in the camp. They equal the smuggled documentary evidence in providing visible proof of the crimes perpetrated in Auschwitz.

Evacuation

The last stage of the horrifying ordeal of the women prisoners of Auschwitz was evacuation of the camp. From August 1944 to January 1945, more than 30,000 women were deported to camps in the German interior as part of the first phase of evacuation. On January 17, 1945, 18,672 women reported for the last roll call in Birkenau, Auschwitz, and the satellite camps. The next day, the vast majority of these women embarked on the evacuation journey, which has become known as the death march.

For sick women and those unable to keep up with the furious pace of the march, these evacuations amounted to a last ruthless selection. The evacuation routes were strewn with the bodies of women prisoners shot by escorting SS personnel or killed by their rifle butts. In Wodzislaw Slaski and Gliwice, which served as assembly points for the prisoners, the women were loaded onto open freight cars and deported, most to Bergen-Belsen and Ravensbrück, where ultimately about 10,000 women ended up. Countless women perished along the way or after arrival. Some 4,000 sick and emaciated women who had been left behind were liberated with the arrival of the Soviet Army at Auschwitz.

NOTES

This essay draws on Nazi documentary materials and related publications, especially works by Danuta Czech, Franciszek Piper, Tadeusz Iwaszko, Lechoslaw Ceba, Andrzej Strezelecki, Anna Pawelczynska, and others. I have also relied extensively on memoirs of former prisoners (Seweryna Szmaglewska, Margita Svalbova, Krystyna Justa, Krstyna Zywulska, Antonia Piatkowska, Janina Komenda, Halina Birnbaum, Jenny Spitzer, Maria Slisz-Oyrzynska, among others), as well as on numerous accounts, reminiscences, and testimonies to be found in the Auschwitz-Birkenau State Museum in the following collections: Affidavits/Declarations, Reminiscences, Trial of Höss, and Trials of Members of the Auschwitz Camp Staff.

1. *Memoirs of Rudolf Höss, Commandant of Auschwitz* (in Polish) (Krakow, 1965), p. 139.

2. Seweryna Szmaglewska, *Smoke over Birkenau* (in Polish) (Krakow, 1946), p. 16.

3. Archives of the Auschwitz-Birkenau State Museum (ASAM), collection Affidavits/Declarations, vol. 87, card 88.

4. Halina Birnbaum, *Hope Dies Last* (in Polish) (Warsaw, 1988), pp. 138, 139.

5. Szmaglewska, pp. 123–24.

6. Note by Zalman Lewenthal, in *Amidst a Nightmare of Crime* (Oswiecim, 1973), pp. 142, 146.

7. ASAM, Materials on the camp resistance movement, vol. 1, card 41, vol. 4, cards 162–66.

17

Children

HELENA KUBICA

Among the crimes that the Nazis committed against humanity, the enormity of the wrongs perpetrated against children and young people stands out in singular tragic dimension. During the Second World War, children lost their lives in many ways and in many places, but the largest number of them perished in the Nazi concentration camps and centers of mass murder.

Auschwitz, which combined both functions—extermination through work and by immediate murder—played a major part, and Jewish children deported to Auschwitz constituted the overwhelming majority of the young people who were put to death by the Nazi regime. Broadly speaking, children and juveniles were placed in the camp as victims of the Nazi plan to exterminate the Jews; as victims of the plan to isolate and exterminate Gypsies; because they cooperated or took part in the resistance movement, which spread throughout occupied Poland and the Soviet Union; because they were included in the arrest and deportation of entire families; because they were part of the civilian population deported after the outbreak of the Warsaw revolt in 1944; or because they were born in Auschwitz.

The lack of preserved and available documentation about the atrocities makes it difficult to determine the precise number of children incarcerated or murdered in Auschwitz. The Nazis went to great lengths to erase the traces of their deeds, mainly by destroying documents, particularly in the last stage of the war. As a rule, children who were unfit for work were killed immediately upon arrival without undergoing any registration; the few who were registered and put to work did not live long.

Only fragmentary information is available concerning the children prisoners. For example, employment records of prisoners in Auschwitz reveal that on April 23, 1944, there were 2,846 male children (not counting the Gypsy camp). On August 21, there were 779 boys under the age of 14. On October 2 and 3, the male and female camps in Birkenau housed 2,510 children of both sexes.

Other documents indicate that on January 10, 1945, several days before the final evacuation of the camp, there were still 940 children of both sexes under the age of 14 on the grounds of the various subcamps of Birkenau. Shortly before the liberation of the camp on January 26, 435 boys and girls still remained in one of the sections of the women's camp at Birkenau.[1]

Partially preserved documents contain only the names or camp serial numbers of over 18,000 Jewish, Gypsy, Polish, Russian, and other children and juveniles under the age of 17.[2] In general, it may be concluded that during the first stage of the camp's existence, the proportion of registered children and young people was very low. But over time their numbers grew steadily, reaching the highest level in 1944.

Jewish Children

Children of Jewish origin were deported to the camp with their families because they were Jewish. Such deportations took place under the framework of the "final solution of the Jewish question" as early as the first months of 1942. As a rule, the children were put to death in the gas chambers upon arrival.

The first transports of Jewish deportees comprised Polish Jews from Upper Silesia, mostly from Sosnowiec. Upon arrival, without undergoing any registration, they went straight to the provisory gas chambers set up in two peasant houses in Birkenau (bunkers 1 and 2), which were put into operation in the first half of 1942.

As the camp expanded and the demand for labor grew, a few transports of Jews from Slovakia and France were brought to the camp in their entirety and registered. The transports, especially the ones from Slovakia, included juveniles and even children under age 14. Partially preserved transport lists for the period from April 17 to July 17, 1942, encompassing 8,749 men— mostly Slovak Jews deported to the camp in various transports—indicate that 656 of the deportees were children (the youngest were 11 or 12 years old) and adolescents. They did not stay in the camp for long; by the first half of 1942, most of them had perished.[3]

Among the Jewish women from Slovakia were many juvenile girls. That is borne out by information in the preserved list of the first transport to

Auschwitz from Poprad on March 25, 1942, among other sources. This transport comprised 999 women, of whom 116 were 16 or 17 years old. One girl was only 14.[4]

Beginning in July 1942, Jewish transports routinely went through selection upon arrival. The young, healthy, and able-bodied men and women were selected for labor. The remaining deportees, above all children, mothers with small children, and pregnant women, were consigned to death in the gas chambers without any registration.

The total number of Jewish children deported to and murdered in Auschwitz is impossible to determine. However, one is able to shed light on the scale of the deportations by analyzing the preserved transport lists that include the ages of the deportees.

For France, the lists of names of Jews transported from the transit camp at Drancy and other localities have been preserved almost entirely. Deportation of French Jews began on March 27, 1942, and ended on August 11, 1944. A total of 71 transports comprised 69,119 persons, including at least 9,820 children and juveniles under age 17. Of these youngsters, 7,368 were under age 14. The largest number of children arrived in 1942 during July, August, and September. For example, in the August 19 transport, more than half (582) of the 1,000 deportees were children. In the August 26 transport, 553 of the 1,057 deportees were children.[5]

The lists of names of Jewish deportees from Belgium also have been preserved almost entirely. Deportations from Belgium commenced in 1942 and continued until 1944. Among the 24,906 Belgian Jews deported to Auschwitz in 27 transports, there were 4,654 children and juveniles under age 16. One example is the September 1, 1942, transport that carried 1,000 persons, of whom 344 were children. Another is the September 26, 1942, transport that carried 1,742 persons, including 523 children.[6]

Documents pertaining to the transports of Jews from Germany and Austria to Auschwitz also have been preserved.[7] Nearly all these transports were supervised by the Berlin Gestapo. Among the 20,000 deportees shipped to Auschwitz from 1942 to 1945, more than 2,500 were children and juveniles. Berlin transport 32, which departed on March 3, 1943, with 158 Jews from Norway in addition to German Jews, included 22 children under 14. (Altogether, 84 Norwegian children and juveniles under 17 lost their lives in the camp.) Austrian Jews were usually shipped to Auschwitz via the Terezin ghetto. Only 200 persons, including 15 children under age 14, traveled directly from Vienna to Auschwitz from March 3, 1943, to September 1, 1944.

Beginning in July 1942, transports of Jews from the Netherlands began arriving in large numbers, mainly via the transit camp at Westerbork. From 1942 through 1944, the total number of Jewish deportees from Holland reached about 60,000 persons in 68 transports. Of the 31,662 deportees in 36 transports analyzed statistically by the Dutch Red Cross, 4,903 were children and juveniles under age 17.[8]

No documents have been preserved that enable us to estimate the number of children brought to Auschwitz in the transports that carried Polish Jews. There is no doubt, however, that they were second in number only to the Hungarian Jews. Similarly, no documents have survived regarding the transports of Jews from Yugoslavia to Auschwitz for the period August 8, 1942, to August 21, 1944. Partially preserved camp documents indicate, however, that 63 Yugoslavian Jewish children and juveniles were registered in the camp, of whom 12 survived until liberation.

Late in 1942 and throughout 1943, numerous transports arrived from the ghetto camp at Theresienstadt, in Czechoslovakia. Initially, the deportees in these transports were treated like other Jewish deportees. After selection, most of them, including children, were gassed. However, beginning in September 1943, deportees from Terezin did not undergo any selections and were placed in the family camp that was set up in Birkenau, apparently for camouflaging purposes. In September 1943, the so-called Familienlager Theresienstadt housed about 5,000 persons, including 1,040 children and juveniles. Of this number, 760 were between two months and 14 years old.

Prisoners in the family camp were accorded better treatment than most other prisoners. In contrast to other Jewish prisoners, they did not undergo selections. In addition, the camp authorities designated two blocks for children and set up a kindergarten of sorts for the youngest and a school for the older children—an extraordinary phenomenon in the camp. The kindergarten pupils were taught songs and poems, and the older children between the ages of six and ten studied in three groups. Older boys were allowed to publish a school magazine on packing paper they managed to secure. And the camp authorities even allowed the young prisoners to organize a puppet theater and to present plays twice a week on a simple stage in the barracks. The kindergarten pupils received better food than other inmates. Their soup was cooked separately, and occasionally they received larger rations of beet marmalade, margarine, even small pieces of butter.

One transport that rolled into the camp from Terezin on October 7, 1943, was unusual. It contained 1,260 children with 53 guardians. The children were Polish Jews who had been sent to Terezin on August 24, 1943, from the Bialystok ghetto, where the SS was busy suppressing an uprising during the liquidation phase of the ghetto. The children were due to be exchanged for German prisoners of war. The exchange failed to materialize, however, and the children were sent to Auschwitz.

In September 1943, about 5,000 more Jews from the Terezin ghetto were placed in the camp, increasing the number of children and juveniles by 568 (including 467 children under age 14). Six months later, on the night of March 8–9, 1944, the family camp of Terezin Jews was partially liquidated, and 3,791 men, women, and children who had arrived on the September transports were trucked off to the Birkenau gas chambers. The final liquidation of the family camp was completed on July 11 and 12, 1944, when the remaining 7,000 Jews, including children, were murdered.

Nearly completely preserved transport lists enable us to conclude that in 1942–44, 46,099 persons were deported to Auschwitz from Terezin, including at least 6,460 children and juveniles under age 17 and 5,067 children under 14. Only a few of them survived. Others perished either immediately upon arrival or after several months.[9]

Deportation of Jews from Greece began in the middle of March 1943. Most of the transports originated in Salonika. During 1944, three transports carrying Jews originated in Athens and Rhodes. From March 15 to August 7, 1943, 48,633 Greek Jews from Salonika arrived at Auschwitz; only 11,747 of them were placed in the camp after selections were made. The remainder, who constituted nearly 80 percent of the deportees, were put to death in the gas chambers, including about 12,000 children.[10] In 1944, about 6,000 more Jews from Athens and the islands of Corfu and Rhodes were deported to Auschwitz; a considerable number of them were children.

Auschwitz-bound transports of Italian Jews also carried children. Deportation of the Jewish population from Italy began in the second half of 1943 and reached its peak in 1944. The first transport, carrying 1,030 Jews from Rome, reached Auschwitz on October 23, 1944. Aboard were 296 children and juveniles under age 17. One hundred ninety-three of the children were under 10 years old, and 20 were infants less than a year old.[11] The last transport of Italian Jews arrived on October 28, 1944. Altogether, more than 7,400 persons were deported from Italy in 1943 and 1944. Except for the first transport from Rome, no documents exist to indicate the number of children among the Jewish-Italian deportees.

In the middle of May 1944, mass deportations of Jews from Hungary to Auschwitz began. Less than two months later, about 438,000 Hungarian Jews had arrived at the camp. Mass transports of Hungarian Jews were exceptional because of the large number of children they carried. This fact has been confirmed by numerous accounts and testimonies by former prisoners, as well as by reports that members of the camp underground were able to dispatch at the time. Unfortunately, a lack of documentation precludes determining the precise number of children and juveniles who arrived in the transports of Jews from Hungary, although it is certain that they constituted a high percentage.

A great majority of the children who were on the transports from Hungary were gassed immediately upon arrival. Beginning in June 1944, some were briefly placed in the so-called transit camps (*Durchgangslager*). That occurred when entire transports were sent directly from the unloading platform to the transit camps without selections. While in the transit camps, most of the children either died owing to the harsh conditions or fell victim to selections. Only a few managed to avoid selection by creating the impression that they were fit for work. Those who did were subsequently transported with the adult prisoners to other camps in the German interior or to Auschwitz satellite camps such as Trzebinia (where a group of 100 boys ages 14 to 17 were sent), or to Jawiszowice (where several dozen boys were sent).[12]

In the second half of 1944, the Auschwitz camp began taking delivery of Jewish deportees from the liquidated labor camps in Kovno and Estonia. These Jewish deportees, who were consigned for extermination, arrived mainly via the Stutthof concentration camp. One example is a July 26, 1944, transport that carryed 524 women and 899 children.[13]

Some transports carried children exclusively. For example, one transport, which arrived in Birkenau from Dachau on August 1, 1944, carried 129 Jewish boys from Kovno ranging in age from eight to 14. Another transport from Kovno, which arrived on September 12, 1944, carried 300 Jewish children, who were put to death in the gas chambers the same day.[14]

These estimates allow us to conclude that at least 43,000 of the children and juveniles under age 17 who perished in Auschwitz had arrived in transports from France, Belgium, the Netherlands, Germany, Austria, Norway, Greece, the Terezin ghetto, Italy, and the Soviet Union. However, no figures are available that pertain to the largest groups of Jewish children—those sent to Auschwitz with their families from Hungary (438,000 persons) and Poland (300,000). Similarly, no data are available on the number of children who were among the Jewish deportees from Slovakia and Yugoslavia. But we can conclude that children and juveniles constituted roughly 20 percent of these arrivals, or 185,000.

Gypsy Children

In addition to Jews, the extermination plan put into effect by the Third Reich included Gypsies, who, in SS chief Heinrich Himmler's opinion, "should be removed from Europe as a race of little value." In December 1942, Himmler issued an order whereby nearly all the Gypsies living in the Reich and the Protectorate of Bohemia and Moravia, regardless of age or gender, should be rounded up and incarcerated in a concentration camp for the duration of the war.[15] In accordance with an executive order of January 29, 1943, the first transports of Gypsy families and their property— mainly from Germany, the Protectorate of Bohemia and Moravia, and Austria—began rolling into the BIIe sector of the Birkenau camp in February 1943.

From February 26, 1943, to July 21, 1944, nearly 21,000 men, women, and children were placed in the Gypsy family camp. This figure does not include the 1,700 Gypsies who were brought from the Bialystok region and—without undergoing registration—were gassed immediately because they were suspected of being infected with typhus. Analysis of the registration records that were kept in the Gypsy camp reveals that of the more than 20,000 Gypsies who were registered, nearly 6,000 were children under age 14, including 363 babies born in the camp.[16]

In the summer of 1943, on orders of Dr. Josef Mengele, the camp physician, one of the barracks in the Gypsy camp was designated as a nursery and another as a kindergarten of sorts. The barracks housed children under age six who were put under the care of several women prisoners. The children were divided into three groups, and each group received slightly different food. After some time, however, the special feeding arrangements were stopped. The interior of the kindergarten blocks boasted whitewashed walls decorated with colorful drawings. The SS men often photographed or filmed the children as they played in the adjacent playground.

Beginning about the end of May 1944, the Gypsy camp was gradually liquidated. It had already been seriously depopulated by inmate deaths from hunger and disease, as well as by selections of prisoners suspected of typhus. As part of the liquidation of the camp, the authorities moved a number of men, women, and children—mostly German Gypsies—to the main camp, Auschwitz I. On August 2, the surviving 1,408 persons in this group, including 105 boys ranging in age from nine to 14, were shipped to camps in the German interior. The remaining prisoners in the Gypsy camp at Birkenau—nearly 3,000 men, women, and children—were put to death in the gas chamber of crematorium V. The Gypsy camp was finally liquidated.[17]

A group of 800 Gypsy boys and girls who had been shipped to the Buchenwald concentration camp were brought back to Auschwitz on October 10, 1944, and gassed.[18]

Polish Children

The first transports of Polish deportees rolled into Auschwitz in June, July, and August 1940. They carried adults from various prisons, adults who had been rounded up on the streets, and juvenile boys, including school students and scouts. Partially preserved lists of names of the initial Polish deportees brought from Tarnow, Wisnicz, Silesia, Krakow, and Warsaw during this period reveal that at least 100 of the 3,000 prisoners were boys 14 to 17.[19]

In August 1940, the camp authorities separated some of the young prisoners from the adults. They were assigned to a special block (5) and to the bricklaying school (*Mauerschule*), which was organized specifically for them. The arrangement lasted only six months. In the spring of 1941, the school was abolished and the youngsters were assigned to various labor squads. Most of them perished shortly thereafter.

Additional transports of male prisoners included boys under age 17, and even some 13- and 14-year-olds. This fact is borne out by the partially preserved lists of prisoners who were registered upon arrival. The registry (*Zuganglisten*) contains, among other information, the prisoners' dates of birth. The lists indicate, for example, that on February 1, 1941, a transport that originated in Warsaw carried 596 prisoners, including 39 juveniles. Transports that arrived on April 5 and 7, also carried large groups of juvenile prisoners, including some 14-year-olds.[20]

The first transports of Polish women prisoners began arriving in Auschwitz in April 1942. Along with women deportees, they carried girl scouts and school students who had been arrested for collaborating with the resistance against the repressive measures the Germans were instituting against the Polish youth. On December 13, entire Polish families that had been expelled from the Zamosc region, which was designated for German settlers, started arriving from the resettlement camp in Zamosc. They arrived in three transports, on December 13 and 16, 1942, and February 5, 1943. The transports carried 1,301 persons, including at least 119 children and juveniles of both sexes.[21]

The boys met an especially tragic fate in the camp. After spending several weeks with the male prisoners on the grounds of Birkenau camp BIb, they were transferred to infirmary ward 20 in the main Auschwitz camp. There, on orders of the camp authorities, they were murdered with phenol injections. This "pinprick" operation, as the prisoners called it, did not include the girls. But they were decimated by the horrible unsanitary conditions that prevailed in Birkenau.

The next large consignment of Polish youth consisted of children and juveniles who arrived with scores of adult prisoners in the aftermath of the outbreak of the Warsaw revolt in August 1944. Four transports arrived in Auschwitz-Birkenau from the Pruszkow transit camp on August 12 and September 4, 13, and 17. Of more than 13,000 men and women from Warsaw, at least 1,400 boys and girls under age 17 were placed in the camp, including 684 children whose ages ranged from several months to 14 years.[22]

Incomplete documentation prevents us from determining with any degree of accuracy the exact number of children and juveniles who were detained in block 11 to await summary trial by the Gestapo, then sentenced to death or incarcerated in the camp.

Children from Belorussia and the Ukraine

In 1943 and 1944, Soviet children were also deported to the camp in line with Himmler's order of January 6, 1943, which said that "in the course of operations against the 'bands' [partisans], men, women, and children suspected of connections with the bands are to be collected and dispatched in assembly transport to the camp in Lublin or Auschwitz."[23]

Following Nazi Germany's attack on the Soviet Union, the Einsatzkommandos operating in the occupied eastern territories, particularly the notorious Einsatzkommando 9, rounded up entire families in the areas covered by pacification operations. The families were taken primarily from Belorussia (especially from the Minsk and Vitebsk regions) and Ukraine (especially Lwow) and deported in transports to various camps.

At least 15 transports carrying civilians from the occupied areas of the Soviet Union were sent to Auschwitz. The transports that carried the largest number of children were from Vitebsk (on September 9, October 22, and November 23, 1943) and Minsk (on December 4, 1943).

Soviet children also arrived in Auschwitz in evacuation transports from Majdanek in April 1944 and from the Stutthof concentration camp. In some cases, juvenile prisoners ranging in age from 11 to 17 were among the Soviet prisoners of war who were sent to the POW camp that existed at Auschwitz from October 7, 1941, to March 1, 1942. In addition, an undetermined number of Soviet children arrived with adult prisoners in assembly transports that originated in various regions of the Third Reich.

A lack of documents precludes determining the precise number of Soviet children who were sent to Auschwitz. But taking into account only the four transports from Vitebsk and Minsk, for which partial estimates are available, we may conclude that the transports carried at least 900 children and juveniles.[24]

Children Born in the Camp

After the camp for women was established in Auschwitz on March 26, 1942, many women who were pregnant when they arrived in the camp gave birth there. Unfortunately, the precise number of children born in the camp cannot be determined, because not all births were recorded in the camp registration books.

During the early period of the women's camp, probably up to mid-1943, children born in the camp were not registered at all. Newborns were killed either by injecting them with phenol or by drowning. Others died after several days because of malnutrition, disease, or the cold. The privilege of keeping newborn children was first granted to Gypsy women when the family camp was established. In the women's camp, the practice of killing non-Jewish babies was discontinued in June 1943. Nonetheless, most newborns died of malnutrition or from the unsanitary and primitive hygienic conditions soon after birth.

Many infants were classified by SS doctors as suitable for Germanization in accordance with the established racial criteria. Such children did not undergo registration. Rather, they were separated from their mothers, quarantined for preliminary anthropological examinations, then dispatched to the branches of the Resettlement Bureau in Lodz, Naklo, or Potulice, or to the centers of Lebensborn, an organization that dealt with the Germanization of children.[25]

The few children who managed to survive for longer periods were registered as "newly arrived" and were assigned camp serial numbers. In most cases, their numbers were tattooed on their thighs or buttocks. When a birth occurred, the Camp Registry Office (Standesamt II) would be notified, and the place of birth would be recorded as "Auschwitz-Kassernstrasse."[26] Available camp documents reveal that the first camp serial number was assigned to a baby in the women's camp on September 18, 1943.[27]

Children born to Jewish prisoners in the women's camp were not registered but were killed immediately. Even though all the women prisoner-physicians, midwives, and nurses maintained that the largest number of births occurred among Jewish women, only eight births to Jewish women were recorded. Preserved camp documents indicate that the first Jewish newborn was recorded and registered on February 21, 1944.

Camp documents for 1943–45 and documentation from the campaign to aid released prisoners contain records of only 650 children born in the women's camp and the Gypsy family camp.[28] This figure does not include Jewish children born in the so-called *Durchganglagere*, because, apart from accounts of former women prisoners, no relevant documents have been preserved.

Living Conditions

The fate of children and adolescents incarcerated in the Auschwitz camp, especially in the years 1940–43, did not differ much from that of adult prisoners. Boys and girls, regardless of whether they were Jewish or not, were placed together with adults and assigned primarily to the labor force. Teenage boys were put to work in coal mines, in road construction, and in removing rubble. They also worked in the camp at physically demanding jobs. In the men's camp in Birkenau, boys were harnessed to heavy wagons, called *Rolwagen*, in place of horses. In the women's camp, teenagers, even girls under 14, worked in agricultural labor squads.

In addition to exhausting work, which was frequently beyond the physical abilities of the malnourished teenagers, the boys and girls were often subjected to brutal treatment, ingenious tortures, and punishments for even the smallest offenses. They were sentenced to penal labor squads, incarcerated in the bunkers of block 11 ("death row"), even executed by shooting. Among the inmates incarcerated in the camp prison were 58 boys under age 17, including a 13-year-old Jewish prisoner, Hirsh Jablonski, who was executed by shooting in May 1943 under orders from the camp Gestapo.[29]

One of the severest forms of punishment involved hanging the offender from a post for several hours with his hands twisted behind his back. This punishment was applied to juvenile as well as adult prisoners. A 16-year-old Pole, Czeslaw Kempisty, was punished in this fashion for throwing several turnips, which he was unloading from a wagon, to famished Soviet prisoners of war as they passed by on their way to work.

In addition to official punishments, juvenile prisoners of both sexes were exposed to beatings and other kinds of brutal treatment by the camp functionaries of the SS and by sadistic fellow prisoners. One 17-year-old Jewish prisoner from Hungary, Benkel Faivel, was shot in the head by an SS man for trying to pass a piece of bread to a woman prisoner. A 13-year-old Jew, Halina Grynstein, was shot in the shoulder for approaching the camp fence to exchange words with another woman prisoner.

The middle of 1943 brough a change in the treatment of non-Jewish children. While Jewish children continued to be ruthlessly murdered in the gas chambers upon their arrival in the mass transports, children of non-Jewish origin, who were either born in the camp or deported there, were registered and allowed to live. However, their life expectancy was very short because of the living conditions.

With the influx of transports of civilians from the occupied territories of the Soviet Union, especially from September 1943 on, large numbers of children were assigned to the women's camp in Birkenau. Children over three years of age were separated from their mothers and assigned to two separate blocks in the BIa section. Smaller children were allowed to remain with their mothers.

Inmates of the children's blocks were gradually shipped out in transports to Lodz or Potulice for Germanization. In early November 1943, as many as 542 children were sent to the resettlement camp at Potulice.[30] Very few Russian children remained in the camp. Those children who did remain fell victim to disease and died due to the unsanitary living conditions. Although the children were assigned to special blocks, living conditions were no better than in other parts of the camp.

In the second half of 1944, a large number of Polish children arrived in transports with civilian adults from Warsaw. Girls from age two to 16 and boys under nine were separated from their mothers and put in a separate block on the grounds of the women's camp. The older boys were sent to the male prisoners' camp, where they were assigned to rooms.

The children's diet did not differ much from that of adult prisoners. They were rationed black coffee or herb extract, black bread with margarine, turnip soup, and unpeeled boiled potatoes. Only the smaller children received thin slices of white bread and tiny pieces of butter. By not allocating milk or nourishing meals for infants, the camp authorities in effect condemned them to death by hunger.

Children in the camp sick room and those subjected to criminal medical experiments enjoyed somewhat better living conditions and nourishment. Jewish twins, midgets, and children afflicted with physical abnormalities were selected from the transports consigned to destruction and placed at the disposal of doctors—especially Josef Mengele—as material for medical experiments. They too were placed in special barracks, and in the second half of 1944 constituted the second largest group of children in the camp. They were not put to work but remained in the exclusive care of Mengele.

Twins were not the only children subjected to criminal experiments. Teenage Jewish girls were sterilized and boys were castrated. Experiments conducted on Polish and Russian children involved putting drops of an unknown liquid into their eyes, which caused them to redden, swell, and suppurate. In some cases the experiments resulted in partial or complete loss of sight. Among the babies, it almost always meant death.

Medical experiments also were conducted on the Auschwitz children after they were transferred to other camps. For example, in December 1944, a group of 20 Jewish children ranging in age from five to 12 were transferred from Birkenau to the Neuengamme concentration camp, where they served as guinea pigs for SS doctor Kurt Heissmeyer in his research on tuberculosis. Toward the end of the war, on April 20, 1945, they were murdered by hanging from heating pipes in a school on Bullenhuserdamm Street, in Hamburg.[31]

The most common diseases among the children were pneumonia, starvation-induced diarrhea, extensive ulceration, scabies, scarlet fever, diphtheria, and measles. The most devastating were typhoid fever, typhus, and tuberculosis. Many Gypsy children suffered from ascites, caused by starvation. Mengele evinced special interest in the disease and even assigned one block for patients with ascites on whom he conducted experiments—usually ending in death.[32]

Although many of the children died from disease and starvation, the main reason for their high mortality rate was direct extermination in the gas chambers. Until November 1944, when gassing was discontinued, Jewish children faced the constant danger of being selected and sent to the gas chambers with the sick and emaciated adult prisoners. When selecting children for gassing, the German doctors not only took into account their health and degree of emaciation but also their height.[33]

The method of killing by phenol injections into the heart was used on Jewish and non-Jewish children, especially before the gas chambers were put into operation. Later, murder by injection was used mainly on Jewish and Gypsy children subjected to medical experiments.

The extermination of children prisoners, as well as the mass transfers to other camps, especially when the camp was being gradually evacuated, left few children survivors on the day of liberation. After the last evacuation transports had departed, the children who remained in the camp with the sick prisoners and those who were unfit for marching were assembled in the women's camp by the prisoner medical staff. Former prisoner Stanislawa Jankowska made notes that indicate that on January 26, 1945 (one day before the liberation of the camp), 435 children and juveniles of both sexes remained in the camp.[34]

The children who were liberated from Auschwitz-Birkenau were extremely emaciated. The older children who had been put to work suffered from frostbitten extremities. Most of them were transferred to Soviet field hospitals, which were set up on the grounds of the former main camp, or to the camp hospital of the Polish Red Cross directed by Dr. Jozef Bellert.

After examining a group of 180 children, ranging in age from six months to 14 years, a judicial-medical commission determined that most of them suffered from diseases that they had contracted in the camp. Sixty percent were afflicted with vitamin deficiency and emaciation; 40 percent suffered from tuberculosis. The children had lost between 5 kg and 17 kg of weight, a staggering figure considering that they had arrived there in the second half of 1944 and stayed in the camp for only three to six months.[35] Most of the survivors were Jewish children who had been subjected to medical experiments and children from Warsaw.

But liberation did not necessarily mean an end to the children's suffering. Not all of them could return to their homes and resume normal life. Many of their parents either had perished in Auschwitz or were still incarcerated in other camps in the Third Reich to which they had been transferred in evacuation transports. In most cases, the youngest children did not know who they were or their place of birth.

In addition to having lost their parents and homes, many children sustained permanent health disabilities. They left the camp in states of extreme physical and psychological deprivation. Instead of continuing their studies like their luckier peers, they had to recuperate. Many spent years in hospitals, in sanatoria, or at home and handicapped. Incarceration in the camp left many of them with permanent neuroses or with tuberculosis, anemia, or circulatory, respiratory, or kidney disease. The incidence of health disabilities among former child prisoners was five times higher than that of their peers who had not gone through the hell of Auschwitz. This fact brings into sharp relief the devastating effects that the camps had on the children who were lucky enough to survive them.

NOTES

1. Archives of the Auschwitz-Birkenau State Museum (ASAM), call no. D-Au-4/20, inventory no. 155087, file 25—miscellaneous; collection Recollections, vol. 61a, card 19.

2. These documents include incomplete lists of names of new arrivals (*Zugangsliste*) in non-Jewish and Jewish transports; daily prisoner inventory books in the male camp for January 19 to August 19, 1942; main inventory books of the Gypsy camp—men and women; numerical and name files of Auschwitz-Birkenau prisoners—in ASAM; materials "UWZ Potulice"; daily employment records of male and female prisoners in Auschwitz II-Birkenau; personal records of prisoners (*Personalbogen*); the death certificates book (*Sterbebuch Band*); the numerical file of male prisoners (*Nummerbuch*); files of the Soviet Commission for Investigation of German Crimes in the Auschwitz Concentration Camp, as well as materials of the Polish Red Cross concerning liberated prisoners; materials of the camp resistance movement; testimonies and affidavits of former prisoners—in ASAM; list of names of prisoners of the subcamp at Trzebinia; lists of names of transports from Theresienstadt to Auschwitz; Auschwitz-Birkenau, *KL Koncentracijske taborisce: Collective Study* (Maribor, 1982), photocopies in ASAM.

3. ASAM, call no. O-AuI-2, vol. 1, 2—transport lists of Jews, April 17–July 17, 1942.

4. ASAM, call no. RSHA-3/128, inventory no. 155590.

5. ASAM, call no. D-RF-3/1–74, vol. 1–26—lists of transports from Drancy.

6. Serge Klarsfeld, *Maxime Steinberg: Memorial de la déportation des Juifs de Belgique* (Brussels, 1982), pp. 22–23.

7. ASAM, call no. D-RF-3/121/1–16—Berlin Gestapo, Auschwitz-Transporte; call no. D-RF-3/119/1—Gestapo-Transportlisten, Auschwitz–Transporte.

8. ASAM, collection Studies, vol. 26, transports of Jews from the Netherlands to Auschwitz.

9. ASAM, call no. D-RF-3/84 to 87, vol. 1–27—photocopies of transport lists of Jews from the Terezin ghetto to Auschwitz in 1942–44. The roster of children and juveniles remains incomplete, since some photocopies are practically illegible. As a result, it is impossible to determine how many children and juveniles were in the group of 5,499 persons.

10. Danuta Czech, "Deportation and Extermination of Greek Jews in the Auschwitz Concentration Camp" (in Polish), *Zeszyty Oswiecimskie*, 1969, no. 11, pp. 16–22. Miriam Novitch, "The Fate of Jewish Children in Greece" (in Polish), in

Children and Juveniles in the Second World War (Warsaw, 1982), p. 81.

11. Liliana Picciotto Fargin, *L'occupazione tedesca e qli ebrei di Roma* (Milan, 1979), pp. 43–73.

12. ASAM, collection Trzebinia, microfilm no. 1340/7,8,9; collection Brzeszcze, file I, card 218.

13. Archives of the Stutthof Museum (ASM), collection Commandant's Orders, call no. I-I-i, no. 49.

14. ASAM, Materials of the camp resistance movement, vol. 7, card 460; see also ASM, microfilm call no. 264—photocopy of a cable from the Stutthof commandant, P. W. Hoppe, to SS-WVHA, and call no. 1-II-14—prisoner registry book.

15. Bulletin of the Main Commission for the Investigation of Nazi Crimes in Poland (Warsaw, 1952), vol. 7, p. 163.

16. ASAM, call no. D-AuII-3/1/1, D-AuII-3/2/1—Ledger of the male and female Gypsy camp, call no. D-AuI-3a, vol. 6—Stärkemeldung AuII-FKL—dates July 17 and 28, 1944.

17. ASAM, collection Höss Trial, vol. 1, card 26; vol. 5, card 31; vol. 6, card 43.

18. Note of Zalman Lewenthal, in *Amidst a Nightmare of Crime* (in Polish) (Oswiecim, 1973), p. 193.

19. Irena Strzelecka, "First Poles in Auschwitz" (in Polish), *Zeszyty Oswiecimskie*, 1983, no. 18, pp. 69–144; ASAM, Numerical records of the Polish Red Cross, inventory number 1507.

20. ASAM, collection Zugangsliste, vols. 1–5. Lists of newly arrived prisoners for the period January 7 to December 22, 1941.

21. Computations on the basis of documents and materials in ASAM.

22. ASAM, call no. D-RO/92, vol. 8a—Numerical inventory of men sent from Warsaw to Auschwitz after the outbreak of armed uprising, compiled clandestinely by prisoners in the camp; call no. D-R0/93, vol. 8b—an incomplete list of names of women sent to the camp from Warsaw after the outbreak of the uprising.

23. Nuremberg document NO-2031.

24. ASAM, call no. Mat/1345, vol. 108c, cards 131 to 150—Inventory of Soviet children brought to the camp in 1943 from Vitebsk and Minsk.

25. Lebensborn, established on December 12, 1935, on the initiative of Himmler, was entrusted with, among other things, the task of Germanization of children from the east. This mission was assigned to this institution in executive order no. 67/I of the Reichskommissar for the Consolidation of Germanhood, of February 19, 1942. Lebensborn placed children with foster families and special institutions, arranged adoptions, issued testimonials and false birth certificates, changed first and family names, and ran its own registration office.

26. ASAM, collection Geburtsurkunde, call no. D-AuI-2/1,2,3.

27. ASAM, collection Resistance Movement Materials, vol. 20b, c—Transport lists for men and women compiled clandestinely by men and women prisoners on the basis of the Zugangsliste.

28. According to accounts and recollections of former women prisoners who served on the staff of the camp sick room, the number of births was much larger.

29. "Reproduction of the 'Bunker Book,'" *Zeszyty Oswiecimskie*, 1957, no. 1.

30. ASAM, collection Files of the Resettlement Bureau—the Potulice Camp (UWZ Lager-Potulitz), call no. IZ-2/1–5, vol. 1; IZ-2/5–8, vol. 1a.

31. Gunther Schwarberg, *Der SS-Arzt und die Kinder* (Hamburg, 1979).

32. ASAM, call no. Hygiene Institute, file 41, microfiche no. 1143/69.

33. ASAM, collection Statements, vol. 117, cards 7–8.

34. ASAM, collection Reminiscences, vol. 61a.

35. ASAM, call no. IZ (Inne Zespoly—other collections), 1/3, cards 39–42, expert opinion issued by the Special Commission of the Investigation of Nazi Crimes in Poland.

18

The Family Camp

NILI KEREN

One of the most extraordinary phenomena of the implementation of the Nazi "final solution" in death camps was a special family camp established in September 1943 for prisoners who had been brought to Auschwitz-Birkenau from Theresienstadt. These 5,000 Jewish prisoners were spared the customary selection process and the subsequent extermination of those "unfit for work." Instead, the newly arrived were placed in a separate camp, designated BIIb, located not far from the main entrance gate. They were allowed to keep their civilian clothes, their hair was not cut, and women, men, and children were allowed to remain together. Although the "camp elder" (*Lageralteste*) was a German criminal prisoner, all other official duties remained in the hands of Jewish prisoners. Living conditions in this camp, however, were as bad as in others, and about 1,000 died during the first six months.

In December 1943, another transport of 5,000 Jews arrived from Theresienstadt; their reception and living conditions afterward were identical to those of the first transport. No one knew why Theresienstadt prisoners were accorded privileged treatment and assigned to a separate camp. Most believed that their fate would also be different.

On March 7, 1944, exactly six months after the arrival of the first transport to Birkenau, the "special" prisoners were taken together to the gas chambers and murdered during the night, without undergoing selection. Shortly before they were gassed, the victims were directed to send postcards to relatives who had stayed behind in Theresienstadt and in other places; the postcards were dated March 25, i.e., two weeks after their senders were no longer among the living.

Two more transports from Theresienstadt joined the surviving remnants of the December transport. By that time it had become clear that each transport was assigned a life expectancy of six months, since names of all prisoners were annotated with the symbol SB6, i.e., "special treatment (*Sonderbehandlung*) after six months." In keeping with this directive, in July 1944, six months after the arrival of the December transport, its prisoners were gassed; this time, however, the inmates went through a selection, and the entire camp was liquidated.

The "family camp" at Birkenau lasted only ten months. Having fulfilled its mission, it was liquidated. What then was the purpose behind the camp's existence? Documents and correspondence between the International Red Cross and Adolf Eichmann's office[1] indicate that the Germans established the camp to refute reports of mass extermination of Jews by offering "proof" to the contrary. The Nazis organized visits of Red Cross delegations to Theresienstadt, produced postcards sent from Birkenau to relatives in various places, and planned for a visit by a Red Cross delegation to Birkenau as part of their deception plan. The Jewish inmates of BIIb were held as living proof that reports about Auschwitz had been without foundation.[2]

The Red Cross delegation visited Theresienstadt on June 23, 1944, and was scheduled to go on to Birkenau. However, Red Cross officials were satisfied with the first part of their inspection; their hosts convinced them that Theresienstadt was the final destination and no transports departed from there. Certain that Red Cross officials were convinced about the purpose of Theresienstadt, the Nazis no longer needed the family camp and therefore could proceed with liquidating the entire camp in July.[3]

Only a handful of the September transport prisoners survived. Testimony about the first days of the camp was given by survivors of the subsequent transports. No one had known the destination. The horror of travel in cramped cattle cars and their arrival in the camp in the middle of the night left the prisoners profoundly shaken—an experience described in numerous accounts. New prisoners were marched off, whereas the elderly and the weak remained by the roadside. Disinfection, registration, tattooing of numbers, and encounters with "old-timers" increased the prevailing confusion and disorientation.

Inside the wooden barracks that served as the family camp, where they first experienced the congested bare bunks, the reality of their destination slowly dawned on the new arrivals. Several weeks later, rumors about gas chambers and ovens would become a fixture in their consciousness. For the time being, however, this information did not bear on their fate; they soon became accustomed to the daily routine of roll calls and punishments, hunger and deprivation.

The new prisoners grew emaciated; their behavior changed gradually, so that, as we learn from the testimony of a prisoner who arrived in the next transport,

> These people had changed completely their behavior. We had known each other, we had been friends, after all, and one of them had become Blockalteste, a person in charge of a block with 400 people or more. Someone approached him as a friend, but he told him: "We don't play games here," and started making a speech: "You've come to a place from which you will not return." The people we had known became unrecognizable. Those I had known as civilized persons, behaved like savages, and it was difficult to explain the change that had come over them. . . .[4]

> This young man from the first transport beat up his friend's father for a trivial reason. Was it because he broke ranks, or did not manage to fix his shoes as required . . . to think that both were movement members. . . .[5]

Among the prisoners of the September 1943 transport was Freddy Hirsch, a widely admired educator from Theresienstadt. As part of his efforts to improve the living conditions of children, he was among the first to be sent to Birkenau, which gave rise to many questions. Most testimonies and other accounts state that Hirsch was sent to Birkenau as punishment for violating the Nazi ban against ghetto inmates entering the special camp established for the children from Bialystok brought to Theresienstadt in the summer of 1943. While this may have been the official reason behind his inclusion in the September transport, it may not have been the only reason.[6] If the Reich Main Security Office did, in fact, plan to establish a special family camp for Czech Jews from Theresienstadt to display to Red Cross representatives, it needed people such as Freddy Hirsch to help stage the "show."

Although Hirsch could not have been aware of the Nazi plans, it would have been typical of him to use his assigned post to improve life for children who arrived in Birkenau. Special conditions in the camp, especially the presence of parents, siblings, and other relatives, did not deceive him, and he had a good idea of the fate in store for camp inmates. The Germans appointed him head of the children's block, a position he exploited to continue the work he had performed in Theresienstadt, caring for and educating hundreds of children who found themselves in Birkenau. Although no Nazi document refers to the exceptional treatment of the Jewish children in the family camp, the intent behind the decision to set up the facility indicates that the Germans were keenly interested in meeting Hirsch halfway.

Hirsch sought to create for the children a separate block which would function as a social-educational-treatment facility, modeled after the "children's house" in Theresienstadt. Block 31 was assigned for this purpose, and Hirsch was allowed to take under his care children under 14. Nazi authorities encouraged activities for children in this block and took steps to improve their diet. The children received more nourishing soup, which often contained such delicacies as meat. They received larger bread rations, sugar and jam, and occasionally such prizes as white bread and milk. To prisoners from other camps in Birkenau who chanced to enter the family camp, the entire spectacle would have appeared bizarre and puzzling, since there were practically no other Jewish children in Birkenau except for those selected by Josef Mengele for his medical experiments or those who had lied about their age to get into the camp with their parents. Moreover, the sight of children with unshaven heads who wore "civilian" clothes was practically unprecedented in the camp. All this was taking place when starvation and the mortality rate increased each week among adult prisoners in the family camp.

Organization of the Children's Block

Hirsch served as the "block elder" of the children's block. He appointed staff for teaching as well as guidance and treatment. Even though the Nazis set 14 as the maximum age, Hirsch managed to bring in older boys and girls under various pretenses to work as assistants, messengers, and so on. He also increased the number of workers in the block, since he knew that living conditions under his management were better than those in other sections of the camp where prisoners were put to back-breaking work. He attempted to recruit workers with previous experience with children; everyone deemed capable of constructive and sustained educational work was recruited to the children's block.

Hirsch chose as headmistress Miriam Edelstein, wife of Jacob Edelstein, the elder of Jews in Theresienstadt, who had been sent to Birkenau with his fellow inmates but was kept apart from other Czech Jews. Miriam and her son Arieh ended up in the family camp. Hanka Epstein served as Hirsch's deputy.

No available testimony provides the precise number of the children in block 31. However, on the basis of the existing materials, we can assume that during the day about 500 children remained in the block.

Needless to say, the children's block was not built especially for this purpose. It was an ordinary camp living block, divided into sections by wooden bunks which were usually designated for sleeping. The children were divided into small groups, mostly by age, and each group occupied one such section, which also doubled as a classroom. The block operated from early morning until evening. At night, children stayed with their fathers or mothers, according to gender. They ate their meals in the block. Being in the children's block did not exempt them from roll call. However, unlike the adult prisoners, who reported for roll call twice a day in front of their barracks in all weather conditions, often for long hours, the children were allowed to report inside their block, a comparative luxury in the camp.

Hirsch refrained from scheduling obligatory educational programs, since the staff was not provided with any means to carry out regular schooling or other educational activities. There was no reason to make plans in advance. Yet the staff worked with a single purpose, to hide from their charges the reality of Birkenau: mass killings in gas chambers. The children's block was located close to the main entrance, far from the gas chambers and ovens at the other end of the camp. The truth gradually reached the prisoners of the family camp, especially since the smoke and the stench of burning bodies could not be concealed. The best the teaching staff could do was to keep these subjects off the daily agenda of the children. Given the privileged conditions in the children's block, the task of maintaining an illusion about their fate was somewhat easier.

The educational staff sought to uphold the humanity of their charges and to shield them from the gruesome realities faced by ordinary prisoners. Thus they made a tremendous effort to ensure that the morning ablutions would take place, even when the coldest winter days froze the water in the pipes, and tried to obtain clothes for the children that would lend a semblance of normality to their life. As one prisoner wrote,

> Shivering with cold, they made their way to the washing rooms. The cold was so fierce (minus 30 degrees C) that the puddles in the passage had turned into sheets of ice which broke under the children's soles. They took off their upper clothes and washed in the foul water which gave off such a powerful stench that the SS men were prohibited to use it for washing their eating utensils. The night's freezing temperatures covered the faucets with white frost. The children kept moving their arms and dried themselves with a single towel which all of them shared. . . [7]

Hirsch held physical activities in high regard; he himself had engaged in sports at the Ha-Gibor (youth sports movement) stadium in Prague and later in Theresienstadt. During his term as director of the children's block, and later, the teachers frequently organized sports activities for the children, including gymnastics, games, even soccer and handball competitions. To try to maintain physical and mental health in the heart of the Birkenau death camp was the goal pursued.

Daily Routine in the Children's Block

The children would arrive at block 31 early in the morning. Their breakfast was brought by children carrying pots and crates of food.[8] Accompanied by their guardians, they would wash and perform morning calisthenics, then receive their first meal of the day.

Afterward, they went to their groups. Each group with its teachers and guardians went to its designated section of the block to spend three hours studying. In the afternoon, three more hours were devoted to sports activities and games until roll call. After roll call and supper, the children were allowed to visit their parents, and they remained with their families for the rest of the night.

Daily routine in the children's block was not rigorously adhered to. Children were permitted to spend time with their parents, even at the expense of curricular activities. In any event, this was not a frequent occurrence until March 1944, when the September transport was put to death. Afterward, children had less trust, their mood grew gloomier, and they sought to spend more time with their parents. At that time the children had their own lodgings, which probably prompted them to seek the company of their parents even at the expense of peer activities. As one prisoner stated later,

> We would wander around the camp, and met adults, not like in Theresienstadt. I spent long periods of time at my mother's bed. She told me a great deal about the house in Prague, made me remember our address, and revealed to me that some of our belongings had been stored with our neighbor in Prague. We talked a lot how we would all get together again and go back home. Our guardians did not prevent us from staying with our parents; they even let us skip classes. . . .[9]

Children's Studies at Birkenau

Educators and guardians, some of whom had already worked with children in Theresienstadt, taught the pupils in block 31 without the aid of books or notebooks. Their most important assets were memory, imagination, and the gift to tell stories and organize quizzes and games.

As a rule, every person on the staff who wanted to teach some subject, be it history, Judaic studies, or geography, had to make do without books, relying on memory only. Whether or not the class turned out to be a success depended largely, of course, on the instructor's talent and ability to impose discipline on the group. It must be kept in mind that each group sat on wooden bunks arranged in a circle around the teacher, and next to it sat another group. Thus each group listened to at least three lectures: one of its own instructor, and two from the instructors who taught their groups on both sides.[10] One prisoner stated later:

> I remember Otto Kraus . . . who used to sit, and he was a person who knew how to tell stories, he sat among us and told us the contents of a book, but not the way some people who relate one book in a quarter of an hour. With him it took hours. These classes have etched themselves so deeply on my mind, that even now I am not sure whether I heard it or read it. . . . Avi Fisher was also like that. He was in charge of a group of pupils, and told them stories. We listened. He too was a man who knew how to tell stories. . . .[11]

Every teacher tried to enrich the children's minds with information from his or her own special field of knowledge. Avi Fisher, who was interested in astronomy and history, described fascinating phenomena in the realm of astronomy and outer space to the children. He also told them stories about faraway countries and related historical events. The children liked his descriptions of prewar life in summer camps during the school vacations. The older children could remember this experience from before the war, whereas the younger ones were given the opportunity to daydream about a life they hoped to experience in the future. Teachers often switched their study groups; this was nicknamed "library book replacement," since each teacher served as a living book of sorts, and the children would borrow a different "book" from time to time. Thus it was possible to diversify the curriculum by changing the stories and descriptions.[12]

Despite overwhelming odds, eight books found their way to the children's block, including H. G. Wells's *Brief History of the World*, a Russian language textbook, and an analytical geometry text. Fisher used the geometry book to divert the children's attention by making them solve mathematical problems during crises.[13] Every evening the books were locked in the room of the block elder, together with other valuables, such as medicines. These priceless objects were put in the care of one of the assistants, Ditta Polkova, who would hide them in a different place every night, according to a schedule prepared in advance. Ditta was one of the teenagers over 14 whom Hirsch kept in the block to assist the teaching staff, thereby exempting them from the forced labor required of other prisoners.

One girl pupil was a gifted painter. Before long, she was given permission to paint on the walls of the block and even issued appropriate materials for this purpose, with the approval of Dr. Mengele. As one prisoner noted, "She started off by painting grass and greenery on the block's wall, and soon enough the entire wall turned into a window into another world. She attended to every detail in her painting which turned out to be simple but very clear." The grass kept growing and spreading every day. When the children arrived at the kindergarten, they stopped in front of the painted wall and started counting the daisies and bell-flowers above their heads.[14] The girl went on to paint other walls with motifs from children's tales, including Snow White and the Seven Dwarfs, which was staged as a play by the children.

Avi Fisher, Otto Kraus, and the rest of the staff knew they must find as many interesting and diverting ways as possible to engage the children's attention during long hours of the day. These included songs and games which could be played without disturbing other study groups occupying the same block. They invented a word play game which opened with a sentence, usually taken from a textbook or a story told to the children, who were expected then to fill in a missing word; this prompted them to remember words, places, and names of animals and plants tha. the youngest children had never had the opportunity to see.

The children were not always willing to go back to study after lunch. Fisher solved the problem by mounting a brick chimney located in the middle of the block and leading the group in singing. The children liked his comic talents enormously, and soon he would be surrounded by a crowd of children who sat on the floor. The song they liked most was the French children's song "Alouette." Not a mere song, it involved a whole game of movement. The singing was active, loud, even screaming, and very joyous. Fisher directed with his hands, while someone would beat the rhythm on a piece of tin. Engrossed in the song, the children could forget the time, the place, and the suffering in their lives. "Alouette" was followed by Czech folk songs. All the children became one voice; they sang like people who were alive. As Fisher recounter later,

> Once in a while a kapo, or a prisoner [who was a] skilled worker from one of the men's blocks, or an SS guard wandered onto the scene. They did not understand the words, but clapped their hands along with the others all the same. Most of the children had been born in Czechoslovakia, but even those whose mother tongue was Dutch or German learned the Czech songs and knew both the melody and the lyrics. On such occasions, the barracks became a safe ship sailing through the vast spaces of the ocean, and the scent of home rose from the singing.[15]

As part of these extracurricular activities, the children staged a play entitled "Five Minutes in the Robinson's Kingdom," a local paraphrase of the story of Robinson Crusoe. The play was written by one of the teachers, Jirzi Frenkel. In addition to the two main characters, Robinson Crusoe and Friday, children played the sailors and monkeys who climbed an improvised palm tree.[16]

In early March 1944, the September transport had been six months in the family camp. All those included in this transport were ordered to report for transfer to another camp. The prisoners harbored hopes that they would be removed from Birkenau. First, they were transferred to a nearby camp for quarantine. While they waited, a number of prisoners who belonged to the international underground active in Birkenau learned that thousands of Czech Jews were scheduled to be killed in the gas chambers on March 7. At this stage, a few Czech prisoners enjoyed relative freedom of movement between various camps, and they had helped organize the underground network. Among those consigned to perdition, eyes were turned toward Freddy Hirsch. When approached with a request that he lead the underground action and resistance of the prisoners of the September transport, his first reply was: what would happen to the children? He agonized over the possibility that a decision to revolt might send his charges to certain death. He asked for time to think. He went into seclusion, and while there he took his life, apparently by poisoning his own food.

On March 7, 1944, without any official warning, all prisoners of the September transport were loaded onto trucks which, instead of driving out of the gates of Birkenau, traveled straight to crematorium III, where all the victims were gassed.

Before his departure from the family camp, Hirsch had transferred his duties in the children's block to Josef Lichtenstein.[17] Honze Bremer (Dov Barnea) became his deputy. The staff members who had been murdered in the gas chambers were replaced by other educators and teachers from the December transport, whose life expectancy was already known—six months from the time of their arrival in Birkenau.

Lichtenstein and his staff attempted to restore a semblance of routine to the life of the remaining children. They accomplished this task to some extent, despite the gaping hole left by the death of pupils and teachers, and above all of Hirsch, who had been adored by the children. The activities followed the established pattern: studies, games, singing, and spectacles. One of the most memorable events was the Passover Seder organized in block 31 in April 1944. Since the children and most of the staff were not familiar with the rules of the ceremony, they improvised in order to suffuse the event with a traditional aura. The children were told the story of Exodus, of the crossing of the Red Sea and leaving the house of bondage to freedom. It was clear that the story cast a spell over them. Ota Kraus taught them the "four questions" (sung during the Passover Seder), which they sang with enthusiasm. As Kraus wrote in his diary,

> They did not observe all the rules of the ceremony as prescribed by the traditions. The Seder itself took place in the afternoon, with ersatz matzot and wine.

The Passover plate was passed from hand to hand, binding all the groups together. True, they drank tea instead of wine, and certainly no prescribed leg joint. But despite everything, even though they lived in the world of fantasy, it was an original Passover Seder. . . .

As long as they believed in miracles, not everything had yet been lost. Afterward, an improvised children's choir sang the song about happiness and freedom from the Ninth Symphony of Beethoven. All the block's residents joined the song. Over three hundred children and adults sang together "All men are brothers."[18]

According to testimonies, the sound of the song reached the ears of Dr. Mengele, who had arrived at the block. He knew the melody and the words but had no idea that the singers were celebrating Passover. When he entered, everybody fell silent. Mengele nodded his head at Lichtenstein, implying that the singing could continue. That night, April 7, a Czech prisoner named Slavek Lederer escaped from the camp to freedom.[19]

Children and the Realities of the Camp

The staff in the children's block sought to reduce the children's contact with the prisoners whose appearance and conduct bore the indelible marks of their experience in the camp. Most prisoners were prepared to do anything for additional food, clothing, shoes, cigarettes, or other articles which could provide them with relief, or at least an illusion of relief, from the condition of constant hunger and deprivation. The staff believed that by occupying the children with studies and social and sports activities during the day, they would succeed in making them forget the smoke billowing from the smokestacks and the long columns of prisoners streaming incessantly into Birkenau. The staff was aware that the children moved about in the camp, spent nights in their parents' barracks, and met with other prisoners, which exposed them to the realities of the camp. But they carried on with their efforts.

Early on, the staff decided to refrain from using words such as *smokestack* and *gas* in their conversations and to suppress all reports or knowledge of these subjects. However, this proved to be too much to bear. The educators and teachers found themselves unable to refrain from discussing these issues among themselves, and the children overheard conversations in their parents' barracks.

About a month following the liquidation of the September transport, a boy, aged 11, named Stiepan, staged a skit, which he had written and rehearsed together with his friends. Here is Avi Fisher's account:

I remember that one of them was in a store where he was asked to pay money, and he wanted to give cigarettes instead. In general, he behaved like an Auschwitz prisoner, whose behavior appeared incomprehensible to people leading normal lives. Convinced his customer was mad, the storekeeper called for an ambulance. The ambulance (represented by a simple wheelbarrow) pulled in, and when the boy, i.e., the actor who acted the adult character, who also happened to be the author of the skit, was being loaded on it, he refused, and resisted, screaming: "I want to go by foot, don't get me in the car! I don't want to go to the gas!" The children responded with laughter. For the first time, I knew full well that this secret, which we had tried so much to suppress and had thought we succeeded, the secret was out and every child knew it.[20]

Adult prisoners, many of whom were parents of pupils in the children's block, were pleased that there existed a place where their offspring could lead a semblance of normal life. The presence of children injected some vitality into the camp; it even managed to produce smiles on the faces of adult prisoners who were slowly wasting away. Some prisoners from other camps, such as skilled workers who could enter the camp while on duty, invented excuses for visiting the children's block; the sight of so many children playing, singing, and studying rejuvenated them, and offered an opportunity to forget their camp existence, even briefly. One of these prisoners, a Pole, occasionally brought to the block a book which he had happened to come across, in order to enrich the meager library collection.

Ties of a different kind evolved during the second phase of the camp's existence. Some children quickly realized the material advantages they had and, knowing the needs of adult prisoners, started trading with them. One former prisoner recounted:

> The children were very smart and would sell clothes. . . . I remember one child to whom we gave clothes three times a week, but he kept going barefoot and unclothed, since he would sell everything. The child was very smart and he bought food for his entire family.[21]

Such phenomena touched off debates on moral education among the staff. As Kraus stated,

> Should we raise an outcry and die like the young Antigone, or go on stealing and ignore others in order to save one's own skin? . . . Should we teach them to tell the truth or lie? Thou shall not cheat! Thou shall not steal! Love thy neighbor! Shouldn't we teach them how to survive in this jungle? . . . Be honest, noble and help others [he quoted a line from a German poet and burst out laughing]. Schiller is of no consequence whatsoever inside the concentration camp; how long can we go on playing the game of "as if"?[22]

Despite the negative phenomena, there were numerous cases of mutual help and regard for fellow inmates which stood out. As Fisher recalled,

> Every day one of them contributed a spoon of soup for another child. This allocation was an orderly arrangement. A different child every day. Their explanation was very convincing and very successful. They said: "We hardly feel it if there is one spoon of soup less in our meal, but the other child receives a double ration, and he can eat a proper meal once at least."[23]

The Liquidation of the Children's Block

The children's block was liquidated step by step. The first, most difficult stage occurred on March 7, 1944, when all prisoners of the September 1943 transport were gassed. (On the way to the gas chambers, they sang Hatikva and the Czech national anthem.)[24] Although nothing was mentioned explicitly, those who survived knew that their educators and dear friends had been murdered and their bodies incinerated in ovens.

By then, the educators knew that their fate and the fate of others had been sealed and that they would die six months following their arrival at the camp. The countdown had begun, and although the intensive educational activity did not indicate it, awareness of the end lurked under the surface. Within the children's block, the small inmates began discussing plans for resistance. Some of the educators who were let in on it felt that it gave them more strength to go on.[25]

In May, another transport from Theresienstadt arrived at Birkenau. Hundreds of new children joined the block, which soon became a scene of bustling activity. By that time children no longer lived with their parents. In addition to block 31, they had a special block that served as living quarters and could meet with their parents during the day, whenever they wanted to.

The six months allotted to the December transport were almost up. On July 1, 1944, Mengele appeared in the camp, and the selection of men, women, and children commenced. One survivor told about it:

> We were told to get undressed, leaving only the lower part of our bodies with the clothes on, and pass by him one by one. One of my good friends, Harry Goldenberg, who was in front of me in line, was told to step to the right, where a small group of prisoners had already been standing. The rabbi was sent to the left. I too was told to step to the left. I returned to Dr. Mengele and sobbing asked him to let me remain with my friends. At first he shook his head in refusal, but a moment later he smiled and said, "OK, go to the right, you too!" So, I found myself in a group of 98 children, ranging in age from 12 to 17 years. Immediately afterward, our group was separated from the others, and two hours

later we were removed from the block. Thereupon, ranged in columns, we were taken to the block's gate. My mother stood on the roadside and I could part from her. We left the camp and turned toward the ovens. Some distance off, we turned left, in the direction of the Gypsy camp, and from there we were told to run on the double to the sauna, that is the bath.[26]

Most women, men, and children, with the exception of those selected for work in other camps, were led straight to the gas chambers. The entire children's block was liquidated. The Czech family camp, no longer needed, had been emptied of its inhabitants.

NOTES

1. Otto Dov Kulka, "Ghetto within Extermination Camp" (in Hebrew), in *Nazi Concentration Camps* (Yad Vashem, 1984), pp. 249–60.
2. Ibid., p. 259.
3. Leni Yahil, "Danish Jews in Theresienstadt" (in Hebrew), *Yalkut Moreshet*, 1965, no. 4, pp. 65–87.
4. Dov Barnea, Oral Documentation Section, Institute for Contemporary Jewry, Hebrew University of Jerusalem.
5. Ibid.
6. See later paragraphs.
7. Ota Kraus, Diary (in Hebrew), MS., Natanya, 1990.
8. Miroslav Karny, "Testimony from Auschwitz" (in Hebrew), in Bienau File, Terezin Archives, Givat Haim, Ihud.
9. Eli Bachner, Oral Documentation Section.
10. Avi Ofir (Fisher), Oral Documentation Section.
11. Karny. Harry (Kraus), Oral Documentation Section.
12. Ota Kraus, statement given to the author.
13. Ofir.
14. Kraus, Diary, p. 55.
15. Ofir.
16. Barnea.
17. Yosef Lichtenstein ("Sefel"), was a member of He-Chalutz movement and one of the educators in the children's block.
18. Kraus, Diary.
19. On the escape of Slavek Lederer, see Otto Kulka, "Five Escapes from Auschwitz" (in Hebrew), *Moreshet*, 1964, no. 3.
20. Ofir. Also Esther Milo, oral testimony; Ota Kraus, statement given to the author.
21. Barnea.
22. Kraus.
23. Ofir.
24. Filip Müller, in "Claude Lanzmann, 'Shoah,'" *Kinneret*, 1986, pp. 213–16. See also Rudolf Vrba, "I Cannot Forgive," *Bantham*, 1964, pp. 190–92.
25. Karny. See also Ofir; Kraus, Diary.
26. Bachner.

19

Gypsies

YEHUDA BAUER

For the Nazis, Gypsies posed first a social and subsequently an ideological problem. If ever there was an Aryan population, surely it was the Gypsies. Their Indo-European history can be traced to the fifth century, when their clans headed westward from northwest India. According to some researchers, one stop on their migratory journey, a settlement at Gype near Modon in what is now Greece, may have been the source of the term *Gypsy*.[1] European Gypsies now call themselves Roma (humans).

By the 14th century, Gypsies had arrived in Western Europe. They did not settle on land, an impossibility for newcomers to feudal Europe, but became itinerant craftsmen and petty traders: tinkers, iron-, silver-, and goldsmiths, horse traders, and so on. As landless wanderers, they were soon marginalized and persecuted in the most brutal fashion. The Central and West European Gypsy tribes who called themselves the Sinti (from the Sindh River, in India) or the Manush (men, humans), were occasional targets of attempts to eliminate them or to kidnap their children to be raised as Christians. Gypsies were frequently subjected to eviction, criminalization, whipping, and forced labor. After the Diet of Freiburg in Germany in 1498, their lives were officially declared to be forfeit.

Over the centuries, anti-Gypsy prejudice in Central Europe and Germany resulted in both legal and illegal discrimination and persecution, partly forcing the Gypsies into a semicriminal existence. Large numbers must have perished in these persecutions between the 15th and 19th centuries, but others fled in search of relative security.

With the rise of the Third Reich, harassment of Gypsies continued. Gypsies were classified as "asocials." Being asocial was a serious crime in a Nazi-fied society that insisted on regimentation based on settled existences. More important, the Nazis saw their "asocial" behavior as a genetically induced, unchangeable characteristic. They were defined as "parasites" or as "a peculiar form of the human species who are incapable of development and came about by mutation."[2]

These ideological quirks may have reflected practical problems as well. The Gypsy population was small; a report to SS chief Heinrich Himmler in 1941 indicated that there were 28,000 Sinti in Germany and 11,000 in Austria (predominantly of the Lalleri tribe).[3] But they formed, from a bureaucratic point of view, an inefficiently used labor potential; local authorities had to pay for social help, educational facilities, and so forth for the wanderers. Gypsies were accused of petty crimes, reflecting the hostility of the settled German population. An administrative decree of the Prussian Ministry of the Interior in 1936 spoke of the Gypsy "plague" and of the Gypsies as thieves, beggars, and swindlers.[4] A number of racist Nazi authors wrote learned books and articles about the Gypsies and their unassimilability to the German *Volk*.

The solution Nazi ideology found for all these problems was to argue that the Gypsies were no longer "pure" Gypsy Aryans but *Mischlinge*, or mixed-bloods. The definition of who was a Gypsy often ran parallel to the definition of Jews.

In 1936, in the course of a roundup of so-called asocials, about 400 Gypsies were sent to Dachau concentration camp. Until 1938, however, Gypsies could follow their traditional occupations in Germany more or less unhindered, though after 1937 every effort was made to deport Gypsies who were not German subjects or to prevent such people from entering Germany.

A racist ideologue with medical background, Dr. Robert Ritter, was empowered to set up the Research Office for the Science of Inheritance, later the Research Office for Race Hygiene and Population Biology.[5] Ritter was to examine the whole German Gypsy population for its racial characteristics; his findings were to determine Nazi policy. Ritter examined some 20,000 Roma and determined that about 90 percent were Mischlinge. He proposed to separate the Gypsies from the German population, separate the Mischlinge from the "pure" Gypsies, and send the Mischlinge to forced-labor camps, where they would be sterilized. Still, both types of Gypsies were considered "asocial." These ideas were by no means kept secret. Ritter presented them in 1937 at an international population congress in Paris.

A decree by Himmler on December 14, 1937, provided for preventive arrest of people who had not committed any illegal act but were endangering the community by their asocial behavior. The list for administrative enforcement published April 4, 1938, included "vagabonds (Gypsies)" along with beggars and prostitutes. A further Himmler decree (issued later but predated to December 8, 1938) promised to solve the Gypsy question "in accordance with the essence of their race." On March 15, 1939, Himmler declared that while Germany respected other races, a strict separation should be enforced between the "Gypsy plague" and Germans and between half-breeds and "pure" Gypsies. The police would deal with the problem. These measures appear to have been related to the tendency of the SS to put a maximum of new asocial prisoners in its camps, which were being converted to economic enterprises employing slave labor.

Probably 8,000 of the 11,000 Gypsies in Austria were members of the so-called Ungrika (Lalleri) tribe in the Burgenland, the eastern Austrian province bordering on Hungary. They had been living there since the 18th century as a settled village proletariat, some of whom were musicians, helpers in hunts, etc. Relations with the Austrian peasants were generally good, because the Gypsies fulfilled an important social function. After the "Anschluss," Gypsy children were forbidden to go to school, and the Gypsies were disenfranchised. In November 1940, the Nazis established a family concentration camp for Gypsies at Lackenbach in the Burgenland. By October 1941, 2,335 people were interned there. In November 1941, two transports of 1,000 Gypsies each arrived in Lodz, where they met the fate of other Gypsies who were deported there. It is likely that most of the 8,000 Burgenland Gypsies were murdered during the war, but we do not have exact figures. Many were deported to Auschwitz in 1943.[6]

On September 21, 1939, in the course of the conquest of Poland, Reinhard Heydrich, chief of the RSHA (Reich Main Security Office), issued orders regarding Jews which also included the provision that 30,000 German Gypsies (along with Poles and Jews from the newly acquired west Polish territories) should be deported to Poland, an edict that would have included most of the Reich's Gypsies. Over time, the policy toward the Roma became more brutal. In the autumn of 1941, 5,007 Austrian Gypsies, largely of the Lalleri tribe, were deported to the Lodz ghetto, then gassed at Chelmno in early 1942.

In April 1941, Ritter and his race hygiene office released their findings on Gypsies. Of the 18,922 Gypsies classified by Ritter, 1,079 were defined as "pure" Gypsies, 6,992 as "more Gypsy than German," 2,976 as half-breeds, 2,992 as more German than Gypsy, 2,231 as uncertain, and 2,652 as "Germans who behaved like Gypsies."[7] Ritter's definitions paralleled those applied to Jews: "A Gypsy is a person who, as a descendant of Gypsies, has at least three purely Gypsy grandparents. Moreover, a Gypsy half-breed is a person who has less than three Gypsies among his grandparents. In addition, a Gypsy half-breed is also a person who has two Gypsy half-breeds among his grandparents." Ritter defined these "half-breeds" as "highly unbalanced, characterless, unpredictable, unreliable, as well as lazy or disturbed and irritable, or in other words disinclined to work and asocial," especially if they carried within themselves "also from the local (i.e., German) side low-grade hereditary qualities."[8]

A year later, in May 1942, Gypsies were put under the same labor and social laws as the Jews.[9] Himmler issued a clarification on October 13, 1942, relating to Gypsy chiefs who would supervise the pure Sinti, for whom a certain freedom of movement would be allowed. According to a document of January 11, 1943, 13,000 Sinti and 1,017 Lalleri would be thus considered.[10]

As for all the other Gypsies, Himmler issued a decree on December 16, 1942, providing for their deportation to Auschwitz, with the exception of socially adapted former Wehrmacht soldiers (all Gypsies were supposed to have been discharged from the army after 1940, but practical implementation did not come on a large scale until 1942–43) and war industry workers in important positions. The RSHA issued an administrative order to implement this decree on January 29, 1943.

Orders regarding Gypsies, especially orders to be executed by organizations such as the Wehrmacht, were not always followed. There is evidence that some Gypsies, or part-Gypsies, were let alone. Others managed to hide their identity, which was easier for Gypsies than for Jews. In addition, the definitions contained in the decree were rather confusing. The order was to apply to "Gypsy Mischlinge, Roma Gypsies, and members of clans of Balkan origins who are not of German blood." This apparently meant that all non-Sinti Gypsies and all Mischlinge in Germany should be deported. Whether the order was to apply to Gypsies outside the official Reich boundaries—in Western Europe, Poland, Yugoslavia, Russia, etc.—was unclear.

Treatment of Gypsies in the various European countries differed considerably. In Bohemia and Moravia, which were part of the Reich, Gypsies shared the fate of the German Gypsies: discrimination, concentration, and annihilation. The number of Gypsies who were not caught in this process remains undetermined.

In Slovakia, which was half-independent, only desultory attempts were made to concentrate some of the wandering Gypsies in forced labor camps. As far as one can tell, Slovakian Gypsies were not deported. Hundreds were brutally murdered in a number of villages during the occupation of Slovakia by German troops after the failure of the Slovak national uprising in October 1944.[11]

For France, there is testimony that some 30,000 were interned under the supervision of the Secretariat for Jewish Affairs of the Vichy government. Many or most of them were later sent to camps, including Dachau, Ravensbrück, and Buchenwald. One estimate claims that 15,150 of them died, while 40,000 appear to have survived in French camps. Five hundred of the 600 Gypsies in Belgium are reported to have died in Polish camps.[12]

The situation in Holland is instructive. After the failure of the local Nazi police to concentrate the Gypsies in late March 1943 as they had been ordered, they received new orders in May to concentrate all "wandering" Gypsies. Because of exceptions, only 1,150 out of 2,700–3,000 wandering Gypsies were affected. Many of them fled in time or sold their wagons and thus were no longer considered wanderers. On May 16, 1944, 565 persons were arrested in their wagons, of whom 245 were deported to Birkenau via the Jewish camp of Westerbork.[13]

Some figures for Croatia, where the local Ustasha movement targeted Gypsies along with Serbs and Jews, report 90,000 Roma victims in local Ustasha murder camps, but another source puts the number at 26,000 (out of 27,000). In Serbia, there is no doubt that Gypsies, along with Jews, were murdered in retaliation for the Serb uprising against the Nazis.[14]

Some Italian Roma were sent to camps in Germany after the German occupation of the country in September 1943, but most escaped. For Hungary, one source claims that 30,000 were sent to German death camps, and only 3,000 returned.[15] While no evidence exists to substantiate that figure, there is evidence that in the last stages of the war, the fascist government of Ferenc Szalasi did try to concentrate and deport Gypsies in some provinces, without much success. The large Gypsy contingent in Romania (at least 280,000) was not attacked en masse, but about 25,000 of them were dumped in Transnistria, according to one source.[16]

In the Baltic States and the Soviet Union, Roma were murdered by some of the Einsatzgruppen, according to their reports. The Wehrmacht Field Police, in a communication of August 25, 1942, stressed the need to ruthlessly "exterminate" bands of wandering Gypsies.[17] In May 1943, Alfred Rosenberg, in charge of the Eastern Territories, suggested that Roma should be concentrated in camps and settlements but not treated the same as Jews. But Himmler would not permit the intrusion of another authority in what he considered to be his own area of competence. His order of November 15, 1943, determined that "sedentary Gypsies and part-Gypsies are to be treated as citizens of the country. Nomadic Gypsies and part-Gypsies are to be placed on the same level as Jews and placed in concentration camps. The police commanders will decide in cases of doubt who is a Gypsy."[18]

While the order applied only to the occupied Soviet areas, it seems to indicate a trend of thinking among top-level Nazi officials. Some sedentary Roma were drafted into labor brigades or sent to concentration camps, but the same fate befell other Soviet citizens as well. Kenrick estimates the number of Roma murdered in the USSR at about 35,000. That excludes Gypsies who were murdered by the Einsatzgruppen, especially in the south

(Einsatzgruppe D under Otto Ohlendorf, who stated in his postwar trial that his group murdered tens of thousands of Gypsies). As far as we know, only a few Soviet Gypsies were sent to Auschwitz.[19]

There is information about Roma being sent to Jewish ghettos but kept separate from the Jews. We do not know whether they were sedentary or not, nor what their numbers were; nor do we know anything about their lives while in the ghettos. In most cases, we also have no information about their ultimate fate. They apparently constituted a small percentage of Polish Gypsies. It is possible that they were the wandering Gypsies Himmler referred to in the case of the USSR.[20]

Himmler's order regarding the USSR and the possibility that a similar policy might have been followed elsewhere contradict the other Himmler policy of allowing the "pure" Gypsies a wandering existence of sorts within the Reich confines. This latter policy, however, was challenged by Martin Bormann, Hitler's secretary, who was appalled at the possibility that wandering Gypsies would continue to be part of the German landscape. It seems that the problem was not discussed further and that the whole Gypsy "problem" was for Himmler and most other Nazis only a minor irritant. Since Nazis often solved minor social irritants by murder, this is apparently what happened to many of the Gypsies.

If this analysis is correct, a picture emerges of the Nazi policy toward the Gypsies. An originally Aryan population, so the policy went, had been spoiled by admixture of non-Gypsy blood and had therefore acquired hereditary asocial characteristics. In the Reich, their asocial behavior constituted a problem to be solved by police means, sterilization, and murder, primarily of those defined as half-breeds. What would happen to the "pure" minority was a matter for further discussion. In the territories controlled by the Reich, wandering Gypsies constituted an irritant that would be often removed by murder. Sedentary Gypsies, by and large, were not important enough to bother about. Gypsies caught by police would be shipped to concentration camps.

As German power declined, there was a tendency to utilize Gypsy manpower for military means, and some Gypsies interned in camps were used for this purpose, just as Nazi policy dictated the same use for German criminals interned in camps. How was this policy implemented in Auschwitz?

There is no evidence that Roma were sent to the Auschwitz concentration camp complex (or the gassing establishment at Auschwitz-Birkenau) before 1943. In the agreement signed on September 18, 1942, between Himmler and Nazi Justice Minister Otto Thierack, Gypsies were included among those groups whose members, if sentenced by regular German courts, were to be handed over to the SS for "annihilation through labor"; they appeared in third place, after security cases and Jews.[21] But during the remainder of 1942, this agreemen apparently did not lead to any large-scale deportations to Auschwitz.

The Auschwitz *Kalendarium*[22] contains a notation for July 1942 that the total of those who had been killed in the camp was 4,124, of whom one was a Gypsy. On December 7, 1942, two Czech Gypsies escaped; one, Ignatz Mrnka of Banova, was recaptured on January 12, 1943, and the other, Franz Denhel, apparently managed to hide. Both had arrived at Auschwitz in a transport of 59 males from Bohemia, and it is unclear whether the others were Gypsies. The two escapees apparently had been marked as "asocials" by the SS because they were Gypsies. On April 7, a Polish woman, Stefania Ciuron, a Gypsy who had been sent to Auschwitz on February 12, fled from the camp and was apparently never caught.[23]

On January 29, 1943, an RSHA decree ordered the deportation of German Gypsies to Auschwitz. It is unclear whether this decree abolished the former provision by Himmler to preserve the racially "pure" Sinti and Roma of Germany. The general impression remains of a lack of clarity in Nazi thinking regarding the Gypsy "problem."

On February 26, 1943, the first transport of German Gypsies arrived in Auschwitz, containing a few families. They were placed in Birkenau IIe, a section of the Birkenau extension of Auschwitz that was to become the Gypsy family camp but which at that stage had not been completed. A second transport arrived on March 1. These two were followed by transports on March 3 and 5 (two transports). In these four transports, 828 Sinti and Roma from Germany were included, 391 males and 437 females.[24]

The major transports of Gypsies arrived in Auschwitz between March and May 1943, but smaller groups and a couple of larger ones were sent intermittently in the autumn of 1943 and until May 1944. Smaller groups and individuals were sent to Auschwitz in between these dates. One last group (18 persons from Vitebsk in Russia) arrived on June 17, 1944.

According to the *Kalendarium,* the larger groups consisted of 32 transports from Germany, four from what the *Kalendarium* calls Czechoslovakia, three from Poland (among them, on May 12, 1943, a transport with 971 persons), one from Germany and Hungary, one from Yugoslavia (on December 2, with 77 persons), and three mixed transports (on March 7 from Germany, Yugoslavia, Poland, and Czechoslovakia; on March 17 from Germany, Czechoslovakia, and Poland; and on January 17, 1944, from France, Belgium, Holland, Germany, and Norway). With no evidence that any Roma were deported from Slovakia to Auschwitz, it would seem that when Czechoslovakia is mentioned, Bohemia and Moravia are meant. These areas were under a German protectorate and were considered by the Nazis as part of the Reich.[25]

The great majority of the Roma sent to Auschwitz—13,080, according to one source[26]—were Sinti from Germany and Lalleri and others from Austria and the Protectorate. Numbers from each of the other countries were small, with the exception of one large transport from Poland. There is no indication how or why these Gypsies were arrested or whether there was a policy of seeking them out, and if so, why this policy did not succeed or was not executed energetically. While a large proportion of the Gypsy population of the extended Reich was sent to Auschwitz, only very small numbers of Gypsies from the rest of Europe were affected. On the other hand, that these small numbers were included seems to indicate a trend toward an emerging policy on all Gypsies.

Almost all the Roma were interned in the BIIe Gypsy family camp at Birkenau. Writings on the subject do not explain why the Nazis treated the Gypsies differently from other arrestees, who were not housed in family camps, with the exception of the Theresienstadt Jewish family camp. As to the Theresienstadt Jews, there is sufficient documentary evidence that Nazis considered a possible Red Cross visit to Auschwitz in their decision-making. As far as the Roma are concerned, such considerations played no part. No documentary evidence is available to help solve the question.

But it would be a mistake to assume that the Gypsy family camp was unaffected by "normal" procedures at Auschwitz. On March 22, 1943, 1,700 Roma men, women, and children who had arrived in transports in the previous few weeks but had not been registered because of illness (mainly typhoid) were murdered by gassing. A second mass gassing of Roma occurred on May 25, 1943, when 1,035 persons were murdered; they were ill, mostly with typhoid.

Others continued to be kept in the family camp. Perhaps this policy was adopted due to a lack of clarity among Nazi bureaucrats about the Roma. They were obviously viewed as hereditary asocials, yet hesitation about them continued. By the end of 1943, 18,736 Roma had been interned in the BIIe camp, of whom at least 2,735 were later murdered by gassing.

Danuta Czech argues in the *Kalendarium*[27] that Himmler decided on the liquidation of the Gypsy family camp during his visit to Auschwitz in the summer of 1943, a visit that ended with the removal of Rudolf Höss as camp commandant. However, the first major attempt at liquidating the family camp did not occur until May 1944, or about nine months later. If Himmler said something about the Gypsies in the summer of 1943, it was not followed through on.

A number of Roma were among the individuals held at Auschwitz who tried, usually unsuccessfully, to escape. No known attempt has been made to find and interview individuals who did manage to escape.

In the spring of 1944, a number of Roma in Auschwitz were sent elsewhere. Thus on April 15, 1,357 men and women were sent to Buchenwald and Ravensbrück (the women's camp). Others were transferred to the main labor camps.

Accommodations in the Gypsy camp were in long, primitive wooden barracks, each of which had a smokestack at either end. Between the smokestacks, running the whole length of the barrack, was a thick pipe, which also served as a kind of table. On both sides of the pipe stood three-tiered wooden beds, on each of which a Gypsy family was accommodated. The inmates separated the beds with blankets which they had brought with them.

We know little about the internal organization of the Gypsy camp, but apparently the inmates organized in accordance with Roma custom in clans and families, trying to keep their culture intact as much as possible. SS attempts to make the Gypsies adjust to German order met with little success, and the Germans desisted from trying to turn the families into ordinary Auschwitz camp "material." The Gypsies played music and had circuslike performances, despite the hunger, disease, and deprivation. Under the deplorable unhygienic conditions, a rare sickness prevailed—noma—whose symptoms are somewhat akin to leprosy. The main sufferers were children and the aged.

On May 15, 1944, for unknown reasons, the camp command decided to murder the remaining 6,000 Roma in BIIe. The German commander of the family camp, Georg Bonigut, apparently disagreed with the decision and informed some of his Roma acquaintances of the fate that was awaiting them. On May 16, the SS surrounded the camp, intending to lead the inmates to the gas chambers. They were met by Roma armed with knives, iron pipes, and the like, and it was clear that there would be a fight. The Germans retreated, and the liquidation was temporarily postponed. On other occasions, when they met with organized resistance, the SS never hesitated to use brute force. Clearly, the weapons in the hands of the inmates did not pose any major threat to the well-armed Germans. Yet they desisted, perhaps owing to the general uncertainty and hesitancy surrounding the whole Gypsy "problem."[28]

On May 25, the SS separated out 1,500 Roma for work, and removed them from the family camp. On August 2, 1,408 more men and women were selected for work, and most of the remaining Gypsy men, women, and children were gassed.

Only a few Roma were housed in Auschwitz after that. Camp records show that on September 9, 1944, one Roma was sent from Auschwitz to Buchenwald. On October 5, 1,188 Gypsy inmates were transferred to Auschwitz from Buchenwald, apparently persons who were physically exhausted and destined to be killed. Most likely, all were gassed.

It appears that 2,735 Gypsies were murdered at Auschwitz in March and May 1943; 2,897 on August 2, 1944; and 800 probably on October 5, for a total of 6,432, out of 20,946 Gypsies registered in the two main books (*Hauptbücher*) covering the Gypsies that were found in Auschwitz after liberation. Subtracting the number gassed and those transferred elsewhere (probably at least 4,000) from the total registered, some 10,000 Gypsies remain unaccounted for. The most likely explanation is that illness, deprivation, and individual or small-scale acts of murder caused their demise. This supposition appears to be borne out by the few Gypsy postwar testimonies. The number of survivors, those transferred out of Auschwitz and alive at the war's end, is unknown.

An additional question arises: what happened to the German and Austrian Gypsies who were not deported to Auschwitz? According to Ritter's figures, there were 25,955 German Sinti Gypsies (not including 2,652 Germans "behaving like Gypsies"), and the number of Austrian Gypsies was estimated at 11,000, for a total of some 37,000. With 2,500 of these Gypsies deported to Poland in 1938–40 and 3,000 interned in Austrian camps (most all of whom were eventually killed), 5,000 sent to Lodz and gassed at Chelmno, and 13,000 deported to Auschwitz and killed there, we derive a total of up to 23,500 German and Austrian Gypsies killed. That would leave 13,500 unaccounted for. They may be the 14,017 Sinti and Lalleri defined by Himmler as pure or nearly pure Gypsies who would be spared.

As the war drew to its close and the German military situation became more and more desperate, the Nazis used some of the concentration camp inmates, as well as German criminal prisoners and Gypsies, as cannon fodder. According to one testimony, some 4,000 Gypsies were recruited into the Wehrmacht in these last stages. Only 700 survived.[29] One must regard this testimony with great caution until more documentary evidence emerges.

The murder of Gypsies in Auschwitz must be viewed from two perspectives: the fate that the Nazis prepared for the Gypsies generally and the fate of the Gypsies in the framework of Auschwitz.

While clear parallels existed with the plight of the Jews, it is precisely these parallels that also point to the major differences between the fate of the two groups. The Gypsies were defined in much the same way as the Jews were, but for opposite purposes, at least in theory. The "pure" Gypsies were, initially, to be spared as a separate, originally Aryan group, while the Mischlinge were destined for extermination. In the case of the Jews, all were to be murdered, except some grades of Mischlinge, who were to be sterilized or even let alone. There was logic in this, from a National Socialist ideological point of view, as the Jewish "race" had to be completely eliminated but not the "pure" Aryan Gypsies.

But Nazi thinking about the Gypsy problem was hopelessly muddled. "Pure" as well as Mischlinge Gypsies in Germany were considered genetically "asocial." Ritter and others argued in favor of their sterilization. The Nazis' Gypsy "problem" thus had both racial and social aspects. In the case of the wandering Gypsies, there was the additional irritant of old prejudices and

practical considerations of administrators and soldiers who did not like groups
of wanderers threatening their communications. To them, differentiations
between racially pure and less pure wanderers must have been unimportant.
In a social-psychological environment such as that, irritations were solved by
murder. When wanderers were encountered, they were often annihilated;
settled Gypsies were not disturbed. Nazis also differentiated between Gypsies in Germany and those elsewhere, because Gypsies in the occupied countries, especially in the East, did not pose a "racial" danger to Germans.

The second perspective is that of the fate of the Gypsies in Auschwitz.
Only a minority of German, Austrian, and Czech Gypsies and a tiny minority of non-German Gypsies were sent to Auschwitz, but their fate
became a symbol for the general fate of the Gypsies. That the Germans
kept the Gypsies alive in family groups for almost a year and a half without
separating men from women indicates that no decision as to their fate had
been made when they were sent to the camp. If there had been a plan to
murder them, it would not have taken the SS that long to do so.

Yet, while the fate of the Gypsies at camp BIIe hung in the balance, they
were treated just as badly as the other prisoners, and in some ways worse.
There were very few privileged Gypsies. Most suffered from the terrible
deprivation, hunger, disease, and humiliation. Evidence shows that in camps
such as Ravensbrück, Gypsies were also subjects of medical experiments.
An unknown number of men and women were sterilized. In Auschwitz, Dr.
Josef Mengele conducted his notorious experiments on Gypsies as well as
Jews. All or most of the Gypsy twins used in his experiments were killed,
whereas at least some Jewish twins survived. Dr. Carl Clauberg's medical
experiments at Auschwitz involved Gypsy women.

While Jews were the lowest group in Auschwitz, Gypsies were a very
close second. Relations between the two groups varied. Jewish prisoner doctors and nurses in the Gypsy camp made some personal contacts. On the
whole, however, the Gypsies were mainly separated in their camps and regarded every Gadja (non-Gypsy) with suspicion and hostility, and there
were occasional clashes, induced by the horrible camp conditions.

One of the few Gypsy testimonies may provide insight into the psychology of the Gypsies at Auschwitz. The published interview, with an un-
named Sintitsa (a Sinti woman), was unedited, and so it retains the German
slang used by the woman.[30]

"So, we were then living up there at Lehnerz with my parents," the woman
said. "I was married, my sister was married, my brother, he was 15, not quite
16 and Mrs. Wagner's little one was 13 and they worked [in a factory]." The
two boys were arrested but escaped from prison, and the police came and re-
arrested the brother, beating him up in front of his weeping mother. Then
"they" came and arrested the mother and the witness's sister, with her eight-

month-old baby. The witness hid but was found and arrested for resistance to authority, "because I prevented them from beating up the boy. I did not resist. It was forbidden to move, in those days. We were forbidden to move, only to the workplace and back home, not to the left, not to the right, no pub, we could not enter anywhere, we had to sign our names to that."

The witness was deported to Auschwitz in the early spring of 1943 and received the number Z-3890. She was put into the women's camp, along with her mother and sister. She had blood in her lungs and was put into the hospital, "which was worse than a stable. The lice crawled all over our faces; I have never seen so many lice. In the blankets with which we had to cover ourselves they were as thick as nuts. I suddenly saw that my mother had come; they brought my mother, too. She wasn't there long; she died. She cried for water. I couldn't give her any; I was forbidden to get near the water. My mother then lay in my bed with me; they brought her to me, [she had] high fever, and then my mother died."

Her brothers, her father, her husband, and her three children—aged ten, eight, and six—were in the family camp. Another Gypsy woman suggested to her that she should volunteer to be a nurse in the family camp, where the woman prisoner-doctor was a Gypsy, too. Though she could hardly stand on her feet, the witness asked the other woman to help her get the job. She managed somehow to pass the examination by an SS doctor and became a nurse. When she was taken to the family camp, she saw her father.

So I asked where the children were. So he said, they are in block 30. I can't forget that. And he asked about my mother, and so I said she was dead. And I asked for the children, for my brothers and so on, and he didn't know, they were not with him. And the SS came and tore me away from my father and brought me to the block. . . and so I worked with the camp doctors, they were prisoners, too, Jews. And they were good to us, yes, they helped us a lot.

And so I was in there for a day, not quite, I went out again and went to the block where my children were. They were only skin and bone, unrecognizable. They lay there, one can say, already dying. And so I said to my father, bring the children to the sick bay, bring the children in, I said, I will see what I can do. Had they come in there earlier, it might have made a difference. And so my father brought in the eldest the next day, she was ten. And when I saw her, she could not speak a word anymore. She only lay there, her eyes open, and not a word. Could only lie there, was more dead than. . . only breathed. So I spoke to her, [she did not speak] a word, then she died. They simply threw her there, with the other corpses. My own child.

And so one after the other. The one, she was six, was already dead when I came there. I did not see her anymore. Not long after, the other one died too. They were only skin and bones. Skin and bones, nothing else, one could count the ribs. The eyes so deep in the head. The children were dead, all three.

My father came into the sick bay, also died. Two uncles were in there, a cousin; and one of the uncles with all his family, and Mrs. Wagner, she had nine children, seven of them died in there. Seven, they came to me, I saw it myself. One of them was my sister-in-law, she was married to my brother. And then my father was dead, and I was just skin and bones, I could hardly stand. I only prayed that I should die, I could hardly live anymore. And if I had not had my strong religion, I would have killed myself. I am being honest. But I couldn't. Well, so I recovered a bit through the other women who spoke to me, "you have still siblings who need you," and so on.

In reading testimonies, it becomes clear that the fate of individual Roma deported to Auschwitz paralleled that of the Jews. However, it was not the same. There were no young Jewish children in the camp, with a few exceptions, as they and a large proportion of the women and the elderly were murdered upon arrival. The Gypsies saw their helpless family members die in the family camp one by one, from hunger and disease. Others were mutilated by sterilization or tortured in medical experiments.

The fate of the Gypsies in Auschwitz and elsewhere has been little reported, and the reports have often been stereotyped. Most researchers note that lack of information can be attributed to the suspicion and distrust with which the Gypsies, based on their collective experience, view the Gadja. Gypsies also would have had difficulty discussing aspects of their experience, since some of the basic taboos in Gypsy culture were violated at Auschwitz and elsewhere regarding standards of cleanliness and sexual contact. The sterilizations performed on many Gypsies were part of this violation. Most Gypsies could not relate their stories involving these tortures; as a result, most kept silent and thus increased the effects of the massive trauma they had undergone. In addition, very few Gypsies became members of the intellectual community, in Germany or elsewhere, so that too few from among their own number sought information about what happened to them. Even today, most of the research done on the fate of Gypsies is the work of non-Gypsies, especially Jews.

NOTES

1. Rüdiger Vossen, ed., *Zigeuner* (Frankfurt am Main, 1983), pp. 22–23.
2. Dr. Robert Ritter, quoted in Joachim Hohmann, "Der Völkermord an Zigeunern," lecture delivered at the Paris conference "La Politique Nazis d'Extermination," p. 3.
3. Statistics here closely follow my article "Jews, Gypsies and Slavs," in *UNESCO Yearbook on Peace and Conflict Studies* (Paris, 1985), esp. pp. 81–86, and the literature cited therein.

4. Ibid., p. 5.

5. "Rassenhygienische und bevölkerungsbiologische Forschungsstätte," *Gesell-schaft für bedrohte Völker* (Göttingen-Vienna, 1981).

6. Claudia Mayerhofer, *Dorfzigeuner* (Vienna, 1987); Erika Thurner, *Nationalso-zialismus und Zigeuner in Österreich* (Vienna-Salzburg, 1983).

7. Cf. Tilman Zülch, ed., *In Auschwitz vergast, bis heute verfolgt* (Hamburg, 1979), p. 67.

8. Hohmann lecture, p. 17, quoting the Informationsdienst des Rassenpolitis-chen Amtes der NSDAP, April 20, 1941.

9. Ibid., p. 23. quoting the Informationsdienst des Rassenpolitischen Amtes der NSDAP, May 20, 1942.

10. Ibid., pp. 85–86.

11. Ctibor Necas, *Nad osudem céskych a slovenskych Cikánu v letech 1939–1945* (Brno, 1981).

12. Donald Kenrick and Grattan Puxon, *The Destiny of Europe's Gypsies* (London, 1972), pp. 103–7; Vossen, p. 85; Sybil Milton, "Occupation Policy in Belgium and France," in Michael Berenbaum, ed., *A Mosaic of Victims: Non-Jews Persecuted and Murdered by the Nazis* (New York, 1990), pp. 80–87.

13. Michael Zimmermann, *Verfolgt, vertrieben, vernichtet* (Essen, 1989), pp. 62–63.

14. Menachem Shelah, "Genocide in Satellite Croatia during the Second World War," in Berenbaum, pp. 20–36; Christopher R. Browning, "Germans and Serbs: The Emergence of Nazi Antipartisan Policies in 1941," in ibid., pp. 64–73.

15. Kenrick and Puxon, pp. 125–27; Joachim S. Hohmann, *Geschichte der Zigeu-nerverfolgung in Deutschland* (Frankfurt, 1988), pp. 171–72. Hohmann states that there were 275,000 Gypsies in Hungary and Hungarian Transylvania and that there was a sterilization program in place in Hungary starting in 1942. The evidence is not con-vincing.

16. Kenrick and Puxon, pp. 128–30; Hohmann, *Geschichte*, p. 171.

17. Kenrick and Puxon, pp. 146–50.

18. Ibid., p. 150. Hohmann. *Geschichte*, p. 172, claims that East European Gyp-sies were included in the genocide wholesale, with the deportation eastward of the German Gypsies. I can find no proof of this.

19. Kenrick and Puxon, p. 149.

20. Jerzy Ficowski, a Polish writer who has tried to trace the fate of the Polish Gypsies, tells us that most of them fell victim to mass murders outside the concen-tration camps, committed by the Feldgendarmerie, the Gestapo, the SS, and Ukrai-nian fascists (Ficowski, "Die Vernichtung," in Zülch, pp. 91–112). This is a rather inexact description. Gypsies brought into the Warsaw ghetto were murdered at Tre-blinka, but we have no list of ghettos in which Gypsies lived alongside Jews (with the exception of Lodz). Interestingly, Ficowski says (p. 93) that in Volhynia, for-merly in eastern Poland, where there was a Ukrainian majority, "only" Polish Gyp-sies were murdered (some 3,000–4,000); Ukrainian Gypsies were left alone. Small groups of Gypsies were brought to Majdanek and to the extermination camp of Belzec (a group of 20 persons is mentioned). The upshot is, according to Ficowski, that of the 18,000–20,000 Gypsies living in prewar Poland, only 5,000–6,000 sur-vived. Ficowski's claim is, it seems, not conclusive, as there are many more Gypsies in Poland today than there would be if only 5,000–6,000 had survived the war. Cf. Jerzy Ficowski, "The Fate of the Polish Gypsies," in Jack N. Porter, ed., *Genocide and Human Rights* (Washington, D.C., 1982,) pp. 166–77.

21. PS-654, Nuremberg Trial Documents. In the future, Gypsies and others who had transgressed would be handed over not to the courts but to the SS directly.

22. Danuta Czech, ed., *Kalendarium der Ereignisse im Konzentrationslager Auschwitz Birkenau 1939–1945* (Hamburg, 1989), p. 263. The material on which the *Kalendarium* was based includes lists prepared at the behest of the Nazis, lists and reports illegally copied by inmate clerks and preserved, documents abandoned when the Nazis retreated from Auschwitz in January 1945, and other materials, including testimonies of survivors. See the editor's introduction, pp. 7–14.

23. Ibid., p. 354.

24. Ibid., pp. 423, 426, 429, 432, 433.

25. Ibid., passim. On May 12, 1944, 39 children arrived from the Catholic children's institution of St. Josefspflege at Mulfingen, despite efforts of the sisters there to prevent the tragedy. The children had been examined by Eva Justin, Ritter's aide, who first gained the children's trust, then registered and checked them, then caused them to be deported to Auschwitz. Justin died a respected German academic. Cf., Johannes Meister, "Die Zigeunerkinder von der St. Josefspflege in Mulfingen," in *Zeitschrift für Sozialgeschichte des 20 und 21 Jahrhunderts* 2, no. 2 (April 1987).

26. Zülch, p. 315.

27. Czech, pp. 374–75.

28. Ibid., pp. 774–75.

29. Testimony of Julius Hadosi, in Anita Geigges and Bernhard W. Witte, *Zigeuner Heute* (Bernheim, 1979), p. 276; see also Kenrick and Puxon, pp. 162–65.

30. The testimony was published by Roland Schopf in Joachim S. Hohmann and Ronald Schopf *Zigeunerleben* (Darmstadt, 1980), pp. 125–41. The interviewer was Eva Maria Parusel, and the testimony was included in a paper written in Fulda in 1976.

20

Hungarian Jews

RANDOLPH L. BRAHAM

The Pre-Occupation Era

Nazi treatment of Hungarian Jews represents a unique chapter in the history of the Holocaust. Although the Jews in Hungary, a nation allied with Germany, were subjected to severe economic restrictions, discriminatory legislation, and a series of violent actions during the early years of the war, they remained relatively well off until Germany occupied Hungary on March 19, 1944.[1]

Like the conservative-aristocratic leaders of the country, the Hungarian Jews lived under the illusion of immunity and were, for the most part, oblivious to the destruction around them. After German occupation in the late stage of the war, however, this last large and relatively intact community of nearly 800,000 Jews was subjected to the most ruthless, speedy, and concentrated destruction process of the war.[2] Within a few months, all of the Jews in Hungary, with the exception of those in Budapest, were sent to concentrations camps, mainly Auschwitz.

The Nazis isolated, expropriated, marked, placed in ghettos, and deported Jews to Auschwitz with unparalleled speed and efficiency on the eve of the Allied victory—even though the secrets of Auschwitz were already widely known in the outside world. Upon arriving in Hungary, the SS and the Eichmann-Sonderkommando put to work the expertise and the well-oiled machinery of destruction that they had acquired while implementing the "final solution" in Nazi-dominated Europe during the previous two years. They were successful in carrying out their mission in Hungary with unanticipated speed and efficiency largely because of the interplay of several factors, including the passivity and the abandonment of the Jews by the local non-Jewish population, the indifference of the international community, and, above all, the wholehearted cooperation of the Quisling government of Döme Sztójay, the former Hungarian minister in Berlin. It was this government, appointed with the consent of Miklós Horthy, the long-reigning regent of Hungary, that placed the instruments of state power—the police, gendarmerie, and civil service—at the disposal of the SS.

The "solution" of the Jewish question in Hungary was envisioned at the Wannsee Conference of January 20, 1942, in accordance with the ideas incorporated in the German Foreign Office's memorandum of December 8, 1941. The Germans were encouraged by the many antisemitic statements of Prime Minister Miklós Kállay, who was inaugurated in March 1942, and began a systematic and increasingly forceful campaign to induce Hungary, a loyal member and beneficiary of the Axis alliance, to embrace the "final solution" program.[3]

The Germans were not aware, however, that Kállay's anti-Jewish pronouncements were calculated largely to appease the Nazi elements at home and abroad. A "civilized anti-Semite" who crystallized the views and aspirations of the ruling conservative-aristocratic gentry, Kállay was disposed to reduce or perhaps even eliminate the Jews' influence in business, industry, and the professions. But he found any and all suggestions for a physical solution repugnant. He was firm and consistent in rejecting the Germans' persistent demands that the Jews be sent to ghettos and deported. He argued that the Jewish question in Hungary did not lend itself to as easy a solution as it did in the Third Reich because of the proportionately larger number of Jews in Hungary, and because of the important role that Jews played in the national economy, which was mainly in the service of Germany.

The pressure on Hungary became relentless during the second half of 1942 when the systematic extermination of European Jews was in full swing. Hungary's radical Right extremists, who played secondary roles in Hungary's military and political establishments, were interested in emulating Germany's anti-Jewish policy. Under a plan discussed with a leading member of the Eichmann-Sonderkommando, the extremists were ready to follow up the "resettlement" of the "Galician Jews" with the deportation of all other Jews.[4] Heinrich Himmler, head of the Reich Main Security Office (Reichssicherheitshauptamt), agreed with the plan, promptly approved it, and assigned the Foreign Office to implement it. Although the plan was advanced without the knowledge or consent of Kállay, the Germans used it as a basis to "solve" the Jewish question after the German occupation of Hungary.

Following the destruction of the German and Hungarian armies at Stalingrad and Voronezh early in 1943, the Kállay government began to change its domestic and military policies. The changes acquired momentum after Italy was extricated from the Axis alliance in July 1943. In a series of dramatic moves, the Kállay government changed the political landscape of the country within a short time. It recognized the Badoglio government, purged the foreign service of the openly pro-Nazi elements, allowed a partial relaxation of censorship, brought the officers responsible for the Délvidék massacres to trial, and relaxed the grip on the Jews.

Irritated as the Germans were with these measures, they were particularly incensed over certain decisions they deemed threatening to their military and security interests. The Kállay government was resolved to extricate Hungary from the war. Toward that goal, it established contact with the Allies and demanded that the Germans cooperate in the withdrawal of the Hungarian armed forces from the front, ostensibly to defend the country from the rapidly advancing Soviet Army. Hitler's fear that the Kállay regime was determined to emulate Italy was well-founded, and induced him to occupy Hungary. The destruction of Hungarian Jewry—a major ideological objective of the Nazis—was a significant component of his decision.[5]

The German occupation of Hungary made it possible for the German and Hungarian radicals and Nazis to unite forces in their effort to liquidate the Hungarian Jews. They proceeded at lightning speed, exploiting the "legal" facade provided by the Horthy-Hitler-Schloss-Klessheim negotiations of March 17-18, 1944. Under an agreement with Hitler, Horthy consented to supply Germany with a few hundred thousand Jewish "workers." That action and Horthy's decision to continue as regent played into the hands of the Nazis, who were eager to maintain the facade of Hungarian sovereignty to assure stability, to maximize the German exploitation of Hungary's economic and military resources, and above all, to facilitate the smooth implementation of the "final solution."

The Post-Occupation Era

The SS began anti-Jewish operations concurrently with the German occupation of Hungary. Supplied with enemy lists prepared by their agents in Hungary, the SS arrested and held hostage the country's leading anti-Nazi political and economic figures, including the conservative-aristocratic elite on whom the Jews largely depended for their safety, the Jewish and Jewish-Christian leaders of business and industry, and many prominent artists and journalists. The SS also arrested a large number of Jews who happened to be in or around bus and railway stations and boat terminals. The thousands of

Jews arrested in these "individual actions" (*Einzelaktionen*) were interned with the hostages in Kistarcsa, Sárvár, and other camps. They were among the first to be deported to Auschwitz in late April, prior to the countrywide movement to put Jews in ghettos.

The SS assumed jurisdiction over the Jewish community almost immediately after arriving in Hungary. It did so with the tacit consent of the Hungarian authorities, who advised the Jewish leadership to cooperate with the Germans. To ensure the effective implementation of their objectives, the Eichmann-Sonderkommando provided for the subordination of all Jewish communities to the Central Jewish Council (Központi Zsidó Tanács), which was established with the involvement of the traditional leaders of Hungarian Jews. The council, against its will, became one of the many instruments the Nazis employed in the anti-Jewish drive.[6]

The SS units, including the Eichmann-Sonderkommando, the Gestapo, and the various intelligence and security police forces, were relatively small. Because of their limited numbers, they could not possibly have carried out their sinister designs without the aid of the Hungarians. The unanticipated enthusiasm with which the Sztójay government supported the anti-Jewish drive impressed even the members of the Sonderkommando.

Within a week after its inauguration on March 22, the Sztójay government adopted the "legislative" framework for the isolation and expropriation of the Jews. This was followed by two crucial decrees enacted early in April. One required Jews to wear the Star of David to identify and separate them from the Christian population. The other was a highly confidential decree addressed to the leading officials of the gendarmerie, police, and state administration that called for the ghettoization, deportation, and concentration of the Jews.[7]

The anti-Jewish drive was directed centrally by a team that included the leading figures of the Eichmann-Sonderkommando and Hungarian officials assigned by the Ministry of the Interior. The techniques used to round up, expropriate, and put Jews in ghettos were in accordance with the team's master plan and were basically the same all over the country. Jewish leaders in each community were ordered to provide detailed lists of all Jews and their exact addresses. On the ghettoization dates established at the county meetings, the roundups began. They were carried out with the help of civilian, police, and gendarmerie elements, who relied primarily on the lists that the Jewish community leaders had provided. In hamlets, villages, and smaller district towns, the roundups were carried out almost exclusively by gendarmes. In the larger cities, the ghettoization was the responsibility of the police who acted in concert with local civil servants. In many cities, police units were assisted by gendarmes especially assigned for that purpose, local Nyilas (Hungarian Nazi) elements, and "volunteers" from the local rightist and "patriotic" groups, including the Levente paramilitary youth organization.

Typically, the Jews were awakened at dawn and given only a few minutes to pack food and essential clothing and bedding not to exceed 50 kilograms per person. Many Jews who had been alerted to the impending disaster spent the previous night packing or making contingency plans. The gendarme and police units were usually accompanied by civilians, including teachers and civil servants, who were organized into special committees for the expropriation of the Jews. The Jews were forced to surrender all their valuables and property before they were transferred to the local ghetto. Jews from small rural communities were often initially concentrated in the district seats—in ghettos situated in and around local synagogues and community buildings. After a few weeks, all Jews were transferred to the entrainment and deportation centers, usually the county seats.

The ghettos were virtually sealed off by wooden or barbed-wire fences, and windows facing the Christian sections were whitewashed. The Jews were forced to pay all the expenses associated with the ghettos. In many communities, they had to pay in advance. In other communities, the central government compensated town and city officials for their expenses with the wealth that was confiscated from the Jews. While the Jews were confined to the ghettos, local Christian entrepreneurs exploited many of them for agricultural and industrial labor. They also were in great demand by the Germans for housekeeping and other services. The Jews often volunteered for such work with the false expectation that it could help them escape deportation.

To ensure the orderly and effective implementation of the "final solution" program, the de-Jewification experts divided Hungary into six operational zones, each encompassing one or two of the gendarmerie districts into which the country was divided.[8] The anti-Jewish operations in the zones were carried out in accordance with decisions made at conferences held just prior to their launching. These conferences were usually attended by the leading members of the German and Hungarian de-Jewification teams; the top officials of the county, district, and city administrations; and the heads of the police and gendarmerie commands active in each zone.

The roundup and concentration of the Jews in zone one began on April 16, 1944, the first day of Passover. The drive was technically "illegal" because the decree to put the Jews in the ghettos was not issued until April 28.

Although the Jews in the ghettos were isolated and deprived of all means of communication and transportation, Jews in the other parts of the country soon learned about the ominous developments and became apprehensive. Their restlessness and fear grew with rumors about their own possible ultimate fate. These fears were based on accounts of many Polish and Slovak refugees who were savvy about the realities of the "final solution," and on news reports from various clandestine sources.

The top leadership of Hungarian Jewry had more reason to fear the worst. At the end of April or early in May, they received reports by two Hungarian-speaking Slovak escapees from Auschwitz about the realities of the death camp and about the feverish preparations that the SS was making in anticipation of the arrival of the Jewish transports from Hungary.[9]

Lulling the Jews into Submission

Following the start of the anti-Jewish operations in zone one, the public relations experts of the de-Jewification squad began a well-orchestrated and fairly effective campaign to mislead the masses and assuage the fears of the Jews. They justified the operations as necessary precautionary measures designed to protect the security of the country in areas identified as military operational zones. The Jews outside the affected zone, especially the Magyarized Jews, were at first inclined to accept the draconian measures as "rational" in light of the Nazis' identification of the Jews as "Bolshevik allies." When the ghettoization drive was extended to zone two, the Jews of northern Transylvania were "assured" that they were merely being relocated to Kenyérmezo or Mezotur, where they would be put to work on agricultural and industrial projects for the duration of the war. Many of the Jews of Trianon Hungary in turn were assured that measures applied against the unassimilated, basically Yiddish-speaking Jews would not be enacted against them because they were loyal, patriotic, and fully Magyarized Jews.

The Jewish masses, unaware of what had happened elsewhere in Nazi-dominated Europe, also drew comfort for possible salvation from negotiations that some Jewish leaders conducted with the SS on the subject of an emigration option. Neither they nor their leaders were fully aware, however, that the "negotiations" initiated by the SS, including the notorious proposal for exchanging "trucks for blood," were apparently designed to mislead the Jews and to reap material and ideological benefits for the "final solution" program.[10]

When the deportations began on May 15, 1944, the Germans adopted additional deceptive measures to ensure the smooth and uninterrupted implementation of their program. Partially to counteract the impact of the Auschwitz Protocols and to calm the Jews, the SS authorized—for the first time in the history of the camp—the taking of pictures of one of the Hungarian transports. It is quite probable that the Nazis originally wanted to use the pictures selectively to support the fiction that the Hungarian Jews were merely being resettled in Poland.[11]

To further deceive the Jews and the world about the ultimate fate of the deportees, the Germans produced a documentary contrasting their "humanity" with the barbarism of the Hungarians. The documentary revealed the humane and generous treatment the deportees received at the hands of the Germans upon their arrival in Kassa, the railway hub used as a transfer point, in contrast to the brutal behavior of the cock-feathered Hungarian gendarmes who were in charge of the entrainment and deportation of the Jews.

To deceive those still left in the country after the first waves of mass deportations to Auschwitz, the Germans also arranged for the delivery of postcards to friends and relatives of many of the deportees. Postmarked "Waldsee," a fictitious geographic name, the cryptic messages ("Arrived safely. I am well") were often from victims forced to write just before they were gassed.

Preparatory Work in Auschwitz

In anticipation of the daily arrivals of 12,000 to 14,000 Jews from Hungary, the SS administration of Auschwitz revamped and expanded the extermination machinery of the camp. By the time the first transports arrived on May 16, the machinery of destruction was ready to ensure a regular, effective, and continuous assembly-line operation at a scale and speed never before employed.

The SS staff was reinforced, and additional "experts" were assigned to the camp. Among them was SS-Obersturmführer Karl Höcker, who was transferred from Maidanek early in May 1944 to serve as adjutant to Richard Bär, the camp commander. Höcker was reportedly the SS plenipotentiary for the resettling of the Jews from Hungary (Bevollmächtigter der SS für die Umsiedlung der Juden aus Ungarn). In that capacity, he "set the extermination machinery in motion during the time of the Hungarian transports."[12] About the same time, Hauptscharführer Otto Moll, a murderously cruel officer, was transferred from the Gleiwitz auxiliary camp to serve as "manager" in Auschwitz. His primary task was to plan and supervise the efficient extermination of the masses of Hungarian Jews. The former Auschwitz commandant, Rudolf Höss, arrived back in Auschwitz temporarily to supervise the whole action.

With the Soviet forces fast approaching Romania, time was of the essence. A large number of prisoners were employed to bring the destruction machinery up to date. Under Moll's direction, the crematoria were renovated: the furnaces were relined, the chimneys were strengthened with iron bands, the loading and unloading ramps were completed with a three-track railway system that provided a direct link to the death factories, and large pits were dug in the immediate vicinity of the gas chambers for the burning of the large number of corpses that the crematoria could not handle. Each pit was 40 to 50 meters long, 8 m wide, and 2 m deep. At the bottom of each pit, a channel was dug in the center to make possible the "harvesting" of the fat exuding from the burning corpses for reuse as fuel in the cremation process. At the height of the deportations from Hungary nine such pits were in operation, in addition to the crematoria. The strength of the two Jewish Sonderkommando units serving the gas chambers was increased from 224 to 860, and the "Canada" commando, in charge of sorting the loot, was increased to more than 2,000.

Mass Deportations to Auschwitz

In zone one, Carpatho-Ruthenia and northeastern Hungary, the mass deportation of the Jews began at dawn on May 15. After many weeks in overcrowded ghettos (mainly in brick yards or out in the open), deprived of food and sanitary facilities, and brutalized by gendarmes and policemen in search of valuables, many Jews, while apprehensive and depressed, boarded the trains in the desperate hope that their unknown destination would be better. Their wishful thinking was sustained by natural psychological instincts of survival and by rumors spread by their tormentors. The Jews, accompanied by gendarmes, were taken to the railway station along streets that were sealed off by the police. Before they boarded the trains, their last remaining valuables were taken from them.

The night before, more than 6,300 Jews had boarded the first two transports in the ghettos of Nyíregyháza and Munkács. They arrived in Auschwitz on May 16. The transports from Hungary usually reached Auschwitz in three or four days, if unmolested by local partisans or by the Allies.

The deportation schedule called for three or four trains per day. Each train contained approximately 3,000 to 3,500 Jews. The victims were crammed 70 to 90 per freight car, which was supplied with two buckets: one filled with water and the other empty, for excrement. The doors of the freight cars were padlocked, the barred windows almost hermetically sealed. The trains were accompanied and guarded by Hungarian gendarmes until their arrival in Kassa, where the gendarmes were replaced by the SS.

The inhumane overcrowding of the freight cars and the late spring heat caused many of the Jews, especially the ill and elderly, to die en route, mostly of suffocation. Those who survived the trip arrived exhausted and emaciated. They were lethargic, apathetic, and quiet—relieved just to be able to breathe fresh air. Above all, having traveled for days in the brutally hot, sealed freight cars with little or no water, most were plagued by raging thirst. The thought of water was such a preoccupation that they could not focus on the realities around them. Their weakened condition brought on by prolonged thirst was part of the carefully planned, preprogrammed suffering they were to endure before being gassed. The SS aimed to paralyze the victims' ability to notice things and their will to resist. Their restlessness on the ramp while waiting to be processed was usually subdued by promises of water or soup after the "disinfecting showers."

The processing of Hungarian Jews was similar to that of other transports from Nazi-occupied Europe. For political, ideological, and practical reasons, a large percentage of the Hungarians was selected for gassing. Selection on the ramp was carried out by a number of SS officers and doctors, including Dr. Josef Mengele. One of Mengele's closest associates on the ramp was Dr. Victor Capesius, the camp pharmacist and Romanian national whose command of the Hungarian and Romanian languages proved useful in dealing with the deportees from Hungary, especially northern Transylvania.

The road from the ramp to the gas chambers led past long barbed-wire fences. An eyewitness described the procession.

> Long columns of those who during the selection had been chosen for the walk to the gas chambers struggled along the dusty roads, exhausted and in low spirits, mothers pushing prams, taking the older children by the hand. The young helped and supported the old and sick. Some had strayed into this procession because on the ramp they had implored the SS not to separate them from their frail and helpless relatives.[13]

The extermination operation was organized on an assembly-line basis using the most up-to-date method of mass killing. After the gassing, the bodies were processed by the inmates of the Sonderkommando and any valuable materials were contributed to the advancement of the economic interests of the Third Reich. Teeth were extracted for the gold and silver in them, orifices were searched for hidden valuables, and the women's hair was cut off. After these operations, the corpses were released for cremation. The incineration period lasted an average of five to six hours. The ashes were crushed to fine powder on a 60-by-15-meter concrete platform before being dispersed or dumped into the Vistula.

At all hours there were thousands of Hungarian Jews waiting their turn outside the crematoria and along the roads between the camps. A former member of the Sonderkommando described the scene.

> While the body carriers dragged the dead outside [the gas chambers], a new crowd of people was already waiting, unsuspecting, in the wood. . . . They had to wait patiently until the dead had been taken out of the gas chambers and the items left in the changing room had been removed.[14]

There were occasions, albeit few, when Hungarian Jews, sensing the danger awaiting them, tried to escape to the nearby forest. They were hunted down by the SS and shot in the glare of spotlights.[15]

By the end of June 1944, so many transports were arriving from Hungary that new camp facilities had to be set up. Mountains of luggage accumulated in the warehouses and on the ramps. The SS personnel, like the Jewish commandos, were reduced to a state of complete exhaustion—the former because of their engagement in life-and-death decisions classifying the new arrivals, the latter because they had to work day and night to sort the loot and to carry the gassed bodies to the crematoria and burning pits.

Accounting of the Deportations

The Hungarian and German agencies involved in the liquidation of the Hungarian Jews prepared detailed progress reports on their activities. The office of Otto Winkelmann, the higher SS and police leader in Hungary, forwarded reports of the SS to the Reich Main Security Office in Berlin. Edmund Veesenmayer, the Führer's plenipotentiary in Budapest, forwarded reports to the German Foreign Office. On June 13, 1944, Veesenmayer reported that by June 7, a total of 289,357 Jews had been "transported to their destination" from zones one and two in 92 trains, each with 45 freight cars.

The completion of operations in zone three (northern Hungary) was reported on June 30. With the deportation of 50,805 Jews from this zone, the number of deportees rose to 340,162. Following the completion of the campaign in zone four (southern Hungary), the number of deportees increased to 381,661. Finally, with the deportation of 55,741 Jews from zone five (western Hungary and the suburbs of Budapest) by July 9, Veesenmayer reported on July 13 that 437,402 Jews had been taken "to their destination."[16]

The roundup and deportation of the Jews from the towns surrounding Budapest on July 8 and 9 was "illegal," for Horthy had halted the "further transfer of Jewish workers to Germany" on July 7. This regent's decision, which saved the Jews of Budapest, was based on many domestic and international factors. Domestically, Horthy was subjected to increasing pressure by the heads of the Christian churches and the more moderate conservative political and governmental figures of the country. In the international sphere, the regent was also urged to halt the anti-Jewish drive by some of the most prominent leaders of the world, including President Roosevelt, the king of Sweden, and Pope Pius XII. Like the rest of the free world, these leaders were shocked by the speed and brutality with which the Jews of Hungary were being deported and destroyed. The realities of the "final solution" program in Hungary were first revealed in Switzerland and Sweden, where the leading newspapers published accounts based on the Auschwitz Protocols late in June 1944. But perhaps the most decisive factor underlying Horthy's belated decision to halt the deportations was the military one. At that time, the Allies were already firmly entrenched in Normandy and were in the process of liberating France. The Soviet Army was fast approaching Hungary.

The official halt to the deportations notwithstanding, the SS and its Hungarian accomplices continued to smuggle out transports to Auschwitz almost until the gas chambers and crematoria were destroyed in late fall 1944. One of the largest of these transports left the Kistarcsa internment camp on July 19 carrying 1,220 Jews. It was followed by the deportation of approximately 1,500 Jews from the Sárvár internment camp on July 25.[17]

From Auschwitz to Other Camps

Of approximately 438,000 Hungarian Jews deported to Auschwitz from May 15 to July 9, 1944, about 10 percent were determined to be fit for labor. Some were retained to work in Auschwitz itself; the remainder were dispersed to 386 camps in the Nazi empire. The largest groups were concentrated in the notorious camps of Bergen-Belsen, Buchenwald, Dachau, Gross-Rosen, Günskirchen, Mauthausen, Neuengamme, Ravensbrück, and Sachsenhausen. Like Auschwitz, several of those camps had subcamps.

The number of Hungarian Jews in Auschwitz continued to decline following the periodic selections and transfers. By the time the camp was evacuated in January 1945, only a few thousand were left. Most of them were transferred on long death marches to other camps in the central and western parts of the fast-crumbling Third Reich.[18] Few who were evacuated survived until the liberation in April and May 1945.

NOTES

1. During the pre-Occupation era, the Jews of Hungary were subjected to a series of discriminatory laws that affected every aspect of their lives. The period also witnessed several violent actions against Hungarian Jews, including the massacre of nearly 16,000 "alien" Jews at Kamenets-Podolsk in August 1941; the murder of nearly 1,000 Jews in the so-called Delvidek area early in 1942; and the killing of thousands of labor servicemen, especially in the Ukraine and German-occupied Serbia. For details, see Randolph L. Braham, *The Politics of Genocide* (New York, 1981), pp. 118–361.

2. According to the census of 1941, Hungary had a Jewish population of 725,005, representing 4.94 percent of the total population of 14,683,323. Under the

antisemitic laws then in effect, approximately 100,000 converts and Christians of Jewish origin were also identified as racial Jews.

3. During the interwar period, Hungary had pursued a revisionist foreign policy in conjunction with the Third Reich. It was thanks to this policy that Hungary doubled its territory in 1938–41, having acquired the Felvidek (Upper Province) and Carpatho-Ruthenia from Czechoslovakia in November 1938 and March 1939, respectively; Northern Transylvania from Romania in August 1940; and the so-called Delvidek area from Yugoslavia in April 1941. For details, consult Braham, chaps. 4 and 5.

4. For details on the various deportation schemes advanced by Hungarian Right radicals, see ibid., pp. 274–84.

5. For details on the antecedents of and the forces involved in the occupation, see ibid., pp. 362–99, and Gyorgy Ranki, *1944. marcius 19. Magyarorszag nemet megszallasa* (March 19, 1944: The German occupation of Hungary) (Budapest, 1978).

6. As elsewhere in Nazi-dominated Europe, the role played by the Central Jewish Council was quite controversial. For details on its composition and activities, see Braham, chap. 14.

7. For the English translation of Decree 6163/1944, which was issued over the signature of Laszlo Baky on April 7, 1944, see ibid., pp. 529–31. The decree was accompanied by several appendices detailing the procedures for the expropriation, roundup, ghettoization, and concentration of the Jews.

8. For details on the areas covered by the ten gendarmerie districts and the six anti-Jewish operational zones, see ibid., pp. 408–12 and 536, respectively.

9. The Auschwitz Protocols were based on the accounts of Alfred Wetzler and Rudolf Vrba (Walter Rosenberg), who succeeded in escaping from Auschwitz on April 7, 1944. The Hungarian Jewish leaders and the leaders of the Hungarian and world Christian community received copies of the reports shortly after they were completed toward the end of the month. Their contents were not shared with either the Jewish or the Christian masses of Hungary. For details on this controversial chapter of the Holocaust in Hungary, see ibid., pp. 691–731.

10. For details on the nature and implications of these negotiations, see ibid., chap. 29.

11. The album containing these pictures was found by a survivor who had been deported from the ghetto of Beregszasz. The album is in Yad Vashem's possession. For some details on the background and debate surrounding the album, see Randolph L. Braham, "Photographer as Historian: The Auschwitz Album," *Shoah*, Fall-Winter 1983–84, pp. 20–23.

12. Bernd Naumann, *Auschwitz: A Report on the Proceedings against Robert Karl Ludwig Mulka and Others before the Court at Frankfurt* (New York, 1966).

13. Filip Müller, *Auschwitz Inferno* (London, 1979), pp. 133–34.

14. Ibid., pp. 139–40.

15. For accounts of such incidents, see Danuta Czech, *Auschwitz Chronicle, 1939–1945* (New York, 1990), pp. 636, 776. Hungarian Jews were involved in the revolt of October 7, 1944, when, as the largest contingent of the 300 Sonderkommando workers who had been selected for liquidation, they attacked the SS guards and set one crematorium afire. Ibid., pp. 725–26. See also Müller, pp. 153–56, 159–60.

16. For the reports by Edmund Veesenmayer, see Randolph L. Braham, *The Destruction of Hungarian Jewry: A Documentary Account* (New York, 1963), Documents 174, 182, 193, and 286. For reports by Lieutenant-Colonel Laszlo Ferenczy, see Braham, *Politics*, chaps. 19–22.

17. For details on the deportations from the Kistarcsa and Sarvar internment camps, see Braham, *Politics,* chap. 25. For the identification of several smaller so-called SIPO-SD transports taken to Auschwitz from Hungary during summer and fall 1944, see Czech, pp. 669, 688, 713, 735. See also Sari Reuveni, "Mishlochim meyuhadim verakavot meucharot me'Hungaria le'Auschwitz be'shanah 1944" (Special transports and late trains from Hungary to Auschwitz in 1944), *Yalkut Moreshet,* 1985 (May), pp. 123–34.

18. Most of the surviving Hungarian Jews were taken to Buchenwald. For statistical details on the victims held in Auschwitz during the last few months of its operation, see Czech, pp. 687, 778, 782.

21

Auschwitz—A Psychological Perspective

LEO EITINGER

Although many scientists and clinicians have shown much interest in the perpetrators of the crimes at Auschwitz and the acts of aggression they committed, my line of research has been concerned more with the victims of Nazi aggression—perhaps because I myself was one of the victims. How have these victims reacted to and coped with the maltreatment to which they were subjected? What have been the long-term effects of serious aggression, and what kind of help might be offered these victims?

The prisoners in Auschwitz came from nearly all the countries of Europe —from northern Norway to southern Greece, from western France to eastern Poland and Russia. They were Jews and non-Jews from social backgrounds and political persuasions as diverse as their geographic origins. Some were highly qualified artists and scientists, high-ranking civil servants and industrialists. Others were average artisans, craftsmen, businessmen. A few were asocial and violent criminals. They had different life experiences and different encounters with the Nazis before they arrived at Auschwitz, and they had different expectations as they entered the camp. Norwegian Jews, for example, had experienced little persecution; they had spent the first two years of the war supported by neighbors and virtually unmolested by the Germans. Polish Jews, on the other hand, had been persecuted and degraded in ghettos and forced-labor camps, and had been the victims of pogroms and transports before they were deported to Auschwitz. In short, there were many differences among the prisoners.

Regardless of these differences, arrival at Auschwitz was a shock deliberately provoked by the SS guards to make the prisoners confused, apprehensive, anxious, uneasy, and unable to think or reason in normal and rational ways. After the deportees to Auschwitz underwent several days' journey in closed, dark, overcrowded cattle cars without food, water, or hygienic facilities, the train would jolt to a halt and the doors would open suddenly. The prisoners' first impressions were armed SS men shouting unintelligibly, dogs barking, and some shadowy, bleak, and scared-looking persons in striped uniforms bustling around trying to communicate something that none of the newcomers could understand. The SS men drove everyone out of the cattle cars, bellowing and beating the new prisoners blindly and indiscriminately. Their mission was to create a panic situation. It took some time for the prisoners to understand that they were to leave their luggage in the cattle cars, and that those who had taken their rucksacks or suitcases with them should abandon them immediately on the railway platform.

The next stage was to line up in long rows, men and women separately, and pass inspection by an SS officer, who again divided the newcomers into two groups by pointing to the left or right. Young and able-bodied prisoners were sent to one side, old and sick persons and children to the other. The newcomers did not have a chance to think about what was going on. They were either pushed onto trucks or into a marching group. They were directed either to the gas chambers or into the camp. The newcomers did not yet know that all their strength would be exploited until it was totally drained. Then they would be sent to the gas chambers or killed another way.

The final series of tribulations that the newcomers underwent was during the admittance procedure. Before going into the bath, the prisoners had to hand over all their personal belongings—money and valuables such as wedding rings, personal clothing, and photographs. The SS did not even pretend that they would return anything to the Jewish prisoners. Everything was collected without receipt. This action, which told the Jewish prisoner that they had reached the last stop, was not practiced with non-Jewish prisoners. The illusion of probable survival was maintained for non-Jews.

The stay in Auschwitz was beyond human comprehension. German author Friedrich Hebbel (1813–69) described it in a nearly prophetic way as "a situation where everybody is bound to lose one's reason or one has no reason to lose." Psychologically one can view the experiences of Auschwitz from the prism of a "crisis." An emotional crisis occurs when a person is put into a situation in which the usual problem-solving mechanisms are insufficient, ineffective, or both. The crisis produces a complex set of emotions and symptoms that unfold in somewhat predictable "phases" over a specific period. The natural course of a crisis depends on an individual's capacity to mobilize available resources and the presence or lack of support persons or support systems (during and after the crisis). In cases in which an individual's vulnerability is high, resources and support are lacking, and the precipitating events are overwhelming—as in the case of the Auschwitz imprisonments—the personality may disintegrate or break down.

The phases of every crisis follow a pattern. According to the crisis theory, an Auschwitz prisoner's traumatic experiences would follow this psychological paradigm: the shock phase—arrival at Auschwitz; the reaction phase—life in Auschwitz with all its realities and stress situations as prisoners use all the coping mechanisms they can muster to deal with events and survive; the recoil phase—after the liberation, when prisoners use new psychological mechanisms in an attempt to decrease their symptoms, find ways to adapt to their new freedom, and reconstruct their lives.

The Shock Phase

During this first phase, victims may appear confused and shaky, or they may seem composed, cool, and not visibly affected, even though their inner psyches are suffused with perplexity, helplessness, and chaos. When exposed to several unpredictable situations that they cannot change or stop, most people appear apathetic and act like automatons, obeying orders without thinking. Contact with reality is reduced. Everything seems somehow unreal, and the meaning of what is going on around them is somewhat reduced.

The Nazis knew how to exploit these predictable changes in human behavior. It is more than likely that this exploitation was the main reason that practically none of the many prisoner groups (including many Soviet prisoners of war) tried to resist. With victims thus disorganized, the SS could carry out the most debasing procedures, such as "deverminization," which included shaving hair on the head, under the arms, and intimate parts of the body. Male prisoners shaved men and women who were forced to stand on stools, surrounded by SS (controllers) or bemused onlookers. The victims' shock reactions were also the main reason why during this phase almost none of the prisoners tried to commit suicide, which would be a logical outcome of a purely intellectual assessment of the situation.

The shock phase usually lasted until the newcomers were transported to their blocks, had numbers tattooed on their arms, received their prison uniform, and were transformed from human beings into "prison numbers."

The Reaction Phase

After the Auschwitz prisoners "awakened" from the shock phase, even greater problems began. In the ensuing reaction phase, the prisoners had to face the realities of daily life in the camp and find psychological mechanisms to cope with them.[1] The hardships of Auschwitz were manifold; only a few can be mentioned here.

Disruption of the Family

Arrests and roundups (evacuations of the various ghettos) and admission to Auschwitz were carried out with total disregard for family ties. Entire communities were uprooted, social networks were disrupted, and personal identity was dismembered. Those who came to Auschwitz with their families learned quickly what the separation into lines and groups and the good-byes on the railway platform meant. In this atmosphere of brutality, there was no opportunity to mourn. During this phase, repression was the only way to cope.

Feelings of Insecurity

Behavior in Auschwitz was distorted and unpredictable. That only heightened the feelings of insecurity and helplessness in each individual. The rules were senseless, capricious, and often contradictory.[2] They were as hard to predict as they were to follow. They were often unrelated to the realities of camp life. Dehumanization and degradation added to the feeling of one's own worthlessness and insecurity. Insecurity was caused by the fact that one's own life was in constant danger. That was vividly demonstrated by the fact that every prisoner was a victim of random violence or deliberate cruelty. Nothing was less important or less valuable than the life of a prisoner, and nothing was more important than a prisoner's presence at roll call, dead or alive. The *number* of prisoners was all-important.

Jewish prisoners had the most difficult time, and the heaviest and most degrading jobs. They were slated for annihilation through forced labor. Because they ranked at the very bottom of the prisoner hierarchy in Auschwitz (and all other concentration camps), they had the most difficulty in securing the lighter jobs that increased the chances for survival. Thus the number of those who succumbed to exhaustion, sickness, and starvation was highest among the Jewish prisoners. Their possibilities to cope were minimal.

Harsh Forced Labor

Under the constant and ruthless supervision of the *Kapos* ("privileged" prisoners who functioned as heads of work gangs), forced labor was routinely combined with beatings and other kinds of ill treatment. That only added to the prisoners' psychic stress—continuous stress caused by the recurring macabre deaths that the prisoners witnessed and by the constant anticipation of their own deaths. Old, weak, and sick prisoners were selected regularly for execution, sometimes on a daily basis. Death permeated the atmosphere of Auschwitz and Birkenau; its stench was everywhere.

Starvation

A lack of nutrition dominated the life of nearly all Auschwitz prisoners. That was not a somatic problem only. Research on hunger disease has shown that over extended periods, starvation can cause impaired memory, reduced initiative, fatigue, drowsiness, and irritability. These symptoms are usually followed by indifference, dullness, and apathy. The last phase of starvation was known in the camp as the muselman state—when all mental processes are retarded and normal reactions cease.[3] In the case of many of the Auschwitz prisoners, this condition seemed to be largely of psychic origin. In many cases, death followed. Life ceased to interest the prisoners and they gave up hope.

Hunger reduces resistance to infection and thereby weakens the general health. Survival is dependent on motivation. One must be strongly determined to survive, but hunger itself reduces the ability to be consciously determined. The feeling of constant overwhelming hunger counteracts motivation and leaves its victims apathetic.[4]

Deprivation of Basic Needs

Deprivation of hygienic facilities, of privacy, and of appropriate medical care was routine. Prisoners were unable to wash daily or to change underwear at regular intervals. This was the case in Auschwitz and especially in Birkenau and many of the subcamps. Normal problem-solving capabilities were insufficient to deal with the daily routine of debasement and dehumanization.

Coping

In the face of never-ending adversities, the prisoners had to find new ways to adjust. At Auschwitz, coping meant surviving. The ways the prisoners chose to cope depended on their situation and available alternatives, and on their personality, level of maturity, moral fiber, and strength. Unfortunately, far too little is known about those who did *not* survive, such as the kind of psychological mechanisms they used and the immediate reasons for their deaths.

A Norwegian Example

Although Norwegian Jews constituted only a tiny minority in Auschwitz, they provide some interesting, though incomplete, answers. Their unfamiliarity with the Nazi system and their poor knowledge of the main languages used in Auschwitz proved detrimental to their survival, as shown by the following statistical data. The Nazis started arresting Jews in Norway in the fall of 1942. In November, 530 Jews were deported. Of those, 473 were born in Norway and 57 were refugees from Central Europe. There were no further transports until February 1943, when the next Jewish transport was dispatched. It consisted of 284 persons. Of those, 258 were Norwegian born and 26 were Jewish refugees from central Europe. Out of the first transport in November, nine (1.6 percent) survived, seven Norwegian Jews and two former refugees. From the second transport, six (3.2 percent) survived, three Norwegians and three former refugees. After the second transport, 11 refugees who had been in hiding in Norway were found and deported to Auschwitz, seven of whom (63 percent) survived. The figures tell a clear story. There were two decisive factors that made it difficult for those on the first Norwegian transport to cope—devastating mistreatment of prisoners and the extremely harsh winter of 1942–43.

Two other examples shed light on other sides of the problem that the Norwegian Jews faced. Two brothers, 18 and 25 years of age, had been fortunate enough to be sent to the same block in Auschwitz. On the second day, the younger brother did not understand an order and the block elder punished him by kicking and beating him. His brother felt obliged to help and told the block elder to leave his brother alone. The block elder summoned two "colleagues," who beat both brothers to death.

In another example, a merchant about 30 years of age, who had been deported to Auschwitz from Norway in August 1942, managed to survive his first winter in a nearly miraculous way. When he heard about the transport from Norway in the spring of 1943, he inquired about the fate of his wife and children and was told that indeed they had been on that transport. With that news, his powers of resistance broke down. The next day he went to the camp hospital and was found too weak for further work. He was killed immediately by an injection of carbolic acid into the heart.

The first theory of coping with aggression in concentration camps was set forth by Bruno Bettelheim in 1943.[5] He maintained that most of the long-term prisoners coped with the violence and aggression they encountered by identifying with the aggressors.[6] Some prisoners in Auschwitz did identify with their aggressors. This occurred, for example, when the SS guards delegated some of their unlimited power to certain prisoners. Yet any change of regime in the camp or any transport to another camp or subcamp could result in the dethronement of these "super-prisoners," often drastically and with fatal results. Interviews with about 1,500 ex-prisoners in Norway and Israel support the fact that identifying with the aggressor proved to be a negative coping mechanism which eventually led to the destruction of those prisoners or, in the few cases where they survived, to deep pathological personality changes.

Positive coping in Auschwitz meant surviving without becoming completely demoralized by "selling out" to the SS—that is, becoming their spy or their tool by helping them maltreat or even kill fellow prisoners. Mutual help among prisoners in their successful ability to cope should not be underestimated. Studies by Elmer Luchterhand have shown that stable pairing was the most common type of interpersonal relationship that occurred among successful copers.[7] Most of them developed a sharing and helping relationship with another person. The pair was their basic unit of survival. Luchterhand was also able to show that it was the split between criminal and noncriminal prisoners that most decisively influenced the development of the prisoners' social system.

Luchterhand's findings conform to a high degree with interviews I have conducted with former prisoners. But even the list of successful coping mechanisms derived from interviews should be approached cautiously. If one survivor says that he survived because he used a particular psychological mechanism, it is likely that others used similar survival mechanisms without success. These reservations must be kept in mind when considering the problem of coping.

During my interviews with Auschwitz survivors in Israel, it became clear that the majority who adjusted well after the war—those who were able to work and reestablish good interpersonal relationships—credit their survival to their ability to make decisions. Prisoners in Auschwitz were essentially powerless. Yet prisoners were helped by the feeling that they had at least some power over themselves. Survivors have given varying descriptions of the efforts they undertook or the decisions they made that facilitated survival: systematically saving one's strength, never giving up, helping others and receiving help, and dealing correctly with the daily ration of bread. "Correctly" could mean eating every crumb of bread immediately upon receiving it, not risking death by keeping a crust of bread in the pocket. "Correctly" could also mean the opposite, that is, dividing the bread into two, three, or four portions and never eating more than one portion at any one time, despite one's ravenous hunger. As one survivor put it, "They had a reserve to fall back on, and this was just as important as feeling satisfied."[8]

Physician and nurse prisoners who had been fortunate enough to get positions in Auschwitz where they could maintain their personal norms and values by continuing their prearrest occupation and thus work for and help others had the best chances to survive and to avoid Auschwitz's ethically devastating atmosphere. (Inevitably, though, there were some among the medical personnel who abused their positions for personal gain.)

In Auschwitz, disregard for family ties was total. So it was special when close family members could stay together and help each other—if not in a material way, at least by mutual moral support. Elie Wiesel's description of the importance of his father's presence with him in Auschwitz is a moving testimony to this.[9]

Denial was another coping strategy. It could be disastrous when prisoners in Auschwitz denied the grim realities of the daily duties, such as the very real necessity for daily vermin control. Yet to a certain extent, denial could be lifesaving if it helped a prisoner at least to act as though dangerous situations and severe anxieties did not exist. Otherwise, accepting the logic of fatalism in Auschwitz could lead to the only logical consequence of an impossible situation—suicide.

The ongoing struggle to survive from day to day was complicated, and depended on many factors. Yet the unfortunate prisoners had no influence on the complex factors that determined their daily fate. There were, however, small areas where individual strategies—the allocation of defensive resources at one's disposal—could be of decisive importance. Evidence of this is limited, however. There is only the testimony of survivors.

Many former prisoners believe that they survived only because it was of vital importance to them to tell their stories of suffering and survival.[10] Others believe they survived through mere chance or luck regardless of any individual action on their part. When comparing groups of survivors who actively mobilized coping mechanisms with those who ascribed their survival to chance, the former turn out to have suffered fewer postwar psychiatric complications than the latter. In other words, coping mechanisms that enhanced the individual's contact with a group or were based on intact and positive value systems, such as retaining self-respect,[11] proved important not only in determining immediate survival but also in determining postwar reactions.

Suicide in Auschwitz has been discussed from a psychological point of view on different occasions. It has often been asserted that suicide was rare. That, however, cannot be proved. There are no data on how many of the prisoners who were shot while trying to escape actually were attempting suicide. Nor do we have data on how many prisoners threw themselves on the electrically charged barbed-wire fences that surrounded the camps. And no one knows how many prisoners went to medical examinations with the intention of ending their lives. Investigations done after the war are hardly representative. No figures are available.

The Recoil Phase

Though using a psychological paradigm to help explain the general phenomena of crisis is instructive, the Auschwitz crisis is not really analogous to other crisis experiences and thus the standard psychological paradigms are not always relevant. Incarceration at Auschwitz was extreme in every respect—impossible to imagine, impossible to understand, impossible to compare with other events, and difficult to portray. Human nature, however, follows its own course; and even after the most terrible trauma, a victim will try to overcome past horrors during the recoil phase. This phase is psychologically characterized by fairly successful implementation of new coping mechanisms. That results in a decrease in symptoms and a gradual resumption of normal functioning. That in turn leads to reorganization, or the final reconstructive phase in which the victim begins dealing with the personal meaning of the traumatization. Such was the case with most of the Auschwitz survivors.

When liberation came, most of those left at Auschwitz after the death marches were too weak to move or even to be aware of what was happening. Awakening from the nightmare was sometimes even more painful than captivity. After initial improvements in their physical condition, the mental abilities to think and to feel returned. When that happened, Jewish former prisoners could no longer repress what had happened, and the reality was agonizing. My studies of Auschwitz survivors living in Israel show that 80 to 90 percent lost most of their closest relatives. Three out of four lost their entire family.[12] Studies I conducted in Norway show that six of the 11 surviving Norwegian-born Jews were the sole survivors of their immediate families. All had lost at least two close relatives.[13]

Whereas many former prisoners were sent home after liberation (often after long delays and difficulties),[14] the newly released Jewish prisoners from Eastern Europe had no one to return to and nowhere to go. Their old life had ended, and they had no idea what to do with the new life they had so unexpectedly been given. The situation was similar for former Auschwitz prisoners who had been liberated after surviving death marches and transport to other camps. They had to remain in what were relabeled as "displaced persons" (DP) camps. International organizations took care of them and tried to put meaning into their lives. Without belittling the efforts of these organizations, it must be recognized that individuals were of little importance to large international organizations. These individuals still had no right to decide for themselves or to determine their own fate. Now "displaced persons," they were brought up before boards from various countries that decided whether they could be considered eligible for immigration.

Many Jewish survivors had no wish to be dependent on others' decisions or to live on charity any longer. As a result of their experience and destiny, many expressed their views and attitudes and decided to be organized and active for their national aims, which was in their opinion the way to achieve their rehabilitation as individuals. Many tried to make their own way to Palestine, where they expected to find a solution to all their problems. Some were admitted by the British administration, but the majority were stopped en route and put in yet another internment camp, in Cyprus. Only when the State of Israel was established did it become possible for these surviving Jews to emigrate there and start a new life.[15]

Jewish former prisoners who left the camps and returned to their home-towns in Eastern Europe were, in most cases, confronted with rejection and hate. Their homes were in ruins, and the possibility of finding new means of subsistence was minimal. They were often the only survivors of a large family; they felt isolated and often had no contact with hostile neighbors who showed no understanding of their plight. They could not understand their new surroundings, which were different from the world they had dreamed of in the camp. No wonder that many sought a new country where they could start a new life. And no wonder that Israel, for many of them, seemed to be the place designated by fate as the solution to all their problems. But many of the new immigrants had unrealistic ideas of what Israel had to offer. Their awakening to reality was not easy.

Others preferred to emigrate to countries such as the United States, Canada, and Australia, hoping to find secure and quiet lives there. All of them had to adjust to strange new surroundings, learn new languages, absorb new laws, and build new lives. The complete breakdown of former family and community ties inevitably caused radical changes in their conceptions of themselves and their environments.

None of the general practitioners, psychiatrists, psychologists, and social workers who aided the survivors knew much about the traumas the survivors had lived through. When they learned what had happened, they couldn't believe it. Yael Danieli[16] described how a "conspiracy of silence" evolved between the therapists and their patients. Many different factors influenced the experts' evaluations of psychological and psychosomatic reactions of the survivors.[17]

Several authors[18] have documented the feelings of guilt endured by survivors of Auschwitz, because, unlike most of their family members and friends, they were still alive. In the emotionally overloaded atmosphere of the first postwar years, when the Nazis' attempted extermination of the Jewish people in Europe and the failure of the Allies to act to prevent it became common knowledge, the attitude of Jewish psychiatrists could not be an "objective" one. It is possible that the postwar importance attached to the "severe and persisting guilt complex" as a central symptom of the survivor syndrome may have its roots in unconscious guilt feelings that therapists projected on their survivor patients.[19]

The main psychological symptoms experienced by Auschwitz survivors were anxiety, sleep disturbances, and nightmares. Affective disturbances with emotional lability, dysphoria, and depression were also common. Hyperirritability and feelings of inner tension with hyperalertness and exaggerated startle response were not infrequent. In other cases, apathy stemming from the camp experiences continued in the form of reduction of affect and loss of initiative.

Most observers describe Auschwitz survivors as not having dramatized or appealed for help in a hysterical way. The most common impression was that of a "winged" individual, a person who was not capable of enjoying life adequately. In more extreme cases, the individuals seemed to be merely existing; they were alive, did what work had to be done, but found no joy in life. They were not the same after the war; something essential had changed.[20]

The Jewish Auschwitz survivors who remained in Europe after the war were a tiny minority that felt isolated to a degree rarely experienced before by any group of people.[21] There were no graves to mark the burial place of the deceased; the dead had literally disappeared without a trace. In one sense, Auschwitz has become a symbol for all the missing graves of European Jews.[22]

Many of the Auschwitz survivors have been characterized by the concentration camp or survivor syndrome. The symptoms that this syndrome comprise were described with variations in different countries. The largest and most systematic studies were performed in Denmark[23] and Norway.[24] The following symptoms were considered the basis for the concentration camp survivor symdrome: failing memory and difficulty in concentration; nervousness, irritability, restlessness; fatigue; sleep disturbances; headaches; emotional instability; dysphoric moodiness; vertigo; loss of initiative; vegetative lability; and feelings of insufficiency. If four or fewer of these symptoms were reported, we did not regard the syndrome as being present. We excluded nightmares and anxiety because they were present in all the interviewed survivors.

Some authors stressed other symptoms, such as survivor guilt, repressed aggression, depression, premature aging, asthenia, and organic brain damage. Many studies were uncontrolled; sometimes the case histories of only one or very few survivors were studied. Character traits found in one or two persons sometimes were considered "typical for survivors" without any proof that these symptons could be ascribed to the stay in Auschwitz. Theories about the syndrome's etiology vary among the authors of the postwar literature.[25] To delve into the question of which author has identified the correct etiology or symptoms of the concentration camp syndrome is futile. Variations in the symptoms may be traced to the choice of those examined[26] and to the theoretical orientation of the investigators.[27] Furthermore, the complex nature of the populations in question and the difference in degrees of trauma and extent of loss of sociopsychological and interhuman relationships also help explain the differences in published findings. The variation in findings applies to the many uncontrolled case studies where quite accidental, more-or-less common character traits have been ascribed to the survivors of concentration camps.

Sometimes the term *survivor* is not even properly delineated. To compare people who spent years amid the horrors of Auschwitz with people who escaped from Germany in 1933, or with those who lived safely in the United States during the war but felt like "vicarious survivors" after the war, is to grossly underestimate the impact of long-lasting and excessive traumatization, the effect of which has been proved by numerous investigations all over the world.

Studies of randomly selected samples of concentration camp survivors conclude that there are long-term consequences from the stress experience of the Holocaust.[28] (The literature on survivors has grown so large that it is impossible to quote individual authors, and one must refer to bibliographies.)[29] Unfortunately, the findings of gross pathology in Auschwitz survivors have been frequently misinterpreted and construed to imply that their pathological reactions (or rather their normal reactions to pathological situations) persist unchanged forever. Such a view disregards not only the capability of human beings to adapt but also the regenerative powers of the ego. Many survivors have discovered coping mechanisms in their new surroundings, many have found their place in postwar societies, and many have successfully integrated their past trauma into present reality. Many survivors have strived once again to be an active part of a family and a community, to belong and to create. Unfortunately, many intrapersonal difficulties were only repressed, not solved. Investigations into the unconscious clearly demonstrate that scars are present.

The extreme traumatization of Auschwitz inflicted deep wounds on the prisoners. These wounds have slowly healed, but studies show that even after 45 years the scars are still present. The psychic wounds hurt and sometimes reopen. The strength to deny or fight old memories diminishes during serious illness and when vitality is reduced by other causes, such as old age.[30]

The stress experienced by prisoners of Auschwitz has shown that human beings can undergo extreme traumatic experiences, become deeply impaired, and yet retain the ability to rehabilitate their egos. Former prisoners continue to exhibit increased vulnerability to stress situations, but they also show a greater sensitivity toward fellow humans, a greater capacity for empathy, and a greater appreciation for the higher values in life.[31] Sometimes persistent traumatic memories return in reinforced strength. With the passage of time, health deteriorates, mental capacities dwindle, and life increasingly loses its meaning. Help for the survivors of Auschwitz is then more important than ever.

NOTES

1. D. Hamburg and J. Adams, "A Perspective of Coping Behavior," *Archives of General Psychiatry* 17 (1967), pp. 277–84.

2. Paul Chodoff, "Depression and Guilt among Concentration Camp Survivors," *Existential Psychiatry* 7 (1970), pp. 19–26.

3. P. Helweg-Larsen et al., "Famine Disease in German Concentration Camps: Complications and Sequels," *Acta Psychiatrica et Neurologica Scandinavica,* Supplement 83 (1952).

4. It seems appropriate to refer here to a special study carried out from February to July 1942. The study included 70 adult clinic patients, about 40 children, and some 40 people seen as private patients. The adults had been kept on a very low calorie diet, with small amounts of protein and fat, for several months, some even for years. According to the data obtained, the 800-calorie diet contained 3 g of fat and 20 to 30 g of vegetable protein. It consisted of dark bread, rye flour, kasha, potatoes, traces of butter, lard, oil, sugar, and a plateful of soup. It contained mostly carbohydrates and was grossly deficient in vitamins. It is a sign of human and intellectual heroism that the coldly factual report of this study was written in 1942 by a group of doctors at what was called the "hospital" in the Warsaw ghetto. All these doctors suffered the same conditions as their patients, and only four of the 28 doctors who conducted the investigations survived the war. At great personal risk, they managed to smuggle out their findings. A part disappeared during the war, but the most important section was published in Myron Winick, ed., *Hunger Disease: Studies by the Jewish Physicians in the Warsaw Ghetto* (New York, 1979).

5. Bruno Bettelheim, "Individual and Mass Behavior in Extreme Situations," *Journal of Abnormal Social Psychology* 38 (1943), pp. 417–52.

6. Bettelheim's description is based on a camp experience before the war which little resembled the realities of Auschwitz during the war.

7. E. Luchterhand, "Early and Late Effects of Imprisonment in Nazi Concentration Camps," *Social Psychiatry* 5 (1970), p. 110.

8. Leo Eitinger, *Concentration Camp Survivors in Norway and Israel* (Oslo, 1964).

9. Elie Wiesel, *Night* (New York, 1958).

10. P. Schmolling, "Human Reactions to the Nazi Concentration Camps," *Journal of Human Stress* 10 (1974), pp. 108–20.

11. Leo Eitinger, "Coping with Aggression," *Mental Health and Society* 1 (1974), pp. 297–301.

12. Eitinger, *Concentration Camp Survivors.*

13. Leo Eitinger, "On Being a Psychiatrist and a Survivor," in Alvin H. Rosenfeld and Irving Greenberg, eds., *Confronting the Holocaust: The Impact of Elie Wiesel* (Bloomington, 1978), pp. 186–99.

14. Primo Levi, *The Truce* (London, 1965).

15. Leo Eitinger, "Jewish Concentration Camp Survivors in the Post-War World," *Danish Medical Bulletin* 27 (1980), pp. 232–35.

16. Yael Danieli, "Therapists' Difficulties in Treating Survivors of the Nazi Holocaust and Their Children," Ph.D. dissertation, New York University, 1981.

17. D. C. Hertz and H. Freyberger, "Factors Influencing the Evaluation of Psychological and Psychosomatic Reactions in Survivors of the Nazi Persecution," *Journal of Psychosomatic Research* 26 (1982), pp. 83–89.

18. Chodoff, "Depression and Guilt among Concentration Camp Survivors," and W. G. Niederland, "The Problem of the Survivor," *Journal of Hillside Hospital* 10 (1961), pp. 233–47.

19. Leo Eitinger and E. Major, "Stress of the Holocaust," in Leo Goldberger and Shlomo Breznitz, eds., *Handbook of Stress*, 2d ed. (New York, 1993).

20. Eitinger, *Concentration Camp Survivors*.

21. U. H. Peters, "Die psychischen Folgen der Verfolgung: Das Uberlebenden-Syndrom," *Fortschritte der Neurologie-Psychiatric* 57 (1989), pp. 169–218.

22. Carol Rittner and John K. Roth, *Memory Offended: The Auschwitz Convent Controversy* (New York, 1991).

23. Knud Herman and Thygesen Paus, "KZ-syndromet," *Ugeskrift for Laeger* 116 (1954), pp. 825–36.

24. Axel Strom, ed., *Norwegian Concentration Camp Survivors* (Oslo and New York, 1968.)

25. Eitinger, *Concentration Camp Survivors;* Leo Eitinger, "A Follow-Up Study of the Norwegian Concentration Camp Survivors' Mortality and Morbidity," *Israeli Annals of Psychiatry and Related Disciplines* 11 (1973), pp. 199–208; H. Krystal, ed., *Massive Psychic Trauma* (New York, 1968); Niederland, "The Problem of the Survivor"; H. Szwarc, "The Premature Aging of Former KZ-Prisoners," in *Zeitschrift für Aktersforscing* 40 (1985), pp. 209–12.

26. Leo Eitinger, R. Krell, and M. Rieck, *The Psychological and Medical Effects of Concentration Camps and Related Persecutions: A Research Bibliography* (Vancouver, 1985).

27. Paul Chodoff, "Late Effects of the Concentration Camp Syndrome," *Archives of General Psychiatry* 8 (1963), pp. 323–33; K. D. Hoppe, "Chronic Reactive Aggression in Survivors of Severe Persecution," *Comprehensive Psychiatry* 12 (1971), pp. 230–37; J. Kestenberg, "The Psychological Consequences of Punitive Institutions," *Israel Journal of Psychiatry and Related Sciences* 18 (1981), pp. 15–30.

28. W. W Eaton, J. J. Sigal, and M. Weinfeld, "Impairment in Holocaust Survivors after 33 Years: Data from an Unbiased Community Sample," *American Journal of Psychiatry* 139 (1982), pp. 773–77; I. Levav and J. H. Abrahamson, "Emotional Distress among Concentration Camp Survivors: A Community Study in Jerusalem," *Psychological Medicine* 14 (1984), pp. 215–18.

29. Leo Eitinger, "Psychological and Medical Effects of Concentration Camps," *Research Bibliography* (Haifa, 1981); Eitinger, Krell, and Rieck.

30. Levav and Abrahamson; S. Fenig and I. Levav, "Demoralization and Social Supports among Holocaust Survivors," *Journal of Nervous and Mental Disease* 179 (1991), pp. 167–72; S. Robinson et al., "The Late Effects of Nazi Persecution among Elderly Holocaust Survivors," *Acta Psychiatrica Scandinavica* 82 (1991), pp. 311–15; J. Rosen et al., "Sleep Disturbances in Survivors of the Nazi Holocaust," *American Journal of Psychiatry* 148 (1991), pp. 62–66.

31. H. Dasberg, "Trauma in Israel," in H. Dasberg et al., eds., *Society and Trauma of War* (Assen-Maastricht, 1987), pp. 1–13, 59, 60.

Part V

The Resistance

No study of Auschwitz could be complete without understanding the anti-Nazi resistance, which occurred even in the concentration camps. Such resistance required elaborate and careful organization. It did not emerge without disciplined planning and a long period of political activity carried out even in the shadows of gas chambers. Hermann Langbein, a participant in the resistance, describes the political organization, its structure, motivations, and activities, the relationship between various political movements in the camps, contacts with the outside, and the operations undertaken at Auschwitz—which ranged from blowing up crematoria at Birkenau to organized escapes.

There were very few escapes from Auschwitz. Henryk Swiebocki tells why. He details the security arrangements surrounding Auschwitz, the limitations on escape routes, and the handicaps prisoners faced. Their heads shaven, arms tattooed, dressed in camp fatigue, they could be easily identified. And those they left behind faced "collective responsibility." Prisoners were subject to almost endless roll calls in the cold of winter or the heat of summer. Random death penalties were often imposed, and thus every escaping prisoner knew that one or another of his fellow inmates might be condemned to death. Solidarity often restrained inmates from fleeing. Escapes involved planning and cooperation, but also good fortune and opportune timing. Each escape was an adventure, as Swiebocki details.

The *Sonderkommando* worked in the shadow of the ovens and the crematoria. It was their task to force victims into the gas chambers, load their bodies into the ovens, then dispose of the residue. During their brief assignment, they were well fed before joining those that went before them in the gas chambers. Several members of the commando units buried diaries in the fall of 1944 before they were put to death. Nathan Cohen examines the writings of three of them and the fragments of memory they left behind. This material is significant, especially because it is contemporaneous with the events and unfiltered by the passage of time.

Michael Berenbaum

The Auschwitz Underground

HERMANN LANGBEIN

Prisoners in every Nazi concentration camp sought ways to diminish the absolute terror of the SS. In Auschwitz—more than in any other camp—those who dared to think about resistance had to concentrate on saving lives, because unlike the destruction camps of Sobibor, Treblinka, and Belzec, Auschwitz had a large working prisoner population.

Several factors make it difficult to fully reconstruct resistance activities in the camp. Most participants and witnesses did not survive. Some groups claimed credit for the success of resistance activities and, not infrequently, tried to deny that distinction to others. And, finally, the army of SS informants throughout the camp during its duration meant that secrecy about resistance activities was essential.

Only those prisoners who survived the arrival process without strong psychological damage and those who were in work situations where they did not suffer from chronic hunger could hope to mount any form of resistance to the murderous apparatus of the SS. That was a very small minority. Any thoughts of resistance, for example, were beyond the horizon of the lifeless "*Muselman*" or the prisoners on their way to becoming "*Muselmänner*." Even the large number of prisoners who were not mainly preoccupied with hunger and finding food had lost the courage and motivation to help save others from the killing machinery. All too often they watched as someone they had managed to slip out of the deadly "selection" process—at great danger to themselves—was marked for death during the next selection. Such numbing experiences caused many prisoners to abandon any thoughts of resistance and to concentrate on keeping themselves alive. In spite of these limitations, efforts were made to save lives; there were forms of resistance.

Any prisoner who had access to the clerks' offices and to the indexes could tell from the death lists which satellite camps had the worst living conditions. New prisoners were always needed in those places where many died. For example, prisoner requisitions were especially numerous for camps that supplied laborers for the most demanding work, such as the coal mines of the IG Farben factory. The camp leadership as a rule requested that Jews be transferred to those camps. When a prisoner in the clerk's office was ordered to prepare a transfer of prisoners to a satellite camp for the next morning, the SS gave only general directions and the number of prisoners to be transferred. It was up to the clerk to put the transport list together. If an experienced inmate learned of an upcoming transfer and knew a prisoner who worked in the clerk's office, he could sometimes arrange to see the list. If he found that an acquaintance was scheduled for transfer, he could beg his connection to strike the name from the list. With luck, this worked. However, the given number always had to be met. That meant that the clerk had to choose an unknown inmate to be transferred to a camp where there would be little chance for survival.

If an inmate nurse in the infirmary learned from a friend who worked in the SS quarters that a selection of all those who did not appear to be ready for work was planned for the next day in the HKB (hospital), he could—if he had the courage and the necessary connections—hide a few individuals from his section of the HKB and spare them the gas chamber. Of course, he could save only a few from the murderous selection. Such opportunities posed dilemmas. Whom to help? And whom to send to their deaths?

The inmates' infirmary always lacked the most needed medicines. But some inmates managed to smuggle them into the camp. The civilian Polish population outside the camp frequently helped in procuring medicines. Sometimes, inmates were able to acquire them from the Canada storage rooms, where the belongings of the victims were kept. When medicine did reach the HKB, it was up to the inmate nurse or doctor to decide who would receive it. Because there was never enough medicine to go around, the medical staff found itself in a difficult situation. As Dr. Robert Waitz put it, the choice was "either to do nothing, which was a solution dictated by cowardice, or to become an activist."

Inmate doctors faced an even worse dilemma in the HKB of the women's camp. In the first years of the camp, any woman who managed to conceal the fact that she was pregnant long enough to give birth was killed with her baby. To spare the lives of pregnant women, the inmate doctors gave secret abortions regardless of the stage of pregnancy. The camp administration was strictest when it came to Jews. If a Jewish woman managed to secretly de-liver a baby under unimaginably primitive conditions, the child had to die to save the mother because it was impossible to keep a newborn hidden from the camp administration. "All the poison in the camp was set aside for this purpose, and it still was not enough," recalled Lucie Adelsberger, a Jewish doctor from Berlin. "Some mothers," she recollected, "could not forgive either themselves or us." Another doctor, Olga Lengyel, wrote years later that "the Germans made us into murderers."

Other opportunities were available to those who risked taking part in resistance activities. Any inmate who held a position of responsibility, be it kapo, block elder, clerk, nurse, or doctor, enjoyed numerous privileges and was shielded from the worst conditions, such as chronic hunger and the ceaseless fear of being beaten. These inmates were also in positions to learn more about how the camp administration worked. But they could never ignore the fact that, as privileged members of the camp, they were accomplices to the SS. Some, mostly the political prisoners, used their privilege for personal gain. Others used the available opportunities to stand up against the apparatus of the camp leadership whenever possible.

No resistance group, however, could mitigate the largest death campaign—the gassing of those Jews who were deported by the Reich Main Security Office (RSHA), declared unfit for work, and sent immediately to death.

Before Auschwitz became, in addition to a concentration camp, a death camp in 1942, primarily Poles, especially members of the Polish intelligentsia, were interned there. It was a goal of the National Socialists to eliminate the "dangerous" Polish elite and to bring the standard of the Polish people down to a base level. The first resistance groups were therefore comprised of Poles, with Polish officers often in charge. Witold Pilecki, known in Auschwitz as Tomasz Serafinski, was the leader of one such group. Problems arose when attempts were made to coordinate the work of the different Polish-officer groups because Pilecki was only a captain, and others held higher rank. Each group had five members who were sworn to secrecy. The rules of secrecy, however, were not strictly followed in the beginning. One group of older members was assigned to light work in the potato-peeling detachment, where they spoke, perhaps too freely, among themselves. Kazimierz Smolen recalled that the members of this group were given the important assignment of getting information about the concentration camp to the outside—a mission that became more important when Auschwitz was converted to a death camp. The group did have some success. As early as March 18, 1941, a communiqué from the group reached the London-based Polish government-in-exile. But the members of the Polish resistance groups paid heavily for their loose conduct. The political department of the camp learned of their activities and locked up and tortured many members. On January 25 and October 11, 1943, the SS shot 54 resistance-group members.

When RSHA transports began to arrive in Auschwitz in the spring of 1942, Auschwitz became the largest death camp, and the responsibility of those who had the strength to mount resistance efforts increased greatly. The arrival of the transports also changed the composition of the prisoner population. Whereas Poles accounted for 30.1 percent of the inmate population in May 1943, their numbers dropped to 22.3 percent in August 1944. As citizens of other nations arrived at the camp, the inmates who as Jews wore the Star of David rose to 57.4 percent in May 1943 and to 64.6 percent by August 1944. But because the Jews suffered the worst living conditions, they were the least likely to be physically able to mount resistance efforts.

When an international assembly of those with the courage and ability to resist was formed, it was the Poles who played the most active roles. They had been in the camp the longest and possessed camp "smarts," a prerequisite for every resistance activity. They also had been able to gain important positions in the infirmary and in the clerks' offices—key roles for resistance activities. Finally, the Poles had the best—and practically the only—chance to make contact with other Poles who worked in the camp and who lived in the area around the camp.

A detachment of Poles who worked in the Rajsko nursery near the main camp organized an operation to smuggle lifesaving medicine into the camp. A moving letter smuggled out of the camp in 1942 by Edward Biernacki sheds light on the extent of his activities: "In June, July, and August, I brought roughly 7,500 cc of injectable medicine into the camp infirmary as well as 70 series of typhus vaccine. Other work of the same type and its results are surely considerable. You can be sure that your wishes and hopes are not being disappointed. For your willingness to sacrifice and your thoughts, once more: God will repay you."

In November 1942, the Polish resistance members reported to their friends in Krakow that the medicine officially dispensed by the SS pharmacist covered 20 percent of their needs. Another 10 percent could be stolen, or "organized," in the camp—apparently from the Canada storage area. That meant that 70 percent of the camp's medicinal needs had to be smuggled into the camp. One can read in a surviving report that "percentagewise, we have mostly Poles [among the sick], perhaps 50 percent. We help only these."

A resistance group made up of Austrians, French, Poles, Czechs, and Germans and including both Jews and non-Jews was formed under the command of Ernst Burger, an Austrian who was sent to Auschwitz in December 1941. Czechs and Poles who had fought in the international brigades in Spain took especially active roles in the group. They were accustomed to cooperating over international borders and had language skills that eased contacts. Members with Communist party backgrounds had been raised under regimes of strict discipline and knew the value of secrecy.

In August 1942, 17 prisoners were brought to Auschwitz from Dachau. The personnel office of the prisoner quarters had requested them to help fight the typhus epidemic that was raging through Auschwitz. It had even spread to the SS troops and the civilian population. At the time, I myself was an Auschwitz prisoner and had been appointed clerk to Dr. Eduard Wirths, the new SS garrison physician. My appointment opened a new channel of communication that was enhanced by Wirths's intention to change camp health conditions in the wake of the epidemic. Almost without exception the 17 new inmates were Germans (or Austrians whom the SS considered German). Many of them had gained resistance experience working against the camp administration in Dachau. Wladyslaw Fejkiel, a Polish doctor familiar with the HKB in the main camp, believed that the transferred inmates had worked a "sort of revolution" at Dachau. The new inmates quickly made contact with Burger's group and with me.

While in prison in Krakow after the war, Auschwitz Commandant Rudolf Höss characterized Wirths as "very soft and good-natured and definitely needed strong support. . . . The whole business of the destruction of the Jews went against his moral scruples, about which he often confided in me. He often favored the inmate doctors; often I even had the impression that he treated them like colleagues." Wirths was, in fact, the first SS garrison physician to trust inmate doctors with managerial positions in the infirmary, against the general rule that inmate doctors were not to be made part of the HKB personnel. Wirths was opposed to the practice of giving prisoners who were incarcerated for criminal activities nearly unlimited power over political prisoners. So instead of using Germans with the green stripes of criminal prisoners, he installed the Germans from Dachau, who wore the red stripes of political prisoners, as camp elders in the main camp HKB and in all the inmate infirmaries under his command.

The central office had urgently bid Wirths to fight the typhus epidemic. Owing in part to the epidemic, the mortality rate among registered prisoners for the third quarter of 1942 was 20.5 percent per month. As Wirths puzzled over how to fight the rising tide of typhus, he was told that the first thing he had to do was to stop the inmates' fear of the infirmary.

That fear was justified. An inmate who could no longer drag himself to work would first report himself sick. He would be examined by an inmate doctor in the evening after the roll call, spend the night in a room in block 28, and be brought before Dr. Friedrich Entress, the SS physician in the HKB for the main camp. The inmate doctor on duty would record his diagnosis on an index card, which also listed the patient's identification number and prisoner type. With only a quick glance, Entress would decide if the patient could be ready to work again in a short time. Only then did he decide whether to admit the patient to the HKB. If it appeared that the patient would not be able to return to work or—more important—if the patient was listed as Jewish on the index card, Entress would order that the patient "be given a shot." Next, the patient would be taken to infection block 20 of the HKB and killed with an injection of phenol in the heart. A report that the Polish resistance managed to send to Krakow maintained that an average 30 to 60 people per day were "given a shot." Of this number, four to six were usually Polish. Most of the rest were Jewish, a fact that was known in the camp. Thus prisoners avoided the HKB as long as was physically possible. Their avoidance was a major cause of the rapid spread of contagious diseases in the camp.

During his postwar trial before a U.S. military tribunal, Entress said that a central order commanded the killing of the "incurably insane, incurably tuberculitic, and those continually unable to work." Although Entress overstepped these bounds daily, he reported to Wirths, his superior, that the patients had tuberculosis. With help from the new camp senior of the HKB, I was able to prove to Wirths that Entress had never examined the patients for tuberculosis. As a result, Entress was transferred to an outlying camp and the injections were appreciably reduced. A message smuggled out of Auschwitz in May 1943 reads: "General easing of tension. The sick are remaining in the infirmary till a complete recovery and return of their strength." The fear of reporting sick had diminished, and the conditions needed to fight the battle against the typhus epidemic had improved.

The Polish resistance movement anchored in the HKB realized the importance of cooperation among all those working to improve living conditions in the camp. Thus the disparate groups made contact and shortly thereafter they began to cooperate with each other.

The key meeting took place on May 1, 1943. It was a National Socialist holiday, and many SS members had taken the day off. As a result, only a few work detachments were sent out. The meeting was attended by representatives from the Polish officers' group and by Jozef Cyrankiewicz, who represented another Polish resistance group. Many of the Poles considered Cyrankiewicz to be an official of the Krakow Socialist party. The purpose of the meeting was to mount a unified resistance. During the meeting, some argued against working with Germans or Austrians because they spoke the language of the killers. More than a few Poles expressed antisemitic prejudices and maintained that it was dangerous to work with Jews because they could not hold up under torture. It is to Cryankiewicz's credit that he successfully overcame such tendencies among his countrymen.

The international leadership of the united movement, called Battle Group Auschwitz, consisted of two Poles and two Austrians. Although their activities centered on the main camp, they did have contact with some outlying camps, especially the largest—Buna (Monowitz). Their contact there was a group of politically unified Germans and Austrians who had been transferred in the fall of 1942 from Buchenwald when that camp was made all Jewish. At Buna (Monowitz), the group members had managed to assume the most important positions in the HKB. It was more difficult for Battle Group Auschwitz to maintain contact with Birkenau, the largest camp complex. But resistance groups were active there as well. For example, in the women's camp in Birkenau, groups of French and Czechoslovakian women, including Czech Jews, became allies to successfully fight the murderous methods of the camp administration.

An unusual resistance group that was devoted almost exclusively to saving lives was organized by Jews who were transferred to Auschwitz from Theresienstadt in September 1943. The men, women, and children were incarcerated together in a section of Birkenau without going through the usual selection process. A group of young Zionists (youth movement activists) from Theresienstadt proposed that a block be equipped for use by children eight to 14 years old. Freddy Hirsch, an inmate with the demeanor of a gym teacher, impressed the SS with his ability to instill discipline with a whistle. The SS permitted the block to be established, and a school of sorts was set up and classes were organized. The administration eventually showed off the facility to visitors. The resistance groups in Birkenau knew that the SS planned to gas the Theresienstadt family camp in six months. They suggested that Hirsch—the strongest authority in that section of camp—organize a revolt when the time came. But Hirsch apparently chose suicide, and most of the other family camp members went to the gas chambers. A few youths, however, were separated from the others at the last moment, spared because SS personnel had grown fond of them.

Every group that tried to help deflect the worst measures, improve conditions, or gather information had to contend with an army of informers fielded by the Political Division, as the camp Gestapo was known. For their protection, it was necessary for the resistance groups to uncover and, when necessary, kill informants. Commandant Höss wrote of successes that Battle Group Auschwitz enjoyed in this regard in the main camp: "It was hardly possible to maintain [informants] in the infirmary." The Political Division knew that the center of the resistance lay in the HKB. As a result, it tried to place as many informants there as possible.

As in every concentration camp, the prisoners who worked in the Auschwitz munitions factories, including the Union Werke, attempted sabotage whenever possible. Their theory was that the enemy should get as few weapons as possible from their slaves. The SS reacted with extreme violence to every attempt at sabotage. For example, a prisoner named Tuschenschneider in the chemical factory in the satellite camp at Blechhammer took a piece of wire to bind up his shoe so he would not stand out from the other workers when marching home. A German overseer observed this and wrote down his number and the number of a Greek Jew who also saw the "sabotage." They were hanged along with their Kapo, a young Frenchman, in January 1945.

Despite such deterrence measures, prisoners made attempts at true sabotage. Roger Abada, a Frenchman, recalled that it was possible to set up systematic sabotage that the officials at the German munitions factories (DAW) could not track down. Their efforts reduced production by 50 percent in a few months. Sometimes efforts to sabotage defense businesses were spontaneous, and sometimes they were planned. Whenever possible, Battle Group Auschwitz placed specialists in enterprises where qualified employees were requested, and where sabotage seemed feasible. The success of activities in the Union, a munitions factory, which employed women, is evident from complaints that the grenades produced in the factory did not explode. A group of prisoners from the Laurahutte satellite camp who worked in the technical bureau of the Rhine metal factory of AG Dusseldorf found a way to damage the mechanisms of the artillery after it had been inspected. Thus their sabotage was not detected. Prisoners who dismantled damaged aircraft in Birkenau systematically destroyed equipment and instruments that could otherwise have been reused.

After the Polish and international prisoners merged, Battle Group Auschwitz was chiefly led by Polish, German, and other political prisoners, who sought ways to influence individual SS members. Occasionally, spontaneous human emotion came into play. This was especially common when an SS member learned that a prisoner was his countryman; then the prisoner was able to use the kinship to advance the resistance. Dr. Otto Wolken, for example, was classified as "unable to work" at the arrival selections. When an SS man heard that Wolken spoke an Austrian dialect, he asked where he came from. Wolken told him, "From Vienna." The SS man replied, "Aha. A countryman. I am from Linz," and pulled him out of the group destined for immediate gassing. An SS man learned that Renee Jellinek came from his home city of Drunn and arranged for her to be transferred to the nursing personnel, which saved her life. A relationship that could almost be called friendship arose between Heinz Lewin, a Jew who played in the Birkenau men's band, and Joachim Wolff, an SS officer. Wolff, who was described as civil, often attended the band practices, where he learned that Lewin, like himself, came from Halle, in Saale. When Wolff returned from vacations, he would tell Lewin how things were at home and describe the effects of the bombings.

Once the prisoners realized the value of personal contacts with fellow countrymen, they sought to expand them. Katharina Princz learned that a 50-year-old SS man named Nagel came from Bratislava, as did she. Nagel spoke Hungarian with her and other women from the area, and eventually he promised to smuggle mail and deliver packages for her. Two Austrian SS members helped a fellow countryman smuggle out illegal correspondence in return for items the prisoners could steal. Thus goods could be "organized" from Canada and other sources that not only helped the prisoners but also led to the corruption of the guards. SS officer Sepp Spanner, one of the two Austrian SS members, said that he had spoken to and later helped prisoners whom he heard speaking with an Austrian accent. Of course these cases were exceptional and related mostly to prisoners of German origins.

The resistance groups used the opportunities that their SS sources offered to initiate further contacts. As Zalman Lewenthal, chronicler of the special detachment, described in an account of the camp that he buried near the crematorium, a group of activists from his detachment was able to smuggle reports and "no small sum of money" to the resistance movement in the camp.

Jozef Cyrankiewicz and Stanislaw Klodzinski wrote up-to-date reports, and Battle Group Auschwitz sent them to Krakow with the help of Polish civilians who worked in the camp. The information was sent to the Polish government-in-exile in London by means of a hidden radio transmitter. The leaked information, in conjunction with the no longer concealable corruption of leading SS officers, led to a change of Auschwitz commandants. SS man Wilhelm Boger, the well-informed right hand of the Political Division, said on July 5, 1945, while in U.S. detention, that "as the mass deaths in Auschwitz were made known to the world in the fall of 1943, changes were suddenly made in the leadership of the camp." Rudolf Höss was replaced as commandant by Arthur Liebehenschel. Höss, however, was placed in the central management of concentration camps. The change in command was made known on November 11, with the new commandant's first order.

Opportunities for the resistance movement to influence the top rungs of the camp administration increased with the change in camp leadership. Liebehenschel agreed with Wirths that criminals should not be given unlimited power over other prisoners. He arranged for the "green" camp elder to be replaced by a German political prisoner who had been incarcerated in concentration camps since 1933. The new camp elder in turn ensured that beatings by his subordinate block elders would cease, or at least be greatly reduced. However, Liebehenschel could enact such changes in the main camp only because Auschwitz was divided into three parts after Höss left. Birkenau was renamed Auschwitz II, and Monowitz and another satellite camp were combined as Auschwitz III. Each had its own commandant.

The worse the situation on the front became for the Germans, the better the chances to coerce SS members to help the prisoners. Eventually prisoners from Battle Group Auschwitz made contact with a young SS block leader and induced him to join them in escaping and fleeing to a group of Polish partisans who were operating south of Auschwitz. The SS man was considered reliable because he came from East Prussia, an area being threatened by Russian troops. It was understandable why he would want to leave Auschwitz. Although the SS man repeatedly delayed the time of the escape, he did help the prisoners tremendously by furnishing them with an SS uniform and the passcard that was needed by any SS person who wanted to lead prisoners out through the series of guard posts. The escape took place without him. A Battle Group member, dressed in the SS uniform, led his fellow prisoners, dressed in their zebra suits, through the guard posts. A meeting point, where the escapees were to be given clothes and weapons, was agreed upon with the partisans. The goal was to initiate a coordinated action between the partisans and the prisoners to fight the Nazis as soon as the Soviet troops neared Auschwitz. Whenever possible, the partisans were to spare the Auschwitz inmates from the fate of the prisoners of the concentration camp at Majdanek. As Soviet troops approached Majdanek in July 1944, the SS killed most of the inmates. Those who survived were marched to Auschwitz. Of more than 1,000 evacuees, only 837 arrived back in Auschwitz on July 28. The rest were murdered during the march.

While that escape was being planned and repeatedly delayed, Battle Group Auschwitz was planning another more extensive escape. An SS man named Frank was to smuggle out five prisoners on October 27, 1944, in a chest disguised as a wash transport. The group comprised four Poles and the Austrian Ernst Burger, a leader of Battle Group Auschwitz since the beginning. The resistance had been in contact with Frank since the summer of 1944. He had reported to them on the strength of the troops and functioned as a contact with the Polish underground organization outside the camp. It is not known if Frank was the same SS block leader who was involved with another escape planned for that summer; nor is it known why Frank persuaded another SS man to join the escape. The other SS man was the weak link in the chain of secrecy. He betrayed the escape, and the prisoners were taken from the chest, tortured, and finally hanged in front of the roll call. Frank was placed before an SS tribunal and shot. Plans for any coordinated resistance upon the approach of Soviet troops were thus defeated.

Detailed reports about Auschwitz and the mass destruction of Jews and other prisoners was sent to the outside world with the help of civilians who worked beside prisoners in the factories and who broke the command not to make contact with the prisoners. Of the more than 2,000 secret messages that are extant today, approximately 350 were sent by Battle Group Auschwitz.

The prisoners knew that the SS members listened to the BBC. And they knew that broadcasts that included information about Auschwitz had a noticeable effect on the SS. Prisoners who worked in the SS quarters used SS health records to prepare a list of names and numbers of those SS members who were particularly active in the destruction apparatus. The list, sent to London through the Polish underground in Krakow, was broadcast by the BBC along with a warning that persons on the list would be held responsible for the mass crimes perpetrated in Auschwitz. After the program was broadcast in early 1944, the prisoners sensed a nervousness among the SS. It was later learned, for example, that Gerhard Lachmann of the Political Department received a paybook under another name. His real name had been on this list.

A report to the chief of the security police dated July 5, 1944, made resistance members aware of a telegram that was intercepted on its way to London from the special service of the Foreign Office in the British Embassy in Bern. It contained news of the deportation of Hungarian Jews to "Birkenau on Oswiecim in Oberschlesien," and was accompanied by numbers and a reference to "the four crematoria in Birkenau." It also included a suggestion that the Allies bomb the train tracks from Hungary to Birkenau and "the facilities of the death camps." Such a suggestion had been made by Battle Group Auschwitz.

In addition to such reports, the Allies were able to get concrete information from Auschwitz escapees who had seen the killing machinery. One of these escapees was Jerzy Tabeau, a Polish medical student who escaped from the camp on November 19, 1943. Later, in Krakow, he wrote a detailed 19-page report on Auschwitz, which was circulated among the Allies under the title "The Report of a Polish Major." Two Slovakian Jews, Alfred Wetzler and Walter Rosenberg (Rudolf Vrba), escaped on April 7, 1944, and reached Slovakia. Owing to their camp experience and their recent duties as block clerks, they were able to write a detailed report illustrated with sketches that they drew as they prepared to flee. Their report, which spoke chiefly of the massive destruction campaign against Jews, was supplemented by information from Polish Jews Czeslaw Mordowicz and Arnost Rosin, who fled from Birkenau on May 27, 1944. The reports reached the Allies, who reacted with hesitation and only later cleared them for publication.

The British public reacted more quickly to a communication from Battle Group Auschwitz, which reached London on September 6, 1944, by the usual Krakow route. It told of the camp administration's plan to destroy the camp by means of artillery and aerial bombardment upon the approach of Soviet troops. The SS called this "the Moll plan" after Otto Moll, head of the crematoria and gas chambers. It is probable, but not certain, that the publication of this communication in England was one of the reasons why the Moll plan was never put into effect.

Battle Group Auschwitz also organized multiple escapes of prisoners who were in particular danger. Because it was possible to overcome antisemitic tendencies both in their own ranks and in the Polish underground that took in the escapees, many Jewish prisoners in Auschwitz owed their lives to such escapes.

A report from the chief of the Sipo (security police) at Katowice dated December 18, 1944, reveals how the security police office assessed the activities of the resistance in and around this camp. The Sipo knew that Cyrankiewicz, "commandant" of the Polish underground in the camp, used the pseudonym "Red" to contact the underground outside the camp. The Sipo also knew of the group's work concerning situation reports, details about new and transferred prisoners, camp structures, guard personnel and assessments of individual SS men, inmate organizations, future plans, and preparations for escapes.

Adelaide Hautval performed an act of resistance that was unique in the history of the Nazi concentration camps. A gynecologist, she was the daughter of an evangelical pastor in Lothringen. She had complained of the Germans' poor handling of Jewish women in a French prison. The SS reaction was swift: "If she wants to defend Jews, then let her share their fate." She was deported to Auschwitz. The SS garrison physician put her in experimental block 10 in the main camp, where she was to work in the sterilization experiments on Jewish women begun by Carl Clauberg. When Hautval saw what was being done there, she refused to take part. The garrison physician asked if she knew that Jews were, essentially, subhuman. She answered that there were various kinds of people, some different from her, some different from him. Through a combination of luck and help from inmates of the HKB, Hautval survived.

Battle Group Auschwitz was helped by the fact that some prisoners were allowed to receive packages. The order to allow deliveries was given to concentration camp commandants on October 30, 1942, in an effort to keep up the strength of the workers in the armament industries. Jews, Gypsies, and Russians were not allowed to receive packages. In February 1943, packages began to arrive in large numbers. On June 20, 1943, Stanislaw Klodzinski asked the Polish underground on behalf of the Battle Group to send prisoner addresses to foreign countries so that packages could be sent to Auschwitz—when possible through the International Red Cross. In addition to the concrete help provided by the foodstuffs that arrived, prisoners hoped that "the Germans will be shown that the whole world knows what is going on in Auschwitz." Lists of inmates and their prison numbers were collected. It was decided to include the addresses of Germans in the camp as well as Czechs and others. Although the SS confiscated many of the packages, the campaign did have an effect.

"We were convinced that we would never come out of this hell, and we wanted the world to know everything" was the motivation for Vera Foltynov, a Jewish Czechoslovakian communist, to smuggle plans of the Birkenau crematorium and its built-in gas chamber to Czechoslovakia. Like her friends Waleri Walova (also a Jewish Czechoslovakian communist) and Krystyna Horczak (a Pole), she worked in the central site supervision office of the Waffen SS.

I had similar reasons for smuggling to comrades in Vienna the numbers of those who had been taken to the garrison at Auschwitz and murdered. As clerk for the SS garrison physician, I was able to collect the number of prisoners killed from the quarterly and monthly reports that the physician routinely sent to Berlin-Oranienburg. The lowest number (2.3 percent of the total prisoner population) was recorded in the October 1943 report. The figure climbed to 10 percent in March 1944. In Vienna, Otto Langbein and his friends copied a pamphlet that contained information about the death camp and put copies in mailboxes and between the pages of telephone books in long-distance phone booths.

It is important to stress that all the steps of resistance that were taken cannot be included here because many cannot be confirmed. The number of resistance efforts that cannot be reported because there are no surviving witnesses or participants remains a mystery. Little is known about the resistance attempts of those who were immediately selected for the gas chamber. It will never be known how many desperate acts occurred before the poison gas took effect. Only a few have been documented. On May 25, 1944, a few hundred Hungarian Jews attempted to hide in the ditches and undergrowth around the gas chambers. The SS hunted them down with flashlights and shot them. Three days later, a similar escape was attempted with the same results. Battle Group Auschwitz reported the incident to Krakow.

The most clearly documented resistance effort was an act of desperation that took place in the crematorium on October 23, 1943. Former prisoners Arie Fuks and Kazimierz Smolen testified on the subject in the Frankfurt Auschwitz trial. Fuks said that he heard his detachment captain say that a Jewish woman, a dancer from Warsaw, refused to go from the dressing room into the gas chamber and was subsequently threatened by SS man Schillinger. She grabbed his pistol, shot and killed him, and wounded another SS man in the leg. Smolen, who worked in the records department of the Political Department at the time, said he had heard of the event and knew the name of the wounded SS member, Wilhelm Emmerich. Most prisoners learned that Schillinger had died while en route to the hospital at Katowice through an order from the commandant to give him an honorable obituary.

Jerzy Tabeau described the event in his "Report of a Polish Major":

> 1,800 Polish Jews arrived from Bergen-Belsen on an RSHA transport; they had passes with them allowing them to travel to Latin American countries. They were part of the so-called "exchange Jews." . . . Only after their arrival on the

off-loading ramp did they realize that they had been brought to Auschwitz [and not to a place from which they could leave the country, as they had been told] . . . . Men and women were separated on the ramp. . . . After inspecting the travel documents and making the announcement that a disinfection was mandatory before further travel, the SS led the women to the dressing room. The order to undress disquieted the women; the SS, however, began collecting their rings and watches. A woman who recognized that she was in a hopeless situation flung an article of discarded clothing over the SS-Oberscharführer Schillinger's head, tore his pistol away from him and shot him three times. She also shot at the SS-Unterscharführer Emmerich. The other women fell on the SS with their bare hands; one received a bite wound on the nose, another's face was scratched. . . . Some of the women were shot down, the rest were led into the gas chambers and killed. Schillinger died on the way to the hospital. Emmerich eventually recovered his health; his leg, however, was lamed.

In retaliation, the SS guard posts opened up with random machinegun fire the next day. Thirteen prisoners were killed, four wounded seriously, and 42 slightly wounded. Tabeau's source is unknown, and no one from the RSHA transport survived to tell the story.

Höss testified in Nuremberg about this desperate effort, stating that

a transport from Belsen arrived. After roughly two-thirds, mostly men, were in the gas chambers, a mutiny broke out among the last third in the dressing room. Three or four SS underofficers entered the room with weapons in order to speed up the undressing. . . . Lighting wire was ripped out, the SS [were] attacked, one [was] stabbed to death, and all [were] relieved of their weapons. As it was completely dark in the room, a wild gun battle ensued between the guard post at the exit and the prisoners inside. On my arrival, I locked the doors, ended the gassing of the first two-thirds, and went into the room with flashlights and guards; we drove the prisoners into a corner from which we led them out one at a time to an adjacent room, where they were shot with small-caliber pistols by my command.

In the document buried by Zalman Lewenthl, he stated that this rebellion was triggered by a young Jew. Although details of the incident differ, there is one constant among the accounts: on October 23, 1943, a Jew executed an SS man who was participating in mass murder.

After the SS converted Auschwitz to a death camp, it assigned prisoners to a special detachment, the Sonderkommando, to work in the crematoria and gas chambers. The prisoners they chose were mostly strong young people who didn't know the camp because they had just arrived on an RSHA transport. Under orders from Adolf Eichmann, most Sonderkommando members were killed after every death campaign because they bore Nazi secrets. Only skilled workers, such as stokers, mechanics, and inmate officials, were exempted, according to Höss's testimony at the Warsaw tribunal.

The inmates' knowledge of the SS policy of killing put unimaginable psychological pressure on their daily work. On December 3, 1942, 300 members of the special detachment were murdered in a gas chamber. It had most likely been revealed that the night shift kapo, a Slovakian Jew named Weiss, had planned an escape. The traitor was beaten to death by members of the night shift before they were gassed. A countryman of Weiss who had contact with the Sonderkommandos reported that the next day the SS "formed a new special detachment of Jews deported from Sosnowitz."

Plans among detachment members to revolt, escape, and rebel remained alive, however. Lewenthal wrote about why it was so hard to come to a final decision to take a rebellious action: "There was always someone who felt tied to the camp, one because of the good food [members of the special detachment had the chance to "organize" more than enough extra food], another because of a girl he loved."

Head kapo Kaminski, who was deported to Auschwitz in a transport of Jews from Bialystok in the summer of 1942 and assigned to the special detachment, played an extraordinary role. Dov Paisikovic described Kaminski as small, of above-average intelligence, and between 30 and 40 years of age (old for a member of the detachment). Lewenthal wrote that as preparation for the most intensive death campaign—against the Hungarian Jews— "simply the entire detachment, regardless of which shift or class one belonged to, with no exceptions, not even from the worst, pushed to finally end this work." The replacement of Commandant Liebenschel (assessed as "too soft" by the central SS office) and the return of Höss to Auschwitz on May 8, 1944, fully empowered to carry out the death campaign, were strong signals to the prisoners. Additionally, the number of inmate members of the Sonderkommando was increased. Its highest documented level was 952 prisoners. More than half were Hungarian Jews, 200 were Greek Jews, and the remainder were Jews from Poland, France, and Czechoslovakia. After the death campaign against the Hungarian Jews, the size of the special detachment was reduced, as was the routine. Two hundred prisoners from the special detachment were killed with Zyklon B on September 23. The SS tried to keep the truth about the killings from the special detachment members by telling them that the murdered members had been transferred to the outlying camp at Gleiwitz (Gliwice). The detachment, however, learned the truth.

At that time, Kaminski, who had prepared a revolt along with two Greek Jews, decided to wait no longer. One of the Greeks, said to be named Alexander Hereirra (or Errera), pressed the resistance movement in the camp to initiate a coordinated operation. Lewenthal wrote:

We began to put an appropriate pressure on the camp [he apparently meant the resistance in the camp] so that they would understand that it was now high time. Unfortunately, the date was pushed back from day to day. All of our detachments are of the opinion that we are in much more danger than all the other prisoners in the camp, even more than the Jews in the camp. We believed that the Germans would erase every trace of their crimes to date. The only way they could do this was through the extermination of all our detachments. The large offensive had begun. We could see that the Russians were daily drawing nearer. Others [apparently people in the camp resistance] came to the conclusion . . . that it would be better to wait until the front was closer, until . . . the disorganization of the German military was greater. From their perspective they were right, all the more so since they did not feel directly threatened with destruction.

The leadership of Battle Group Auschwitz evidently had realized that even after a successful coordinated breakout, there was no chance to house, care for, or give a decent chance of survival to as many people as might escape. Therefore a massive escape effort could only be justified if Soviet troops were in the immediate area.

A Jewish group of resistance members, including Union workers, supported the revolt by smuggling out gunpowder on women who worked in the powder pavilion. Although the young Jewish women who worked there were very strictly supervised, Roza Robota, a 23-year-old member of the group, found ways for the women to smuggle out tiny amounts each time they left work. Wrobel, a Polish Jew assigned to the special detachment, received the powder, and a Russian technician named Borodin fashioned a kind of hand grenade. Porebski, an electrician who had access to the special detachment through his work, acted as liaison between them and the resistance members in the camp. He described the crude armaments as "small lead containers, filled with powder, small stones, crumbled bricks, and a fuse."

Kaminski, the kapo, did not live to see the revolt. It appears that he was betrayed. The SS grew suspicious and shot him, letting it be known in the Sonderkommando that he was shot because he tried to kill an SS member. But plans for the revolt continued. Members of the special detachments of all four Birkenau crematoria were to break out simultaneously and attempt to destroy the crematoria. In the event, however, it happened differently.

On Saturday, October 7, 1944, the Sonderkommando received a report from Battle Group Auschwitz that another 300 members were soon to be "removed" (killed). At that time the total strength of the detachment was 663. The 300 (whose names had been released by the SS) decided to revolt. A German kapo surprised the conspirators at midday and threatened to expose them. The conspirators immediately killed him and began a rebellion in crematorium IV without the planned simultaneous actions. Lewenthal described the revolt, although he was not an eyewitness because he was working in another crematorium. When the SS came to take the 300 away, "they showed incredible courage, in that they would not move. They raised a loud cry, and threw themselves on the guards with hammers and axes, wounding a few of them and beating the rest with whatever they could, and threw stones at them."

Further details of this heroic rebellion, the only major rebellion in the history of Auschwitz, cannot be exactly recounted. None of the members of the special detachment in crematorium IV survived. It is known, however, that the rebels blew up and set crematorium IV on fire. The members of the special detachment in crematorium II heard the explosion, saw the flames, and managed to overpower the German kapo and throw him, still alive, into one of the ovens. "Without a doubt he deserved this, perhaps this death was too easy for him," Lewenthal wrote. They also threw an SS member, whom they had disarmed, into an oven and beat another SS member to death. They tore down the fence around the crematorium and the wire entanglement that separated them from the women's camp and broke out.

Sonderkommando members in the other crematoria were surprised by the timing of the outbreak. "Without preparation, without the help of the prisoners of the entire camp, and in broad daylight, it was difficult even to believe that someone, even a single individual, would be able to save himself. Therefore we had to wait. Perhaps this would continue until evening, and then, if we thought it urgent, we would do it." These are the words Lewenthal used to describe the situation from his vantage point in crematorium III. He added: "It was not easy to hold back the Russians who were with us." Alarms rang out, and the SS immediately moved to cut off the escapees' route. The escapees barricaded themselves in a barn in Rajsko. The SS set it on fire and slaughtered everyone. Members of the inmates' fire department who turned out to extinguish the blaze in crematorium IV witnessed the slaughter of all the special detachment members near the crematorium. Later the firefighters had to extinguish the barn in Rajsko.

The ranks of the Sonderkommando had been reduced to 212 prisoners; 451 members had been killed in the rebellion. The SS reported that three SS officers were dead. One of the few surviving Sonderkommando members recalled that 12 SS members were wounded. Crematorium IV could never be used again for gassing.

Most of the organizers of the planned revolt were killed after the breakout. Zalman Gradowski, from Luna in the district of Grodno, buried a document near the crematorium just as Lewenthal had. He wrote that he had buried it "under the ashes, the most certain place where one will excavate in order to find traces of the millions of murdered people. We of the special detachment have long sought to bring an end to the horrible work we were made to do under pain of death." His notes were dated September 6, 1944, one month before the rebellion.

Jankiel Handelsman and Josel Warszawski (whose name was really Dorebus), who had been deported to Auschwitz on an RSHA transport from France, both died in the revolt. Warszawski, born in 1906, had been an active communist in Poland and France. Handelsman, born in 1908, was locked in a bunker after the rebellion and evidently died as a result of torture. Lewenthal also named other members of the revolt: Lajb Panusz (Herszko) and Ajyzyk Kalniak, both from Lomza; Lajb Langfus, born in Warsaw and deported to Auschwitz from Makow Mazowieki; and Jozef Deresinski from Luna in Grodno. A Greek who survived the special detachment, a professor from the University of Athens, also named Greek Jews Baruch, Burdo, Carasso, Ardite, and Jachon.

The Political Department was enraged. Surviving members of the Sonderkommando were captured and tortured. And the SS sought to find out how the powder that was used to blow up crematorium IV had made its way from the Union factory to the special detachment. Three Jews who worked in the factory—Ella Gartner, Ester Wajsblum, and Regina Safirszty—were locked in the bunker on October 10. Roza Robota, from the stock camp, was also locked in the bunker on the accusation that she had organized the smuggling of the powder to Birkenau. They resisted every torture. On January 6, 1945, the four women were hanged with other prisoners in attendance. It was the last execution at Auschwitz. On January 18, the approaching Soviet troops forced the SS to evacuate the camp.

Prisoner Escapes

HENRYK SWIEBOCKI

Their lives constantly in danger, under conditions of permanent uncertainty, the prisoners of Auschwitz sought deliverance wherever they could. For many, escape appeared the only option. The will to save their life, combined with yearning for freedom with their families and for their native land, especially among the Poles, played a crucial part in the decision to attempt to escape. However, the desire to save one's life was not always a chief motive. In rare cases, other considerations also played a part, including the determination to smuggle out evidence of the SS crimes, to inform the outside world about the camp, and to establish contact with various resistance movements.

In practice, every escape attempt posed a Herculean challenge. In addition to the powerful presence of SS guards, the camp boasted a sophisticated security system, constantly being improved by the Germans. Thus prisoners who approached the electrified fence that ringed the camp and who entered the so-called neutral zone risked being shot without warning by SS guards manning watchtowers, which formed the so-called small guard chain. The outer security zone, called the area of interest of the Auschwitz concentration camp, encircled the electrified fence. Intensively policed, this huge tract of land, covering about 40 square kilometers, had been emptied of the local Polish population except for a handful of skilled workers and their families—mostly miners and railroad workers deemed indispensable for the German war economy. Next to the camp, a special "restricted area" was established. Entering or leaving it was permitted only to bearers of a special document issued by the camp commandant. Numerous signs reading "Forbidden zone!

Violators shot without warning!" were posted throughout. A special SS settlement, inhabited by families of the SS Auschwitz personnel, a community hostile to prisoners, was established in the camp's vicinity. A similar attitude characterized the Volksdeutsche from the Ukraine, Wallachia, Moldova, Bessarabia, and Semgorod, who were settled on the farms of Poles expelled from the area.

With the discovery of a prisoner's escape, SS men immediately were put on alert and set off in pursuit. The first sites to be searched were roadside ditches and groves. In addition to motorized troops, the SS unleashed specially trained hounds. Security around the camp and the surrounding protection zone was reinforced by posting SS sentries on the watchtowers forming the so-called large guard chain, positioned several hundred meters to several kilometers from the camp fence. Shifts of SS guards manned the towers for three days and nights. Only on the fourth day, or earlier if the escaping prisoner was captured, were the guards of the large guard chain recalled.

Escaping prisoners had little chance to get away. First, their appearance—shaven head, camp fatigues—and the number tattooed on their arms made them easy to spot and identify. Second, non-Polish prisoners were in unfamiliar terrain and could not speak the language of the local population. Third, upon discovery of an escape, camp authorities immediately notified the Gestapo, the criminal police (Kripo), and border police (Greko). Armed with information about the escaped prisoners, their camp serial numbers, and the date of escape, German police were thorough and meticulous in checks they conducted within their jurisdiction. Fourth, the names of the escaped prisoners were entered into lists of wanted persons forwarded to all police stations. All these measures, especially the latter two, enabled the Germans to apprehend escapees long after their escape, even at some distance.

Prisoners deciding to escape must have been fully aware that once captured, their fate was sealed. In most cases the penalty was death. However, before being put to death (by shooting, hanging, or starvation), the victim was subjected to gruesome interrogation by the Gestapo, aimed at obtaining information about the escape itself and any accomplices. Reprisals were unleashed against other prisoners as well. In their efforts to stamp out escapes, camp authorities resorted to collective responsibility, applied in various forms. One technique was a roll call lasting for many hours (the longest took 19 hours on July 6–7, 1940), during which prisoners had to stand at attention, squat, or kneel in the mud (in Birkenau, for example), regardless of weather or season.

Another form of collective responsibility was the death penalty against prisoners in the same work squad (*Kommando*), or who lived in the same block or barracks as the escapee. Usually 10 prisoners would be selected for death, but in some cases even more died. Death by starvation was particularly horrible; it was applied in the bunkers of block 11 ("the death block") in the main camp of Auschwitz I. In 1941, Father Maximilian (Rajmund) Kolbe, a Polish priest of the Dominican order, stepped forward to save the life of another prisoner condemned to death by starvation. Kolbe died on August 14, 1941; the prisoner he volunteered to replace, Franciszek Gajowniczek, survived the camp.

Reprisals for escapes were not confined to prisoners and were often unleashed against civilians living in the vicinity. Those suspected of having assisted escapees were incarcerated in the camp, often with their families. In some cases, the parents of the escaped prisoner were arrested and put in the camp, until, so they were told, the escapee was found. The principle of collective responsibility was applied up to the second half of 1943; later, collective punishment was used sporadically. For many prisoners contemplating escape, it proved an insurmountable barrier.

However, one circumstance worked to the advantage of an escapee, namely, the fact that many prisoners worked in the vast area outside the camp. Prospects for escape from an out-of-camp workplace were much better than from within the camp itself. SS guards could not keep close and constant watch on all prisoners. In some situations, prisoners managed to put the SS men off their guard by taking advantage of the terrain. Most escapes originated outside the camp.

Attitudes of the local population played a crucial part in the success of escape attempts. Residents living near the camp, both those not uprooted from the "interests area" and those who lived outside it, assisted escapees on many occasions and took part in organizing escapes notwithstanding the risk and danger involved. In 1940, the Auschwitz commandant reported to the high SS and police leader in Breslau that "the local population is fanatically Polish, and, as has been ascertained by intelligence sources, prepared to take any action against the hated SS camp personnel. Every prisoner who managed to escape can count on help the moment he reaches the wall of a first Polish farmstead."[1]

Members of Polish resistance organizations active near the camp were drawn from the local population. The resistance devoted most of its efforts to providing material assistance to the prisoners, especially by smuggling food and medicines into the camp. The resistance also helped to establish contacts between Polish prisoners and their relatives outside the camp and extended assistance to escapees. Various resistance organizations also served as conduits of clandestine communication with the camp, smuggling letters and reports about the crimes of the SS out of the camp.[2]

Other circumstances also worked to an escapee's benefit. Beginning in 1942, when Auschwitz functioned as the center of annihilation of European

Jews, their belongings were stored in camp depots and from there dispatched to various destinations in the Reich. Prisoners planning to escape could sometimes gain illicit access to the plundered property in order to outfit themselves with civilian clothes, footwear, and other indispensable articles. Money, gold, and diamonds that belonged to murdered Jews also found their way into the hands of prisoners, who used them to bribe SS personnel to help them escape or at least to turn a blind eye at the critical moment. This, however, entailed enormous risk of betrayal or extortion.

The first escape in the history of Auschwitz came on July 6, 1940, when Polish prisoner Tadeusz Wiejowski managed to get away. He was assisted by five other Poles employed as civilian workers by a German construction firm working on the grounds of the recently established camp. Dressed in the clothes of one of these workers, Wiejowski walked out in their company. Furnished with money and food by the civilian workers, he left the area by freight train. Two days later, his accomplices were arrested and, following a cruel interrogation, were sentenced to death, later commuted to three floggings and incarceration in the camp. Only one of them, Boleslaw Bicz, survived, but he died shortly after the war.[3]

Many others followed Wiejowski's example by seizing opportunities and often displaying great cunning and ingenuity. They escaped individually and in groups. Many escapes were spontaneous affairs, executed ad hoc, but there were also numerous attempts that required a great deal of planning. The latter stood a much better chance of success, especially when assisted by the Polish resistance and the local population. Sometimes external help was the key factor in successful attempts, especially in 1943–44, when the number of escapees from Auschwitz rose sharply.

Preparations for escape included setting the date and planning the mode and routes, including such details as meeting points with resistance contacts. Civilian clothes, wigs, supplements to SS uniforms, identity documents, and other articles needed by escapees were smuggled into the camp. Props and disguises varied, depending on whether escaping prisoners planned to get away disguised as civilian workers or SS men. Sometimes hand-drawn maps with the escape route were provided to escapees. Messages smuggled out of Auschwitz give glimpses into these preparations.

> Dear Mrs. Jadzka: The man with the wicker should wait for us on Tuesday, Wednesday, and Thursday from 10 A.M. till 1 P.M. There will be four of us. I will be dressed in a uniform. Others have three pairs of civilian trousers and three caps. I need a cap size 57, four jackets, and one pair of trousers. I have no civilian [clothes]. Let me go over it once again: one complete suit of clothes for me, one cap and three jackets. The place as we agreed. Skidzin. To be on the safe side, please send once more a provisional plan on Monday and a reply whether the date suits you. In case of pouring rain at 8 o'clock, the whole ven-

ture is put on hold automatically. But if it just drizzles we go. I have to have your reply on Monday, because in view of recent events, I don't know how things are outside. So we agree on the 10th of this month, Tuesday, from 10 A.M. to 1 P.M. at Skidzin, as marked on the plan. Respectfully, Kucz.[4]

August 14. "Viper." This group must leave the camp. Alert on the Bobrek bridge for 20 days. Increased alert from midnight to 3 A.M. The main concern is shelter during the day, so that they can march during the night. Please tell Anna Cieliczko, Zakopane, GG, Parkstrasse 935, to leave the premises immediately; they are looking for her. She must be helped and has to leave. Greetings, Staszek. [5]

There will be four of us. . . . When you are ready I'll give you the date. The important thing is to find out what is the best route, where there are fewer troops, so that they won't bother us. We'll have overalls as workers should. Now, as to the papers. Werka had done our papers with photographs. Get them from her; this would be the best thing to do. . . . Please write to me what would be the best route once we leave the grove where we have met, beginning the Wola road, a little farther away from the railway station. This would be the first sally port, where we could set up a meeting. Please describe in detail the next step, as well as recognition signals which would enable us to understand each other.[6]

Alfons, November 25, 1944. Please give a meeting point for one person on the Auschwitz-Kochlowice-Katowice route, along with a plan and a password. Eventually, from that point on he can travel by bicycle. In any event, things should be ready either on Thursday or Friday (for Romek). Lech is charged with preparing papers and a wig for him on Monday. Kisses, Staklo.[7]

The resistance secured escape routes through a network of liaisons. If the attempt was successful, the escapee was transferred to the care of contact persons using an appropriate password. But assistance did not end at this point. The next, and very important, stage was to shelter the escapees for a period to enable them to recuperate. Depending on their physical condition, the recovery period lasted from several days to several weeks. This time was used to prepare forged identity papers and the so-called work cards, which legalized their status under the occupation. Afterward, the escapees were assigned, in consideration of their wishes, either to resistance work near the camp or to partisan units operating in the mountains. Others were transported to the Polish General Government, where they went into hiding or joined the ranks of the Polish underground.

In many cases, prisoners escaped from Auschwitz disguised as SS men. Thus on December 29, 1942, three Poles—Jan Komski, Boleslaw Kuczbara, and Mieczyslaw Januszewski—and one German, Otto Kussel, made a successful escape. They left riding in a horse-driven cart, under the escort of Kuczbara, who wore an SS uniform. Undisturbed at SS checkpoints, they managed to cross the guard chain.[8]

Their escape was planned and prepared in coordination with accomplices outside the camp. The letter to Mrs. Jadzka quoted earlier was one of many such messages between these prisoners and the members of resistance organizations operating outside. Details were agreed upon, dates set only to be postponed, new times suggested, the escape route changed. Ultimately, it was decided that the attempt would be made on December 29. The escaping prisoners were to reach Broszkowice, which had been emptied of its residents and was due to become part of the camp. There, in one of the houses, a Polish woman, Janina Kajtoch, who had been active in assisting escaping prisoners, stashed civilian clothes for the escapees. It was she who had smuggled into the camp a map with the designated escape route. According to plan, having crossed the guard chain, the four prisoners headed for Broszkowice. The map guided them to the house, where they found civilian clothes in the attic. Thus disguised, they were led by Andrzej Harat, a member of the Home Army cell operating near the camp, to Libiaz near Auschwitz, where he hid them in his house. Later, the escapees were smuggled into the General Government.

All were eventually captured. Baras (Komski) and Januszewski were arrested in Krakow during a street roundup, Kuczbara and Kussel fell into German hands in Warsaw. Baras (Komski) was again incarcerated in Auschwitz, although camp authorities did not recognize him as an escapee. He spent the war in a succession of camps and survived. Januszewski probably committed suicide while being transported back to Auschwitz, since he did not reach the camp. Kussel was reincarcerated in the camp on September 25, 1943, and subsequently transferred to the Flössenburg concentration camp. He survived the war. Kuczbara was killed during the war.[9]

Half a year earlier, four Polish prisoners made a daring escape from the SS food depot, located in the vicinity of the main camp. On Saturday afternoon, June 20, 1940, they made their way through a manhole into the basement of the closed depot building, which was guarded by an SS man. They went through the boiler room, using keys made earlier to fit the locks, then broke into the storage room containing SS uniforms and into the weapons and ammunition depot. Dressed in the uniforms and armed, they removed a passenger car from the nearby garage and drove away. They managed to pass through the SS checkpoint and leave the area around the camp undisturbed. Subsequently, they reached the General Government. One of these escapees in all likelihood was killed in Warsaw; the other three survived the war.[10]

Another Polish prisoner, Jerzy Bielecki, escaped dressed in an SS uniform together with a Jewish woman prisoner, Cyla Cybulska. Bielecki was furnished with the uniform by another prisoner, Tadeusz Srogi, who worked in the clothing depot of the SS. The latter also provided him with an SS pass. On July 21, 1944, Bielecki, disguised as an SS man, appeared in the headquarters building where Cybulska was employed. He presented himself to the SS woman supervisor as a functionary of the camp Gestapo and ordered her to deliver to him woman prisoner 29558, whom he was to escort to interrogation. The SS supervisor failed to see through the disguise and carried out the order. Bielecki escorted Cybulska out of the restricted camp zone. At the SS checkpoint, he used a forged pass. After walking for 10 nights, they reached the border of the General Government and managed to cross it uneventfully. Cybulska was sheltered by a Polish family in the village of Przemeczany near Raclawice; Bielecki joined a Home Army partisan unit. Both survived the war. Later, Bielecki was awarded the Medal of the Righteous among the Nations of the World by Yad Vashem in Jerusalem for helping Jews during the war.[11]

This escape method was also followed by Polish prisoner Edward Galinski and Mala Zimmetbaum, a Polish Jew who arrived in Auschwitz on a transport from the Malines camp in Belgium. Their attempt, however, ended tragically. Galinski bought a uniform from an SS man. Zimmetbaum, who worked as a runner and interpreter for the SS and had access to the SS guard room, managed to obtain a blank pass. On June 24, 1944, Galinski, disguised as an SS man, led Zimmetbaum out of the restricted camp zone. At the SS checkpoint, he used the forged pass. About two weeks later, however, the two escapees were apprehended by a German border patrol in the Beskid Zywiecki mountain region. They were returned to the camp and after interrogation were sentenced to death. They were executed on September 15, 1944.[12]

Two other Polish prisoners, Antoni Wykret and Henryk Kwiatkowski, used SS uniforms to escape on September 9, 1944, together with three companions, also Poles. Then on September 28, two German-speaking Poles, Leonard Zawadzki and Alfons Szumanski, used the same ruse to escape, taking along four other Polish prisoners. Both attempts were made following thorough preparations. Fellow prisoners employed in SS depots and the camp print shop supplied them with uniforms and blank SS passes. All details of the operation, including meetings with contact persons, were coordinated with the leader of the Home Army's Sosienka partisan unit, Jan Wawrzyczek. A series of messages was transmitted by Zofia Zdrowak, a Home Army liaison who operated in the camp zone, maintaining underground contact with prisoners. All the participants later joined partisan units of the Home Army: the Sosienka unit operating near the camp and the Garbnik unit in the mountains of Beskid Zywiecki. That year, there were about 30 Auschwitz escapees in these two units.[13]

In testimony after the war, Wawrzyczek said that a number of non-Polish escapees also served under him in the Sosienka unit, including Josef Prim, a Jew from Brno; Vasil Mlavic, a Yugoslav; and two Soviets, Georgei Nikorov and Andrey Pavli. Prim, who escaped from the Jawischowitz satellite camp in the winter of 1943, was found by partisans and remained under their care for seven months before recovering. Mlavic escaped, taking advantage of the confusion caused by a brief skirmish between partisans and the SS escort.[14]

The Jaroslaw Dabrowski partisan unit, under the command of the pro-communist Polish People's Army, also operated in the area near the camp. In 1944, three escaped Soviet prisoners of war fought in its ranks: Piotr Novikov, Vasily Novikov, and Jan Szulik.[15]

Escapees from Auschwitz who joined the partisan units operating in the vicinity of the camp often displayed uncommon bravery. On October 18, 1944, Polish escapees S. Furdyna and Antoni Wykret, disguised as SS men, intercepted a horse cart carrying two prisoners and three guards. Passing themselves off as functionaries of the camp Gestapo, they conducted a thorough search of the cart, examined the pass of the SS guard, and told him they were taking the prisoners with them for interrogation by the Gestapo. Two of these liberated prisoners, Stanislaw Zygula and Marian Szayer, later joined the Sosienka unit.[16] In all probability, this incident prompted the commandant of Auschwitz, Richard Bär, to issue a garrison order on November 7, 1944, that reads, in part: "Due to the fact that the Polish resistance movement [the Home Army] enters the Auschwitz concentration camp sphere of interest in SS and Wehrmacht uniforms, a tighter control of all SS and Wehrmacht personnel is required."[17]

Occasionally, escapes took place with the collaboration of SS personnel. For example, Jewish prisoner Siegfried (Vitezslav) Lederer, brought to Auschwitz from the Theresienstadt ghetto, was assisted in his escape by SS man Viktor Pestek, a German from Romania, who was regarded by prisoners as a decent person. Disguised as an SS man, Lederer left Auschwitz-Birkenau on April 4, 1944, accompanied by Pestek. They traveled by train to Prague, successfully passing through border controls. Later, Lederer reached the Theresienstadt ghetto to inform others about the fate of the Jews in Auschwitz. He joined the Czech resistance and survived the war. But Pestek met a tragic fate. Upon his to return to Auschwitz with a view to organizing another escape, he was arrested by the SS. Following a savage interrogation, he was shot on October 8, 1944.[18]

It must be kept in mind that escape attempts involving the collaboration of the SS were very risky. Exposure could be expected at any time. Two Jewish prisoners, Daniel Ostbaum, an active member of the underground organization of Sonderkommando prisoners at Birkenau, and Fero Langer fell victims to the provocation of an SS man named Dobrovolny, a Volksdeutsche from Slovakia. Sometime in 1944, he led them several kilometers outside the camp and shot them.[19]

Another escape attempt, undertaken by five prisoners active in the camp resistance, also ended in tragedy. The plotters were an Austrian and four

Poles. The escape was planned for October 27, 1944. According to the plan, two bribed SS men would smuggle the prisoners out of the camp inside a truck carrying dirty laundry to Bielsko. The truck was then to stop in the woods, near the village of Leki, where the escapees were to be handed over to the underground contact. As it turned out, however, one of the SS men informed the camp Gestapo about the attempt. On October 27, the truck with the prisoners inside did leave the camp gate but then stopped at the barrier and the checkpoint booth, where armed SS men climbed inside. The truck then turned around and pulled up to block 11. The hiding prisoners were removed and incarcerated in the bunkers of this block. All of them took poison. Two died, and the other three were resuscitated. Later, two other Austrian prisoners who had assisted in preparing the escape were placed in the bunkers. Following interrogation, all five remaining prisoners were hanged on December 30—just weeks before liberation of the camp.[20]

Many escapes involved the preparation of hiding places or bunkers outside the camp fence, near places where the prisoners worked. On a set day, the escapees hid in them. They were often assisted by their fellow prisoners, who camouflaged the terrain and the hideout itself, scattering rough tobacco and pouring turpentine around the area to throw SS dogs off the scent. The escaping prisoners remained in hiding for three days—the duration of the state of alert declared by the SS after escapes. During this time, the SS manned the posts on the guard towers. When the alert was over and the guards were recalled, the escaping prisoners left their hideout and moved on. Such a technique was used by two Jewish prisoners—Alfred Klahr from Austria and Stefan Bratkowski from Poland—in June 1944. The escape, aimed at establishing contact with the communist Polish Workers' party and the Soviet Army, began in a hideout at the Deutsche Ausrüstungswerke (DAW), near the main camp. Assisted by the Polish resistance operating in the area, the two escapees succeeded in reaching Warsaw. But they did not survive the war. Both were killed in Warsaw; Bratkowski fell in combat during the Warsaw uprising.[21]

It was difficult for Jewish prisoners to escape from the camp, mainly because they could not rely on the help of relatives or friends in Poland. They were further hampered by limited contacts with Polish resistance and underground organizations. It was also difficult for other prisoners who did not speak Polish and had no relatives in the country to escape.

The DAW also served as a launching pad for the escape of two other prisoners, both Polish and members of the international prisoner resistance. On June 27, 1944, they hid in a small concrete basement. They left this hiding place the next day and moved on to meet with underground contacts of the Polish Socialist party, which operated in the area. They were smuggled to Krakow, then returned to the area to engage in assistance activities to prisoners. On October 27, 1944, one of the escapees, Konstanty Jagiello, was killed in a battle with SS men in the village of Leki-Zasole while taking delivery of escaped prisoners.[22]

In the second half of July 1944, two Jewish members of the international prisoner organization escaped from a hiding place prepared in advance. They were Josef (Pepi) Meisel of Austria and Shimon Zajdow-Wojnarek of Poland. Once in the hands of resistance contacts near the camp, they were smuggled to Krakow and passed on to the local branch of the Polish Socialist party. They were given shelter initially with a family in Krakow and later outside the city. Both survived the war.[23]

Prisoners of Auschwitz II-Birkenau escaped using similar methods. In the middle of July 1944, four Polish prisoners escaped using a bunker prepared in advance in the sector nicknamed "Mexico." The escapees managed to leave the camp area and met the contact, Sylwester Pawel of Chelmko, who led them to a tugboat anchored on the Vistula River at Gromiec, near Auschwitz. Captain Stanislaw Szydlowski and his Polish crew hid the escapees in a special recess, and having passed border controls, brought them to the Dabie harbor near Krakow. Then the escapees embarked on a small passenger vessel, which shipped them to Nowy Korczyn. From there they reached a partisan unit of the Home Army and in its ranks fought the German occupation forces in the Kielce, Miechow, and Jedrzejow regions.[24]

Several months earlier, two Slovak Jews—Alfred Wetzler and Walter Rosenberg, who later adopted the name Rudolf Vrba—made a successful escape from Birkenau.[25]

Czeslaw Mordowicz, a Polish Jew, and Arnost Rosin, a Jew from Slovakia, also escaped. On May 27, 1944 they hid outside the camp fence in a bunker they had dug in the gravel works. The next evening, the bunker was destroyed and the two men hiding in it were covered with earth. They managed to claw their way out and succeeded in getting past the SS guards and leaving the restricted area. Later, they reached the Slovakian town of Liptovsky Svaty Mikulas, where they met with officials of the Slovak Jewish Council and church authorities and gave them a detailed account of the camp and mass murders in the Birkenau gas chambers. The report was smuggled to the West. Both escapees survived the war, although for Mordowicz the escape did not mark the end of his ordeal. In the fall of 1944, he was arrested in Bratislava and again sent to Auschwitz. Fortunately for him, he was not recognized by the SS. He was subsequently transferred to another camp and lived there until its liberation.[26]

On November 19, 1943, two Polish prisoners pulled off an extraordinary escape. They short-circuited the electrified fence, extinguishing the illumination, then cut the barbed wire and got out. The surprised and confused SS sentries on the guard towers opened fire—which, however, could not be very effective in complete darkness. The escapees managed to traverse the camp zone. One of them, Jerzy Tabeau, reached Krakow and the protection of the local underground. The other, Jerzy Cieliczko, went into hiding in Zakopane and later joined a partisan unit. He fell in combat against German troops. Tabeau fought in the ranks of partisan units of the underground Polish Socialist party until the end of the war. On the instructions of the Polish resistance, he compiled a report on Auschwitz in Krakow in late 1943 and early 1944. He described events in the camp from the spring of 1942 to the fall of 1943, referring also to the first years of the camp's existence. Polish resistance smuggled his report to the West in the first half of 1944. Together with other such reports, it was published in the brochure "German Extermination Camps—Auschwitz and Birkenau" as "The Report of a Polish Major." Tabeau's account was known in this form for many years in the historiography of the Nazi occupation.[27]

Those reports were not the only ones compiled by escaped prisoners. A bi-weekly publication, *Reports from France*, issued by the French Mission of Information in London, published in its September 15–October 1, 1944, issue a six-page story, "The Camp at Drancy and the Extermination Camps in Poland." It was a report about the camps compiled by an anonymous Jewish escapee from Auschwitz. After incarceration in the Drancy camp, he was deported together with his family to Auschwitz II-Birkenau. He listed his wife and daughter as probably killed in the gas chambers. Sometime after his arrival, he was transferred to the Jaworzno satellite camp (Neu-Dachs), from which he escaped. The escape took place in the coal mine where prisoners of the satellite camp worked. Information contained in his report indicates that the escape was carried out on September 7, 1943.[28] From cables sent by camp authorities, we learn that on that date two Jewish prisoners escaped from Jaworzno: Charles Zussmann, 31, a Frenchman, and Itzik Rosenblatt, 24, a Pole. Rosenblatt was captured shortly thereafter and brought back to the camp on September 9.[29] Lack of information about the capture of Zussmann suggests that he authored the report published in London.

Although unpublished during the war, reports compiled by Polish escapees Witold Pilecki and Stanislaw Chybinski are of special interest. Pilecki, a member of the Polish resistance, became known as a voluntary prisoner of Auschwitz. He deliberately let himself be captured during a street roundup carried out by the Germans in Warsaw in September 1940 in order to get into the camp and organize prisoner resistance. Incarcerated under the name Tomasz Serafinski, he became one of the commanders of the camp underground organization affiliated with the Home Army as early as 1940. On the night of April 27, 1943, he and two other Poles escaped from the camp bakery, having earlier blocked the door of an SS post. Once free, he was active in the Polish Home Army in Warsaw and compiled reports about the camp. In *Six Faces of Courage*, published in London in 1978, Michael Foot portrayed Pilecki as one of the major figures in the European resistance.[30] The second report author, Stanislaw Chybinski, escaped on May 20, 1943, together with two other Poles while doing surveying work in the camp zone. That summer, after his escape, he wrote a report, "Pictures from Auschwitz," which was delivered to the Polish resistance. Later, he fought with the Home Army in the camp zone.[31]

On July 28, 1942, three women prisoners escaped from the so-called penal camp at Budy: Alicia Zarytkiewicz, Paulina Gorska, and Erica Krause. Zarytkiewicz was Polish; the other women were designated as Germans. Taking advantage of the temporary absence of an SS guard, the three women threw a blanket over the barbed-wire fence and climbed outside. A lunar eclipse occurred as the prisoners were negotiating the fence. After reaching the nearby woods, the three escapees went separate ways. Zarytkiewicz reached Krakow, where she contacted the local resistance organization. Krause was captured and brought back to Auschwitz; in August 1944 she was transferred to the Ravensbrück concentration camp.[32]

Several other escape attempts were made at the Budy penal camp. The largest took place on the evening of December 29, 1942, when nine Russian women made a run for freedom. Their fate remains unknown.[33]

Some prisoners tried their luck using tunnels. One such attempt took place in the summer of 1944 in the Eintrachthutte satellite camp at Swietochowice. The would-be escapees dug a tunnel that originated in a barrack under construction and terminated in a trench outside the camp, in the vicinity of a guard tower. The trench served as an air-raid shelter for SS personnel. The excavation work took two months. On the night of July 3, the diggers reached the trench and prisoners began getting out in groups of three. As the third group was getting away, the SS sentry in the watchtower sounded the alarm. However, the dark night favored the prisoners, and two Poles and seven Russians got away. Later, two of the men joined partisan units of the Peasant Battalions in the Ryczon region, and another joined the Home Army in the Pilica River region. One, Leib Ziziemski, a Polish Jew, was captured on July 13, 1944, near Bielsko and was incarcerated again in Auschwitz. Miraculously, he survived the camp and the war.[34]

A similar attempt, in which about 30 prisoners of the Neu-Dachs satellite camp at Jaworzno took part in the second half of 1943, ended tragically. A *Kapo* noticed the excavation works at the tunnel originating from one of the barracks and ending in a nearby grove and immediately notified the SS. As a result, the camp authorities arrested several dozen prisoners, some of whom were sentenced to hard labor in the penal unit at Birkenau. The remainder were put in bunkers; 19 were selected for execution (11 Poles and eight Czechs) and were hanged on December 6, 1943.[35]

Prisoners also escaped from German industrial plants that employed them. One such incident took place in 1944 in the IG Farbenindustrie chemical works at the village of Dwory near Auschwitz, the location of the satellite camp Auschwitz III-Monowitz. A Polish civilian worker, Jozef Wrona of Nowa Wies, who was active in helping prisoners, organized the escape of two Jewish prisoners from Germany: Max Drimmer and Hermann Scheingesicht. On June 20, during the lunch break, Wrona hid them in one of the plant storage rooms in a recess filled with glass wool. The next evening, he returned to the hiding place, removed the glass wool, dressed the two prisoners in civilian clothes, and led them out of the plant. Later, he hid them in his house in Nowa Wies, where they stayed until November 15, 1944. At that time, Wrona was already wanted by the Gestapo; before he went into hiding he found shelter for his protégés at the house of his friends near Rybnik. Drimmer and Scheingesicht remained there until liberation. In 1990, Yad Vashem awarded Wrona the Medal of the Righteous among the Nations of the World for his help to Jews, including the two escapees.[36]

Prisoners also attempted mass escapes during revolts. One such incident occurred on June 10, 1942, among prisoners of the penal unit for men at Birkenau. On May 27, 1942, about 400 Polish political prisoners, brought to Auschwitz in 1940 and 1941 in transports from Warsaw and Krakow, were incorporated into the penal unit. Every several days, 10 to 20 prisoners were selected to be shot. Faced with the prospect of annihilation of the entire group, the prisoners decided to attempt a mass breakout. The escape was to begin after the signal announcing the end of work and return to the camp. At that time, the prisoners were digging a drainage trench. On the appointed day, the detail work ended earlier than usual due to rain. The plan went awry: only nine of some 50 prisoners involved in the undertaking managed to escape. Two were captured four days later about 25 kilometers from Auschwitz. They were brought back to the camp and shot a month later. The escape cost many other lives. During the chase, 13 prisoners were shot, and the next day the SS shot 20 and gassed about 320 Polish prisoners from the penal unit in reprisal.[37]

On June 13, 1942, three Polish prisoners—Marian Mykala, Zygmunt Piotrkowski, and Franciszek Sykosz—who worked outside the camp cutting willow twigs on the banks of the Sola River overpowered their SS guard, grabbed his weapon, killed him and fled. Since their capture is not mentioned in the extant camp documents, it is assumed that the attempt was successful. In reprisal for the killing of the SS man, about 10 Polish residents of Auschwitz were shot in the camp.[38]

Another revolt involving a mass breakout took place on November 6, 1942, at Birkenau. It was carried out by several dozen Soviet prisoners assigned by camp authorities to help search for a prisoner who did not show up at roll call. The search was conducted on the grounds of a sector still under construction. Taking advantage of dusk and fog, the prisoners ran in the direction of SS posts, broke through them, and fled to the nearby woods. Later they moved on. In the course of the pursuit launched by the SS, many of them were shot or captured. However, several prisoners, including Andrei Alexandrovich Pogozhev, Victor Kuznetsov, and Pavel Stenkin, managed to slip away. Two weeks later, Pogozhev and Kuznetsov were apprehended by German gendarmes near Rybnik, but they were not recognized as escapees from Auschwitz. They were placed in the Lamsdorf camp for prisoners of war. Stenkin met a similar fate and was placed in the Heydebreck camp. He managed to escape, broke through the front lines, and rejoined the Soviet Army. Later, he took part in the final assault on Berlin.[39]

The most famous uprising in the history of the camp was the revolt of Jewish *Sonderkommando*, who serviced the crematoria of Auschwitz II-Birkenau. Facing annihilation, on October 7, 1944, they staged an armed revolt in crematorium IV. The doomed Jews set afire and dynamited the crematorium and fled to the nearby woods. When prisoners in crematorium II heard shooting and saw the crematorium burning, they fell upon their German Oberkapo and threw him—alive—into the burning oven. Another SS man met the same fate. Then they made their escape attempt. The notes of Zalman Leventhal, a Sonderkommando worker whose manuscript was unearthed after the war on the grounds near the crematoria, contain this passage relating to the incident:

> They couldn't wait any longer; every minute counted because armed guards were getting closer. Quickly they divided among themselves everything they had prepared for the last moment. Then they cut the wires and all of them fled beyond the sentry lines. While escaping, they showed a great sense of responsibility and dedication. In the last minutes, when their lives hung in the balance with each passing second, they paused to carry out their last mission: cutting the wires of the fence of the neighboring women's camp to enable the women there to escape. Unfortunately, they couldn't accomplish much. All they did was to run several kilometers away from the camp before being surrounded by other sentries.[40]

The escapees barricaded themselves in a barn in the village of Rajsko. The pursuing SS men set fire to the barn and murdered the escaping prisoners. Prisoners who put up a fight in the grove near crematorium IV were massacred. All in all, 250 prisoners were killed in the fighting. The SS lost three men killed and over a dozen wounded. In reprisal, 200 more Sonderkommando prisoners were shot by the Germans after the revolt.[41]

Escapes attempted during the liquidation and evacuation of the camp in January 1945 constitute a separate chapter in the history of prisoners' escapes from Auschwitz. Several tens of thousands of prisoners were evacuated in the first transports on foot. They headed westward in long columns escorted by SS men, marching in the direction of Wodzislaw and Gliwice. Some evacuees attempted to escape, especially when the columns passed through villages, small settlements, and towns. Other preferred locations were groves, woods, and hilly terrain. They tried their luck during stopovers. Many were felled by SS bullets. German police also captured escapees and shot them. However, considerable numbers succeeded in getting away. Many of them were sheltered by local Poles in houses, barns, sheds, and haystacks, where they remained until liberation.

Anna Tytoniak, a Pole, escaped while her column was passing through Brzeszcze and found shelter with the Plaskur family. Later, the Plaskurs' relatives put her up in Zywiec, where she survived until liberation. Krystyna Zywulska, a Polish Jew, also escaped while her column was passing through Brzeszcze. Romualda Ciesielska managed to get away at Jawiszowice, where the Weglarz family gave her shelter. Two other Poles also escaped at the same village.[42]

Many prisoner escape attempts were made at Poreba, whose residents helped or actually hid several dozen men and women prisoners. Among the latter were two Jewish women, Anna Mysliborska and Maria Teichman, who were offered shelter by Gertruda Pustelnik until liberation, and two Polish women, Danuta Mikusz and Walentyna Konopska. Two Sonderkommando prisoners, Shlomo Dragon and Henryk Tauber, both Jews, escaped in the vicinity of Pszczyna. Another Sonderkommando prisoner, Alter Feinsilberg, got away at Jastrzebie, together with another Jewish prisoner, Henryk Goldshal; both were offered shelter by Marta Bialecka.[43] In the same locality, three Polish women also ran for freedom. Two hid with the Kemny family until liberation. Anna Koczur, a resident of Jastrzebie, sheltered 13 escaped men and women in her house, including Nadezhda Tsvetkova from Belorussia. In Wodzislaw, the Lassok family hid eight women prisoners who escaped from their evacuation column.[44] The Hanak family of Kamien, near Rybnik, offered shelter to two Jewish prisoners. In the village of Wilcza near Rybnik, the Frohlich family, together with Rozalia Kalabis, sheltered Shalom Lindenbaum and his father until liberation.[45]

In Leszczyny, near Rybnik, the Jurytko family sheltered 14 Jewish prisoners who escaped from the evacuation transport and hid in their barn and cowshed. Upon departure, the grateful escapees left their hosts a note:

> We the undersigned, escapees from KL Auschwitz, wish it to be known that Bruno Jurytko sheltered us at the risk of his own life and the lives of his family members. For eight days he fed us, offered lodgings and all needed assistance. He did all this at the time when German troops and the SS were in pursuit of

escapees throughout the area. In so doing, he saved our lives, without any material benefits, acting as a decent human being.

The note concludes with 14 signatures, some of which remain illegible. However, each signature was accompanied by a camp number (B-1926, A5289, B-3215, 177704, 128012, 46751, B-8304, 19708, B-2154, B-9925, 117592, 105674, 105205, 171509), as well as each escapee's place of origin: Radomsko, Palis, Kielce, Antwerp, Rejowiec Lubelski, Garbatka, Lodz, Biala Podlaska, Plock, Lodz, Amsterdam, Berlin, Berlin, Vienna.[46]

NOTES

1. Archives of the Auschwitz-Birkenau State Museum (ASAM), file of the escape of Tadeusz Wiejowski, D-Aul-1/13, card 25. The quoted passage is from a letter of July 19, 1940, from R. Höss to Erich von dem Bach-Zelewski.

2. See Henryk Swiebocki, "Assistance to Auschwitz Prisoners by the Camp Zone Resistance Movement" (in Polish), *Zeszyty Oswiecimskie* 19 (1988).

3. ASAM, Höss Trial, vol. 3, cards 32–35, testimony of Boleslaw Bicz; file of the escape of Tadeusz Wiejowski, cards 22–23 (letter of July 19, 1940, from Höss to dem Bach-Zelewski); cards 5–8 (letter of August 3, 1940, from the chief of the camp Gestapo to the chief of the Gestapo in the Third Reich, Heinrich Müller); collection Affidavits, vol. 42, card 73, account by Stanislaw Krep-Trojecki. See also Danuta Czech, *Kalendarium der Ereignisse im Konzentrationslager Auschwitz-Birkenau 1939–1945* (Reinbek bei Hamburg, 1989), pp. 40–41, 44–46, 56–57.

4. ASAM, files of the camp resistance (Mat.RO), vol. 10, card 10, letter of November 10, 1942, from prisoner Boleslaw Kuczbara to a member of the camp zone resistance organization of the Home Army, Helena Stupka, alias Jadzka.

5. ASAM, Mat.RO, vol. 1, card 38, passage from a letter of 1944 from prisoner Stanislaw Zygula to a liaison person of the camp zone resistance organization of the Home Army, Bronislawa Dluciak.

6. ASAM, Mat.RO, vol. 9, card 55, fragment from a message of 1944 from prisoner Stanislaw Zygula to a liaison person of the camp zone resistance organization of the Home Army, Bronislawa Dluciak.

7. ASAM, Mat.RO, vol. 3, card 203, encrypted communication of November 25, 1944, from prisoner S. Klodzinski, alias Staklo, to a member of the camp zone resistance organization of the Polish Socialist party, Marian Gach, alias Alfons.

8. ASAM, cables concerning prisoner escapes, Kriminalpolizei Hohensalza (Inowroclaw), A-Au-I-1, card 9, dealing with the escape of O. Kussel, J. Baras (Komski), B. Kuczbara, and M. Januszewski; collection Affidavits, vol. 71, cards 66–68, account by former prisoner Jan Komski.

9. Janina Kajtoch, "I Knew People of Good Will" (in Polish), in *Chimneys: Auschwitz 1940–1945* (Warsaw, 1962), pp. 330–34; Jozef Garlinski, *Fighting Auschwitz* (London, 1975), pp. 163–64, 269, 273; ASAM, collection Affidavits, vol. 68, card 127, account by Helena Stupka; collection Reminiscences, vol. 54, cards 52, 55–57, Andrzej Harat, "Reminiscences from the Time of Occupation" (in Polish).

10. ASAM, files of Gestapo Lodz (Litzmannstadt), IZ-8/3, cards 67, 67a (cables concerning the escape of prisoners K. Piechowski, S. G. Jaster, J. Lempart, E. Bendera); collection Affidavits, vol. 4, cards 572–77, vol. 27, cards 66–70, vol. 67, cards 169–73, accounts by former prisoners Jozef Lempart, E. Bendera, K. Piechowski; Garlinski, pp. 271–72.

11. ASAM, files of Gestapo Lodz (Litzmannstadt), IZ-8/4a, cards 67, 68, cables concerning the escape of C. Stawiski (Cybulska) and J. Bielecki; collection Affidavits, vol. 16, cards 57–61, vol. 104, cards 104–8, vol. 52, cards 126–28, accounts by former prisoners J. Bielecki, Cyla Zacharowicz-Cybulska, Tadeusz Srogi.

12. ASAM, files of Gestapo Lodz (Litzmannstadt), IZ-8/4a, cards 20–23 (cables concerning the escape of M. Zimmetbaum and E. Galinski); "Wieslaw Kielar, Edek and Mala" (in Polish), *Zeszyty Oswiecimskie* 5 (1961), pp. 109–19; Tomasz Sobanski, *Fluchtwege aus Auschwitz* (Warsaw, 1980), pp. 65–76; see also Czech, pp. 805, 879.

13. ASAM, collection Affidavits, vol. 4, cards 504–6, vol. 65, cards 58–60, vol. 12, cards 175–78, vol. 16, cards 70–71, vol. 52, card 125, vol. 11, cards 12–13, accounts by former prisoners St. Malinski and St. Zakrzewski, H. Kwiatkowski, J. Prejzner, W. Maliszewski, T. Srogi, Z. Zdrowak; T. Sobanski, pp. 163–69; see also Swiebocki, pp. 99–100, 113.

14. ASAM, collection Affidavits, vol. 14, cards 17–18, account by Jan Wawrzyczek.

15. Stanislaw Walach, *Partisan Nights* (in Polish) (Krakow, 1970), p. 302; ASAM, collection Affidavits, vol. 4, card 534, account by F. Szlachcic.

16. ASAM, collection Affidavits, vol. 4, cards 440–44, account by former prisoner Stanislaw Zygula; see also Sobanski, pp. 170–78. On December 3, 1944, prisoners S. Furdyna and M. Szayer were killed in a skirmish with SS men at Brzeszcze-Budy. A. Wykret was captured but managed to escape from the car transporting him back to Auschwitz and survived the war; see Sobanski, pp. 176–78.

17. ASAM, collection Trial of the Auschwitz SS personnel, vol. 39, cards 236–37, Standorsonderbefehl, November 7, 1944.

18. ASAM, files of Gestapo Lodz (Litzmannstadt), IZ-8/4a, cards 61–63 (cable concerning the escape of S. Lederer); Hermann Langbein, *Menschen in Auschwitz* (Vienna, 1972), pp. 497–500; Erich Kulka, "Escapes of Jewish Prisoners from Auschwitz-Birkenau and Their Attempts to Stop the Mass Extermination," in *The Nazi Concentration Camps: Proceedings of the Fourth Yad Vashem International Historical Conference* (Jerusalem, 1984), pp. 406, 497; H. G. Adler, *Theresienstadt 1941–1945* (Tübingen, 1955), p. 152; see also ASAM, files of trials of SS men, vol. 196a, card 554, Mat. 1487 (concerning the execution of V. Pestek).

19. Filip Müller, *Sonderbehandlung: Drei Jahre in den Krematorien und Gaskammern von Auschwitz* (Munich, 1979), pp. 88–89; Kulka, pp. 405–6; Perkowska-Szczypiorska, *The Diary of a Runner for the Resistance* (in Polish) (Warsaw, 1962), pp. 228–30; ASAM, collection Affidavits, vol. 14, card 23, account by former prisoner Alter Feinsilberg.

20. Sobanski, pp. 207–17; Czech, pp. 917, 953, 954; see also Langbein, pp. 493–94; ASAM, Mat.RO. vol. 3, cards 193–94, letters smuggled out of the camp from Jozef Cyrankiewicz (October 28, 1944) and S. Klodzinski (November 2, 1944) to the Polish resistance.

21. ASAM, files of Gestapo Lodz (Litzmannstadt), IZ-8/4a, cards 5–6, cable concerning the escape of prisoners L. Lokmanis (Klahr) and S. Bratkowski; Tadeusz Iwaszko, "Haftlingsfluchen aus dem KL Auschwitz," *Hefte von Auschwitz* 1964, p. 33.

22. ASAM, files of Gestapo Lodz (Litzmannstadt), IZ-8/4a, cards 25–26 (cable concerning the escape of K. Jagiello and T. Sobanski); Sobanski, pp. 79–86, 207–8, 212–14.

23. ASAM, files of Gestapo Lodz (Litzmannstadt), IZ-8/4a, cards 73–74, cable concerning the escape of J. Meisel and S. Zajdow; collection Affidavits, vol. 41, cards 52–54, vol. 99, card 6, vol. 99, cards 34–42, accounts by former prisoner J. Meisel, L. Motyka, S. Zajdow-Wojnarek; see also Iwaszko, pp. 32–33.

24. ASAM, files of Gestapo Lodz (Litzmannstadt), IZ-8/4a, cards 58–59 (cable concerning the escape of R. Kordek and Z. Michalak); collection Affidavits, vol. 67, cards 73–74, vol. 85, cards 120–21, vol. 86, cards 28–29, 31–34, vol. 89, cards 11–12, accounts by former prisoner J. Papuga and by Sylwester Pawel, J. Nosek, and S. Sosin; see also R. Kordek, "The Way Back" (in Polish), in *Escapes to Freedom: Reminiscences of Poles from the Time of War and Occupation* (Poznan, 1980), pp. 376–419; Sobanski, pp. 102–14.

25. For more information on Vrba and Wetzler, see chap. 25.

26. ASAM, files of Gestapo Lodz (Litzmannstadt), IZ-8/4, cards 118, 119 (cable concerning the escape of C. Mordowicz and A. Rosin); collection Affidavits, vol. 50, card 103, 107–11, account by former prisoner C. Mordowicz; Martin Gilbert, *Auschwitz und die Allierten* (Munich, 1982), pp. 253, 272, 273, 424, 425; Erich Kulka, "Five Escapes from Auschwitz," in *They Fought Back: The Story of the Jewish Resistance in Nazi Europe* (New York, 1975), pp. 208, 209.

27. ASAM, files of Gestapo Lodz (Litzmannstadt), IZ-8/3a, card 113 (cable concerning the escape of J. Wesolowski [Tabeau] and R. Cieliczka); collection Affidavits, vol. 98, cards 4, 5, 12–24, 27–31, account by former prisoner J. Tabeau; Mat.RO. vol. 5a, cards 307–32 (report by J. Tabeau); M. Gilbert, p. 276.

28. Polish Institute and the General Sikorski Museum, London, archives, call no. A.12 73/5, copy of article "The Camp at Drancy and the Extermination Camps in Poland."

29. ASAM, files of Gestapo Lodz (Litzmannstadt), IZ-8/2, cards 165–67 (cables concerning the escape of C. Zussmann and I. Rosenblatt, the capture of the latter, and his reincarceration).

30. ASAM, cables concerning prisoner escapes, cards 116–18 (on the escape of prisoners T. Serafinski [Pilecki], J. Reto [Redzej], and E. Ciesielski); collection Reminiscences, vol. 130, cards 3–14, and vol. 183, cards 4–71 (report by Witold Pilecki, compiled after his escape), and vol. 130, cards 16–120 (postwar account by Witold Pilecki); Garlinski, pp. 163–73, 265, 266; E. Ciesielski, *Auschwitz Reminiscences* (in Polish) (Krakow, 1968), pp. 112–78.

31. Cables concerning prisoner escapes, card 145 (on the escape of S. Chybinski, J. Rotter [Basinski], and K. Jarzebowski); Mat.RO. vol. 5b, cards 343–401 (S. Chybinski's report, "Pictures from Auschwitz"), vol. 34, cards 55, 57–58, 60, 80–82; cf. Swiebocki, pp. 53–54.

32. ASAM, files of Gestapo Lodz (Litzmannstadt), IZ-8/3, cards 84, 84a (cable concerning the escapes of A. Zarytkiewicz, P. Gorska, E. Krause); collection Affidavits, vol. 11, cards 26–27, account by former prisoner Alicja Zarytkiewicz; T. Iwaszko, "Fluchten weiblicher Haftlinge aus dem KL Auschwitz," *Hefte von Auschwitz* 18 (1990), pp. 158–60.

33. ASAM, files of Gestapo Sieradz, IZ/10, inventory no. 155988, card 4 (letter of January 5, 1943, from Gestapo Litzmannstadt, notifying the Sieradz branch about the escape of Russian women prisoners).

34. ASAM, Meldeblatt, 3, D-Au-1, cards 334–336 (Meldeblatt der Staatspolizeileitstelle Breslau IIF, no. 15, dated July 15, 1944, contains names of the escapees); Franciszek Piper, "Das Nebenlager 'Eintrachthutte,'" *Hefte von Auschwitz* 17 (1985), pp. 133–37; Ber Mark, *The Scrolls of Auschwitz* (Tel Aviv, 1985), p. 110.

35. Franciszek Piper, "Das Nebenlager 'Deu-Nachs,'" *Hefte von Auschwitz* 12 (1970), pp. 100–101; ASAM, the Bunker Book, part 11, D-Aul-3, cards 54–56 (entries of death of 19 prisoners).

36. ASAM, collection Affidavits, vol. L25, cards 37–49, account by Jozef Wrona and addenda, including photocopy of the Honorary Diploma of Yad Vashem, letters from Max Drimer and Hermann Schine (Scheingesicht), and press clippings.

37. ASAM, files of Gestapo Lodz (Litzmannstadt), IZ-8/3, cards 52–60 (cables concerning the escape of prisoners from the penal unit), IZ-8/2, cards 50, 121 (cables concerning the capture of A. Buczynski and E. Stoczewski); Teresa Ceglowska, "Strafkompanien im KL Auschwitz," *Hefte von Auschwitz* 17 (1985), pp. 183–85; Czech, p. 248.

38. ASAM, files of Gestapo Lodz (Litzmannstadt), IZ-8/3, cards 62–64 (cables concerning the escape of M. Mykala and F. Syrkosz); ASAM, collection Affidavits, vol. 22, cards 13, 14, vol. 22, cards 121, 122, vol. 99, cards 147, 148, accounts by residents of Oswiecim (Auschwitz): Anna Zieba, Andrzej Gebultowski, and Waleria Adamczyk; Czech, p. 227.

39. ASAM, collection Affidavits, vol. 19, cards 11–14, letter of May 17, 1962, from former prisoner Andrei Alexandrovich Pogozhev (according to him, the following also escaped in the course of the revolt: Andrey Zaitsev, Nikolai Gavorov, Ivan Zimin, and Nikolai Pisarev); Sobanski, pp. 142–51; Michal Stepanovicz Zbochen, "The Anti-Nazi Resistance in the Auschwitz Camp Zone" (in Russian), in *Modern and Recent History* 3 (1965), p. 112.

40. Zalman Leventhal Handschrift, in "Inmitten des Grauenvollen Verbrechenen: Handschriften von Mitgliedern des Sonderkommandos," *Hefte von Auschwitz* 13 (1972) pp. 179–80.

41. Ibid., pp. 178–81; Czech, pp. 898–900; cf. Müller, pp. 250–57.

42. ASAM, collection Affidavits, vol. 12, cards 201–4, vol. 22, cards 130–31, vol. 20, card 31, accounts by former prisoners Anna Tytoniak, Romualda Ciesielska, Franciszek Dusik; Krystyna Zywulska, *I Survived Auschwitz* (in Polish) (Warsaw, 1960), pp. 335–38.

43. ASAM, collection Affidavits, vol. 67, card 33, vol. 113, cards 29–36 (account by former woman prisoner Danuta Mikusz, and note of September 4, 1985, concerning assistance to the escapees, confirmed by former prisoner Alter Feinsilberg); Höss Trial, vol. 11, card 116, testimony of former prisoner Shlomo Dragon; Andrzej Strzelecki, *Evacuation, Liquidation. and Liberation of KL Auschwitz* (in Polish) (Oswiecim, 1982), pp. 184–85.

44. ASAM, collection Affidavits, vol. 119, cards 173–74, vol. 89b, card 487, accounts by former women prisoners Roza Gajowczak-Dryjanska and Ernestyna Lassok-Bonarek; Strzelecki, p. 187.

45. ASAM, collection Affidavits, vol. 129, cards 202–4, vol. 122, cards 79–81, vol. 123, cards 44–45, vol. 123, cards 52–54, accounts by Ryszard Hanek, former prisoners Shalom Lindenbaum, Dorota Kuc, and Lucja Rduch.

46. ASAM, collection Affidavits, vol. 120, cards 41–43 (account by Bronislawa Jurytko), cards 43a–43b (copy of a document with the signatures of the rescued Jews), card 43c (article by Lukasz Wywrzykowski, "Even the Stone Can Have Pity" [in Polish], *Dziennik Zachodni* 77 [April 1–4, 1988]).

24

Diaries of the Sonderkommando

NATHAN COHEN

Between 1945 and 1970, six diaries and fragments of notes written in Yiddish by three members of the Auschwitz *Sonderkommando* were found hidden near the crematoria in Birkenau.[1] These diaries were written by men who knew that they had no hope of remaining alive. Only their testimony could survive them and reach the free world. Each diary was composed by a man of distinct personality, who emphasized a different aspect of life "in the heart of hell." Each according to his own style and his own world view presented the frightful reality that was exclusively his. No one in the camp but the Sonderkommando—and certainly no one outside it—could have known of their experiences.

Out of a sense of historic mission imposed upon them—Zalman Gradowski, Zalman Leventhal, and Dayan Langfus—the three joined together to document on paper their lives during the Holocaust: the ghetto, deportation, arrival in Auschwitz, and their work in the Sonderkommando. They buried their writings in different types of protective utensils near crematoria, hoping that the day would come when they would be found and read. They apparently had an unknown number of partners whose writings have not yet been discovered.

All three writers were from traditional backgrounds, and each had something distinctive to say about his experience with the Sonderkommando. The three were also participants in the resistance; two of them took active roles. This essay surveys the documents and the writing styles and attempts to portray the character of the authors.[2]

Zalman Gradowski

Born about 1910 into a family of merchants and scholars in Suvalk, on the border of Lithuania and Poland, Zalman Gradowski studied in the Tifereth Bachurim Yeshivah and was a well-known figure among the city's youth. He was connected with the Betar movement and was active in Revisionist circles in the city. After completing his studies, he worked with his father, who was a merchant and businessman. He married and moved to Lona, in the Bialystok region. According to his brother-in-law, the Yiddish author David Stard, Gradowski did some writing before the war but did not seem to have a promising future as an author. An ardent Zionist, Gradowski intended to emigrate with his family to Israel in the summer of 1940. However, because of the war, he was unable to realize his plans.

At the time of the Soviet annexation in 1941, Gradowski was serving as a clerk in a government company. In November 1942, the Jews of Lona were moved to a transit camp in Kalabosin, near Grodna, and from there were transported to Auschwitz by train. Gradowski arrived at Auschwitz with his mother, wife, two sisters, brother-in-law, and father-in-law, who were taken immediately to the gas chambers on the morning of December 8, 1942.[3] The Germans put Gradowski into the Sonderkommando unit, the prisoners who serviced the crematoria. Over time, he became an underground activist who took part in the revolt in crematorium IV on October 7, 1944.

Yaakov Freimark, a fellow inmate who helped smuggle bottles of benzine and demolition materials into the crematoria, revealed in testimony that one day when he was bringing the slop pails to the crematorium where Gradowski worked, Gradowski gave him a gold medallion with "Sh'ma Israel" etched on it and ordered him to leave the place immediately. A short time after Freimark left, he heard the echoes of the rebel Sonderkommando's shots. Freimark also witnessed Gradowski's hanging the next day. According to Freimark, Gradowski was cruelly tortured and his skull crushed.

It is not known exactly when or how Gradowski wrote his notes. His first manuscript was found on March 5, 1945, near Birkenau's crematoria by a delegation of the Soviet Commission for the Investigation of Nazi War Crimes. The manuscript was stored in a flat German-made bottle 18 centimeters long and 10 centimeters wide, which was sealed with a padded metal cork. The commission took the document to the Medical-Military Museum in Leningrad. Ber Mark, the noted historian and director of the Jewish Historical Institute in Warsaw, had access to the material.[4] He reported that the notebook had originally contained 90 partially numbered pages measuring 9.5 by 14.5 centimeters. Several pages apparently had been torn off, for when the notebook was found, it had only 81 pages. Each page contained 20 to 30 lines of writing. A letter by the author, dated September 6, 1944, was attached to the notebook.

Gradowski's notes are written in black ink and for the most part can be deciphered. The notes open with a call to the men of the free world, living a life of secure peace, to join the writer on a "tour" of his path of torture. He calls on his imaginary reader to see how a civilized people has joined hands with Satan to become a murderous phenomenon whose like the world has never known. Gradowski writes that this nation of Satan's servants is bringing the Jews of the entire world to the altar to sacrifice them before their pagan Aryan god, in whose eyes the blood of Jews is very dear and whose intent is that no Jews should remain in the world. The murder is being conducted, Gradowski writes, with the greatest efficiency, for "the greater the culture, the greater the murderer . . . and the greater the development, the more terrible the deeds."[5]

These words are followed by a detailed description of the November 1942 transport from Kalabosin, which Gradowski terms an expulsion unprecedented in Jewish history, whose goal was annihilation. He describes the deportation from Kalabosin, the torturous train journey through Treblinka and Warsaw, and the arrival at Auschwitz. His writings detail the selection, the first shock of parting from family members, and the processing of the "happy ones" who were to remain alive. Those who were chosen to stay alive were sent to a barracks in the camp, where they totally lost their identities and personalities and became automatons doing whatever the murderers commanded them. At each stage of the "tour," Gradowski scolds his imaginary companions and tells his readers that the time to break down has still not come, for the next vision will be more terrible than the last. The notes conclude with an announcement that the long-awaited Sonderkommando rebellion is liable to break out any day and for that reason he is hiding the document with the hope that it will be discovered in the future.

The words remind the reader of the images of the journey to hell in Dante's *Divine Comedy*. It is possible that Gradowski was acquainted with Dante's work and used it as a model. But it is just as possible that the terrible reality Gradowski lived was so unique that it could only be envisioned in Dante's fictional creation.

The first page of the notebook is written in Russian, Polish, German, and French. It proclaims, "Show an interest in this document. It contains rich material for the historian." The letter attached to the notebook says that the written material is being buried in a pit with the ashes of the victims burned by the Sonderkommando, whose dead members are being interred alongside their victims. Gradowski calls on the finder to continue digging in the area because dozens of other manuscripts have been buried there, apparently by other members of the Sonderkommando and by Gradowski himself. The members of the Sonderkommando, in Gradowski's words, also have scattered around the place a very large number of teeth, in order to leave traces of the millions of people murdered. The rebels have lost all hope of surviving, and for a long time have been preparing an uprising, which is about to break out despite attempts by other groups of prisoners to keep them from actively resisting. Gradowski finishes the letter with a call to consider his writings when judging the tormented men of the Sonder-kommando, who have been forced to do horrifying work. The notes conclude with the announcement that the revolt is imminent.

Gradowski's second manuscript, found among the ruins of the ovens in the summer of 1945 by a Pole, reached the hands of Chaim Walnerman, a native of Oswiecim, who emigrated to Israel in 1947. It was not published until the end of the 1970s, when Walnerman printed the writings in a private edition titled *In the Heart of Hell.* This manuscript consists of three parts: "A Moonlit Night," "The Czech Transport," and "The Parting."[6] The notes were written in a rich literary language and inversive style. One would expect a man in Gradowski's circumstances to write in simple, practical language, which would have been enough to horrify the reader. Therefore, there is room to assume that the style of the notes is the author's customary form of expression, that he did not intend to give his words any special poetic character. Even if this inference is true, it still does not make it easier for the reader to understand Gradowski's notes.

The language is ambiguous; the repeated use of a moon motif is especially prominent in the first chapter. This chapter is a lyrical dirge in which the writer turns to the moon and pours out penetrating questions about the fate of the Jewish people. Gradowski does not understand how the moon dares to show herself above the hell of Auschwitz without demonstrating the slightest identification with the people being tortured to death below. The use of the moon motif allows the reader to imagine various things concerning what the moon represents. It is known that the writer was, and in a certain sense remained, an observant Jew. His appeal then may have been to one of the Hosts of Heaven as a substitute for a direct appeal to God or as a substitute for a defiance of God. On the other hand, we cannot rule out that this is really an appeal directed to the moon—which rules the "kingdom of the night"— and tears the writer's eyes out by illuminating the darkness and death enveloping his tormented life. Gradowski sees in the moon a cruel being, and hates her indifference, even as he cannot ignore her beauty. The writer also refers several times to his personal fate and his feelings about the members of his family who were killed. Gradowski summarizes his life in the camp: "The dark night is my friend, tears and screams are my songs, the fire of sacrifice is my light, the atmosphere of death is my perfume. Hell is my home."[7]

In the second chapter, "The Czech Transport," Gradowski mourns the fate of his people and the spiritual depths they have reached. He refers to the extermination of the first group of prisoners from the *Familienlager* BIIb, the family camp erected at Birkenau in September 1943 to contain the first 5,000 Jews from Theresienstadt.[8] The usual "welcoming ceremony"—selection—was not carried out with those who entered Birkenau on that transport. Instead, they were immediately taken as families to an area especially set aside for them. In December 1943, an additional shipment of 5,000 persons arrived. On March 7, 1944, the entire September shipment was murdered without selection. In May 1944, another 10,000 arrived at the family camp, and in July the entire camp was liquidated.

Gradowski characterizes the condemned people in the family camp in a sentimental way. They had been favored with "special conditions" in the camp, then suddenly were condemned to death, incapable of comprehending their fate. Gradowski described each stage of preparation for murder: the arrival of the condemned, their entrance in the undressing room, and their obedience to each order that culminated in their mechanical murder by the Germans. Afterward, the Sonderkommando removed the bodies and burned them. The writer likens the burning of bodies to actions carried out in hell (the title of the book was taken from this description). Gradowski expresses bitterness at the victims' apathy and submissiveness. He had expected that those taken to die would carry out some violent action against the Sonderkommando or the Germans. But after being severed from their families, the victims were helpless and obedient. When other family members arrived later, they entered the gas chambers with expressions of joy on their faces. At the end of the chapter, Gradowski describes the process of burning the bodies. Within 20 minutes, a living, thinking, and acting person was turned into a pile of ashes.

In the third chapter, "The Parting," the writer presents the complex and terrifying existence of the Sonderkommando, who were required to send their comrades to death. In September 1944, 200 members of the Sonderkommando were taken to the main camp of Auschwitz for execution. Gradowski had spoken of himself and his comrades as "We, the Brothers of the Sonderkommando,"[9] and expressed the hope that when they faced selection, the reservoir of hatred and revenge would explode. Yet that did not happen when the 200 were taken to their deaths. Those who remained felt as if a piece of sky over them had become even more pale. Those "happy ones" who survived were embarrassed to look at each other, and felt as though a part of their bodies had been amputated. Gradowski feels even more helpless than before. He faces a future without hope. He knows of no way to overcome the psychological block that prevents him and his companions from rebelling and committing suicide.

Each of the chapters opens with an introduction in which the writer asks the person who finds his work to memorialize the events and writings and to preserve the memory of the members of his family who perished. The introduction to the "The Parting" closes with numbers which, when added together, equal the numerical value of the letters in the writer's name.

Freimark, Gradowski's fellow inmate, was a native of Gradowski's hometown. He was assigned to work in "Canada," the unit where inmates' belongings were handled. In his testimony about the Sonderkommando and Gradowski, Freimark indicated that it was very difficult to make contact with the members of the Sonderkommando. He and Gradowski decided to stay in touch by setting a time to meet on their way to empty slop pails. Freimark mentioned that Gradowski's clothes always had a strong odor of smoke and charred flesh and that Gradowski himself seemed healthy and fat. In their hasty meetings, Gradowski would describe the help that members of the Sonderkommando gave to other prisoners and the responsibility he felt to throw bread to a hungry prisoner. After the Sonderkommando were relocated to an area near the crematoria, contact between the two men was less frequent. Freimark said that Gradowski used to assert that he would someday wipe out his sins and those of his comrades with his blood.[10]

Zalman Leventhal

From the testimony of his brother, which appears in Ber Mark's *Scrolls of Auschwitz*, it becomes clear that Zalman Leventhal was born in 1918 in Tschechanov, Poland, the fourth of seven brothers and sisters. He went to his city's grade school and later traveled to Warsaw to study in yeshiva. When the war broke out, he returned home. The liquidation of Tschechanov's Jews began in November 1942, and on December 10, Leventhal and his family were deported to Birkenau. At first he was given various jobs, but after a Sonderkommando team was murdered—an informer had revealed escape plans[11]—Leventhal was made a member of the Sonderkommando on January 10, 1943.

Leventhal's manuscript, containing more than 100 pages, was found in a glass jar in 1962 in the area of crematorium III in such a state of dampness and decay that it was almost impossible to read. The unnumbered pages had become separated and were out of order. It was time-consuming work to reconstruct the order of the pages, and the text is probably still out of order in a few places.

Leventhal's writing differs both in style and content from the other two recorders. It is neither ordered nor planned. His words are simple and direct, written from a storm of feelings. The writing is associative and, at times, repetitive. Leventhal pays little attention to style or form. He describes himself as a simple man who in the past did not mix much with people. Sometimes he deviates from continuity to spend time on a certain subject. He often expresses his opinions about things and does not recoil from criticism, even from his Sonderkommando colleagues.

Leventhal, too, begins his record with the story of the persecution of Jews solely because of their origin and religion. He describes the expulsion from his city, the train journey to Auschwitz, the cruel treatment en route by the Poles, and the joy the Poles showed over the Jews' affliction. He, too, depicts the arrival at Auschwitz and the time it took the inmates to realize the bitter truth about the fate of their families. He tried to figure out why he and his comrades were allowed to live. He concluded that "they want to live at any price."[12] He too, in his words, was too weak to fight the instinct to live.

The document uniquely describes the history of the Sonderkommando underground in Birkenau. Leventhal mentions both Gradowski and Langfus. He also tells the story of the courage of Stanislaw Kaminski, the *Kapo* who was among the planners of the first rebellion and helped smuggle demolition equipment into the area of the ovens. Kaminski was put to death on August 8, 1944,[13] after he was informed on by the Polish kapo in charge, Mietek Morawa. Leventhal pays special attention to two Jewish Socialist activists of Polish descent who arrived at Auschwitz from France in 1943— Yossel Warszawski (originally Yossel Darembus) and Yankel Handelsman. The two actively planned and executed the Sonderkommando uprising. Leventhal writes that as a provincial person he could never properly appreciate the acts of men like these.

In his description of relationships among the prisoners, Leventhal does not spare those who lost their humanity or forbade their comrades to carry out underground sabotage actions or to escape. It was as though these persons had become accustomed to what they were doing and had made peace with what was going on around them. To illustrate the inner conflict in his soul, Leventhal emphasizes that there were comrades who preferred to end their lives. He said that when he looked around him, he could state conclusively, "Only those from the second rank remain, the lower ones, a few simple people. The better ones, the more refined, the milder, are gone." He could not stand it.[14] Leventhal notes that Langfus was among the religiously observant prisoners who showed great humanity and guarded a high moral standard as much as possible. But because such prisoners were few in number and scattered widely, they were swallowed up and disappeared among all the rest.[15]

Leventhal judges some prisoners in the camp harshly, especially Russian and Polish members of the general underground. These prisoners tried from the beginning to prevent his comrades from revolting, on the pretext that

Auschwitz was about to be liberated. They ignored the fact that the Germans would liquidate the Sonderkommando before liberation to erase all traces of mass murder. The Sonderkommando aided the general underground in the camp by supplying equipment, money, and documents, Leventhal states, but received nothing concrete in return. The Polish prisoners were the worst of all. They expressed their anti-Semitism at every opportunity. The underground got a little help from a group of Soviet POWs who joined them in the spring of 1944, and especially from a group of Jewish women prisoners who worked in the Union factory and risked their lives to smuggle demolition materials to the area of the incinerators. The most famous of these female prisoners was Rosa Robota, from Leventhal's hometown, who was caught, brutally tortured, and put to death by hanging by the Germans after the uprising.[16]

On the day the revolt broke out, October 7, 1944, Leventhal was delayed in crematorium III and was not present when it took place. So his reports of the events that day are not especially accurate. Nevertheless, his personal evaluation of what happened is of great importance. The document is signed and dated October 10, 1944. The date of Leventhal's death is not known. Leventhal dedicates the diary to the memory of his comrades in the underground—Yossel Warszawski, Zalman Gradowski, Leyb Isaac Kalniak, Yosef Derevinski, Leyb Langfus, and Yankel Handelsman.

Another manuscript signed by Leventhal was found in 1961 with a diary from Lodz.[17] This second document was written in crematorium III between August 15 and 19, 1944. Leventhal briefly details the terror in which he and his comrades lived and the danger that hung over the camp every day. The Germans were not prepared to allow even one Jew to remain alive. He writes that he felt a responsibility to ensure that the diary be saved. He also mentions that other hidden manuscripts were in the area of the crematorium. At the end of the piece, he writes that if his words are read in the future by someone who was not a member of the Sonderkommando, they are not capable of reflecting the complete truth, for the reality that the Sonderkommando lived was much more horrible. He mentions the Warsaw ghetto uprising and asks why others condemned to death did not behave more like the members of the uprising.

Leyb Langfus

It was not an easy task to identify the writings of the Dayan Leyb Langfus. In 1952, a search delegation sent by the Polish ruling party found a diary in the crematorium III area signed "A.Y.R.A." and passed it on to the archive of the Jewish Historical Institute in Warsaw. It starts in 1943 and ends November 26, 1944. One part of the manuscript includes detailed descriptions of events at which the writer was present. Most of the diary is written with great restraint in a reportorial style, although at times the writer cannot hold back evaluations of his own. The author speaks only once in the first person.[18] A last will and testament, which comes at the end, is the part written in the first person. Still, the writer does not identify himself or give any details about himself or his family. Another section of the diary contains evidence collected from a man who succeeded in escaping from Belzec only to find himself at Birkenau.[19]

As a result of research begun by Ber Mark and continued by his wife, it became clear that the writer of the diary was a person the prisoners called "the Makover Dayan," Leyb Langfus, the Dayan from Makov-Mazovietsk. The signature letters on the document are the initials of the writer's name, Arye Yehuda Regel Arucha. Regel Arucha is Hebrew for "long foot" (Langfus).

Manuscript comparisons have found that this author was also responsible for three other documents, which were found together with Leventhal's second piece. The three documents include two reports of executions, one of 600 children and the other of 3,000 women, and a numerical list, in Polish, of prisoners who were exterminated by gas between October 9 and 24, 1944, in crematoria II, III, and V.

Immediately after the war, still another manuscript was found in a glass jar in the same place. It was taken and kept in the finder's home in Oswiecim until October 1970, when the finder took it to the Auschwitz-Birkenau State Museum. This manuscript contains 52 unbound pages measuring 4.3 by 6.6 inches. Because of poor storage conditions, most of the pages have become almost entirely illegible. This document includes a number of unsigned pieces by the same writer. But because of its title, "The Expulsion," its reference to the name Leyb by his wife,[20] and a reference to Makov, it is clear that the author was Langfus. The manuscript includes a history of the liquidation of the Makov-Mazovietsk ghetto on November 18, 1942, and details about the removal to the city of Mlava, the train journey to Auschwitz, and the arrival in Birkenau.

In the first chapter, the writer describes the prevailing feeling of desolation and helplessness at home and throughout the city just before the expulsion to the concentration camp, whose true significance the victims had apparently guessed. He mentions that his stand then was that it was better to die as men, and add a fourth graveyard to the three already in the city, than to fall into the hands of the Germans. The writer goes on to describe the events as though he were an outside observer. This document makes it clear that the writer had a wife and a son. He mentions his family in only one sentence as he describes the selection upon arrival at Auschwitz.

The subjects and the descriptions in this work are identical to Gradowski's first piece. It is possible that the authors agreed beforehand on the contents of their writings.

The original document is in the Auschwitz museum, and there is only a partial translation into Polish (the Yiddish original can no longer be deciphered). Separate pages were not always in order, something especially noticeable at the end of the notes.

Langfus was born in Warsaw and studied in the Zusmir Yeshivah. In the mid-1930s, he married the daughter of the Dayan Shmuel Yosef Rosenthal of Makov-Mazovietsk. After the Dayan died, his son-in-law took his place. At the outbreak of the Second World War, the rabbi of the city fled to Warsaw. Langfus became his successor.

According to the testimony of a comrade in the Judenrat, Langfus insisted from the very beginning that the Germans could not be believed and must be opposed. In November 1942, the Jews were sent from Makov-Mazovietsk to Mlava, and from there, at the beginning of December—the time of Leventhal's arrival—to Auschwitz. Langfus's wife and son were sent immediately to the gas chambers.

Langfus was taken to be a Sonderkommando but did not burn bodies; instead, he disinfected and prepared women's hair for shipment to Germany.[21] According to his writings, he was present in the crematorium area until the condemned were driven into the death chamber. He would then leave the place.

Leventhal describes the Dayan as an intelligent man of pleasant habits, but it was hard for Leventhal to share the Dayan's acceptance of the divine decree.[22] Yet Langfus was an enlightened man. He wrote objectively and was reticent to express a personal appraisal of events or behavior. He was an active member of the Sonderkommandos' underground,[23] and even in his writings about the liquidation of the ghetto, he expresses his disappointment that the Jews of the city did not choose to die there rather than allow themselves to be deported. Clearly, Langfus did not believe in passively accepting his fate even if he did not challenge the divine decree.

Langfus's writings describe events and situations that he witnessed when he was in the crematorium's undressing room, where the victims took off their clothing before walking into the gas chambers. For example, he tells of the Rebbitzin from Stropkov, who, before she entered the gas chamber, asked the master of the universe to forgive the Rebbe from Belz, who calmed the Jews of Hungary concerning what was about to happen, then escaped to Palestine.[24] In another writing, he describes a group of Hasidim from Hungary, who after saying *Vidui*, the final confession, invited the Sonderkommando to drink a last *L'Chaim* with them. This event so touched the heart of one of the prisoners that for hours he cried and called to his comrades, "We have burned enough Jews! Let us destroy everything, and go together to sanctify God's name!"[25] In contrast to this description, the Dayan reports that when a transport of children from Shavli arrived in November 1943, one of the children came up to a member of the Sonderkommando and said to him, "You are a Jew! How can you drive such sweet children in to be gassed, just so you can stay alive? Is your life among a band of murderers really dearer to you than the lives of so many Jewish sacrifices?"[26]

Langfus's central composition, which includes testimony from the Belzec camp, is dated November 26, 1944. In the last section, he indicates that the prisoners were then busy dismantling the ovens in order to take them to Germany (Sachsenhausen and Mauthausen). He asks the finder to gather all the writings signed with the initials A.Y.R.A. and to print them under the title "The Horrors of Murder." He also writes that he and another 170 comrades from the Sonderkommando are being taken to a "shower" (gas chamber) and are about to be put to death.

The three authors of these works did not nurture any hope that they would escape from the abyss. They well understood that Germany soon faced defeat but that they themselves would not survive. Therefore they saw in the planned revolt an action of supreme importance, which had to be carried out at any price. As to the future, it was clear to them that the war would end, the world would return to its routine, and the Jewish people would continue to exist, perhaps even in a land of their own. The act of writing, in the shadow of the ovens, was for the members of the Sonderkommando a means of preserving their own sanity and of leaving a legacy for the free world. The world must know something about the experiences of terror that they were living through day by day and hour by hour. It was clear to them that their period would be researched and that many would show interest in what had happened in the camp. Therefore, each was careful to emphasize that other writings were to be found there as well. They were sure they would be found, read, and studied. In this way, they would achieve their goal.

NOTES

1. The Sonderkommando members' writings were first printed, in a Polish translation, in the periodicals of the Auschwitz-Birkenau State Museum and the Jewish Historical Institute in Warsaw. There were, however, discrepancies between the originals (more precisely, the originals as later published outside Poland) and the Polish publications; an article by M. Piekarz, "The Rebbitzin from Stropkov on the Belzer Rebbe's Promise and Two Opposing Outlooks on the Lesson of the Decrees," *Kivunim* 24 (1984), pp. 59–60, relates directly to these discrepencies. I therefore have

chosen to use mainly material printed in Israel and cited in two books. My first source is Zalman Gradowski, *In the Heart of Hell* (Jerusalem, 1944); a transcription of Gradowski's manuscript is in the Yad Vashem Archives, designated MJ 1793. My second source is Ber Mark, *The Scrolls of Auschwitz* (Tel Aviv, 1977). Manuscripts by the three Sonderkommando members were examined by Mark and his wife and included in his book: Zalman Gradowski, "A Record," pp. 286–350; Leyb Langfus, "Horrors of Murder," "The 600 Children," "The 3,000 Naked Ones," and "List," pp. 351–76; and Zalman Leventhal, "Records," pp. 377–430 (the latter includes 94 pages from Leventhal's notebook, which originally contained more; references to this notebook are based on the original pagination), and Leventhal, "Supplement to the Lodz Manuscript," pp. 430–35. I have also consulted an additional document by Langfus published only in a Polish translation, in *Wsrod koszmarnej zbrodni—rekopisy wiezniow Sonderkommando odnalezione w Oswiecimiu* (Oswiecim, 1971), pp. 73–123.

2. Biographical details are from several sources. For Gradowski, I consulted the introductions by C. Wasserman, D. Stard, and Y. Wijgodski to Gradowski's *In the Heart of Hell;* Mark's *Scrolls of Auschwitz* (index listings); *Suvalk Yizkor Book* (New York, 1961), pp. 396–407; and the testimony of Yaakov Freimark, Yad Vashem Archives 03/2270. For Leventhal, I consulted Mark and *Biuletyn Zydowskiego Instytutu Historycznego* (1968), nos. 65–66, pp. 211–12. For Langfus, I relied on Mark and an interview I conducted in Jerusalem on February 29, 1988, with Milton Buki, a former Sonderkommando member.

3. Gradowski, *In the Heart of Hell*, p. 21.

4. Ber Mark, "O pamietniku Zalmana Gradowskiego czlonka Sonderkommando w obozie koncentracyjnym Oswiecim," *Biuletyn Zydowskiego Instytutu Historycznego* 1971, pp. 171–73.

5. Gradowski, "A Record," p. 292.

6. The order of the writings apparently was decided by Walnerman, because on the microfilm at Yad Vashem, the order is slightly different from the way it is in the book.

7. Gradowski, *In the Heart of Hell*, p. 24.

8. For further information on the family camp, see A. D. Kulka, "A Ghetto in the Extermination Camp," *The Nazi Concentration Camps* (Jerusalem, 1984), pp. 249–60, and chap. 18 in this volume.

9. Gradowski, *In the Heart of Hell*, p. 89.

10. O. Kraus and E. Kulka, *The Auschwitz Death Factory* (Jerusalem, 1961), p. 234; H. Langbein, *Menschen in Auschwitz* (Vienna, 1972), pp. 231–32. In memoir literature, Gradowski is mentioned for the first time in the book of Kraus and Kulka, as one of the organizers of the Sonderkommando revolt. The two knew of him only through hearsay, and gave his name incorrectly, "S. Grandowski." Hermann Langbein and Jozef Garlinski also mentioned Gradowski in their books as a leader of the revolt.

11. J. Garlinski, *Fighting Auschwitz* (London, 1976), p. 239.

12. See additional details in Kraus and Kulka, p. 144.

13. Leventhal, "Records," p. 33; Mark, pp. 233–34; Kraus and Kulka, pp. 231–32; Garlinski, p. 238. Freimark also mentioned in his testimony the special and exceptional figure of the kapo Kaminski.

14. Leventhal, "Records," p. 39.

15. Ibid., p. 86; see also F. Müller, *Eyewitness Auschwitz* (New York, 1979), pp. 65–66.

16. On Rosa Robota, see Mark, pp. 249–56; *Tchechanov Community in Its Destruction* (Tel Aviv, 1952), pp. 31–33; *Yizkor Book of the Tchechanov Jewish Community* (Tel

Aviv, 1962), pp. 387–91; Y. Gutman, *Men and Ashes* (Merchavia, 1957), pp. 147–51.

17. The diary was published in Polish by the Committee for Investigation of Nazi War Crimes in Poland, under the title *Szukajcie w Popiolach* (Lodz, 1965).

18. Langfus, *Wsrod Koszmarnej Zbrodni*, p. 99. The identification of the writer as Leyb Langfus was confirmed in my presence by Milton Buki.

19. Langfus, "Horrors of Murder" et al., p. 361.

20. Mark, p. 280.

21. See Müller, pp. 56–67. Similarly, Milton Buki mentioned in my presence that Langfus did not take part in removing the bodies and burning them but spent most of the time at the entrance of the bunker as a gatekeeper.

22. Leventhal "Horrors of Murder" et al., pp. 36, 78.

23. As Leventhal mentions and as stated by Langbein, p. 233, and Garlinski, p. 239.

24. Langfus, "Horrors of Murder" et al., p. 356.

25. Ibid., p. 351.

26. Ibid., p. 358.

Part *VI*

Auschwitz and the Outside World

MARTIN GILBERT details information regarding Auschwitz received in the West from couriers and spies and follows the trail of this information as it seeped into the consciousness of those formulating war policy. He also examines what the Jewish community in the Free World knew and how it responded to the information received.

Walter Laqueur has termed the wartime knowledge of the Holocaust a "terrible secret." Detail after exacting detail was known, and yet little was done to forestall the killing process. Gilbert documents the painfully slow process by which the West learned of Auschwitz and of the killing center at Birkenau. On December 8, 1941, gassing began at Chelmno. On January 20, 1942, the decision to kill all Jews was announced at a meeting convened by Reinhard Heydrich at Wannsee. By February 9, preliminary reports of gassing were received in the West. Yet the special role of Auschwitz remained unknown. Gilbert argues that the very nature of the camp as a multidimensional complex—slave-labor, concentration, and death camp—concealed its most lethal purpose. In May, June, and July 1942, as the deportations from the ghettos in Poland began, reports of massive killing were circulating—Sobibor, Belzec, and Treblinka were named, but not Auschwitz. In the West, deportations to the death camps became known as the "unknown destination, somewhere in Poland."

Only on November 5, 1943, was Birkenau named by the Polish underground. The escapes of Auschwitz inmates in April and May 1944 brought a detailed outline of the camp's operation to the attention of people in the West. This increased knowledge coincided with the deportation and murder of Hungarian Jews. But it did not lead to concerted action to help those incarcerated.

The most important and most famous of the escapes from Auschwitz was that of Walter Rosenberg (also known as Rudolph Vrba) and Alfred Wetzler in the spring of 1944. As messengers of the underground, they wrote a report in Slovakia bringing authoritative information to the West regarding Auschwitz. Miroslav Karny's depiction of the content of their report and its consequences is rich in historical detail. Though based on historical documentation, it rivals a gripping work of fiction. Rosenberg had worked on the ramp at Auschwitz, where he had witnessed the arrival and disposition of transport after transport. The documentation regarding Auschwitz offered by Rosenberg and Wetzler described in unflinching detail the mechanism that was used in Auschwitz-Birkenau. It made clear the methods that were employed, including gassing, and documented how mass murder was technologically possible. It described the construction, installation, organization, management, and security surrounding Auschwitz, as well as the everyday life of its prisoners.

The reaction to the report, composed in Zilina at the end of April 1944, was uneven. It provoked Rabbi Weissmandel to action in Slovakia, pleading for bombing of the camp and the rail lines leading to it. Its publication was delayed in Budapest in the weeks before the deportation of Hungarian Jews to Auschwitz began. The report was translated into German within a matter of days, transmitted to the Vatican in May, even broadcast over radio channels. Still, six months later the report had not been made public in the United States despite the pleadings of John Pehle, who directed the War Refugee Board. When he attempted to make the information public, Elmer Davis, who headed the Office of War Information, insisted that it not be published: nobody would believe the report, and therefore the American public would cease to believe other war information.

The refusal of the Allies to bomb Auschwitz has come to symbolize the general indifference of the bystanders to the plight of the victims. David S. Wyman has researched the full record of why Auschwitz wasn't bombed. Wyman describes the misleading statements of the Roosevelt administration, the repeated requests from Jewish leaders in the United States and abroad, the pleas of those survivors of Auschwitz who escaped the camp, and the pressure generated by the War Refugee Board to bomb Auschwitz. He depicts the war-effort priorities that diverted resources and commanded attention. The grandson of two Protestant ministers, Wyman was led by his exploration of U.S. responses to the Holocaust to painful conclusions.

In the spring of 1944, the escapees had brought full knowledge of the Auschwitz camp to the attention of the West, but the deportation of Hungarian Jews had begun. The Allies controlled the skies, and repeated requests were made by responsible sources, including the War Refugee Board, to bomb Auschwitz and its rail lines. The responses Wyman documents were either disingenuous or ill-informed: it was impracticable and would require the diversion of considerable air support. The true story is that on ten days between July and October, a total of 2,700 bombers flew on missions quite near Auschwitz. But no bombs were dropped there; no effort was made to end the killing. The same request was made in London. British Prime Minister Winston Churchill had approved the bombing and maps had been supplied by the Jewish Agency, but the plan was buried in the Foreign Office. Meanwhile the killing continued. By the time Auschwitz was liberated in January 1945, it was too late for most of the prisoners.

What happened to the perpetrators? Aleksander Lasik describes the postwar trials that brought a few of them to justice. Of the seven thousand SS personnel who served at Auschwitz, only a thousand faced judicial proceedings. For the most part, the sentences were light and the results meager. Lasik describes the quest for information and for justice and the ambiguous results of the trials, including their impact on the German people. The quest for justice, he concludes, "has now passed to the historians."

Lawrence Langer, a student of literature, began to study the Holocaust in order to explore the depths of the literary imagination. The more deeply he immersed himself in the story of the Holocaust, the more he switched perspectives. He soon focused his exclusive attention on the Holocaust and used literature as an entrée into the experience. Here he reviews the literature of Auschwitz and concludes that it exists to help us navigate the voyage into the abyss. Unlike Elie Wiesel, who believes that only those who were there will ever know what it was like, Langer gleans from the writings and the testimony of those who were there the essence of a disorienting event, the heart of an abnormal universe which shatters our complacency and disrupts our sense of meaning, order, and purpose. Langer believes that the more we search for meaning, the more we must confront its absence. He forces us to confront the severed connection between the pre-Auschwitz world and its aftermath. Auschwitz, Langer concludes, refutes creator, creation, and creature. Those who live in its aftermath must confront the void.

Michael Berenbaum

What Was Known and When

MARTIN GILBERT

On November 27, 1941, the World Jewish Congress in Geneva reported to Jerusalem that Jews who managed to escape what it described as the massacres, starvation, and oppression of Europe's ghettos no doubt were going to be sent somewhere overseas, outside Europe altogether. This report was typical of the misinformation reaching the West that winter. There were no German plans to send Jews out of Europe. Even as this report reached Jerusalem, the comprehensive plan under discussion in Berlin was for the murder of Jews living west of the Ribbentrop-Molotov Line. It would be accomplished by deporting them to death camps, where they would be killed in gas chambers or vans.

The camp sites chosen for the reception and murder of the deported Jews were in remote areas: four in German-occupied Poland and one in German-occupied Soviet territory. The first to be operational was in a wood near Chelmno, a village in western Poland. The first deportees were sent to Chelmno and killed in gas vans on December 8, 1941. In all, 2,300 Jews were murdered that day at Chelmno. In the following months, at least a thousand were killed there each day, most of them brought by train from the Lodz ghetto and the towns around Lodz, until as many as 400,000 had been slaughtered.

News of this final phase of the destruction of European Jewry did not reach the West for six months. The news that did arrive early in 1942 related to events that had taken place four months before. On February 9, two months after the establishment of Chelmno, the British Legation in Bern sent to London a report that had reached Switzerland: young Jews were being taken to Germany from throughout Nazi Europe "for gas experiments." The Foreign Office asked its representatives in Bern if the report could be confirmed. On February 18, the answer came that the legation had consulted "a prominent local private banker," a leading member of the Jewish community at Basle. He, too, had heard of such a report from a "visitor" who had come to Basle from Vienna, but this visitor could not confirm the report. These experiments had, in fact, taken place four months earlier, at Bernberg, southwest of Berlin.

During the 15 months following the opening of Chelmno, a period which coincided with the high point of German military mastery of Europe—when the Reich dominated from the North Cape to Cape Matapan and from Cape Finisterre to the Caucasus—more than two million Jews were murdered at the five Nazi death camps of Chelmno, Belzec, Sobibor, and Treblinka in Poland, and Maly Trostenets in the Soviet Union. They included tens of thousands of Western European Jews, many of them Polish-born, who were rounded up and deported eastward by train. Others were sent to Kovno in Soviet Lithuania and Riga in Soviet Latvia, where they were killed at the sites of earlier mass murders of local Jews.

In March 1942, yet another death camp was set up across the main railway line from the existing concentration camp at Auschwitz, which handled mostly Polish prisoners. Tens of thousands of Poles had been imprisoned at Auschwitz and many murdered since June 1940. Beginning in 1942, mass extermination installations were located at nearby Birkenau.

Several factors helped the Germans maintain the secrecy of their killings at Birkenau. No map since 1919 had shown the German name, for the area had then become a part of Poland. In 1942, back in German hands, the area had several hundred German factories that had been relocated there; like the existing coal mines, they required slave labor on a substantial scale. Not every Jewish deportee to Birkenau was to be murdered. While the children, the elderly, and the sick were taken straight from the deportation trains to the gas chambers, several hundred able-bodied men and women from each train (sometimes as many as 500 in a train with 1,000 deportees) were sepa- rated from those to be killed and were sent to barracks, from which they would go each day to their slave-labor tasks.

The existence of so vast a slave-labor population proved one of the most effective means of hiding the main purpose of Birkenau. The confusion grew out of the fact that Birkenau lay within the administrative area of an existing concentration camp, Auschwitz (in Polish, Oswiecim), where regular prisoners faced the worst rigors of punishment, including torture and execution. Those who, in 1942 and 1943, heard the name Auschwitz in connection with the destination of Jewish deportees already knew the name well: they had heard it through the frequent publications of the Polish government-in-exile in London, as a terrible place of punishment, but not—for it had not been up to that point—a place of mass murder.

On March 12, 1942, German railway authorities completed their Auschwitz-Birkenau timetable for the months ahead. Four days later, Zionist representative Richard Lichtheim, in reporting from Geneva to London on the imminent start of deportation of 70,000 Jews from Slovakia, described the deportees' destination as "a ghetto near the Polish border." It was, of course, not a ghetto at all. The first Jewish deportees arrived on March 26, 1942. The first gassing of Jewish deportees at Auschwitz took place on May 4.

During the next two years, trains brought Jews to Auschwitz-Birkenau from all over Europe. But for those two years, their destination was regularly reported to officials in Jerusalem, London, and New York as "somewhere in the East," or Poland, or, most frequently, "an unknown destination." According to information conveyed by the underground, a Polish prisoner who escaped from Auschwitz in November 1943 delivered a detailed report on the camp, including the process of mass destruction in Birkenau. Hermann Langbein mentions the case in his essay in this volume (chapter 21). Jerzy Tabeau, a Polish medical student, escaped from the camps on November 19, 1943. Later, in Krakow, he wrote a detailed 19-page report on Auschwitz which was circulated among the Allies under the title "The Report of a Polish Major." We have no evidence that the contents of the report in regard to Birkenau were published in the international press or were made known to the general public.

On May 13, nine days after the first Jewish deportees were gassed at Auschwitz, a traveler from Budapest, on his way through Switzerland to South America, told the Jewish representatives there, who at once alerted Jerusalem, that 20,000 Slovak Jews had already been sent, as he put it, "to Poland." What had happened to them there "is not yet known." Further confusion was created by these reports: although Auschwitz, like Chelmno, had been inside Poland between the wars, in 1939 it had been annexed to Germany, as part of Ost-Ober-Schlesien, and as such appeared inside the German border on all wartime maps. Thus Jews reported sent "to Poland" in the report of May 13 were looked for in Poland, especially Treblinka, on the outskirts of Warsaw. Treblinka is important in the discussion of the secrecy preserved by Birkenau because, from mid-1942, it was the camp most widely mentioned in Western accounts. It appeared to be the main camp of destruction and dominated the reports reaching the West in the summer of 1942.

The Bund Report from Warsaw, which reached London in June 1942 and was broadcast at once over the BBC, sought to give a comprehensive summary of what was known to the Jews of Warsaw at the time of its compilation, sometime in May. The report mentioned Chelmno, and, thanks to the escapee Yakov Grajanowsky, who had told his tale in Warsaw, it described the killings at Chelmno in detail. Of the deportation of 25,000 Jews from Lublin (a deportation which, we now know, was primarily to Belzec), the report could only venture the phrase "carried off to an 'unknown destination' in sealed railway cars." Auschwitz-Birkenau was not mentioned in the report. But when it was being compiled at the end of April or early May, no more than 1,000 of the 6,000 Jewish deportees there had been murdered.

Between May 5 and May 11, 1942, about 5,200 Jews from the Zaglembia towns of Dabrowa-Gornisca, Bedzin, Zawierce, and Sosnowiec were murdered at Auschwitz-Birkenau in the gas chamber of bunker 1 (called the "little red house"). This terrible news does not appear in any report sent to the West in the next two years. Nonetheless, rumors abounded, and many contained horrible details. On June 24, the Polish Ministry of Foreign Affairs in London reported rumors circulating in Warsaw "that Jews are used in testing of poisonous gasses." It did not say where this was taking place. At a World Jewish Congress press conference in London on June 29, Dr. Schwarzbart said a million Polish Jews had been murdered in death camps, but he made no mention of Auschwitz.

On July 1, the *Polish Fortnightly Review*, published in London, mentioned Sobibor for the first time and reported the murder of tens of thousands of Jews there. In the same issue, a full report on Oswiecim referred only to the fate of non-Jewish Poles. This report confirmed that Auschwitz was a punishment camp for Poles. Among the experiments tried on the prisoners there, it said, "is the use of poison gas." No mention was made of Jewish inmates or of Jewish victims. Two weeks later, on July 16, the *Polish News Review*, distributed in London, wrote of Jews being murdered in "large gas stations" set up in Poland. But the only region mentioned was "the Lublin district," that is, Sobibor and Belzec.

Among the large Jewish communities murdered almost in their entirety at Birkenau between May 1942 and April 1943 was that of Salonika (more than 40,000 murdered). More than 44,000 Jews from the "model" ghetto of Theresienstadt were also deported to Birkenau and killed, as were tens of thousands of Jews from Slovakia, France, Belgium and Holland. Not one of these deportations was associated with Auschwitz in any of the reports reaching the West. What was known, and widely reported, especially from France, Belgium, and Holland, were the roundups and deportations. On August 3, 1942, the *Times* of London included the Jews of Slovenia in its account of the most recent deportations. From Holland, it reported, 600 Jews were said to be deported every day (this figure was an exaggeration). But where were they being deported to? According to the *Times*, "These exiles are herded together in Poland in conditions of degradation and misery. Their eventual fate is either extermination or wretched survival in the vast eastern ghetto around Lublin, beyond the pale of the German Reich."

On August 8, the *Times* reported widespread French indignation at the deportation of Jews from France "to an unknown destination." A second article in the same column told of a report that had just reached London of Nazi brutality toward Dutch Jews. Whole families were awakened in the early morning, ordered to take food for three days and marched to the station. They were then sent huddled together in trains "which leave for an unknown destination." The actual destination was Auschwitz-Birkenau. It was still an unknown destination as far as the Jewish deportations were concerned. Ironically, however, the very next item in the same column of the *Times* that morning named the true destination: the Oswiecim concentration camp. But it named the camp not in connection with the Jewish deportations but as the place to which 540 non-Jewish Poles were being sent as a result of a wave of sabotage "spreading all through Poland."

The "unknown destination" still had not been connected with Auschwitz-Birkenau. Nor was Auschwitz mentioned in a message passed to Switzerland that August and then sent on to the West through Gerhard Riegner, of the World Jewish Congress. Riegner's informant told him that "in the Führer's headquarters, a plan has been discussed, and is under consideration, according to which all Jews in countries occupied or controlled by Germany, numbering 3.5 to 4 million, should, after deportation and concentration in the east, be at one blow exterminated." Again the location is blurred, and the plan is said to be still "under consideration." In fact, as we now know, this plan had passed its consideration phase at least eight months earlier.

Throughout the period when Birkenau was operational, more than 120 of Germany's 200 top-secret radio circuits were being picked up by radio in Britain and decrypted at Bletchley Park. These circuits included German Army, Navy, Air Force, and concentration camp circuits. Among the circuits picked up for a relatively short period were those to the concentration camp directorate in Berlin. These messages, which came from several concentration camps, were decrypted at Bletchley from the spring of 1942 until February 1943. They listed the number of inmates each day and the daily "departures by any means."

There was no mention at all of gas in the daily concentration camp messages that were sent from Auschwitz to Berlin. The Auschwitz figure of inmates stood at about 20,000. This was the figure for the Auschwitz main camp. Birkenau was not mentioned in the tallies; nor do the numbers at Birkenau at any one time—seldom less than 70,000 and often considerably more—appear in any of the tallies. Walter Laqueur stated in his foreword to *Auschwitz Chronicle* (1990), the English translation of Danuta Czech's *Kalendarium*, that at Bletchley there were "reports monitored day after day of 4,000 people arriving in the evening, of whom less than 1,000 were still alive the following morning." That is not so. No such reports of deaths were decrypted, or indeed sent, by this method. The deaths referred to in the decrypts were ascribed mainly to typhus and spotted fever; also, though less often, to shootings and hangings. These referred to the Auschwitz main camp and to Polish prisoners, not Jewish deportees.

The phrase used in these decrypts, "departures by any means," did not refer exclusively, or indeed primarily, to deaths. There was a constant transfer from both Auschwitz and Birkenau to other camps. The slave-labor system of the region depended upon such transfers. In 1943, Auschwitz and Birkenau received a total of 150,000 prisoners, of whom 20,000 were in fact transferred to other places. Thus the image of a labor camp was enhanced, not diminished, by the decrypts of constant movement. Even these decrypts ceased in February 1943.

On August 15, 1942, Richard Lichtheim, the Zionist representative in Geneva, noted down in a memorandum information brought by two eyewitnesses, one a Jew and one a non-Jew, who had just reached Switzerland from Poland, one having arrived only the previous day. One paragraph of Lichtheim's memorandum reported, tersely and accurately: "Jews deported from Germany, Belgium, Holland, France, and Slovakia are sent to be butchered, while Aryans deported to the east from Holland and France are genuinely used for work." Once more, even amid a mass of facts and the names of dozens of mass-murder sites elsewhere, including Belzec, there was no mention of Auschwitz or Birkenau.

On August 27, the United States consul in Geneva sent the State Department details of the continuing deportations from France. His source was a well-informed U.S. citizen who had just returned from Vichy. In mid-August, he said, 3,500 Jews had been deported eastward from camps in Vichy France. He added that "new orders announce that between August 23 and mid-September, 15,000 others will meet the same fate." What was that fate? According to the American, deportation meant either forced labor or slow extermination in the Jewish "reservation in Poland." There was no mention of Auschwitz or any other camp. According to this report, the murder of the Jews was taking place primarily by slow starvation in the eastern ghettos.

Less than two weeks after this report, the main article on the imperial and foreign page of the *Times* was headed "Vichy's Jewish Victims—Children Deported to Germany." The article told of the "unabated ruthlessness" of the deportation campaign. Women and children, it stated, were "suddenly notified" that they could visit their relatives in various internment camps and were then "forced to accompany the deportees without being given any opportunity to make preparations." According to this detailed report, "a train containing 4,000 Jewish children, unaccompanied, without identification papers or even distinguishing marks, left Lyons for Germany." Where in Germany was not known. It was Auschwitz.

Although the destination of the deportees wasn't known, the impact of the news from France was considerable. On September 8, British Prime Minister Winston Churchill referred to the deportations during the course of a comprehensive parliamentary survey of the war situation. The "brutal persecutions" in which the Germans had indulged "in every land into which their armies have broken," he told the House of Commons, had recently been augmented by what he described as "the most bestial, the most squalid and the most senseless of all their offences. When the hour of liberation strikes in Europe, as strike it will, it will also be the hour of retribution."

On May 26, 1943, one year and three weeks after the first systematic gassing of Jewish deportees at Auschwitz, a report appeared in the *Times*, from its correspondent in Istanbul (who was in touch with the Jewish Agency representatives there), which told of the deportation of 50,000 Jews from Salonika "to Poland" and gave a detailed and moving eyewitness account of the cattle wagons in which the Jews had been deported. At a place in Yugoslavia, the report stated, the Jews had been taken to a camp where they had been "disinfected" and their heads, including those of the women, shaved. From there, the report ended, "the survivors were sent to Krakow, where all trace of them has been lost." They had, in fact, been taken to Birkenau, near Krakow, where most of them had been gassed. Once more, the names Birkenau and Auschwitz didn't appear in the report. The phrase "where all trace of them had been lost" is a reminder, not only of how an effort to trace a destination had failed but also of the secrecy with which the Germans deliberately enshrouded all such movements.

Five days later, on June 1, under the heading "Nazi Brutality to Jews," the *Times* diplomatic correspondent did give the camp's Polish name, Oswiecim, as having been mentioned in several reports as the destination for Jews from Krakow. The Krakow ghetto, he said, had been "emptied," a thousand Jews having been murdered in the streets and houses, the others "taken off to the Oswiecim concentration camp." The correspondent did not know what had become of the deportees there. Nor did he know the destination of Jews deported from several other Polish towns "under conditions harder than life can bear for long," and, he added, "the journeys are often very long." Where these long journeys were to, no one seemed to know.

The unknown destination kept its secret in part because it was more than one destination and because Jews deported from the same deportation centers were sent to different death camps. Thus throughout April and May 1943, a total of 20,000 Dutch Jews were deported by train from Westerbork camp in Holland. Their destination was unknown to the Dutch Jewish authorities and to Allied agents and neutral observers. It was not Auschwitz but Sobibor. But the gas chambers of Birkenau were never idle. On June 25, 1943, more than a thousand French Jews, having been deported from Drancy, reached the camp; half were gassed that same day. And although the deportations of Dutch Jews to Sobibor ended on July 20, they resumed, on August 24, to Auschwitz.

Between August 24 and November 16, more than 8,000 Dutch Jews were deported to Auschwitz, the majority of whom were gassed. Yet Auschwitz was still unmentioned in the almost daily messages of fear and alarm that were reaching the Jewish and Allied leaders. The concern that summer was with labor camps and the growth of the slave-labor camp system. Thus on July 2, Riegner telegraphed to the Czechoslovak government-in-exile in London, for transmission to the World Jewish Congress: "We receive alarming reports from camps in Upper Silesia. A French deportee worker reports large concentrations of Frenchmen, English prisoners-of-war, ordinary convicts and Jews in labor camps." Riegner's report continued:

> Large factories with accommodation for workers are being constructed directly above coal mines for the purpose of producing synthetic rubber. 36,000 men work on one building site; 24,000 on another one. Among them are several thousand Jewish deportees between the ages of 16 and 24 who are treated worst. Guards carry leather whips with which they constantly beat their victims. The deportees are still dressed in the clothes they wore when arrested, which are completely tattered by now. Their daily food ration consists of two small portions of soup, a hundred grams of bread and some black coffee. They sleep on the bare soil, so crowded together that it is impossible to stretch. The ill and injured receive no medical attention. The rate of mortality is so high that in some camps the Jewish personnel has been entirely replaced many times over. Non-Jewish workers are forbidden any contact with the Jews.

This news was alarming. It was also accurate, as far as the labor camps of Upper Silesia were concerned. But it made no mention of Auschwitz, which lay at the center of the Upper Silesian camp system, or of Birkenau, which was the scene of daily gassings and killings of a never-ending flow of deportees, several thousands of whom were indeed sent to the labor camps that Riegner had so graphically described. Throughout 1943, similar confusion and lack of knowledge continued. On May 19, 1943, during a debate in the House of Commons about Jewish refugees, the deportations were described in graphic detail. Yet the only camp mentioned by name was Treblinka. Of the Jews of Belgium, who were in fact being deported to Auschwitz, it was said that they had been deported "to concentration camps in Poland and in Germany." Two months after this debate, on July 20, 1943, the Jewish Agency representatives in Istanbul sent Jerusalem a digest of the messages which they had recently received from Europe. The deportees from Theresienstadt, the messages stated, had started on a journey "of which none knew the end."

The Istanbul message also brought disturbing news about the Jews of Zagreb, the capital of the Axis state of Croatia. A message had reached Istanbul two months earlier that no more than 400 Jews, including a mere 45 children, were left of the once-flourishing Jewish community of many thousands. These thousands, the message stated, had "moved to take up residence in the suburb of Kever." Kever was Hebrew for "grave." Now there was more news. Of the 400 survivors of two months earlier, 350 had been deported "to an unknown destination."

The fullest account up to that time of the mass murders came in a letter sent from the Polish town of Bedzin on July 17, 1943, by four young Zionists. As soon as their letter, smuggled across Nazi-dominated Europe, reached Istanbul in mid-August, the scale of slaughter was confirmed. Their letter told of 80,000 Jews from German-annexed or -incorporated western Poland who had been gassed at Chelmno. As for the cities of Warsaw, Lublin, Czestochowa, and Krakow, "today there are no longer any Jews." They had been exterminated in Treblinka, the "famous extermination camp," as the letter described it, not only for Polish Jews but also for Jews from Holland, Belgium, and elsewhere.

The letter of July 17 went on to tell of how all the Jews of the Lublin region had been gassed in Belzec and Sobibor. The letter then stated that only in East Upper Silesia, where Bedzin was located, were Jews still living in "something resembling human conditions." But even there, things were changing. Three weeks earlier, 7,000 Jews had been "transferred" from Bedzin and had been killed in Auschwitz..According to the letter, "There they were killed by shooting and burning." There was no mention of gas. Nor was there any mention of deportations to Auschwitz from any other towns.

For several months, few Jews in Bedzin had been among those who had managed to receive South American passports from Switzerland. But in their letter of July 17, the four young Zionists noted that those who had received these protective documents had "simply vanished." At first it had been thought that they were safe, "but we now know that they were sent to Auschwitz."

Three days later, a further letter was sent from Istanbul to Jerusalem. It had been sent to Turkey from Bratislava just over three months earlier, and it too mentioned Auschwitz, but not as a center of mass murder. Instead, the letter referred to what it called "those main centers" to which men and women had been sent, and named three: "Auschwitz in Upper Silesia," "Birkenau in Upper Silesia," and "Lublin." The letter went on to explain that "the life in these camps is that of protective custody."

The Nazis still hoped to maintain the impression that Birkenau was not a death camp. On September 6, 1943, two trains were sent there from the Theresienstadt ghetto, arriving on the following day. On arrival, no selection at all was made for the gas chambers. Nor were the men and women sent to separate camps. Instead, the 5,007 deportees were taken to a special area of Birkenau, 30 stables, and allowed to live together in a kind of family camp as they had done previously in Theresienstadt. No SS doctors appeared, as in other barracks, to select the sick and weak for gassing. Instead, the deportees were encouraged to send postcards to relatives and friends in Theresienstadt and in Czechoslovakia. The senders' address on these cards was given as "Birkenau, bei Neuberun, Ost Oberschlesien."

Neu Berun was a small town more than five miles northwest of Birkenau. Its name was chosen deliberately by the Nazis so that no one receiving a card from the family camp would link it with the standard letter-heading "Konzentrationslager Auschwitz o/s" used by other Birkenau prisons on the rare occasions when they were given permission to write. Thus Birkenau's identity was kept separate from Auschwitz and appeared to be quite a different location. The message of these postcards was clear, and in the case of the 5,000 Theresienstadt deportees, accurate. They had indeed been deported, and deported to Birkenau, but they were still alive.

Three factual reports, enclosed in a message brought by courier to Istanbul from Bratislava on September 11, 1943, and at once passed on to Jerusalem, London, and New York, provided further confirmation of a deliberate Nazi plan to murder all Jews. The Bratislava report noted that "today we know that Sobibor, Malkinia-Treblinka, Belzec, and Auschwitz are liquidation camps" where, in order to produce "the semblance of a labor camp," small work forces were maintained. That was why, the report added, "from time to time a few individuals could send us a sign of life." Auschwitz had now been mentioned twice in three months as a place of the murder of deportees. But it had been given no prominence. As for Birkenau, from which so many postcards were being dispatched, it had not been named at all.

On November 5, 1943, the name Birkenau, as opposed to Auschwitz, first appeared in a telegram from Geneva. It was in a message from Riegner to the Czechoslovak government-in-exile in London and to his World Jewish Congress colleagues there. The message stated that "transports out of Theresienstadt have recently shown a marked increase. Between July 15 and September 30, 6,800 Czech Jews—among others—were deported from Theresienstadt to Birkenau. They were put aboard the deportation trains under cover of mounted machine-guns ready for firing." This was the Czech family camp.

On March 14, 1944, the Polish government-in-exile in London published a full account of the killing of Jews at Lvov-Janowska camp. This account made a considerable impact, stirring efforts to publicize the fate of Jews still believed to be alive in the Lvov region. Most, in fact, had been deported a year earlier to Belzec and murdered.

On the day after that report was published in London, the truth about Auschwitz was "revealed" yet again, in Istanbul. The source was the Polish underground, and the details were published in Istanbul in a newspaper, *Polska pod Okupacja Niemiecka,* issued by the Polish consul general in Istanbul, A. N. Kurcyusz. According to Kurcyusz, 850,000 Jews had been gassed at Auschwitz between the summer of 1942 and the autumn of 1943, among them 60,000 from Greece, 60,000 from France, Belgium, and Holland, and 501,000 from Slovakia, Bohemia, and Moravia. In addition, Kurcyusz noted, some 15,000 Jews from the Polish cities of Bedzin and Sosnowiec had been gassed in Auschwitz during the summer of 1943. These figures were far larger than any that had yet been published in the West for the number of Jews gassed at Auschwitz and larger than what is now considered to be the real number of gassed victims during this period. The report made clear the precise location of the "unknown destination," but it did not mention Birkenau, the name that had been associated with the Theresienstadt deportations. This report seems to have been completely ignored by both the Allied and Jewish representatives in Istanbul. No copy of it appears to have been sent on to London, Washington, or Jerusalem. The facts, at last so fully reported, remained as secret as if they had never been published.

On March 24, two weeks after this obscure and unpublicized Polish report, U.S. President Franklin D. Roosevelt warned of dire penalties for anyone who participated in what he called "deportations of the Jews to their death in Poland." Where in Poland he did not say. Roosevelt's warning was followed six days later by a strong warning by British Foreign Secretary Anthony Eden to all satellite governments "who expel citizens to destinations named by Berlin." Such expulsions were, he said, "tantamount to assisting in inhuman persecutions and slaughter."

On March 3, the inmates of the Czech family camp at Birkenau were told to write postcards asking for food parcels. They were made to date these postcards March 25, 26, or 27. Then, on March 7, they were taken from their barracks to the gas chambers and killed. A second Czech family camp was then established with new deportees from Theresienstadt. Two Czechoslovak Jews, Rudolph Vrba and Alfred Wetzler, who had been working at Auschwitz since the summer of 1942, realized that the fate of the second family camp would be the same as the first. On April 7, they hid in one of the work areas between the first and second perimeter fences, in the first phase of their plan to escape from the camp and to work their way southward.

As Vrba and Wetzler lay in their hiding place within sight of the huts of Birkenau, the Jewish representatives in Geneva were telling two U.S. diplomats in Switzerland what they knew of the fate of European Jewry. Riegner and Lichtheim, who headed the delegation, reported for more than an hour on the most recent news that had reached them. They spoke about what they called the "tragic fate" of the Jews of Europe. Riegner handed over two photographs. One showed "the dead bodies of the Jews of Transnistria," Romanian Jews who had been deported eastward in the autumn of 1941, and the other showed what Riegner called "one of the death chambers in Treblinka." This second photograph, said Riegner, "was corroborating evidence to the report lately issued by Polish circles and describing the death camp at Treblinka." Once again, there was no mention of Auschwitz or of Birkenau. Not even their names appear in the report of this long meeting. Yet the gas chambers there had already been in operation for nearly two years.

As Vrba, Wetzler, and their terrible information began the journey southward, the SS was making plans to build two more gas chambers at Birkenau. Reaching the Slovak town of Zilina on April 25, Vrba and Wetzler gave detailed figures, which had been collected systematically in the camp since the summer of 1942 and which Vrba had committed to memory, of the number of deportees murdered since May 1942. These figures made clear just how many of the French, Dutch, Belgian, Slovak, Greek, and other Jews, hither-to known only to have been sent to an "unknown destination," had not only been sent to Auschwitz but had also been murdered there. The two men also described in detail the selections and gassing process and the deaths by brutality and starvation. They made no reference in their report to the imminent fate of Hungarian Jewry; indeed, they left Birkenau a month before the arrival of the first transports from Hungary. But their escape was known by the SS, which sent numerous telegrams seeking to find them.

On April 25, the very day on which Vrba and Wetzler were telling their story to the Jewish leaders in Zilina, Adolf Eichmann, the Nazi who directed Jewish operations, gave the Hungarian Jewish leadership in Budapest a Gestapo offer to negotiate "goods for blood" to avoid the death camps altogether in return for a substantial payment. On that fateful day, two events thus coincided: the truth about Birkenau had reached those who had the ability to make it known to the potential victims, and the offer had been made to negotiate "goods for blood."

On May 27, seven weeks after the escape of Vrba and Wetzler, a Polish Jew, Czeslaw Mordowicz, and a Czech Jew, Arnost Rosin, also escaped. They had been at Birkenau during the first 10 days of the killing of Hungarian Jewish deportees and were thus able to describe the arrival of the Hungarian Jews and the pits at Birkenau in which, for many days, "corpses were burned day and night."

On June 6, 1944, Anglo-American forces landed in Normandy. The Soviet Army was on the border of Hungary. The Nazi deportations from Western

Europe had not been completed. In France, although 83,000 Jews had been deported and murdered, mostly at Auschwitz, 200,000 were still alive, many being hidden from deportation. Ten days after the Normandy landings, Lichtheim, asked by Jerusalem about the fate of several hundred Polish Jews interned at Vittel in France, about whom there had been concern and international activity since April, was able to report from Geneva only that "they had been sent elsewhere," and that "the name of the place was not revealed." The place was Birkenau.

The Vrba-Wetzler report reached Switzerland two days later, on June 18. Now not just the name of the place was revealed; it was also shown to be the place that had so often figured as "the unknown destination" or as "somewhere in Poland." On realizing the meaning of the Vrba-Wetzler revelations, Lichtheim wrote at once to Jerusalem and New York: "We now know exactly what has happened and where it has happened." "Very large numbers" of European Jews been killed "systematically" not only in what he referred to as "the well-known death camps in Poland (Treblinka, etc.)" but also in "similar establishments situated near or in the labor camp of Birkenau in Upper Silesia." Lichtheim added:

> There is a labor camp in Birkenau just as in many other places of Upper Silesia, and there are still many thousands of Jews working there and in neighbouring places (Jawischowitz, etc.). But apart from the labor camps proper, there is a forest of birch trees near Birkenau (Brzezinka) where the first large-scale killings took place in a rather "primitive" manner, while later on they were carried out in the camp of B itself with all the apparatus needed for this purpose, i.e., in specially constructed buildings with gas chambers and crematoria.

Lichtheim went on to point out that according to the new report, "many hundreds of thousands" of Polish Jews had been sent to Birkenau and "similar" numbers of other Jews had either been deported first to Poland or "directly sent to Birkenau in well-known cattle trucks from Germany, France, Belgium, Holland, Greece, etc.," and that all of these deportees had been "killed in these establishments."

Neither Vrba and Wetzler nor Lichtheim made any reference to the deportation of Hungarian Jews. But on June 23 a letter reached Chaim Pazner in Geneva from Moshe Kraus, director of the Palestine Office in Budapest, stating that between May 15 and June 19, more than 430,000 Jews had been deported from the Hungarian provinces to Birkenau. The truth about Birkenau having been revealed in Geneva five days earlier, there could now be no doubt whatsoever about the fate of the Hungarian deportees: not only their destination but also their destruction was now obvious. Kraus went on to warn that another 350,000 Jews had been assembled near Budapest, awaiting deportation. This statement made his letter not a mere account of what had already occurred but a call to action.

The news at once was passed by Pazner to the Jewish Agency. At the same time, a British diplomat in Switzerland, Elizabeth Wiskemann, and the U.S. War Refugee Board representative there, Roswell McClelland, both sent full telegraphic accounts to their respective capitals. The British account, signed by the minister to Switzerland, Clifford Norton, contained a suggestion that a massive air raid should be threatened on Budapest against all government buildings connected with the deportation of Jews. In London, on July 6, Chaim Weizmann (who had just flown to London from Palestine) and Moshe Sharett, secretary of the Jewish Agency's Political Department, asked Eden for a series of urgent measures, including broadcast warnings to Hungarian railway workers. "I am entirely in accord with making the biggest outcry possible" was Churchill's reaction as soon as he was shown the requests on July 7, and broadcasts to Hungary were begun at once. The Jewish Agency also asked Eden on July 6 for bombing of the railway lines from Hungary to Auschwitz. Churchill's immediate response to this was positive and emphatic: "Get anything out of the air force you can, and invoke me if necessary."

Following a heavy bombing raid over Budapest on July 2 by a U.S. Air Force mission totally unconnected with the Auschwitz bombing request and the heavy diplomatic pressure from many sources, Miklos Horthy, the regent of Hungary, demanded a halt to any further deportations. The raid had been severe in its effect on the Hungarian capital and was thought by the Hungarian leaders to be directly connected to the Norton-Wiskemamn telegram of June 26. The Germans could not continue the deportations without full Hungarian police and railway participation. After two days of argument, the Germans deferred to Horthy's demand, having no manpower at their disposal to resist it. More than 200,000 Hungarian Jews thereby were saved from deportation by train to Auschwitz.

That the Germans quickly switched their deportation efforts from the remaining Jews in Hungary to the 40,000 surviving Jews of the Lodz ghetto in Poland and other non-Hungarian deportation points was a fact not then known. Deportations continued, once more behind a mask of secrecy, for three more months. When Soviet forces reached Auschwitz in January 1945, they found human and documentary evidence of the true nature of the camp. But it was not until May that Moscow published an account of what the Soviets had found there. As always, Auschwitz was still cursed by the problem of delay of knowledge, by concealment of truth.

26

The Vrba and Wetzler Report

MIROSLAV KARNY

As far as the Polish historian Tadeusz Iwaszko was able to learn, of the 667 Auschwitz prisoners who attempted to escape, 270 failed and paid with their lives. No documentation of the fate of the other 397 has been found, so it may be conjectured that many of these escapes were successful.[1] One may consider the escape of Alfred Wetzler and Walter Rosenberg to be one of the most important because of the revelations contained in the report they wrote in Zilina at the end of April 1944. In the historical literature it is known as the Vrba and Wetzler report because Walter Rosenberg used the name Rudolf Vrba on the false documents that were drafted for him in Slovakia after the escape.

On April 7, 1944, at 8:33 in the evening, the commander of the Auschwitz II-Birkenau concentration camp, SS-Sturmbannführer Hartjenstein, was notified by teleprinter that two Jews under preventive arrest, Walter Rosenberg and Alfred Wetzler, had escaped and had not been apprehended. Rosenberg, who was born on September 11, 1924, in Topolcany, in western Slovakia, had been committed to the camp on June 30, 1942, by the Reich Main Security Office (RSHA). Wetzler, who was born on May 10, 1918, in Trnara, also in western Slovakia, had been sent to Birkenau by the same office on April 13, 1942.[2]

As a matter of fact, at the time the message was sent out, neither prisoner had yet escaped from the camp. Both were hiding on the camp grounds in a prepared hiding place under a pile of wooden planks at the horse stables that were used as prisoners' living quarters, in the third sector of Birkenau, called "Mexico" in the camp jargon. They did not leave their hiding place until April 10.[3]

Eighteen days passed before Vrba and Wetzler reached Zilina, after a distressful journey during which death was waiting for them at every turn. Their Jewish colleagues in Zilina then made it possible for them to draw up a detailed report on Auschwitz and Birkenau, the largest subsidiary camp of Auschwitz.[4]

Though Vrba and Wetzler were the authors of the report,[5] it was, in fact, the work of many dozens of Auschwitz prisoners who at great risk collected top-secret information on the camp crematoria, and created the conditions for the escape. Keeping files on the camp's activities was punishable by torture and death. In spite of the risks involved, Vrba and Wetzler secured help from many parts of the camp, including the *Sonderkommando* prisoners who worked at the gas chambers. Their report could not have been written without such help.[6]

By the time of the escape, the fact that millions of persons were being slaughtered under the Nazis' genocide plans was known to many all over the world; it had been verified on numerous occasions, and the report drawn up in Zilina only confirmed that fact. The report was unique for other reasons. It described the extermination mechanism that was used in Auschwitz-Birkenau in unflinching detail. It made clear the Germans' methods of industrialized slaughter. It explained with eyewitness clarity the technical mystery of how it was possible to annihilate millions of people. It horrified its readers with its revelations about the essentially simple annihilation mechanism that the Nazis used, and about the hitherto unprecedented and inconceivable opportunities for genocide that the Nazis exploited.

An historian with a knowledge of the vast amount of research that has been conducted on the subject of Auschwitz—the archives, the documents, the records relating to actions at law, and the memoirs of prisoners and captors—must respect the phenomenal amount and kind of material that these two brave Auschwitz prisoners managed to collect and report.[7] They described the camp with absolute accuracy: its construction, the installations, the organization of camp management and security, the categories of prisoners, the system of prison numbers, the everyday life of the prisoners, the prisoners' accommodations and diet, the labor displacement, how the headquarters dealt with prisoner escapes, how the camp conditions themselves were the cause of deaths, the selections on the arrival platform and in the camp, and the shootings, injections, and gassings. Only such a sober, factual description could bring people who did not personally experience it to believe the unbelievable—the monstrosity of the Auschwitz crime. Vrba and Wetzler evidently understood this and acted accordingly in April 1944. Their dispassionate work required a maximum of self-denial and an extraordinary effort to suppress the emotions aroused by the suffering they had endured.

The Vrba and Wetzler report is an invaluable historical document because it provides facts that were known only by the prisoners, few of whom lived to see liberation. The authors reveal, for example, that a great number of discharge forms were filled out for prisoners who were killed in the gas chambers. Such information shows one of the methods by which the official statistics about the death rate in the concentration camp were falsified.[8]

Oscar Krasnansky-Karmiel, who translated the report into German as the authors wrote it in Slovak, claimed in a foreword to the report that the authors did not include "anything from other persons"—in other words, that they witnessed everything they wrote about firsthand. That may not be the case. An essential passage of the report is based, for example, on information about arriving transports and the fate of their passengers. Although the authors could have learned much of this information firsthand, they were, in many instances, dependent on information from others. In addition, each of their informants could have observed only a small part of the events. It was the policy of the camp headquarters to create an artificial state of chaos to preclude observation of the extermination process. The complexity of the Auschwitz concentration and extermination camp, along with its associated camps, also precluded prisoners from witnessing the camp's activities in their entirety.

Only a small percentage of the prisoners who passed through the camp were registered. Among prisoners not registered were those sent to the gas chambers directly from the arrival platform, those classified as "in stock" (*Depothäftlinge*) who were in Auschwitz for a short time and died there, and those transferred for labor displacement to other camps. It is understandable, under these circumstances, that Vrba and Wetzler could not have gathered entirely authentic figures concerning the total number of victims in Auschwitz, nor about the number of prisoners who were deported from particular countries to Auschwitz. Their account estimates that 1,765,000 Jewish prisoners were exterminated in Auschwitz between April 1942 and April 1944. More recent historical research indicates that their estimate was too high. One researcher has estimated that the total number of Auschwitz victims during the entire time the camp was in existence was 1,471,000 persons, of whom 1,353,000 were Jewish.[9] According to another estimate, at least 1,100,000 persons were exterminated, of whom at least 960,000 were Jewish.[10]

The Vrba and Wetzler report does not claim to be just a historical document, nor merely an epitaph for Auschwitz victims. Whereas the Sonderkommando prisoners buried their testimonies without the hope of ever speaking freely about their plight,[11] this report, written by the two prisoners who escaped to Slovakia, had a different purpose: to warn people and to arouse them to action.

The report was written and translated no later than April 28, 1944. By the end of that month it was available to the leading Jewish officials in Bratislava and in Budapest, which at the time had been occupied for six weeks by the German Wehrmacht and SS. Leaders of Hungary's Jews decided to delay publicizing the report for a number of reasons. According to U.S. historian Randolph L. Braham, they began to circulate the report confidentially to a small circle of people sometime after the second half of June.[12] By that time more than 300,000 Hungarian Jews had been deported to Auschwitz, and of that number, only 10 percent were still alive.

A different attitude was held by members of the underground, the so-called working group in Bratislava led by Rabbi Michael Dov Weissmandel and Gisi Fleischmann. It considered the Vrba and Wetzler report as a most pressing appeal to the entire human race to put an end to further industrialized slaughter. The group provided one copy of the report to Giuseppe Burzio, the Vatican chargé d'affaires in Bratislava. On May 22, he sent it to the Vatican, but it didn't reach its destination until five months later, in the second half of October. That fact is evident from the official Vatican edition of the document.[13] Vatican State Secretary Domenico Tardini did not ask one of the men working in the office of the secretary to make an excerpt from the report until October 22. Vatican editors have concluded from that and other documents that the report did not reach the office of the secretary before October.[14]

On May 27, 1944, two other Jewish prisoners, Arnost Rosin and Czeslaw Mordowicz, escaped from Auschwitz and were able to get to Slovakia on June 6. Although they were arrested there, they attained an exemption from prison by payment. They also drew up a report, which included events that had occurred between the time Wetzler and Vrba escaped and the time they escaped. Rosin and Mordowicz gave an account of the first Hungarian transport that arrived in Birkenau on May 10. All the prisoners on that transport were allowed to live, and were forced to write postcards that gave their place of residence as "Waldsee" (Wood Lake). The report also stated that as of May 15, mass transports were arriving by way of the completed railway spur that went straight to the crematorium. Only about 10 percent of the arrivals were selected for the camp. The rest were immediately killed with gas and cremated. The report announced: "The Jews are now being killed with gas in masses as it has never happened up to now even in Birkenau."[15]

Probably about June 20, two of the escapees, Vrba and Mordowicz, accompanied by Oscar Krasnansky-Karmiel, met with a priest at the priest's insistence in the Svaty Jur monastery. They assumed he was Burzio, the Vatican chargé d'affaires. For hours, both escaped prisoners told him about the functioning of the Auschwitz death factory and answered his questions to verify their trustworthiness.[16] It was revealed later that the priest was not Burzio but Mario Martilotti, a member of the Vatican nuncio office in Switzerland, who was temporarily assigned to Bratislava.[17] The editor of the Vatican documents found no evidence that Martilotti's report about the meeting ever reached the Vatican.[18]

Either the same day or a short time after the Auschwitz message sent by Burzio started its five-month journey from Bratislava to the Vatican, Weissmandel decided to send the Vrba and Wetzler report to Switzerland. It was his second attempt. All traces of the first copy sent to Switzerland had been lost.[19] This time he appealed for help to the Slovak resistance movement.

Dr. Jaromir Kopecky, who acted as a diplomatic representative of the Czechoslovak exile government in Switzerland, wrote in his unpublished memoirs that the rabbi of Bratislava, who had received the report from the escaped Auschwitz prisoners, knew about the connection between the Slovak resistance and Kopecky, and thus the report got to his attention.[20] It is true that Kopecky did not name Weissmandel as the source of the report, but it is evident that it was him by virtue of the fact that Kopecky received, together with the Vrba and Wetzler report, a letter addressed to Rabbi Schönfeld in London, signed by D. Weissmandel and G. Fleischmann, delivery of which was to be managed by Kopecky. The letter has a date of May 22, 1944. Thus the report must have been sent, at the earliest, on that day.[21] According to the information from Kopecky, the materials were delivered to him by a contact with the code name "Agenor," Orga Mickova.[22] She confirmed that she had run a courier service under that name; however, in February 1982, she did not remember that particular delivery.[23]

Kopecky showed the Vrba and Wetzler report to his adviser on Jewish affairs, Fritz Ullmann,[24] and to the general secretary of the World Jewish Congress, Gerhart M. Riegner. Of all the information in the dreadful message, the most pressing to them was the date June 20.[25] Vrba and Wetzler described in detail the greatest mass execution of Czechoslovak citizens during the entire six years of German occupation[26]—on March 8, 1944, when 3,792 Czech men, women, and children were sent to the gas chambers in Birkenau. Vrba and Wetzler also warned that the events of March 8 would be repeated on June 20 for a second transport of Czech prisoners.

Kopecky, Riegner, and Ullmann promptly decided to inform the Czech government. Kopecky turned for help to Elizabeth Wiskemann, the British legate in Bern, who managed to send out his 36-line message.[27] Although Kopecky did not specifically name Vrba and Wetzler and probably did not even know their names, he referred to their report and gave details of the peril, requesting that British and U.S. radio stations broadcast the report immediately to prevent further slaughter.

> The report, involving gruesome detailed descriptions of the slaughter, in the gas chambers, of hundreds of thousands of Jews of all nationalities from occupied Europe, informs that the first group of approximately 4,000 Jews that had arrived in Birkenau from Terezin at the beginning of September 1943 was, after six months of quarantine, killed with gas on the 7th of March, 1944. . . . Considering the fact that the first group has been wholly exterminated, the peril menacing with extermination of the second group is to a high degree serious. Please, broadcast promptly the most urgent warning possible to the German murderers who are managing the slaughter in Upper Silesia.

According to the handwritten comment of Wiskemann, the message was sent on June 14.[28] It reached London and was deciphered there the next day.[29]

That evening, the monitoring service of the Reich Protector Office recorded the news of London Radio's broadcast in Czech and Slovak.

> News coming from London informs that German authorities in the Protectorate commanded that 4,000 Jews from the concentration camp of Terezin be executed in the gas chambers. All who participated in the execution of the Jews would be, naturally, called to account.[30]

The following day, London Radio broadcast a more comprehensive transmission and more insistent warning.[31] It is evident from the handwritten comment on the monitoring record that someone from the Reich Protector Office had ordered that the chief of the Central Bureau for Jewish Affairs in Bohemia and Moravia be consulted. He answered in brief: "Larger items departed from here and directly from Slovakia." His answer was dated June 17, and as soon as the following day, the German secretary of state for Bohemia and Moravia, High Police Führer K. H. Frank, left to inspect Terezin. The publicity about Terezin must have proved inconvenient for the man who oversaw the SS camps, Heinrich Himmler, and for the Reich Ministry of Foreign Affairs.[32] A monitor from Prague recorded a warning broadcast from London during the subsequent days. In his material, one can read a long excerpt from a condemning and warning resolution that was ratified by the Czechoslovak State Council in its plenary session on June 19. Berlin also registered responses to the Auschwitz report. The press department of the Foreign Office confidentially spread a Reuters report on the warning of the Czechoslovak government[33] on June 18 and 20. It included the entire text of the State Council resolution taken from the Czech Radio broadcast of the news from its monitoring service.[34] Neither the Prague nor the Berlin translation of the resolution was entirely exact. Although several passages were omitted or distorted, all the important points were included.[35]

The world had now learned of the forthcoming slaughter of thousands of prisoners in the family camp in Birkenau. The authorities in Berlin were aware of this fact. It is not possible to document the influence this knowledge had upon the fate of the family camp in Birkenau. However, it is a fact that June 20 did not turn into another March 8. The revelation of the existence of the family camp published in the Vrba and Wetzler report did not and could not save it. The family camp was built as an alibi, if needed, to show inspectors that the Jews who were deported to the East, allegedly for labor displacement, were alive and reasonably well. Therefore in spring 1944, Himmler permitted the International Red Cross Committee to inspect not only Terezin but also one of the Jewish labor camps,[36] the family camp in Birkenau. On June 23, the International Red Cross Committee delegate, Dr. Maurice Rossel, visited Terezin. The rosy image of the Terezin ghetto drawn by Rossel conflicted with reality but met the needs of German propaganda. In addition, his affirmation that Terezin was the *Endlager* from which no further deportations were made was in direct contradiction to the Vrba and Wetzler report. The Reich Main Security Office waived an inspection of "one Jewish labor camp," and the family camp was no longer necessary. After selection, 3,500 of its prisoners were sent to labor squads and the rest, who had been transported there in December 1943 and May 1944, were murdered in the gas chambers.[37]

After the first urgent wire concerning the family camp, Kopecky sent a comprehensive extract of the Vrba and Wetzler report to the Czechoslovak government-in-exile in London on May 26.[38] He added to it the testimony of another escaped Auschwitz prisoner, Polish major Jerzy Tabeau, which he had also received from Bratislava.[39] At the same time, Kopecky declared that he would send the complete report of the first two escapees to the Ministry of Foreign Affairs by courier, with the assistance of Wiskemann. In addition, he passed one copy to the War Refugee Board representative Roswell McClelland and to the International Red Cross Committee. It is a tragically ironic fact that Kopecky and Riegner passed the complete text of the Vrba and Wetzler report to a member of the International Red Cross Committee, Albert Lombard, and to a representative official, Jean-Etienne Schwarzenberg, on June 23, the same day that Rossel inspected Terezin.[40]

Kopecky also added new information based on data concerning Hungary's Jewish deportations. He noted that 12,000 Jews from the area of Sub-Carpathian Ukraine, Transylvania, and Kosice, where 320,000 Jews had been living, were deported daily and that 5,000 deportees traveled daily by train through Slovakia and 7,000 through Sub-Carpathian Ukraine.[41]

It is generally accepted that at the time Vrba and Wetzler were preparing their escape, it was known in Auschwitz that annihilation mechanisms were being perfected in order to kill hundreds of thousands of Hungary's Jews. It was this knowledge, according to Vrba, that became the main motive for their escape. In addition to saving themselves, they were concerned about warning Hungary's Jews about what awaited them at Auschwitz. "I was attracted by the possibility to cross the plans of the Nazis by revealing them to Hungary's Jewish inhabitants while they were still free," Vrba explained in a letter to British historian Martin Gilbert.[42]

"The Vrba and Wetzler record warned with absolutely understandable words against the impeding annihilation of Hungary's Jews," Canadian historian John S. Conway wrote.[43] But in fact, there is no mention in the Vrba and Wetzler report that preparations were under way for the annihilation of Hungary's Jews. A chronological account in the Vrba and Wetzler report concludes:

> In mid-March, a small group of Jews taken out from their hiding places in Bedzin and Sosnowiec arrived. We came to know from one of them that many of Poland's Jews were being saved in Slovakia and from there to Hungary with the help of Slovakia's Jews.
>
> When the Terezin inhabitant transport was killed with gas [on March 8, 1944], after then we did not have any increase up to the 15th of March, 1944. The camp number decreased, therefore all the men from currently arriving transports, mainly with Holland's Jews, were taken to the camp. We left the camp on the 7th of April, 1944, but we still had heard that big transports of Greece's Jews would arrive.[44]

If Vrba and Wetzler considered it necessary to record rumors about the expected arrival of Greece's Jewish transports, then why wouldn't they have recorded a rumor—had they known it—about the expected transports of hundreds of thousands of Hungary's Jews?

It is certain beyond a shadow of a doubt that saving their own lives was not the only motive for Vrba's and Wetzler's escape. The abundance of information about the Auschwitz death factory that they had collected is indisputable proof of that. Their information-gathering activities only increased the chances that their preparations for escape would be discovered and that they would be punished even more brutally than if their escape had been a mere act of personal salvation. Though they did not know about the imminent Hungarian *Endlosung*, they longed to testify "in order that the astounding Nazi crimes might not keep secret," to warn the world, and to appeal for the salvation of hundreds of thousands of people who were in prisons in Auschwitz and other death camps or would soon arrive at the camps—"And maybe millions," Wetzler wrote in the original version of his memoirs.[45]

Kopecky learned about the tragedy of Hungary's Jews not from the Vrba and Wetzler report but from the Weissmandel and Fleischmann letter, intended for Rabbi Schönfeld. It announced that 12,000 persons were being deported daily from Hungary to Auschwitz, and it sought opportunities to help them.[46]

At the conclusion of his message, Kopecky included suggestions from the Bratislava senders of the Vrba and Wetzler report about which he had consulted with Fritz Ullmann and representatives of Jewish organizations in Geneva: (1) let the Ministry of Foreign Affairs inform other Allied governments, in particular those whose citizens suffer in both camps, and direct a warning to the Germans and Hungarians that the Germans who are in control of these governments will be affected by reprisals; (2) bombard the crematoria, which are distinguishable by high chimneys and guard towers in both camps; (3) bombard the main communications of Slovakia and Sub-Carpathian Ukraine; (4) use the report for a large publicity campaign, but, without giving a source; (5) make public the warnings directed to the Germans and Hungarians; (6) ask the Vatican to make a sharp public condemnation; and (7) let the Ministry of Foreign Affairs inform the Bureau of the World Jewish Congress and the Jewish Agency in London.

On July 4, 1944, the Czechoslovak government handed over Kopecky's excerpt from the report, simply called "Report on Conditions in the Concentration Camps Auschwitz and Birkenau," to the Allied governments, asking them to make a "solemn warning to Hitler's government, which is, beyond any doubt, responsible for these organized, barbarous crimes." It recommended that the Allies bombard the crematoria in both camps and the main railway lines that connected Slovakia and Sub-Carpathian Ukraine with Poland and also had military significance, particularly the bridge at Cop.[47]

Meanwhile, on June 22 or 23, a considerably abbreviated English translation of the Vrba and Wetzler report reached Switzerland. It was sent on June 19 by the head of the Palestinian Bureau in Budapest, Miklos Kraus, along with the report about Hungarian deportations. Romanian diplomat Florian Maniolo was the mediator who passed these documents on to the general consul of Salvador in Bern, George Mantell. From him, they came to the attention of British journalist Walter Garrett.[48]

In four messages, Garrett informed the London central office of his News Service Exchange about the deportation transports of Hungary's Jews to Auschwitz and, based on the Vrba and Wetzler report, painted a dramatic image of what was awaiting these Jews in a place where 1,715,000 Jewish prisoners had already been slaughtered. In this way, the dreadful tragedy of the victims came to light, and an appeal to the world conscience was intensified.[49] In the following 18 days, 383 articles based on data from the Vrba and Wetzler report[50] appeared in the Swiss press and news contained in the report was circulated in other countries.

In spite of that, if one goes through the cartons of press clippings from around the world collected by the Czechoslovak Ministry of Foreign Affairs at the time, one wonders about the distorted publicity and particularly the method of publicizing the news. Articles in the *New York Times* sent by its reporter Daniel T. Brigham from Geneva are typical. The first article, "Inquiry Confirms Nazi Death Camps," which includes a table of the estimated number of victims from different countries, contains only a few sentences from the report that did not suffice to make clear the Auschwitz murder mechanism. In the second article, "The Death Camps Places of Horror," nothing about killing with gas is mentioned, although Vrba and Wetzler had described the operation of the gas chambers in detail. And the article referred to Slovak refugees only in the context of tattooing.[51]

Publication of the report itself was delayed, and the entire report, complete with all its documentaion, never reached the public during the war. Attempts to publish it in Switzerland met with great difficulty. Swiss authorities hesitated for a long time about whether to permit publication. Finally they gave permission,[52] but the published report was shortened considerably, and an insignificant number of copies was printed by a primitive technique, probably on an internal press.[53] The Czechoslovak government's attitude can also be blamed for inadequate publication and distribution of the report. This government failed to publish anything about the July 4 note in the press. Its official paper, *Czechoslovak*, which regularly reported on government discussions, did not even mention the note.

The entire text of the Vrba and Wetzler report, which Kopecky sent to Czechoslovak President Edvard Benes not later than June 26, probably did not reach London for some time. According to historian Martin Gilbert, an unabridged version went through the British legate in Stockholm and on to London on July 26.[54] By that time, the Czechoslovak government had the entire report at its disposal.

The British government replied on July 29 to the Czechoslovak note that accompanied the report. The reply was signed by F. K. Roberts on behalf of the absent minister and addressed to Minister Jan Masaryk. It announced that the British government fully sympathized with the Czechoslovak government in its exasperation over the treatment of Jews in the camps, that it had consulted the United States about this matter, and that it "is taking and will take all the measures possible for salvation that correspond to the successful carrying on of the war."[55]

When the British Foreign Office received the entire text of the Vrba and Wetzler report, the department for refugees became alarmed. "Although a usual Jewish exaggeration is to be taken into account," Ian Henderson commented in a report on August 26, "these statements are dreadful." Gilbert, who has thoroughly gone over the archives of the Foreign Office, notes that none of the officials who received the Czechoslovak document dated July 4, which contained the essential excerpts, or later the report itself, had thought to give either one to the press. Both had been distributed only to those who were in charge of war crime affairs, and these officials had filed them away.[56]

The representative of the War Refugee Board in Switzerland, McClelland, was one of the first to receive, in mid-June 1944, the complete text of the Vrba and Wetzler report from Kopecky. But only a summary could be sent from Bern to Washington. McClelland did not have the opportunity to send the complete report until mid-October. U.S. historian David Wyman, after studying the abundant preserved documentation, concluded that the U.S. Embassy in Bern had assigned little significance to the War Refugee Board. That is evident from the fact that it took the Auschwitz document more than four months to travel from Bern to Washington.[57]

On November 1, 1944, reports of the Auschwitz death factory were brought to the attention of the executive president of the War Refugee Board, John Pehle. He decided to place the Vrba and Wetzler report, supplemented by information from Rosin and Mordowicz and the testimony of Tabeau, at the disposal of the press. However, several wee¹ s were to pass before that happened. In the meantime, a U.S. army journal, *Yank*, asked the War Refugee Board for material for an article about German war crimes. It was given a copy of the Vrba and Wetzler report, but the editors decided not to use it. It was "too Semitic" for them; they required a "less Jewish account" that would not inflame a "latent anti-Semitism in the army."[58]

One day after the War Refugee Board passed copies of the document "German Extermination Camps—Auschwitz and Birkenau"[59] to an editorial board prior to distribution to the press, the head of the Office of War Information, Elmer Davis, called Pehle. He refused to distribute the report. His reasoning was strange: nobody would believe what was written in it and therefore the American public would cease to believe other information from Davis's office about the war.[60] Pehle insisted, and a set of documents was officially released for publication at a press conference at the end of November—almost exactly seven months after the Vrba and Wetzler report was written. According to a dispatch from the Czechoslovak Embassy on November 28, all the prominent newspapers in Washington carried substantial information about the report on Sunday and Monday and cited excerpts from it.[61]

The Soviet offensive was now approaching Auschwitz so quickly that Himmler commanded that the operation of the gas chambers be ceased and that they be disassembled. He was anxious to prevent a repetition of what had happened in the Majdanek concentration camp, when the Soviet Army liberated the camp so quickly that the Nazi criminals had not been able to cover all the traces of their activities.

History sometimes proves tragically ironic. On October 30, 1944, selections on the arrival platform took place for the last time in Auschwitz-Birkenau when 1,689 people from the Terezin transport were sent to the gas chambers. Subsequently, only individuals were killed with gas during selections in the camp. The last 13 women were gassed (or possibly shot) on November 25 in crematorium II.[62] That same day, the Germans began to demolish the crematorium and its gas chambers. Not until that day did the War Refugee Board overcome its hesitation and release the reports of the Auschwitz escapees to the press. Not until that day.

NOTES

1. Tadeusz Iwaszko, "Haftlingsfluchten aus dem Konzentrationslager Auschwitz," in *Hefte von Auschwitz* 7 (1964), p. 49.

2. Archives of the Auschwitz-Birkenau State Museum, APMO4, film 90, shot 66–67.

3. Alfred Wetzler described the story of his escape under the pseudonym Jozef Lanik in *Co Dante nevidel* (Bratislava, 1964). Further editions: *Co Dante nevidel* (Prague, 1966) and *Was Dante nicht sah* (Frankfurt am Main, 1967, and Berlin, 1968). Rudolf Vrba, in cooperation with Alan Bestic, issued his memoir as *I Cannot Forgive* (London, 1963). The German version is *Ich kann nicht vergeben* (Munich, 1964).

4. See Miroslav Karny, "Ein Auschwitz—Bericht und das Schicksal des Theresienstädter Familienlagers," in *Judaica Bohemiae* 21 (1985), no. 1, pp. 9–28.

5. The report is divided into three parts. Wetzler wrote the first part, Wetzler and Vrba the second part together, and Vrba the third part, which described his journey through Majdanek to Auschwitz and his experience in the camp. That is how the division of work was recorded in the first postwar edition of the report, issued in 1946 *(Oswiecim, hrobka styroch milionov l'udi,* Bratislava, p. 74), and Wetzler confirmed it in a letter to the author, April 14, 1982. He emphasized, however, that although each first wrote his passage by himself, later they worked on the whole text together for two or three days, then wrote six more versions. As they worked on it, it was being translated from Slovak into German by Oscar Krasnansky-Karmiel with the assistance of Gisela Steiner. The Slovak text of the report has not been preserved.

6. The full text of the Vrba and Wetzler report was published by John S. Conway in "Der Auschwitz-Bericht von April 1944," in *Zeitgeschichte*, August–September 1981, pp. 313–442. Its text was also published by Heiner Lichtenstein in a supplement to *Warum Auschwitz nicht bombardiet wurde* (Cologne, 1980), but with many modifications made without mentioning that the editor had changed the authentic text. The Auschwitz-Birkenau State Museum is preparing a critical edition of the Vrba and Wetzler report for a special issue of *Zeszyty Oswiecimskie.*

7. Vrba and Wetzler agree that they had learned many data over a long period that they used later in their report. But Wetzler affirms in a letter to the author (1982) that in addition they had carried part of their work around with them in written form hidden in two metal tubes, one of which, with exact layouts of the camp and its extermination mechanisms, was lost during their escape, so that the layouts had to be replaced by mere sketches. In the second tube, there were data about transports (see Lanik, *Co Dante nevidel,* 1964, p. 177). On the other hand, Vrba has stated: "Neither I nor Wetzler carried any notes from Auschwitz-Birkenau. I think these 'written messages' were conjured up because nobody could explain my

personal memotechnical methods, which were the basis of the statistics contained in the V-W report." Vrba's statement is contained in a letter from John S. Conway to the author (1984).

8. See M. Karny, "Vernichtung durch Arbeit: Sterblichkeit in den NS-Kozentrationslagern," in *Beitrage zur nationalsozialistichen Gesundheits-und Sozialpolitik* (Berlin, 1983), pp. 140–45.

9. Georges Wellers, "Essai de détermination du nombre de morts au camp d'Auschwitz," in *Le Monde Juif*, October-December 1983, pp. 127–59.

10. See the essay by Franciszek Piper in this book (chap. 4).

11. Reports of the prisoners in the Sonderkommando were found after the war in the crematoria areas and are published in *Wsrod Koszmarnej Zbrodni—Notatki wiezniow Sonderkommando*, 2d ed. (Oswiecim). German edition: *In mitten des grauenvollen Verbrechens: Handschriften von Mitgliedern des Sonderkommandos* (Auschwitz, 1972).

12. Randolph L. Braham, *The Politics of Genocide* (New York, 1981), p. 712.

13. *Actes et documents du Saint Siège relatifs à la Seconde Guerre Mondiale*, vol. 10 (Vatican City, 1980), document 204, p. 281.

14. Tardini added one observation to the document, which on October 26 had been completed. He inquired whether it was the same report that had arrived from Switzerland. According to the Vatican editors, the inquiry referred to the report sent by the Bern nuncio, Bernardini, on July 28, 1944, which consisted of four pages and told about deportations of Jews to Auschwitz. Ibid., document 279, p. 364.

15. Their report in the German version is reproduced in the supplement of Michael Dov Weissmandel, *Min Hametzar* (New York, 1960). Concerning the history of their escape, see the report of Czeslaw Mordowicz, October 1, 1964, APMO, Zespot Oswiadczenia, bk. 50, pp. 103–11. The Czechoslovak Ministry of Foreign Affairs sent the text of this report in Slovak, dated July 28, 1944, to a member of the State Council, A. Frischeron, on December 18, 1944; AFMZV, LA-D, cart. 190.

16. Vrba, pp. 286–94; Erich Kulka, "Five Escapes from Auschwitz," in *They Fought Back*, ed. Zuri Suhl (New York, 1968), pp. 212–37.

17. John S. Conway, "Fruhe Augenzeugenberichte aus Auschwitz: Glaubwurdigkeit und Wirkungsgeschichte," in *Viertel Jahrshefte für Zeitgeschichte* 1979, no. 2, p. 276

18. *Actes et documents*, p. 281. This finding refutes the widespread interpretation that the message of Burzio reached the Vatican, which then sent its legate to Bratislava to verify it.

19. Martin Gilbert, *Auschwitz and the Allies* (London, 1981), pp. 216–17.

20. I was given a copy of a chapter from Kopecky's unpublished book by the author.

21. The data from Kopecky's memoirs are also confirmed by the record in the papers of the Jewish Agency representative in Geneva, Richard Lichtheim—*Aktenvermerkbetreffend Birkenau und Auschwitz*, June 23, 1944; from the materials of Dr. J. Kopecky. I owe Prof. J. S. Conway thanks for the photocopy of a letter to Schönfeld translated in the Archives of the War Refugee Board.

22. Interview with Dr. J. Kopecky, October 22, 1975.

23. Interview with Orga Mickova, February 4, 1982.

24. Fritz Ullmann was a member of the delegation sent from the Protectorate of Bohemia and Moravia to the 21st Zionist Congress in Geneva in August 1939, and he remained as a representative of the Jewish Agency in Switzerland to look after emigration affairs and to maintain connections between the Protectorate's Jews and the free world. See Ruth Bondy, *Elder of the Jews: Jakob Edelstein of Theresienstadt*

(New York, 1989), p. 152 and Karger Mendel, "Dr. F. J. Ullmann," in *Zeitschrift für die Geschichte der Jüden* 10 (1973), nos. 1–2, pp. 45–48.

25. Letters from Dr. G. M. Riegner of October 5 and December 13, 1983, to the author; also Kopecky's memoirs and Lichtheim's *Aktenvermerk*.

26. See M. Karny, "Terezin a terezinsky rodinny tabor v Osvetimi," in *Terezinske listy* 19 (1991), pp. 9–23; "Terezinsky rodinny tabor v Birkenau," in *Sbornik historicky* 26 (1979), pp. 229–304; "Das Theresienstadter Familienlager in Birkenau," in *Judaica Bohemiae* 15 (1979), pp. 3–26.

27. I owe thanks to Dr. G. M. Riegner for a photocopy of this message and of the documents linked to it from the archives of the War Refugee Board. See also David S. Wyman, *Abandonment of Jews: America and the Holocaust 1941–1945* (New York, 1984), p. 29.

28. E. Wiskemann sent the message to London, and she passed the text of the message together with Kopecky's letter to A. W. Dulles of the U.S. Office of Strategic Services on June 14 with this note: "I have just wired this—could you also? Yours E.W. 14/6." Dulles did not wire the materials to Washington; he passed them on to Roswell McClelland, representative of the War Refugee Board in Switzerland, on June 15.

29. Foreign Office; W. D. Allen announced it by letter no. C8037/1343/12 to the Czechoslovak Ministry of Foreign Affairs on June 16, 1944. The archives of the Federal Ministry of Foreign Affairs (AFMZV), LA-D, carton 190.

30. Records on the broadcasting of London and Moscow radios. State Central Archives in Prague, SUA4., URP. cart. 1170.

31. Ibid. Deviations from the text of Kopecky's message were evidently caused by inaccurate monitoring.

32. See Karny, "Ein Auschwitz," and M. Karny, "Vorgeschichte, Sinn und Folgen des 23 Juni 1944," in *Judaica Bohemiae* 19 (1983), no. 2, pp. 72–98.

33. Central State Archives in Potsdam (ZStAP), now the Federal Archives in Koblenz, collection of films, film 15463, K 348410.

34. Ibid., K 348411–2.

35. Text of a resolution of the State Council, SUA, SR-L, cart. 56, pp. 88–89.

36. Letter of the chief of Security Police and Security Service (signed Mildner 4 on the German Red Cross form on May 17, 1944, with a notification that the Reichsführer SS had permitted both inspections). Bundesarchiv Koblenz (BAK), R 58/89, p. 15.

37. A set of documents referring to its activity related to Terezin was given by the International Red Cross Committee at a meeeting of historians in 1991 ("Documents du Comité International de la Croix-Rouge concernant le ghetto de Theresienstadt"). My study in *Terezinske listy*, no. 20, is dedicated to their analysis.

38. Dispatches 322–25, from June 26, 1944. AFMZV, LA-D, cart. 190, nos. 4950, 4951, 4909, 4910 duv/44.

39. Jerzy Tabeau was imprisoned in Auschwitz under the name Jerzy Weselowski (camp no. 27273). He escaped from the camp on November 19, 1943, and wrote his report in winter 1943–44. He did not come to know how his report had been used until 1981, from the historian Barbara Jaroszova, who presented him a photocopy of the report, written in his own hand, that was kept in the Auschwitz-Birkenau State Museum. Relation of Dr. J. Tabeau on January 14, 1982, APMO, Zespol Oswiadczenia, bk. 98, s. 1–32. I was not able to find out how the report of Tabeau got to Weissmandel, who passed it on to Kopecky. That Kopecky had re-

ceived the report of a Polish major together with the Vrba and Wetzler report is explicitly stated in his message no. 322.

40. Jean-Claude Favez, *Unter Mitarbeit von Genevieve Billeter: Das Internationale Rote Kreuz und das Dritte Reich* (Zurich, 1988), p. 449. Kopecky, together with Riegner, discussed the Vrba and Wetzler report with the International Red Cross Committee once more, and they decided that Schwarzenberg would pass the excerpt from the report to the German Red Cross, ibid., p. 216.

41. Dispatch no. 325, June 26, 1944.

42. Vrba's letter to Gilbert, July 26, 1980, in Gilbert, p. 182. At another time, Vrba wrote: "From Jan. 1944, however, I witnessed unusually extensive technical preparations, designed to step up the intake of this murder machine to 20,000 victims a day. It was no secret in Auschwitz that these extraordinary preparations were designed for the rapid annihilation of Hungary's Jews, who were almost 1,000,000 strong. In March . . . it was evident to us Auschwitz prisoners that the start of this well-prepared action was quite imminent." Vrba, "Footnote to Auschwitz Report," in *Jewish Currents*, March 1966, pp. 23–24.

43. Conway, "Fruhe Augenzeugenberichte," p. 276; also p. 267.

44. The German translation reads: "Mitte Marz kam eine kleine Gruppe von Benzburger und Sosnowitzer Juden, die aus ihren Verstecken ausgehoben wurden. Von einen erfuhren wir, daß sich viele polnische Juden nach der Slowakei und von dort nach Ungarn retten und daß ihnen hierbei die slowakischen Juden helfen. Nach der Vergasung des Theresienstadter Transportes hatten wir bis zum 15. März keinen Zuwachs. Der Lagerstand sank, weshalb dann alle Mannervon fortlaufend ankommenden Transporten von insbesonderehollandischen Juden, in das Lagergebrachtwurden. Wir verliessen das Lager am 7. April 1944 und horten noch, daß große Transporte mit griechischen Juden ankommen."

45. Alfred Wetzler, "Pruhovane karavan," Archive of the Union of Antifascist Fighters (ACSPB), 1963, pp. 143, 147.

46. See n. 21.

47. AFMZV, LA-D, cart. 190. In the letter of safe conduct signed by Hubert Ripka, it was emphasized: "Even if it should happen that the report is incorrect in a few concrete details, for instance, if it exaggerates the number of victims in some cases, it is indisputable that terrible cruelties are being carried out wholesale, systematically, and on a deliberately organized plan." The English text of the whole document was published by Gilbert, pp. 262–64.

48. Werner Rings, *Advokaten des Feindes: Das Abenteuer der politischen Neutralität* (Vienna, Munich, Düsseldorf, 1966), pp. 142–46. Gilbert, pp. 244–45. Later, Mantello expressed regret that he had not received the report in full and that it had come to his attention late. His letter of May 18, 1964, is quoted by Kulka, p. 236.

49. The texts of Garrett's messages of June 24, 1944, were published by Jeno Levai, in *Zsidósors Európaban, Budapest*, pp. 68–71.

50. Rings, pp. 144–46.

51. *New York Times*, July 3 and 6, 1944. SUA, ZTA, carton 1242. AFM ZV-LA-D, cart. 471.

52. Mario D. Fenyo, *Hitler, Horthy, and Hungary* (New Haven, 1972), pp. 188–89.

53. *Die Judenausrottung in Polen: Augenzeugenberichte*, series 3, August 1944.

54. Gilbert, p. 290.

55. F. K. Roberts to J. Masaryk, July 29, 1944. AFMZV, La-D, cart. 190.

56. Gilbert, p. 290. David Allen of the Foreign Office made this final record on

August 15: "I am afraid this looks as though it would not help greatly toward identifying individuals responsible."

57. Wyman, p. 324.

58. A letter from the editors of *Yank* to John Pehle, November 16, 1944, is quoted by Wyman, pp. 324–25.

59. Executive Office of the President, War Refugee Board, Washington, D.C., "German Extermination Camps—Auschwitz and Birkenau," November 1944.

60. Brewster Chamberlin and Marcia Feldman, eds., *The Liberation of the Nazi Concentration Camps 1945* (Washington, D.C.: United States Holocaust Memorial Council, 1987), p. 176. Joseph Borkin, *The Crime and Punishment of I.G. Farben* (New York, 1978) pp. 112–13.

61. AFMZV, LA-D, cart. 190.

62. Danuta Czech, ed., *Kalendarium der Ereignisse im Konzentrationslager Auschwitz-Birkenau 1939–1945* (Reinbek bei Hamburg, 1989), pp. 920 and 933. The information in the *Kalendarium* was originally issued in a series in *Hefte von Auschwitz*. It was stated there that these 13 women prisoners were the last victims of the Auschwitz gas chambers (vol. 8, 1964, p. 88). In the book, it states that they were "unmittelbar getotet." The author thus leaves open the question of how they were murdered.

27

Why Auschwitz Wasn't Bombed

DAVID S. WYMAN

During the spring of 1944, three circumstances combined to make bombing the Auschwitz gas chambers and the rail lines that led to the camp from Hungary critically important and militarily possible.

In mid-April, the Nazis started concentrating Jews in Hungary for deportation to Auschwitz. In late April, two escapees from Auschwitz revealed details of the mass murder taking place at the camp, thus laying bare the fate awaiting the Hungarian Jews. And by May, the U.S. 15th Air Force, which had operated from southern Italy since December 1943, reached full strength and started pounding Axis industrial complexes in Central and East Central Europe. For the first time, Auschwitz and the rail lines that led to it from Hungary were within striking range of Allied bombers.

The two escapees were young Slovak Jews, Rudolf Vrba and Alfred Wetzler. Toward the end of April, they reached the Jewish underground in Slovakia and sounded the alarm that preparations were under way at Auschwitz for exterminating the Hungarian Jews. They dictated a detailed report on the camp's geographic layout, internal conditions, and gassing and cremation techniques.[1]

A copy of the Vrba-Wetzler report reached Budapest by early May. By mid-June, Roswell McClelland, the U.S. War Refugee Board representative in Switzerland, had received a copy. He found it consistent with earlier information that had filtered out. The report was further corroborated by a non-Jewish Polish military officer who also had recently escaped from the camp.[2]

In June, the information made its way into the hands of the Allied governments and began to appear in the Swiss, British, and American press.[3]

By late June 1944, the outside world knew the truth about Auschwitz and had detailed descriptions of its geographic location and layout.

In mid-May, as deportation from the eastern provinces of Hungary started, Jewish leaders in Budapest sent out a plea to bomb the rail route to Poland. The message specified the junction cities of Kosice and Presov and the single-track rail line between the two cities. The Jewish underground in Bratislava, Slovakia, telegraphed the request in code to Isaac Sternbuch, the representative in Switzerland of Vaad Ha-Hatzala, the American Orthodox Jewish rescue committee. The plea reached Sternbuch about May 17.[4]

Sternbuch submitted the message to the military attaché of the U.S. legation in Bern and requested that it be sent through diplomatic lines to the Union of Orthodox Rabbis in New York. A week later, a similar but more urgent telegram arrived from Bratislava. This appeal also went to the military attaché for transmission to New York. More pleas came, and Sternbuch relayed them to the U.S. legation. Yet, by June 22, Sternbuch had received no reply from New York. For unknown reasons, the messages had been blocked, either in Bern or in Washington.[5]

Meanwhile, during the third week of May, Rabbi Michael Weissmandel and Mrs. Gisi Fleischmann, leaders of the Slovak Jewish underground, smuggled a long letter out of Slovakia that described the first deportations from Hungary and stressed the fate awaiting the deportees. In their letter, they appealed for immediate bombing of the main deportation routes, especially the Kosice-Presov railway, and cried to the outside world to "bombard the death halls in Auschwitz." Their letter reached Switzerland, but not until late June.[6]

At about the same time, one of Sternbuch's pleas for railway bombing, transmitted illegally through Polish diplomatic channels, circumvented U.S. censorship and broke through to American Jewish circles.[7] On June 18, Jacob Rosenheim of the New York office of the Agudath Israel World Organization addressed letters to high U.S. government officials, informing them of the ongoing deportations. He submitted that paralysis of the rail traffic from Hungary to Poland could at least slow the annihilation process and implored the government officials to begin bombing the rail junctions of Kosice and Presov immediately.[8]

Rosenheim's appeals were relayed to the War Refugee Board. On June 21, John Pehle, executive director of the WRB, transmitted the request to the War Department. Three days later, he discussed it with Assistant Secretary of War John J. McCloy. McCloy agreed to look into it.[9]

In fact, the War Department had started to consider the proposal the day before, and on Saturday afternoon, June 24, the proposal arrived at the Operations Division, the arm of the department charged with strategic planning and direction of operations. On Monday, the Operations Division ruled against the proposed bombing, stating that the suggestion was "impracticable" because "it could be executed only by diversion of considerable air support essential to the success of our forces now engaged in decisive operations."[10]

Actually, the decision was not based on any analysis of air operations; nor were Air Force commanders in Europe consulted. Rather, the rejection came directly out of a confidential War Department policy established in Washington nearly five months earlier.

In late January 1944, shortly after President Roosevelt established the War Refugee Board, the board requested British help in carrying out its rescue program. The British government was reluctant to cooperate, partly because the presence of the secretary of war on the WRB implied that the armed forces would be used in rescuing refugees. The War Department, in a move to reassure the British on this issue, set down the following policy:

> It is not contemplated that units of the armed forces will be employed for the purpose of rescuing victims of enemy oppression unless such rescues are the direct result of military operations conducted with the objective of defeating the armed forces of the enemy.[11]

This policy effectively removed the War Department from participation in rescue efforts.

Another of the WRB's earliest moves was an attempt to arrange for some cooperation from U.S. military commanders in the war theaters. In late January 1944, the board proposed through McCloy that the War Department send a message to war theater commanders instructing them to do what was possible, consistent with the successful prosecution of the war, to assist the government's policy of rescue.[12]

Although the executive order that established the WRB specifically mandated such cooperation, the military leadership in Washington balked at dispatching the message. McCloy referred the proposal to the Office of the Chief of Staff after jotting on it, "I am very chary of getting the Army involved in this while the war is on."[13] The War Department's decision crystallized in February in an internal memorandum, which stated that "we must constantly bear in mind, however, that the most effective relief which can be given victims of enemy persecution is to insure the speedy defeat of the Axis."[14] In concrete terms, this meant that the military had decided to avoid rescue or relief activities.

In late June, when the Operations Division received Rosenheim's proposal to bomb rail points between Hungary and Auschwitz, it drew these two earlier pronouncements from the files and used them as the basis for its decision:

The War Department is of the opinion that the suggested air operation is impracticable for the reason that it could be executed only by diversion of considerable air support essential to the success of our forces now engaged in decisive operations. The War Department fully appreciates the humanitarian importance of the suggested operation. However, after due consideration of the problem, it is considered that the most effective relief to victims of enemy persecution is the early defeat of the Axis, an undertaking to which we must devote every resource at our disposal.[15]

Thus two confidential policy statements, generated several months earlier, were used to rule out the proposal to bomb the Kosice-Presov railroad. This decision then served as a precedent for rejecting all subsequent requests. The War Department simply claimed it had already considered such operations and found them infeasible.

In fact, when the War Department formed its basic policy on rescue the previous February, it knowingly and secretly decided not to comply with the executive order that established the War Refugee Board. The record of a crucial meeting of mid-level War Department officials shows that Colonel Harrison Gerhardt, McCloy's executive assistant, advised Colonel Thomas Davis of the Operations Division's Logistics Group to "read from the executive order, in which it is stated that the War, State and Treasury Departments will cooperate to the fullest extent." Davis responded, "I cannot see why the Army has anything to do with it whatsoever." Later in the meeting, Davis insisted, "We are over there to win the war and not to take care of refugees." Gerhardt replied, "The President doesn't think so. He thinks relief is a part of winning the war." At the end of the discussion, Davis crystallized the problem and its solution:

> The hook in the executive order is in paragraph 3 [the section that required the War, State, and Treasury departments to execute WRB programs]. Obviously there will be continuing pressure from some quarters to enlarge the sphere of this thing. I think that we should make our position fairly inelastic.[16]

Davis's view prevailed. In direct contradiction to the president's executive order, the War Department unilaterally decided against involving the military in rescue. It was this policy—never disclosed outside the War Department—that extinguished Rosenheim's plea for railroad bombing.

Before McCloy could advise Pehle of the decision on Rosenheim's proposal, another request reached the WRB through its representative in Switzerland. A cablegram from McClelland on June 24 summarized the information that he had received concerning the Hungarian deportations. It also listed the five main railroad deportation routes and pointed out:

It is urged by all sources of this information in Slovakia and Hungary that vital sections of these lines especially bridges along ONE [the Csap, Kosice, Presov route] be bombed as the only possible means of slowing down or stopping future deportations.[17]

Pehle, not aware that the War Department had already ruled against Rosenheim's request, relayed McClelland's cablegram to McCloy on June 29. The chance for approval of a proposal to bomb five rail systems was minute; indeed, it received no separate consideration. The official War Department reply simply adapted the Operations Division's language rejecting the earlier Rosenheim proposal to fit the new, expanded bombing request. McCloy signed it on July 4.[18]

Calls for bombing the deportation rail lines continued to come to Washington. But starting early in July, appeals for Air Force action to impede the mass murders increasingly centered on destruction of the Auschwitz gas chambers. Even before the first of these proposals reached Washington, Benjamin Akzin of the WRB staff was arguing for strikes on Auschwitz. He held that bombing the killing installations would, at least for a time, appreciably slow the slaughter.[19]

By mid-July, Pehle and the WRB board decided to press the military on the question. But a careful plan to do so apparently went awry, for no formal approach took place, though Pehle and McCloy did discuss the issue sometime during the summer of 1944. Their conversation must have dampened Pehle's interest in the project, because he informed Henry Morgenthau, Jr., the secretary of the treasury, in September that the board had decided not to refer the proposal to the War Department.[20]

Late in July, the Emergency Committee to Save the Jewish People of Europe wrote President Roosevelt calling for bombing the deportation railroads and the gas chambers.[21] The letter emphasized that the railroads were also used for military traffic and that an attack on Auschwitz could open the way for inmates to escape and join the resistance forces. Therefore both proposed actions would assist, not hamper, the war effort. Nothing at all came of this overture.

The next proposal, issued from the World Jewish Congress in New York, went directly to the War Department. On August 9, A. Leon Kubowitzki sent McCloy a message that he had recently received from Ernest Frischer of the Czech government-in-exile. It called for bombing the Auschwitz gas chambers and the deportation railroads.[22]

The War Department's reply, signed by McCloy and dated August 14, followed a familiar pattern:

I refer to your letter of August 9 in which you request consideration of a proposal made by Mr. Ernest Frischer that certain installations and railroad centers be bombed.

The War Department has been approached by the War Refugee Board, which raised the question of the practicability of this suggestion. After a study it became apparent that such an operation could be executed only by the diversion of considerable air support essential to the success of our forces now engaged in decisive operations elsewhere and would in any case be of such doubtful efficacy that it would not warrant the use of our resources. There has been considerable opinion to the effect that such an effort, even if practicable, might provoke even more vindictive action by the Germans.

The War Department fully appreciates the humanitarian motives which prompted the suggested operation, but for the reasons stated above, it has not been felt that it can or should be undertaken, at least at this time.[23]

Meanwhile, the only significant approach ever made to the British government on the bombing issue had nearly run its course—unsuccessfully, despite the support of Prime Minister Winston Churchill and Foreign Secretary Anthony Eden. On July 6, two days after McCloy wrote to the War Refugee Board rejecting the first of the U.S. bombing proposals, Chaim Weizmann and Moshe Shertok conferred with Eden. Acting for the Jewish Agency and at the suggestion of its representatives in Budapest, Geneva, and Jerusalem, the two Zionist leaders presented Eden with a list of proposals for attempting to save the remaining Hungarian Jews. Included was a request that "the railway-line leading from Budapest to Birkenau, and the death-camps at Birkenau and other places, should be bombed." Eden agreed to transmit the bombing proposals to the Air Ministry.[24]

That same day, Eden wrote to Churchill expressing support for the bombing requests. Churchill answered him the following day: "You and I are in entire agreement. Get anything out of the Air Force you can, and invoke me if necessary." Eden at once sent the proposals to the secretary of state for air, Sir Archibald Sinclair. "Could you let me know," he wrote, "how the Air Ministry view the feasibility of these proposals? I very much hope that it will be possible to do something. I have the authority of the Prime Minister to say that he agrees."

The Weizmann-Shertok request, which had started off so rapidly, began to bog down in the meshes of the Air Ministry and the Foreign Office. Sinclair did reply to Eden on July 15, declaring that bombing the railways was "out of our power" because the targets were too distant; the camps also were too far away for RAF heavy bombers to reach. He further replied that although it was very unlikely, there was a possibility that U.S. bombers could reach the camps. He said he would raise the issue with the U.S. authorities.

Eden, very displeased with Sinclair's answer, characterized it as "unhelpful" and jotted in its margin, "He was asked to act."

But neither Eden nor Churchill followed up on the matter; the Air Ministry officials and especially the Foreign Office officials tied it up for the next several weeks. Foreign Office personnel, in internal deliberations, questioned the workability, the value, and even the need for the plan. (They assumed that a reported stoppage in the deportations from Hungary meant that the mass killing had ended at Auschwitz.)

At the beginning of August, the Air Ministry staff asked the Foreign Office to furnish maps and detailed plans of the camps so the air staff could look into the feasibility of striking them. Two weeks later, the Foreign Office mentioned the request to the Jewish Agency. Within hours, the Jewish Agency procured the material from the Polish government-in-exile in London and transmitted it to the Foreign Office.

At that point, however, the Foreign Office decided to put an end to the plan altogether. Instead of sending the maps and plans to the Air Ministry, they were shunted off to the Foreign Office files. The Foreign Office subsequently turned down the bombing proposals on the grounds that the "technical difficulties involved" in carrying out the missions were too great and the reported cessation of the deportations from Hungary had ended the need for the bombings. In fact, the mass killing was continuing at Auschwitz. That was the reason why the Jewish Agency continued to press for bombing. And the question of technical difficulties had never really been addressed, partly because the Air Ministry had not been given the maps and plans of the camps. On September 1, Richard Law, acting for the Foreign Office, wrote to both Weizmann and Sir Archibald Sinclair informing them that the proposal had been rejected.

In Washington, meanwhile, pressures were building again for bombing the railroads, this time the lines between Auschwitz and Budapest, where the last large enclave of Hungarian Jews was threatened with deportation. During September, entreaties came from Vaad Ha-Hatzala, of the American Orthodox Jewish Rescue Committee. Rabbi Abraham Kalmanowitz, anxious for the appeal to reach the WRB as soon as possible, telephoned WRB staff member Benjamin Akzin, even though it was the Sabbath. When Akzin relayed the rabbi's plea to Pehle, he also spelled out his own dissatisfaction with the War Department's inaction regarding the bombing requests. Akzin maintained that the WRB had been "created precisely in order to overcome the inertia and—in some cases—the insufficient interest of the old-established agencies" concerning the rescue of Jews.[25] Pointing to the Allies' air superiority at the time, Akzin pressed for a direct approach to President Roosevelt to seek orders for immediate bombing of the deportation rail lines. But the board did not move on the appeal.

On the other crucial bombing issue—air strikes on Auschwitz—the WRB did act, but with hesitation. Near the end of September, members of the Polish exile government and British Jewish groups went to James Mann, the WRB representative in London, with information that the Nazis were increasing the pace of extermination. They urged the WRB board to explore again the possibility of bombing the killing chambers. Mann cabled their plea to Washington. Other messages that reached the board at the time reported Nazi threats to exterminate thousands of camp inmates as the Soviet Army forced the Germans back across Poland. Pehle decided to raise the issue once more, though not forcibly. He transmitted the substance of Mann's dispatch to McCloy "for such consideration as it may be worth."[26]

McCloy's office apparently didn't consider the matter important enough to discuss it with the Operations Division, nor even to reply to the WRB. Gerhardt recommended that "no action be taken on this, since the matter has been fully presented several times previously."[27] McCloy let his assistant's recommendation stand.

The last attempt to persuade the War Department to bomb Auschwitz came soon after the full text of the Auschwitz escapees' reports finally reached Washington on November 1. The detailed chronicles of horror jolted the board and shocked Pehle into writing a strong letter to McCloy urging destruction of the killing installations. Pehle also pointed out the military advantages of bombing the industrial sites at Auschwitz simultaneously.[28]

Pehle's appeal went from McCloy's office to the Operations Division, which rejected the proposal on the grounds that air power should not be diverted from vital "industrial target systems" and that Auschwitz was "not a part of these target systems."[29] In reality, it was. The Operations Division was either uninformed or untruthful. It also explained that destruction of the killing facilities would require heavy bombers, medium bombers, or low-flying or dive-bombing airplanes. It then made two misleading statements, which indicated that the mission was either technically impossible or inordinately risky:

> The target [Auschwitz] is beyond the maximum range of medium bombardment, divebombers and fighter bombers located in United Kingdom, France or Italy.

> Use of heavy bombardment from United Kingdom bases would necessitate a round trip flight unescorted of approximately 2000 miles over enemy territory.[30]

The first statement was false; Mitchell medium bombers and Lightning dive bombers had sufficient range to strike Auschwitz from Italy, as did British Mosquito fighter bombers. The second statement muddled the issue. Why omit the airfields in Italy? Heavy bombers could reach Auschwitz from there with no unusual difficulties. The bases in the United Kingdom, however, were substantially farther from Auschwitz and not relevant to the mission under consideration.

No further requests were made for bombing Auschwitz. Unknown to the outside world, in November 1944, SS Chief Heinrich Himmler ordered the killing machinery destroyed. On January 27, 1945, the Soviet Army captured the Auschwitz camp.

Thus the War Department consistently turned down proposals to bomb Auschwitz and the rail lines leading to it. The chief military reason given was that such proposals were "impracticable" because they required the "diversion of considerable air support essential to the success of our forces now engaged in decisive operations elsewhere."[31] Was this reason valid? The answer is no.

From March 1944 on, the Allies controlled the skies over Europe. Beginning in early May, the Italy-based 15th Air Force had the range and capability to strike the relevant targets. In fact, during the same days in late June that the War Department was refusing the first requests to bomb railways, a fleet of 15th Air Force bombers was waiting for proper flying conditions to attack oil refineries near Auschwitz. This mission, which took place on July 7, saw 452 bombers travel along and across two of the five deportation rail lines. On June 26, 71 Flying Fortresses on another bombing run passed by the other three rail lines, crossing one and flying within 30 miles of the other two.[32]

As for Auschwitz, as early as January 1944, Allied bombing strategists were analyzing it as a potential target because of the synthetic oil and rubber installations connected to the camp. Two months later, the huge Blechhammer oil-refining complex, 47 miles from Auschwitz, came under careful study. Early in May, General Ira C. Eaker, commander of Allied air forces in Italy, pointed out that strikes on Blechhammer could be carried out simultaneously with attacks on war industries at Auschwitz and Odertal.[33]

By May 1944, the 15th Air Force had turned its primary attention to oil targets. Throughout the summer, as their involvement with the invasion of France lessened, the British-based U.S. Eighth Air Force and the Royal Air Force increasingly joined in. Most observers, then and now, have agreed that the close attention paid to oil in 1944 and 1945 was one of the most decisive factors in Germany's defeat. Loss of oil gradually strangled the Third Reich's military operations.[34]

In late June, the 15th Air Force was about to move the "oil war" into Upper Silesia, where Germany had created a major synthetic-oil industry based on the vast coal resources there. Eight important oil plants were clustered within a rough half-circle 35 miles in radius, with Auschwitz near the northeast end of the arc and Blechhammer near the northwest end. Blechhammer was the main target. Fleets ranging from 102 to 357 heavy bombers hit it on ten occasions between July 7 and November 20. But Blechhammer was not the only industrial target. All eight plants shook under the impact of tons of high explosives. Among them was the industrial section of Auschwitz itself.[35]

Late in the morning on Sunday, August 20, 127 Flying Fortresses, escorted by 100 Mustang fighters, dropped 1,336 500-pound high-explosive bombs on the factory areas of Auschwitz, less than five miles east of the gas chambers. The weather was excellent, making conditions nearly ideal for accurate visual bombing. Antiaircraft fire and the 19 German fighter planes there were ineffective. Only one U.S. bomber went down; no Mustangs were hit. All five bomber groups reported success in striking the target area.[36]

Again, on September 13, a force of heavy bombers rained destruction on the factory areas of Auschwitz. The 96 Liberators encountered no German aircraft, but heavy ground fire brought three of them down. As before, no attempt was made to strike the killing installations, though a stray bomb damaged the rail spur to the gas chambers.[37]

On December 18 and again on December 26, U.S. bombers pounded the Auschwitz industries.[38]

Beginning in early July, air strikes in the area were extensive. For example, two days after the first raid on Auschwitz, 261 Flying Fortresses and Liberators bombed the Blechhammer and Odertal oil refineries. Many of them passed within forty miles of Auschwitz soon after leaving their targets. On August 27, another 350 heavy bombers struck Blechhammer. Two days after that, 218 hit Moravska Ostrava and Oderberg (Bohumin), both within 45 miles of Auschwitz.[39] Not long before, on August 7, heavy bombers carried out attacks on both sides of Auschwitz on the same day: 357 had bombed Blechhammer and 55 had hit Trzebinia, only 13 miles northeast of Auschwitz.[40]

It would be no exaggeration, therefore, to characterize the area around Auschwitz, including Auschwitz itself, as a hotbed of U.S. bombing activity from August 7 to August 29. Yet on August 14, the War Department wrote that bombing Auschwitz would be possible only by diversion of air power from "decisive operations elsewhere."[41]

A question remains: would the proposed bombing raids have been, as the War Department maintained, of "doubtful efficacy"?

In the case of railroad lines, the answer is not clear-cut. Railroad bombing had its problems and was the subject of long-lasting disputes within the Allied military. Successful severing of rail routes necessitated close observation of the cut lines and frequent bombing, since repairs took only a few days. While railroad bombing could be very effective for targets assigned a continuing commitment of air power, in the midst of the war no one expected diversion of that kind of military force for rescue purposes.[42]

It might also be argued that railroad bombing would not have helped after July 8, 1944—the day on which the last mass deportations from Hungary to Auschwitz took place. The argument is convincing with regard to the three deportation railways farthest from Budapest, because most Jews outside the capital were gone by then. But more than 200,000 Jews remained in Budapest. And they faced the constant danger that the transports to Auschwitz might be resumed. This threat meant that the other two deportation railways, which would have been used to carry Jews from Budapest to Auschwitz, remained critically important.

In this situation, the United States could readily have demonstrated concern for the Jews. Without risking more than minute cost to the war effort, the War Department could have agreed to stand ready, if deportations resumed, to spare some bomb tonnage for those two railroads, provided bombers were already scheduled to fly near them on regular war missions. As it happened, on ten different days from July through October, a total of 2,700 bombers traveled along or within easy reach of both rail lines on the way to targets in the Blechhammer-Auschwitz region.[43]

In fact, deportations from Budapest appeared imminent in late August, and another appeal for railroad bombing was sent to Washington through Sternbuch, in Switzerland. On September 13, the answer came back to Bern. The War Department considered the operation impossible. Yet on that very day, 324 American heavy bombers flew from Italy to the Silesian targets. En route, they passed within six miles of one of the railways. On the way back, they rendezvoused directly above the other. As they regrouped, some of them dropped leftover bombs on the freight yard below and, entirely by coincidence, cut the main rail line.[44]

As to the "efficacy" of bombing Auschwitz itself, there is no doubt that destruction of the gas chambers and crematoria would have saved many lives. Mass murder continued at Auschwitz until the gas chambers were closed in November 1944. Throughout the summer and fall, transports kept coming from many parts of Europe, carrying tens of thousands of Jews to their deaths.[45]

Could the death factories have been located from the air? The four large gassing-cremation installations stood in two pairs. Two of the extermination buildings were 340 feet long, the others two-thirds that length. Chimneys towered over them. Beginning in April 1944, detailed aerial reconnaissance photographs of Auschwitz-Birkenau were available at the U.S. Air Force headquarters in Italy. And descriptions of the structures and of the camp's layout, supplied by escapees, were in Washington by early July 1944.[46]

Officials in Washington thus had data on the killing installations, their locations, and their purpose. But they relayed none of this information to the Air Force command in Italy, where Air Force personnel had aerial photographs of the extermination buildings but had no inkling of what they were and no reason to examine them closely, because their attention was focused on the industrial areas five miles away.[47]

Could aerial bombing have been precise enough to knock out the mass-murder buildings? Definitely yes. One procedure would have been for some of the heavy bombers on one of the large Auschwitz strikes to swing over to the Birkenau side and blast the killing facilities. Heavy bombers flying at their normal 20,000 to 26,000 feet could have destroyed the buildings. But complete accuracy was rarely possible from such heights. Some of the bombs probably would have struck the nearby Birkenau barracks.

Jewish leaders in Europe and the United States, assuming that the use of heavy bombers would result in the death of some inmates, wrestled with the moral problem. Most concluded that loss of life under the circumstances was justifiable. They were aware that about 90 percent of the Jews were gassed on arrival at Auschwitz. They also realized that most who were spared for the work camps struggled daily through a hellish, famished existence as slave laborers and were worn out in a matter of weeks and dispatched to the gas chambers. The bombing might have killed some of them, but it could have halted or slowed the mass murder.[48]

We know now that many Auschwitz prisoners shared their viewpoint. Olga Lengyel, a Birkenau survivor, recalled after the war that she and the inmates she knew hoped for an air raid. "If the Allies could blow up the crematory ovens! The pace of the extermination would at least be slowed."[49] Two sisters, Hungarian Jews who were in Birkenau when the Auschwitz industrial areas were hit, told of the prisoners in their section praying for the bombers to blast the gas chambers. They were more than ready to die for that.[50]

Heavy bombers were not, however, the only choice. A small number of Mitchell medium bombers, which hit with more accuracy from lower altitudes, could have flown with one of the missions to Auschwitz.[51] An even more precise alternative would have been dive-bombing. A few Lightning (P-38) dive-bombers could have knocked out the murder buildings without danger to the inmates at Birkenau. P-38s proved they were capable of such a distant assignment on June 10, 1944, when they dive-bombed oil refineries at Ploesti.[52]

The most effective means of all for destroying the killing installations would have been to dispatch about 20 British Mosquitoes to Auschwitz, a project that could have been arranged with the RAF. This fast fighter bomber had ample range for the mission, and its technique of bombing at very low altitudes had proven extremely precise. In February 1944, for instance, 19 Mosquitoes set out to break open a prison at Amiens to free members of the French resistance held there for execution. The first two waves of the attack struck with such accuracy, smashing the main wall and the guardhouses, that the last six planes did not bomb. In Pehle's November appeal for bombing Auschwitz, he pointed out the similarity to the Amiens mission. The War Department denied that any parallel existed, but in fact the Amiens attack required greater precision and had to be carried out in very bad winter weather.[53]

If the killing installations had been destroyed at that stage of the war, it would have been practically impossible for the hard-pressed Germans to rebuild them. The original construction, carried out in a time of more readily available labor, transportation, and materials, had taken eight months. Without gas chambers and crematoria, the Nazis would have been forced to reassess the extermination program. Operation of the gas chambers, which killed 2,000 persons in less than half an hour, required only a limited number of SS personnel, whereas killing tens of thousands by gunfire would have tied down a large military force. The Nazis also would have had to face the body-disposal problem, an obstacle that caused serious difficulty until the huge crematoria were built.[54]

The basic principle behind the War Department's rejection of the bombing proposals was that military resources could not be diverted to nonmilitary objectives. The logic of this position was extremely forceful in a world at war. But this policy was not nearly as ironbound as the War Department indicated in its replies to the bombing requests. Exceptions occurred quite often, many of them for humanitarian purposes. For instance, the Allied military moved 100,000 non-Jewish Polish, Yugoslav, and Greek civilians to safety in Africa and the Middle East, and maintained them in camps there. Again, the U.S. and British armies in Italy supplied tens of thousands of refugees with food, shelter, and medical care.[55]

The war effort was deflected for other decent purposes as well. Kyoto, the ancient capital of Japan and a center of culture and art, was on the Air Force target list. In spring 1945, Secretary of War Henry L. Stimson asked McCloy, "Would you consider me a sentimental old man if I removed Kyoto from the target cities?" McCloy encouraged him to do so. The Air Force command argued against the decision but adhered to it. On another occasion, McCloy himself prevented the planned bombing of Rothenburg, a German town noted for its medieval architecture.[56] As Soviet forces neared Warsaw at the beginning of August 1944, the Polish Home Army (a non-Communist resistance force linked to the Polish government-in-exile in London) rose against the Germans. The Soviet advance suddenly stopped, however, and the Red Army remained about ten kilometers from Warsaw for weeks while the Nazis decimated the unaided and poorly supplied Polish fighters.[57] Polish officials in London put intense pressure on the British government to do something about the situation. Although Air Marshal Sir John Slessor, the RAF commander in Italy, argued that supply flights to Warsaw from Italy would result in a "prohibitive rate of loss" and "could not possibly affect the issue of the war one way or another," his government ordered the missions run. Despite heavy losses, Slessor concluded that the effort had "achieved practically nothing."[58]

The United States did not participate in the Italy-based missions to Warsaw. But Roosevelt, under heavy pressure from Churchill, ordered U.S. bombers in Britain to join the effort. On September 18, 107 Flying Fortresses dropped 1,284 containers of arms and supplies on Warsaw and continued on to bases in Russia. At most, 288 containers reached the Home Army. The Germans took the rest.[59] The cost of the mission was low in numbers of aircraft lost but extremely high in the amount of air power kept out of regular operations. To deliver 288 (or fewer) containers to a military force known to be defeated, more than a hundred heavy bombers were tied up for nine days.[60] An Air Force intelligence officer, reporting on the U.S. part in the Warsaw airdrops, acknowledged that the president, the War Department, and the Air Force had realized that "the Partisan fight was a losing one" and that "large numbers of planes would be tied up for long periods of time and lost to the main strategic effort against Germany." Still, all those involved concurred in the decision to go forward, "despite the lack of a firm commitment" to the Polish government by the United States.[61]

Why did the United States divert such a large amount of bombing capacity during a crucial phase of the oil campaign? The report explained: "Despite the tangible cost which far outweighed the tangible results achieved, it is concluded that this mission was amply justified. . . . America kept faith with its Ally. . . . America wanted to, tried, and did help within her means and possibilities."[62] The Warsaw airdrop was executed only by the diversion of considerable air power to a totally impractical project. But the United States had demonstrated its deep concern for the plight of a devastated friend.[63]

If, when the first request for bombing Auschwitz reached the Operations Division, it had inquired of the air command overseas, it would have found the 15th Air Force on the verge of a major bombing campaign in the region around Auschwitz. Instead, the Operations Division never looked into the possibilities. From July through November 1944, more than 2,800 bombers struck Blechhammer and other targets close to Auschwitz. The industrial area of Auschwitz itself was hit twice. Yet the War Department rejected every proposal to bomb the railroads or the death camp on the basis of its initial, unsupported assertion that the plan was "impracticable" because it would require "diversion of considerable air support."[64]

It is evident that the diversion explanation was no more than an excuse. The real reason the proposals were refused was the War Department's prior decision that rescue was not to be a part of its mission—the president's order establishing the War Refugee Board notwithstanding. To the U.S.

military, Europe's Jews represented an extraneous problem and an unwanted burden.

But a final question remains. How could it be that the governments of the two great Western democracies knew that a place existed where 2,000 helpless human beings could be killed every 30 minutes, knew that such killings actually did occur over and over again, and yet did not feel driven to search for some way to wipe such a scourge from the earth?

NOTES

1. Rudolf Vrba and Alan Bestic, *I Cannot Forgive* (New York, 1964), pp. 198, 231–34, 247–49; War Refugee Board, *German Extermination Camps* (Washington, D.C., 1944).

2. Vrba and Bestic, pp. 249–50; Randolph L. Braham, *The Politics of Genocide: The Holocaust in Hungary* (New York, 1981), p. 1014; Livia Rothkirchen, *The Destruction of Slovak Jewry: A Documentary History* (Jerusalem, 1961), p. xli; Dulles to McClelland, June 15, 1944, with enclosures, McClelland to Pehle, October 12, 1944, box 61, Extermination Camps, War Refugee Board Records, Franklin D. Roosevelt Library (cited hereafter as WRB Records); Gerhart Riegner to David Wyman, May 25, 1977; Morgenthau Diaries, Franklin D. Roosevelt Library, book 750, pp. 354–60, book 751, p. 239, book 800, p. 193; "War Refugee Board History," p. 447, box 110, WRB Records.

3. *Wiener Library Bulletin* 27 (1973–74), p. 42; *Manchester Guardian*, June 27, 1944, pp. 4, 8, June 28, 1944, p. 8; *New York Times*, June 20, 1944, p. 5.

4. "Explanation of wire from our friends in Slovakia" (n.d.) with attached telegram, box 62, Union of Orthodox Rabbis (January–June 1944), WRB Records.

5. "Just now a second telegramme" [May 23, 1944], with attached telegram, McClelland to de Jong, May 25, 1944, with enclosure, Harrison to Secretary of State, June 2, 1944, Sternbuch to McClelland, June 22, 1944, box 62, Union of Orthodox Rabbis, WRB Records.

6. MB and GFl, "We are sending you," May 22, 1944, box 61, Extermination Camps, WRB Records; Riegner to Wyman, May 25, 1977.

7. Paraphrase of cable [June 12, 1944] attached to Hilldring to OPD, June 23, 1944, OPD 383.7, sec. II, case 21, record group 165 (War Department General and Special Staffs), National Archives; Polityka, August 9, 1975; *Polish Review* 22–24 (1977), p. 14.

8. Rosenheim to Morgenthau, Hull, Stimson, June 18, 1944, box 35, Hungary 5, WRB Records.

9. Office of Assistant Secretary of War to War Refugee Board, June 20, 1944, ASW 400.38 War Refugee Board (box 151), Assistant Secretary of War Files, record group 107, National Archives; Hilldring to OPD, June 23, 1944, OPD 383.7, sec. II, case 21, record group 165 , National Archives; Pehle, Memo for the Files, June 24, 1944, box 35, Hungary 5, WRB Records.

10. Ray Cline, *Washington Command Post: The Operations Division* (Washington, D.C., 1951), p. ix; CAD D/F (Hilldring to OPD), June 23, 1944, including date

stamps, CAD 383.7 (1) (1–21–43) sec. 2, record group 165, National Archives; all of file OPD 383.7, sec. II, case 21, record group 165, National Archives.

11. U.S. State Department, *Foreign Relations of the United States 1944* (Washington, D.C., 1966), vol. 1, pp. 987–90; Morgenthau Diaries, Franklin D. Roosevelt Library, bk. 699, p. 22; TRH, Memo for Record [June 26, 1944], OPD 383.7, sec. II, case 21, record group 165, National Archives; Pasco to Gailey, February 7, 1944, Handy to Chief of Staff, February 8, 1944, JHC, Memo for Record (n.d.), OPD 334.8, WRB, sec. I, case 1, record group 165, National Archives.

12. TRH, Memo for Record [June 26 , 1944], OPD 383.7, sec. II, case 21, record group 165, National Archives; Morgenthau to McCloy, January 28 , 1944, ASW 400. 38 War Refugee Board (box 151), record group 107, National Archives.

13. Note from McCloy to McNarney penciled on top margin of Morgenthau to McCloy, January 28, 1944, ASW 400. 38 War Refugee Board (box 151), record group 107, National Archives.

14. The executive order charged the War Refugee Board with carrying out "the policy of this Government [which is] to take all measures within its power to rescue the victims of enemy oppression who are in imminent danger of death and otherwise to afford such victims all possible relief and assistance consistent with the successful prosecution of the war." The order also specified, "It shall be the duty of the State, Treasury and War Departments, within their respective spheres, to execute at the request of the Board, the plans and programs [developed by the board]." McNarney to Assistant Secretary of War, February 6, 1944, ASW 400. 38 War Refugee Board (box 151), record group 107, National Archives.

15. OPD D/F (Hull to CAD), June 26, 1944, OPD 383.7, sec. II, case 21, record group 165, National Archives.

16. Gerhardt, Memo for the Subcommittee, February 11, 1944, meeting held at 4:00, February 11, 1944, ASW 400. 38 War Refugee Board (box 151), record group 107, National Archives.

17. Harrison to Secretary of State, June 24, 1944, ASW 400. 38 Jews, record group 107, National Archives.

18. Pehle to McCloy, June 29, 1944, HAG to McCloy, July 3, 1944, McCloy to Pehle, July 4, 1944, ASW 400.38 Jews, record group 107, National Archives.

19. Akzin to Lesser, June 29, 1944, box 35, Hungary 5, WRB Records.

20. Summary of Steps, July 13, 1944, Pehle to Stettinius, July 13, 1944, draft memos to Secretary of War, to the President, and to Stimson, July 13, 1944, Pehle to Morgenthau, September 6, 1944, box 34, Hungary 1, WRB Records; Pehle to McCloy, October 3, 1944, box 35, Hungary 5, WRB Records.

21. Smertenko to Roosevelt, July 24, 1944, State Department decimal file 840.48 Refugees/7–2444, National Archives.

22. Kubowitzki to McCloy, August 9, 1944, ASW 400.38 Countries-C-D-E-F (box 151), record group 107, National Archives.

23. McCloy to Kubowitzki, August 14, 1944, ASW 400.38 Countries-C-D-E-F (box 151), record group 107, National Archives. The study mentioned by McCloy had never been made.

24. This paragraph and the five paragraphs that follow it are based on information in Bernard Wasserstein, *Britain and the Jews of Europe 1939–1945* (London, 1979), pp. 307–20, and Martin Gilbert, *Auschwitz and the Allies* (New York, 1981), pp. 269–73, 284–85, 303–7.

25. Akzin to Pehle, September 2, 1944, box 35, Hungary 5, WRB Records; Kalmanowitz to Pehle, September 11, 1944, box 36, Hungary 6, WRB Records.

26. Winant to Secretary of State, September 29, 1944, Proskauer to Pehle, September 26, 1944, Union of Orthodox Rabbis and Vaad Hahatzala to Pehle, September 26, 1944, box 18, Poland 1, WRB Records; Pehle to McCloy, October 3, 1944, ASW 400.38 Jews, record group 107, National Archives.

27. HAG to McCloy, October 5, 1944, ASW 400.38 Jews, record group 107, National Archives.

28. Mannon to Pehle, November 16, 1944, Hodel, Memorandum, November 2, 1944, Pehle to McCloy, November 8, 1944, box 6, German Extermination Camps, WRB Records; interview of John Pehle by Laurence Jarvik, October 16, 1978.

29. OPD Routing Form, November 8, 1944, OPD 000.5, sec. 3, case 53, record group 165, National Archives; Hull to Assistant Secretary of War, November 14, 1944, ASW 400.38 Countries-Germany, record group 107, National Archives.

30. Hull to Assistant Secretary of War, November 14, 1944, McCloy to Pehle, November 18, 1944, ASW 400.38 Countries-Germany, record group 107, National Archives.

31. McCloy to Pehle, July 4, 1944, ASW 400.38 Jews, record group 107, National Archives; McCloy to Kubowitzki, August 14, 1944, ASW 400.38 Countries-C-D-E-F (box 151), record group 107, National Archives.

32. Wesley Craven and James Cate, eds., *The Army Air Forces in World War II*, vol. 3 (Chicago, 1951), pp. xii, 47, 66, 283, 792–93; Charles Webster and Noble Frankland, *The Strategic Air Offensive against Germany 1939–1945*, vol. 3 (London, 1961), pp. 132–33, 136; James Sunderman, ed., *World War II in the Air: Europe* (New York, 1963), p. 174; Eaker to Spaatz (CS440IE), May 8, 1944, box 143, "Operational Planning: Attacks against Oil Targets," Carl A. Spaatz Papers, Library of Congress (cited hereafter as Spaatz Papers); Eaker to Spaatz (CS719IE), June 27, 1944, box 35, Cables June 44, Spaatz Papers; U.S. 15th Air Force, "Complete Summary of Operations, 1 November 1943–8 May 1945," record group 243 (U.S. Strategic Bombing Survey), National Archives; U.S. 15th Air Force Mission Reports, microfilm reel A6465 (July 7, 1944), frames 1029, 1031, 1040, 1050, 1052, 1138, 1178, Albert F. Simpson Historical Research Center, Maxwell Air Force Base, Alabama (cited hereafter as Mission Reports); Glenn Infield, *The Poltava Affair* (New York, 1973), p. 166.

33. Aiming Points Reports, Oswiecim, January 21, 1944, Blechhammer North and South, March 15, 1944, sec. 4-lg (141, 142, 163), record group 243, National Archives; Spaatz to Eaker (586), April 27, 1944, Eaker to Spaatz (CS440IE), May 8, 1944, box 143, "Operational Planning: Attacks Against Oil Targets," Spaatz Papers. The Air Force made reconnaissance photographs of the Auschwitz complex on April 4, 1944, and had a map of it available in May 1944. (Mission Reports, microfilm reel A6494, frame 1602).

34. Craven and Cate, vol. 3, pp. 177–79, 292–96, 645, 794–96; Webster and Frankland, vol. 3, pp. 46–47, 237–40.

35. Craven and Cate, vol. 3, pp. 177–78; Webster and Frankland, vol. 3, facing p. 47; U.S. 15th Air Force, "Complete Summary of Operations, 1 November 1943–8 May 1945," record group 243, National Archives; Infield, *The Poltava Affair* p. 181; *Kansas City Star*, August 21, 1944, p. 4.

36. U.S. 15th Air Force, Daily Operations, August 1944, record group 243, National Archives; U.S. 15th Air Force, "Complete Summary of Operations, 1 November 1943–8 May 1945," record group 243, National Archives; Synthetic Oil Plant of I.G. Farben at Oswiecim (n.d.), GS 5612, record group 243, National Archives.

37. U.S. 15th Air Force, Daily Operations, September 1944, record group 243, National Archives; Synthetic Oil Plant of I.G. Farben at Oswiecim (n.d.), GS 5612,

record group 243, National Archives; Kazimierz Smolen, ed., *Hefte von Auschwitz*, vol. 8 (Krakow, 1964), p. 66.

38. U.S. 15th Air Force, Daily Operations, December 1944, record group 243, National Archives.

39. U.S. 15th Air Force, Daily Operations, August 1944, record group 243, National Archives; U.S. 15th Air Force, "Complete Summary of Operations, 1 November 1943–8 May 1945," record group 243, National Archives.

40. U.S. 15th Air Force, Daily Operations, July and August 1944, record group 243, National Archives; U.S. 15th Air Force, "Complete Summary of Operations, 1 November 1943–8 May 1945," record group 243, National Archives; Mission Reports, microfilm reel A6473 (August 22, 1944), frame 595; Infield, p. 181.

41. McCloy to Kubowitzki, August 14, 1944, ASW 400.38 Countries-C-D-E-F (box 151), record group 107, National Archives.

42. Craven and Cate, vol. 3, pp. 72–79, 149–62, 371–72, 405, 473, 652, 655, 736, 746; Webster and Frankland, vol. 3, p. 260; Hilary Saunders, *Royal Air Force, 1939–1945*, vol. 3 (London, 1954), pp. 223–25.

43. U.S. 15th Air Force, "Complete Summary of Operations, 1 November 1943–8 May 1945," record group 243, National Archives; Mission Reports, microfilm reel A6465 (July 7, 1944), frames 1029, 1031, 1040, 1050, 1178, reel A6473 (August 20, 1944), frames 172–73, 178, 214, reel A6473 (August 22, 1944), frames 583, 595, 606, 816, reel A6474 (August 27, 1944), frames 730, 733, 741, 746, reel A6477 (September 13, 1944) frames 623, 651, reel A6481 (October 13, 1944), frames 740, 775, 942, 957, reel A6481 (October 14, 1944), frames 1412, 1441, 1446, reel A6482 (October 17, 1944), frame 658.

44. Sternbuch to Vaad Ha-Hatzala, August 28, 1944, September 13, 1944, box 20, Vaad Ha-Hatzala Papers, Yeshiva University Archives, New York; Mission Reports, microfilm reel A6477 (September 13, 1944), frames 623, 651; U.S. 15th Air Force, "Complete Summary of Operations, 1 November 1943–8 May 1945," record group 243, National Archives; Interpretation Report no. DB 214, September 16, 1944 (Vrutky), GS 5612, record group 243, National Archives.

45. Kazimierz Smolen et al., *Selected Problems from the History of KL Auschwitz*, vol. 1 (Oswiecim, 1967), pp. 209–13.

46. Jan Sehn, *German Crimes in Poland*, vol. 1 (Warsaw, 1946), pp. 84–85, 88, fig. 7; War Refugee Board, *German Extermination Camps*, pp. 6, 7, 15, 22; Jozef Garlinski, *Fighting Auschwitz* (London, 1975), pp. 77, 89; Otto Kraus and Erich Kulka, *The Death Factory* (London and New York, 1966), p. 15, fig. 2; Morgenthau Diaries, Franklin D. Roosevelt Library, bk. 750, pp. 184–88, 354–60; *New York Times*, February 24, 1979, p. 2; *Studies in Intelligence*, Winter 1978–79, pp. 11–29; *Military Intelligence*, January 1983, pp. 50–55.

47. Synthetic Oil Plant of I.G. Farben at Oswiecim (n.d.), GS 5612, record group 243, National Archives; *Military Intelligence*, January 1983, pp. 50–55.

48. Morgenthau Diaries, Franklin D. Roosevelt Library, bk. 750, pp. 184–88, 354–60.

49. Olga Lengyel, *Five Chimneys* (Chicago, 1947), pp. 123, 155–56.

50. Claire Barker, interview with David Wyman, April 17, 1977; Claire Barker to David Wyman, April 18, 1978. Other examples: Pelagia Lewinska, *Twenty Months at Auschwitz* (New York, 1968), p. 21; *Jewish Observer*, January 1979, p. 45; *Commentary*, July 1978, pp. 9–10.

51. Sunderman, pp. 320–21; Craven and Cate, vol. 3, pp. 376–77, 382–83, 399.

52. Craven and Cate, vol. 3, p. 283; Mission Reports, Narrative Report, Mission no. 702, 82 Fighter Group (June 10, 1944).

53. Philip Birtles, *Mosquito* (London, 1980), pp. 20–25, 57, 88–95, 135–40, 145–46, 183–85; Sunderman, pp. 324–27; Saunders, vol. 3, pp. 91–92, 406; *New York Times*, October 29, 1944, p. 7; Pehle to McCloy, November 8, 1944, McCloy to Pehle, November 18, 1944, ASW 400.38 Countries-Germany, record group 107, National Archives. At least 44 Mosquitoes were stationed at Allied air bases in Italy in June 1944 (E. A. Munday, Air Historical Branch, Ministry of Defence, London, to David Wyman, March 29, 1983).

54. Smolen, vol. 1, pp. 22, 193–94, 200–201; War Refugee Board, *German Extermination Camps*, p. 16, part 2, p. 13; Sehn, vol. 1, pp. 85–86; Filip Friedman, *This Was Oswiecim* (London, 1946), pp. 54–55.

55. Office of War Information Press Release, June 13, 1944, box 4, Camps, WRB Records; Hilldring to McCloy, January 25, 1944, ASW 400.38 War Refugee Board, record group 107, National Archives; Ackermann to Murphy, May 5, 1944, Ackermann to Pehle, May 11, 1944, box 1, Ackermann, WRB Records.

56. *Japan Quarterly*, Fall 1975, pp. 340–45; *Harper's*, February 1947, p. 105; *Amherst: The College and Its Alumni*, Winter 1976, p. 31.

57. Craven and Cate, vol. 3, p. 316; Infield, chap. 13; John Slessor, *The Central Blue* (New York, 1957), pp. 612–13, 620–21; James M. Burns, *Roosevelt: The Soldier of Freedom* (New York, 1970), pp. 534–35.

58. Slessor, pp. 614–20; *Observer* (London), August 16, 1964, p. 9; Craven and Cate, vol. 3, p. 316.

59. Winston Churchill, *The Second World War: Triumph and Tragedy* (Boston, 1953), pp. 128–45; Craven and Cate, vol. 3, p. 317; Warsaw Dropping Operations [October 9, 1944], Anderson to Kuter, September 24, 1944, box 182, Subject File—Operations—Warsaw Dropping Ops, Spaatz Papers.

60. Anderson to Kuter, September 24, 1944, Warsaw Dropping Operations [October 9, 1944], box 182, Subject File—Operations—Warsaw Dropping Ops, Spaatz Papers; McDonald to Deputy Commanding General, Operations, October 14, 1944, box 139, Neutral and Occupied Countries: Poland, Spaatz Papers.

61. McDonald to Deputy Commanding General, Operations, October 14, 1944, box 139, Neutral and Occupied Countries: Poland, Spaatz Papers.

62. Ibid.

63. Roosevelt's role in the effort for the Warsaw Poles is clearly documented, but evidence is lacking as to whether he was ever consulted on the question of bombing Auschwitz and the railroads to it. Burns, pp. 534–35; Churchill, pp. 135, 139–44; Craven and Cate, vol. 3, p. 317; Anderson to Kuter, September 24, 1944, Warsaw Dropping Operations [October 9, 1944], box 182, Subject File—Operations—Warsaw Dropping Ops, Spaatz Papers; *Washington Post*, April 17, 1983, pp. D1–D2; telephone conversations Morton Mintz and David Wyman, March 25, 1983, and April 5, 1983.

64. Hull to Assistant Secretary of War, November 14, 1944, ASW 400.38 Countries-Germany, record group 107, National Archives; U.S. 15th Air Force, "Complete Summary of Operations, 1 November 1943–8 May 1945," record group 243, National Archives; Infield, p. 181; Mission Reports, microfilm reel A6473 (August 20, 1944), frames 170, 172.

28

Postwar Prosecution of the Auschwitz SS

ALEKSANDER LASIK

In the 50 years since the crushing defeat of one of the bloodiest dictatorships in human history, only a small proportion of Nazi criminals has been put on trial, a smaller proportion has been sentenced, and a still smaller percentage has served full sentences. Some who could be charged with war crimes are still alive and at large.[1] Only when all investigations and legal proceedings have been completed and all relevant sources are made available to historians will it be possible to draw a complete picture of the punishment of Nazi criminals. But the available, if incomplete, data convey a simple truth: in general, the postwar battle for justice has been lost. This conclusion is borne out by an analysis of the fate of the personnel of the largest concentration camp, the primary arena for the murder of European Jews, Auschwitz.

More than a dozen publications on this subject have dealt mostly with the trial of the founder and first commandant of the Auschwitz camp, Rudolf Höss, and 40 camp personnel before the Supreme National Tribunal in Poland[2] as well as the 1960s trial in Frankfurt am Main in Germany.[3] Apart from Hermann Langbein's *Der Auschwitz Prozess: Eine Dokumentation*, containing a partial list of punitive measures against SS men from Auschwitz, existing literature provides no comprehensive treatment of this subject. The present essay attempts to fill this lacuna in historical research, at least in part, without claiming to be the definitive study of this matter.

The Number of SS Personnel

Our analysis begins with determining the number of SS personnel in Auschwitz who could be prosecuted for committing war crimes and crimes against humanity.

The number of personnel assigned to Auschwitz at any one time depended on a number of factors. The most important of these factors were the following: the size of the prisoner population, as determined by the nature of the tasks assigned to the camp by the Reichsführer-SS Heinrich Himmler and the policymaking echelons of the SS; the establishment in 1942 of the extermination camp at Birkenau, the largest murder site of the Holocaust, near Auschwitz; and evacuation of other concentration camps close to the front lines, as well as the liquidation of Auschwitz itself in January 1945.

Shifts in staff size were dramatic. In January 1941, the staff numbered about 700 SS men. On January 15, 1945, 12 days before the liberation of the camp by Soviet troops, there were 4,480 SS men and 71 SS women supervisors (SS-Aufseherinnen).[4]

These figures, however, provide nothing more than a static picture. In fact, Auschwitz experienced considerable fluctuation in SS personnel size in the years 1940-45. Based on an analysis of available camp documents, we have been able to assemble personal files of nearly 6,500 members of the Auschwitz SS personnel. Assuming that an incomplete data-base resulted in an error in the range of 10 percent, we may conclude that a total of 7,000 to 7,200 SS men and women supervisors served in Auschwitz.

Speaking in absolute numbers, the entire staff was replaced almost twice. Approximately 20 percent of the total went on to serve in front-line divisions of the Waffen SS, mainly with the Fifth SS Viking Armored Division and the Sixth SS Nord Mountain Division. That yields a figure of 1,500 SS men sent mostly to the eastern front. Assuming that half of them fell in combat—a rather high estimate—we may conclude that about 6,500 former members of the Auschwitz SS personnel survived the capitulation of the Third Reich. This approximate, though plausible, figure provides us with a basis for discussion.

The SS Structure

The structure of SS power and authority is vitally important to our assessment of the efficiency of the postwar prosecution of crimes perpetrated in the camp. This information enables us to ascertain whether, in sentencing criminals, courts considered the positions held by the defendants and the brutality and criminal nature of their responsibilities within the camp hierarchy of power. This is important information since, in many cases, no witnesses were present who could testify as to the guilt of individual defendants or explain how the position of a certain SS member in the camp apparatus of terror affected his or her behavior toward prisoners. We can also draw conclusions on the efficiency of the prosecution with regard to the number of defendants put on trial and the substantive issues addressed in their trials.

Beginning in the second half of the 1930s, the Nazis implemented an identical organizational structure for the SS in all concentration camps. Camp personnel were divided into three sectors: camp administration, officials of SS firms operating in the camps and branches of central SS offices, and guard forces—the largest contingent of the SS camp personnel.

Camp administration comprised (beginning in February 1942), seven basic departments (*Abteilungen*), designated by Roman numerals. Department I—Headquarters (Abteilung I—Kommandantur), headed by the adjutant of the camp commandant, was generally responsible for the SS personnel, means of transport and communications, and censorship of prisoners' mail. Except for small working groups, SS personnel working for Department I had no direct contact with prisoners. Some, however, took part in direct extermination. For example, drivers from the car pool transported sick and weak victims, those consigned for quick extermination, to the gas chambers.

Department II—Political Department (Abteilung II—Politische Abteilung) evoked the greatest fear among prisoners. Its employees were in direct contact with prisoners from the moment of registration in the camp until the prisoners' death. Its functionaries conducted interrogations which often led to the death of the victims and decided which prisoners should be put to death. Furthermore, Department II officials functioned as a Gestapo branch in the camp and processed transports of victims consigned for immediate extermination, which made them, in effect, overseers of the efficiency of the Holocaust. All functionaries of Department II took direct part in the mass murder. SS men in charge of the crematoria were responsible to its chief through the agency known as the Registry Office (Standesamt).

Department III—Camp Administration (Abteilung III—Schutzhaftlagerführung) was in charge of prisoner affairs, including supervision of prisoners in their living quarters. The department supervisor (Schutzhaftlagerführer, Lagerführer), who also served as permanent deputy of the commandant during his absence, had under him SS personnel in charge of counting prisoners in the camp (Rapportführer), who supervised SS personnel in charge of prisoner blocks (Blockführer). All Department III functionaries had direct contact with prisoners and, along with their counterparts in the Political Department, constituted a crucial link in the apparatus of terror. They were personally involved in the murder of prisoners or issued orders to this effect to prisoners in assigned official duties. In addition, as guards on the unloading platform, they took delivery of the victims of the Holocaust, whom they subsequently escorted to the gas chambers. One task of Department IIIa—Prisoner Employment (Abteilung IIIa—Arbeitseinsatz), a separate unit within Department III, was organizing and overseeing the work of prisoners. At its core were the leaders of prisoner labor squads (Kommandoführer), who were in direct and daily contact with prisoners in places of work, ensuring the implementation of camp goals—the utilization of the slave labor of prisoners and their consequent destruction through work. The behavior of squad leaders toward prisoners varied individually.[5] Only some members of this department volunteered for "special operations" on the unloading platforms in Birkenau.

Department IV—Administration-Economy (Abteilung IV—Verwaltung) boasted the most elaborate organizational structure. It supplied the entire camp (both SS personnel and prisoners) with food and clothing, administered housing, supervised work in laundries and baths, controlled storage depots, maintained camp equipment, and ran the printing press. In addition, Department IV was in charge of camp finances, including deposits of prisoners' property; it plundered the property of the victims of extermination. Its functionaries maintained daily contact with work squads of prisoners employed by various organizational agencies of the department; their conduct toward prisoners varied. Many SS personnel, with the help of some prisoners, abused their powers and engaged in embezzlement, even ordinary theft, of everything from food to diamonds. The department itself collaborated in mass extermination, both by delivering the Zyklon B gas to the camp and overseeing the organized plunder of the property of the victims.

Department V—Camp Physician (Abteilung V—Standortarzt), comprised three sections: general-medical, dental, and pharmacy. It provided medical attention, in the ordinary meaning of the term, for SS personnel alone; its tasks with regard to the prisoner population had nothing to do with the duties and responsibilities spelled out in the medical oath. Camp doctors often performed selections of prisoners, and those they designated as unfit for work were murdered in the gas chambers or put to death by injecting poisonous substances into the heart; the injections were performed by subordinate medics of the SS (SDG). In preparation for mass murder, SS doctors selected the victims and confirmed their subsequent deaths in the gas chambers. Their assistants, members of the disinfection squad trained in handling gaseous poisons, poured Zyklon B into the gas chambers. The dental section of Department V extracted false teeth made of precious metals from the bodies of the victims. Department V also conveyed the melted gold and platinum to the Central Medical Depot of the SS and from there to the Reichsbank. Functionaries of the medical service were in constant contact with prisoners and almost without exception took an active part in their extermination, engaging also in various experiments on them.

The last and smallest was Department VI—Welfare, Schooling, and Training of SS forces (Abteilung VI—Fürsorge, Schulung, und Truppenbetreuung). It consisted of several SS men charged with organizing training sessions for SS personnel, especially in ideological matters and cultural activities. To control access to information, the department did not employ prisoners. Its functionaries did not have official contact with the prisoner population.

The second sector comprised SS personnel employed by SS-owned firms which operated in Auschwitz.[6] Their responsibilities and the scope of their control over prisoners were roughly comparable to those of the functionaries of Department IIIa. The same applies to SS personnel employed in the Auschwitz branches of central SS institutions: the Building Inspectorate and the Hygiene Institute of the Waffen-SS and the Police in Rajsk. The prerogatives and authority of the latter were similar to that of functionaries of Department V, the SS medical service.

The most numerous group, comprising roughly 85 percent of the entire SS personnel in Auschwitz, were SS men serving as guards. They were assigned the task of isolating the camp grounds, guarding the sealed camp, and escorting, supervising, and guarding prisoners working in open areas. Labor squad guards were in daily contact with the prisoners, and to increase their chances of commendation, promotion, or being granted a special leave, they often shot prisoners under the pretext of thwarting an attempted escape.

During mass extermination, prisoner escape, or such special actions as the revolt of the Sonderkommando prisoners, the guards secured the unloading platform and the camp and searched or pursued prisoners. As a group, the guard served as manpower pool for various operations of the camp administration.

In 1942, with the arrival of the first group of women prisoners, SS women supervisors appeared in the camp. The scope of their power and authority vis-à-vis women prisoners was identical to that of functionaries of Department III and IIIa with regard to men. Together with their SS male counterparts, they took part on an equal basis in the murder of victims of the Holocaust.

Geography of Searches and Extraditions

As mentioned, roughly 20 percent of SS personnel in the camp were sent to the front. At that time, both the SS Viking and Nord divisions operated on the eastern front, where some of the former functionaries of the Auschwitz camp fell in combat or were captured by Soviet troops. Assuming that half died and half were captured, we may conclude that at least 5,500 SS men who had served in Auschwitz found shelter in western occupation zones. This figure seems plausible, especially in view of the fact that during the last days of the Nazi regime, both SS personnel and active members of National Socialist party did everything possible to avoid capture by the Soviet Army.

Since no studies based on Soviet archival sources have been conducted, it has been difficult to determine to what extent Soviet intelligence services attempted to identify SS personnel who had served in concentration camps from among those taken prisoner. We do know that many prisoners were shipped to the eastern and northern territories of the Soviet Union, where their service files were probably not subjected to close scrutiny. Also, this author has no information about Soviet trials of Auschwitz SS personnel or extradition of any of them to another country.[7]

Authorities in the U.S., British, and French occupation zones took steps to seek out persons suspected of having committed war crimes and crimes against humanity. Once detained as a result of either positive identification or denunciation, a suspect was sent to one of the many internment camps, where military intelligence officials examined the suspect's wartime career. Individuals were sought out and matched against interdiction lists compiled during the war. The results of these searches were conveyed to military representatives stationed in the western occupation zones, to enable them to seek extradition of war criminals, especially those who operated in territories occupied by the Third Reich. But this system collapsed in 1949 with the establishment of the Federal Republic of Germany (West Germany) and, later, the formation of the German Democratic Republic (East Germany). Politicians lost interest in prosecuting war criminals as the Cold War extended its sway over Europe and the world.

Until archival sources are available to historians, we cannot estimate the number of SS personnel from Auschwitz identified and interned in the western occupation zones or the number who went into hiding in the Soviet occupation zone, later transformed into East Germany.

Prosecuting Nazi Criminals

Since international law did not foresee the occurrence of genocide, especially on such a colossal scale, legal foundations and regulations had to be laid to prosecute and pass sentence against Nazi war criminals. The origins of this law can be found in the Moscow Declaration of October 30, 1943, in which the former Allies—the United States, Great Britain, and the Soviet Union—formulated the project of prosecuting and sentencing Nazi criminals. The work of assembling prosecuting apparatus, collecting materials, and preparing legal and court material lasted several years.

The International Nuremberg Tribunal on September 30 and October 1, 1946, declared, among other things, that the SS was a criminal organization and gave international legal status to the courts instituting legal proceedings against war criminals and crimes against humanity, thus recognizing their verdicts as legally valid. This act was later reaffirmed by a resolution of the General Assembly of the United Nations.

Trials of Auschwitz SS Personnel in Poland

Thanks to the work of the Polish Military Mission and the Polish government, at least 1,000 former members of the Auschwitz SS were extradited to Poland in the years 1946–48. On the basis of a decree promulgated on September 12, 1944, special penal courts were appointed.[8] On January 22, 1946, a special act appointed the Supreme National Tribunal, which was charged with trying the most important criminals extradited to Poland.[9] Between March 11 and 29, 1947, in Warsaw, it brought to trial the camp's first commandant, Höss, and from November 24 to December 16, 1947, in Krakow, it tried 40 members of the Auschwitz SS force.

These two trials met with considerable response in Poland and worldwide, since they revealed the dimensions of the crime perpetrated in Auschwitz. Höss and 23 defendants in the Krakow trial were sentenced to death (two of them were pardoned later), six received life sentences, seven were sentenced to 15 years in prison, and three received sentences of ten, five, and three years. One SS man was acquitted.

Other members of the Auschwitz SS personnel extradited to Poland were tried by district courts in Krakow, Wadowice, Raciborz, Cieszyn, Sosnowiec, Gliwice, Bytom, and Katowice. The trial records available to this author indicate that legal action was taken against 602 persons, of whom 590 were sentenced; 11 died awaiting trial, and in one case, proceedings were discontinued. Death sentences were passed against six SS men and two SS women supervisors (1.4 percent of all district court rulings), three SS men were sentenced to life in prison (0.5 percent of all rulings), six were acquitted (1 percent), and the remaining defendants received sentences ranging from six months to 15 years in prison (97.1 percent).

These data give no information about the authority wielded by the defendants in the camp structure of power, which should have been considered when passing sentences. The largest proportion of the 631 SS men convicted and sentenced by Polish courts were guards—426 defendants (67.5 percent). The next largest group of defendants—166, or 26.3 percent—included former functionaries of one of the seven departments of the camp administration. The remaining 37 former SS men had worked for SS firms or for central offices of this organization operating in Auschwitz (5.9 percent). In addition, two former camp commandants, Höss and Arthur Liebehenschel, stood trial in Poland.

One striking conclusion undoubtedly is the lenient sentencing of SS men who had worked for Departments II, III, and V, departments which took part in extermination of registered prisoners or were implicated directly in mass murder. This may be indicative of the Polish courts' desire to refrain from seeking revenge or passing sentences according to the principle of collective responsibility; however, it may also mean that the prosecution lacked full understanding of the functioning of the camp structure of power or the importance of the positions held by the defendants. Thus the most common sentence was three years in prison (passed against 32.3 percent of the defendants), mainly on the grounds that the defendant had been a member of the SS.

Haste and the assembly-line style of many of the judicial proceedings resulted in manifest errors, which led to acquittal or lenient sentencing for defendants who had major responsibility for terrorizing prisoners and contributed actively to the death of hundreds of thousands of people brought to Auschwitz for immediate extermination.

One striking example of this judicial approach was the release of SS Sturmbannführer Wilhelm Burger after five years in a Polish prison. Burger had been head of the Administration-Economy Department in Auschwitz and subsequently chief of Department DIV (administration) in SS-WVHA. Other examples are the cases of SS Hauptsturmführer Otto Brossmann, leader of the first and second guard companies in Monowitz and Lagerführer of the large satellite camp Blechhammer in Blachownia, who was ultimately acquitted by the court in Krakow in 1950, following numerous appeals; SS-Hauptsturmführer Karl Tauber, director of the camp dental clinic, sentenced to four years in prison; SS-Unterscharführer Alois Frey, who had served as Lagerführer of the Gunthergrube satellite camp at Ledziny, convicted and sentenced to six years in prison by the court in

Krakow; SS-Hauptscharführer Bernhard Walter, former head of the Criminal Identification Department (Erkennungsdienst), a subdivision of the Political Department, who in conversations with prisoners had admitted to having executed by shooting several hundred persons at the "Death Wall" in the courtyards of block 11, and was sentenced to three years in prison; and SS-Hauptscharführer Werner Hahn, chief of the "Canada" complex in Birkenau, a notorious sadist and criminal, who received a sentence of eight years.

Trials in West Germany

The creation in 1949 of the Federal Republic of Germany resulted in transferring the prosecution and punishment of members of the Auschwitz SS personnel to the court system of that country. Foreign countries could demand extradition of persons suspected of having committed war crimes and crimes against humanity, but for former Auschwitz functionaries, such steps proved futile. Although police and magistrates continued to prosecute Nazi criminals, results were meager, despite indications that at least several hundred former Auschwitz personnel lived, either openly or in hiding, within the borders of West Germany.

In any event, in the years 1949–80, more than a dozen former SS personnel were tried before German tribunals. In many cases, suspects could not face trial owing to their advanced age or poor health. Thus, for example, SS-Brigadeführer Carl Clauberg, who had performed sterilization experiments on women prisoners in block 10, was arrested by the Soviets at the end of the war, tried in 1948 in the Soviet Union, sentenced to 25 years' imprisonment, and repatriated to Germany in 1955. For a time he practiced medicine under his own name and boasted of his scholarly achievements. He was arrested again but died awaiting trial in Kiel in 1957. The last Auschwitz commandant, SS-Sturmbannführer Richard Bär, identified and arrested in 1960, also died in detention during preparations for his trial.

Of all the trials which took place in West Germany, the best known were the four Frankfurt trials, conducted in 1963–76 in Frankfurt am Main. The first trial lasted from December 20, 1963, to August 20, 1965. Initially, the indictment was brought against 23 SS personnel and one former prisoner assigned official duties in the camp. However, following the death of Bär and dismissal of the case against a former SS medic, Hans Nierzwicki, who could not be put on trial owing to ill health, only 22 defendants were tried. They were two adjutants of the commandant who had served as heads of Department I; five functionaries of Department II; one Lagerführer of Auschwitz I, together with four other SS functionaries of Department III; one functionary of Department IV; eight employees of Department V; and one former prisoner assigned official duties.

After the protracted trial, interrupted by various procedural snags, six of the defendants, including the former prisoner assigned official duties, were sentenced to life in prison. Eleven defendants were given sentences ranging from three to 20 years. The cases of two defendants were dropped owing to illness, and three former SS men won acquittal.

In the second Frankfurt trial, indictments were brought against three defendants: Burger, former head of Department IV, ultimately sentenced to eight years; former SS medic Gerhard Neubert, who had already been tried in the first Frankfurt trial, sentenced to three and one-half years; and a former functionary of Department III, sentenced to life in prison.

A total of 23 defendants, including two former prisoners with official duties, were scheduled to be included in the third trial, but ultimately, only two defendants, the former prisoners, stood trial, from August 30, 1967, to June 14, 1968.

The fourth Frankfurt trial, which lasted from December 18, 1973, to February 3, 1976, involved only two defendants. However, the case against one was discontinued in November 1974 and the case against the other in 1976.

In addition to the Frankfurt trials, proceedings were instituted against individual former members of the SS personnel, but with inconsequential outcomes.

Trials in Other Countries

Other countries which could be expected to take legal steps against former SS personnel from Auschwitz after 1949 were Austria and East Germany. However, efforts to prosecute Nazi criminals in these countries brought even more meager results. In Austria, for example, two former SS officers who had served with the building management were tried in 1972 and acquitted. In several other cases, which involved former functionaries of Departments III and IV, proceedings ended even before the trial could take place. In 1966, authorities in East Germany, under pressure from public opinion, brought to trial a former SS doctor, who until then had practiced medicine under his own name in East Berlin. The defendant received a death sentence. We may only guess that many former SS men lived undisturbed in that country.

Three trials took place in two other countries: two in Czechoslovakia (one SS medic and one SS woman supervisor) and one in the Netherlands (a former functionary of an SS firm which operated in Auschwitz). In Czecho-slovakia, the courts handed down death sentences, which were carried out; the defendant in Holland was given two years in prison.

Other Trials of 55 Auschwitz Personnel

Apart from legal proceedings against former SS personnel in Auschwitz in-dicted for their activities in the camp, some appeared as defendants in more than a dozen trials in 1945–48; the indictments, however, did not involve the Auschwitz period. These were trials of SS personnel from other camps conducted by U.S., British, and French tribunals.

The most famous was the 1945 trial of SS personnel of the Bergen-Belsen concentration camp before the British tribunal. It concluded with a death sentence (exclusively for crimes committed in Bergen-Belsen) against the following defendants: SS-Hauptsturmbannführer Josef Kremer, who had served as adjutant of Höss in Auschwitz and in 1944 as adjutant of the com-mandant of Auschwitz II-Birkenau; SS Hauptsturmbannführer Franz Hoss-ler, who had held the post of Lagerführer of Auschwitz I and Auschwitz II—supervisor of the women's camp; Peter Weingartner, former functionary of Department III; Irma Grese, former SS woman supervisor; and the SS woman superintendent (SS-Oberaufseherin), Elisabeth Volkenrath.

In November 1945, the U.S. tribunal tried members of the SS Dachau personnel, including SS-Obersturmführer Vinzenz Schottl, who had served as Schutzlagerführer in Auschwitz III-Monowitz, and SS Hauptscharführer Otto Moll, a notorious sadist and head of crematoria in Birkenau. Both re-ceived death sentences and were executed.

In another trial of Buchenwald personnel conducted before the U.S. tri-bunal, SS-Obersturmführer Hans Merbach, former leader of the company of dog guides (Hundestaffel) from Auschwitz, was sentenced to death. In the trial of SS personnel of the Neuengamme concentration camp conducted before the British tribunal, the defendants included SS Obersturmführer Anton Thumann, who for several weeks had served as Lagerführer in Birke-nau, and two SS physicians: SS-Hauptsturmführer Alfred Trzebinski and SS-Obersturmführer Bruno Kitt. All three received death sentences.

In the trial of SS servicemen from the Natzweiler concentration camp before the French tribunal, two defendants had served in Auschwitz: SS-Sturmbannführer Fritz Hartjenstein, former commandant of Auschwitz II-Birkenau, and SS-Hauptsturmführer Walter Schmidetzki, in charge of depots where belongings of the murdered Birkenau victims were stored. In this case, too, death sentences were passed. In a trial involving former SS personnel of the Mittelbau-Dora concentration camp, SS Obersturmführer

Hans Moser, former company leader in Auschwitz, was sentenced to death. In the trial of SS personnel of the Ravensbrück concentration camp, one defendant was a former SS woman superintendent from Auschwitz, Johanna Langenfeld, who also received a death sentence.

Other significant trials included the 1979 trial of members of the SS personnel of the Lublin-Majdanek camp, which took place in Düsseldorf. Charges were brought against, among others, two SS women superintendents, Rosemarie Suss-Reischl and Charlotte Wollert-Mayer, and against a former block leader in Auschwitz, SS-Rottenführer Heinz Willain. Willain received a prison sentence; the other defendants were acquitted.

This survey may be treated as a balance sheet of the postwar prosecution and punishment of former members of SS personnel from Auschwitz. Taking into account several suicides, including those of two SS physicians, Eduard Wirths and Heinz Thilo, we may conclude that only about 10 percent of the former Auschwitz SS personnel stood trial in various countries, although not all of them were charged with crimes committed in Auschwitz.

Generally speaking, Nazi war criminals were not pursued consistently, and large-scale prosecution took place only in the immediate postwar period. Sentences were not free of evident errors, while legal proceedings in West Germany dragged on for years, often bogging down in procedural details. The situation in Austria in this regard was even worse. In the 1950s, trials of SS guard force members who had taken an active part in mass murders of prisoners during evacuation marches were discontinued. Thus the campaign to bring to justice those responsible for the deaths of the Auschwitz victims, including the mass murders of Jews, is no longer in the hands of courts. It is now a matter for historians.

NOTES

1. One example is Alois Brunner, a former associate of Adolf Eichmann, who lives in Damascus.

2. See, for example, J. Gumkowski and T. Kulakowski, *Zbrodniarze hitlerowscy przed Najwyzszym Trybunalem Narodowym* (Nazi criminals before the Supreme National Tribunal) (Warsaw, 1967); T. Cyprian and J. Sawicki, *Siedem procesow przed Najwyzszym Trybunalem Narodowym* (Seven trials before the Supreme National Tribunal) (Poznan, 1962).

3. See, for example, H. Langbein, *Der Auschwitz Prozess: Eine Documentation* (Vienna, Frankfurt am Main, Zurich, 1965); B. Naumann, *Auschwitz: Bericht über die Strafsache gegen Mulka u.a. vor dem Schwurgericht Frankfurt* (Frankfurt am Main, 1965).

4. Archives of the Main Commission for the Investigation of Nazi Crimes in Poland, microfilm collection, frame 00051, call no. M-891.

5. This variety is reflected in the reminiscences of former prisoners who served in labor squads.

6. Firms operating in Auschwitz included Deutsche Lebensmitteln GmbH, Deutsche Ausrustungswerke, Deutsche Erd- und Steinwerke GmbH, and Golleschauer Portland-Zement AG.

7. In his book, Langbein mentions a trial of a number of SS men in the Soviet Union, without, however, offering any details.

8. K. Smolen, "Karanie zbrodniarzy oswiecimskich" (Punishment of Auschwitz criminals), in *Oswiecim: Hitlerowski oboz masowej zaglady* (Auschwitz: A Nazi Mass Extermination Camp) (Warsaw, 1987), pp. 169–70.

9. For a broad discussion of the status and legal acts defining the jurisdisction of the Supreme National Tribunal in Poland, see Cyprian and Sawicki, pp. ix–xxviii.

29

The Literature of Auschwitz

LAWRENCE LANGER

In the beginning was the testimony. Any study of the literature of Auschwitz may start with judicial versions of the way it was, based on eyewitness accounts. But it can never end there.

Readers of the proceedings of the so-called Auschwitz trial of former camp guards that ran for 20 months (and which I attended for a few days in the summer of 1964) will discover not a narrative leading to insight and understanding but a futile dispute between accusers and accused. The prisoners in the dock denied virtually everything. Mulka was not there when the prosecution says he was; Kaduk never shot anyone; Boger only used his infamous torture instrument, the "Boger swing," on rare occasions; Klehr was on leave during Christmas 1942, when he was charged with murdering inmates by injecting phenol into their hearts. Guilt exists, but the agent is always someone else. Little in this bizarre courtroom drama leads to a unified vision of the place we call Auschwitz. Scenes remain episodic and anecdotal; scenarios never coalesce; characters stay vague, as protagonists dissolve into helpless victims (through no failure of will, to be sure, but the tyranny of circumstance), while antagonists collapse into mistaken identities or innocent puppets maneuvered from afar.

What awareness can emerge from an incident like the following, which casts its net of censure so widely that we strain to unsnarl the agents from the victims? A group of prisoners was excavating a ditch filled with water. A witness testified that SS men forced them to leap into the ditch. "They had to jump into the water and swim. Then they ordered a prisoner named Isaac—he was called Isaac the Strong in the camp—to drown his comrades.

Finally they also ordered him to kill his own father. In the act of drowning his father, Isaac went berserk and started to scream. So Stark [one of the SS guards on trial] shot Isaac in the water." Faced with the accusation, Stark denied his role: "I have nothing to say, because I was not present at any of the incidents the witness described."[1] Such painful testimony may carry the conviction of truth, despite Stark's dissent, but by its very nature the judicial process does not allow it to remain unchallenged. The defense promptly began to discredit the witness with witnesses of its own, whose evidence may indeed be false—the court is dubious—but how can we ever know? At the moment when Isaac the Strong became Isaac the Mad, he crossed a frontier separating the normal world from the abnormal universe of Auschwitz, leaving us beyond the barrier, musing on the chance of ever entering into its reality ourselves.

The literature of Auschwitz exists to help us navigate that voyage. It is a perilous journey but a crucial one if we are ever to admit how little the idea of justice helps us in our efforts to pierce the dark core of that death-camp experience. We must confront it on *its* terms, not ours, leaving behind traditional casts of characters with their Isaacs the Strong, and the heroism and tragedy implicit in such titles. In our search for the *meaning* of Auschwitz, to our dismay, we meet often only its absence; what we have to forgo to establish contact with such barren terrain is the theme that absorbs most writers who venture into it.

Not all commentators, of course, agree that the terrain is so barren, or that we must forgo so much in order to wander there. The leading exponent of the view that in spite of Auschwitz, life and suffering are unconditionally meaningful is Viktor Frankl, whose *Man's Search for Meaning* is still probably the most widely read text on the subject. Frankl's strategy is to minimize the atrocities he himself survived and to stress the connections between pre- and post-Auschwitz reality. Unintentionally confirming the wish of his persecutors, he leaves his fellow victims anonymous, while naming and quoting instead a long list of explorers of the human spiritual condition, including Spinoza, Schopenhauer, Tolstoy, Dostoyevsky, Rilke, Nietzsche, and Thomas Mann. The reader is thus prompted to believe, for example, that Tolstoy's Christian novel *Resurrection* or Dostoyevsky's Christian declaration—"There is only one thing that I dread: not to be worthy of my sufferings"—is somehow relevant to the Jewish victims of Auschwitz.[2]

Frankl manages to transform his ordeal in Auschwitz into a renewed encounter with the literary and philosophical giants who preceded its emergence, thus preserving the intellectual and spiritual traditions they championed, and his own legacy as an heir to their minds. He uncovers truth by assertion, not analysis, as if the word were an eternally valid bulwark against the dehumanizing assaults of physical violence. Many witnesses in the courtroom at Frankfurt would have been bewildered by the scriptural finality of Frankl's proclamation that "if there is a meaning in life at all, then there must be a meaning in suffering."[3]

Frankl's language invites us, indeed requires us, to dismiss the petitions of despair before we confront them. Consider the testimony of Joseph Glück, who happened to be on the witness stand when I was present in the courtroom. I recall the figure of a shrunken, elderly Jewish man who seemed crushed and exhausted by his memories, though he had not yet begun to recite them. He whispered hesitantly, seemingly intimidated by the large hall (where the proceedings had been moved when the room in the Palace of Justice proved too small), by the ranks of the accused and their lawyers, and by the crowd of spectators. He had been deported to Auschwitz from Klausenburg with 2,800 other Jews, 400 of whom had been selected for work upon arrival. The rest had been sent directly to the gas chambers, including his wife, two children, mother, sister and her two children, brother, mother-in-law, and sister-in-law. His situation was certainly not unique, but his statements stunned the audience.

Asked if he is the sole survivor, Glück replies, "Yes." Naumann reports: "For a moment the word hovers over the courtroom, irrevocable but uncertain to whom and where it should turn so that it might not only be heard but also comprehended. The old man sits motionless."[4] No one is foolish enough to ask him if there is meaning in his suffering, or whether he feels worthy of it. The judge shuffles the papers in front of him. Everyone there, including me, grapples with the question of how to translate his simple affirmative—a word haunting the air like a scrap of animated anguish—into a shareable experience. This instant remains vivid to me because it was one of the first times that I asked myself how a literature of Auschwitz, and of the Holocaust in general, might ever achieve such a goal.

That is the focus of our inquiry. From the multiple talents that have addressed themselves to this issue emerges a complex, at times contradictory, vision of a way of existing that continues to elude precise definition. For example, against Frankl's insistence on the power of literature and philosophy to sustain the inner self during the camp ordeal, we have the contrary view of Jean Améry, a classic exposition of the futility of literary memory once it entered the precincts of Auschwitz. Because the mind in Auschwitz collided not merely with death but with the kind of dying peculiar to an extermination camp, normal responses lost their value. The intellectual was left suddenly defenseless: "Death lay before him, and in him the spirit was still stirring; the latter confronted the former and tried—in vain, to say it straight off—to exemplify its dignity."[5] Frankl argues that Auschwitz challenged the individual to rise above his outward fate, furnishing him "with the chance of achieving something through his own suffering."[6]

Améry insists that both fate and suffering disappeared from the vocabulary of Auschwitz, as did death itself, to be replaced by the single fear, shared by all, of *how* one would die: "Dying was omnipresent; death vanished from sight."[7]

Foreseeing the bleakness of a future without the heritage of his literary past, Frankl seems to have decided to treat Auschwitz as a temporary anomaly rather than a permanent rupture. His pledge to inner freedom and the life of the spirit flows from that choice. For Améry, entering the world of Auschwitz, as he reflected on it afterward, left him with a totally different vista of past *and* future.

> The first result was always the total collapse of the *esthetic* view of death. What I am saying is familiar [though less so, one suspects, than Améry believed]. The intellectual, and especially the intellectual of German education and culture, bears the esthetic view of death within him. It was his legacy from the distant past, at the very latest from the time of German romanticism. It can be more or less characterized by the names Novalis, Schopenhauer, Wagner, and Thomas Mann. For death in its literary, philosophic, or musical form there was no place in Auschwitz. No bridge led from death in Auschwitz to *Death in Venice*. Every poetic evocation of death became intolerable, whether it was Hesse's "Dear Brother Death" or that of Rilke, who said: "Oh Lord, give each his own death." The esthetic view of death had revealed itself to the intellectual as part of an esthetic *mode of life*; where the latter had been all but forgotten, the former was nothing but an elegant trifle. In the camp no Tristan music accompanied death, only the roaring of the SS and the Kapos.[8]

A major function of the literature of Auschwitz is to help us discard the moral, philosophical, and literary systems created by what Améry calls the "esthetic mode of life," systems defining character and conduct and the tragic sense itself. That becomes especially necessary when they bar the world of Auschwitz from our efforts to enter its realm.

How are we to understand Améry's avowal that in Auschwitz the intellect "nullified itself when at almost every step it ran into its uncrossable borders"? The results were devastating. "The axes of its traditional frames of reference then shattered. Beauty: that was an illusion. Knowledge: that turned out to be a game with ideas."[9] In the presence of this warning, we struggle to prevent our own discourse about Auschwitz from becoming merely a game with ideas.

One way out of the dilemma is to accept the threatening possibility of how easily Auschwitz reduced earnest pleas like Rilke's "Oh Lord, give each his own death" to nothing but elegant trifles, utterly irrelevant to the modes of survival available in the camp. Our reluctant surrender of what Améry calls the esthetic mode of life is an admission of the powerful role it plays in shaping the conduct and belief of Western civilization, and of how bereft we appear without its support, and of the social and economic "modes" that accompany it.

The arriver at Auschwitz entered a world of sensation, not mind: the roar of the SS and kapos; the bursts of flame and smoke spiraling from chimneys; the rank smell of charred flesh. In a remarkable little-known story called "Phantoms, My Companions," Auschwitz survivor Charlotte Delbo enacts this encounter as her narrator journeys by boxcar toward Auschwitz, accompanied by leading characters of the French dramatic repertoire, from Molière to Giraudoux. One by one, frightened by the uncertainties looming before them, they leap from the train, until when it arrives and the doors are thrown open, only Alceste, the Misanthrope, remains. He gazes wildly at the bleak, obscure landscape, and disappears, leaving the narrator to the world of corrosive sensation that the esthetic mode of life had done nothing to prepare Alceste for. Denied the options of art, the narrator faces her doom alone.

Dialogue is the heart of drama; Molière's Misanthrope is disgusted by the social pretensions and hypocrisy that pass for talk among his peers. As Améry describes the content of dialogues in Auschwitz, however, we begin to glimpse how thoroughly camp reality disarmed traditional notions of the esthetic mode of life, how useless an Alceste would be to counsel or rebuke in such a place. "Inmates carried on conversations about how long it probably takes for the gas in the gas chambers to do its job. One speculated on the painfulness of death by phenol injection. Were you to wish yourself a blow to the skull or a slow death through exhaustion in the infirmary?"[10] The literature of Auschwitz makes constant inroads on our assumptions not only about the esthetic mode of life (which the quoted passage reduces to incoherence) but also about the actuality on which it is based. The universe of dying that was Auschwitz yearns for a language purified of the taint of normality.

Primo Levi, who more than anyone else wrote and rewrote the experience of Auschwitz in search of its significance for him and for us, evokes that instant when at war's end the world of the living faced in embarrassed silence the world of the surviving dead. He tries to analyze the internal content of that momentous meeting, as the first four Soviet soldiers to enter Auschwitz gaze at Levi and his gaunt comrades.

> They did not greet us, nor did they smile; they seemed oppressed not only by compassion, but by a confused restraint, which sealed their lips and bound their eyes to the funereal scene. It was that shame we knew so well, the shame that drowned us after the selections, and every time we had to watch, or submit to, some outrage: the shame the Germans did not know, that the just man experiences at another man's crime; the feeling of guilt that such a crime should exist, that it should have been introduced irrevocably into the world of things that exist, and that his will for good should have proved too weak or null, and should not have availed in defense.[11]

Inversions cancel meaning here, then challenge its rebirth in the desolate and arid moral soil of Auschwitz. Liberators "oppressed" by compassion; victims shamed by the crimes they witnessed, but did not commit; the innocent feeling guilty, the criminal unashamed; but most of all, the visible failure of good to carry out its historic mission of unmasking and overwhelming evil—such inversions discredit the traditional power of language and the meaning it is accustomed to serve.

More than any other commentator, Levi spent his life trying to explain the nature of the contamination that was Auschwitz. It represented a stain not just on individuals but on time and history too. The Auschwitz trial was concerned with what was done and by whom. The premise behind it was that identifying guilt and punishing crime would make a difference in a society based on order. But for Levi, the reach of the moral chaos that nurtured Auschwitz was so vast that justice could not begin to embrace or define its limits. That was a task for the writer, as Levi shows.

> So for us even the hour of liberty rang out grave and muffled, and filled our souls with joy and yet with a painful sense of pudency, so that we should have liked to wash our consciences and our memories clean from the foulness that lay upon them; and also with anguish because we felt that this should never happen, that now nothing could ever happen good and pure enough to rub out our past, and that the scars of the outrage would remain within us for ever, and in the memories of those who saw it, and in the places where it occurred, and in the stories that we should tell of it.[12]

Levi is honest enough to concede that moral fatigue at the hour of liberty may have been the initial source of this daunting vision. But when he wrote about it soon after war's end, he found the language to confirm its deep and permanent impact on our time.

> Because, and this is the awful privilege of our generation and of my people, no one better than us has ever been able to grasp the incurable nature of the offense, that spreads like a contagion. It is foolish to think that human justice can eradicate it. It is an inexhaustible fount of evil; it breaks the body and the spirit of the submerged, it stifles them and renders them abject; it returns as ignominy upon the oppressors, it perpetuates itself as hatred among the survivors, and swarms around in a thousand ways against the very will of all, as a thirst for revenge, as a moral capitulation, as denial, as weariness, as renunciation.[13]

Some literature of Auschwitz, in a desperate retreat from charges like these about the infection spreading from the very existence of the place, seeks vindication in a counter vision that would restore moral health to the victims, imposing shame and accusation upon the culprits alone. It resists

Levi's acute but paradoxical sense that shame and *self*-accusation, however unwarranted, nonetheless remained a burden for him and many of his fellow former prisoners throughout their lives—in the end, a burden that consumed and probably destroyed him.

The unendurable truths of Auschwitz that Levi expounded with such courage and distinction do not merge easily with traditional literary forms. Thirty years ago Rolf Hochhuth's bold historical drama *The Deputy* (1963) burst upon the literary scene in a scandal of controversy. Today it reads like a tame piece of theater indeed, though when I saw it in Vienna in 1964, Hochhuth's setting of the last act in Auschwitz itself seemed a dazzling and agonizing innovation. It testified to how little the imagination must have been prepared then for a literature of Auschwitz.

Hochhuth himself paid tribute to this idea in some preliminary remarks in the printed text, revealing his conviction—common at the time, but less so, one hopes, today—that we "lack the imaginative faculties to be able to envision Auschwitz."[14] So much commentary currently exists on the camp (including this volume), that such an attitude now appears naive and even antiquated. But it was a protective device, one thankfully discarded by artists greater than Hochhuth like Tadeusz Borowski and Charlotte Delbo.

In his efforts to realize Auschwitz on the stage, Hochhuth dismisses documentary naturalism as a stylistic principle, concluding that "no matter how closely we adhere to historical facts, the speech, scene, and events on the stage will be altogether surrealistic."[15] This is a perfectly legitimate point of view; Elie Wiesel describes his arrival at Auschwitz amid the flames of burning pits as a visionary nightmare. But when Hochhuth shifts from setting to character, he lapses into figures so conventional that he sacrifices any surrealistic effect achieved by the vague movements of the doomed toward the gas chambers in the dim recesses of the stage. The Priest and the Doctor are so clearly defined as adversaries in the contest between Good and Evil that they dwindle into allegory, a fruition fatal to *any* adequate representation of Auschwitz in art.

The confrontation between the Priest and the Doctor reflects, on a smaller scale, the epic encounters between Milton's Satan and God, though Auschwitz has altered the theological balance. The Priest becomes a tragic martyr, improbably choosing to share the fate of the Jews, while the Doctor, the spirit of cynical negation, betrays his ancestry in Ivan Karamazov's devil, a less sinister but equally contemptuous literary prototype. His obvious real model is Dr. Mengele, though Hochhuth is not interested in developing a reliable portrait of that notorious figure. He succumbs instead to the blandishments of literary precedents, offering a familiar metaphysical dispute between the ruthless nihilism of the Doctor and the compassion of the Priest, weakened by the failure of the Pope and the Catholic hierarchy to assert their spiritual force in opposition to the powers of destruction.

Sounding more like Dostoyevsky's Grand Inquisitor than a character from a play about Auschwitz, the Doctor unwittingly reveals his literary origins:

> The truth is, Auschwitz refutes
> creator, creation, and the creature.
> Life as an idea is dead.
> This may well be the beginning
> of a great new era,
> a redemption from suffering.
> From this point of view only one crime
> remains: cursed be he who creates life.
> I cremate life.[16]

The commonplace disguised as the profound may betray the limitations of the Doctor's intellect, since his voice falls far short of Ivan Karamazov's mighty indictment of God's world that still beguiles readers into accepting it as Dostoyevsky's position too. The real point of *The Deputy* is to charge the Church with a spiritual timidity that was partly responsible for enabling the historic designs of the Third Reich to end in the gas chambers of Auschwitz. But the verbal premises on which the structure of the play is built—good, evil, conscience, truth, spirit, love—do not carry us very far into the daily tensions and moral conflicts of life in Auschwitz itself; nor do they illuminate the natures of men like Mengele, whose elusive motives are hidden behind the taunting, caustic facade of the Doctor's single-minded voice.

A play that discards the metaphysics of Auschwitz as a theme and turns instead to what we might call its materiality is Peter Weiss's *Investigation* (1965), whose content derives almost wholly from testimony at the trial in Frankfurt mentioned earlier. By blending and shaping statements from witnesses and the accused into a carefully organized pattern, Weiss creates from the futile courtroom dispute a fresh vision of the clash in Auschwitz between moral space and destructive place. Although naked testimony may lead the imagination only into confusion, silence, and despair, the form imposed on it by Weiss achieves the opposite effects. Guards and officers in the end indict themselves by their own relentless but transparently false denials of complicity, while the language of the victims finally sheds a terrifying light on the ordeals they succumbed to—or wretchedly survived.

Weiss's drama confirms the difficulty, not to say impossibility, of creating a literature of Auschwitz by relying purely on the powers of invention. In the cast of characters he identifies each of the "accused" in his play by their real names, since it is these particular agents of mass murder we need to understand, not their dramatic prototypes. The witnesses, on the other hand, remain anonymous, spokesmen and spokeswomen for the vast numbers who are unable to speak for themselves (although a few of the witnesses represent the voices of former SS members not on trial, who worked in various administrative capacities in the camp). The imagination is drawn into the landscape of Auschwitz by states of feeling inspired by the testimony, condensed evidence that slowly moves us from a sense of how things were to an encounter with what they implied.

Unlike Hochhuth, Weiss does not present Auschwitz as a harrowing inferno, alienating us through the awesomeness of the atrocities committed there. One of his witnesses insists:

> We must drop the lofty view
> that the camp world
> is incomprehensible to us
> We all knew the society
> that produced a government
> capable of creating such camps

Earlier, the same witness had insisted:

> When we talk of our experience nowadays
> with people who were never in a camp
> there is always something
> inconceivable to them about it
> And yet they are the same people
> who in the camp were prisoners and guards[17]

Weiss lowers the barriers of the unimaginable, however, not merely by the statements of his witnesses but chiefly by the studied arrangement of the 11 multipart "Songs" that compose the scenes of his drama. Beginning with the "Song of the Platform" and the "Song of the Camp" and ending with the "Song of Zyklon B" (the chemical agent of extermination) and the "Song of the Fire Ovens" (the site of physical annihilation), Weiss gradually narrows the space separating the imagination from the camp, leading us from the ramp to the barrack, through various execution sites like the Black Wall (outside) and the cells of block 11 (indoors), to the gas chambers and the body's final confined destination, the crematorium. The victim's shrinking fate is thus duplicated by the sequence of the testimonies, which in their quest for literal truth have made available through the shaping pen of the dramatist the imagined truth of Auschwitz too.

Unfortunately, the literature of Auschwitz can also be used for political purposes. One distressing enigma of Weiss's text is his refusal to identify the Jews as the primary victims of the murder machinery in the camp, although attentive readers could not possibly mistake his references to the six million "persecuted" or to those "killed for racial reasons." Because the events of

Auschwitz are still anchored firmly in historical memory, mention of Mengele and Zyklon B and the crematorium are enough to remind us of the destruction of European Jewry. Weiss's universalizing tendency, however, may become more of a problem for future generations, for whom the allusive power of these brief labels will have lost their specific, not to say metaphorical, value. Fortunately, Weiss's play will not be the only source of Holocaust actuality for those generations, for whom the literature of Auschwitz will consist, as it does for us, of a multiplicity of voices and points of view to guide us through its dismal labyrinth.

The boundaries separating the historical moment from its imaginative portrayal may be instructively studied in Elie Wiesel's *Night*, still one of the most concisely powerful narratives of the Auschwitz experience. Although widely read as an autobiographical memoir, *Night* also continues to be classified and critically acclaimed as a novel, and not without reason. Because it is a written text, *Night* suffers the curbs and enjoys the privileges of art, from which courtroom testimony or any oral account of the Auschwitz ordeal is exempt. Art in its essence invites us to see life other than as it literally was, since all art, even the most objective naturalism, requires selection and composition, thus altering the purity (or in this instance, the impurity) of the original event.

In one of its aspects, Wiesel's text is a study of fathers and sons in Auschwitz, with all inmates being the children of God the Father. That lifts the narrative, to its credit to be sure, beyond the constraints of autobiography into the realm of imagined fiction. Nothing is more "literary" or stylized in the story than the young boy's denunciation of God's world and the implied renunciation of its creator, the seeds of which are nurtured by passages in Dostoyevsky and Camus, in addition to the conditions of Auschwitz itself.

The literature of Auschwitz is thus bound by its historical context in a way that most other literature is not. Within the above-mentioned constraints, it faces the challenge familiar to all serious writers: finding an appropriate tone and point of view, a suitable angle of vision, a valid and convincing center of consciousness through which to filter the trial of atrocity. Although extravagantly fictionalized historical material about the Holocaust (as in Leslie Epstein's *King of the Jews*) may alienate some readers, a subtly imagined center of consciousness, invented or not, can draw them against their will into the net of human abuse, where their own sense of normal reality struggles to escape from the lure.

One of the finest examples we have of such a strategy is Tadeusz Borowski's collection *This Way for the Gas, Ladies and Gentlemen*, published in Poland in 1959, though many of its stories were written shortly after the war when Borowski was in his early 20s. Dismissing Hochhuth's premise that we lack the imaginative faculties to be able to envision Auschwitz (formulated, ironically, years *after* Borowski's suicide in 1951), Borowski chronicles the divorce between reader expectation and inmate behavior through a casual and understated first-person narrative style. His narrators disarm us with the simplicity of their opening gambits, feigning a disinterest that is slowly undone by subsequent events. He refuses to supply us with guidelines for the inhuman tour we are about to begin, teasing our curiosity with hints of disorder that gradually invade our lingering innocence.

"All of us walked around naked," begins one of his stories, leaving his reader to wonder whether the speaker is Adam in the Garden of Eden or the resident of a nudist colony. The narrative then eases us into the place we call Auschwitz: "The delousing is finally over, and the striped suits are back from the tanks of Zyklon B solution, an efficient killer of lice in clothing. . . . The clinical clues are puzzling, but not yet sinister, until the sentence finishes: "and of men in gas chambers."[18] Generations from now, this passage may require footnoting; when Borowski wrote it, it needed only assent. What he forces us to assent to, however, violates every value that civilization presumes to cherish; Borowski's stories portray the systematic mutilation of such values in the Auschwitz he knew and experienced.

One test of a literature of Auschwitz is its candor in imitating the atmosphere of moral and physical mutilation that the Germans deliberately created in the camps. The notions of heroism and villainy so central to Frankl and Hochhuth in their visions of Auschwitz vanish from Borowski's literary horizon. Andrzej Wirth, a Polish commentator on Borowski's art, helps us understand why; Borowski's scenario, he argues, has nothing to do with the classical conception based on the necessity of choice between two systems of value. The hero of Borowski's stories is a hero *deprived of all choice.* He finds himself in a situation without choice because every choice is base. The tragedy lies not in the necessity of choosing but in the impossibility of making a choice.[19]

When the goal of moral being is not virtue, but staying alive, then our sense of character loses its mooring in literature, scripture, or philosophy and succumbs to circumstance—the awful predicament that Borowski energizes in his Auschwitz stories.

In the culture of coping that defined existence in the death camp, the survivor depended for his life—at least for a brief time—on the death of someone else. If the tragic figure is one who through action or attitude rebels against his destiny, what are we to make of one of Borowski's narrators, who helps drive victims from the cattle cars, unloads their belongings, watches them being led off to the gas chambers, feels rage at his involvement in their fate instead of pride at his mastery of his own, and finds in an attack of nausea little relief from an environment that dehumanizes everyone—

murderer, victim, and survivor? Life gestures are contaminated by death or become death gestures themselves.

The narrator spends his rage in impotent silence, bereft of meaningful choice: "The air is filled with ghastly cries, the earth trembles beneath me, I can feel sticky moisture on my eyelids. My throat is completely dry." Earlier he had broken his silence by explaining to some Greek inmates in what he called "crematorium Esperanto" the challenge that lay before the Canada commando where they worked: "Transport kommen, alle Krematorium, compris?"

In the global idiom of mass murder, words do not dignify and communication brings neither community nor communion. He is victim himself of what he calls the only permissible form of charity in Auschwitz, the camp law dictating that "people going to their death must be deceived to the very end."[20]

Among his most important contributions to the literature of Auschwitz are Borowski's portraits of what Primo Levi would later call the "functionary-prisoners" in the camp, those squad leaders or kapos or other inmates who through luck or manipulation joined the internal power hierarchy and thus entered the gray zone of its moral life, prolonging their own temporary survival amid the murder of others—before them, around them, often in their place. People staying alive, he suggests, must also be "self-deceived" about the origin of their survival, although the very consciousness of this fact lurks menacingly beneath the facade of indifference that usually dominates his narrator's voice. He is concerned with the state of mind bred by being among the "privileged," and the psychological price one pays to remain there.

The internal power hierarchy in Auschwitz was neither exclusively male nor non-Jewish, though this is the prevailing rule in Borowski's fictional vision. Sara Nomberg-Przytyk's *Auschwitz: True Tales from a Grotesque Land,* a series of interconnected stories, chronicles the odyssey of a Jewish woman who joins the ranks of female functionary prisoners before our eyes, learning through the process what one must discard of one's civilized moral and psychological baggage in order to gain and retain that status. Although she will be low down in the hierarchy, Nomberg-Przytyk's narrator is not blind to the gray zone she is soon to enter.

> The SS men saw the splendor in which the camp functionaries lived, but all this took place with their silent approval. It was a devilish system in which the SS men and the functionaries were united by a chain of cruelty. The contrast between their splendor and our misery kept them constantly aware of what they stood to lose in the event that they failed to carry out the orders of the SS men. They used whatever methods were necessary to assure their own survival

and their relatively comfortable way of life. If the voice of conscience chanced to awake in them, they would quiet it continuously with the same arguments: "We suffered so much in the first few years. We lived through those hard times. Now we are not going to die for the sake of some dirty *Zugang* [new arrival]."[21]

Such a passage may tempt us to believe that selfishness and brutality were the vital conditions for staying alive in this milieu, but the narrator discovers that motives in Auschwitz were far more baffling, controlled not by some inner system of values but by circumstances unrelated to one's will.

She remembers thinking, for example, "that in Auschwitz there was nothing more important than trying to help your fellow sufferers and yet, at the same time, how immoral it was to decide whose suffering should be alleviated and whose should continue unabated. Who had given us the right to condemn or to save another? In Auschwitz there was no fairness in the merciless struggle for survival. Those with scruples died isolated and abandoned. That was the new order of the concentration camp."[22] This is what Wirth meant when he suggested that in Borowski's Auschwitz all choices were base, including the decision to aid a fellow sufferer. If the literature of Auschwitz can help us understand nothing more than this troubling but truthful paradox, it will have vindicated its vexing challenge to the imagination.

In October 1944, Nomberg-Przytyk's narrator is working as a clerk in the hospital barrack. One evening, while she and her comrades are discussing the difference between conscious and unconscious death, the other clerk in the infirmary interrupts with a story that freezes the momentum of their abstract debate. She tells of a group of 156 Polish girls from Krakow, who had been sent to the clinic, so they thought, for examination before being shipped to work in Germany. "They were talking loudly, laughing, never dreaming that they had been horribly deceived and that the *leichenauto* [vehicle serving as a hearse] was coming for them in about an hour." Clearly they are "fellow sufferers" who, as the functionary prisoners know, are about to be killed by phenol injection. How does one define one's human role at a moment like this? "Perhaps I should shout it out to them," says the speaker, "'Calm down! Don't laugh. You are living corpses, and in a few hours nothing will be left of you but ashes!' Then what? Then we attendants would go to the gas chambers and the women would die anyway."[23] Suddenly the question "Is it better for a human being to know that he is about to die?" assumes dimensions of complexity that no prior system of belief allows us to simplify.

Nomberg-Przytyk shares Borowski's talent for sketching the rupture between Auschwitz reality and conjectures about it—the prisoners' and our own. "We didn't tell them the truth," the speaker says, "not out of fear for our own lives, but because we truly did not know what would be the least painful way for the young women to die. . . . If we told them what was in store for them, then a struggle for life would ensue. In their attempt to run from death they would find only loneliness, because their friends, seeking to preserve their own lives, would refuse to help them."[24] Difficult as it is for us to imagine, not to say concede, mutual support becomes an academic question when the issue is death by phenol injection. Courage and truth itself shrivel into privileged virtues reserved for those living beyond the ominous shadows of the gas chamber.

In this instance, the women themselves eventually discover what is in store for them, and a terrible outcry erupts. They are surrounded, beaten, then each girl "was dragged screaming, by two SS men, into the presence of Mengele," who presumably administers the fatal injection. Some of the remaining victims try to run away. "Then the dogs were set on them. Their deaths were completely different from the deaths of the first batch of women who went to their deaths unknowing. Who knows which death was more difficult, but the first group seemed to die more peacefully." This story, called "The Verdict," suspends judgment but goads the reader into the role of juror through its conclusion: "'I still don't know whether we should have told the women about the death that was waiting for them. What do you think?' None of us said anything."[25]

The reader is left speechless, too, silenced by the sorrowful if contrary fates of victims *and* survivors. Is there such a notion as "complicity through the eyes," by which a witness is diminished simply because of what she has seen? When Nomberg-Przytyk's narrator is freed, she does not rejoice. "I felt comfortable, warm and clean," she admits. "But I was not happy. I did not know why. Again and again I repeated to myself the refrain: 'Be happy, you are free.' But this did not help. I was sad. Sadness strangled me."[26] Her response will seem odd only to those who have not immersed themselves in the literature of Auschwitz, where they are forced to discover how closely woven, morally and emotionally, are the stories of those whom Primo Levi, in a striking image, has called "the drowned and the saved."

If the saved remain tainted in their memories by the misfortune of the drowned, this is one of the melancholy bequests of the camp experience. "It was a logical consequence of the system," wrote Levi, "an inhuman regime spreads and extends its inhumanity in all directions, also and especially downward; unless it meets with resistance and exceptionally strong characters, it corrupts its victims and its opponents as well."[27] A corollary "logical consequence" of Auschwitz, to be extracted by the diligent moralist, is unfortunately this. There was no rein on the shame, humiliation, and torment that the Germans could inflict on their prey, no check to their malice, brutality, lust for ruin. Their talent for atrocity was unlimited. Goodness, on the other hand, was curbed among the victims at every turn by fear, hunger, thirst, confusion, illness, and despair. The *will* to compassion may have remained intact, but its power to oppose the ungoverned ferocity of the camps faltered before the sterile cruelty inherent in the system.

Few writers in the tradition of Auschwitz convey this painful truth with the dense immediacy of Charlotte Delbo, whose trilogy *Auschwitz et après* (Auschwitz and after) explores the fragmenting of the self and the uncoupling of its milieu that were the most enduring legacies of the camp experience.[28] For Delbo, Auschwitz was simply a place of unnatural, premature dying; her art represents a resolute search for a prose and poetry equal to this dismal fact. In her vision, the self is inseparable from the cold, hunger, and exhaustion that slowly erode its substance, until the crust of dignity formerly enclosing a human being loses its protective value and decays. She insists that we join her in witnessing what remains, as she and her fellow prisoners peer from a barrack window:

> At first we are not sure what we see. It is difficult at first to distinguish them from the snow. The yard is full of them. Naked. Lying close to each other on the snow. White, a white that looks bluish against the snow. Their heads are shaven, their pubic hairs are straight and stiff. The corpses are frozen. White with brown nails. Their upturned toes are truly ridiculous. Terrible, ridiculous.[29]

Is unaccommodated woman no more than this? Behind the logical consequences of Primo Levi's Auschwitz, legitimate as they are, lies the physical assault on the body that mirrored its indelible nucleus.

Into the heart of this nucleus Delbo's incantatory prose lures us, groping toward images to match the abrupt reversals implicit in her theme.

> Standing, wrapped in a blanket, a child, a little boy. A tiny shaven head, a face in which the jaws and the brow ridge stand out. Barefoot, he jumps up and down without stopping, with a frenzied movement that makes one think of that of savages dancing. He wants to wave his arms too to keep warm. The blanket slips open. It is a woman. A skeleton of a woman. She is naked. One can see her ribs and hip bones. She pulls the blanket up on her shoulders and continues to dance. A mechanical dance. A dancing skeleton of a woman. Her feet are small, thin and bare in the snow. There are living, dancing skeletons.[30]

This is a true art of revelation, though not in the familiar sense. Unlike Frankl, Delbo has no qualms about exposing a culture built on mistaken identities, enticed by traditions of enlightenment and romanticism into forming idealized versions of the inviolable self. Auschwitz has disfigured those traditions, leading Delbo to focus on the violated human form, and to ask how such fragmentation might be integrated into the ambitions of future generations.

The irony of such a quest, not to say question, does not escape Delbo herself. She follows her description of the living, dancing skeleton with an early example of what has become a postmodern fashion—a self-reflexive admission of the artifice of art: "And now I am sitting in a café writing this story—for this is turning into a story."[31] Can a literature of Auschwitz *ever* span the chasm between what we were and what the camp's very existence has made us a part of? Throughout her narrative, Delbo pays tribute to the women friends who supported her at those moments when she felt unable to go on, as if one impulse of her story was to reaffirm the strength of human community despite the assault of Auschwitz on its spirit. But in the end, this support proves a wan comfort; she records the collapse of identity, the "failure" of character, the splintered unity, the merging of women with a mute, unfruitful earth.

The last vignette in *None of Us Will Return* is called "Springtime," an ironic dirge to the season of renewal from whose solace Delbo and her friends seem endlessly barred.

> All these lumps of flesh which had lost the pinkness and the life of flesh were strewn about in the dusty dried mud, were completing the process of withering and decomposing in the sunlight. All this brownish, purplish, gray flesh blended in so well with the dusty soil that it required an effort to pick out the women there, to make out empty breasts amid this puckered skin that hung from women's chests.

As Delbo the artist composes, her characters "decompose," and this is the challenge that a literature of Auschwitz will always have to face. The realities of the camp continue to contradict the premises of form and of language itself, resulting in a split that may in fact define the bond between the writer and this material, and our possible access to it.

In the second volume of her Auschwitz trilogy, *Une Connaissance inutile* (A useless knowledge), Delbo offers a distilled variant on this dilemma:

> I'm back from another world
> to this world
> that I didn't leave
> and I don't know
> which is real
> tell me have I come back
> from that other world?
> As for me
> I'm still there
> and I'm dying
> back there

every day a bit more
I die again
the death of all those who died
and I no longer know what's real
in this world
from the other world-back-there
now
I no longer know
when I'm dreaming
and when
I'm not dreaming.[32]

We have only to compare the returns of Odysseus and Aeneas from their "other world-back-there" with Delbo's to see how radically a demythologized literature of Auschwitz differs from traditional epic encounters with the realm of death. Odysseus carefully keeps the dead from profaning his living person, while Aeneas comes back from his visit to the underworld with a happy prophecy of a future civilization. Neither would understand Delbo's doom-laden line, "I die again / the death of all those who died," a line that stretches the circle of its recruits to include its audience as well.

The experience of Auschwitz, like all of the Holocaust, cannot be left behind. Nor do we return from our encounter with its literature unblemished. Instead, like Delbo, Levi, and all the rest, we face the necessary burden of adjustment. When Delbo admits, "I return / from beyond knowledge / now I need to unlearn / otherwise it's clear / I couldn't go on living," she intends not to slight her past but to invite us to share with her the twin vision that a journey through Auschwitz has etched on our culture. We pay a price for learning how to imagine what happened; then we add to our debt by feigning that beyond those mounds of corpses and heaps of ashes a chaste future is still feasible: "because it would be too stupid / in the end," as Delbo agrees, "for so many to have died / and for you to live / without making something of your life." But she frames this with a more somber paradox, one that echoes hollowly through the Holocaust universe, leaving us little but a bleak query to kindle hope:

I've spoken with death
so
I know
how useless were so many things we learned
but I gained this knowledge at the price of suffering
so great
I wonder
if it was worth it.[33]

NOTES

1. Bernd Naumann, *Auschwitz: A Report on the Proceedings against Robert Karl Ludwig Mulka and Others before the Court at Frankfurt*, trans. Jean Steinberg (London, 1966), pp. 146, 147.

2. Viktor Frankl, *Man's Search for Meaning*, rev. and updated ed. (New York, 1984), p. 87.

3. Ibid., p. 88.

4. Naumann, p. 217.

5. Jean Améry, *At the Mind's Limits: Contemplations by a Survivor on Auschwitz and Its Realities*, trans. Sidney and Stella P. Rosenfeld (New York, 1986), p. 16.

6. Frankl, p. 89.

7. Améry, p. 17.

8. Ibid., pp. 16–17.

9. Ibid., p. 19.

10. Ibid., p. 17.

11. Primo Levi, *The Reawakening: A Liberated Prisoner's Long March Home through East Europe*, trans. Stuart Woolf (New York, 1965), p. 12. Although the book did not appear in Italy until 1963, Levi says he finished writing it in 1947.

12. Ibid., pp. 12–13.

13. Ibid., p. 13.

14. Rolf Hochhuth, *The Deputy*, trans. Richard and Clara Winston (New York, 1964), p. 222.

15. Ibid.

16. Ibid., p. 249.

17. Peter Weiss, *The Investigation*, trans. Jon Swan and Ulu Grosbard (New York, 1966), pp. 108, 107–8.

18. Tadeusz Borowski, *This Way for the Gas, Ladies and Gentlemen*, trans. Barbara Vedder (New York, 1967), p. 29.

19. Andrzej Wirth, "A Discovery of Tragedy: The Incomplete Account of Tadeusz Borowski," trans. Adam Czerniawki, *Polish Review* 12 (Summer 1967), p. 45.

20. Ibid., pp. 41, 35, 37. In some of my comments on Borowski, I draw on passages from my *Versions of Survival: The Holocaust and the Human Spirit* (Albany, 1982).

21. Sara Nomberg-Przytyk, *Auschwitz: True Tales from a Grotesque Land*, trans. Roslyn Hirsch (Chapel Hill, N.C., 1985), pp. 20–21.

22. Ibid., pp. 45–46.

23. Ibid., p. 111.

24. Ibid., p. 112.

25. Ibid., p. 113.

26. Ibid., pp. 153–54.

27. Primo Levi, *The Drowned and the Saved*, trans. Raymond Rosenthal (New York, 1988), p. 112.

28. Only one part of the trilogy, *None of Us Will Return*, exists in an English version. Rosette Lamont's translation of all three parts awaits publication at this writing. Her translation of *Days and Memory*, a separate volume also partly concerned with Delbo's Auschwitz experience, was published by Marlboro Press in 1990.

29. Charlotte Delbo, *None of Us Will Return*, trans. John Githens (New York, 1968), p. 20.

30. Ibid., p. 31.

31. Ibid.

32. Charlotte Delbo, *Une Connaissance inutile* (Paris, 1970), pp. 183–84. My translations.

33. Ibid., pp. 191, 190, 185.

INDEX